MW01248825

CANADA YEAR BOOK 1994

*Published by authority of the Minister
responsible for Statistics Canada*

*© Minister of Industry,
Science and Technology, 1993*

*Available by mail from
Publication Sales and Services
Statistics Canada
Ottawa, Canada
K1A 0T6*

*Every attempt has been made to identify and credit sources for photographs. The publisher
would appreciate receiving information as to any inaccuracies in the credits for
subsequent editions.*

*Catalogue No. 11-402E/1994
ISBN 0-660-15186-3*

*The Canada Year Book is edited and prepared in the Communications Division of
Statistics Canada.*

Production and composition: Dissemination Division, Statistics Canada

Printing: D.W. Friesen & Sons Ltd., Altona, Manitoba

Cover design: Neville Smith

Design concept and direction: Aviva Furman and Neville Smith

Book design: Cheryl Vincent

*Cover photography: John de Visser / CMCP
             David Reede / First Light
             Darwin Wiggett / First Light*

The cover
*The photographs on the cover of the 1994 Canada Year Book bring together vital Canadian
motifs: John de Visser's photo interpretation of Niagara Falls reminds us of its unending
energy, its mysterious beauty; Darwin Wiggett's automobile lights zigzag across the landscape,
evoking a sense of speed, of the vastness of this country. On the back cover, David Reede's
Prairie grain fields link us to the land and to its beauty.*

*The sun and the moon on the front and back cover embody the passage of time. As cyclical as
the Year Book itself, their shapes run through the volume as motifs that interplay with other
graphic elements to celebrate change and progress.*

*Selected quotes were printed with permission from McClelland & Stewart Inc., Stoddart
Publishing Co. Limited, CBS Entertainment, the Estate of Robert W. Service, and
David F. Pelly in Canadian Geographic Magazine.*

Note of Appreciation

*Canada owes the success of its statistical system to a long-standing cooperation involving
Statistics Canada, the citizens of Canada, its businesses and governments. Accurate and timely
statistical information could not be produced without their continued cooperation and goodwill.*

The paper used in this publication is alkaline.

As Statistics Canada celebrates its 75th anniversary, I am pleased to introduce the 1994 edition of the **Canada Year Book***.*

A venerable publishing tradition in Canada, and a highlight of Statistics Canada's publishing program, it offers much to praise and celebrate. In existence since the founding of Canada in 1867, the **Year Book** *stands as a record of Canadian achievement and development.*

Each edition bring to readers a wealth of information on the social, economic, demographic, cultural and political life of Canada, and each edition offers us the chance to present information in a way that we can all relate to and understand.

The **Canada Year Book** *offers an on-going testimony of the wealth and beauty of Canada, of its values as a nation and its place in the world community. I take great pleasure in recommending it to all interested in understanding and knowing more about this great country of ours.*

Ivan P. Fellegi
Chief Statistician of Canada

ACKNOWLEDGEMENTS

The heart and guiding light of the **1994 Canada Year Book** has been Tanis Browning-Shelp, new to the Canada Year Book editorial team as Project Manager. Together with Ms. Browning-Shelp and Wayne Smith, Director of Communications and mentor for the project, I am honoured to thank the many people who have committed their time, energy and imagination to this book.

My special thanks to the English and French editorial teams, who broke new ground in research and writing. On the English team: Dave Blais, Dawne Carleton, Philip Cross, Duncan Currie, David Gonczol, Liz Hart, Carroll Holland, Sarah Hubbard, Keane Shore, Lauren Walker and Daniel Woolford. On the French team, headed by Senior Editor Denis Bernard: André Girard and Margo Nobert. Special thanks also to Linda Mac Donald who guided a 'Niagara Falls' of paper, and to David Scrimshaw for a fresh and creative look at tables, charts and graphs.

A new management group came together to guide the **1994 Year Book**. For their mix of far-ranging vision and close attention to the bottom line, particular appreciation is extended to Denis Desjardins, Martin Podehl, David Roy and Wayne Smith.

For handling the daunting task of co-ordinating development, typesetting and printing contracting, many thanks to Louis Boucher and Johanne Beauseigle; thanks also to the development team, headed by Marc Pelchat and consisting of Guy Berthiaume, Benoît Fontaine, Pierre Groulx and Rachel Mondou; to the typesetting team, headed by Diane Joanisse and consisting of Suzanne Beauchamp, Ghislaine Desgagné, Jean-Marie Lacombe, Rosemarie Andrews, Sue Lineger, Ginette Meilleur, Hélène Paquin, Louise Simard, Danielle Soucy-Collin and Ann Trépanier; and to Jacques Tessier and Carol Misener for printing liaison.

For their superlative work and commitment, many thanks to the Systems and Production team, headed by Diane Leblanc and consisting of Elaine Brassard, Chantal Cléroux, Natacha Cousineau, Anne Gervais, Richard Lane, Josée Leblanc, Lise Paquette and Karen Temple.

For innovative marketing and a decisive sales strategy, thanks to Katherine Bonner and Suzanne Joberty. Thanks also to Alain Mazet of the Secretary of State for translation services.

Many thanks to Neville Smith and Aviva Furman for art direction and design; to Cheryl Vincent for her dedicated and imaginative approach to the principal design work; to Christian Labarthe for creative typography; to Frank Mayrs for photographic research and selection that 'tells the story'; to John McCraken for skilful design co-ordination; and to Renée Saumure for solid graphic direction.

*Many thanks also to the group of experts within Statistics Canada who assisted in identifying key trends and acted as principal advisors for the **Canada Year Book**. They are: Philip Cross, Jean Dumas, Iain McKellar, Craig Mckie and Garnett Picot. The **Canada Year Book** draws on the contributions of hundreds of experts both within Statistics Canada and throughout the government and the private sector. Statistics Canada is greatly honoured to thank all contributors and referees for their time and help in assembling the* **1994 Canada Year Book**.

Jonina Wood
Editor-in-Chief
Canada Year Book

The **Canada Year Book** has guided readers to a better understanding and knowledge of Canada since it was first printed in 1867. In that year, it chronicled the political, vital and trade statistics of the day, and 'public events of interest'. It was a first for its time and it literally defined the concept of a year book for Canada.

Since then, it has grown and matured, becoming in the process one of Canada's most comprehensive reference resources. Collectively, the year books printed since 1867 form a library on the life of Canada and offer testimony to the political, economic, demographic and cultural changes of the last 126 years.

The **1994 Canada Year Book** continues the tradition. With 22 chapters on all dimensions of life in Canada, this is a book intended for everyone. Each chapter features a mix of statistics and narrative to present readers with trends and developments of the day. The **Year Book** also offers its traditional complement of charts, graphs and tables.

What's New...

For the first time, the **Year Book** features colour photographs on the life of the country, in addition to its series of black and white photographs drawn largely from the National Archives of Canada and the Canadian Museum of Contemporary Photography.

Continuing an innovation from the **1992 Year Book**, the 1994 edition also presents a series of more than 100 feature articles. Interesting, sometimes off-beat, but always informative, these are stories on events in Canada today.

Where Does The Information Come From?

*While the **Year Book** draws largely on the resources of Statistics Canada, it also has a nation-wide network of contributors who provide the **Year Book** editorial team with invaluable advice, guidance and information. The **Year Book** is indebted to this network of contributors.*

*Reference years for **Year Book** statistics vary. For some subjects, the most recent statistics available may be from 1993. Others may date from the late 1980s, in the absence of more up-to-date sources. In 1991, Statistics Canada conducted its Census of Population and Census of Agriculture and we are pleased to be able to present many highlights gleaned from them. For a list of further readings and sources, readers can refer to the end of each chapter.*

Keys To Finding What You Want

*The **1994 Canada Year Book** features an expanded index as a first stop in the search for specifics. A series of tables accompanies each chapter, in addition to the charts and graphs which complement the text. These are also indexed, in terms of subject matter. The Table of Contents will guide you to 22 chapters, grouped under larger headings: The Land, The People, The Nation, The Economy, and Arts and Leisure.*

Three appendices include a list of Statistics Canada's network of Regional Reference Centres, a key to metric conversion, and captions and credits for all colour photographs featured in the Year Book.

A Celebratory Note

*In this edition of the **Year Book**, we note the celebratory mood of Statistics Canada. In 1993, as the **Year Book** was being prepared for press, the Agency celebrated its 75th anniversary as Canada's national statistical agency.*

Today, some 75 years since it first came into being, Statistics Canada is the country's largest publishing house, producing some 900 titles every year, in print, on computer tapes, on CDs and in maps. With a national network of Regional Reference Centres, it has became a permanent and enduring part of Canadian life.

An Invitation

*We invite readers of the **Canada Year Book** to write to us if they have any comments or suggestions for the improvement of this book. We can be reached at the following address:*

Canada Year Book 1994

Communications Division

Statistics Canada

R.H. Coats Building

Tunney's Pasture

Ottawa, Canada

KIA OT6

CONTENTS

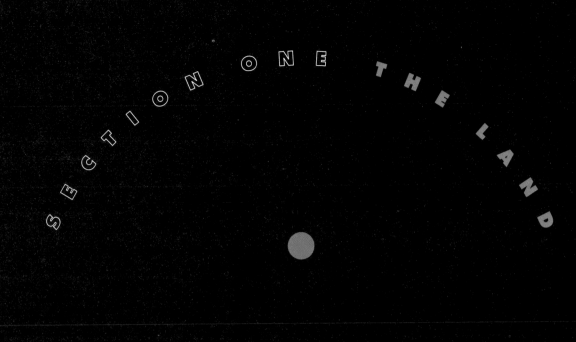

SECTION ONE THE LAND

CHAPTER ONE

PHYSICAL SETTING

INTRODUCTION

THE POETRY OF THE LAND There is an old Mohawk saying that the people do not make the land, it is the land that makes the people. Indeed, few nations have been so profoundly conditioned by the forces of nature as Canada. The reality of the land is overwhelming; its magnitude, its rugged terrain, and its climatic extremes all shape the fundamental attitudes of its 27 million inhabitants. For some, Canada's landscapes kindle a deep and spiritual bond with the earth, exemplified in the country's literature and art. Canada's poets and writers — Antonine Maillet, W.O. Mitchell, Margaret Laurence, Robert Service and Gilles Vigneault to name a few — set their stories against backdrops of harsh northern winters, wild prairie skies, lush West Coast rain forests, noble mountain ranges or the salty breezes of the St. Lawrence River and Maritime provinces. For painters such as the Group of Seven, Emily Carr, Alex Colville and Marc-Aurèle de Foy Suzor-Coté, Canada's landscapes are a palette of colour: stunning yellow prairies, rich green forests, vibrant autumn leaves, cool blue lakes and rivers, and dazzling winter fields of white.

For others, the land has generously provided countless natural resources that have governed the course of industry and commerce. From the early days of the fur trade, through the Klondike rush for gold, to today's forestry, mining and energy industries, the land has nurtured the growth of a strong nation.

This chapter tours the country from east to west; from its Atlantic harbours, over the stubborn rocks of the Precambrian Shield, across the prairies, through the narrow passes of the Rockies to the Pacific, then north to the immense tundra and up to the icy shores of the Arctic Ocean.

PHYSICAL GEOGRAPHY

Canada's northernmost point, Cape Columbia on Ellesmere Island, is only 768 kilometres from the North Pole. Its southernmost point, Lake Erie's Middle Island, shares roughly the same latitude as Rome and the French Riviera. Between these two points are over 4 600 kilometres of mostly wilderness and wildlife. The greatest east-west distance stretches over 5 500 kilometres from Cape Spear, Newfoundland, to the Yukon–Alaska border.

With shores on three oceans, the Atlantic, Pacific and the Arctic, Canada has the world's longest coastline at almost 244 000 kilometres. Much of this is formed by islands. Canada also encompasses the offshore areas of the Canadian continental margin; including Hudson Bay, these areas cover more than 6.5 million square kilometres.

The country's 10 million square kilometres of territory may be described in terms of its 15 ecological regions, its 39 natural regions, or its 17 geological provinces. Generally, though, there are six regions: the Appalachian region, the Precambrian Shield, the Great Lakes-St. Lawrence Lowlands, the Interior Plains, the Western Cordillera and the Arctic Islands.

THE APPALACHIAN REGION The Appalachian region encompasses the provinces of Newfoundland, Prince Edward Island, Nova Scotia, New Brunswick and parts of Quebec. The Appalachian Mountains were formed almost 300 million years ago by folds in the earth's surface. Over the ages the mountains have been worn down by glaciers, wind and water; their highest elevation, in Gaspe's Shickshock Mountains, is under 1 300 metres. Generally, the region is heavily wooded with mixed sugar maple and spruce forests.

THE GREAT LAKES-ST. LAWRENCE LOWLANDS Nestled between the Appalachians and the Precambrian Shield is the smallest, yet most productive agricultural area in the country. The Great Lakes-St. Lawrence Lowlands region covers about the same amount of area as Newfoundland as it stretches from Quebec City to the banks of Lake Huron. Mixed forests of sugar maple and spruce sprout out of its rich, sedimentary soils.

Kaj R. Svensson / Viewpoints West

Basalt Columns, Brandywine Falls, British Columbia.

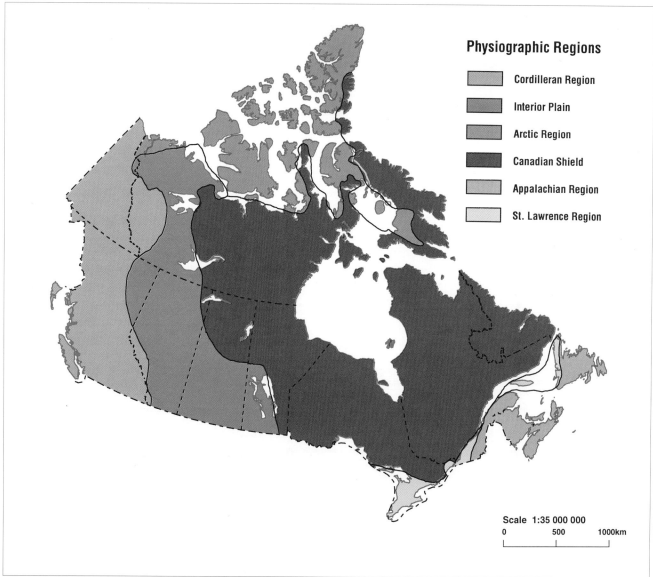

Physiographic Regions

- Cordilleran Region
- Interior Plain
- Arctic Region
- Canadian Shield
- Appalachian Region
- St. Lawrence Region

Scale 1:35 000 000

0   500   1000km

From *The New Canadian Oxford Atlas* by Walter G. Kemball. Maps© Oxford University Press. Reproduced by permission of the publisher.

Canada's physiographic regions.

T H E   P R E C A M B R I A N   S H I E L D Also known commonly as the Canadian Shield, this stony, silent mask of Precambrian rock is the dominant geological feature of the country. Comprising nearly half of Canada's total area, the shield creeps south from Baffin Island, coils around Hudson Bay, covering almost all of Quebec and Ontario, through the northern sections of Manitoba and Saskatchewan, rising up again to the eastern two-thirds of the Northwest Territories. The shield is a country of deep forests, rocky outcrops, and countless lakes and rivers. Known for its sheer inhospitality, its combination of rock, bog and scant layers of soil limits travel and makes settlement and farming virtually impossible. Almost one-quarter of the world's fresh water is concentrated in these lakes and rivers.

In the South, white pine, spruce and fir thrive in the long growing season. In the far North the cold climate is too harsh for trees, but in a brief, six-week summer, the land bursts to life with a rich covering of mosses, short grasses and desert-like plants that grow, bloom and fade very quickly.

THE INTERIOR PLAINS In stark contrast to the rocky shield, the fertile Interior Plains are a seemingly endless expanse of land and sky. In describing his entry to this area from the east, author Al Purdy wrote "It's like coming out of a dark room — to leave the hills and leafless forests of an Ontario countryside on a dull April day, to find yourself under the white blaze of a Saskatchewan sky."

The Interior Plains are not completely flat; they rise almost one kilometre in three shallow steps from Manitoba to Alberta. Northward, they spread up through the Mackenzie River Valley to the Arctic Ocean. Early explorers named this region after the French word *prairie*, meaning 'meadow'.

During the last Ice Age, the area was flattened by glaciers as they ground their way back and forth across the face of the region. Topsoil, clay and minerals were scraped off the mask of the Canadian Shield and deposited in the central part of the plains, leaving the soil in this area ideal for agriculture, especially grain farming.

The dry southwest — in the southernmost parts of Alberta and Saskatchewan — features a desert-like sweep of short grasses. To the north, are more fertile grasslands; higher rainfall has created millions of small ponds, providing breeding grounds for half of North America's ducks, geese, swans and pelicans.

THE WESTERN CORDILLERA

The Western Cordillera is a vast, rocky spine of mountains that hug the Pacific coastline to the south as far as the tip of South America. Canada's portion of the Cordillera embraces the western border of Alberta, most of British Columbia and all of the Yukon Territory as it stretches 2 400 kilometres from the 49th parallel north to the Arctic Ocean. The highest range in this tangle of mountains is the Rockies, known for their spectacular crests, plunging gorges and blue-green lakes. Approached from the east, these mountains rise in a formidable barrier, offering limited routes to the west side. Only the Fraser River Valley and the gap at Prince Rupert, British Columbia allow the Trans-Canada highway and the rail systems to pass.

A valley of plateaus, plains and low rolling mountains fill the central part of the region. This mild and sunny area offers fertile soils and is well known for its vineyards and fruit and vegetable farms.

In the enviably moderate climate on the West Coast, the land is covered by dense rain forest. The trees grow to tremendous heights: some thousand-year-old Douglas firs tower more than 90 metres high and can be as much as 5 metres in diameter.

By comparison, the northern parts of the Western Cordillera are strikingly harsh. Inland, as the region stretches to the north, the temperatures are among the coldest in North America.

THE ARCTIC REGION North of Canada's mainland lie hundreds of islands in the Arctic Ocean. In a great triangle of naked, rolling, lake-dotted plains, broken only by scattered ranges of worn hills and regions of grey rock and gravel, this area spans 2 800 kilometres from east to west, and stretches 1 800 kilometres up to the northern tip of Canada.

Here the ground remains permanently frozen to a depth of almost half a kilometre, making development difficult and farming impossible. Often called 'the Barrens', this land has surprising vitality. In a brief but productive six-week summer, the area surface bursts into colour with a covering of mosses, lichens, dwarf shrubs and grasses. Millions of scattered ponds form protective breeding grounds for thousands of species of insects and birds. For a short time the lulling silence of the land is broken with a deafening symphony of mating calls and territorial squabbles.

Perhaps the most striking characteristic of the North is the heavenly aurora borealis — the northern lights. They often appear as ghostly curtains, billowing green and white in the northern skies. Occasionally they erupt into a kaleidoscope of purple, red and yellow shimmering across the sky. Most of these auroras occur between 100 and 250 kilometres above the earth's surface, where the atmosphere is thin enough to glow like the gas in a fluorescent lamp as electrical currents from the sun speed through space at speeds of up to 4 million kilometres per hour, a phenomenon known as the solar wind. Because of the orientation of the earth's magnetic field, Canada, especially the North, is the most favoured nation on the planet for aurora watching.

John de Visser / CMCP

Near Dauphin, Manitoba.

ECONOMIC GEOGRAPHY

Politically, Canada comprises 10 provinces and 2 territories. Each province administers its own natural resources. In the Yukon and Northwest Territories, resources — except for game — are administered federally because of the extent and remoteness of the territories and their sparse population.

ON THE HOMESTEAD Only about 10% of Canada is permanently settled, and only Prince Edward Island is completely occupied. Large parts of the interior of Nova Scotia, New Brunswick and the Gaspé Peninsula are unpopulated. Around the New-foundland coast and on the shores of the St. Lawrence River below Quebec City, settlement occurs only in narrow bands.

About 60% of the country's population lives between the Canada–US border and a 1 000-kilometre east-west line running from Quebec City to Sault Ste Marie, Ontario. Nearly 40% of the population lives in the metropolitan areas of Quebec, Montreal, Ottawa-Hull, Toronto, Hamilton, London, St. Catharines-Niagara, Windsor and Kitchener.

Canada's largest tract of continuous settlement winds through Manitoba, Saskatchewan and Alberta, occupying over 6% of Canada's area and boasting five major cities: Edmonton, Calgary, Winnipeg, Saska-toon and Regina. North of this mainly agricultural block, astride the Alberta–British Columbia border, is the Peace River district, an agricultural area stretching to the 57th parallel.

The southern half of British Columbia is settled in interconnecting strips in valleys between the mountain ranges. Population is dense in the lower mainland around Vancouver.

A number of remote settlements lie in the North, the largest of which are in Ontario and Quebec between the 47th and 50th parallels in the Clay Belt-Abitibi area. Outside these urban-rural blocks are smaller settlements based on mining, forest industries, transportation, administration, defence, hunting and fishing.

NEWFOUNDLAND Canada's youngest and most easterly province joined Confederation in 1949. In the Appalachian region, the Island of Newfoundland is covered by forested hills and low mountains and dotted with innumerable ponds and swamps. Its rugged, rocky coastlines are sprinkled with coves and isolated fishing villages.

St. John's, the capital, lies on the eastern coast of the Avalon Peninsula. Other urban areas are Corner Brook on the west coast and Grand Falls in the central part of the island. Remote from the country, the island has its own time zone 30 minutes ahead of the Maritime provinces.

Labrador, the larger area of Newfoundland, is connected to the mainland. Bordering the North Atlantic Coast to Hudson Strait, Labrador extends inland about 750 kilometres. A striking mosaic of Appalachian rocks, wetlands and lakes, Labrador has rugged coastline headlands rising out of the sea. In the extreme north, the Torngat Mountains rise to a peak of 1 652 metres at Mount Caubvik. The Torngats are totally barren — some peaks even harbour small glaciers. Many Labrador rivers feature numerous waterfalls and the river valleys are well-forested. Coastal waters abound in fish, and the Precambrian rocks are rich in iron ore.

Newfoundland's economy, once dependent upon fishing, now focuses on extracting and processing natural resources. Iron ore is the dominant commodity, followed by zinc and asbestos. Food processing and the paper industries are the main manufacturing sectors.

PRINCE EDWARD ISLAND Canada's smallest province is a rust coloured island cradled in the Gulf of St. Lawrence, east of New Brunswick and north of Nova Scotia. Prince Edward Island's gently

rolling landscapes peak at about 140 metres above sea level. The coast is gently sculpted by bays and inlets running inland. To writer Phil Jenkins, "the island seems to be one large farm, populated either by cows or potatoes, surrounded by water and divided by reddish lanes lined with lupins."

Charlottetown is the provincial capital and largest urban area.

Agriculture is indeed the mainstay of the island — dairy cows and livestock graze in pastures alternating with famous PEI potato fields. Along with some mixed grains, 70% of the island is given over to growing potatoes. Charlottetown, Cavendish, and the sandy provincial beaches draw healthy crowds of tourists each summer.

NOVA SCOTIA Nova Scotia is a peninsula connected to the rest of the country by the Isthmus of Chignecto, a strip of land only 20 kilometres wide. No part of the province is more than 50 kilometres from the sea; its shores front the Bay of Fundy, the Atlantic Ocean, the Gulf of St. Lawrence and the Northumberland Strait. The northeastern portion, Cape Breton Island, is separated from the mainland by the Strait of Canso, traversed by a permanent causeway. Cape Breton Island is almost cut in half from northeast to southwest by the saltwater Bras d'Or Lake. While a wooded upland rises in the north, the mainland is mostly flat. The Atlantic side is rocky, with dozens of bays, inlets, coves and harbours that have been deeply carved by the sea.

The two large urban areas are Halifax-Dartmouth and Sydney-Glace Bay. Halifax, the capital, is a bustling industrial centre nestled in one of the world's most accessible natural harbours.

Not surprisingly, Nova Scotia's fishery is the largest in the North Atlantic. The principal species are lobster, cod, scallop, and haddock. About 10% of the land is agricultural, mostly in the Annapolis Valley and northern Nova Scotia. These areas are important for their fruit, particularly apples, and dairy farming. Coal is the province's principal mineral, yet gypsum and salt production also take place. Manufacturing is varied and includes food processing, rubber and plastics, paper and wood products and transportation equipment.

CANADA'S CLIMATE

Canadians have learned to pay attention to climatic extremes. Futile attempts to start a car at −30°C and tongue-lolling summer heat have shaped the national psyche. At the same time, the fruits of modern technology — climate-controlled shopping malls and inter-connected office complexes — have insulated Canadians from the extremes of heat and cold, allowing us to enjoy each season in its less forgiving moments.

Canada's climate varies considerably from region to region. In the extreme north, the temperature rises above 0°C for only a few months each year. Most Canadians, however, live within 300 kilometres of the country's southern border, where mild springs, warm summers and crisp autumns prevail at least 8 months out of 12.

The climate in Canada changes with each season as the hours of sunlight increase and decrease and as North America's weather systems shift. The terrain — mountain ranges, plains and bodies of water — also plays an important role in shaping the climate of each region of the country.

THE WEST COAST

The West Coast of British Columbia has the most temperate climate in Canada, thanks to mild, moist Pacific Ocean airstreams. As the moist air rises over the mountains, it cools and precipitation falls on the westward mountain slopes — usually as rain at lower altitudes and snow at higher ones. The valleys between the mountain ranges receive much less precipitation and experience warm arid summers.

THE PRAIRIES

The Prairies, which extend from the Rocky Mountains east to Winnipeg, Manitoba, make up the Canadian section of the vast North American Great Plain. Cold winters and hot summers are the norm here, with relatively light precipitation no matter what the season. For instance, in southern Saskatchewan, annual precipitation averages less than 350 millimetres (mm) compared with 1 110 mm in Vancouver.

GREAT LAKES/ST. LAWRENCE

More than half the Canadian population lives close to the Great Lakes or along the St. Lawrence River. Here, winter brings heavy snowfalls. Spring can be fleeting and somewhat unpredictable. Summers tend to be longer and more humid than in other parts of Canada. Mean daily temperatures reach close to 20°C from mid-June to mid-September with week-long heat waves in the 30s a common occurrence.

ATLANTIC CANADA

The combined influence of air masses from northern and eastern Canada and the United States with air currents off the ocean give this region one of the most variable climates anywhere in the country. In winter, temperatures can seesaw widely as arctic air is replaced by maritime air from passing storms. Snowfall can be heavy, particularly in New Brunswick, and fog is common in spring and summer, especially in Newfoundland. The warmest months are July and August, when mean temperatures range from 16-18°C.

THE BOREAL FOREST

Spanning the entire country immediately north of the Prairies, the Great Lakes and the St. Lawrence River is the boreal forest. Snow usually covers the ground here for more than half the year. Precipitation is light, except along the Labrador coast where Atlantic storms exert an influence.

THE HIGH ARCTIC

Further north above the tree line lies the High Arctic, where temperatures in many areas might climb above freezing for only a few weeks in July/August. A few feet below the delicate-looking but tenacious vegetation that grows in the summer, the ground remains frozen year-round.

Mike Hawkes / Environment Canada

Tornado!

NEW BRUNSWICK   New Brunswick's extensive coast banks the Chaleur Bay on the north, the Gulf of St. Lawrence and Northumberland Strait on the east, and the Bay of Fundy on the south. A northwestern plateau, 300 to 450 metres above sea level, is deeply divided by valleys sloping to the Saint John River that flows south for over 650 kilometres. While much of the province's soil is rocky and unsuitable for agriculture, the Saint John River Valley forms a fertile oasis. Generous rainfall produces a prolific forest growth throughout the province.

The Bay of Fundy, between New Brunswick and Nova Scotia, boasts the world's highest tides — they average 10 metres and rise as high as 17 metres, high enough to easily swallow a five-storey building.

New Brunswick's capital is Fredericton. Saint John, at the mouth of the Saint John River, is the principal port and industrial centre.

Agriculture is varied. The upper Saint John River Valley produces potatoes, and the lower valley is important for dairy and beef cattle, poultry, pork and vegetables. Food processing, and the paper and wood industries are the major forms of economic activity. Zinc, potash and lead are important in mining. Lobster and crab are the principal species in the province's fishery.

QUEBEC   Quebec is Canada's largest province. With about 80% of its area covered by the Canadian Shield, Quebec is dotted with hundreds of lakes, woods and tumbling plateaus. The low mountains of the Appalachian region lie south of the St. Lawrence River. A slim strip along the southeastern boundary of Quebec contains the flat surface and fertile soils of the Great Lakes-St. Lawrence region.

Quebec, the provincial capital, was founded by Samuel de Champlain in 1608. Montreal is the province's largest city, and one of North America's great industrial, commercial and financial centres.

About one-quarter of Canadian manufacturing takes place in Quebec. Paper, primary metals and food processing dominate this sector. Quebec is one of the world's leading producers of asbestos and is also a major producer of gold, iron ore and copper.

Robert Bourdeau / CMCP

Lake Superior, Ontario.

Hydroelectric power makes an important contribution to the provincial economy.

Quebec's agriculture focuses mainly on dairy and livestock.

ONTARIO Canada's second largest and most populous province banks the freshwater shores of the Great Lakes and the saltwater shores of Hudson Bay and James Bay. The rocky Canadian Shield dominates most of the province. In Canada's early days, a favourable climate, fertile soil and ease of travel made the Southern Lowland-Great Lakes area important for agriculture; today it is one of the world's great industrial agglomerations. Toronto, the provincial capital, falls within Canada's largest metropolitan area, with almost 4 million inhabitants.

Ontario is the heart of Canadian manufacturing, accounting for about half of the country's total. The manufacture of transportation equipment such as cars and trucks is the largest single industry. Other important industries include chemicals and chemical products, electrical and electronic products, food, primary metals and fabricated metal products. Although Ontario ranks second among the provinces in the value of its total mineral production, it leads in production of metals including nickel, copper, gold, uranium and zinc.

Ontario has the largest farming sector in Canada. Livestock and dairy farming predominate, but small grains, fruit and vegetables are important cash crops. The freshwater fishery, conducted primarily in the Great Lakes, has declined because of pollution and overfishing.

MAJOR WEATHER RECORDS AND EVENTS

THE WARMEST AND THE COLDEST

In Canada, wide variances in temperature occur from season to season and coast to coast. The highest temperature ever recorded in Canada was 45°C at Midale and Yellow Grass, Saskatchewan, on July 5, 1937. The lowest temperature of −63°C was observed at Snag, Yukon, on February 3, 1947.

HEAT WAVES AND COLD SPELLS

While day-to-day changes in weather conditions are the norm, sometimes one type of weather will lock in for days or weeks at a time. Such was the case when Canada's most intense heat wave struck the western and central regions of the country in July 1936. For a week and a half, humid 37°C temperatures prevailed. Crops were destroyed and 780 people died from the heat.

Although heat waves rarely last long, cold spells can last several weeks. One of the longest cold spells on record hit Saskatoon in 1936. The temperature stayed below −18°C for 58 consecutive days from January 3 until March 1. The most extreme change in temperature took place in January, 1962 in Pincher Creek, Alberta, when a warm, dry wind known as a "Chinook" brought the temperature up from −19°C to 22°C in one hour!

THE WETTEST AND THE DRIEST

As moist air from the Pacific Ocean meets the mountainous coastline of British Columbia, downpours are the inevitable result. In fact, apart from short-duration rainfall, all Canadian records for the greatest amount of precipitation are for locations on the West Coast. Henderson Lake on Vancouver Island set the Canadian record of 8 100 millimetres (mm) annual precipitation in 1931. Revelstoke Mount Copeland in the BC mountain interior holds the distinction of receiving the most snowfall in a single season — 2 400 centimetres (cm) in the winter of 1971-72.

Canada's Arctic has been called a frozen desert — and for good reason. While much of the North is covered in snow for many months throughout the year, precipitation can average less than 100 mm a year across the Arctic's western and central islands. Arctic Bay in the Northwest Territories holds the record for the lowest annual amount of precipitation — 12.7 mm in 1949.

FLOODS AND DROUGHTS

Most floods are caused by sudden and intense downpours. The most severe flood in Canadian history occurred on October 14-15, 1954, when Hurricane Hazel brought 214 mm of rain to the Toronto region in just 72 hours. The Don and Humber rivers and the Etobicoke Creek flooded, killing 80 and causing the equivalent of over $100 million in damage in today's dollars. Spring snowmelt has also been the cause of many of Canada's worst floods. For instance, in 1950, the Red River in Manitoba rose 10 metres above normal, submerging one-fifth of Winnipeg and forcing the evacuation of 100,000 people.

Too little water has been a recurring problem on the Prairies since the soil was first tilled. The most serious drought came in the 1930s. Between 1933 and 1937, the region received only 60% of its normal rainfall. The drought of the 1980s equalled that of the 1930s in duration and intensity, reducing grain exports by $4 billion in 1988 alone.

STORMY WEATHER

No region of Canada is secure from the fury of winter blasts and blizzards. Intense winter storms are frequently accompanied by numbing cold, ice or heavy snow. For the residents of Newfoundland, the blizzard of 1959 was one of the worst on record. The storm, which struck on February 16, took six lives, left 70,000 Newfoundlanders without power, crippled telephone service, and blocked highways and roads with drifts 5 metres high.

In the summer months, thunderstorms are frequent afternoon occurrences across much of the southern part of the country. Southwestern Ontario holds the distinction of having the highest average number of thunderstorm days at 34. This also is the region most frequently hit by tornadoes (an average of 21 each year). On May 31, 1985, eight tornadoes moved across southern Ontario, causing $100 million in property damage and killing 12. Tornadoes also occur in the West. On July 31, 1987, one hit Edmonton, Alberta, killing 27, injuring over 200, leaving 400 homeless and causing more than $250 million in damage.

In terms of property alone, the most expensive natural catastrophe in Canadian history was a violent hailstorm that struck Calgary on September 7, 1991. Insurance companies eventually paid about $400 million to repair over 65,000 cars, 60,000 homes and businesses, and a number of aircraft.

MANITOBA Manitoba is the country's geographical heartland. The northern Precambrian mask is heavily glaciated, and its major rivers, the Nelson and the Churchill, flow into Hudson Bay. Its southern flat plain is the lowest of the three step-like formations of the Interior Plains Region. Floored by deep fertile clay soils left by glacial lakes, the region is separated from the Saskatchewan Plain along its western boundary by the Manitoba Escarpment, a narrow belt of hilly terrain.

Winnipeg, the capital, is the industrial centre of Manitoba. Here, two extremes of climate occur. In winter, Winnipeg is the coldest major city in Canada — its January mean temperature is –18.3°C. In summer, the city swelters in the relentless, desert-like heat.

Manitoba's economy is built on agriculture. Wheat and other grain crops are most important, followed by livestock. There is also a small commercial freshwater fishery out of Lake Winnipeg. The province's manufacturing is varied, led by food processing and transportation equipment. Mineral production is mainly metals, especially nickel, copper and zinc.

SASKATCHEWAN Two-thirds of Saskatchewan fall within Canada's Interior Plains. The second step of the prairie formation, the Saskatchewan Plain, has deep fertile soil. The highest of the prairie steps extends from the slope of the Missouri Coteau. The Cypress Hills rise above this level. Cutting across the lowland are the branches of the Saskatchewan River that flow to Lake Winnipeg.

Regina, the capital, and Saskatoon serve mainly as distribution centres for surrounding areas.

Known as the 'bread basket of the nation', Saskatchewan's leading industry is agriculture, dominated by wheat and other grains. Saskatchewan is a major world producer of potash, used in chemical fertilizers. Other important minerals include fuels such as crude oil and natural gas, and metals, most notably uranium. The manufacturing sector is relatively small but varied.

ALBERTA With the famous Rocky Mountains rising on its western border, Alberta lies mainly in the interior plains. The winter climate is highly variable.

The famous Chinook, a warm southwestern wind sweeping down the eastern slopes of the Rockies can raise the temperature by as much as 15°C in one hour.

The two largest cities, Calgary and the capital, Edmonton, are located in one of Canada's richest oil and gas producing areas.

Alberta accounts for about half the value of minerals produced in Canada. Almost all of this comes from fuels — petroleum, natural gas and its byproducts, and coal. The province's grain and livestock production is also important. Chemicals, chemical products and food are the leading commodities in Alberta's diversified manufacturing sector.

BRITISH COLUMBIA Essayist Eric Nicol once wrote that ''British Columbians like to think of their province as a large body of land entirely surrounded by envy.'' Nestled between summit and seashore, British Columbia is set apart from the rest of the country by the Rocky Mountains. The provincial interior is marked off by the Rocky Mountain Trench containing the headwaters of the Kootenay, Columbia, Fraser, Peace and Liard rivers. Westward, the landscape is lower and broader and the effects of glaciation are not as spectacular. In the western section, the Coast Mountains extend southward from the St. Elias Mountains where the loftiest peaks on the continent thrust out of glistening icefields.

The inner passage adjacent to the coast — the Strait of Georgia, Queen Charlotte Strait and Hecate Strait — is one of the finest natural waterways in the world. Vancouver Island rises steeply from a rocky coastline; in the Queen Charlotte Islands, individual mountain ranges are separated by deep, narrow valleys.

Vancouver, the largest city, is a rapidly growing industrial centre and seaport. Victoria, the capital, clings to the southern tip of Vancouver Island.

British Columbia's economy thrives on its natural resources. The forest industry is particularly important, both as a primary activity and as the largest component of the province's manufacturing sector. Lumber is the main forest product, but pulp and paper production is also substantial. Food processing and

Kaj R. Svensson / Viewpoints West

Boston Bar Creek, British Columbia.

Thomas Kitchin / First Light

Dinosaur Provincial Park, Alberta.

Canada has no fewer than ten World Heritage Sites that rank with the likes of the pyramids of Egypt, the Galapagos Islands, and the ancient city of Damascus in Syria. They have been recognized by the United Nations Educational, Scientific and Cultural Organization (UNESCO), which by 1992 had carefully reviewed and designated only 359 such sites in the world.

The sites fall into two categories: natural and cultural. In Canada, natural sites include:

▲ *Kluane National Park in the Yukon, known for some of the world's largest ice fields outside polar regions and a spectacular range of mountain environments;*

▲ *The Canadian Rocky Mountain Parks (and three provincial parks), in Alberta and British Columbia, which hold significant fossil sites, lakes and river systems, and some 360 animal and bird species;*

▲ *The desert badlands of Dinosaur Provincial Park Alberta, with their stunning deposits of Upper Cretaceous dinosaur fossils;*

▲ *Wood Buffalo National Park in Alberta and the Northwest Territories, with the largest undisturbed meadows left in North America, one of the world's finest inland river deltas, salt plains, and endangered bison, crane and falcon species; and*

▲ *Nahanni National Park* Northwest Territories, with nearly 5 000 square kilometres of wilderness, including the South Nahanni watershed and canyon system, tundra-capped mountains, caves and the spectacular 90-metre Virginia Falls, twice the height of Niagara Falls.

The cultural sites include:

▲ *Anthony Island* (South Moresby), in British Columbia, for its Haida Indian totem poles and mortuary columns in Ninstits Village — one of the most impressive and remarkable Coastal Indian sites in the Pacific Northwest;

▲ *Gros Morne National Park* Newfoundland, for evidence of human cultural history from the Stone Age Maritime Archaic tradition, through Dorset Eskimo, to visits by Norse seafarers, French and Basque whalers, Jacques Cartier, and Captain James Cook;

▲ *L'Anse aux Meadows National Historic Park* Newfoundland, since it is the site of the oldest known European settlement in the New World, a Viking colony dating to the 11th century and the legendary Norseman Leif Erikkson;

▲ *The Historic District of Quebec* as the best remaining example in North America of original walled fortifications from the 17th, 18th and 19th centuries; and

▲ *Head-Smashed-In Bison Jump* Alberta, as the oldest and best-preserved bison jump in North America, probably used by native peoples to hunt bison as early as 8000 B.C.

Natural World Heritage Sites are outstanding examples of major stages in the earth's evolution, of ongoing geological processes, biological evolution, or of the foremost natural habitats of threatened animal or plant species.

Cultural sites meet tests of authenticity for unique artistic or creative masterpieces; long-time influence over a cultural area of the world; unique testimony to a lost civilization; outstanding examples of human cultural settlements; or tangible association with events or ideas of universal significance.

Canada played a major role in setting up the World Heritage Convention, which outlines how sites are chosen, sets up a site preservation fund for 123 member states, and promotes heritage conservation worldwide.

primary metals are other important manufacturing industries. The province's extensive minerals sector is dominated by fuels such as coal, natural gas and petroleum, and metals in the form of copper and gold.

Livestock, specialty crops and fruit are the major agricultural products in British Columbia. In its extensive fishery — Canada's largest — salmon makes up over half the landed value. Herring is also important.

YUKON TERRITORY Of this magnificent land, Robert Service once wrote: ''. . . there's the land (have you seen it?) / It's the cussedest land that I know, / from the big, dizzy mountains that screen it / To the deep, deathlike valleys below / some say God was tired when He made it: / Some say it's a fine land to shun; / maybe: but there's some as would trade it / For no land on earth — I'm one.'' This may be a common sentiment among the residents of the Yukon. Indeed, Yukoners refer to the rest of the country as ''the outside.''

North and slightly west of British Columbia, the Yukon Territory is a triangle of plateaus and mountain ranges bounded by the Northwest Territories and Alaska. Its only coast extends along the Arctic Ocean west of the Mackenzie River Delta. Between the Coast Mountains on the west and the Mackenzie Mountains on the east lies a plateau of rough, irregularly rolling upland. Numerous river valleys cut through the territory. In the southwest, many peaks of the St. Elias Mountains soar to heights of over 4 000 metres. The highest point in Canada, Mount Logan (5 959 metres), is located in this mountain range.

The entire territory is above latitude 60° north; part extends beyond the Arctic Circle. The Alaska Highway links the region with British Columbia and Alberta. The capital and main urban centre is Whitehorse.

Mining is the chief economic activity in the Yukon, with zinc, lead and gold as the dominant commodities. During the summer periods, tourism is a major source of revenue. Every summer hundreds of hotels, motels and campgrounds welcome travellers from all over the world who are drawn to the mysterious 'land of the midnight sun', the last frontier of North America.

NORTHWEST TERRITORIES
The Northwest Territories include all Canadian territory north of the 60th parallel, except for the Yukon and the northwestern tip of Quebec and Labrador. All islands south of the 60th parallel in Hudson Bay and James Bay are also part of the Territories. This vast area, more than one-third of Canada, is characterized by extremes in topography, flora and fauna, and climate; permafrost occurs throughout the Territories.

East of the mountain fringe along the Yukon boundary, the mainland plains slope down to Hudson Bay and northeast to the Arctic Archipelago. The interior plains of the central continent stretch to the Arctic Ocean. Across the low-lying mainland flows the Mackenzie River, linking Great Slave Lake and Great Bear Lake to the Arctic Ocean.

Images of the North as barren wilderness are misleading. The North is home to many fur-bearing animals, crystal clear lakes stocked with many species of fish, and plant life which is shocking in summer with its profuse brilliance. The tundra is almost treeless; although the occasional dwarf willow, only a few inches high, stands in defiance of the icy environment. Up to several hundred years old, the dwarf willow, with its fascinating shapes, brings to mind the Japanese bonsai. Yet, unlike the bonsai, the willow has been twisted into freakish configurations by the snow, ice and wind, rather than through the direction of a gardener. A cover of muskeg and countless lakes and swamps appear in the northeast of the mainland. In the Archipelago, high mountain ranges lie north to south across Baffin, Devon and Ellesmere islands.

Yellowknife, the capital, sits on the north shore of Great Slave Lake. Only the Mackenzie Delta and Great Slave Lake areas are accessible by road from the rest of Canada. In the eastern Arctic, the focal point is Iqaluit (formerly Frobisher Bay).

As in the Yukon Territory, the Northwest Territories' mining industry is large, dominated by zinc, gold and petroleum. Fur and fisheries, mainstays for the native population, are exploited commercially on a small scale.

Thomas Davies / National Gallery of Canada

A View on the River La Puce near Quebec, North America.

INLAND WATERS

Each year millions of tonnes of water fall on the land as rain and snow. Some of this water evaporates; some is stored in lakes, groundwater reservoirs and glaciers; but much more runs off into rivers or streams to the oceans. The Atlantic and Pacific coastal regions receive the most precipitation (100-140 centimetres), followed by Ontario and Quebec (65-90 centimetres) and the semi-arid Prairie region (40-55 centimetres). Canada's northland receives the least precipitation (15-40 centimetres).

About 30% of Canada's annual precipitation falls as snow, much of which stays frozen until spring. This chilly blanket is vital for maintaining soil moisture. At spring thaw, rivers swell with the sudden snowmelt, often flooding their banks.

Though Canada is known as a land of abundant water, certain areas of the country, especially in Alberta's southern prairies, are arid and dry because of limited rainfall and because almost half of Canada's river water flows northward. Farmers in such areas welcome rainy periods. A long summer drought can devastate an entire year's crops.

About 8% of Canada is covered by lakes and rivers, which contain enough water to flood the entire nation to a depth of two metres. This surface water is the source of about 90% of the country's supply of fresh water.

Lakes regulate river flow by smoothing out peaks at flood times and sustaining streamflow during dry seasons. The Great Lakes are among the largest freshwater bodies in the world, covering almost 250 000 square kilometres, 36% in Canada and 64% in the United States.

Lionel Stevenson / Camera Art

Trees and fields, Prince Edward Island.

Groundwater and alpine glaciers contribute to stream-flow. In the Prairies, groundwater is the principal source of streams during extended dry periods. In the hot summer months, glaciers contribute up to 25% of the flow of the Saskatchewan and Athabasca rivers.

The main measure of a country's water supply is its renewable water flow in rivers. Annually, Canada's rivers discharge roughly 105 000 cubic metres per second, nearly 9% of the world's renewable water supply and about 60% of Canada's mean annual precipitation.

Nearly half of the 8 900 kilometre Canada–United States border (including Alaska) lies along or across water bodies. Drainage basins along the border are economically important to both countries.

The Atlantic drainage basin is dominated by the Great Lakes-St. Lawrence system, which carries ocean-going vessels into the heart of North America and is one of the world's largest single freshwater reserves. These lakes are so vast they can absorb large variations in water flow while maintaining uniform outflow.

The Hudson Bay drainage basin is the largest in area, but sparse rainfall in its western region places it behind the Atlantic drainage basin in river flow. This basin supports agriculture to the west and hydro-electric development on the rivers surrounding Hudson Bay.

The mighty Mackenzie, one of the world's longest rivers, dominates the Arctic drainage basin. The river flows from the head of the Finlay River to the Arctic Ocean, draining an immense area in the three western

ACTION ON THE FRASER RIVER

A growing population and increased industrial activity have taken their toll on British Columbia's Fraser River basin. Dams, sewage, and industrial and agricultural pollution are affecting the basin's delicate ecosystem and damaging the salmon stocks, plants, birds and other wildlife that once thrived in its waters and along its shores.

However, a recent plan to nurse the basin back to health may mean the worst is over. In 1991, the federal government unveiled the Fraser River Action Plan (FRAP), a six-year, $100 million initiative to arrest and reverse environmental damage to the Fraser River and its 238 000 square kilometre drainage basin.

Covering more than 25% of the province, the basin supports almost 2 million people — 63% of BC's population — and the bulk of BC's economic activity, including forestry, mining, farming and tourism. It also produces more salmon than any other river system in the world, and is a key resting stop for millions of migratory birds.

Under the new plan, partnerships for managing the basin will be struck with provincial and local governments; aboriginal, environmental and community groups; and industry and labour.

Planners are also seeking to enhance the wildlife habitat and to increase the salmon population to its historic level of abundance.

To do this, they plan to clean up pollution by cutting the discharge of harmful liquid waste by 30% by 1997, and to drastically reduce the release of persistent toxins into the river by the year 2000.

Efforts to increase the ailing salmon population were already showing results even before FRAP was put in place. Around 1900, annual sockeye salmon runs in the Fraser River basin averaged more than 34 million. From 1975 to 1986, they had dropped to an average of less than 8 million fish. But in 1989 and 1990, the runs were up again to an average of 22 million fish — the largest runs since 1913.

provinces and the northern territories. Except for a 26-kilometre portage in Alberta, barge navigation is possible from Fort McMurray on the Athabasca River to the mouth of the Mackenzie, a distance of 2 700 kilometres.

Rivers in the **Pacific drainage basin** rise in the mountains of the Cordilleran region and flow to the Pacific Ocean through steep canyons and over innumerable falls and rapids. These rivers provide power for large hydroelectric developments and, in season, swarm with salmon returning inland to their spawning grounds.

USES OF INLAND WATER All economic activities use fresh water in some way. Of total fresh water withdrawal in 1986, mining accounted for roughly 2%, agriculture 8%, municipalities 11%, and manufacturing 19%. The greatest guzzler of water is the energy sector, accounting for 60% of freshwater use. In 1986 roughly 80 thermal electric plants, including 18 nuclear plants, used a staggering volume of water — equivalent to 54 days of continuous flow over Niagara Falls.

Water use is classified in either of two categories: consumptive, or non-consumptive. Agriculture, for example, is a consumptive user — the water is not returned to its original source after use. Non-consumptive uses, such as manufacturing or mining, return the water to its original source after use.

Dams built across large rivers capture the power of rushing water to provide electricity. Hydroelectricity accommodates about two-thirds of Canada's electrical needs. While this 'non-consumptive' use of water has been heralded as an environmentally clean energy source, dams are known to cause large-scale changes to aquatic and terrestrial ecosystems, including shrinkage of habitat for plants and animals that need fast-flowing water.

Along with fisheries operations and major transportation and shipping routes, Canada's vast network of rivers and lakes provide many recreational opportunities for Canadians. Water recreation occurs in many forms — swimming, fishing, skating, canoeing or simply resting by the water's edge — and in many places — remote northern communities or protected provincial or national parks and in or near major city centres. The country's inland waters are home for many species of wildlife.

COASTAL WATERS

Canada's coastline on the mainland and offshore islands is the world's longest at nearly 244 000 kilometres. The country's coastal waters support valuable biological resources such as fish, crustaceans, marine mammals and seaweeds. These waters are also important for transportation, and their mineral resources in the seafloor below.

Under the 1982 Law of the Sea Convention, which has been signed by Canada, but not yet proclaimed as international law, a country has less control over waters as distance from shore increases.

In internal waters — fiords, or deep bays, for example — foreigners have no rights and Canada's jurisdiction over these areas is much the same as it is on *terra firma*.

In the territorial sea, which extends up to 22.2 kilometres from the coast, foreigners have only right of innocent passage, otherwise Canada has all rights to the area.

In the exclusive economic zone, which extends up to 370 kilometres from the coast, Canada's coastal state has exclusive rights to manage the fishery and to exploit non-renewable resources on or under the seabed. The coastal state also controls pollution.

ATLANTIC Over time, the sea along the Atlantic Coast has inundated valleys, lower portions of the Appalachian Mountains, and the Canadian Shield. The width of the submerged continental shelf varies from 60 to 280 nautical miles (111 to 519 kilometres), and the outer edge varies in depth from 183 to 366 metres. The overall gradient of the Atlantic continental shelf is slight, but it is studded with shoals, plateaus, banks, ridges and islands. Deep channels and gullies cut into the shelf. Large areas undergo constant change because of the continuous deposit of materials eroded by rivers, wave action, wind and ice.

NORTHERN NATIONAL PARKS

Canada's northern national parks seem to have been created especially for lovers of the great outdoors. Natural areas protected by the federal government and managed by Environment Canada, these parks give Canadians the opportunity to appreciate the land, vegetation and wildlife as nature made them and provide for the continuation of traditional uses by aboriginal peoples.

To date, the federal government has protected seven areas in the Yukon and Northwest Territories under the National Parks Act. Only four, however, have been named as national parks: Wood Buffalo, Northern Yukon, Aulavik and Northern Baffin Island. The remaining four — Kluane, Nahanni, Auyuittuq and Ellesmere Island — are national park reserves, as their status is subject to the outcome of land claims negotiations that are currently under way between governments and aboriginal people.

Parks are not created overnight, but are the result of a lengthy process that can take from 10 to 15 years or even longer. The goal is to represent each of Canada's 39 natural regions in the national parks system. First, a comprehensive study of the region's land resources is made to identify representative natural areas. Once a potential park area is selected, a feasibility study is conducted, including an investigation of the current and potential uses of the area and extensive public consultations. If the proposal is feasible and has public support, a park agreement is negotiated involving aboriginal organizations and the territorial government.

According to Canada's Green Plan, the federal government will complete the national parks system by the year 2000. This will require seven more national parks to be established in northern Canada. Current proposals include: Old Crow Flats in the Yukon, and North Baffin, Bluenose, Wager Bay and the east arm of Great Slave Lake in the Northwest Territories.

THE SUNBURN SCALE

If Canadians are sporting wider-brimmed hats and thicker sunscreen in summer, there's a reason. Health advisories say damaging levels of ultraviolet (UV) radiation are reaching the ground. Because of this, in May 1992, the UV Index became part of our daily summer weather reports.

The index will tell you, on a scale of 0 to 10, what the strength of the day's UV rays are and predict the time it will take to sunburn. The higher the number, the better the idea of sun protection becomes. The highest UV levels are recorded in mid-day in the tropics, and typically, they would be a 10 on the UV Index. Here's how it works:

UV INDEX	CATEGORY	SUN BURN TIME
over 9	extreme	less than 15 minutes
7 — 9	high	about 20 minutes
4 — 7	moderate	about 30 minutes
0 — 4	low	more than one hour

UV refers to the sun's 'burning' rays, which increase the risk of skin cancer and eye cataracts. The earth's ozone layer absorbs much of the sun's UV in the upper atmosphere. Now, such culprits as industrial chemicals and other air pollutants are thinning the ozone layer. Ozone levels are down by 6% over the Arctic, and down by as much as 4% across the rest of Canada.

HUDSON BAY AND HUDSON STRAIT Hudson Bay is a shallow inland sea 822 324 square kilometres in area with an average depth of about 128 metres, and a maximum depth in the centre of the bay of 258 metres. Hudson Strait separates Baffin Island from the continental coast and connects Hudson bay with the Atlantic Ocean. It is 796 kilometres long and from 69 to 222 kilometres wide; its greatest depth of 880 metres is close inside the Atlantic entrance. While great irregularities in the seafloor exist, there are few navigational hazards, except in inshore waters.

PACIFIC The continental shelf of the Pacific is strikingly different from other marine zones of Canada. The hydrography of British Columbia is characterized by bold, abrupt relief — a repetition of the mountain landscape. Numerous inlets penetrate the mountainous coasts for distances of 93 to 139 kilometres; these are usually a nautical mile or two wide with deep canyon-like sides. From the islet-strewn coast, the continental shelf extends from 50 to 100 nautical miles (93 to 185 kilometres) to its limit at depths of about 366 metres. The seafloor drops rapidly from the western slopes of Vancouver Island and the Queen Charlotte Islands. These detached land masses are the dominant features of the shelf. Numerous shoals and pinnacle rocks necessitate cautious navigation.

ARCTIC To the north of Canada is part of the great continental shelf surrounding the Arctic Ocean. On this submerged plateau lie Greenland, all the Arctic islands of Canada, and most of the Arctic islands of Europe and Asia.

The floor of the submerged continental margin varies from nearly flat to gently undulating, with isolated rises and hollows. Most of it slants seaward, with an abrupt break at the outer edge to the continental slope. From the Alaskan border to the mouth of the Mackenzie River, the shelf is shallow; its outer edge is 40 nautical miles (74 kilometres) offshore at a depth of about 64 metres. Near the western edge of the Mackenzie River Delta, the shelf is indented by the deep Mackenzie Trough (formerly known as the Herschel Sea Canyon) the head of which comes within 15 nautical miles (28 kilometres) of the coast. The submerged portion of the Mackenzie Delta forms a great pock-marked

John Sylvester / First Light

Frost on birch trees, Prince Edward Island.

undersea plain, most of it less than 55 metres deep. This plain is 250 miles (402 kilometres) long and up to 75 nautical miles (139 kilometres) wide. North and east of it, the continental shelf is more deeply submerged. Most of the well-defined continental shoulder is over 549 metres deep; this gives way to a smooth continental slope extending to the Canada Basin at about 3 658 metres.

The deeply submerged continental shelf runs along the entire west coast of the Canadian Arctic Archipelago from Banks Island to Greenland. Major channels between the islands have flat floors at about the same depth as the shelf. Local irregularities may be the result of glacial action. The only deep indentation is a sinuous canyon that heads off Robeson Channel close to Greenland. A series of steps marks the submerged sides of the Archipelago channels, and the slopes on the islands' western shores.

ISLANDS

In the North, Canada's largest islands lie within the Canadian Arctic region, extending from the islands in James Bay to Ellesmere Island, which reaches 83° north. With an area of 507 451 square kilometres, Baffin Island is Canada's largest island — almost 90 times the size of Prince Edward Island.

The largest West Coast islands are Vancouver Island and the Queen Charlotte Islands; but the coastal waters are studded with many smaller rocky islands. On the East Coast, the largest islands are the Island of Newfoundland, Prince Edward Island, Cape Breton Island, Grand Manan and Campobello islands of New Brunswick, and Anticosti Island and the Îles-de-la-Madeleine of Quebec.

SNOW BY ANY NAME

Into every Canadian's life, it seems, at least a little snow must fall. Most live with it, or in it, for a third or more of each year, and even the inhabitants of the temperate West Coast get an occasional storm. It follows that we don't lack colourful descriptions for the white stuff. Skiers describe their playgrounds in terms of ''powder,'' ''corn'' or ''hardpack,'' winter's pedestrians may wade through ''slush'' or ''drifts,'' and weather forecasters routinely speak of ''flurries,'' ''squalls'' or ''blizzards.''

But the most numerous and precise names come, arguably, from the Inuit, some of the country's first inhabitants. Because they live along the fringes of the Arctic, their lives are acutely affected by snow for long periods. In a land where hunting, travel and shelter — indeed, survival — have depended on constantly changing snow conditions, it's vital to communicate these conditions precisely.

The Inuit have a rainbow of names for snow, describing the way it looks as it falls, its appearance on the ground, and ways to use it. For instance, snow that is being melted for drinking water and snow used to build snow houses have different labels.

These words are taken from dialects of the Inuktitut language, which is part of the Eskimo-Aleut language family. Mostly spoken in the eastern Arctic, it may nonetheless hold options for Canadians looking for other ways to refer to powder, slush, or ''that white stuff''. To that end, the following list is offered:

▲ **Aniu:** Snow for making water (by melting, to drink or for cooking purposes).

▲ **Aniugaviniq:** Very hard, compressed and frozen snow.

▲ **Apigianngaut:** The very first snowfall of autumn.

▲ **Apijaq:** Snow covered by bad weather.

▲ **Aput:** Snow on the ground.

▲ **Isiriartaq:** Snow that falls yellow or reddened, as though it were smoked as it fell.

▲ **Atsakaaq:** Ball of snow made by rolling snow on the ground (unlike hand-made snowball).

▲ **Katakartanaq:** Snow with a hard crust that gives way under footsteps.

▲ **Kavisilaq:** Snow roughened by rain and frost.

▲	*Kinirtaq:*	Compact, damp snow; with a consistency like bannock or sourdough (bread dough). Of a thick consistency having little water. Describes dough, molasses, or damp snow that is compact because it is soaked, but which has lost some of its water.
▲	*Mannguq:*	Melting snow.
▲	*Masak:*	Wet falling snow (but not snow on the ground).
▲	*Masavuq:*	Soft snow falls.
▲	*Masaaqijuq:*	Soft snow is falling.
▲	*Matsaaq:*	Snow soaked in water; half-melted (either on the ground or in a billy can over a fire).
▲	*Natiruvaaq:*	Fine snow carried by the wind or deposited by the wind; drifting snow.
▲	*Pukaangajuq:*	Snow that is sufficiently crystallized; good enough to make a snow house.
▲	*Pukak or Pukaq:*	Crystalline snow that breaks down, that separates and looks like coarse salt (often found on the ground, when digging down beneath other levels of snow).
▲	*Qannialaaq:*	Light falling snow.
▲	*Qannik:*	Snow which falls; snow flakes.
▲	*Qiasuqaq:*	Snow that has thawed and then become refrozen with an iced surface.
▲	*Qiqumaaq:*	Snow with a frozen surface, usually found after a light spring thaw.

Other Inuktitut words related to snow include **allaatautik, amittukaaq, ammalukitaak** *and* **tulluk**, *all of which describe types of snowshoes; and* **piirsituq** *or* **pirsituq**, *which mean, simply, ''it is snowing.''*

Darwin R. Wiggett / First Light

Red Rock Coulee, Alberta.

Notable islands in inland water include Manitoulin Island in Lake Huron, the Thirty Thousand Islands of Georgian Bay, and the Thousand Islands in the outlet from Lake Ontario into the St. Lawrence River.

TIME ZONES

Canada has six time zones. The most easterly, Newfoundland standard time, is three hours and 30 minutes behind Co-ordinated Universal Time (UTC). The most westerly, Pacific standard time, is eight hours behind UTC. From east to west, the remaining zones are called Atlantic, eastern, central and mountain. For daylight saving time, clocks across the country (except in Saskatchewan) are set forward one hour on the first Sunday in April. On the last Sunday in October, the nation's clocks are reset to standard time.

GOVERNMENT SURVEYING, MAPPING AND REMOTE SENSING

Energy, Mines and Resources Canada (EMR) is the federal department responsible for collecting and analyzing data on Canada's diverse land forms. The department's Surveys, Mapping and Remote Sensing Sector produces reliable surveys, maps, remotely-sensed data and geographic information covering the Canadian land mass. The sector promotes the development of geographic information technologies and of related expertise in government, academia and private industry. As a world leader in geomatics, the sector helps to develop Canada's economy and international trade.

The Canada Centre for Surveying is a leader in satellite positioning and other state-of-the-art techniques used to establish positional frameworks that are fundamental to all forms of surveying. The centre oversees surveys on all areas under the Canada Lands Survey Act, including native reserves, national parks, offshore areas and the northern territories. The centre also maintains the border shared by Canada and the United States.

The Canada Centre for Mapping (CCM) is responsible for producing National Topographic System maps, the *National Atlas of Canada*, the *Gazetteer of Canada* series, aeronautical charts and other map products. The centre produces maps in a fully digital environment, from a growing data base of topographic information that has been created and maintained by the Canada Centre for Geomatics. CCM also maintains a national data base on the status, origin and location of over 500,000 physical features and populated places in Canada.

The Canada Centre for Remote Sensing collects data on satellites and develops applications for satellite, airborne and radar data. A number of national and international projects linked to vegetation monitoring, global change research and resource management have fostered Canada's excellent worldwide reputation as a supplier of remote sensing products and services. The centre is also responsible for the ground receiving system and applications development for Canada's RADARSAT satellite, scheduled for launch in 1995.

PROTECTING CANADA'S HERITAGE

ENVIRONMENT CANADA   Environment Canada is the federal government agency that works to achieve a balance between the needs of society and the long-term viability of natural ecosystems.

Toxic substances, especially those that do not readily degrade in the environment, can have a cumulative effect on all living things, including humans.

The Canadian Environmental Protection Act (CEPA), proclaimed on June 28, 1988, is a framework for protecting Canadians from pollution caused by toxic substances. CEPA consolidates the Environmental Contaminants Act, the Canada Water Act, Part III, the Clean Air Act, the Ocean Dumping Control Act and Section 6(2) of the Department of the Environment Act (1979).

CEPA requires that industries and government deal responsibly with the thousands of toxic substances used in products sold in Canada, and with the hundreds of sources of toxic discharges. The legislation improves the federal government's ability to manage use of toxic chemicals by improving enforcement methods and making punishment of polluters tougher — penalties for non-compliance may include fines of up to $1 million per day and imprisonment for up to five years.

ACID RAIN   Acid rain is mainly caused by emissions of sulphur dioxide (SO_2) and nitrogen oxides (NO_x) from power plants and metals smelters. This precipitation has long been a serious pollution problem, especially in Eastern Canada: it kills fish and other aquatic life, injures trees and other plants, and damages buildings and monuments. Quite literally, acid rain has been destroying some of the country's heritage.

Since the mid-1980s, Canada has been fighting acid rain through co-operative efforts between the government and industry. In the late 1980s, the federal government and seven of the easternmost provinces launched a federal-provincial program to cut SO_2 emissions by almost 50% from 1980 levels before 1995. In March 1991, Canada signed the Canada–United States Air Quality Agreement, which commits both countries to co-operate in reducing emissions by fixed amounts within certain time periods. Canada has committed to achieving a cap of 3.2 million tonnes of SO_2 emissions by the year 2000.

OZONE   Ozone layer depletion leads to increased ultraviolet radiation, which has been linked to skin cancer, crop damage and premature aging of various materials. Ozone depletion is caused by emissions of chlorofluorocarbons (CFCs) and other long-lived chlorine-containing and bromine-containing chemicals.

An important participant in the international effort to address this global problem, Canada hosted the meeting resulting in global controls on ozone-depleting substances — the 1987 Montreal Protocol on Substances that Deplete the Ozone Layer. Canada also

Robert Semeniuk / First Light

Bylot Island, Northwest Territories.

helped strengthen this protocol at a 1990 meeting in London, England, and called for tighter phase-out schedules at a 1991 meeting in Copenhagen. Amended schedules now call for a phase-out of halon production and consumption by 1994 and of CFCs, methyl chloroform and carbon tetrachloride production and consumption by 1996. At the Copenhagen meeting, parties to the Montreal Protocol also adopted Canada's proposal to take all practicable measures to minimize emissions of ozone-depleting substances including recovery and recycling programs.

CLIMATE CHANGE Climate change occurs as deforestation, land-use changes, industrial processes and the burning of fossil fuels increase the concentrations of so-called greenhouse gases in the atmosphere.

Carbon dioxide (CO_2) is the most abundant of these climate-controlling gases; half the CO_2 emitted in human history has been emitted in the last 30 years, and emissions continue to rise 4% per decade.

WATER RESOURCES Managing and preserving Canada's freshwater ecosystems is one of the most pressing environmental challenges on the horizon. Some 75% of Canadians rely on surface water for domestic water supply; the remainder rely on groundwater. Both the quality and supply of these water sources is increasingly threatened. Major concerns focus on: surface and groundwater contamination resulting from industrial effluents, agricultural runoff, landfill leachates, poorly treated sewage and long-range transport of airborne contaminants.

Environment Canada's *Green Plan*, released in 1990, outlines the federal government's commitment to finding solutions to some of the problems threatening Canada's aquatic ecosystems. The Drinking Water Safety Act, promised in the *Green Plan*, provides authority for legally enforceable standards for drinking water in areas under federal jurisdiction. Increasingly, federal and provincial governments, environmental non-governmental organizations and individual Canadians are paying more attention to what actually goes into Canada's water supply, rather than on what comes out.

WETLAND CONSERVATION

Wetlands are among the country's most precious landscapes. Not only do they act as sponges, providing protection against flooding, they also function as the land's 'kidneys', filtering water and reducing pollution. Currently, almost 14%, or 127 million hectares of Canada's land surface, is covered by wetlands. However, since European settlement, an astonishingly high percentage of the country's wetlands has been lost to agricultural expansion — including 80% of wetlands in British Columbia's Fraser River Delta, 70% of the prairie wetlands, 70% of the St. Lawrence-Great Lakes Region wetlands, and 65% of Atlantic coastal marshes. Today, pressures are highest on the remaining wetlands in farmlands of the southern areas of Manitoba, Saskatchewan and Alberta.

Wetlands also provide breeding grounds and migration stops for tens of thousands of waterfowl. The North American Waterfowl Management Plan (NAWMP), signed in 1986 by Canada and the United States, calls for the preservation of 15 000 square kilometres of wetlands in the Prairies and the Great Lakes Basin by the year 2000. This agreement will bring seriously declining waterfowl populations back to the level of the 1970s, when the average fall migration was about 100 million birds.

NAWMP will be implemented over a 15-year period. It seeks to restore the mid-continental habitat of mallard and pintail ducks by protecting and improving 1.5 million hectares of waterfowl habitat in Canada and the United States. Additional wetlands will be protected along the lower Mississippi River and the Gulf Coast, on the Pacific Coast, and in California's

Central Valley. Other projects will protect black duck habitat in Eastern Canada and on the East Coast of the United States. The first waterfowl habitat enhancement and protection project under NAWMP was established in the Quill Lakes area of Saskatchewan in 1988.

SUSTAINABLE DEVELOPMENT

Environmental indicators are measures of critical factors that provide information regarding the health of the environment, much in the way that a pulse or a temperature reading indicates the state of a person's health. These indicators, polychlorinated biphenyls (PCBs) levels in seabird eggs, for example, reflect certain aspects of environmental quality. Over time, these factors indicate how the environment is responding to stresses, and to remedial actions taken to relieve stresses.

In 1991, Environment Canada's Indicators Task Force released a preliminary list of environmental indicators that will serve as a starting point for systematic monitoring of changes in the state of Canada's environment.

Environment Canada's role in promoting sustainable development further includes establishing conservation strategies as development blueprints; building a solid base of environmental knowledge; providing information on environmentally sound development; influencing federal programs so that environmental objectives are achieved along with economic ones; and developing policies, methods and tools to help make sustainable development a reality.

STATE OF THE ENVIRONMENT

Since 1986, Environment Canada and Statistics Canada have jointly established a State of the Environment (SOE) reporting system. SOE reporting has been a legislative requirement since the Canadian Environmental Protection Act was proclaimed in June 1988.

Systematic environmental reporting helps to build a reliable bank of information on natural resource use and environmental quality. SOE reporting helps to develop accurate progress reports relating environmental problems, to identify emerging issues and to encourage the sustainable use of natural resources.

NATIONAL PARKS
AND HISTORIC SITES

THE RACE FOR SPACE From small ecological reserves and historic sites, to large national and provincial parks and game sanctuaries, protected areas in Canada all play an important role in preserving our natural and cultural heritage. Currently about 7% of the country has some form of protection. The federal *Green Plan* recommends that Canada set aside 12% of its total area as protected space.

Many factors are considered in assessing the range of protected sites in Canada: the degree of protection necessary in each area; its size and geographic location; and its ecological relevance. Accordingly, 39 land regions and 29 marine regions have been identified as representative of Canada's physical, biological and oceanographic characteristics.

There are also many types of protected areas in Canada — parks, reserves, conservation areas and sanctuaries are a few examples. Each protected area has a different purpose and its own niche in Canada's network of protected areas. The larger areas may contain many different zones that individually fulfil different objectives in one area.

Canada's 36 national terrestrial parks cover over 200 000 square kilometres of territory — almost 2% of the country's area. Two marine parks protect 285 square kilometres of Canada's marine territory.

The first national park was established in the Rocky Mountains near Banff in 1885. Since then, the parks system has expanded to include at least one national park in each province and territory. These parks represent 24 terrestrial regions and 5 marine regions. More than 100 national historic parks and historic sites have also been created, while more than 1,000 persons and events of national significance have been commemorated with plaques or distinctive monuments. Over time, the federal government plans to expand the parks system to include a national park in each of the 39 natural regions.

About 20 million visits a year are recorded in the national parks.

PROVINCIAL PARKS The provinces have also established parks. Some are wilderness areas left in their natural state, but the majority are smaller scenic areas, easily accessible and equipped with camping and picnic facilities. In recent years, some of the provinces and both of the northern territories have joined the federal government in a co-operative program to heighten national recognition and increase protection to rivers and waterways that are ecologically significant, that offer outstanding recreation, or that have historical importance.

SOURCES

Energy Mines and Resources Canada

Environment Canada

Fisheries and Oceans

National Research Council Canada

Statistics Canada

Provincial government departments

FOR FURTHER READING

Selected publications from Statistics Canada

▲ *Canada: A Portrait. Biennial. 11-403E*

▲ *Human Activity and the Environment. 1991. 11-509E*

▲ *Census Divisions and Census Subdivisions, Reference Maps. 1991. Census. 92-319*

▲ *Maps, Census Metropolitan Areas, Census Agglomerations and Census Tracts, 1991. Census. 92-320*

Selected publications from Other Sources

▲ *The State of Canada's Environment. Environment Canada, 1991.*

A wide range of Canadian geographic information and documentation is available from Energy, Mines and Resources Canada. The *National Atlas of Canada* and the *Gazetteer of Canada* series are produced by the Canada Centre for Mapping. Maps, aeronautical charts and air information publications may be purchased from the Canada Map Office. Reproductions of federal aerial photographs as well as custom reproductions, mosaics, microfilm, colour transparencies of selected LANDSAT images and photomaps of certain parts of the country can be obtained from the National Air Photo Library. New types of products such as videodiscs containing maps in analogue form and image maps combining satellite imagery and topographic data are also available from the Canada Map Office.

TABLES

1.1   LAND AND FRESHWATER AREA

	Land km²	Freshwater km²	Total km²	Percentage of total area
Newfoundland	371 690	34 030	405 720	4.1
Prince Edward Island	5 660	—	5 660	0.1
Nova Scotia	52 840	2 650	55 490	0.6
New Brunswick	72 090	1 350	73 440	0.7
Quebec	1 356 790	183 890	1 540 680	15.5
Ontario	891 190	177 390	1 068 580	10.7
Manitoba	548 360	101 590	649 950	6.5
Saskatchewan	570 700	81 630	652 330	6.5
Alberta	644 390	16 800	661 190	6.6
British Columbia	929 730	18 070	947 800	9.5
Yukon Territory	478 970	4 480	483 450	4.8
Northwest Territories	3 293 020	133 300	3 426 320	34.4
Canada	9 215 430	755 180	9 970 610	100.0

1.2   PRINCIPAL HEIGHTS

Province and height	Elevation m	Province and height	Elevation m
NEWFOUNDLAND		QUEBEC (concluded)	
Torngat Mountains		Mont Gosford	1 192
Mount Caubvick[1] (highest point in Nfld.)	1 652	Mont Richardson	1 185
Cirque Mountain	1 568	Mont Mégantic	1 105
Mealy Mountains		Les Laurentides	
Unnamed peak (53°37' 58°33')	1 176	Unnamed peak (47°19' 70°50')	1 166
Kaumajet Mountains		Mont Tremblant	968
Bishops Mitre	1 113	Mont Sainte-Anne	800
Long Range Mountains		Mont Sir-Wilfrid	783
Lewis Hills	814	Monts Otish	
Gros Morne	806	Unnamed peak (52°19' 71°27')	1 135
		Collines Montérégiennes	
PRINCE EDWARD ISLAND		Mont Brome	533
Highest point			
Queen's County (46°20' 63°25')	142	ONTARIO	
		Ishpatina Ridge (highest point in Ont.)	693
NOVA SCOTIA		Ogidaki Mountain	665
Highest point		Batchawana Mountain	653
Cape Breton Highlands (46°42' 60°36')	532	Tip Top Mountain	640
		Niagara Escarpment	
NEW BRUNSWICK		Blue Mountains	541
Mount Carleton (highest point in NB)	817	Osler Bluff	526
Wilkinson Mountain	785	Caledon Mountain	427
QUEBEC		MANITOBA	
Monts Torngat		Baldy Mountain (highest point in Man.)	832
Mont D'Iberville (highest point in Que.)	1 652	Highest point in Porcupine Hills	823
Les Appalaches		Riding Mountain	610
Mont Jacques-Cartier	1 268		

1.2 PRINCIPAL HEIGHTS (concluded)

Province and height	Elevation m	Province and height	Elevation m
SASKATCHEWAN		BRITISH COLUMBIA (concluded)	
Cypress Hills (highest point in Sask.)	1 468	Purcell Mountains	
Wood Mountain	1 013	Mount Farnham	3 481
Vermilion Hills	785	Monashee Mountains	
		Torii Mountain	3 429
ALBERTA			
Rocky Mountains		YUKON TERRITORY	
Mount Columbia (highest point on Alta.-BC boundary)	3 747	St. Elias Mountains	
North Twin	3 733	Mount Logan (highest point in Canada)	5 959
Mount Alberta	3 620	Mount St. Elias (on Alaska-Yukon boundary)	5 489
Mount Assiniboine (on Alta.-BC boundary)	3 618	Mount Lucania	5 226
Mount Forbes	3 612	King Peak	5 173
South Twin	3 581	Mount Steele	5 067
Mount Temple	3 547	Mount Wood	4 838
Mount Brazeau	3 525	Mount Vancouver (on Alaska-Yukon boundary)	4 785
Snow Dome (on Alta.-BC boundary)	3 520	Mount Macaulay	4 663
Mount Lyell (on Alta.-BC boundary)	3 504	Mount Hubbard (on Alaska-Yukon boundary)	4 577
Mount Athabasca	3 491		
Mount King Edward (on Alta.-BC boundary)	3 490	NORTHWEST TERRITORIES	
Mount Kitchener	3 490	Mackenzie Mountains	
		Unnamed peak (61°52' 127°42')	
BRITISH COLUMBIA		(highest point in NWT)	2 773
St. Elias Mountains		Mount Sir James MacBrien	2 762
Fairweather Mountain (highest point		Ellesmere Island	
on Alaska-BC boundary)	4 663	Barbeau Peak	2 616
Coast Mountains		Baffin Island	
Mount Waddington	4 016	Mount Odin	2 147
Rocky Mountains		Devon Island	
Mount Robson	3 954	Summit Devon Ice Cap	1 920
Mount Columbia (on Alta.-BC boundary)	3 747	Franklin Mountains	
Mount Clemcnceau	3 642	Cap Mountain	1 577
Mount Assiniboine (on Alta.-BC boundary)	3 618	Mount Clark	1 462
Mount Goodsir: North Tower	3 581	Pointed Mountain	1 405
Mount Goodsir: South Tower	3 520	Nahanni Butte	1 396
Snow Dome (on Alta.-BC boundary)	3 520	Banks Island	
Mount Bryce	3 507	Durham Heights	732
Selkirk Mountains		Victoria Island	
Mount Sir Sandford	3 522	Unnamed peak	655
Cariboo Mountains			
Mount Sir Wilfrid Laurier	3 520		

[1] *Mount Caubvick is also known as Mont D'Iberville in Quebec.*

1.3 THE GREAT LAKES

	Elevation[1] m	Length km	Breadth km	Maximum depth m	Total area km²	Area on Canadian side of boundary km²
Superior	184	563	257	405	82 100	28 700
Michigan	176	494	190	281	57 800	—
Huron	177	332	295	229	59 600	36 000
Erie	174	388	92	64	25 700	12 800
Ontario	75	311	85	244	18 960	10 000

[1] *Long-term mean 1860–1972; International Great Lakes Datum, 1955.*

1.4 PRINCIPAL LAKES[1] EXCEEDING 600 KM[2]

Province and lake	Elevation m	Area km[2]	Province and lake	Elevation m	Area km[2]
NEWFOUNDLAND AND LABRADOR			**SASKATCHEWAN (concluded)**		
Smallwood Reservoir	471	6 527	Lac La Rouge	364	1 413
Melville Lake	tidal	3 069	Peter Pond Lake	421	778
			Doré Lake	459	640
NOVA SCOTIA					
Bras d'Or Lake	tidal	1 099	**ALBERTA**		
			Lake Clair	213	1 436
QUEBEC			Lesser Slave Lake	577	1 168
Lac Mistassini	372	2 335			
Réservoir Manicouagan	360	1 942	**BRITISH COLUMBIA**		
Réservoir Gouin	404	1 570	Williston Lake	671	1 761
Lac à l'Eau-Claire	241	1 383	Atlin Lake[2]	668	775
Lac Bienville	426	1 249			
Lac Saint-Jean	98	1 003	**YUKON TERRITORY**		
Réservoir Pipmuacan	396	978	Kluane Lake	409	781
Lac Minto	168	761			
Réservoir Cabonga	361	677	**NORTHWEST TERRITORIES**		
			Great Bear Lake[3]	156	31 328
ONTARIO			Great Slave Lake	156	28 568
Lake Nipigon	320	4 848	Nettilling Lake	30	5 542
Lake of the Woods[2] (total 4 472)	323	3 150	Dubawnt Lake	236	3 833
Lac Seul	357	1 657	Amadjuak Lake	113	3 115
Lake Abitibi[2]	265	931	Nueltin Lake	278	2 279
Lake Nipissing	196	832	Baker Lake	2	1 887
Lake Simcoe	219	744	Lac la Martre	265	1 776
Rainy Lake (total 932)	338	741	Yathkyed Lake	140	1 449
Big Trout Lake	213	661	Kasba Lake	336	1 341
Lake St. Clair (total 1 210)	175	490	Aberdeen Lake	80	1 100
			Napaktulik Lake	381	1 080
MANITOBA			MacKay Lake	431	1 061
Lake Winnipeg	217	24 387	Garry Lake	148	976
Lake Winnipegosis	254	5 374	Contwoyto Lake	564	957
Lake Manitoba	248	4 624	Hottah Lake	180	918
Southern Indian Lake	254	2 247	Aylmer Lake	375	847
Cedar Lake	253	1 353	Nonacho Lake	354	784
Island Lake	227	1 223	Clinton-Colden Lake	375	737
Gods Lake	178	1 151	Selwyn Lake	398	717
Cross Lake	207	755	Point Lake	375	701
Playgreen Lake	217	657	Ennadai Lake	311	681
			Wholdaia Lake	364	678
SASKATCHEWAN			Tulemalu Lake	279	668
Lake Athabasca	213	7 935	Kamilukuak Lake	266	638
Reindeer Lake	377	6 650	Lac de Gras	396	633
Wollaston Lake	398	2 681	Buffalo Lake	265	612
Cree Lake	487	1 434	Kaminak Lake	53	600

[1] *Excludes Great Lakes, see Table 1.3.*
[2] *Spans provincial or territorial boundary. Listed under province or territory containing larger portion.*
[3] *Largest lake wholly in Canada.*

1.5 PRINCIPAL RIVERS AND THEIR TRIBUTARIES

Drainage basin and river	Drainage area km²	Length km
FLOWING INTO THE PACIFIC OCEAN		
Yukon (mouth to head of Nisutlin)	. .	3 185
(International Boundary to head of Nisutlin)	323 800	1 149
Porcupine	61 400	721
Stewart	51 000	644
Pelly	51 000	608
Teslin	35 500	393
White	38 000	265
Columbia (mouth to head of Columbia Lake)	. .	2 000
(International Boundary to head of Columbia Lake)	102 800	801
Kootenay	37 700	780
Kettle (to head of Holmes Lake)	4 700	336
Okanagan (to head of Okanagan Lake)	21 600	314
Fraser	232 300	1 370
Thompson (to head of North Thompson)	55 400	489
North Thompson	20 700	338
South Thompson (to head of Shuswap)	17 800	332
Nechako (to head of Eutsuk Lake)	47 100	462
Stuart (to head of Driftwood)	16 200	415
Skeena	54 400	579
Stikine	49 800	539
Nass	21 100	380
FLOWING INTO THE ARCTIC OCEAN		
Mackenzie (to head of Finlay)	1 805 200	4 241
Peace (to head of Finlay)	302 500	1 923
Smoky	51 300	492
Athabasca	95 300	1 231
Pembina	12 900	547
Liard	277 100	1 115
South Nahanni	36 300	563
Fort Nelson (to head of Sikanni Chief)	55 900	517
Petitot	. .	404
Hay	48 200	702
Peel (mouth of west Channel to head of Ogilvie)	73 600	684
Arctic Red	. .	499
Slave (from Peace River to Great Slave Lake)	616 400	415
Fond du Lac (to outlet of Wollaston Lake)	66 800	277
Back (to outlet of Muskox Lake)	106 500	974
Coppermine	. .	845
Anderson	. .	692
Horton	. .	618
FLOWING INTO HUDSON BAY AND HUDSON STRAIT		
Nelson (to head of Bow)	892 300	2 575
(to outlet of Lake Winnipeg)	802 900	644
Saskatchewan (to head of Bow)	334 100	1 939
South Saskatchewan (to head of Bow)	144 300	1 392
Red Deer	45 100	724
Bow	26 200	587
Oldman	26 700	362
North Saskatchewan	12 800	1 287
Battle (to head of Pigeon Lake)	30 300	570
Red (to head of Sheyenne)	138 600	877
Assiniboine	160 600	1 070
Winnipeg (to head of Firesteel)	106 500	813
English	52 300	615

1.5 PRINCIPAL RIVERS AND THEIR TRIBUTARIES (concluded)

Drainage basin and river	Drainage area km²	Length km
FLOWING INTO HUDSON BAY AND HUDSON STRAIT (concluded)		
Fairford (to head of Manitoba Red Deer)	80 300	684
Churchill (to head of Churchill Lake)	281 300	1 609
Beaver (to outlet of Beaver Lake)	. .	491
Severn (to head of Black Birch)	102 800	982
Albany (to head of Cat)	135 200	982
Thelon	142 400	904
Dubawnt	57 500	842
La Grande-Rivière (Fort George River)	97 600	893
Koksoak (to head of Caniapiscau)	133 400	874
Nottaway (via Bell to head of Mégiscane)	65 800	776
Rupert (to head of Témiscamie)	43 400	763
Eastmain	46 400	756
Attawapiskat (to head of Bow Lake)	50 500	748
Kazan (to head of Ennadai Lake)	71 500	732
Grande rivière de la Baleine	42 700	724
George	41 700	565
Moose (to head of Mattagami)	108 500	547
Abitibi (to head of Louis Lake)	29 500	547
Mattagami (to head of Minisinakwa Lake)	37 000	443
Missinaibi	23 500	426
Harricana/Harricanaw	29 300	533
Hayes	108 000	483
aux Feuilles	42 500	480
Winisk	67 300	475
Broadback	20 800	450
à la Baleine	31 900	428
de Povungnituk	28 500	389
Innuksuac	11 400	385
Petite rivière de la Baleine	15 900	380
Arnaud	49 500	377
Nastapoca	13 400	360
Kogaluc	11 600	304
FLOWING INTO THE ATLANTIC OCEAN		
St. Lawrence River	839 200	3 058
Nipigon (to head of Ombabika)	25 400	209
Spanish	14 000	338
Trent (to head of Irondale)	12 400	402
Ottawa River	146 300	1 271
Gatineau	23 700	386
du Lièvre	. .	330
Saguenay (to head of Péribonca)	88 000	698
Péribonca	28 200	451
Mistassini	21 900	298
Chamouchouane	. .	266
Saint-Maurice	43 300	563
Manicouagan (to head of Mouchalagane)	45 800	560
aux Outardes	19 000	499
Romaine	14 350	496
Betsiamites (to head of Manouanis)	18 700	444
Moisie	19 200	410
St-Augustin	9 900	233
Richelieu (to mouth of Lake Champlain)	3 800	171
Churchill (to head of Ashuanipi)	79 800	856
Saint John	35 500	673
Little Mecatina	19 600	547
Natashquan	16 100	410

1.6 AREAS OF MAJOR[1] SEA ISLANDS, BY REGION (SQUARE KILOMETERS)

	Area		Area
Baffin Island	507 451	Arctic Islands south of Queen Elizabeth Islands (but north of the Arctic Circle)[2] (concluded)	
Queen Elizabeth Islands		Richards	2 165
Ellesmere	196 236	Air Force	1 720
Devon	55 247	Wales	1 137
Axel Heiberg	43 178	Rowley	1 090
Melville	42 149		
Bathurst	16 042	Northwest Territories south of the Arctic Circle	
Prince Patrick	15 848	Southampton[3]	41 214
Ellef Ringnes	11 295	Coats[3]	5 498
Cornwallis	6 995	Mansel[3]	3 180
Amund Ringnes	5 255	Akimski[3]	3 001
Mackenzie King	5 048	Flaherty[3]	1 585
Borden	2 794	Nottingham[4]	1 372
Cornwall	2 258	Resolution[4]	1 015
Eglinton	1 541		
Graham	1 378	Pacific Coast	
Lougheed	1 308	Vancouver	31 285
Byam Martin	1 150	Graham	6 361
Île Vanier	1 126	Moresby	2 608
Cameron	1 059	Princess Royal	2 251
		Pitt	1 375
Arctic Islands south of Queen Elizabeth Islands (but north of the Arctic Circle)[2]		Atlantic Coast and gulf of St. Lawrence	
Victoria	217 291	Newfoundland and Labrador	
Banks	70 028	Newfoundland (main island)	108 860
Prince of Wales	33 339	Gulf of St. Lawrence	
Somerset	24 786	Cape Breton	10 311
King William	13 111	Anticosti	7 941
Bylot	11 067	Prince Edward	5 620
Prince Charles	9 521	Bay of Fundy	
Stefansson	4 463	Grand Manan	137

[1] *A major island has a land area greater than 130 km², a minor island less than that.*
[2] *There are no islands over 130 km² in the Yukon Territory.*
[3] *Keewatin District.*
[4] *Franklin District.*

1.7 NATIONAL PARKS

Park and year established	Area km²	Location	Description
Banff 1885	6 640.8	Western Alberta, on east slope of Rocky Mountains	Scenic mountain area, Banff and Lake Louise resorts. Mineral hot springs. Summer and winter sports. Commercial accommodation. Campgrounds.
Yoho 1886	1 313.1	Eastern British Columbia, on west slope of Rockies	Mountain peaks, waterfalls and lakes. Yoho and Kicking Horse valleys. Commercial accommodation. Campgrounds.
Glacier 1886	1 349.4	Eastern British Columbia in the Selkirk Mountains	Alpine region, towering peaks, glaciers and forests. Climbing, ski touring, camping.
Waterton Lakes 1895	525.8	Southern Alberta, adjoining Glacier Park in Montana	Mountainous area with peaks and lakes. Commercial accommodation. Campgrounds.
Jasper 1907	10 878.0	Western Alberta, on east slope of Rockies	1 000 km of trails. Icefields, lakes. Mineral hot springs. Summer and winter sports. Commercial accommodation. Campgrounds.
Elk Island 1913	194.3	Central Alberta	Fenced preserve with large herds of buffalo, deer, elk and moose. Summer and winter sports. Campgrounds.
Mount Revelstoke 1914	262.6	Eastern British Columbia, on west slope of Selkirks	Mountain-top plateau, alpine meadows and mountain lakes. No campgrounds.
St. Lawrence Islands 1914	4.1	St. Lawrence River between Brockville and Kingston, Ontario	Mainland area and 17 islands among the Thousand Islands. Accessible by boat from mainland points. Campgrounds.
Point Pelee 1918	15.5	On Lake Erie, south-western Ontario	Wildlife. Beaches, marsh area, southern flora, nature trails. Staging ground for migratory birds.
Kootenay 1920	1 377.9	Southeast British Columbia, on west slope of Rockies	Includes section of Banff-Windemere Highway. Broad valleys, deep canyons, mineral hot springs. Commercial accommodation nearby. Campgrounds.
Wood Buffalo 1922	44 807.0	Alberta and Northwest Territories	Forests and open plains. Mainly a wildlife sanctuary. Largest herds of free roaming bison in world. Accessible from Fort Smith, NWT. Campgrounds.
Prince Albert 1927	3 847.6	Central Saskatchewan	Forest region. Lakes and streams. Summer and winter recreation. Commercial accommodation. Campgrounds.

1.7 NATIONAL PARKS (continued)

Park and year established	Area km²	Location	Description
Riding Mountain 1929	2 975.9	Southwest Manitoba	Wildlife sanctuary on escarpment. Lakes. Commercial accommodation. Campgrounds. Summer and winter recreation.
Georgian Bay Islands 1929	14.2	In Georgian Bay, near Honey Harbour, Ontario	Accessible by boat. Unusual geological formations on Flowerpot Island. Campgrounds. Picnic areas.
Cape Breton Highlands 1936	950.5	Northern Cape Breton Island, Nova Scotia	Rugged Atlantic coastline. Fine seascapes. Commercial accommodation. Campgrounds.
Prince Edward Island 1937	18.1	North shore, Prince Edward Island	Tennis, golf, bathing beaches. Commercial accommodation. Campgrounds.
Fundy 1948	205.9	On Bay of Fundy in New Brunswick	Forested region, wildlife, rugged terrain. Commercial accommodation. Campgrounds. Winter and summer recreation.
Terra Nova 1957	396.5	On Bonavista Bay, New- foundland (North of St. John's)	Maritime area, rocky headlands and forests. Sport fishing. Commercial accommodation. Campgrounds.
Kejimkujik 1968	381.5	South-central Nova Scotia	Inland park. Lakes and Rivers. Hiking, canoeing, campgrounds, swimming, inter- pretation program, picnic area. Historic Micmac Indian petroglyphs.
Kouchibouguac 1969	238.8	100 km north of Moncton, New Brunswick	Sheltered from the sea by a 25km sweep of sand dunes. Rivers and lagoons invite explorers in canoes, rowboats and kayaks.
Pacific Rim (Reserve) 1970	499.6	306 km northwest of Victoria, British Columbia	Ocean meets rain forest and sandy beaches at Park. Surfing. Hiking through the mighty forest.
Forillon 1970	240.4	724 km northeast of Quebec City, Quebec	Steep limestone cliffs off the Gaspé coast plunge into the Gulf of St. Lawrence at the Park. Walking and hiking trails.
La Mauricie 1970	543.9	200 km northeast of Montreal, Quebec	Rolling hills, lakes and fast-running rivers. Canoe routes with wilderness campgrounds and areas for tents and recreational vehicles. Beaches, lookouts and walking trails.
Kluane (Reserve) 1972	22 015.0	158 km west of Whitehorse, Yukon Territory (on the Alaska Highway)	Sitting on Canada's westernmost border, is the home of icefields, glaciers, and our highest mountains. Warm temperatures from mid-June to August. Tents and recreation vehicles use the campground at Kathleen Lake.

1.7   NATIONAL PARKS (continued)

Park and year established	Area km²	Location	Description
Nahanni (Reserve) 1972	4 765.6	Southwest corner of the Northwest Territories	First natural site named to the UNESCO World Heritage List. Wilderness canoeing with white-water adventure on the South Nahanni River. Access by air or water only from Fort Simpson or Watson Lake.
Auyuittuq (Reserve) 1972	21 471.1	Baffin Island, Northwest Territories	Rugged terrain, short, cool summers and long, cold winters. Jet service connects Montreal, Iqaluit (Frobisher Bay) and Pangnirtung; the 31 km by foot, freighter canoe or snowmobile to the Park.
Gros Morne 1973	1 942.5	126 km north of Corner Brook, Newfoundland	Short trails or two-day excursion routes.
Pukaskwa Year of agreement 1978	1 877.8	25 km east of Marathon, Ontario (halfway between Thunder Bay and Sault Ste Marie)	Rugged wilderness, on the north shore of Lake Superior. Campground, sandy beach, and hiking trails.
Grasslands 1981	906.5	100 km south of Swift Current, Saskatchewan	Ranching surrounds the prairie dogs and antelope amid the intriguing Killdeer Badlands and remnant teepee rings of the first residents.
Mingan Archipelago (Reserve) 1984	150.7	200 km east of Sept-Îles, Quebec	Atlantic puffins, rare plants and flowers not found anywhere else in Canada. Unusual rock formations. Guided water tours and primitive camping. Accommodation and other services nearby.
Ivvavik (name changed in 1992) 1984	10 168.4	Yukon Territory	Migration route for the Porcupine herd of barren ground caribou, and North American waterfowl area.
Ellesmere Island (Reserve) 1986	39 500.0	Northeast of Yellowknife, Northwest Territories (the most northerly lands in Canada)	Region of perpetual ice and snow, with tenacious flora and fauna.
Bruce Peninsula 1987	270.0	Near Georgian Bay, Ontario	Dense forest of cedar, balsam, fir, spruce, birch and aspen. Breeding birds, wildlife and rarely seen Massasauga rattlesnakes. Hiking and swimming as well.
Gwaii Haanas Archipelago (Reserve) 1988	1 470.4	Southern portion of the Queen Charlotte Islands, British Columbia Wilderness area (accessible only by floatplane, helicopter or boat)	Numerous bays and small islands. Natural hot-springs, volcanic and limestone rock. Sitka spruce, western red cedar and hemlock. Seabird colonies.

1.7 NATIONAL PARKS (concluded)

Park and year established	Area km²	Location	Description
Northern Baffin Island (withdrawal order signed) 1992	22 252.0	North-west Territories Canada's Eastern Arctic	Result of the Nunavut Land Claim Agreement. Area special for its rugged landscapes, its diversity of arctic vegetation and wildlife resources, and its rich cultural heritage.
Aulavik (Banks Island) 1992	12 275.0	Northwest Territories, the most westerly island in the Canadian Arctic Archipelago	Deeply-cut river canyons and rugged, desert-like badlands. One of the highest concentrations of muskoxen in the world. (40,000)

1.8 PROVINCIAL PARKS

	Number of parks	Total area (developed area) km²	Types of Park	Number of camping parks
Newfoundland and Labrador	93	4 394	Natural environment Outdoor recreation Natural scenic attractions Wilderness and ecological reserves Waterway parks Park reserves	41
Prince Edward Island	31	15 (9)	Campgrounds Resorts Beaches Picnic Roadside rest sites Heritage Water skiing Natural area	14
Nova Scotia	122	218 (90)	Campgrounds Picnic Beach Roadside rest sites Wildlife Historic	21
New Brunswick	48	249 (45)	Recreation Picnic Campgrounds Beach Resource	. .

1.8 PROVINCIAL PARKS (concluded)

	Number of parks	Total area (developed area) km²	Types of Park	Number of camping parks
Quebec	50	71 00	Tourist Wilderness preserves Hunting and fishing preserves Salmon streams Campgrounds	26
Ontario	261	63 284	Wilderness area Natural environment Waterway Nature Reserve Recreation Historical	97
Manitoba	147	15 000	Wilderness area Natural environment Heritage Recreation Special use Wayside	86
Saskatchewan	31	9 080	Wilderness area Natural environment Recreation Historic	21
Alberta	115	12 514	Wilderness area Recreation	170
British Columbia	390	53 359	Wilderness area Recreation Natural environment Marine	170 170

1.9   SOME CANADIAN EXTREMES

Largest province	Quebec (1 540 680 km^2)
Smallest province	Prince Edward Island (5 660 km^2)
Northernmost community	Grise Fiord, Ellesmere Island, Northwest Territories (76°25'N)
Southernmost community	Pelee Island South, Ontario (41°25'N)
Easternmost community	Blackhead, St. John's District, Newfoundland (52°39'W)
Westernmost community	Beaver Creek, Yukon Territory (140°52'W)
Highest city	Rossland, British Columbia (1 056 m at railroad station)
Highest community	Lake Louise, Alberta (1 540 m)
Deepest lake	Great Slave Lake, Northwest Territories (614 m)
Highest waterfall	Della Falls, British Columbia (440 m — more than one leap)
Greatest waterfall by volume	Horseshoe Falls, Niagara River, Ontario (5 365 m^3/s)
Northernmost ice-free port	Stewart, British Columbia (55°56'N)

Sources
Energy, Mines and Resources Canada
Environment Canada
Respective Provincial Government Departments

THOMAS KITCHIN / FIRST LIGHT

CHAPTER TWO

FORESTS, FISH AND WILDLIFE

INTRODUCTION

It is somehow fitting that it was a Canadian, Maurice Strong, who was Secretary General of the United Nations Conference on the Human Environment in 1972 — generally regarded as the beginning of the environmental movement — and of the subsequent conference on environment and development in 1992. Canadians have always had strong links with their environment. Indeed, Canada's primary resources have formed and continue to form the backbone of its economy.

Development of this economy, however, has led to pollution in the Great Lakes, smog in the cities, and contamination of ground water and soil. Canadians are now becoming aware that the nation's economic vitality depends on creating sustainable development — economic growth while still protecting Canada's rich natural resources.

FORESTS

Canada's forests represent about 10% of the world's total forest area. Forests are essential to ecological processes, including climate control and soil conservation, and are also home to innumerable species of animals and plants. For these reasons, and to ensure the viability of Canada's forest industries, Canada's forests must be managed wisely. In the past 10 years, forest management activities have more than doubled.

Despite heavy harvesting by early traders and settlers, forests — mainly coniferous — still cover 45% of the country's total land area. A national forest inventory is conducted every five years by Forestry Canada in co-operation with provincial and territorial agencies. The most recent estimates (1991) show 416 hectares of inventoried forest land. Of this, 250 million hectares are productive, that is, available for growing and harvesting timber. Provincial Crown forest land was 88% of the productive total, leaving 2.5% under federal jurisdiction, and 9.5% in private ownership. Private lands include small woodlots and larger, industrial freehold parcels.

Preliminary estimates indicate that there are 1,764 highly protected federal and provincial sites (27 million hectares) within Canada's forest land boundaries. Under the 1990 *Green Plan*, the Government of Canada has stated its intention to set aside 12% of the nation as protected space.

The forest industry consists of logging, wood and paper industries. Canada is a world leader in many forest products. For example, it is the world's largest producer of newsprint, the second largest producer of pulp and the third largest producer of sawn lumber.

Canada's main sources of wood are the inventoried, non-reserved forest lands south of 60° north latitude. At 215 million hectares, they represent nearly 88% of Canada's productive forest lands. This extensive woodland permits the forest industry not only to compete internationally but also to contribute substantially to the wealth of every province and territory.

Together, the logging, wood and paper sectors account for about 10% of Canada's value added (the value of goods less the costs incurred in their production) for goods-producing industries. With a trade surplus of $18.1 billion in 1991, the forest industry is a major contributor to Canada's positive trade balance.

The forest industry is concentrated in British Columbia, Quebec and Ontario. In 1990, the combined value added for these provinces was $16.3 billion, about 84% of the national total.

The output of the forest industry, after rising steadily from 1982 to 1989, dropped in 1990. Shipments decreased 6.8% from 1989 to $46.9 billion, but this was still 80% higher than in 1982 when the upward trend began. All three sectors declined in 1990; logging was down 6.7%; wood 6.5% and paper 7.0%. Employment declined 6.3%, representing a loss of 18,500 jobs in communities whose livelihood depends on the forest sector.

The downturn in economic activity continued throughout 1991. Sawmill production declined by 5.0% and real output for the group was more than 10% below the 1990 level. The first signs of any recovery did not appear until the second quarter of 1992 when real output for the group showed a marginal 0.8% increase over the 1991 levels.

Thomas Kitchin / First Light

Grizzly bear.

Janet Dwyer / First Light

Purple Loosestrife — deceptively beautiful.

It appears to be every inch the exotic European beauty. **Lythrum salicaria**, *or purple loosestrife, stands one to two metres high topped with a striking stalk of pink or purple flowers. Travellers may be charmed when they see it at the roadside, and their chances of seeing it are good in many parts of the country.*

But Canadian environment, agriculture and wetland specialists are desperately seeking ways to control it. Purple loosestrife, away from its home in Europe, is an overbearing, tenacious and unwelcome guest.

At the same time it has no natural enemies — animal, fish or insect — at least native to Canada. But Agriculture Canada scientists are working on a plan to breed European insect varieties that are known to feed on different parts of the plant. As of 1993, no herbicides had been approved for use against it, and pulling it up by hand is only practical when small numbers of plants are involved.

The problem with purple loosestrife is that it grows and spreads faster than any native plant species. The origin of this plant is buried in the murk of botanical history, but it is thought to have crossed the ocean from Europe to North America; it first appeared in Quebec in the mid-1800s. Its seed may have stowed away in the holds of ships bound for Canada, or perhaps been hidden in the matted coats of imported sheep. Eighteenth century gardeners sometimes cultivated it as a decorative plant and nursery keepers sold it commercially. At one time, beekeepers even promoted it as a honey plant.

A single purple loosestrife plant produces as many as 2.7 million seeds a season. As well, it can spread by sprouting new plants from tiny pieces of stem and root after it is torn up or mowed. Where purple loosestrife takes root, wetlands, normally home to many forms of wildlife, fall silent. No native animals are known to feed on the plant; birds do not nest among its firm, densely packed stalks; and fish cannot survive in water choked with its roots. It can strangle freshwater and saltwater marshes, beaches, ponds, stream banks, farm dugouts, irrigation and navigation canals, and lowland pastures, dominating or displacing native plants. It even flourishes in sewage treatment ponds.

Botanists have been watching purple loosestrife for close to a century but it only became a headache during the 1980s. In 1990, awareness of the problem rose as the media began reporting it heavily.

Quebec, Ontario and Manitoba are the provinces most seriously affected. The Maritime provinces — New Brunswick, Nova Scotia, and Prince Edward Island — all have spreading purple loosestrife populations and it is also present in Newfoundland. Experts think small localized infestations in Saskatchewan and Alberta can be controlled. It is present in British Columbia watersheds, but was only recognized as a serious problem in 1992. No purple loosestrife has been reported in Yukon and the Northwest Territories.

Purple loosestrife is also worrisome for global reasons. Canada's 1.3 million square kilometres of wetlands comprise almost 25% of the world's total. These lands act as natural water purifiers, protect shorelines, reduce and control flooding, and shelter many kinds of waterfowl, plants, animals, reptiles and fish. They are also important sources of oxygen, and have a vital part to play in maintaining climate.

Locally, communities near wetlands benefit economically from activities such as hunting, fishing, trapping, tourism and recreation and from forest products and agricultural products such as berries and wild rice. In Canada, these economic spinoffs are estimated to exceed $10 billion annually.

Experts concluded in 1992 that bio-controls had the best chances of slowing or halting purple loosestrife's spread. Three varieties of European insects, two of them leaf-eating beetles and the third a root-mining weevil, show promise. Tests in Europe and the United States and follow-up studies in Canada suggest that these will not harm native plant or animal species. In large enough numbers, and perhaps joined by other approved imported insect varieties, they may counter the beautiful, but unwelcome, invader.

...FOREST FOR THE TREES

One of the enduring pictures of Canada is of a country rich in stands of dark evergreens growing right to the edges of wilderness lakes and rivers. Indeed, Canada's forests cover more than half of the country's land area, and represent one-tenth of the world's total forested area.

In addition to being a beautiful part of Canada, they contribute to its economy. In 1992, forest resources generated employment for almost 730,000 Canadians and contributed $18.8 billion to Canada's balance of trade.

Trees are harvested at a rate of about 1 million hectares a year. Recently, government and forest product companies have replanted about half the harvested area each year with tree seeds or seedlings, but not all replanted areas successfully regenerate into forests. Harvests are increasingly managed to promote natural regeneration. As well, replanted forests, unlike the originals, sometimes contain trees of only one age and species.

Sustaining the industry's contribution to the economy depends in part on maintaining the supply of timber.

The annual allowable cut for a forested area is the amount of timber that can be harvested each year without diminishing the long-term sustainability of the forest. For example, for a tree species that requires an average of 80 years to reach maturity, one-eightieth of the forested area can be harvested annually if the harvested areas regenerate sufficiently. Canada's estimated annual allowable cut is 252 million cubic metres.

Uncertainty about future supply has led many Canadians to question whether current harvest rates are in fact sustainable.

Recent studies indicate that the national timber supply is sustainable over the next 30 to 60 years. Nevertheless, regional supplies vary considerably and some local shortages have been identified. Over the longer term, further developments in silviculture (the growing and tending of trees) and technology should help sustain Canada's forest resources.

FEDERAL JURISDICTION The federal government owns about 95 million hectares of forest, but most of this land is in the Yukon or Northwest Territories and is unsuitable for commercial timber production. Of the 5.9 million hectares of federally-owned forest outside the Yukon and Northwest Territories, most is taken up by national parks, military reserves or Indian lands (which account for 1.4 million hectares). Because the federal government has primary or shared jurisdiction over fiscal management, regional development, trade and tariffs, transportation and environment, at least six federal departments have a major interest in forestry.

Forestry Canada The principal federal forestry agency, Forestry Canada, is responsible for the integrated management of Canada's forest resources to meet the economic, social and environmental needs of present and future generations of Canadians.

The department plays a major role in implementing the government's *Green Plan*. For example, working together with the National Community Tree Foundation, Forestry Canada will oversee the planting of

325 million trees in Canadian cities and towns over a six-year period. All Canadians are invited to participate in this program to offset the effects of global warming.

In co-operation with Environment Canada, Forestry Canada continues to focus attention on the problem of atmospheric change, including acid rain and its effects on the long-term sustainability of the forest resource.

The department uses sophisticated satellite technology to maintain its comprehensive national forest inventory, and to improve methods of forecasting, detecting and suppressing forest fires.

Forestry Canada works together with the provinces and private industry to achieve these aims.

Forest development initiatives worth more than $445 million have been negotiated between Forestry Canada and the provinces to encourage long-term forest management planning, improved forestry data, renewal of current harvests by provinces and industry, integrated resource management, human resource development, public awareness, co-funding arrangements and technology transfer.

Forestry Canada gave more than $92 million in grants and contributions to universities and forestry organizations in 1992-93 for research and development. The department's concerns include cost-effective forest management and protection, chemical and biological pest control, pesticide application technology, the environmental impact of forest practices, tree genetics, the use of biotechnology to improve growth and yields, and research on forest ecology.

PROVINCIAL JURISDICTION

The provinces own 296 million hectares or 87% of the forests south of 60° north latitude. The remaining 13% is reserved for national parks or held privately. The Constitution Act, 1867 specifies that the provinces are responsible for managing their public lands and the timber on these lands.

With economically accessible timber resources fully allocated in most provinces, arrangements between provincial governments and the forest industry for harvesting timber on provincial Crown lands are

tending to emphasize industry's management responsibilities. Increasingly, forests are being managed for both timber and non-timber values. Several provinces have made a commitment to set aside more forested lands in parks and reserves, and harvesting rates are being adjusted to reflect changing patterns in the use of forest resources. In Ontario and British Columbia, long-term cutting rights are currently under review.

Forest Fires: Percent of Forest Land[1] Burned

[1] Inventoried forest land.

Local communities are getting more involved — and are having more say — in forest management through programs such as the Community Forests Initiative in Ontario. British Columbia has established a commission on resources and the environment to develop a process for resolving conflicts over land use. Provincial governments and associations of professional foresters have developed or revised codes of ethics on forest management. Several provinces have initiated forestry-related educational programs for aboriginal peoples, and sought ways, including co-management of Crown lands, to increase their involvement in forest management.

PROTECTING THE FOREST Every year, fire, pests and disease destroy as many trees as are harvested in Canada's forests.

Reducing timber losses and other forest damage caused by fires, insect infestations and disease epidemics continues to be a major goal of forestry agencies.

Fire Forest fires caused by lightning burn the most area, and consequently many provinces have automated lightning detection networks. Provincial governments have also stepped up public awareness campaigns to decrease the number of human-caused forest fires. To improve fire response capability, aerial and ground patrols, lookout towers and improved heat detection equipment are being used. Several provinces have early fire detection and intervention programs. Many of these use computerized systems, allowing firefighters to pinpoint hazardous areas and to predict the behaviour of fires.

To fight large fires, most provinces use Canadair CL-215 water bombers — the only aircraft in the world specifically designed to be a water-scooping fire bomber. Also used are other fixed-wing aircraft, and specially equipped helicopters. However, the mainstays of firefighting efforts are regular firefighting crews, backed by trained auxiliary crews. Most provinces work with Winnipeg's Canadian Interagency Forest Fire Centre, which co-ordinates personnel and equipment-sharing when provinces or territories need help. A national group has been formed to standardize training, making inter-agency firefighting more effective.

Insects and Disease As with fires, insect infestations take a heavy toll on Canada's forests. Spruce budworm is the most widespread forest pest, but in Eastern Canada, tent caterpillar and gypsy moth infestations are also common, as are hemlock looper infestations. In British Columbia, pine-bark beetles and Douglas-fir tussock moths have caused extensive damage in the past.

However, sophisticated control programs have decreased the damage caused by most major forest pests. For example, spruce budworm infestation affected 16.5 million hectares of Quebec forest in 1981; in 1990, this had declined to 870 000 hectares. This decrease is due, in part, to strategic spraying programs, which increasingly use biological insecticides such as fenitrothian.

FOREST REGENERATION Conventional forest harvesting methods allow for natural regeneration of just over half of harvested areas, but improved cutting methods are being developed to allow more of the land to regenerate naturally. Artificial regeneration by planting and seeding occurs on the remaining area. The scale of replanting efforts is immense: in 1991, Quebec and British Columbia planted 209 million and 230 million trees respectively, while Ontario planted nearly 150 million. The area planted and seeded has increased from 211 000 hectares in 1980 to 505 000 hectares in 1991.

Reforestation efforts in this country have increased dramatically since the 1970s. Every province has stepped up funding for reforestation while increasing the involvement of the forest industry. Most provinces provide nursery stock for the reforestation of burned areas and for the backlog of lands insufficiently stocked by natural regeneration. Some provinces, however, have encouraged private nurseries and seed orchards rather than expanding their own capacity.

In recent years, attention has turned from increasing the size of reforestation programs to ensuring cost-effectiveness. Many provinces are increasing their use of containerized seedling stocks and have instituted quality control for nurseries and for tree planting. They are also developing silvicultural treatments for specific site conditions and are genetically improving planting stock.

Tony Beck / GeoStock

Capelin — some seabirds feed on these small smelt-like fish and cod fishermen use them for bait.

Tree improvement is receiving increasing emphasis. This approach includes thinning, spacing, clearing and pruning. The provinces with the largest planting programs fund research and applied tree improvement programs; the other provinces rely on Forestry Canada and universities for research information. Cooperative tree improvement councils have been formed by industry and government in several provinces. As a result, seed collection areas and seed orchards have been established throughout Canada to produce and collect superior tree seed.

FISHERIES

With the largest coastline in the world and thousands of rivers and lakes, Canada has for centuries benefited from prosperous fisheries. In some parts of the country, the industry has sustained whole communities for

generations. In 1989, the total Canadian catch was 1.6 million tonnes, worth approximately $1.5 billion. This represented a 0.3% decrease over the 1988 catch. A slight decrease was registered in 1990.

Canada is one of the world's largest exporters of fish products, in terms of value. In 1990, Canada exported three-quarters of its product — 625 000 tonnes worth $2.6 billion. The United States accounted for the largest share (54%) of exports, followed by Japan and the European Economic Community. The most popular export items were cod, herring, crab, lobster and scallop from the Atlantic Coast, and halibut and salmon from the Pacific Coast.

Atlantic Canada In many parts of the region, fisheries have long been the mainstay of economic life. In 1989, the region's catch represented some 75% of Canada's total catch and 64% of landed value.

COD-FORSAKEN WATERS

When John Cabot explored Canada's Atlantic Coast in the 15th century, codfish were so numerous that he scooped them from sea to ship in open baskets. In later years, Newfoundlanders in coastal towns and villages simply called cod 'fish'. Their existences depended so utterly on that single species that they rarely thought of any other.

Today some cod stocks have declined to very low levels. In 1992, Newfoundlanders were deeply shaken when the federal government imposed an unprecedented two-year ban on the commercial Northern cod fishery extending from southern Labrador to the northern Grand Banks, formerly one of the richest areas on the Atlantic Coast. Government promised emergency assistance payments to fishermen, processing workers and boat owners. There were further promises of more comprehensive compensation and voluntary job retraining programs to follow.

The chief cause seems to have been unusual ocean conditions, mainly much colder water temperatures through 1991. Since 1986, the cod stock had been stressed by overfishing, mostly by foreign vessels. Spanish and Portuguese boats, particularly, fished just outside Canada's 200-mile (370-kilometre) zone, and in 1991, accounted for more than a quarter of the total cod catch.

Fishing has historically been one of the Atlantic provinces' largest employers. By early 1992, the total value of Canada's Atlantic fisheries approached $1 billion annually. Cod alone accounted for nearly a third of the weight of the total catch. Overall, 61,000 fishery workers sailed about half that many fishing vessels from hundreds of coastal communities in Quebec, Newfoundland, New Brunswick, Nova Scotia and Prince Edward Island. Another 30,000 people worked in about 1,000 fish processing plants in these provinces.

In the century before 1950, the annual catch taken by small boats and traditional means from the Atlantic waters off Newfoundland averaged about 250 000 tonnes. But then fishermen began to buy bigger vessels with more range, new nets and power equipment, and electronic navigation. Modern European vessels moved in as well. By 1968, the total Northern cod catch peaked at 800 000 tonnes, more than three times the traditional level. But at the same time, inshore fishers' share of the catch fell to its lowest level in all the centuries they had plied Newfoundland's waters.

In 1977, Canada declared a 200-mile (370-kilometre) fishing zone to extend its jurisdiction over fish stocks important to Canadian fishers. In the decade following, scientific evidence suggested that the cod stocks were rebounding. However, in 1989 scientists realized Northern cod stocks had not rebuilt as fast as they had thought. Rather than the five-fold increase they had thought at first, the population had in fact tripled by 1982 and then declined a little.

In 1991, the population fell drastically again, the total stock size by about a half, and the very important spawning stock by about two-thirds.

Scientific assessments to determine how large a fishery to allow after the moratorium are continuing. However, reduced quotas will probably be the rule for several years, so that the cod can regenerate.

By the end of 1992, the federal government had introduced new conservation measures and stricter enforcement to protect small fish and spawning stocks. As well, fishing fleets were required to set up plans to ensure that they caught fewer small fish.

Experts say the fishing industry needs restructuring in order to attain sustainability — in other words, one which matches the size of the cod stock. Ultimately, a significant number of fishery workers will need to retrain for jobs outside of the fishery that supported their lives.

In Newfoundland, the fishing industry accounted for 6.7% of the province's Gross Domestic Product (GDP) in 1988-89, and employed close to 29,000 licensed commercial fishers, with fish plants supplying another 10,000 person-years of employment. By 1991, the number of registered fishers had dropped to below 25,000.

In Nova Scotia, the annual catch grew slightly from 490 000 tonnes in 1988 to 491 000 tonnes in 1989. The value of the 1989 catch was also slightly higher than in the previous year, reaching $437 million. After processing, Nova Scotia fish products were worth about $930 million, with lobster being the most important harvested species. In 1991, there were over 16,000 registered fishers in Nova Scotia.

In New Brunswick, the fisheries are one of the largest industries, worth about $300 million annually. Aquaculture of salmon, with some oysters and mussels, is worth $72 million annually. In 1991, New Brunswick fisheries employed 7,721 registered fishers.

Prince Edward Island's catch was worth $69 million in 1991, rising to $185 million when the value of processing and services are added. Lobster accounted for 20% of the catch. Aquaculture of oysters, mussels and rainbow trout is still small-scale, but increasingly significant. The Island counted over 5,000 fishers in 1991.

Given the significance of the fisheries to the region, a decline in levels of certain traditional Atlantic groundfish stocks — particularly cod — is having serious economic consequences. The decline is due primarily to ecological factors that have reduced the stock by half, and the spawning stock by three-quarters.

As a result of the devastating decline in the stock of Northern cod off the east coast of Newfoundland and Labrador, a two-year moratorium on the Northern cod fishery was announced in 1992 to allow for recovery of the resource.

Emergency assistance payments were made to fishers and plant workers affected by the moratorium.

Western Canada In the western provinces, sport and commercial fishing are major sources of revenue. British Columbia has one of the largest commercial

fisheries in Canada, with a landed value of $480 million in 1990. After processing, the catch was worth $948 million. Five species of Pacific salmon are the mainstay of the industry. Other fish caught alongshore and in the deep-sea fisheries include herring, halibut, cod, sole and a variety of shellfish. Freshwater sport fishing is also an important industry in the province, generating $456 million in revenues in 1990.

Extensive restocking is protecting British Columbia's fisheries. In 1990, the province's five hatcheries produced more than 11 million fish, and a conservation fund established in 1981 has provided more than $6 million for 232 fish habitat protection and improvement projects.

Many provinces put funds from resource-related recreation into managing that resource. In Alberta, part of the revenue for improving habitat protection and resource management comes from sport fishing licences. Alberta's commercial fishing harvest is mostly lake whitefish valued at $1.6 million in 1989.

Manitoba's fishing industry generated more than 14 000 tonnes of product in 1989. The major commercial catches are walleye and sauger. Anglers spent $66.7 million in Manitoba in 1990 on bait, lodges, outfitters and camps. Although fishing is an important source of food for Manitobans living in remote areas and for some native peoples, between 80% and 90% of the fish caught in the province is exported.

Central Canada Ontario has the largest freshwater fishery in North America, with annual commercial landings of about 25 000 tonnes, worth approximately $50 million before processing and $150 million afterwards. The main species harvested from the province's lakes, streams and rivers are smelt, yellow perch, walleye and lake whitefish. More than 90% of the harvest comes from the Great Lakes, mostly from Lake Erie. Ontario also has the largest sport fishing industry among the provinces, with expenditures on fishing trips totalling about $1.1 billion in 1990.

Quebec had a decline in landed commercial volume which fell in 1991 to 71 000 tonnes from 74 000 tonnes in 1990. However, the value of processing plant shipments rose to $85 million in 1991 from $74 million in 1990. To cope with contraction phases in the industry, the province initiated a five-year restructuring program in 1990 that will consolidate the fishing fleet and the processing sector. The program is designed to re-establish a balance between the province's resources and its processing capacity, stabilize the financial situation of fishers and renew the province's resources.

FISHERIES MANAGEMENT

Canada's oceans and inland waters have always been important to the country's growth. For this reason, Canada's *Green Plan* calls for the development of a National Sustainable Fisheries Policy and Action Plan. Enforcement against overfishing and pollution of fish habitat is also being strengthened.

Seacoast and inland fisheries were singled out in the Constitution Act of 1867 as an exclusive responsibility of the new federal government. Today, the federal government still has jurisdiction over Canada's fisheries, although the management of freshwater fisheries has been delegated to the provinces.

The Department of Fisheries and Oceans conserves, develops and regulates Canada's coastal and fresh-water fisheries. The department also conducts fisheries and oceanographic research, publishes charts and tide tables for Canada's waters, and represents Canada in international agreements on fisheries management and marine research.

The federal government also inspects fish and fishery products destined for interprovincial or international trade. In the national parks, fisheries are managed by the Canadian Parks Service.

Federal-provincial agreements have led to a close relationship between provincial departments responsible for fisheries and the federal Department of Fisheries and Oceans. For example, in Quebec the provincial government administers freshwater fish and fish that migrate between salt and freshwater, while marine fisheries are managed by the federal government. In British Columbia, the fisheries for marine species and for salmon that migrate between the sea and freshwater are managed federally, while the provincial government manages freshwater fisheries.

Licences for sport fishing are usually distributed by provincial or territorial governments which retain the revenue collected. Many are putting these revenues into fish conservation projects.

In the sport fishing sector, federal and provincial government programs focus on habitat protection and enhancement. Commercial sector priorities include monitoring and protecting fish stocks, encouraging rationalization of fisheries to increase competitiveness, and funding and promoting aquaculture programs.

International fisheries Much of the damage done to aquatic resources is the result of over-harvesting. This is due to social and economic pressures, domestic and international competition and insufficient knowledge. Problems under Canada's control are corrected as conditions warrant, but resources shared with other nations must be managed jointly.

Through membership in 10 international fisheries commissions and an international council, Canada co-operates with many nations to obtain scientific data and to formulate policies for developing and conserving fisheries. Canada is also a member of the fisheries committee of the United Nations Food and Agriculture Organization and of the Codex Alimentarius Commission, concerned with world food quality standards. In 1950, Canada joined nine other countries in signing the International Convention for the Northwest Atlantic Fisheries.

Canada extended its fishing zones from 12 to 200 nautical miles (22 to 370 kilometres) in January 1977. Negotiations then began to revise multilateral agreements, and a new international organization, the Northwest Atlantic Fisheries Organization (NAFO) was established to regulate fishing outside the 200-mile (370-kilometre) limit. Canada also co-operates with other countries in conserving high seas fisheries resources elsewhere through research and international agreements.

WILDLIFE

In addition to being an integral part of all ecosystems, wild organisms provide significant benefits to people. More than 90% of Canadians participate in wildlife-related activities such as nature photography, wildlife

Tony Beck / GeoStock

Snowy owl.

watching, bird feeding, hunting, fishing, subsistence use and so on. The expenditures on these activities contribute $11.5 billion to Canada's Gross Domestic Product and sustain 284,000 jobs. In addition, many visitors come to Canada to view wildlife, especially the birds and large mammals.

Although Canada still has impressive wildlife populations, including a large proportion of the world's stock of mountain sheep, wolves and grizzly bears, many animal populations have shrunk or even disappeared since Confederation. These losses are due in part to

overhunting in the days before hunting restrictions, and in part to habitat loss, which continues to this day. Agriculture, forestry, and urbanization are still changing the landscape. Certain habitats are already scarce: vast areas of the country's grasslands have been cultivated and more than half of Atlantic coastal wetlands have been drained by people. These trends are difficult to reverse.

In 1990, the provinces, territories and federal government adopted a new Wildlife Policy for Canada. This policy redefines the term *wildlife* to include all wild organisms — including wild plants, invertebrates, micro-organisms, as well as the fishes, amphibians, reptiles, birds and mammals traditionally regarded as wildlife. This was done to provide a comprehensive set of policies guiding the management of Canada's wild species, including those not covered by existing policies, and also to encourage an ecosystem approach to conservation.

FEDERAL JURISDICTION As a natural resource, wildlife falls under provincial jurisdiction. However, in 1973, the Canada Wildlife Act was passed enabling the federal government to work when appropriate with the co-operation of the provinces in research, conservation, and interpretation of all species of non-domestic animals. Also, the federal government has special responsibilities to protect and manage marine species and certain migratory birds, and to conserve wildlife and habitat of national or international importance. This includes species that are endangered or that migrate across provincial or national boundaries, and wetlands of international importance as waterfowl habitat. The new Wild Animal and Plant Protection and Regulation of International and Interprovincial Trade Act received Royal Assent in December 1992. Once in place, the Act will dramatically improve Canada's ability to crack down on illegal trade in wildlife, both internationally and interprovincially.

The Canadian Wildlife Service (CWS) has its origins in the hiring in 1918 of an ornithologist to administer the provisions of the Migratory Birds Convention Act. The Migratory Birds Convention is a treaty negotiated with the United States in 1916 to protect a number of species of birds that migrate each year between the two countries. CWS continues to administer the Act today as a part of Environment Canada.

For those migratory birds that are hunted, CWS works with the provincial wildlife agencies to establish annual revisions of hunting seasons, bag limits, and hunting practices affecting migratory birds. These revisions are based on annual surveys of breeding waterfowl (ducks, geese and swans), done in co-operation with the United States Fish and Wildlife Service, and by annual surveys of waterfowl hunters in Canada to establish the numbers and kinds of birds they kill.

The foundation of CWS's conservation work is its long-standing program of research in wildlife ecology. The results of this research provide the basis for managing and protecting migratory bird populations and their habitats, and for the conservation of other nationally important wildlife. CWS scientists have provided information over the years for the conservation of waterfowl, northern caribou, polar bears, seabirds, shorebirds, and a number of threatened or endangered species. This research includes fieldwork in remote places, and a number of techniques such as the banding of birds and the radio-tracking of large mammals.

CWS's ecological research also contributes to an understanding of the impacts of major development projects and of the effects of widespread human-caused changes, such as the increased acidity of rain and snow.

The CWS endangered species program involves co-ordinating the national effort of government and non-government organizations to identify and recover species at risk. Recovery plans have been instituted for the whooping crane, wood bison, peregrine falcon, piping plover, Baird's sparrow, burrowing owl, Peary caribou, and about 20 other species. In recent years, the white pelican and the tundra subspecies of the peregrine falcon have recovered and have been removed from the list of threatened species. CWS also contributes to international efforts to protect endangered species. The Convention on International Trade in Endangered Species of Wild Flora and Fauna (CITES) is an attempt to protect endangered species by regulating trade in over 15 000 species of wild plants and animals and their parts or derivatives. Canada is a party to CITES, and CWS is responsible for implementing CITES in Canada.

Through research on the effects of toxic chemicals on wildlife, CWS identifies those chemicals used in industry or to control pests that have damaging effects on wildlife. Through advice to national regulatory agencies, it has helped to have those damaging effects reduced. In addition, CWS monitoring of the levels and effects of toxic chemicals in wildlife populations has provided useful indicators of environmental quality.

Habitat protection is another important part of CWS's work. The North American Waterfowl Management Plan (NAWMP), signed by Canada and the United

Stephen Homer / First Light

Puffin sanctuary, Witless Bay, Newfoundland.

Every summer over a million pairs of seabirds converge on the east coast of Newfoundland's Avalon Peninsula. They're headed for the Witless Bay Ecological Reserve, comprised of three small islands located between the communities of Bay Bulls and Bauline.

Newfoundland has one of the largest concentrations of seabirds in the world, and the Witless Bay reserve is home to the largest Atlantic puffin colony in North America, and the second largest Leach's storm-petrel colony in the world. The birds are lured there to feed on capelin, a tiny fish that runs in huge numbers from about mid-June to mid-July, attracting baleen whales, fishermen, and of course, puffins.

Witless Bay, like most seabird colonies, has many different species of birds nesting close together, each species claiming their separate area from just above the tide line to the furthest inland points of the islands. Bird experts conjecture that their turf ownership is decided according to a hidden plan.

Atlantic puffins, or sea parrots, are colourful and stately. They spend their time in the water, or near the nesting burrows they make near the tops of steep grassy slopes. Leach's storm-petrels, on the other hand, are secretive little birds that arrive at night to avoid predators, and nest in burrows in the peaty ground of evergreen forests on the islands.

Kittiwakes, also called tickle-aces, build at least one nest for their eggs, and sometimes two or three, on little outcrops too small for other nesting species. Common murres, and their cousins, thick-billed murres, lay a single pointed egg on the bare rocks near the sea.

Other varieties that nest among the cliffs, boulders and grasses include herring gulls, black-backed gulls, black guillemots (sea pigeons) and razorbills (tinkers). Surrounding waters are an important wintering area for common eiders, king eiders, thick-billed murres and dovekies.

Concentrating in colonies gives seabirds many protective advantages, but it also makes them very vulnerable to human interference, drops in food levels, commercial fishing activity (which can inadvertently catch diving birds in nets) and marine pollution.

Because the Witless Bay Ecological Reserve is so important to replenishing these bird species' numbers each year, Newfoundland's provincial government has been protecting it since 1964. Few humans can actually set foot on the islands and none go without a permit issued by the province, restricting them to specific small areas. Commercial fishing and even boat traffic are restricted. However, it is possible to tour the reserve by water in local boats, as long as the inhabitants of these colourful and important seabird breeding grounds are not disturbed.

States in 1986, focuses on maintaining and restoring wetlands (including nearby upland areas that are important to wetland ecosystems).

NAWMP established its first project to enhance waterfowl habitat in the Quill Lakes area of Saskatchewan in 1988. Five co-operative projects involving public and private agencies are now operating in Canada. One of them, the Prairie Habitat Joint Venture, will restore 1.5 million hectares of waterfowl habitat on the Canadian prairies at a cost of $800 million over the next 15 years. Nesting and migration habitat in Eastern Canada will also be protected at a cost of $200 million through the Eastern Habitat Joint Venture. The Pacific Coast Joint Venture aims to protect about 119 000 hectares. Other projects will concentrate on habitat for Arctic-nesting geese and for duck species in Eastern Canada.

To further protect habitat, especially for migratory birds, CWS administers more than 40 National Wildlife Areas and over 100 Migratory Bird Sanctuaries. A number of co-operative wildlife areas are managed jointly by CWS and the provinces.

PROVINCIAL AND TERRITORIAL JURISDICTION Wildlife management protects wildlife from becoming endangered or extinct, sustains populations and conserves natural habitat. The provinces monitor populations of game and non-game species that are not migratory birds, promote public awareness of wildlife conservation strategies and regulate hunting and fishing. They encourage wise resource use through hunting, trapping and fishing education programs.

Each province has its own method of carrying out this mandate. In Newfoundland and Labrador, research and management programs cover moose, caribou, black bear, lynx, ptarmigan, peregrine falcon, snowshoe and Arctic hare, ruffed and spruce grouse, mink, beaver and Arctic fox.

Many provinces are teaming up with private wildlife conservation groups. On Prince Edward Island, two five-year agreements have been signed by the province and Wildlife Habitat Canada. The first agreement resulted in integrated management of a watershed,

benefiting fish and wildlife; the second protects and enhances the province's wetlands. A five year wetlands development and management agreement has also been signed with Ducks Unlimited Canada.

Nova Scotia emphasizes wetlands management through enhancement, research and inventory programs in conjunction with the North American Waterfowl Management Plan (NAWMP). In 1990, the province signed a conservation agreement with its native people.

Agreements with Wildlife Canada and Ducks Unlimited Canada have contributed to expanded programs in New Brunswick's wetland, coastal and forested habitat. Harvest management controls populations of deer, moose, bear, grouse, snowshoe hare and various furbearers. In 1990, the Antlerless Deer Permit Management Program was introduced to improve control over the reproductive component of the deer herd.

Quebec has adopted a new law to protect threatened and vulnerable species; the habitat of designated species will also be protected. As well, the province has amended its laws to bar any activity likely to affect essential elements of animal or fish habitat. The province has given conservation priority to 11 wildlife habitats; these include white-tailed deer gathering areas, caribou calving and migration areas, waterfowl gathering areas, moose grounds and fish habitats. Aerial inventories, radio tracking and harvest records keep track of animal populations and ensure that hunting, trapping and fishing are conducted responsibly.

Ontario's wildlife management plan includes a release program for peregrine falcons, surveys of bald eagles, and various studies to improve management of the habitats of endangered, threatened and vulnerable species. Wetlands throughout southern Ontario are being evaluated and rated, and significant wetlands will be acquired for special management. The Community Wildlife Involvement Program funds group and individual projects to improve wildlife habitat. Hunter and trapper education programs are mandatory in Ontario. The province's management of fur-bearing mammals is based on an area-specific licensing system, with seasons determined by quotas. Moose and deer populations are managed by controlling the number, age and gender of animals harvested.

Horst Baender / Image Finders

Big Horn Sheep ram, near Jasper, Alberta.

In Manitoba, the past five years have seen some encouraging progress in the field of wildlife management: the peregrine falcon population is recovering and ferruginous hawks appear to be firmly established in the province. The Endangered Species Act was recently proclaimed, affording greater protection for Manitoba's endangered and threatened species. Through a variety of habitat improvement techniques funded by the NAWMP, Manitoba has reversed the fall in nesting duck populations which had reached record low levels during the dry 1980s. Another successful new initiative is the Critical Wildlife Habitat Program which has established the Tall-grass Prairie Preserve. The Waterhen Wood Bison Project, co-managed by the provincial government and aboriginal peoples, has resulted in the births of the first wild bison in Manitoba since the mid-1800s. This trend to new partnerships in wildlife management is expected to continue.

Saskatchewan uses hunting and fishing licence revenues to purchase critical wildlife habitat and to fund habitat development projects. The Saskatchewan Upland Habitat Protection, Enhancement and Restoration (SUPER) program was launched in 1988 to protect upland habitat in agricultural regions. In 1990, the Saskatchewan Wetland Conservation Corporation was created to administer and co-ordinate the province's participation in the NAWMP.

Alberta, too, devotes part of its hunting revenues to enhancing and developing wildlife habitat. Annual

questionnaires monitor harvested game and fur-bearing species, and hunting seasons are carefully regulated. Wildlife recreation is promoted through initiatives such as the Watchable Wildlife Program. Trappers grossed $2.8 million in 1991-92 from the province's fur-bearing animals.

The diversity of British Columbia's physical setting, climate and vegetation enable the province to support a greater variety and abundance of wildlife than any other province or territory: the province is home to 448 species of birds, 143 species of mammals, 19 species of reptiles and 20 species of amphibians; over 295 bird species breed in the province, of which 162 breed nowhere else in the country. The province has recently completed a strategic plan for managing wildlife into the next century. The plan aims to ensure that wildlife resources will continue to provide exceptional recreational opportunities — estimated to be worth over $1 billion to the provincial economy — and to support employment throughout the province.

The Yukon Fish and Wildlife Branch regulates and licences the harvesting of wildlife, and conducts habitat and wildlife protection inventories and research in co-operation with First Nations, wildlife users and the public.

In the Northwest Territories, the Department of Renewable Resources conducts surveys of Dall's sheep and wood bison, radio-collars barren-ground caribou and tags polar bears.

THE FUR INDUSTRY

For the past several years, the production and value of pelts has decreased. Canadian production of raw furs was valued at $42.2 million in 1990-91, down 19.7% from $52.5 million in 1989-90. Of the 1990-91 total, $26.7 million came from farm pelts and $15.5 million from wildlife pelts.

Fur Farming Mink is the most important species raised on fur farms. The peak year was 1967 when 1,359 mink farms produced nearly 2 million pelts. In 1991, pelt production was about 900,000 from 302 farms. The average value of pelts was $22.21, down from $25.79 in 1990.

TRAFFIC IN EXTINCTION

An illegal world-wide trade in live and dead animals, and animal parts, reaches into Canada in many ways. One federal customs officer opened a computer case to find it stuffed with dozens of drugged and dead cockatoos that suffocated while being smuggled for pets. Falcons illegally caught in Canada have reportedly been sold for $30,000 each in the Arab world, where falconers have decimated the birds of prey in that part of the world. Canadian black bears' gall bladders, weighing less than 150 grams, are said to sell for up to $20,000 each in Asia and the Orient, where they are prized ingredients in traditional medicines. In one incident in 1991, Canadian police caught two dealers with 173 bear gall bladders.

World-wide, this illegal traffic in wild animals and animal parts is believed to be a multi-million dollar business. It has been compared with the illegal drug trade: both are organized, cruel, and yield high profits. Until recently, though, there was comparatively little risk in smuggling illegally-obtained animals or animal parts across Canadian borders. That's changing.

In 1975, to combat this illegal trade, Canada was among the first countries to ratify the Convention on International Trade in Endangered Species of Wild Flora and Fauna (CITES), which regulates international trade in wild animals and plants. More than 100 nations have now signed on to regulate trade in over 40,000 of the world's most threatened species. In late 1992 Canada's parliament also enacted the Wild Animal and Plant Protection and Regulation of International and Interprovincial Trade Act. The act still permits controlled movement of selected exotic plant and animal species for legitimate reasons — for scientific study, in travelling zoos, circuses or plant exhibitions, or if they adhere to foreign conservation laws, but bans less legitimate uses. Under it, stiff fines for convictions range up to $150,000 for individuals and $300,000 for corporations, and prison terms run as high as five years.

In some societies the traffic in illegal species is fuelled by culturally-bound demands, and in others by local need for the income provided by poaching. Controlling it poses huge difficulties, especially since wildlife and wildlife parts may be smuggled in or on practically anything, including the human body. Experts say it is a major reason that large numbers of rare animals and plants around the globe are being threatened.

Loss of the world's biological diversity may weaken the interrelationships between all living things in ways that we can only guess at. Since European settlers arrived in Canada, for instance, nine species of fish and animals have become extinct here, 106 others are threatened or endangered, and a further 111 are considered vulnerable. Eleven others no longer exist in this country, but still live elsewhere. Because Canada is a northern country with relatively little biological diversity, this is cause for concern. Because there are fewer kinds of plant and animal life here than in other parts of the globe, each kind is a larger part of the interlocking ecosystem.

Of course, illegal trade isn't the only thing that threatens this diversity. In Canada, some extinctions have been caused by over-hunting, and some by destruction of wildlife habitat for cities, roads, or farmland. Industrial, agricultural and household chemicals can affect the environment in many ways, and acid rain, caused by industrial smog, has the potential to kill off ponds, wetlands, forests and soil, home to both plants and animals.

The rate at which species are vanishing is accelerating everywhere. In the days of dinosaurs, about one species of animal became extinct every thousand years. By 1900 it had become about one species a year. Biologists currently estimate that it stands at one to three animal species a day. Some predict that by the end of the century, human activity will kill off one species an hour, a pace that will have wiped out 15% of all species now living. Preventing traffic in rare and endangered species is a step toward slowing this headlong rush.

Lionel Stevenson / Camera Art

The harbour at St. John's, Newfoundland — a fishermen's refuge for centuries.

Ontario, Nova Scotia, British Columbia and Quebec were the principal producers of mink in 1990-91. Although some mink are raised in every province, newcomers to the business are rare because start-up requires a high capital outlay.

The market for all long-haired pelts improved in the 1970s and prices rose sharply, reaching a high of $364.42 per pelt in 1978. From 1971 to 1991, the number of fox farms increased from 39 to 664. In 1991, farm production of fox pelts decreased 48.9% to 40,517; pelts were valued at $46.27. As is the case with farm-produced fox and mink pelts, the trapping of wildlife for their pelts has decreased over the past few years.

The Atlantic Seal Hunt Harvesting seals is an important source of income in Newfoundland and Labrador, the Îles-de-la-Madeleine, the Quebec north shore and the Arctic. Its significance is greater than the relatively small dollar returns might suggest since there are few income-earning activities available during the seal hunt period.

In 1982, the European market for seal products collapsed as a result of seal hunt protests. In 1983, the European Community banned imports of products from whitecoat harp seals and blueback hooded seals. The seal harvest declined drastically in 1984, prompting the federal government to appoint a royal commission on seals and the sealing industry in Canada.

As a consequence of the commission, the government announced a new seal policy in 1987 which prohibits commercial harvests of whitecoats and bluebacks and the use of vessels over 19.81 metres long, and phases out the technique of catching seals with nets. Today, the seal harvest is less than one-third of the total allowable catch of 186,000 harp seals and is conducted largely by land-based sealers in Newfoundland, the north shore of Quebec and the Îles-de-la-Madeleine.

Harvested seals are used for meat, fur, leather and oil. The harp seal is the main species. More than 3 million of these seals now inhabit the northwest Atlantic and their numbers are believed to be increasing.

SOURCES

Environment Canada — Canadian Wildlife Service

Fisheries and Oceans

Forestry Canada

Statistics Canada

Provincial and territorial governments

FOR FURTHER READING

Selected publications from Statistics Canada

▲ *Pulpwood and Wood Residue Statistics. Monthly. 25-001*

▲ *Shipments of Solid Fuel Burning Heating Products. Quarterly. 25-002*

▲ *Logging Industry. Annual. 25-201*

▲ *Canadian Forestry Statistics. Annual. 25-202*

▲ *Fur Production. Annual. 23-207*

▲ *Report on Fur Farms. Annual. 23-208*

Selected publications from Other Sources

▲ *The Federal Policy on Wetland Conservation. Environment Canada, 1991.*

▲ *A Wildlife Policy for Canada. Canadian Wildlife Service, 1990.*

TABLES

2.1 CANADA'S FOREST INVENTORY, 1991

| | Inventoried forest land ('000 km²) | | | | | Volume³ ('000 000 m²) | | |
	Inventoried forest land[1]	Productive forest land[2]				Softwoods	Hardwoods	Total
		Crown provincial	Crown federal	Private and others	Total			
Newfoundland	225	110	1	2	113	487	38	526
Prince Edward Island	3	..	1	3	3	16	10	26
Nova Scotia	39	10	..	26	37	155	106	261
New Brunswick	61	29	1	30	60	417	205	622
Quebec	825	480	2	66	548	3 089	1 221	4 310
Ontario	580	364	3	56	423	2 389	693	3 083
Manitoba	263	138	3	11	152	597	315	912
Saskatchewan	288	118	5	4	126	445	429	874
Alberta	382	225	17	15	257	1 907	1 155	3 063
British Columbia	605	491	4	21	517	9 872	711	10 583
Yukon	275	74	1	..	75	572	66	638
Northwest Territories	614	119	24	..	143	336	137	474
Canada	4 163	2 159	61	234	2 454	20 285	5 086	25 372

[1] *Land primarily intended for growing, or currently supporting, forest. Includes productive forest land and reserved forest land not available by law for production (as in national parks, some provincial parks, game refuges, water conservation areas, nature preserves and military areas).*
[2] *Productive forest land available for growing and harvesting forest crops. Excludes reserved forest land not available by law.*
[3] *Merchantable volume on productive forest land.*

2.2 FOREST FIRE LOSSES

| | 1989 | | 1990 | | 1991 | |
	Number of fires	Area burned ha	Number of fires	Area burned ha	Number of fires	Area burned ha
Newfoundland	192	68 156	197	47 317	166	65 374
Prince Edward Island	30	195	38	102	48	119
Nova Scotia	425	462	498	1 068	733	1 776
New Brunswick	392	343	377	6 114	656	3 325
Quebec	1,167	2 109 512	851	83 343	1,216	438 328
Ontario	2,430	403 886	1,614	183 693	2,560	318 883
Manitoba	1,226	3 567 948	570	16 365	673	106 585
Saskatchewan	1,020	470 510	897	187 349	762	239 374
Alberta	795	6 411	1,296	30 534	923	6 172
British Columbia	3,520	25 381	3,255	75 778	2,023	30 912
Yukon	244	328 347	154	169 601	187	129 370
Northwest Territories	613	577 585	236	104 616	331	225 470
National parks	131	834	128	25 041	56	1 224
Canada	12,185	7 559 570	10,111	930 921	10,334	1 566 912

2.3 TREES HARVESTED (HECTARES)

	1989		1990		1991	
	Clearcut	Total harvested	Clearcut	Total harvested	Clearcut	Total harvested
Newfoundland	19 449	19 449	29 600	29 600	20 584	20 584
Prince Edward Island	—	2 421	900	2 317	1 114	2 091
Nova Scotia	35 869	36 733	38 830	39 310	36 930	37 566
New Brunswick	90 114	90 114	64 032[e]	696 001[e]	52 707[e]	92 470[e]
Quebec	252 051	342 231	225 624	282 470	192 859	236 816
Ontario	200 293	230 308	209 507	238 213	177 884	199 719
Manitoba	12 205	12 205	10 349	10 349	8 518	8 518
Saskatchewan	22 281	22 281	16 538	16 538	17 242	17 522
Alberta	41 688	41 688	45 000	45 000	50 000	50 160
British Columbia	199 247	218 384	166 565	181 530	174 265	193 654
Yukon	1 554	1 554	366	366	350	350
Northwest Territories	450	450	325	325	467	467
Canada	875 201	1 017 818	807 636	915 618	732 920	859 917

2.4 TREE REPLENISHMENT (HECTARES)

	1989		1990		1991	
	Seeded	Planted with seedlings	Seeded	Planted with seedlings	Seeded	Planted with seedlings
Newfoundland	1 305	3 386	—	3 548	—	2 891
Prince Edward Island	—	744	—	833	—	1 032
Nova Scotia	—	9 760	—	11 255	—	8 198
New Brunswick	—	20 272	69	20 346[e]	32	19 330
Quebec	90	103 140	46	104 323	40	99 550
Ontario	32 969	85 287	27 021	78 098	36 710	83 917
Manitoba	1 579	6 685	5	6 277	2	8 038
Saskatchewan	102	6 004	645	5 367	—	5 915
Alberta	6 653	24 254	9 690	31 862	6 925	33 180
British Columbia	—	174 310	—	209 168	—	199 315
Yukon	—	—	—	—	—	—
Northwest Territories	—	—	—	80	—	39
Canada	42 698	433 842	37 476	471 157	43 709	461 405

2.5 FOREST INDUSTRY, TOTAL ACTIVITY CENSUS VALUE ADDED, 1990 (MILLION DOLLARS)

	Logging	Wood group		Paper group		
		Sawmills	Other wood	Pulp and paper	Other paper	Total
British Columbia	1,524.2	1,740.2	712.8	2,091.4	138.0	6,206.6
Quebec	704.0	526.4	825.9	2,442.6	673.5	5,172.4
Ontario	447.6	234.0	872.7	2,046.2	1,363.1	4,963.6
New Brunswick	230.1	85.9	78.3	468.7	21.1	884.1
Others	291.5	256.1	396.0	990.6	202.3	2,136.5
Canada	3,197.4	2,842.6	2,885.7	8,039.5	2,398.0	19,363.2

2.6 EXPORTS OF WOOD AND PAPER PRODUCTS (MILLION DOLLARS)

	1988	1989	1990	1991
Newsprint	7,299.2	6,507.0	6,461.6	6,494.0
Lumber	5,415.1	5,516.1	5,371.9	5,146.7
Pulp	6,495.8	6,940.3	6,121.0	4,296.9
Other wood	1,082.0	1,055.2	1,070.9	944.1
Other printing paper	285.5	635.6	812.1	786.8
Other paper	1,104.2	1,106.4	1,387.1	1,404.7
Total	21,681.8	21,760.6	21,224.6	19,073.2

2.7 LANDINGS OF SEA AND INLAND FISH AND OTHER SEA PRODUCTS

	1988		1989	
	Quantity[1] t	Landed value $'000	Quantity[1] t	Landed value $'000
Newfoundland	558 358	292,096	521 973	266,359
Prince Edward Island	42 802	68,997	56 931	69,813
Nova Scotia	490 311	436,904	491 485	438,204
New Brunswick	153 361	119,469	168 417	104,935
Quebec	89 337	101,485	82 534	84,686
Ontario	27 591	54,710	26 610	48,123
Manitoba[2]	14 094	25,196	14 699	21,538
Saskatchewan[2]	3 608	4,672	3 904	4,165
Alberta[2]	2 185	2,842	1 594	1,912
British Columbia[2]	265 847	533,559	272 305	416,294
Yukon and Northwest Territories	1 747	2,763	1 954	2,730
Canada	1 649 241	1,642,693	1 642 406	1,458,759
Seafish[3]	1 334 169	1,018,951	1 321 340	963,997
Inland fish	315 072	623,742	321 066	494,762

[1] *Quantity refers to live weight equivalent of landings.*
[2] *Landed value includes final payments to fishers.*
[3] *Quantity includes only fish and shelfish. Landed value also includes marine plants, aquatic mammals, livers, etc.*

2.8 NUMBER OF REGISTERED FISHERS BY PROVINCE

	1989	1990	1991
Sea fisheries			
Newfoundland	29,176	27,905	24,409
Prince Edward Island	5,009	4,970	5,139
Nova Scotia	16,012	15,531	16,300
New Brunswick	7,763	7,544	7,721
Quebec	5,995	5,426	5,303
British Columbia	20,578	20,097	20,000
Total, sea fisheries	84,533	81,473	78,872

2.8 NUMBER OF REGISTERED FISHERS BY PROVINCE (concluded)

	1989	1990	1991
Freshwater fisheries			
New Brunswick	96	96	96
Quebec	241	240	240
Ontario	1,500	1,500	1,500
Prairie provinces and N.W.T.	6,269	6,269	6,269
Total, freshwater fisheries	8,106	8,105	8,105
Total, Canada	92,639	89,578	86,977

2.9 FISH PROCESSING PLANTS AND EMPLOYEES

	1988		1989		1990	
	Establishments	Employees	Establishments	Employees	Establishments	Employees
Newfoundland	112	11,024	110	10,097	109	9,081
Prince Edward Island	20	993	29	1,081	22	1,175
Nova Scotia	121	7,364	126	7,408	119	5,982
New Brunswick	76	4,093	82	4,375	78	3,954
Quebec	42	1,992	36	1,607	49	1,932
Ontario	20	[1]	22	[1]	21	[1]
Manitoba	1	[1]	3	[1]	3	[1]
Saskatchewan	1	[1]	1	[1]	1	[1]
Alberta	1	[1]	1	[1]	1	[1]
British Columbia	59	4,447	62	4,597	57	4,388
Canada	453	31,086	472	30,498	460	27,617

[1] *Confidential, included in Canada total.*

2.10 SPECIES EXTINCT OR AT RISK IN CANADA, 1992

Categories	Mammals	Birds	Fish and marine mammals	Reptiles and amphibians
Extinct[1]	Woodland Caribou (Dawson pop.)	Great Auk Labrador Duck Passenger Pigeon	Blue Walleye Banff Longnose Dace Deepwater Cisco Longjaw Cisco Sea Mink	
Extirpated[2]	Black-footed Ferret Grizzly Bear (Prairie pop.) Swift Fox	Greater Prairie-Chicken	Gravel Chub Paddlefish Gray Whale (Atlantic pop.) Walrus (N.W. Atlantic pop.)	Pygmy Short-horned Lizard
Endangered[3]	Eastern Cougar Peary Caribou (Banks Island pop.) Peary Caribou (High Arctic pop.) Vancouver Island Marmot Wolverine	Eskimo Curlew Harlequin Duck (Eastern pop.) Kirtland's Warbler Loggerhead Shrike (Eastern pop.) Mountain Plover Peregrine Falcon (*Anatum*) Piping Plover Sage Thrasher Spotted Owl Whooping Crane	Acadian Whitefish Aurora Trout Salish Sucker Beluga (St. Lawrence River pop.) Beluga (Ungava Bay pop.) Beluga (SE Baffin Island/Cumberland Sound pop.) Bowhead Whale Right Whale Sea Otter (Pacific Coast)	Blue Racer Lake Erie Water Snake Leatherback Turtle Blanchard's Cricket Frog

[1] *Any species of fauna or flora formerly indigenous to Canada but no longer known to exist.*
[2] *Any indigenous species of fauna or flora no longer known to exist in the wild in Canada but occurring elsewhere.*
[3] *Any indigenous species of fauna or flora that is threatened with imminent extinction or extirpation throughout all or a significant portion of its Canadian range.*

Sources
Canadian Wildlife Service
Fisheries and Oceans Canada
Forestry Canada
Statistics Canada

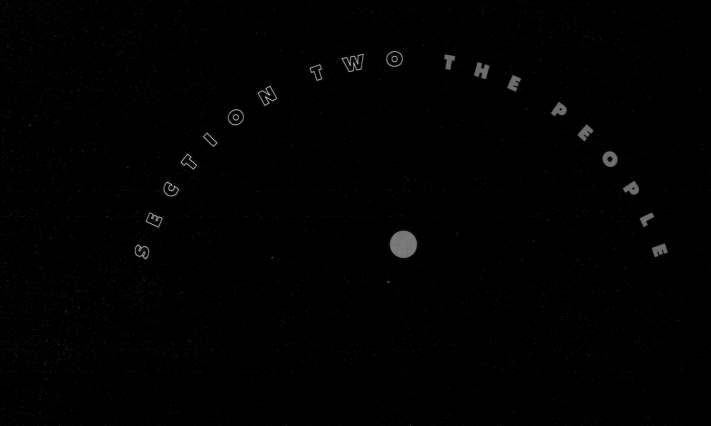

SECTION TWO THE PEOPLE

BRIAN MILNE / FIRST LIGHT

D E M O G R A P H Y

INTRODUCTION

WHERE CANADA STANDS Canada is a huge country, with some 9 million square kilometres of land stretching from Atlantic to Pacific and from within 800 kilometres of the North Pole to a point further south than the Italian city of Naples. But in terms of population, we're rather small. With some 27 million people in 1991, we have about one-third the population of Mexico, a country whose surface area could fit comfortably into Canada four times over.

On the other hand, Canada's population is growing comparatively quickly: at 1.5% in 1990, the rate of population growth was actually the highest in the industrialized world. Europe was running at 0.4%, the United States at 1.1%, and Australia at 1.4%. In contrast, Mexico, a developing country, which may soon be part of a vast economic bloc along with Canada and the United States, was at 2.2%.

Canada is 'younger' than most other industrialized countries, although trends indicate that we are catching up. In 1986, our median age was 31.6; in 1991 it was 33.5. The United States median age was 34.3 the same year, while Sweden's was 37.4 in 1992. Developing countries, on the other hand, have much younger populations. For example, Mexico's median age in 1990 was 19.

In Canada, the total fertility rate (the number of children likely to be borne by one woman in her lifetime) has recently, after decades of decline, shown slow but steady increase. Canada's rate is now higher than that of Europe, slightly lower than that of the United States, but much lower than that of Mexico.

Both marriage and divorce rates were higher in Canada than in Europe in 1991, but both were below the American rates. Mexico had a marriage rate slightly above Canada's but a divorce rate that was much lower.

In 1991, some 186,000 more people entered Canada than left, one-fifth the corresponding figure for the United States, and comparable to the approximately 144,000 more people who left Mexico than entered that year.

The number of Canadians claiming no religious affiliation has nearly tripled over the last 20 years. However, Canadians are more inclined to religion than Europeans, although marginally less so than our American neighbours.

As the world and Canada's place in it continue to change and evolve, so do demographic circumstances within the country. To track the change, Statistics Canada conducts a census every five years; the most recent was held June 4, 1991. Among other things, the census paints the Canadian demographic picture, giving us a clearer idea of who we are, how and where we live, and what changes we may expect to see in the future.

A GROWING AND CHANGING POPULATION

Canada's population has multiplied eightfold in the century-and-a-quarter since Confederation: the 1991 Census of Population counted 27.3 million people in Canada while only 3.4 million — less than the population of Toronto today — were on hand when the country was formed in 1867. At that time, most Canadians were farmers or members of farming families. Today, less than 4% of the population is engaged in agriculture.

Although Canada's population continues to grow in size, the rate of that growth has tended to drop off since the mid-1950s, reaching its lowest point ever in the early 1980s. This tendency has only recently been reversed: between the 1986 and 1991 Censuses, the population grew by 1.8 million people or 7%, considerably more than the growth rate of 4% recorded over the previous five-year period.

Two factors affect the changing size of a population: natural increase (the number of births minus the number of deaths in a given period) and net migration (the difference between the numbers of people entering and leaving the population zone).

Rob Allen

Trick or Treat!

Canada's Population Growth

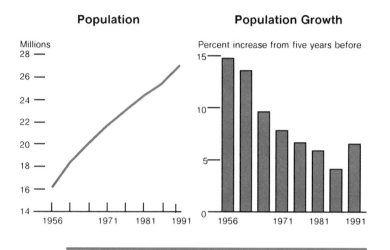

Population

Population Growth

Immigrant Population By Place of Birth

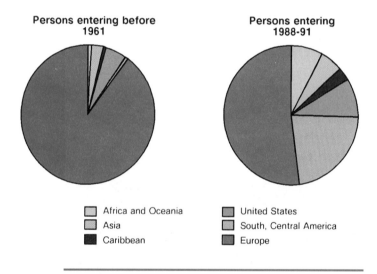

Persons entering before 1961

Persons entering 1988-91

Africa and Oceania
Asia
Caribbean
United States
South, Central America
Europe

IMMIGRATION All kinds of people immigrate to Canada from all parts of the world, ranging from ordinary workers and business people, to refugees or people reuniting with family members. They come from such diverse places as India, Central America, the Horn of Africa and the United Kingdom. Once a person is awarded permanent resident status, they can apply, three years later, for Canadian citizenship. Generally, those coming from countries with many refugees or difficult economic conditions tend to want to become Canadian citizens sooner than does the average immigrant.

As social, political, economic and demographic conditions change, both in Canada and in the rest of the world, immigration policies must be adapted to reflect those changes. When the first Canadian Census of Population after Confederation was taken in 1871, roughly 15% of the country's inhabitants were immigrants (here meaning those born outside Canada). This proportion dropped steadily until the turn of the century, with emigration consistently outpacing immigration. Many of those entering Canada at this time were en route to the United States, where work opportunities were expanding. Those born in Canada also formed part of this exodus.

The proportion of immigrants in the population was considerably higher, around 22%, in the years between 1911 and 1931, owing to the immigration boom that reached a peak in the years preceding World War I and resumed in the years following. This boom was fuelled in part by an energetic campaign on the part of the government to attract settlers to the farmlands of Western Canada — the "Last, Best West" initiative.

In only one decade this century did more people leave than enter the country: the Depression years of the 1930s. After World War II, immigration rose again, as Canada's diversifying economy spurred a demand not for farmers but for skilled industrial workers. They came from Germany, Italy, the Netherlands, Portugal and other European countries, pushing immigration to high levels in the late 1950s. But parallel with this increased immigration came a jump in birth rates — the baby boom of the late 1940s to early 1960s. Although immigration again reached fairly high levels in the late 1960s, and early 1970s, the proportion of immigrants to the population as a whole has for the last 40 years hovered around the 16% mark.

For most of its history, Canada had an immigration policy that included discriminatory provisions against various ethnic groups — for example, the infamous Chinese 'head tax' of 1884-1923, and the virtual suspension of Chinese immigration between 1923 and 1947. Some 35% to 45% of all immigrants admitted to Canada before 1925 were of British origin, and Europe remained the principle supplier of new Canadians until after World War II. However, in 1962 substantial changes made Canada accessible to all, regardless of ethnic origin. In 1967, a points system was initiated to select independent immigrants on the basis of merit; further amendments to the Immigration Act were made in 1976. Partly as a result of all these changes, the majority of Canada's immigrants now come from Asia rather than Europe. The arrival of significant numbers of refugees has also affected immigration patterns, as has the desire of many immigrants to bring their families to Canada.

Notable in the most recent years are the big increases in numbers arriving from Asia, particularly Hong Kong. These increases reflect both the changing social, political and economic climates there (currently a British Colony, Hong Kong will return to Chinese rule in 1997), and Canada's interest in receiving entrepreneurial immigrants.

A new law came into effect in February 1993. This law continues to give priority to the reunification of families, offers protection for refugees who need Canada's help and improves Canada's capacity to select immigrants having particular economic skills or qualifications. It also includes measures to protect Canadian society from those who would abuse its fundamental laws. Refugees fleeing political oppression, war and other forms of civil strife have been made welcome in Canada in increasing numbers over the last decade. In 1986, Canada was awarded the Nansen Medal by the United Nations for its efforts in this regard. What makes Canada's contribution noteworthy is the financial assistance it offers to international refugee organizations and to refugees settling in Canada, as well as the efforts Canada has made on the international stage to help resolve refugee problems all over the world.

CANADA'S TOTAL FERTILITY RATE

In 1990, Canada's total fertility rate stood at 1.8. Demographers tell us that, for a generation to fully replace itself, the fertility rate for that generation must be at least 2.1. In other words, women must give birth to an average of 2.1 children over their lifetimes for the replacement level to be maintained.

Fertility — the rate at which human beings reproduce — is an important topic of study since it underlies the growth and age structure of the population and thus the economic life of the nation.

To measure fertility, demographers often use an index called the total fertility rate. This figure represents the total procreative behaviour of a population in a given year; it corresponds to the number of children a woman would have during her lifetime, if she were to experience the childbearing patterns of a given year.

HEAVEN ON EARTH

Runaway American slaves during the 1850s, hiding in dark and lonely places during their trek north, often sang spirituals about the freedom and safety awaiting them in Canada. They never referred to their destination by name, though — they sang instead about ''heaven''. Heaven was their name for Canada.

Canada is still a land of new beginnings, and almost a quarter of a million immigrants arrive every year from more than 150 countries, attracted by the country's freedoms and opportunities. The 4.3 million immigrants living in Canada at the time of the 1991 Census represented 16% of the total population, a share that has remained pretty steady since the 1951 Census.

If you live in Canada today, odds are high that your neighbours come from another country. In Ontario and British Columbia, those odds are as high as one in four, but vary dramatically elsewhere in the country. In Alberta, for example, immigrants made up 15% of the province's total population, compared with 13% of Manitoba's and 11% of the Yukon Territory's. Quebec and Saskatchewan had far fewer immigrants (9% and 6%, respectively). The Northwest Territories and each of the four Atlantic provinces — traditionally low on the list of preferred destinations — had immigrant populations comprising less then 5% of their territorial and provincial totals.

Like steel to a magnet, new Canadians are drawn to the work, wages and wealth of the big cities, and are more likely than the Canadian-born population to live in one of the country's three largest Census Metropolitan Areas — Toronto, Montreal or Vancouver. Fewer than one-third of all Canadians were living in these cities in 1991, compared with more than half of the country's immigrants. At that time, almost 40% of Toronto's population consisted of immigrants. Vancouver's share, by contrast, was 30%, while Montreal's was 17%.

When a province's total share of immigrants is considered, the pull of large urban centres is nowhere more powerful than in the province of Quebec. In 1991, Montreal was home to 45% of the province's total population, but a staggering 88% of its immigrants. British Columbia, in comparison, had 49% of its total population living in Vancouver in 1991, but 66% of the province's immigrants. Few immigrants are drawn to the urban areas east of Montreal.

Over the years, major urban centres in southern Ontario and the Western provinces have attracted immigrants. In southern Ontario, for example, immigrants in 1991 constituted 24% of Hamilton's population, 22% of Kitchener's and 21% of Windsor's. In Western Canada (excluding Vancouver), Calgary, Alberta, and Victoria, British Columbia, had the highest proportion of immigrants at 20% each, followed by Edmonton, Alberta and Winnipeg, Manitoba, each with 18%.

NATURAL INCREASE Since Confederation, natural increase — the excess of births over deaths in a given period — has accounted for about 80% of Canada's population growth.

In most countries, the rate of natural increase of the human population passes through a process called demographic transition. Before this process begins, high birth rates are countered by high rates of mortality, and population growth is slow. As living conditions, sanitation and health care improve, mortality drops, fertility remains stable and the population grows rapidly. Then, as standards of living continue to rise and birth control becomes more widely available, the birth rate drops too. At the end of the transition, growth is again slow as birth and death rates are low.

At Confederation, Canada's demographic transition was already under way. The birth rate was relatively high, but mortality was already in decline. Since then, Canada's transition process has been fairly typical, except for an unusually sharp drop in the birth rate during the Depression of the 1930s, and an even sharper rise — the baby boom — in the two decades following World War II.

Fertility Ever since Confederation, Canada's total fertility rate has declined steadily, apart from the temporary fluctuations in birth rates already mentioned. In 1921, the fertility rate stood at about 3.5; by the mid-1930s it had dropped to around 2.6. With the baby boom, the rate peaked at almost 4.0 in 1959. In the 1960s it dropped again, and by 1987 was down to about 1.7. However, the next four years showed increases: the 1990 rate was 1.8, the highest in 14 years.

This minor upswing is more noticeable in Quebec, which had a total fertility rate lower than that of the rest of Canada throughout the 1980s.

Mortality In the mid-1800s, Canada's death rate (the number of deaths per year per thousand population) was estimated at between 22 and 25. Mortality was high, and especially so for infants and children: in the 1830s, the infant mortality rate was about 150 per 1,000 live births. By 1921 the crude annual death rate was down to 13 per 1,000 people, and infant mortality was down to 102 per 1,000 births. In 1991, the crude annual death rate was at 7.3 per 1,000 people. The infant mortality rate was 6.8 per 1,000 live births, almost the lowest in the world.

LIFE EXPECTANCY AND AGING As a consequence of the decline in death rates, life expectancy rates in Canada have risen steadily. In 1921, the first year these data were recorded, the average Canadian male could expect to live to about 59, the average female to some months beyond her 60th birthday. In 1990, men could expect to live to 74 and women to 80 and some months.

Canada's population is getting older; in 1991, some 12% of Canadians were aged 65 or older, a full percentage point higher than in 1986. This aging is due partly to increased life expectancy, but more especially to a drop in fertility since the baby boom. With fewer children being brought into the world, and the block of baby boomers heading towards middle age, the average age of the population will continue to push upwards. The tremendous socio-economic challenge that Canada will face in 20 years as a result of this aging is well-documented; what is less well-known is that long before then, improved services will be required for the swelling numbers of seniors born in the 1920s, who are even now entering old age.

Immigrant Population as a Percentage of Canada's Total Population

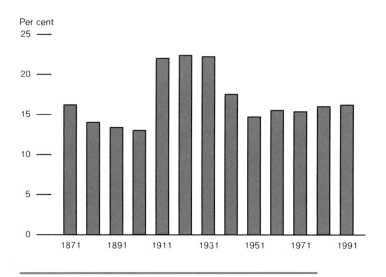

CENSUS METROPOLITAN AREAS

*W*e all have our special names for things and Statistics Canada is no exception. When it gathers information in urban areas or big cities through its census, it calls them Census Metropolitan Areas (CMAs) or Census Agglomerations (CAs).

These share names with cities, but are not the same thing. Both CMA and CA are terms that describe an urbanized core, together with the nearby urban and rural fringe zones which are closely linked with that core economically and socially.

A CA must have an urban core population of at least 10,000 people, based on the previous census.

Once the urban core population reaches 100,000, the CA becomes a CMA.

Vital statistics show that more Canadians were born in 1960 than in any other single year. Since the end of the baby boom in the mid-1960s, the numbers of Canadians born each year have remained relatively stable; at no time have they attained the number born in 1946, the first year of the boom.

WHERE WE HANG OUR HATS

Canada's population is moving. Historically, we have tended to move mostly westward and gravitate towards the big city centres. The country's heartland continues to be Quebec and Ontario: 6 out of 10 Canadians live in these two provinces. However, the distribution of Canada's population among the provinces is still shifting westward, particularly to Ontario from provinces east of there and to British Columbia. This westward shift is especially noticeable if Alberta is included not with the Prairie provinces, as has traditionally been the case, but rather with British Columbia as a western province. In 1991 these two western provinces together accounted for some 21% of Canada's total population, not far behind Quebec's share of around 25%. For many Canadians, one attraction common to southern Ontario and the West Coast as migratory destinations is a relatively mild climate.

Newcomers to Canada have always tended to settle in the more hospitable climates in the south; today, three out of four Canadians live within 150 kilometres of the Canada–United States border. Nevertheless, Canada's northern population is growing. The Yukon Territory, with Canada's smallest total population, had the country's highest growth rate between 1986 and 1991. Both the Yukon and the Northwest Territories, along with British Columbia and Ontario, had population growth rates exceeding the national rate of 8%. The high growth rates in the territories are entirely due to high birth rates, given that between 1986 and 1991 more people moved out of the territories than moved in. Indeed, the 1991 rate of natural increase per 1,000 people for the Yukon was, at 18.9, more than twice the national rate of 8.0, and the rate for the Northwest Territories (25.8) was over three times the national rate. However, these figures can be misleading; in populations as small as those in the territories, even a modest increase in numbers registers as a dramatic leap in percentage.

National Archives of Canada PA 147956

Honeymooning at Niagara Falls: a Canadian tradition.

The other provinces enjoying above-average population growth rates between 1986 and 1991. Ontario and British Columbia had, at the end of this period, rates of natural increase per 1,000 population of 8.2 and 6.9 respectively. Significantly, both provinces are destinations of choice, not only for people moving from one part of Canada to another, but also for immigrants arriving from outside the country.

In 1991, more than half of all Canada's immigrants from abroad had Ontario as their destination. Quebec came second with some 22%, and British Columbia third with about 14%. However, in the same year the net migration out of Quebec was the highest in Canada, as was the net migration into British

Columbia. Ontario also lost out in the interchange of population with British Columbia. Detailed study of these complex migratory flows suggests that whereas immigrants who settle in Ontario tend to stay in that province, immigrants who settle in other provinces are much more likely to move subsequently to Ontario.

The populations of Nova Scotia, New Brunswick, Quebec and Alberta all grew faster in the second half of the 1980s than in the first. Prince Edward Island and Manitoba experienced slower growth in 1986-1991 than in 1981-1986, while Newfoundland and Saskatchewan recorded no growth at all. The population of Newfoundland in 1991 was the same as in 1981, and the population of Saskatchewan

PRIME TIME

John Diefenbaker once said ''if there's snow on the roof, that (doesn't mean) the fire has gone out of the furnace!'' The comment seems particularly apt for Canada's emerging clutch of centenarians. In fact, during the past few years, the 100-plus age group has become the fastest-growing group among elderly people.

Between 1971 and 1991, the number of people aged 100 or older more than tripled, from some 1,100 to 3,700 in the 1991 Census. If current aging trends continue, the number may double in size by 2011.

Until the 1991 Census tracked the increase of 100-year-olds, this group was almost too small to study accurately. What can be said is that these people are beating the odds. When they were born, before the turn of the century, their chances of reaching their 65th birthday were one in three. Their chances of reaching a 100th birthday were infinitesimal — about 0.02%. Yet, between 1986 and 1991, their numbers grew by an astonishing 32%, compared with just 8% growth for the general population.

The first major survey of centenarians was carried out by the **Fondation Ipsen** in France in 1991. It found that these people were remarkably similar in some ways: each had an excellent immune system, a balanced lifestyle free of either deprivation or excess, and a strong personality.

In Canada we also know that reaching 100 may be related to gender. Since the 1960s, women have tended to live longer than men and the latest census shows that the ratio of women to men increases with age. In 1991, close to 80% of all centenarians were women. In 1981, the proportion had been slightly more than 70% women, and in 1961, it had been 64%.

The difference in longevity may explain why only about a tenth of the country's 3,700 centenarians were married in 1991, compared with slightly more than half of the marriageable population as a whole. The older seniors become, the more likely a partner has died.

Whether they are single or married, their distribution roughly parallelled the geographic distribution of Canadians as a whole. For example, in 1991, about 480 centenarians, the largest number concentrated in one area, lived in the Toronto Census Metropolitan Area (CMA); 320 in the Montreal CMA; and 270 in the Vancouver CMA.

Provincially, the picture was much the same. The three provinces with the largest populations were home to the largest numbers of centenarians. Some 1,300 lived in Ontario; some 640 lived in Quebec; and 560 lived in British Columbia.

actually dropped from a record high of slightly over 1 million in 1986 to under 1 million in 1991.

URBANIZATION Canada has over the years become a much more urban society. Back in 1851, only about 13% of the population lived in urban areas. That proportion has climbed virtually continuously ever since. Today, some three out of four Canadians live in urban areas. These may be cities, towns, villages, hamlets, reserves or other centres; to be considered as urban areas, they must have a population of at least 1,000 and a population density of at least 400 per square kilometre. Although the historical trend has been towards increased urbanization across the country, recent figures suggest that the urban-to-rural proportion is stabilizing: the period 1986 to 1991 showed an increase of only one-tenth of a percentage point in the proportion of Canada's population living in urban areas.

Ontario, British Columbia, Alberta and Quebec are all more urbanized than Canada as a whole. The Atlantic region is markedly less urbanized than any other region in Canada except the Northwest Territories, which is the most rural, most sparsely populated and geographically largest area in the country. Surprisingly, Canada's least urbanized province (excluding the Northwest Territories) is also its most densely populated. This apparent paradox is explained by Prince Edward Island's tiny geographical size in comparison with other provinces and territories.

Census Metropolitan Areas (CMAs) Toronto and Montreal are by far Canada's largest CMAs; Montreal's population, although smaller than that of Toronto, was nearly double that of third-place Vancouver in 1991. However, Vancouver's growth rate over the preceding five years was about double that of Montreal, and was second only to that of Oshawa, Ontario. All the CMAs with population growth rates higher than the national rate between 1986 and 1991 are in Ontario and the two western provinces of Alberta and British Columbia.

Immigrants are often attracted to cities. While the combined population of the Montreal, Toronto and Vancouver CMAs in 1991 was less than one-third the population of Canada, more than half of all Canada's immigrants lived in one of those CMAs.

MOVING TO THE 'BURBS'

Most Canadians who live in a big city do not actually live in the heart of the city. The majority make their homes in the surrounding suburbs and bedroom communities, far away from the neon glow of the urban core.

As a result, the populations of these surrounding areas are growing faster than those of the cities they serve.

One way to measure this growth is by comparing the populations of cities with their Census Metropolitan Areas (CMAs). A CMA encompasses all urban and rural areas which are linked to the city's urban core, either socially or economically.

For example, as of June 4, 1991, the city of Ottawa had a population of 313,987 people. The CMA of Ottawa-Hull, however, had a population of 920,857 people. While the city's population grew by 4.4% between 1986 and 1991, the population of the CMA grew by more than 12% — or three times faster — over the same period. The populations of many of Ottawa's outlying communities, such as Cumberland and Kanata, grew by more than 35%.

This trend was evident throughout most of Canada's major cities. For example, the city of Toronto's population grew by 3.8% between 1986 and 1991, but the population of the CMA of Toronto grew by more than 13%. Some outlying communities, such as Richmond Hill and Vaughan, had growth rates of more than 70%.

Moving to the 'burbs' is a lifestyle choice for many Canadians who want to get away from the congestion of the city. But for others, living in the suburbs or outlying areas is a necessity — housing is often more affordable and more available away from the city core.

A WOMAN'S WORK . . .

In many Canadian families, it's the mother who bandages children's scraped knees and soothes the crying, and who may also care for aging parents. Now, a major Statistics Canada study says that women are too busy to carry the full load anymore, and that either care-giving will have to be shared more evenly within households or new arrangements will be needed to support them.

The 1992 report, titled **Gender Inequalities in Caregiving in Canada**, says that some 75% of women, whatever their family status, have sole responsibility for family health care at home, and 13% share it equally with a partner. The balance of women also share responsibility for care, but have the larger share.

As the population ages, demand for care is expected to rise. The report adds that social changes such as a higher divorce rate, more two-income families, greater professional commitments for women and later first pregnancies are making the care-giving role too difficult for women to bear alone.

CMAs tend to keep on growing in population, but some CMAs drop in population over a given period. For example, in the last half of the 1970s, Toronto, Montreal, Vancouver and Ottawa all suffered net losses in population while Calgary and Edmonton gained. But in the following five-year period (1981-1986), the trend was reversed; the four largest CMAs increased in population while Calgary and Edmonton decreased. Such population movements both contribute to and are affected by changing economic conditions in various parts of Canada.

MARRIAGE AND FAMILY LIFE

Over the last 25 years, attitudes to marriage in Canada have changed profoundly. Many Canadians are now postponing or dispensing altogether with marriage in the formal sense. Common-law unions are increasing, while those who do marry are doing so later in life. In 1990, there were 8 divorces for every 20 marriages, compared with 1 divorce for every 20 marriages in 1960. All the signs indicate that marriage, although still part of most people's lives at some time or other, seems to be losing favour in Canada.

A few hundred more Canadian couples married in 1970 than in 1990. But since the population was about one-third bigger in 1990 than 20 years previously, this difference represents a considerable decline in the tendency to marry.

The crude marriage rate — the number of marriages per 1,000 population — has fluctuated over the last 70 years. However, the rate in the 1980s compares to that of the 1960s and indeed the 1920s. On the face of it, this would not appear to indicate that the institution of marriage today is facing a crisis. But the crude marriage rate, while taking into account the total population, does not take into account the numbers of people of marriageable age in that population. In the 1980s, never-married or divorced young adults formed a much larger proportion of the population than in the 1960s. Furthermore, many more marriages now are re-marriages involving divorced people, who have already added their number to the statistics, thereby making deceptively high the total number of marriages over time and hiding a decline in the first marriage rate. So although the number of marriages per 1,000 population in the 1980s is similar to that of other decades, the last 20 years have seen radical changes in the marital behaviour of Canadians.

A more reliable indicator is the total first marriage rate, which takes into account only the marriages of previously single people. This index shows the decline in popularity and the later timing of marriage over the last half-century: standing at the paradoxical level of higher than 1,000 per 1,000 population through most of the 1940s and early 1950s, and above 900 per 1,000 for most of the 1960s, the index stood at just 631 per 1,000 for men and 674 for women in 1989. The paradox is explained by the simultaneous marriages of generations that married early and generations that married later in life.

Over the longer historical perspective, however, a different picture emerges. While marriage in the 1950s and 1960s was early and almost universal, at the time of Confederation Canadians were marrying later and many did not marry at all. While exact comparisons are difficult, it seems that today, Canadians are reverting to the earlier model of late and non-universal marriage, although for different reasons. For example, in 1911 some 35% of men and 20% of women aged 30-34 were still single; in 1966 only 15% and 9% respectively remained single; in 1986 the figures had crept up to 25% and 17% respectively. In that year the mean age at first marriage was 27 for men and nearly 25 for women, compared with 25 and under 23 respectively in 1966.

So Canadians are in some respects returning to marriage patterns of a century ago. However, since that time, many other variables have changed completely. Many more people are divorced and many more live as common-law couples.

DIVORCES Before the liberalization of Canada's divorce laws in 1968, adultery provided the sole grounds for dissolving a marriage, and divorce was rare. However, the new law allowed 16 different grounds for divorce and an immediate surge in divorces took place: the total number of decrees granted in 1969 was more than double the total number granted in 1968.

In recent years, the divorce rate has fluctuated only slightly, although a modest reduction has occurred since 1989.

While interprovincial comparisons are risky, since Canadians move from province to province a good deal, divorce appears to be highest in Alberta, Quebec, Ontario, and British Columbia — Canada's most urbanized provinces. It may well be that the lifestyle imposed by city living is conducive to the breakup of marriages.

Divorces are more common in early marriages; both men and women who marry as teenagers are more likely to divorce than those who marry in their early 20s, who are in turn more likely to divorce than those who marry after the age of 25. This suggests that the current trend toward later marriage could inhibit the rise in divorce rates.

COMMON-LAW UNIONS The number of common-law unions in Canada has more than doubled in the last decade (1981-1991), and increased faster over the last five years than in the previous five.

Population Change, 1986-1991

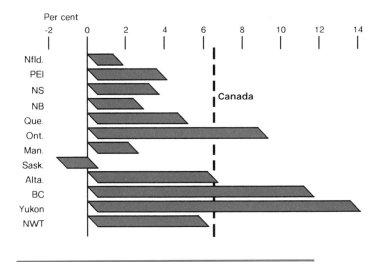

93

Lionel Stevenson / Camera Art

Winter, Charlottetown, Prince Edward Island.

In 1867, at the time of Confederation, most Canadians lived in the country, or along small town main streets.

Today most of us live in town. About 75% of Canadians live in the city or in bedroom communities that form the suburbs.

The rest of us are still out in the country and liking it just fine, according to a new book which looks at life away from the cities. Published in 1992, **Rural and Small Town Canada** *uses data collected by Statistics Canada to paint a picture of life in the country lane.*

What the report finds, however, is that country living can be tough going. Country people, compared to urbanites, have limited social networks, fewer and lesser services, generally make less money, and their social interactions are, well, sparser.

Country people prefer to stay where they are, though. The report says that a substantial 85% of those in the country are happy to stay just where they are, and an 'interesting' 60% of the people who live uptown would rather be further away from the centre of things.

In Canada, the number of rural residents has grown almost continuously since Confederation, even though urban populations have grown much faster. (This rural growth may be partly explained by the fact that Statistics Canada defines rural living in such a way that about a third of Canadians classified as 'rural dwellers' actually live on the fringes of cities.)

When Canada's rural dwellers report to their jobs, they are most likely to work in the service sector or in manufacturing and trade. Agricultural jobs now number less than any one of these, and are still on the decline. Until 1956, farmers made up most of the rural population, but currently they form only about 15% of it.

The average total pay cheque for rural families tends to run around $4,000 a year less than those of city families, but rural families also pay less tax. People in the country tend to have slightly less formal education than city dwellers, but they don't have to put up with higher crime rates. In the late 1980s, violent crime rates were about 15% higher in cities.

In a time when technology and communications connect Canadians in ways previously unknown, we still claim an intangible sense of community that goes with country living. Indeed, the report claims that rural values may create a sense of community sometimes missing in the city.

George Hunter

Louchoux Indian couple, Fort Providence, Northwest Territories.

Clearly, the trend toward this mode of living is gaining momentum. Common-law couples accounted for 6% of all couples in 1981, some 8% in 1986 and 11% in 1991. Indeed, the propensity to live common-law in Canada has increased by 111% (using figures standardized to allow for differences in age structure), and most of this increase came in the last five years. The increase is particularly noticeable in Eastern Canada, which seems to be catching up to the West in this regard.

Common-law living is especially prevalent in Quebec, with British Columbia coming a distant second (this comparison excludes the Yukon and Northwest Territories, since the particular social customs of their high aboriginal populations account for the prevalence of common-law unions in those areas). The rate in Ontario is exceptionally low, and has changed little in the last five years, suggesting that Ontarians prefer unions that are legally sanctioned, even if these may later end in another legal process, that of separation or divorce.

FAMILIES AND HOUSEHOLDS

Family living is still the norm in Canada — almost 85% of the population lived as part of a family in 1991 — but the typical Canadian family, if there is such a thing, continues to undergo a process of change. A generation or two ago, husbands were usually in the workforce, wives at home — no longer. Today the double-income family is more prevalent. Families are smaller, too, although over the last five years the average family size has remained stable (3.1 persons).

The total number of families in Canada increased by 16% between 1981 and 1991, but the growth in two-parent families with children was much smaller (only 6%). In other words, there are many more lone-parent families now than 10 years ago, although the rate of increase is levelling off.

If divorce is one cause of the increase in lone-parent families, another may well be the increasing popularity of the common-law union, since this is easier to dissolve than the legal contract of marriage.

Births to unmarried mothers are on the increase in all parts of Canada. The highest proportion of such births (36% in 1990) is found in Quebec, the lowest (15%) in five first births in Ontario is to an unmarried mother, whereas the figure for Canada as a whole is close to one in three, and for Quebec, almost one in two. The overall increase in births out of wedlock is largely a function of the increase in common-law unions. Many of these births will result in the creation of lone-parent families.

Most lone parents are women, particularly young women aged 15-34. Lone parents are more likely to be divorced or single today than 10 years ago, and less likely to be widowed or separated. The number of married lone parents, although obviously small, has increased. This may be because informal separations are more common nowadays, or perhaps because more married couples are living apart for reasons of work or because one partner is institutionalized.

The proportion of Canadian children living at home that live in lone-parent families is also on the rise, although again the rate of increase is levelling off. Lone-parent families tend to have lower incomes and require more social assistance than two-parent families, so lone-parent children often grow up in closer proximity to the poverty line than do their two-parent peers.

More Canadians are living alone. The number of those in the 25-44 age group living on their own has more than doubled in the last 20 years. However, in 1991 women aged 60 or older still accounted for the majority of Canadians living by themselves.

For the population as a whole, taking age differences into account, the propensity toward solo living has increased by 10% over the last 10 years. During that time, one-person households increased by 29% for single people, 32% for the widowed, and a massive 108% for divorcees.

These increases in double-income families, lone-parent families and solo living suggest that the traditional family, while far from extinct, is under pressure. What is more debatable is whether Canadians are adopting alternative lifestyles as a matter of personal choice or out of sheer necessity.

PORTRAIT OF CANADA

On June 4, 1991, Canada's 17th Census of Population was conducted. With information from 27,296,859 people in 10 million households, the Census provides a new statistical portrait of Canada. Here are some highlights from the 1991 Census.

WE'RE GROWING...

For the first time in 40 years, Canada's growth rate is on the upswing. The Census reported that our population grew by 7.9% since 1986. This increase was due to a combination of increased immigration, decreased emigration and a balanced total of births and deaths.

WE'RE CHANGING...

Although Europeans, at 54%, continued to make up the largest share of immigrants living in Canada in 1991, their proportion has declined steadily from 67% in 1981. During the same period, the percentage of the immigrant population born in Asia almost doubled to reach a high of 25%.

OUR LANGUAGES AT HOME

The number of people whose home language was other than English or French was 2.3 million or 8.4% of the population in 1991, up from 7.5% in 1986. Due to the increased number of recent immigrants who spoke neither English nor French, home languages which grew were Chinese, Spanish and Punjabi while Italian, German and Ukrainian declined.

CANADA'S ABORIGINAL PEOPLE

In 1991, 1,002,675 people reported having aboriginal origins, either as their only ancestry or in combination with other origins, an increase of 41% from 1986. When single and multiple responses are combined, 783,980 people reported North American Indian ancestry, 212,650 reported Métis and 49,255 reported Inuit.

ON LIVING ALONE

More and more Canadians are living alone. In 1961, less than 10% of all private households were one-person households. Three decades later, over 2.3 million people lived alone, some 23% of all private households. The majority (60%) of people living alone were aged 45 or older while only 15% of people living alone were under 30. The percentage of young people aged 15-24 living alone declined from 4% in 1986 to 3% in 1991.

SHE'S THE BOSS

While 9 out of 10 Canadians work for someone else, more Canadians were self-employed in 1991 — they grew by 16% from 1986. Between 1986 and 1991, the number of self-employed women grew faster than the number of men with an increase of 40% in the number of self-employed women with paid employees.

COUNTING EVERYONE IN

The 1991 Census counted 223,410 non-permanent residents; that is, people who held student or employment authorizations, Minister's permits or who were refugee claimants. Over half (56%) of all non-permanent residents lived in Ontario, followed by Quebec (20%) and British Columbia (13%). The major countries of birth of non-permanent residents were Asia (44%), Europe (19%), Central and South America (11%) and Africa (9%).

ON LIVING TOGETHER

In 1991, almost 1.5 million people were living in common-law unions, representing 10% of all Canadian families. Just under two-thirds of both the men and women in these unions had not been married in the past, and 57% were between the ages of 20 and 35.

MORE AND MORE DIVERSE

In 1991, 19.2 million people (71%) reported only one ethnic origin and nearly 8 million people (29%) reported multiple ethnic ancestry. While people with British (28%) and French (23%) backgrounds made up the largest ethnic groups, 31% of the population reported an ethnic background that did not include British or French. This is an increase from 25% in 1986.

While nearly 99% of Canadians can speak one or both of Canada's two official languages, a large proportion of Canadians can carry on conversations in other, 'non-official' languages.

According to the 1991 Census, nearly one in five Canadians can speak a language other than English or French.

Besides our official languages, the most common languages spoken by Canadians were Italian (702,000), German (685,000), Chinese (557,000) and Spanish (402,000). Cree, spoken by almost 94,000 Canadians, was the most common aboriginal language.

Language differences varied widely by region. In the Northwest Territories, where more than half of the residents are aboriginals, almost 50% could speak a language other than English or French. Non-official languages were also common in British Columbia, Manitoba and Ontario, where roughly one-quarter of all residents spoke another language.

At the other end of the scale (and the country), fewer than 4% of those in the Atlantic provinces could carry on a conversation in a language other than English or French.

CAN WE TALK?

To understate the obvious, not all Canadians speak the same language. Canada's First Nations, its aboriginal peoples, speak some 50 languages belonging to 11 distinct linguistic families. The country's large immigrant population has added many other non-European as well as European languages to the linguistic pool. And of course, Canada's two founding nations, the French and the British, have, ever since a French-speaking king named William conquered England in 1066, spoken two languages that were interrelated, sometimes mixed together, and always different.

Yet amid this great diversity, Canadians do communicate with one another. In 1991, less than 2% of the population reported no knowledge of either of Canada's official languages, while 16% (4.4 million people) had knowledge of both English and French, up four full percentage points from the 1951 figure. The 1991 Census also revealed that some 30% of Canadians could converse in two or more languages including non-official ones.

Roughly 6 out of 10 Canadians cite English as their mother tongue (first language learned and still understood). This proportion has fluctuated only slightly over the last 40 years. Anglophones are in the majority in all of Canada's provinces and territories except Quebec, where four out of five are francophones. In neighbouring New Brunswick, one-third of the population claims French as mother tongue, while in the Northwest Territories some 40% report neither English or French as mother tongue but one of several aboriginal languages.

In each province and territory of Canada, the proportion of francophones in the population dropped between 1951 and 1991, and the proportion of francophones to the total population of Canada has been in steady decline throughout that period. Nevertheless, their actual numbers have strengthened considerably, from 4.1 million in 1951 to 6.6 million in 1991. This represents a 63% increase over the period.

The proportion of francophones in the population of Quebec has remained fairly constant, dropping only marginally over the last 40 years. Meanwhile,

Hilda Maxwell / CMCP

Upper Canada Village.

ABORIGINAL LANGUAGES GROUPED BY FAMILY

FAMILY	LANGUAGE	SPEAKERS*
Algonkian (or Algonquian)	Abenaki, Blackfoot, Cree, Delaware, Malecite, Micmac, Montagnais-Naskapi, Ojibwa, Potawatomi	100,000
Athapaskan	Beaver, Carrier, Chilcotin, Chipewyan, Dogrib, Han, Hare, Kasha, Kutchin, Sarcee, Sekani, Slave, Tagish, Tahltan, Tuchone	17,000
Eskimo-Aleut	Inuktitut	16,000
Siouan	Dakota	5,000
Wakashan	Haisla, Heiltsuk, Kwakiutl, Nuuchah-nulth (also known as Nootka), Nitinat	3,400
Salishan	Bella Coola, Comox, Halkomelem, Lillooet, Okanagan, Sechelt, Shuswap, Squamish, Straits, Thompson	3,000

FAMILY	LANGUAGE	SPEAKERS*
Iroquoian	Cayuga, Mohawk, Oneida, Onondaga, Seneca, Tuscarora	2,700
Tsimshian	Coast Tsimshian, Southern Tsimshian, Nass-Gitksan	2,300
Haida	Haida	150
Tlingit	Inland Tlingit	100
Kutenain (or Kootenaian)	Kutenai (or Kootenay)	30-40

Estimates supplied by the Department of Indian Affairs and Northern Development.

LOVE IN A COLD CLIMATE. . .

Falling in love never goes out of style, but the way Canadians act on it is changing. While bridal magazine covers still bear lush photos of traditional weddings, growing proportions of people are no longer going this route. Instead, they are choosing to live together outside of traditional marriage unions.

In Canada in the early 1990s, 'couples unions' — a blanket label for all long-term couples, whether they are married or not — were more common than in the decade before. And although marriage rates declined slightly during the five years previous to the latest census — in 1991, some 77% of all families were based on marriage, compared with 80% some five years before — common-law couples seem to be making up the difference.

In 1981, about 1 in every 16 Canadian couples were living common-law. By the 1991 Census, the number had risen to one in nine. As well, most common-law couples were young: of the more than 1.4 million people living common-law in 1991, some 57% were aged between 20 and 35 years, and close to 64% had never been married.

Common-law relationships also gained popularity among older people. Between 1986 and 1991, they increased by more than 50% among virtually all age groups over 35, and the median age for Canadians who lived common-law rose from about 29 years to 31.

In 1991, close to two-thirds of all people living common-law were single marital status. Divorcees accounted for about a quarter, and separated and widowed Canadians together accounted for about a tenth.

As well, baby boomers may have been more interested in traditional marriage than the generation that followed. During the 1980s, the proportion of young adults who avoided or delayed marrying increased dramatically. In 1991, close to two-thirds of women aged 20 to 24 were single, compared with half of them a decade earlier. During the same period, the percentage of young single men rose from 72% to 82%. Patterns were similar among men and women up to 34 years old.

However, most first common-law relationships are not long term. They end with the partners either marrying or separating. In 1990, Statistics Canada's General Social Survey found that of respondents who had entered their first common-law union during the early 1980s, only 12% of the women and 16% of the men were still living with their first partner.

Rates for families centred around common-law couples were generally highest in the Yukon and Northwest Territories and lowest in the east, but demographers' attempts to quantify the romantic impulse can be viewed in different ways.

Among all Canadians, the highest percentages of common-law families were in the Northwest Territories (22% of all families) and Yukon (20%). The two provinces with the lowest percentages of common-law families were on the East Coast, Newfoundland with 7% and Prince Edward Island with 6%.

But while there were a larger proportion of families based on common-law unions in the North, in absolute numbers more common-law families — 87% of them — lived in Canada's four most highly populated provinces: Quebec (42%), Ontario (25%), British Columbia (12%) and Alberta (8%).

although more anglophones live in Quebec today than were living there in 1951, their share of the total population of the province has gone down about four percentage points. Matching these decreases is a corresponding increase in the proportion of 'allophones', those claiming neither English nor French as mother tongue. Immigration is the main cause of this increase, which echoes a pattern seen across the country, especially in recent years.

Changes in immigration patterns mean that the specific non-official languages most often reported as mother tongue are changing.

Chinese is gaining in strength, while mother tongues of the 'older' immigrant groups are losing ground as successive generations of these groups assimilate to Canada's linguistic majorities.

The non-official languages most often claimed as mother tongue vary in different parts of Canada. According to 1991 data, the Atlantic region's most common non-official mother tongue is Micmac; in Central Canada the most common is Italian; in all three prairie provinces it is German; in British Columbia, Chinese; in the Northwest Territories, Inuktitut; and in the Yukon, the Athapaskan languages of the Dene family. In absolute numbers, very few Canadians east of Quebec speak non-official languages; recent immigration has not been heavy in Atlantic Canada and the aboriginal population, while widespread and growing rapidly, remains relatively small.

CANADA'S ETHNIC DIVERSITY

Ever since the first French and British settlers arrived in the New World and encountered the aboriginal peoples already living here, Canada's population has been ethnically diverse. Responses to the 1991 Census of Population question on ethnic origin indicate that Canada's ethnic mix is becoming increasingly varied.

People with British and French backgrounds still form the largest ethnic groups in Canada. However, more Canadians now claim ethnic origins other than French or British: nearly one-third of the population in 1991 compared to one-quarter in 1986. Conversely, the proportions of people with only French and only British origins both declined.

Of people with neither French nor British origins, the greatest proportion, some 15% of the population, have single European (particularly German, Italian and Ukrainian) ethnic origins. However, the proportion of people with Asian origins rose between 1986 and 1991, from 3.5% to 5.1% (for single origins). This is due largely to increased immigration from Asia in recent years.

Overall, more than 1 million Canadians claimed in 1991 to have aboriginal origins (whether single or multiple origins), a quarter-million more than in 1986. Increased reporting of aboriginal origins may partly be due to the heightened attention that focused on aboriginal issues in the year leading up to the census. Media and other events in society at large do sometimes affect people's responses to census questions; this may explain an increase in the proportion of those — particularly Ontario residents with English as mother tongue — reporting their ethnic origin as 'Canadian'.

Of the country's population, 71% reported single ethnic origins. Quebec recorded the highest proportion of single origins: 92% of its total population. The Yukon had the highest proportion of multiple responses: nearly one-half of its population. In general, new immigrant groups tended to report a higher proportion of single origins, while groups that have been in Canada some time, such as the Scottish, Irish and Northern Europeans (but not the French or Southern Europeans), were more likely to report multiple origins.

REGIONAL DIVERSITY The Atlantic provinces retain their strong British roots; only in New Brunswick did less than half the population report exclusively British origins. Germans and blacks make up the third-largest and fourth-largest ethnic groups in Nova Scotia, and German single responses were among the top five for every province in the Atlantic region.

Three-quarters of Quebec's population, and one-third of New Brunswick's, reported only French origins. Quebec is also home to a number of non-British, non-French ethnic groups; in 1991, the largest Arab and Haitian communities resided in the province. In terms of size, Quebec's communities of persons with Italian, Jewish, Greek, Portuguese, West Asian, Indo-Chinese, Latin/Central/South American, Caribbean

Al Harvey / Masterfile

A stroll in the park, Quebec.

and black origins were second only to those of Ontario. A large majority (85%) of Quebec residents reporting origins other than French or British lived in the Montreal area.

Ontario is ethnically diverse: 40% of the population reported ethnic origins other than British or French. Nearly half of all Canadians having neither French nor British ancestry live in Ontario. Again, this diversity is pronounced in the largest city: Toronto has the highest proportion of non-French, non-British ethnic origins of any Census Metropolitan Area (CMA) in Canada.

Considerable ethnic diversity is also found in the Prairie provinces: origins other than French or British accounted for 47% of the population in Manitoba, 46% in Saskatchewan and 41% in Alberta. As well as relatively large aboriginal populations, these provinces have high concentrations of ethnic groups that immigrated to Canada earlier in the country's history: for example, Germans and Ukrainians.

In British Columbia, 38% reported neither French nor British origins, while 35% reported single British origins, 17% European, and 2% French. One in nine residents (11%) is of Asian origin (1991 figures, single responses).

Only in the Northwest Territories are those of neither British nor French ancestry in the majority: 51% of the population reported single aboriginal origin in 1991. Most of these people are Inuit. In the Yukon, some

19% reported single British origins, making them the largest ethnic group, with single aboriginal origins coming second at around 14%.

KEEPING THE FAITH

While religion has lessened in popularity in Canada over the last 20 years, almost 9 out of 10 Canadians do claim some religious affiliation (88% in 1991). The majority of Canadians who are religious are Roman Catholics, with Protestants coming a close second.

A century ago, almost all Canadians were Christians, and the numbers claiming no religious affiliation were so small as to be negligible. Today, 1 Canadian in 8 has no religion, while 1 in 35 is of a faith that stands outside the Judeo-Christian tradition of the country's founding nations. The most common of these faiths is Islam, followed by Buddhism and Hinduism.

By and large, people in the eastern part of the country are more inclined to religion than those in the West. Of all the provinces and territories, Newfoundland has the highest proportion of Protestants and the lowest proportion of those having no religion. Quebec is the most Catholic province, British Columbia the least. Of those claiming no religion, Ontario has the same proportion as Canada as a whole, while Alberta, British Columbia and the Yukon all have proportions considerably higher than the national average.

SOURCES

Employment and Immigration Canada

Statistics Canada

FOR FURTHER READING

Selected publications from Statistics Canada

▲ *Women in Canada: A Statistical Report. 89-503E*

▲ *The Family in Canada: Selected Highlights. 89-509*

▲ *Immigrants in Canada: Selected Highlights. 89-510*

▲ *Youth in Canada: Selected Highlights. 89-511*

▲ *A Portrait of Seniors in Canada. 89-519*

▲ *A Portrait of Children in Canada. 89-520*

▲ *Canadians in the Pre-Retirement Years: A Profile of People Aged 55-64*, C. Lindsay, M.S. Devereaux. *89-521E*

▲ *Population Estimates and Projections, Census and Intercensal Studies. 91-002 - 91-536E*

▲ *A National Overview, 1991 Census. 93-301*

▲ *The Nation Series, 1991 Census. 93-310 - 93-313D*

Selected publications from Other Sources

▲ *Multicultural Canada: A Graphic Overview. Multiculturalism and Citizenship Canada, 1990.*

TABLES

3.1   MAIN DEMOGRAPHIC INDICATORS, SELECTED COUNTRIES, 1991

	Population on January 1, 1992 '000	Rate of increase per thousand	Births '000	Deaths '000	Natural increase '000	Net migration[1] '000	Infant Mortality rate[2]
Belgium	10,022.0	3.5	126.1	105.2	20.9	14.1e	8.4
Denmark	5,162.1	3.1	64.5	59.5	5.0	10.9	7.3
Germany	80,170.0	5.2	828.3	900.8	−72.5	490.0	7.2e
Greece	10,250.0	4.9	100.0	93.5	6.5	43.5	10.0
Spain	39,055.9	1.6	386.5	338.2	48.3	13.8e	7.8
France	57,206.2	5.5	758.4	526.0	232.4	80.0	7.4
Ireland	3,532.0	3.7	52.7	31.5	21.2	−8.0e	8.2
Italy	57,788.2	0.8	558.8	546.8	11.9	34.9	8.3
Luxembourg	389.8	14.0	5.0	3.7	1.2	4.2	9.2
Netherlands	15,128.6	8.7	198.6	129.9	68.7	62.8	6.5
Portugal	9,845.6	−1.3	116.4	104.4	12.1	25.0	10.8
United Kingdom	57,642.0e	2.7e	792.5	643.1	149.4	6.8e	7.3
Total European Economic Community	346,192.4	3.6	3,987.8	3,842.7	505.1	728.1	7.7
Canada	27,243.0[3]	15.0	411.9	196.1	215.8	186.3	7.0
United States	253,668.0	11.0	4,111.0	2,165.0	1,946.0	857.0	9.2
Mexico	87,241.4	22.0	2,461.8	481.5	1,980.3	−143.6	37.0
North America	337,121.4	...	6,984.9	2,842.6	4,142.3	...	...
Australia	17,652.3	14.0	256.8	118.9	138.0	100.0e	7.2
New Zealand	3,449.6	11.0	60.2	26.5	33.6	5.7	8.3
Japan	120,000.0	5.0	1,223.2	829.5	393.7	257.7	4.4

3.1 MAIN DEMOGRAPHIC INDICATORS, SELECTED COUNTRIES, 1991 (concluded)

	Life expectancy[4]		Total fertility rate[5]	Marriages '000	Marriage rate[6] (per thousand)	Divorce rate '000	Divorce rate (per thousand)
	Men	Women					
Belgium	72.7[e7]	79.4[e7]	1.57	60.8	6.1	20.8	2.1
Denmark	72.0[e7]	77.7[e7]	1.68	30.9	6.0	12.6	2.5
Germany	..	..	1.35[e]	453.3	5.7	176.7[8]	2.2[8]
Greece	73.6[7]	78.6[7]	1.40	62.0	6.1	6.0	0.6
Spain	73.4[7]	80.1[e7]	1.28	219.8	5.6	23.1[8]	0.6[8]
France	73.0	81.1	1.77	280.5	4.9	105.8[7]	1.9[7]
Ireland	71.9[e7]	77.4[e7]	2.18	16.9	4.8	..	..
Italy	73.2[e9]	79.7[e9]	1.26	309.1	5.4	26.5	0.5
Luxembourg	72.3[e7]	78.5[e7]	1.64[e]	2.6	6.7	0.8	2.0
Netherlands	73.7	79.8	1.61	94.9	6.3	28.0	1.9
Portugal	70.2[e7]	77.3[e7]	1.42[e]	71.8	7.3	10.6	1.1
United Kingdom	72.9[e7]	78.5[e7]	1.82[e]	390.0[e]	6.8[e]	167.5[7]	2.9[7]
Total European Economic Community	72.7[9]	79.3[9]	1.56	1,922.5	5.8	580.0	1.7
Canada	74.0	80.6	1.82[7]	188.7	7.0	78.0	2.9
United States	..	..	2.01[8]	2,371.0	9.4	1,187.0	4.7
Mexico	66.5	73.1	3.29	652.4	7.6	49.2	0.6
North America	..	..	..	..	..	..	..
Australia	73.9	80.0	1.91	113.8	6.6	45.6	2.6
New Zealand	71.9	78.0	2.18	23.3	6.8	9.0	2.6
Japan	76.1	82.1	..	742.3	6.0	169.0	1.4

[1] *Difference between immigrants and emigrants.*
[2] *Per thousand live births.*
[3] *Component method estimate based on the 1986 Census, excludes non-residents.*
[4] *In years and tenths of years.*
[5] *Number of children per woman.*
[6] *Per thousand persons.*
[7] *In 1990.*
[8] *In 1989.*
[9] *In 1988.*

3.2 CANADA'S POPULATION[1] (THOUSANDS)

	Nfld.	PEI	NS	NB	Que.	Ont.	Man.
1921	. . .	88.6	523.8	387.9	2,360.5	2,933.7	610.1
1931	. . .	88.0	512.8	408.2	2,874.7	3,431.7	700.1
1941	. . .	95.0	578.0	457.4	3,331.9	3,787.7	729.7
1951	361.4	98.4	642.6	515.7	4,055.7	4,597.6	776.5
1956	415.1	99.3	694.7	554.6	4,628.4	5,404.9	850.0
1961	457.9	104.6	737.0	597.9	5,259.2	6,236.1	921.7
1966	493.4	108.5	756.0	616.8	5,780.8	6,960.9	963.1
1971	522.1	111.6	789.0	634.6	6,027.8	7,703.1	988.2
1976	557.7	118.2	828.6	677.3	6,234.5	8,264.5	1,021.5
1981	567.7	122.5	847.4	696.4	6,438.2	8,624.7	1,026.2
1986	568.3	126.6	873.2	710.4	6,540.2	9,113.0	1,071.2
1987[2]	568.1	127.3	878.0	712.3	6,592.6	9,265.0	1,079.0
1988[2]	568.8	128.5	881.9	714.3	6,640.8	9,431.1	1,084.1
1989[2]	571.1	129.9	888.3	717.8	6,698.2	9,589.6	1,086.3
1990[2]	572.7	130.7	895.1	722.6	6,768.2	9,749.6	1,089.0
1991[2]	575.7	131.2	901.0	727.6	6,847.4	9,917.3	1,094.4
1992[3]	577.5	130.5	906.3	729.3	6,925.2	10,098.6	1,096.8

	Sask.	Alta.	BC	YT	NWT	Canada
1921	757.5	588.5	524.6	4.1	8.1	8,787.4
1931	921.8	731.6	694.3	4.2	9.3	10,376.7
1941	896.0	796.2	817.8	5.0	12.0	11,506.7
1951	831.7	939.5	1,165.2	9.1	16.0	14,009.4
1956	880.7	1,123.1	1,398.5	12.2	19.3	16,080.8
1961	952.2	1,332.0	1,629.1	14.6	23.0	18,265.3
1966	955.4	1,463.2	1,873.7	14.4	28.7	20,014.9
1971	926.2	1,627.9	2,184.6	18.4	34.8	21,568.3
1976	921.3	1,838.0	2,466.6	21.8	42.6	22,992.6
1981	968.3	2,237.3	2,744.2	23.2	45.7	24,341.7
1986	1,010.2	2,375.1	2,889.0	23.5	52.2	25,353.0
1987[2]	1,015.8	2,377.7	2,925.0	24.5	52.0	25,617.3
1988[2]	1,013.5	2,388.7	2,980.2	25.2	52.2	25,909.2
1989[2]	1,006.7	2,425.9	3,048.3	25.5	52.9	26,240.3
1990[2]	997.1	2,473.1	3,132.5	26.0	53.9	26,610.4
1991[2]	994.2	2,521.6	3,212.1	26.7	55.2	27,004.4
1992[3]	993.2	2,562.7	3,297.6	27.9	56.5	27,402.1

[1] *As of June 1.*
[2] *Final postcensal estimates.*
[3] *Updated postcensal estimates.*

3.3 POPULATION GROWTH[1]

Period	Total population growth '000	Births '000	Deaths '000	Natural increase '000	Ratio of natural increase to total growth %	Immi- gration '000	Emi- gration[2] '000	Net migration '000	Ratio of net migration to total growth %	Popula- tion at the end of the Census period '000
1851-1861	793	1,281	670	611	77.0	352	170	182	23.0	3,230
1861-1871	459	1,370	760	610	132.9	260	411	−151	−32.9	3,689
1871-1881	636	1,480	790	690	108.5	350	404	−54	−8.5	4,325
1881-1891	508	1,524	870	654	128.7	680	826	−146	−28.7	4,833
1891-1901	538	1,548	880	668	124.2	250	380	−130	−24.2	5,371
1901-1911	1,836	1,925	900	1,025	55.8	1,550	739	811	44.2	7,207
1911-1921	1,581	2,340	1,070	1,270	80.3	1,400	1,089	311	19.7	8,788
1921-1931	1,589	2,415	1,055	1,360	85.6	1,200	971	229	14.4	10,377
1931-1941	1,130	2,294	1,072	1,222	108.1	149	241	−92	−8.1	11,507
1941-1951[3]	2,141	3,186	1,214	1,972	92.1	548	379	169	7.9	13,648
1951-1956	2,072	2,106	633	1,473	71.1	783	184	599	28.9	16,081
1956-1961	2,157	2,362	687	1,675	77.7	760	278	482	22.3	18,238
1961-1966	1,777	2,249	731	1,518	85.4	539	280	259	14.6	20,015
1966-1971	1,553	1,856	766	1,090	70.2	890	427	463	29.8	21,568
1971-1976	1,425	1,756	822	934	65.5	841	350	491	34.5	22,993
1976-1981	1,350	1,820	842	978	72.4	588	216	372	27.6	24,343
1981-1986	1,011	1,873	885	988	97.7	500	477	23	2.3	25,354
1986-1991	1,754	1,930	945	985	56.2	874	105	769	43.8	27,108

[1] *Includes Newfoundland since 1951.*
[2] *Emigration figures are estimated by the residual method.*
[3] *Data on components of growth shown for 1941–51 were obtained by excluding data for Newfoundland.*

3.4 CANADA'S TOTAL FERTILITY RATE[1]

	1987	1988	1989	1990	Growth 1987-90 in %
Newfoundland	1.57	1.51	1.57	1.55	−1.3
Prince Edward Island	1.86	1.87	1.83	1.92	3.3
Nova Scotia	1.59	1.61	1.66	1.72	8.0
New Brunswick	1.56	1.58	1.61	1.65	5.5
Quebec	1.42	1.48	1.61	1.72	20.8
Ontario	1.68	1.70	1.77	1.82	8.3
Manitoba	1.88	1.89	1.96	1.99	6.0
Saskatchewan	2.04	2.03	2.11	2.11	3.5
Alberta	1.88	1.92	2.00	1.98	5.4
British Columbia	1.71	1.76	1.77	1.81	5.4
Yukon	2.01	2.16	1.98	2.29	14.2
Northwest Territories	3.05	3.16	2.98	3.15	3.1
Canada	1.66	1.69	1.76	1.82	9.8

[1] *Total Fertility Rate is the number of children each women in a population would bear in her lifetime, based on the age-specific fertility rates for a particular year. A generation would be replaced if the number of children born per thousand women was 2,100, that is 2.1 children per woman.*

3.5 CENSUS METROPOLITAN AREAS[1]

	Rank		1986 population	1991 population	Absolute change	Percent change
	1986	1991				
Toronto	1	1	3,431,981[2]	3,893,046	461,065	13.4
Montreal	2	2	2,921,357	3,127,242	205,885	7.0
Vancouver	3	3	1,380,729	1,602,502	221,773	16.1
Ottawa-Hull	4	4	819,263	920,857	101,594	12.4
Edmonton	5	5	774,026[2]	839,924	65,898	8.5
Calgary	6	6	671,453[2]	754,033	82,580	12.3
Winnipeg	7	7	625,304	652,354	27,050	4.3
Quebec	8	8	603,267	645,550	42,283	7.0
Hamilton	9	9	557,029	599,760	42,731	7.7
London	11	10	342,302	381,522	39,220	11.5
St. Catharines-Niagara	10	11	343,258	364,552	21,294	6.2
Kitchener	12	12	311,195	356,421	45,226	14.5
Halifax	13	13	295,922[2]	320,501	24,579	8.3
Victoria	14	14	255,225[2]	287,897	32,672	12.8
Windsor	15	15	253,988	262,075	8,087	3.2
Oshawa	16	16	203,543	240,104	36,561	18.0
Saskatoon	17	17	200,665	210,023	9,358	4.7
Regina	18	18	186,521	191,692	5,171	2.8
St. John's	19	19	161,901	171,859	9,958	6.2
Chicoutimi-Jonquière	20	20	158,468	160,928	2,460	1.6
Sudbury	21	21	148,877	157,613	8,736	5.9
Sherbrooke	22	22	129,960	139,194	9,234	7.1
Trois-Rivières	23	23	128,888	136,303	7,415	5.8
Saint John	24	24	121,265	124,981	3,716	3.1
Thunder Bay	25	25	122,217	124,427	2,210	1.8

[1] The general concept of a census metropolitan area is one of a very large urban area, together with adjacent urban and rural areas which have a high degree of economic and social integration with that urban area.
[2] Adjusted figure due to boundary change.

3.6 DEMOGRAPHIC CHANGE

	Population[1] '000	Total growth '000	Rate per thousand	Births '000	Deaths '000	Natural increase '000	Rate per thousand	Net migration[2]
1981								
Newfoundland	567.2	−1.2	−2.1	10.1	3.2	6.9	12.2	−8.1
Prince Edward Island	122.4	0.1	0.8	1.9	1.0	0.9	7.4	−0.8
Nova Scotia	846.9	2.1	2.5	12.1	7.0	5.1	6.0	−3.0
New Brunswick	695.7	−0.4	−0.6	10.5	5.1	5.4	7.7	−5.8
Quebec	6,412.9	37.4	5.8	95.3	42.7	52.6	8.2	−15.2
Ontario	8,599.7	64.1	7.5	122.2	62.8	59.3	6.9	4.8
Manitoba	1,023.4	6.0	5.9	16.1	8.6	7.4	7.3	−1.4
Saskatchewan	964.1	9.8	10.2	17.2	7.5	9.7	10.0	0.1
Alberta	2,203.6	85.3	38.7	42.6	12.8	29.8	13.5	55.5
British Columbia	2,717.7	56.4	20.8	41.5	19.9	21.6	8.0	34.8
Yukon	22.7	0.9	39.6	0.5	0.1	0.4	17.4	0.5
Northwest Territories	45.0	1.6	35.6	1.3	0.2	1.1	24.6	0.5
Canada	24,221.3	262.1	10.8	371.3	171.0	200.3	8.3	61.8

3.6 DEMOGRAPHIC CHANGE (concluded)

	Population[1] '000	Total growth '000	Rate per thousand	Births '000	Deaths '000	Natural increase '000	Rate per thousand	Net migration[2]
1990								
Newfoundland	571.0	0.8	1.4	7.6	3.9	3.7	6.5	−2.9
Prince Edward Island	130.2	0.1	0.8	2.0	1.1	0.9	6.9	−0.8
Nova Scotia	892.2	6.5	7.3	12.9	7.4	5.5	6.1	1.0
New Brunswick	720.3	4.5	6.2	9.8	5.4	4.4	6.1	0.1
Quebec	6,737.1	75.7	11.2	98.1	48.4	49.7	7.3	26.0
Ontario	9,683.7	162.4	16.8	150.9	70.6	80.3	8.3	82.1
Manitoba	1,086.2	3.6	3.3	17.4	8.9	8.5	7.8	−4.9
Saskatchewan	999.1	−6.6	−6.6	16.1	8.0	8.1	8.1	−14.7
Alberta	2,451.5	50.7	20.7	43.0	14.1	28.9	11.8	21.8
British Columbia	3,101.7	89.6	28.5	45.6	23.6	22.0	7.0	67.6
Yukon	25.9	0.6	23.2	0.6	0.1	0.5	19.3	0.1
Northwest Territories	53.2	1.0	18.8	1.6	0.2	1.4	26.3	−0.4
Canada[3]	26,452.1	388.8	14.7	405.5	191.7	213.8	8.1	175.0
1991								
Newfoundland	571.8	2.4	4.2	7.8	3.9	3.9	6.8	−1.5
Prince Edward Island	130.3	−0.5	−3.8	2.1	1.2	0.9	6.9	−1.4
Nova Scotia	898.7	7.4	8.2	13.0	7.6	5.4	6.0	2.0
New Brunswick	724.8	1.9	2.6	9.9	5.6	4.3	5.9	−2.4
Quebec	6,812.8	82.6	12.1	100.2	48.8	51.4	7.5	31.2
Ontario	9,846.1	192.8	17.6	153.8	72.9	80.9	8.2	91.9
Manitoba	1,089.8	4.4	4.0	17.4	9.0	8.4	7.7	−4.0
Saskatchewan	992.5	−0.2	−0.2	16.2	8.2	8.0	8.1	−8.3
Alberta	2,502.2	47.3	18.9	43.3	14.5	28.8	11.5	18.5
British Columbia	3,191.3	81.7	25.3	46.2	24.0	22.2	6.9	59.5
Yukon	26.5	0.9	34.0	0.6	0.1	0.5	18.9	0.4
Northwest Territories	54.2	1.4	25.8	1.6	0.2	1.4	25.8	0.0
Canada[3]	26,840.9	402.1	15.0	411.9	196.1	215.8	8.0	186.3

[1] As of January 1. Data for 1990 are taken from final postcensal estimates. Calculations are based on unrounded data.
[2] Difference between total growth and natural increase.
[3] Component method estimate based on the 1986 Census, excludes non-residents.

3.7 LAND AREA AND POPULATION DENSITY

	Land area km²	Population per square kilometer				
		1961	1971	1981	1986	1991
Newfoundland	371 635	1.2	1.4	1.5	1.5	1.5
Prince Edward Island	5 660	18.5	19.7	21.6	22.4	22.9
Nova Scotia	52 841	14.0	14.9	16.0	16.5	17.0
New Brunswick	71 569	8.3	8.8	9.7	9.9	10.1
Quebec	1 357 812	3.9	4.4	4.7	4.8	5.1
Ontario	916 734	7.0	8.6	9.4	9.9	11.0
Manitoba	547 704	1.7	1.8	1.9	2.0	2.0
Saskatchewan	570 113	1.6	1.6	1.7	1.8	1.7
Alberta	638 233	2.1	2.5	3.5	3.7	4.0
British Columbia	892 677	1.8	2.4	3.1	3.2	3.7
Yukon	531 844	--	--	--	--	0.1
Northwest Territories	3 246 389	--	--	--	--	--
Canada	9 203 210	1.98	2.34	0.1	2.8	3.0

3.8 IMMIGRANTS ARRIVING, BY PLACE OF BIRTH

	1981		1991		1981-90 Total	
	Number	%	Number	%	Number	%
Europe	44,784	34.8	46,651	20.2	351,511	26.4
Great Britain	18,912	14.7	6,383	2.8	81,460	6.1
Portugal	3,292	2.6	5,837	2.5	38,630	2.9
France	1,681	1.3	2,619	1.1	15,256	1.1
Greece	924	0.7	618	0.3	6,884	0.5
Italy	2,057	1.6	775	0.3	11,196	0.8
Poland	4,093	3.2	15,737	6.8	81,361	6.1
Other	13,825	10.7	14,682	6.4	116,724	8.8
Africa	5,901	4.6	16,530	7.2	72,941	5.5
Asia	50,759	39.5	122,228	53.0	619,089	46.5
Philippines	5,978	4.6	12,626	5.5	67,682	5.1
India	9,415	7.3	14,248	6.2	90,050	6.8
Hong Kong	4,039	3.1	16,425	7.1	96,982	7.3
China	9,798	7.6	20,621	8.9	74,235	5.6
The Middle East	5,409	4.2	24,497	10.6	90,965	6.8
Other	16,120	12.5	33,811	14.7	199,175	15.0
North and Central America	10,183	7.9	18,899	8.2	114,073	8.6
United States	8,695	6.8	5,270	2.3	63,106	4.7
Other	1,488	1.2	13,629	5.9	50,967	3.8
The Caribbean and Bermuda	8,797	6.8	13,046	5.7	89,098	6.7
Australasia	1,020	0.8	735	0.3	5,877	0.4
South America	6,114	4.8	10,468	4.5	67,936	5.1
Oceania	1,024	0.8	2,213	1.0	10,040	0.8
Other	36	--	11	--	375	--
Total	128,618	100.0	230,781	100.0	1,330,940	100.0

3.9 IMMIGRANTS, BY CATEGORY

	1981		1991		1981-90 Total	
	Number	%	Number	%	Number	%
Family Class[1]	51,017	39.7	86,378	37.4	513,380	38.6
Refugees						
Convention refugees	810	0.6	18,374	8.0	62,718	4.7
Designated classes	14,169	11.0	35,027	15.2	159,496	12.0
Aided relatives	17,590	13.7	22,247	9.6	130,751	9.8
Independent immigrants	45,032	35.0	68,755	29.8	464,595	34.9
Total	128,618	100.0	230,781	100.0	1,330,940	100.0

[1] *Close relatives sponsored by a Canadian citizen or permanent resident.*

3.10 POPULATION BY MARITAL STATUS AND SEX, 1991

	Age Groups					
	Total	Under 15	15–19	20–24	25–29	30–34
Total	27,296,860	5,692,555	1,868,635	1,961,870	2,375,540	2,491,045
Male	13,454,580	2,916,905	958,405	985,220	1,182,575	1,237,690
Female	13,842,280	2,775,650	910,230	976,655	1,192,965	1,253,360
Single (never married)	11,398,415	5,692,555	1,816,315	1,435,220	894,540	504,810
Male	6,057,685	2,916,910	946,365	804,085	540,130	300,125
Female	5,340,430	2,775,650	869,950	631,140	354,415	204,690
Married[1]	13,141,085	. . .	49,270	502,945	1,384,875	1,809,790
Male	6,591,945	. . .	10,895	174,775	609,070	868,670
Female	6,549,140	. . .	38,375	328,175	775,805	941,120
Separated	503,600	. . .	1,400	15,310	50,265	73,385
Male	215,820	. . .	480	4,070	17,765	29,830
Female	287,780	. . .	920	11,240	32,495	43,555
Widowed	1,344,695	. . .	860	1,175	2,490	5,735
Male	225,635	. . .	300	335	555	1,215
Female	1,119,065	. . .	560	840	1,935	4,520
Divorced	909,070	. . .	790	7,210	43,370	97,325
Male	363,195	. . .	365	1,960	15,055	37,850
Female	545,870	. . .	425	5,255	28,315	59,475
	35–39	40–44	45–49	50–54	55–59	60–64
Total	2,284,475	2,086,895	1,640,785	1,325,460	1,222,925	1,176,705
Male	1,133,670	1,042,185	824,200	663,285	608,085	571,940
Female	1,150,810	1,044,715	816,580	662,175	614,835	604,765
Single (never married)	291,640	184,600	114,235	81,990	73,870	75,085
Male	168,130	102,565	62,325	44,585	40,290	40,085
Female	123,510	82,030	51,915	37,405	33,575	35,000
Married[1]	1,768,910	1,655,140	1,311,715	1,061,070	960,405	880,035
Male	876,595	842,335	679,265	552,330	506,420	469,840
Female	892,320	812,805	632,450	508,745	453,980	410,195
Separated	76,390	73,100	55,445	39,950	33,395	28,945
Male	32,320	31,875	24,960	18,390	15,365	13,575
Female	44,070	41,220	30,485	21,555	18,030	15,370
Widowed	10,535	18,395	28,045	43,620	74,690	128,145
Male	2,025	3,545	5,010	7,360	12,380	21,290
Female	8,510	14,850	23,030	36,260	62,315	106,855
Divorced	137,005	155,660	131,340	98,825	80,565	64,495
Male	54,600	61,855	52,645	40,615	33,630	27,150
Female	82,405	93,805	78,700	58,210	46,935	37,345

3.10 **POPULATION BY MARITAL STATUS AND SEX, 1991** (concluded)

	Age Groups					
	65-69	70-74	75-79	80-84	85-89	90+
Total	1,073,170	821,900	614,775	376,790	189,490	93,845
Male	492,505	358,955	252,530	140,135	61,250	25,050
Female	580,665	462,945	362,245	236,650	128,235	68,790
Single (never married)	69,315	55,690	47,670	32,800	18,125	9,940
Male	33,930	23,465	17,290	10,185	5,035	2,480
Female	35,385	32,225	30,375	22,615	13,095	7,460
Married[1]	742,210	502,600	309,405	141,805	47,240	13,675
Male	398,500	282,960	186,265	91,670	32,620	9,750
Female	343,705	219,640	123,135	50,135	14,625	3,925
Separated	23,345	15,470	9,695	4,835	1,940	720
Male	10,915	7,255	4,880	2,610	1,115	410
Female	12,430	8,220	4,815	2,225	830	310
Widowed	192,615	223,080	234,600	191,670	120,285	68,750
Male	30,625	35,175	38,630	33,320	21,750	12,120
Female	161,990	187,900	195,970	158,350	98,540	56,630
Divorced	45,695	25,055	13,410	5,680	1,890	765
Male	18,535	10,095	5,465	2,355	740	290
Female	27,160	14,960	7,945	3,325	1,150	470

[1] *Includes persons in common-law unions.*

3.11 NUMBER OF INTERPROVINCIAL MIGRANTS[1], 1991

Province of origin	Province of destination					
	Nfld.	PEI	NS	NB	Que.	Ont.
Newfoundland	. . .	228	2,175	766	393	6,026
Prince Edward Island	182	. . .	1,469	627	159	1,107
Nova Scotia	1,564	681	. . .	2,959	1,170	8,971
New Brunswick	617	551	3,818	. . .	2,588	5,658
Quebec	376	153	1,348	2,473	. . .	26,723
Ontario	6,333	980	8,602	5,297	18,223	. . .
Manitoba	109	82	584	363	876	7,412
Saskatchewan	124	46	356	215	519	2,793
Alberta	910	268	1,735	1,030	1,882	12,136
British Columbia	411	130	1,857	693	2,228	11,489
Yukon	43	—	30	7	31	178
Northwest Territories	98	50	174	47	222	502
Total in	10,767	3,169	22,148	14,477	28,291	82,995
Total out	12,728	4,722	21,161	16,854	40,550	89,599
Net migration	−1,961	−1,553	987	−2,377	−12,259	−6,604

Province of origin	Province of destination					
	Man.	Sask.	Alta.	BC	Yukon	NWT
Newfoundland	284	117	1,413	1,112	39	175
Prince Edward Island	116	73	575	393	—	21
Nova Scotia	688	413	1,951	2,461	47	256
New Brunswick	560	201	1,358	1,349	58	96
Quebec	761	314	3,138	5,021	21	222
Ontario	6,044	2,654	16,921	23,636	183	726
Manitoba	. . .	2,994	6,392	7,290	34	285
Saskatchewan	2,991	. . .	15,250	6,539	171	478
Alberta	3,778	9,167	. . .	30,654	512	1,360
British Columbia	3,279	3,534	21,509	. . .	1,097	628
Yukon	54	25	401	1,029	. . .	94
Northwest Territories	203	161	1,788	818	219	. . .
Total in	18,758	19,653	70,696	80,302	2,381	4,341
Total out	26,421	29,482	63,432	46,855	1,892	4,282
Net migration	−7,663	−9,829	7,264	33,447	489	59

Total number of migrants: 357,978

[1] *From Family Allowance files, January-December, 1991.*

3.12 MARRIAGES, FIRST MARRIAGES AND REMARRIAGES

	Number of marriages	Number of first marriages		Number and proportion of marriages in which at least one spouse had been previously married		Number and proportion of remarriages in which the two spouses had been previously married	
		Males	Females	Number	%	Number	%
1971	191,324	168,944	169,072	31,698	16.6	12,934	40.8
1981	190,082	151,978	154,506	52,340	27.5	21,340	40.8
1990	187,738	143,637	145,350	60,393	32.2	26,094	43.2
1991	172,251	131,996	133,584	55,578	32.3	23,644	42.5

3.13 RELATION BETWEEN THE FORMATION AND LEGAL DISSOLUTION OF COUPLES

	Marriages	Deaths of married persons	Ratio of the number of marriages ended by the death of a spouse to the total number of marriages %	Divorces	Ratio of the number of marriages ended by divorce to the total number of marriages %
1960	130,338	64,553	49.5	6,980	5.4
1981	190,082	83,603	44.0	67,671	35.6
1986	175,518	88,763	50.6	78,160	45.1
1990	187,738	88,997	47.4	78,152	41.6

3.14 NUMBER OF DIVORCES

	1985	1986	1987	1988	1989	1990
Newfoundland	561	610	1,002	884	981	973
Prince Edward Island	213	191	246	260	243	268
Nova Scotia	2,337	2,550	2,640	2,478	2,524	2,347
New Brunswick	1,360	1,700	1,952	1,665	1,647	1,643
Quebec	15,814	18,399	19,315	19,825	19,790	19,405
Ontario[1]	20,854	28,653	38,223	29,873	31,202	28,183
Manitoba	2,314	2,917	3,771	2,998	2,847	2,677
Saskatchewan	1,927	2,395	2,751	2,463	2,451	2,227
Alberta	8,102	9,386	9,170	8,644	8,227	9,314
British Columbia	8,330	11,176	11,697	10,591	10,630	9,649
Yukon and Northwest Territories	168	183	218	191	174	173
Canada	61,980	78,160	90,985	79,872	80,716	76,859
Total Divorce Rate	3,121	3,799	4,314	3,748	3,928	3,827

[1] Data have been adjusted to take account of approximately 2,000 cases granted in Ontario in 1986 and 4,000 in Ontario in each of 1987 and 1988 that are not on the data base due to incomplete information.

3.15 PREVALENCE RATES[1] OF COMMON-LAW UNIONS IN CANADA

	1981	1986	1991
Newfoundland	2.19	3.50	9.34
Prince Edward Island	3.18	5.20	8.51
Nova Scotia	4.92	7.40	10.67
New Brunswick	4.02	6.48	11.04
Quebec	8.13	13.65	21.66
Ontario	5.63	7.20	7.42
Manitoba	5.26	7.03	10.32
Saskatchewan	4.25	6.35	9.57
Alberta	6.61	8.15	11.30
British Columbia	8.12	9.90	13.49
Yukon	15.41	18.30	23.13
Northwest Territories	9.63	14.22	14.76
Canada	6.40	9.18	13.50

[1] *Rate per 100 persons living in couples.*

3.16 FAMILIES

	1981	1986	1991	Increase 1981-1991
Total number of families	6,324,975	6,734,980	7,356,165	
Increase in %	. . .	6.5	9.2	16.3
Number of childless families	2,012,560	2,201,545	2,579,850	
Increase in %	. . .	9.4	17.0	28.2
Number of two-parent families with children	3,598,405	3,679,785	3,821,610	
Increase in %	. . .	2.3	3.9	6.2
Number of single-parent families	714,005	853,640	954,710	
Increase in %	. . .	19.6	11.8	33.7
Ratio of single-parent families to two-parent families in %	19.8	23.2	25.0	
Percentage of single-parent families among all families with children	16.6	18.8	20.0	
Common-law unions	356,610	486,940	725,950	
Increase in %	. . .	36.5	49.1	103.6

3.17 FAMILIES HEADED BY A SINGLE PARENT (PERCENT)

Percent of families with children	1981	1986	1991
Newfoundland	12.7	14.2	15.9
Prince Edward Island	16.7	17.5	18.5
Nova Scotia	17.3	19.0	20.4
New Brunswick	16.8	18.5	19.7
Quebec	17.6	20.8	21.7
Ontario	16.3	17.8	19.3
Manitoba	16.9	18.7	20.4
Saskatchewan	14.6	17.0	18.5
Alberta	15.0	17.6	19.0
British Columbia	17.3	20.1	20.3
Yukon	18.1	21.3	21.7
Northwest Territories	16.4	20.0	20.2
Canada	16.6	18.8	20.0

3.18 POPULATION BY MOTHER TONGUE

	English		French		Other	
	No.	%	No.	%	No.	%
1951						
Newfoundland	357,328	98.9	2,321	0.6	1,767	0.5
Prince Edward Island	89,241	90.7	8,477	8.6	711	0.7
Nova Scotia	588,610	91.6	38,945	6.1	15,029	2.3
New Brunswick	325,412	63.1	185,110	35.9	5,175	1.0
Quebec	558,256	13.8	3,347,030	82.5	150,395	3.7
Ontario	3,755,442	81.7	341,502	7.4	500,598	10.9
Manitoba	467,892	60.3	54,199	7.0	254,450	32.8
Saskatchewan	515,873	62.0	36,815	4.4	279,040	33.5
Alberta	648,413	69.0	34,196	3.6	256,892	27.3
British Columbia	963,920	82.7	19,366	1.7	181,924	15.6
Yukon	6,618	72.8	308	3.4	2,170	23.9
Northwest Territories	3,804	23.8	581	3.6	11,619	72.6
Canada	8,280,809	59.1	4,068,850	29.0	1,659,770	11.8
1991[1]						
Newfoundland	560,236	98.6	2,878	0.5	5,361	0.9
Prince Edward Island	122,209	94.2	5,894	4.5	1,657	1.3
Nova Scotia	841,373	93.5	37,034	4.1	21,533	2.4
New Brunswick	470,943	65.1	243,565	33.6	9,382	1.3
Quebec	664,933	9.6	5,662,695	82.1	568,332	8.2
Ontario	7,700,168	76.4	505,401	5.0	1,879,311	18.6
Manitoba	814,035	74.5	51,146	4.7	226,769	20.8
Saskatchewan	828,775	83.8	22,055	2.2	138,090	14.0
Alberta	2,092,093	82.2	57,886	2.3	395,581	15.5
British Columbia	2,633,823	80.2	51,745	1.6	596,487	18.2
Yukon	24,664	88.7	881	3.2	2,250	8.1
Northwest Territories	31,805	55.1	1,466	2.5	24,399	42.3
Canada	16,785,058	61.5	6,642,643	24.3	3,869,154	14.2

[1] *In order to make the 1991 figures more comparable to those of the previous decenniel census, they have been adjusted and multiple responses have been attributed to specific language groups in the same proportions as in the 1981 Census.*

3.19 POPULATION BY KNOWLEDGE OF OFFICIAL LANGUAGE

	English only		French only		Both english and french		Neither english nor french		Total
	No.	%	No.	%	No.	%	No.	%	No.
1931[1]	6,999,913	67.5	1,779,338	17.1	1,322,370	12.7	275,165	2.7	10,376,786
1941[1]	7,735,486	67.2	2,181,746	19.0	1,474,009	12.8	115,414	1.0	11,506,655
1951[1]	9,031,018	66.2	2,741,659	20.1	1,723,457	12.6	151,879	1.1	13,648,013
1951	9,387,395	67.0	2,741,812	19.6	1,727,447	12.3	152,775	1.1	14,009,429
1961	12,284,762	67.4	3,489,866	19.1	2,231,172	12.2	232,447	1.3	18,238,247
1971	14,469,540	67.1	3,879,255	18.0	2,900,155	13.4	319,360	1.5	21,568,315
1981	16,122,900	66.9	3,987,245	16.6	3,681,960	15.3	291,395	1.2	24,083,495
1991	18,106,760	67.1	4,110,300	15.2	4,398,655	16.3	378,320	1.4	26,994,045

[1] *Excluding Newfoundland.*

3.20 THE RELIGIOUS COMPOSITION OF CANADA (PERCENT)

	1891	1911	1931	1951	1971	1991[1]
Catholic	41.6	39.4	41.3	44.7	47.3	45.7
Roman Catholic	41.6	39.4	39.5	43.3	46.2	45.2
Ukrainian Catholic	—	—	1.8	1.4	1.1	0.5
Protestant	56.5	55.9	54.4	50.9	44.4	36.2
United Church[2]	--	--	19.5	20.5	17.5	11.5
Anglican	13.7	14.5	15.8	14.7	11.8	8.1
Presbyterian[2]	15.9	15.6	8.4	5.6	4.0	2.4
Lutheran	1.4	3.2	3.8	3.2	3.3	2.4
Baptist	6.4	5.3	4.3	3.7	3.1	2.5
Pentecostal	--	--	0.3	0.7	1.0	1.7
Other Protestant[3]	19.1	17.3	2.3	2.5	3.7	7.9
Eastern Orthodox	--	1.2	1.0	1.2	1.5	1.5
Jewish	0.1	1.0	1.5	1.5	1.3	1.2
No Religion[4]		0.4	0.2	0.4	4.3	12.4
Other[5]	1.8	2.0	1.6	1.4	1.2	2.8

[1] *In 1991, inmates of institutions are excluded.*

[2] *Between 1911 and 1931, the United Church denomination was formed through an amalgamation of the Methodists, Congregationalists and about one-half of the Presbyterian group. For 1931 and thereafter, the figures for Presbyterian reflect the segment that did not amalgamate with the United Church.*

[3] *Other Protestant denominations include Methodists and Congregationalists up to 1921, and other denominations such as Adventist, Churches of Christ, Disciples and the Salvation Army. The "Other" group also includes a certain proportion of smaller Protestant denominations.*

[4] *In 1891, "No Religion" is included in "Other". In 1971, the introduction of self-enumeration methodology may have been in part a cause of the larger increase in the proportion of the population reporting "No religion". However, the 1971 and 1991 figures for this group are comparable.*

[5] *In 1981, many of these smaller denominations were disaggregated and are counted in the "Other Protestant" category. The remainder of the "Other" group includes Eastern Non-Christian religions.*

3.21   RELIGIOUS COMPOSITION, 1991 (PERCENT)

	Canada	Nfld	PEI	NS	NB	Quebec	Ontario	Man.	Sask.	Alta.	BC	Yukon	NWT
Catholic	45.7	37.0	47.3	37.2	54.0	86.1	35.5	30.4	32.5	26.5	18.6	20.2	38.2
Roman Catholic	45.2	37.0	47.3	37.2	53.9	86.0	35.1	27.2	30.4	25.4	18.3	20.0	38.0
Ukrainian Catholic	0.5	0.0	0.0	0.0	0.0	0.1	0.4	3.1	2.1	1.0	0.2	0.2	0.1
Protestant	36.2	61.0	48.4	54.1	40.1	5.9	44.4	51.0	53.4	48.4	44.5	43.1	50.0
United Church	11.5	17.3	20.3	17.2	10.5	0.9	14.1	18.6	22.8	16.7	13.0	8.7	5.7
Anglican	8.1	26.2	5.2	14.4	8.5	1.4	10.6	8.7	7.2	6.9	10.1	14.8	32.0
Presbyterian	2.4	0.4	8.6	3.5	1.4	0.3	4.2	1.5	1.2	1.9	2.0	1.3	0.7
Lutheran	2.4	0.1	0.1	1.3	0.2	0.2	2.3	5.1	8.4	5.4	3.3	2.4	1.2
Baptist	2.5	0.2	4.1	11.1	11.3	0.4	2.7	1.9	1.6	2.5	2.6	3.6	1.2
Pentecostal	1.6	7.1	1.0	1.2	3.2	0.4	1.7	2.0	1.8	2.1	2.2	2.2	3.9
Other Protestant	7.9	9.8	9.0	5.5	4.9	2.3	8.8	13.2	10.5	12.9	11.4	10.2	5.2
Eastern Orthodox	1.5	0.1	0.1	0.3	0.1	1.3	1.9	1.9	2.0	1.7	0.7	0.3	0.3
Jewish	1.2	0.0	0.1	0.2	0.1	1.4	1.8	1.3	0.1	0.4	0.5	0.2	0.1
Eastern Non-Christian	2.8	0.3	0.4	0.6	0.3	1.5	3.9	1.6	0.8	3.2	5.1	1.3	0.9
Islam	0.9	0.1	0.0	0.2	0.0	0.7	1.5	0.3	0.1	1.2	0.8	0.1	0.1
Hindu	0.6	0.1	0.0	0.1	0.1	0.2	1.1	0.3	0.2	0.4	0.6	0.1	0.1
Buddhist	0.6	0.0	0.0	0.2	0.1	0.5	0.7	0.5	0.2	0.8	1.1	0.1	0.1
Sikh	0.5	0.0	0.1	0.0	0.0	0.1	0.5	0.3	0.1	0.5	2.3	0.1	0.1
Other Non-Christian	0.1	0.0	0.1	0.1	0.1	0.0	0.1	0.1	0.1	0.1	0.2	0.7	0.4
No Religion[1]	12.7	1.7	3.8	7.7	5.5	3.9	12.7	14.0	11.3	19.9	30.7	35.2	10.7

[1] *Includes Para-religious Groups and others not elsewhere classified.*

3.22 RELIGIOUS COMPOSITION OF SELECTED WORLD REGIONS, 1991

	Region			
	World	Europe	Northern America[1]	Canada
Christian	33.1	82.7	85.4	83.4
Roman Catholic	18.8	52.5	34.7	45.7
Protestant	11.2	23.0	48.6	36.3
Eastern Orthodox	3.1	7.2	2.1	1.5
Eastern Non-Christian	37.8	2.9	4.4	4.0
Islam	17.7	2.5	1.0	1.0
Hindu	13.4	0.0	0.5	0.6
Buddhist	5.7	0.1	0.2	0.7
Other[2]	1.0	0.3	2.7	1.9
Para-religious Groups[3]	8.2	0.3	0.7	0.2
No Religion[4]	20.8	14.0	9.6	12.4
Total	100.0	100.0	100.0	100.0

[1] *Includes USA and Canada.*
[2] *Includes Sikh, Jains, Bahai, Confucian, Shinto, Taoist, Other Eastern Non-Christian and Jewish.*
[3] *Includes Chinese folk religionists, New-Religionists, tribal religionists and other religionists.*
[4] *Includes others not elsewhere classified.*

Sources
Employment and Immigration Canada
Statistics Canada

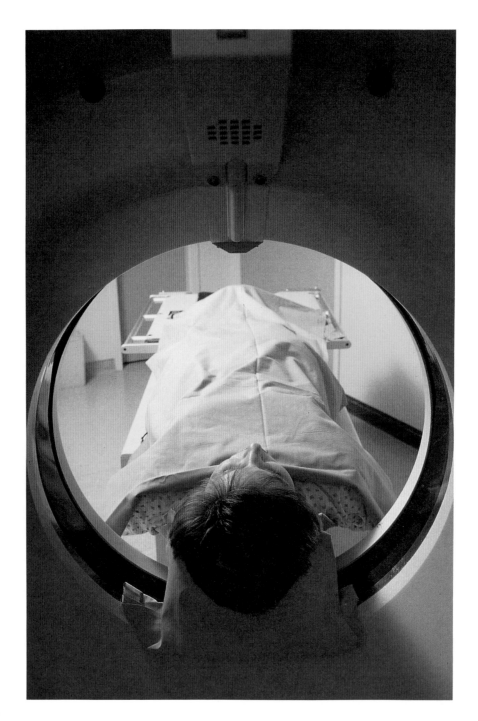

CANAPRESS PHOTO SERVICE

CHAPTER FOUR HEALTH

INTRODUCTION

Canadian spending on personal health services, as a portion of the country's Gross Domestic Product (GDP) is the second highest in the world, after the United States. In 1991, Canadians spent about $67 billion on health services, or about 10% of the GDP, representing average expenditures of $2,474 for every citizen.

Many Canadians are torn between their commitment to a universal medicare system and the reality of meeting escalating costs, which threaten to erode this system. Indeed, health care reform is an issue of public debate and political preoccupation in this country.

To get the maximum value from each health care dollar, health professionals are working toward a more balanced health care system that focuses on illness prevention and health promotion as well as treatment. Health promotion programs are working. More Canadians are recognizing that factors such as lifestyle, diet, unemployment or pollution have a great influence on the health of the individual.

Indeed, Statistics Canada's 1991 General Social Survey indicates that Canadians are taking better care of themselves. Overall, adult consumption of cigarettes and alcohol has declined, and people are getting more exercise and eating healthier foods.

On the other hand, Canada faces important health problems. The number of reported cases of Acquired Immune Deficiency Syndrome (AIDS) is increasing rapidly. Low-income groups have lower life expectancy than other Canadians, as well as higher rates of disability, illness and mental health disorders. A substantial number of Canadians suffer from chronic disease, disability, or emotional stress and lack the community support to cope with these problems.

In the late 1980s, the leading causes of death in Canada were cardiovascular disease, cancer and accidents. However, the mortality rate for childhood cancer has fallen 50% over the past 20 years despite a gradual increase in general incidence of the disease over this period. Improved treatment of leukemia and lymphoma in children accounts for much of this decrease.

To help reduce both the death rate and the severity of injuries sustained in accidents, Health and Welfare Canada established the Canadian Hospitals Injury Reporting and Prevention Program (CHIRPP) in 1989. CHIRPP is an emergency surveillance program that collects data on circumstances in which injuries occur, so that prevention programs can be developed and evaluated.

Hospitalization occurred most commonly as a result of heart disease, stroke, cancer, accidents, respiratory disease and mental disorders. Preventive measures could reduce the incidence of lung cancer and heart disease by up to half; and finding new and more effective ways of preventing illness and injury is an important health priority.

PROMOTING HEALTH One of the cornerstones of effective health care planning is comprehensive, reliable data on the health status and attitudes of a population. In 1985, Health and Welfare Canada conducted Canada's first National Health Promotion Survey. Focusing on how Canadians view their health, the survey covered topics ranging from drug and alcohol use to preventive practices and social support. The survey added to information collected by earlier surveys, and led to the 1986 report, *Achieving Health for All: A Framework for Health Promotion*. This report outlined major health care goals and identified specific issues such as alcohol, tobacco and drug abuse, and mental health.

As *Health for All* pointed out, one way to reduce illness is to change lifestyles. Over the last few decades, many Canadians have improved their diets, stopped smoking and begun to exercise regularly. In 1981, the Canada Fitness Survey found that 56% of Canadians aged 10 and over were physically active; however, less than half of this group were sufficiently active to benefit their cardiovascular health. Strategies to reduce incidence of health problems such as drug and alcohol abuse, AIDS and cardiovascular disease have also changed, and now combine advertising campaigns, research, demonstration projects, education and consultation.

Kay Chernush / The Image Bank

In early 1990, some 1,237 public, private and federal hospitals were operating in Canada.

Thomas Bruckbauer / Image Finders

The implementation of the Tobacco Products Control Act in 1989, for example, made Canada a world leader in tobacco control. The legislation bans advertising and requires large health warning messages on the packaging of all tobacco products. In 1991, about 5.4 million people, 26% of the population aged 15 and over, smoked daily, down from 41% in 1966. However, while the rate among men dropped sharply from 54% in 1966 to 26% in 1991, the percentage of smokers among women dipped only slightly from 28% to 26%.

The federal government helps increase awareness of the benefits of active living through Fitness and Amateur Sport Canada (FAS). This agency has programs for children and youth, senior adults, people with disabilities and employees. As well as co-ordinating programs such as Canada Fitweek, Winteractive International, the Canadian Active Living Challenge and the Quality Daily Physical Education program, FAS conducts research and develops guidelines for training fitness leaders and management volunteers. In 1991-92, FAS contributed $950,000 to the ParticipACTION program's ongoing operations, campaigns and collaborative projects.

CANADA'S HEALTH

LIFE EXPECTANCY Canada's life expectancy is among the highest in the world. Females born between 1985 and 1987 can expect to live for almost 80 years, while males can expect to live for 73 years. Since 1920-22, this is an increase of 19 years for females and 14 years for males.

Women have made much greater gains in life expectancy than men. Back in the early 1920s, women could expect to outlive men by less than two years; by 1985-87, this had more than tripled, although the male–female gap has narrowed slightly over the past decade.

High life expectancy in industrialized countries has come largely from success in combating infectious diseases during the first year of life. Better health care before and after birth, coupled with better nutrition and living standards, led to an 82% drop in the infant mortality rate (deaths under age one as a percentage of all births) from 1951 to 1988.

One consequence of increased life expectancy is that a greater proportion of Canada's population can expect to live to older ages. Again, back in the early 1920s, fewer than 6 out of 10 Canadians could expect to survive to their 65th birthday. By the mid-1980s, this had risen to 8 out of 10. At the oldest ages, the increases in survival are even more striking. In the early 1920s, just over 1 in 10 Canadians could expect to reach their 85th birthday. In 1987, this had increased to more than 3 out of 10.

HEALTH EXPECTANCY While life expectancy indicates the expected number of years of life in all states of health and disability, health expectancy indicates how many of those years can be expected to be lived free of disability.

Current health expectancy in Canada is calculated from the results of the 1986-87 Health and Activity Limitation Survey. According to these calculations,

women can expect to live longer than men, and to have more years free of slight or severe disability. However, a higher percentage of women's lives are likely to be lived with some disability: at birth, disability-free life expectancy represents 84% of total life expectancy for males and 81% for women. By age 65, men can expect that 54% of their remaining lives will be free of disability, while women of the same age can expect to live without disability for 49% of their remaining years. Expected years of life free of severe disability represents 97% of total life expectancy at birth for men, and 94% for women. At age 65, this figure drops to 86% of remaining life expectancy for men, and 78% for women.

Life Expectancy at Birth and Infant Mortality

Life Expectancy at Birth

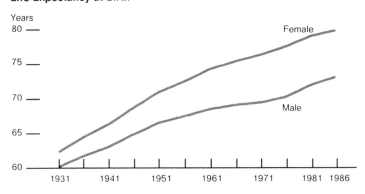

Infant Mortality

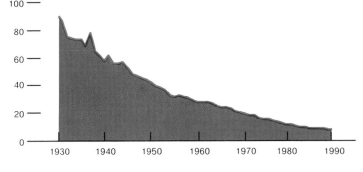

CAUSES OF DEATH Life expectancy has increased throughout this century largely because of a lower incidence of infectious diseases such as tuberculosis and other causes of death that used to take their toll on children and young adults. Among these were premature birth and birth injury, diarrhoeal disease in infants and pneumonia. The majority of Canadians now die at older ages of degenerative diseases such as cardiovascular disease and cancer. The emergence of the epidemic of Acquired Immune Deficiency Syndrome (AIDS) during the 1980s has resulted in recent increases in infectious disease mortality.

In 1990, cardiovascular diseases, including heart diseases and stroke, were responsible for 39% of all deaths. Cancers accounted for a further 27% of deaths, respiratory diseases for 8% and accidents and violence for 7%. Accidental and violent deaths account for a particularly high proportion of deaths among young men — about three-quarters of all deaths of males aged 15 to 24 in 1990.

Between 1980 and 1990, age-standardized mortality rates, which adjust for changes in the age structure of the population, fell substantially in two areas: by 30% for cardiovascular diseases, and 27% for accidental and violent deaths. In the same period, overall cancer

death rates increased slightly for both men and women. Lung cancer death rates continued to rise steeply among women, but levelled out among men in the late 1980s. There was no consistent trend in death rates for respiratory diseases.

Researchers calculate potential years of life lost (PYLL) to gauge the relative impact of the various causes of death. PYLL is calculated by subtracting age at death from 75, the age at which a death can no longer be considered premature.

Cancer is Canada's second leading cause of death at all ages, but it is the leader in PYLL. Accidents and suicides also have a much greater impact on PYLL than on number of deaths. In 1988, these causes accounted for 12% of deaths in the under-75 age groups, but 25% of PYLL.

MORBIDITY Mortality is often caused by degenerative diseases, many of which require long or frequent hospital stays.

For this reason, the leading causes of death are also the leading causes of hospitalization. Morbidity, or illness, is measured in terms of patient-days spent in general and allied special hospitals.

In 1989-90, general and allied hospitals reported 3.6 million separations (hospital discharges or deaths) representing 41.4 million days of care. The hospital separation rate has decreased 10% from 15,755 per 100,000 in 1969 to 14,109 per 100,000 in 1989-90. In the same period, hospital days decreased 14% from 187,234 in 1969 to 161,374 in 1989-90.

In the period from 1969 to 1989-90, age-specific separation rates per 100,000 population decreased for all age groups, except the 65 to 74 and the 75 and older age groups. The rate decreased 29% for the under 15 age group. The rate increased 5% for the 65 to 74 age group and 22% for the 75 and older age group.

DISABILITY Over the years, society's understanding of health has broadened to include mental, physical and social well-being. This change has affected how we define disability.

Causes of Death

1926[1]   1990

Infectious diseases   Respiratory system
Cancers   Perinatal causes
Circulatory system   Accidents/violence
                           Other

[1] Excludes Newfoundland, the Yukon and the Northwest Territories in 1926.

In the past, many people associated disability with crutches and wheelchairs; today we understand that disability includes any condition that hampers a person's day-to-day activities. This could range from total loss of sight to difficulty in tying one's shoes or cutting one's food.

The 1991 Health and Activity Limitation Survey indicated that 4.2 million Canadians — 15.5% of the population — had some degree of disability. While this rate is significantly higher than the 13.2% disability rate measured in 1986, most of the increase occurred among those reporting a mild disability. Of the 1991 total, 6.3% were living in health-related institutions or homes for senior citizens and almost 94% lived in private households. Disability increases with age: almost 7% of children under 15 experience some level of disability, compared to 14% of adults aged 35 to 54 and 46% of those aged 65 and over.

Recent government policies and programs have focused on eliminating the barriers that deny disabled people equal access to facilities and opportunities. The first step in this process is learning more about disabled Canadians and the hurdles they face.

HEALTH CARE SYSTEM Canada's health care system is best described as an interlocking set of 10 provincial and 2 territorial health insurance schemes. Each is universal and publicly funded. As part of the national health care system, each provincial and territorial scheme is linked through adherence to national standards set at the federal level. Under the Constitution Act, 1982 (formerly the British North America Act, 1867), provincial governments have jurisdiction over establishing, maintaining and managing hospitals, asylums, charities and charitable institutions. The federal government is responsible only for establishing and maintaining marine hospitals and quarantines; but in practice federal involvement has been much more extensive.

Because the provinces and territories manage their own health care services, educational programs, health personnel and certification, Canada's health care system is highly decentralized. This means that national networking through advisory committees and professional associations is required to co-ordinate planning and standards.

BREAST IMPLANTS RESTRICTED

Questions about possible health effects related to silicone-gel breast implants have led the federal government to ask manufacturers to provide additional data about their products. In January 1993, the sale of silicone gel-filled breast implants was halted until manufacturers could provide this data.

Critics of silicone gel-filled breast implants are concerned the implants may be linked to an increased risk of diseases such as cancer and arthritis. However, there is no conclusive evidence that these implants pose health problems. Further research is currently being conducted to determine whether these devices pose any health risk.

Breast implants, which replace or augment the internal tissue of a woman's breast, have become increasingly common. Until 1992, between 10,000 and 15,000 of these medical devices were implanted in Canadian women each year. In all, an estimated 150,000 Canadian women currently have breast implants.

The vast majority of breast implants — about 80% — are for cosmetic purposes only. The remaining 20% of such operations are performed to reconstruct breasts lost to disease or injury. Although not currently on the market, sale of silicone-gel breast implants may be permitted on compassionate grounds, or on a case-by-case basis if the alternatives available on the market are not suitable. Conditions which may be considered include replacement for medical reasons, replacement of a temporary tissue expander or reconstruction of a breast lost to disease or injury.

Saline-filled breast implants remain widely available.

CANADIANS ARE SHAPING UP

Statistics Canada's national 'health check-up' has turned up both good and bad news about the health habits of Canadians. According to the findings of the 1991 General Social Survey, the positives outweigh the negatives.

On the smoking front, more and more of us, especially men, are butting out. In 1991, only 26% of men aged 15 and older smoked regularly — less than half of the 54% of men who smoked in 1966.

The smoking rate for women has also declined, but not nearly as much. While 28% of women smoked in 1966, a full 26% of women were still smoking in 1991. If the current trend continues, smoking rates will soon be lower for men than for women. This is already the case for women aged 15 to 19 — in 1991, some 20% of women in this age group were regular smokers, compared to only 12% of men in this age group. In fact, women aged 15 to 19 were more likely to smoke in 1991 than in 1965.

Canadians are watching their intake of alcohol. Those who do drink alcoholic beverages are drinking less. In 1991, some 10% of current drinkers consumed 14 or more drinks per week, compared to nearly 20% in 1978. Generally, men drink more often than women, and tend to consume more alcohol when they do drink.

In addition, the proportion of Canadians who drink has declined. In 1978, close to two-thirds of Canadians consumed one or more drinks per month. By 1991, that was down to 55%.

Besides cutting back on drinking and smoking, many Canadians are improving their health by becoming more active. While younger people tend to be the most active, Canadians of all ages are exercising more. In 1991, some 32% of Canadians aged 15 and older spent their leisure time on physically demanding activities, compared to 27% of Canadians who did so in 1985. Overall, when it comes to burning calories, men tend to be more active than women.

Despite all these changes in Canadian lifestyles, the number of Canadians who are overweight has actually increased. According to Health and Welfare Canada standards, 23% of those aged 20 to 64 were overweight in 1991, compared to only 17% in 1985. Being overweight is much more common among older Canadians, who tend to be less active than younger people.

While men are more likely to be overweight than women, women are more likely to be underweight. In 1991, of women aged less than 45, more were underweight than overweight. Being underweight is especially pronounced among young women — in 1991, only 7% of women aged 20 to 24 were overweight, compared to 25% who weighed too little.

One explanation for women's tendency to be underweight may be that many women perceive their weight differently than men — of women who were surveyed, more than one-third with normal weights believed they weighed too much.

As public awareness of health issues continues to rise, many Canadians look forward to the results of the next national check-up.

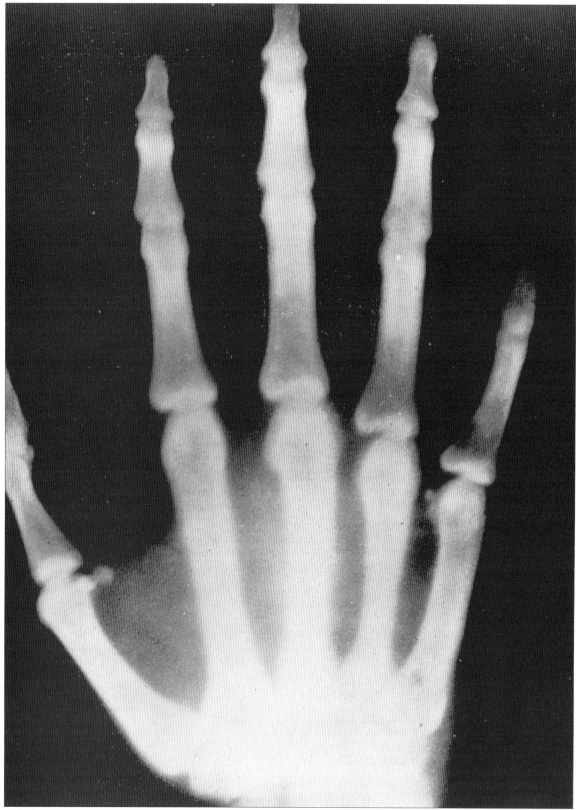

R. O. King and F. Pitcher / National Archives of Canada PA 122914

Photograph of a living hand — one of the first X-rays taken in Canada.

The federal government funds hospital and medical care insurance programs, and grant programs. It also conducts research and information and consultation services. Health and Welfare Canada, the federal health department, provides health services, monitors the working environment of federal public servants, and enforces health regulations for people entering Canada. The department also provides for the health needs of registered Indians and Inuit and for residents of the Yukon Territory through a network of nursing stations, health centres, hospitals and other facilities. In some cases, the department provides funds to native communities to allow them to plan and deliver their own health programs.

Through Health and Welfare Canada, Canada is involved in a number of international health agencies and organizations, including the World Health Organization, the Pan-American Health Organization, the Organization for Economic Co-operation and Development, and other United Nations agencies. To fulfil its international obligations, the department consults, takes part in exchanges and assignments, and enforces regulatory agreements between Canada and other countries.

THE FINANCIAL PICTURE Canada's health costs in the private and government sectors reached nearly $62.7 billion in 1990, an increase of 28.8% from 1987. On a per-person basis, the cost was $2,357 — some $455 more than in 1987, and four times the 1975 figure. From 1960 to 1990, the proportion of the Gross National Product spent on health care increased from 5.5% to 9.7%.

With the introduction of government-operated health care insurance plans across Canada, the overall share of health costs among provincial governments increased from 42% in 1960 to a peak of 76% in 1975. By 1990, this figure had dropped to 72%.

The distribution of health expenditures was relatively stable from 1975 to 1990. Institutional and related services accounted for about 55% of expenditures in 1975, falling gradually to 51% by 1990. Professional services received 22% to 23% of expenditures throughout the period. Spending on drugs and appliances increased from 11% in 1975 to 16% in 1990, while the

'other health expenses' category (which includes public health, capital expenditure, research, and the cost of insuring services) accounted for between 11% and 12% of spending each year.

The Canada Assistance Plan ensures that disadvantaged Canadians receive adequate health care. Through the plan, the federal government pays up to 50% of costs not covered by national hospital and medical care programs. The plan's coverage varies by province, but can include eyeglasses, prosthetic devices, dental services, prescribed drugs, home care services, and nursing home care.

MEDICAL RESEARCH Many facilities and funding sectors play a role in medical research. Hospitals investigate diseases and disabilities and develop and test treatments. Universities focus on the physiological and biochemical bases of health and disease, while industry concentrates on developing new pharmaceutical and medical devices. Federal laboratories set standards and regulations for food, cosmetics, pesticides, drinking water, air, drugs, and for radiation-emitting and medical devices; they also investigate factors affecting the diagnosis and treatment of chronic and infectious diseases.

Funding for scientific research comes from the federal and provincial governments, from private non-profit organizations and from industry. In 1988-89, expenditures on university-based health science research and related scientific activities were $403.6 million. The bulk of this funding (45%) came from the Medical Research Council of Canada. Another 23% came from a variety of voluntary and non-profit organizations, while provincial programs provided 19%. Most research was performed in universities and affiliated teaching hospitals, and in research institutes. Applied research, which includes the development of health care delivery systems, was funded by Health and Welfare Canada (6.6%), and by private and provincial organizations. Foreign sources, such as the National Institutes of Health in the United States, contributed 3.9% of total expenditures.

The Medical Research Council is the largest federal contributor to medical research, with a 1990-91 budget of $241.9 million, an increase of $39.4 million from

1989-90. The council funded 2,249 operating, equipment, group or program grants and 1,519 awards of funds for research personnel.

The National Health Research and Development Program (NHRDP) is also a major federal contributor, providing $30.4 million in 1990-91 for 757 health research projects and related scientific activities. The NHRDP has funded health studies, training and career awards, and national initiatives such as the National AIDS Program and the National Drug Strategy. The NHRDP also works with other agencies and with provincial governments on a number of collaborative funding endeavours, such as investigations of the health effects of exposure to magnetic fields and community health research in the North.

Through transfer payments, the provinces fund the indirect costs of research in universities and hospitals, including costs for facilities and for administration. Direct research costs, such as supplies and equipment, are met by operating grants.

FACILITIES AND SERVICES Canada possesses a network of hospitals supplemented by a broad range of other health services. As of April 1, 1990, some 1,237 public, private and federal hospitals were operating in Canada, as were 6,266 residential care facilities, such as nursing homes.

Acute care hospitals include general hospitals as well as hospitals that specialize in cancer treatment, cardiology, maternity, neurology and orthopedic hospitals. Between 1980 and 1989, beds staffed and in operation in acute care hospitals decreased from 5.4 to 5.0 beds per 1,000 population. In 1989, some 82.7% of these beds were occupied, compared with 80.4% nine years earlier. The proportion of beds designated for long-term care and psychiatric care in acute care hospitals increased from 17.8% in 1980 to 22.7% in 1988. In the same period, in-patient admissions per 1,000 population diminished slightly, while out-patient visits per 1,000 increased substantially along with the proportion of surgeries performed on an out-patient basis.

Between 1980 and 1990, the ratio of physicians-to-population (excluding interns and residents) went down from 650 to 518.

All medically necessary out-patient services are covered by the provincial health insurance plans. Such services include diagnostic services, nursing services, physiotherapy, radiotherapy, emergency and clinical services.

Smaller hospitals typically provide core hospital services — these include medical/surgical services, obstetrics, pediatrics and often intensive care and psychiatric services. Secondary and tertiary referral hospitals, usually located in larger population centres, provide a broader range of specialized and intensive services, such as care for newborn infants with medical problems. Health care services are also available through regional referral plans co-ordinated by each province. Provinces may even join forces occasionally to meet more specialized or rare treatment requirements.

In remote areas, the network of decentralized services includes regional flying ambulances and programs for health promotion, accident prevention and health education. These community and outreach programs are integrated with basic and specialized medical and hospital services.

Rehabilitation and home care services are extensions of core hospital care. They are provided by public and voluntary agencies (including hospitals), by in-patient and out-patient facilities, and by worker compensation board centres. Financed by various federal, provincial and voluntary sources, some rehabilitation and home care services are covered by hospital and medical care insurance. Some programs are oriented to specific diseases; some are attached to hospitals or community centres. Programs range from basic nursing to an array of health and social services.

A vocational rehabilitation program for Canadians with disabilities was initiated in 1952. Since 1973, this program has been administered by Health and Welfare Canada. The federal government shares costs with the provinces for social and vocational assessment; counselling; training; maintenance allowances; tools, books and other equipment; remedial and restorative treatments; and prosthetic and orthotic appliances, wheelchairs and other mobility aids.

Mieke Maas / The Image Bank

Statistics Canada tells us that about 15.5% of Canada's population has some degree of disability.

PERCHANCE TO DREAM...

Shakespeare praised the "sleep that knits up the ravel'd sleeve of care", but as it turns out, a sizeable number of Canadians may wake up feeling frayed. Statistics Canada says that one in five of us has problems sleeping.

Most affected are women, especially lone mothers, elderly people, those looking for work and shift workers.

The news comes to us via the General Social Survey of 1991. The survey found that both men and women actually sleep about seven and a half hours a night on average, but that 28% of women say they find it hard to fall asleep or stay asleep, compared with 19% of men.

Sleep problems are associated with stress, which in turn is likely to be related to low income, pain or health problems. All of these appear to be more common among women than men.

In fact, the link to low incomes was documented. The survey found that women with low incomes were more than twice as likely as women with high incomes to report problems getting to sleep — 41% compared with 20% respectively.

More women experience pain and discomfort than men. The survey reported 22% of women in some kind of discomfort compared with 17% of men.

Women also reported more health problems than men.

Special classes or schools for students with disabilities are usually operated by school boards. Most schools for the deaf and blind are residential schools operated by the provincial government.

HEALTH INSURANCE Canada's nation-wide health insurance system is made up of provincial and territorial plans designed to give all Canadian residents prepaid access to necessary medical care. Provincial and territorial hospital and medical care insurance plans are federally regulated in areas such as the financial extent of coverage, accessibility, portability of benefits and the requirement that the plans be non-profit.

The 1984 Canada Health Act defines the criteria and conditions that each provincial health insurance plan must meet to receive full federal contributions. The Act discourages direct charges to patients for physician and hospital services. The Act is built on the Hospital Insurance and Diagnostic Services Act (1957) and the Medical Care Act (1966-67). The Hospital Insurance and Diagnostic Services Act had made a range of hospital and diagnostic services available at little or no direct cost to the patient. Except in psychiatric and nursing home facilities, these benefits included acute, general, chronic and convalescent hospital services, with some variation by province. The Medical Care Act required the federal government to make payments to provinces and territories operating medical care insurance plans.

In 1990-91, nine provincial medical care insurance plans (no data are available for Prince Edward Island) made $8.1 billion in fee-for-service payments; this included 182 million visits to doctors and 4.6 million surgical procedures. Of the additional 169 million services, more than 113 million were for radiology or laboratory services, with the remaining 56 million consisting of obstetrical, anaesthetic, surgical assistance and other diagnostic and therapeutic services.

Until 1977, the federal contribution was linked to the cost of health services, roughly matching provincial expenditures. The federal contribution now takes the form of block grants and tax transfers to the provinces based on a three-year moving average of the Gross National Product calculated independently of

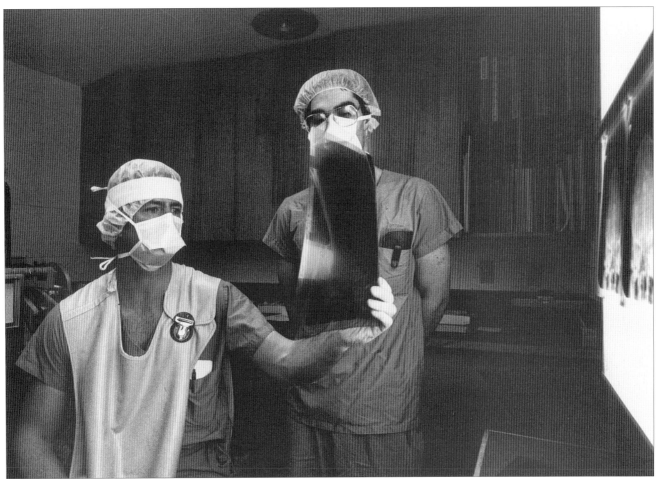

Ted Grant / CMCP

From the photographic series, *A Tribute to Sir William Osler*. Osler, a famous Canadian physician, writer and educator lived from 1849 to 1919.

provincial costs. During the 1980s, the federal government amended the fiscal arrangements five times to limit the growth of Established Programs Financing (EPF) transfers to the provinces. These measures were undertaken in an effort to stem the growth of federal spending in the face of a mounting public debt. Federal contributions are also made toward the cost of certain extended health care services, such as nursing homes and adult residential, ambulatory and home care services.

How the provinces organize, finance and administer their health insurance plans varies. Some administer their plans directly through provincial health departments; other plans are managed by separate public agencies reporting to the provincial health minister. Some provinces have two plans, one controlled by the province and another by a public agency.

Administering these programs is a provincial responsibility. Each province is also free to determine how its share of costs will be financed. Most provinces use general revenues, but Alberta and British Columbia impose premiums, which are reduced for residents with limited income. In Alberta, residents aged 65 years or over are exempt from paying the premium.

The provinces differ slightly in how medical services are delivered and how physicians are paid. However, most physicians are paid on a fee-for-service basis; this accounts for about 95% of the national cost of insured medical services. Other arrangements include uniform per capita fees, salaries, sessional payments, contract services and incentives for practising in medically underserviced areas.

HIV AND AIDS

By early 1993, Health and Welfare Canada had documented 7,770 reported cases of Acquired Immune Deficiency Syndrome (AIDS) in this country, all but 79 of them among adults. Of the total, 5,128 — about two-thirds — had died.

There are very probably more actual cases. Experts at Health and Welfare Canada say delays in reporting, combined with the fact that up to 15% of all cases may never be reported, mean the reported total may be an underestimate. They believe the actual number of AIDS cases that had occured in Canada by early 1993 was closer to 11,000, and projected that by the end of the year, it could be as many as 13,000.

AIDS, described by doctors as a "chronic, progressive disease with life-threatening implications," cannot be spread, like a cold, through a sneeze, or by shaking hands with someone. Only direct exchange of bodily fluids transmits it. This can result from practising certain kinds of sex, sharing hypodermic needles or syringes, or from blood transfusions.

Certain groups are therefore more at risk. The largest group of Canadian AIDS cases, some 78%, have been among people who have taken part in homosexual or bisexual activity. The next-largest group was comprised of people who had heterosexual activity in a high-risk country (for instance areas of Africa where AIDS may have originated) or with a person at risk (8%). Other groups include injectable drug users (2%) and medical patients who receive blood or blood products (4%). Only one case reported in Canada by mid-1993 had resulted from a medical worker being exposed to Human Immunodeficiency Virus (HIV). And about 4% of all cases involve people who don't fit any known risk group.

The risk may be reduced, but not completely removed, by practising safer sex, by sterilizing injection equipment, and through blood products screening programs now in place.

AIDS is preceded by HIV infection, but in Canada, no national registry for HIV-positive cases exists, so the total number of people who are HIV-positive is not known. Medical experts don't know whether everyone who tests positive for HIV eventually develops AIDS. It's also possible that not everyone who becomes infected with

AIDS dies of it. About 8% of persons living with AIDS are long-term survivors, living more than five years after they are diagnosed.

Diagnosing and defining AIDS is difficult. In Canada, a list of 20 infections and malignancies is currently used to define AIDS cases, but it's possible for a person to have severe HIV-related disease and still not fit an AIDS definition.

Moving from the initial HIV infection to advanced AIDS can take years. The only sign a person may notice at the initial HIV infection may be flu-like symptoms for a week or two, and only about 40% develop this symptom. Then they feel normal again. This normal-feeling 'asymptomatic' period may last years before symptomatic HIV infection or AIDS develops — classic literature suggests the median time to an AIDS diagnosis is about 10 years. Some HIV-positive cases still show no symptoms after 14 years. However, it's possible for someone with asymptomatic HIV to infect others without ever feeling ill themselves. And during this time, the virus gradually spreads through the body's cells, weakening its immune system by stages as it does so.

When people are diagnosed with HIV-related diseases early enough, doctors can give them antibiotics, antivirals and other drugs in advance to prevent many of these early symptoms or diseases. It may also be possible to slow the onset of HIV disease somewhat, and preserve some quality of life, by working at taking care of oneself — eating healthily, exercising, avoiding tobacco, alcohol, or drug abuse, and avoiding stress.

By the time severe HIV and/or AIDS sets in, the immune system has become badly compromised. Medicines, which must get help from the immune system to work properly, cannot stop the physical wasting, mental deterioration, cancers and other infections which quicken as the immune system collapses completely.

The median time Canadians have survived once they have contracted AIDS varies from about a year to about 19 months, depending on how the disease is defined. However, the life expectancy after an AIDS diagnosis varies, ranging from days to greater than five years.

Lutz Dille / CMCP

A teenage girl and two boys smoke cigarettes in a laneway, Toronto.

Many provincial plans provide additional benefits. These can include the service of dentists, optometrists, psychologists, chiropractors and podiatrists, as well as home care services, drugs and general preventive medical services. However, these benefits are frequently restricted to certain age groups (for example, dental services for children), or to a maximum value per year. Some Canadians belong to non-government health plans that cover these areas. For example, about 43.5% of the population, or 11.4 million Canadians, were covered by dental insurance in 1989. For disadvantaged Canadians, the Canada Assistance Plan ensures access to adequate medical treatment.

HEALTH PROTECTION   The federal and provincial governments protect the public from unsafe food, drugs and cosmetics, and from unsafe radiation-emitting devices and medical devices. Federal programs also protect Canadians from harmful microbiological agents, environmental pollutants and contaminants, and fraudulent drugs and devices.

Standards for food safety, cleanliness and nutritional quality are determined by laboratory research and by data from Canadian and international sources. These standards cover the use of food additives and the maximum levels of agricultural chemical residues permitted in foods. They are maintained by regular inspections of domestic and imported foods. In addition, all food additives and agricultural chemicals are thoroughly evaluated before they can be used in food sold in Canada.

Manufacturers of new drugs must give government regulators information about the drug, including the results of pre-clinical and clinical studies, and its therapeutic properties and possible side effects. Market approval is governed by assessments of the drug's risks and benefits, and by evaluations of its safety and effectiveness. Once a new drug has reached the market, manufacturers are required to report adverse reactions. Further assessments are conducted to determine whether any reactions are serious enough to signal the need for additional evaluation or action.

To combat disease in Canada, the national laboratory of Health and Welfare Canada monitors seasonal maladies (such as influenza), sexually transmitted diseases, non-communicable diseases and potential disease threats. This surveillance helps identify risk factors and changes in disease patterns. By investigating outbreaks of communicable diseases and by providing laboratory diagnostic services, the department is able to rapidly detect and control infections. In recent years, provincial laboratories have contributed to control of infectious diseases through unique testing agents and through improved procedures for training and for diagnostic quality assurance.

In the environmental health field, government agencies study the effects of potentially hazardous chemical and physical environments. Recent studies have investigated the effects of tobacco smoke, pesticides and household products.

B I O T E C H N O L O G Y Canada is a world leader in biotechnology research and application. Biotechnology is the use of living organisms to provide products and services that can affect everything from the food we eat, to the vaccines we give our children. Its applications are numerous and range from laser beam-activated drugs and the development of anaerobic digestion systems for the treatment of pulp mill effluents, to biological pest controls, bioleaching in the mining sector and the brewing of beer.

In the drug area, 'designer' drugs, tailor-made by the manipulation of genetic material, could replace medicine as we know it today. The discovery of genetic engineering technologies allowed the development of DNA probes, or gene probes, prime diagnostic tools for identifying genetic diseases. Other areas include the production of special antibodies for cancer therapy and prevention of kidney transplant rejection, vaccines, antibiotics, vitamins, anti-hypertensive medication and anti-allergenics. Artificial cells are also being developed for the production of insulin, the replacement of human blood in transfusions, or as building blocks for artificial organs such as livers and kidneys.

Never before has there been such dramatic activity in bioprocessing technologies. However, there are health and environmental safety issues that must be addressed before biotechnological products can be released in the environment or sold as food or used as drugs or vaccines.

A C Q U I R E D   I M M U N E   D E F I C I E N C Y S Y N D R O M E   (A I D S) Since the early 1980s, public health officials have become increasingly concerned about the incidence of AIDS, a virus that attacks the body's immune system. Most persons with AIDS have been exposed to the virus through sexual contact with infected individuals. A small number of people have been infected after receiving blood products or transfusions from donors infected with the virus.

The first case of AIDS in Canada was diagnosed in 1979; since then, incidence has risen rapidly. By April 1993, some 7,770 cases of AIDS had been reported and 5,128 people had died from it.

Health and Welfare Canada's National AIDS Program includes national AIDS surveillance, prevention and public education, clinical trials of drugs and vaccines, epidemiological studies, research, and community-based support. Health and Welfare Canada has ties with many government and non-government organizations, including the World Health Organization and other international agencies. The department also maintains the National Retrovirus Centre and offers state-of-the-art diagnostic services.

PUBLIC HEALTH SERVICES

In urban centres, municipal health departments co-ordinate public health services. In rural regions, most provinces delegate this responsibility to health units. Several provinces provide health services to sparsely populated northern areas. Provincial health departments co-operate with regional and local health authorities to respond to community needs. Voluntary agencies are also an intrinsic part of the community health network, complementing the work of health departments at a grassroots level.

To help educate Canadians on health issues, provincial health departments offer public health consulting services. These include maternal and child health services through clinics and schools and through visits to homes and hospitals. Nutrition consultants work in schools, health and welfare agencies, nursing homes, community centres and other institutions providing diet counselling to special groups, such as diabetics. Other consultants manage accident prevention and health promotion programs.

Public dental health programs focus on preventive care. Dental clinics operated by local health services are usually restricted to low-income and school-age residents. Each province and territory has a dental-care program for welfare recipients. Some provincial governments send dental teams to remote areas, while Health and Welfare Canada provides services to aboriginal peoples. Other programs fund surveys and research, or the training of dentists, dental hygienists, therapists, technicians and assistants.

To help local health agencies and the medical profession protect community health and control infectious disease, each province has a central public health laboratory with branch labs. These labs concentrate on medical testing for hospitals and physicians, and on public-health testing of milk, water and food. Local health authorities organize public immunization clinics for protection against diphtheria, tetanus, polio-myelitis, whooping cough, rubella and measles. Physicians are required by law to report incidents of certain communicable diseases, including tuberculosis, measles and sexually-transmitted diseases. This system alerts public health officials to possible epidemics and helps them gauge the effectiveness of immunization programs. In larger provinces, health departments have special divisions to deal with communicable disease control. In smaller provinces, this function is combined with one or more community health services.

A host of voluntary agencies helps extend government health programs. Historically, these agencies have played a major role in heightening public awareness of health issues, thereby contributing to the development of Canada's health care system. Their close ties with the community make them aware of problems as they emerge, and help them develop quick and innovative responses. The annual value of volunteer services in the health and social services sector is an estimated $1 billion.

In 1990-91, Health and Welfare Canada gave sustaining grants totalling $2.9 million to 49 national voluntary organizations. The department also contributed to research and to other innovative projects.

Voluntary agencies help rehabilitating patients in hospitals, in-patient and out-patient facilities, and worker compensation board centres. Funding comes from various provincial, federal and voluntary agencies.

SOURCES

Health and Welfare Canada

Statistics Canada

FOR FURTHER READING

Selected publications from Statistics Canada

▲ *Health Reports*. Quarterly. 82-003

▲ *Cancer in Canada*. Annual. 82-207. Discontinued, last issue 1983.

▲ *Tuberculosis Statistics, Morbidity and Mortality*. Annual. 82-212. Discontinued, last issue 1986.

▲ *Cardio-vascular Disease in Canada*. 1986. 82-544

▲ *Canadian Youth: Perspectives on their Health*. 1985. 82-545

▲ *Therapeutic Abortions, Canada*. Annual. 82-546

▲ *Report of the Canadian Health and Disability Survey*. 1983-1984, 1986. 82-555

▲ *Annual Return of Hospitals, Hospital Indicators*. Annual. 83-233. Discontinued, last issue 1982/83.

▲ *Mortality, Summary List of Causes, Vital Statistics*, volume III. Annual. 84-206. Discontinued, last issue 1986.

Selected publications from Other Sources

▲ *Achieving Health for All: A Framework for Health Promotion*. Health and Welfare Canada.

▲ *Annual Report 1991-1992*. Health and Welfare Canada.

▲ *Biotechnology Means Business: an Explosion of commercial Activity*. Industry Science and Technology Canada.

▲ *Canadian Cancer Statistics 1992*. Developed by Statistics Canada, Health and Welfare Canada, Provincial Cancer Registries, National Cancer Institute of Canada.

▲ *OECD Health Care Reform Project: National Paper Canada*. Health and Welfare Canada. Presented at Ministers of Health and Finance meeting, June 17-18, 1992.

▲ *A Vital Link: An Overview of Health and the Environment in Canada*. Health and Welfare Canada.

TABLES

4.1   LIFE EXPECTANCY (YEARS)

	Males				Females			
	At birth	20 years	40 years	60 years	At birth	20 years	40 years	60 years
1931	60.00	49.05	31.98	16.29	62.10	49.76	33.02	17.15
1941	62.96	49.57	31.87	16.06	66.30	51.76	33.99	17.62
1951	66.33	50.76	32.45	16.49	70.83	54.41	35.63	18.64
1961	68.35	51.51	32.96	16.73	74.17	56.65	37.45	19.90
1971	69.34	51.71	33.22	16.95	76.36	58.18	38.99	21.39
1976	70.19	52.09	33.59	17.23	77.48	58.95	39.67	21.96
1981	71.88	53.39	34.72	17.96	78.98	60.08	40.73	22.85
1986	73.04	54.27	35.52	18.41	79.73	60.65	41.20	23.17
Gains								
1931-76	10.19	3.04	1.61	0.94	15.38	9.19	6.65	4.81
1931-86	13.04	5.22	3.45	2.12	17.63	10.89	8.18	6.02

4.2   CANADA'S INFANT MORTALITY RATE PER 1,000 LIVE BIRTHS

Year	Male	Female	Both sexes	Year	Male	Female	Both sexes
1921	98.2	77.4	102.1	1981	10.8	8.4	9.6
1931	95.7	76.0	86.0	1986	8.7	7.0	7.9
1941	68.3	53.0	61.1	1987	8.4	6.2	7.3
1951	42.7	34.0	38.5	1988	8.2	6.4	7.2
1961	30.5	23.7	27.2	1989	8.0	6.2	7.1
1971	19.9	15.1	17.5	1990	7.5	6.1	6.8

4.3   INFANT DEATHS AND STILLBIRTHS

	Number			Rate[1]		
	1986	1989	1990	1986	1989	1990
Infant deaths (less than 1 year)	2,938	2,795	2,766	7.9	7.1	6.8
Neonatal deaths						
Less than 7 days	1,577	1,509	1,530	4.2	3.8	3.8
7 days to 27 days	332	319	339	0.9	0.8	0.8
Total, neonatal deaths	1,909	1,828	1,869	5.1	4.7	4.6
Post-neonatal deaths (28 days to 1 year)	1,029	967	897	2.8	2.5	2.2
Stillbirths (28+ weeks gestation)	1,574	1,593	1,598	4.2	4.1	3.9
Perinatal deaths (stillbirths plus deaths at less than 7 days)[1]	3,151	3,102	3,128	8.4	7.9	7.7

[1] *Perinatal rates per 1,000 live- and still-born infants; all other rates per 1,000 live births.*

4.4   LEADING CAUSES OF DEATH, 1990

	Male		Female	
	No.	Rate[1]	No.	Rate[1]
Diseases of the circulatory system	38,823	296.3	36,266	269.0
Cancer	28,865	220.3	23,560	174.8
Respiratory diseases	9,351	71.4	6,921	51.3
Accidents and adverse effects	9,064	69.2	3,993	29.6
Diseases of the digestive system	3,691	28.2	3,303	24.5
Endocrine diseases, etc.	2,533	19.3	2,939	21.8
Diseases of the nervous system	2,275	17.4	2,580	19.1
All other causes	9.358	71.2	8,434	62.7
Total, causes	103,960	793.3	87,996	652.8

[1] *Per 100,000 population.*

4.5   CANCER DEATHS, 1990

Cause	ICD-9[1]	Rank	Number	Percentage	Rate[2]
Males					
Lung	162	1	9,536	33.0	72.8
Prostate	185	2	3,212	11.1	24.5
Colon	153	3	2,216	7.7	16.9
Pancreas	157	4	1,329	4.6	10.1
Site unspecified	199	5	1,313	4.5	10.0
Stomach	151	6	1,305	4.5	10.0
Other of lymphoid and histiocytic tissue	202	7	846	2.9	6.4
Bladder	188	8	821	2.8	6.3
Rectum	154	9	777	2.7	5.9
Brain	191	10	742	2.6	5.7
Total, all cancers	140-208	. . .	28,865	100.0	220.3
Females					
Breast	174	1	4,712	20.0	34.9
Lung	162	2	4,168	17.7	30.9
Colon	153	3	2,215	9.4	16.4
Pancreas	157	4	1,282	5.4	9.5
Ovary	183	5	1,222	5.2	9.1
Site unspecified	199	6	1,160	4.9	8.6
Stomach	151	7	795	3.4	5.9
Other of lymphoid and histiocytic tissue	202	8	763	3.2	5.7
Other and ill-defined sites	159	9	672	2.8	5.0
Rectum	154	10	577	2.5	4.3
Total, all cancers	140-208	. . .	23,560	100.0	174.8

[1] *International Classification of Diseases, 9th Revision.*
[2] *Per 100,000 population.*

4.6 NUMBER OF REPORTED CASES OF SELECTED NOTIFIABLE DISEASES, 1990

	Canada	Nfld.	PEI	NS	NB	Que.	Ont.	Man.	Sask.	Alta.	BC	Yukon	NWT
AIDS	1,183	6	—	17	10	436	437	4	14	83	176	—	—
Amoebiasis	1,965	5	—	13	2	135	1,007	50	69	138	545	1	—
Campylo-bacteriosis	11,817	130	90	223	382	2,151	5,768	—	298	842	1,916	10	7
Chickenpox	20,254	1,338	—	852	170	—	—	—	1,370	14,314	1,702	147	361
Giardiasis	8,786	46	18	119	134	688	3,462	—	649	354	2,235	39	42
Gonococcal infections[1]	13,822	49	10	310	62	1,966	6,148	1,079	903	1,255	1,500	85	455
Hepatitis A	1,939	4	1	4	5	315	412	91	275	274	556	1	1
Hepatitis B	3,001	7	1	115	85	1,039	656	35	34	102	914	10	3
Measles	1,033	3	3	51	12	85	741	—	7	23	107	—	1
Pertussis	8,030	11	31	191	27	1,626	850	117	73	4,851	197	28	28
Salmonellosis[2]	8,947	127	72	336	401	1,962	3,605	310	313	791	991	11	28
Shigellosis	1,652	3	3	12	62	418	530	42	233	117	229	3	—
Syphilis	1,444	2	—	3	26	200	979	13	—	100	120	—	1
Tuberculosis	1,964	8	1	18	32	405	704	95	223	156	270	10	22

[1] Includes all 098 categories except 098.4.
[2] Excludes typhoid 002.0 and paratyphoid 002.1 to 002.9.

4.7 HOSPITAL UTILIZATION

	Discharges		Days of care		Average length of stay Days	Discharges for surgical procedures		Discharges involving surgery %
	Number	Per 100,000 population	Number	Per 100,000 population		Number	Per 100,000 population	
1971	3,568,887	16,587	41,228,313	191,610	11.6	1,617,730	7,518	45.3
1981-82	3,563,350	14,621	43,808,678	179,750	12.3	1,783,416	7,317	50.0
1983-84	3,624,137	14,559	40,828,889	164,020	11.3	1,823,008	7,323	50.3
1985-86	3,653,690	14,708	42,773,844	170,037	11.7	1,832,677	7,285	50.2
1987-88	3,698,664	14,423	43,846,349	170,984	11.9	1,835,716	7,159	49.6
1989-90	3,618,021	14,109	41,381,822	161,374	11.4	1,788,561	6,807	49,4

4.8 THERAPEUTIC ABORTIONS

Residence	Number of therapeutic abortions			Therapeutic abortions per 1,000 females 15-44 years			Therapeutic abortions per 100 live births		
	1986	1989	1990	1986	1989	1990	1986	1989	1990
Newfoundland	367	467	462	2.5	3.2	3.2	4.5	6.0	6.1
Prince Edward Island	13	8	51	0.4	0.3	1.7	0.7	0.4	2.5
Nova Scotia	1,704	2,030	1,871	8.0	9.5	8.7	13.8	16.2	14.5
New Brunswick	358	509	542	2.0	2.9	3.1	3.7	5.3	5.5
Quebec	12,410	13,854	14,438	7.5	8.5	8.8	14.7	15.0	14.7
Ontario	26,928	31,644	31,224	12.1	13.7	13.4	20.1	21.8	20.7
Manitoba	2,568	2,766	2,529	10.2	11.0	10.1	15.1	16.0	14.6
Saskatchewan	1,048	1,339	1,336	4.6	6.0	6.1	6.0	8.0	8.3
Alberta	6,313	6,585	6,621	10.5	10.8	10.8	14.4	15.2	15.4
British Columbia	11,386	11,098	11,518	16.5	15.5	15.8	27.1	25.4	25.2
Yukon	119	136	142	18.9	19.7	20.0	24.6	28.3	25.6
Northwest Territories	248	261	335	19.2	19.0	24.3	16.5	17.6	21.1
Residence not reported	-	8	23	...	...	...	...	...	...
Canada	63,462	70,705	71,092	10.2	11.2	11.2	17.0	18.0	17.5

4.9 HOSPITAL USE FOR MENTAL DISORDERS

	Discharges		Days of care		Average length of stay Days
	Number	Per 100,000 population	Number	Per 100,000 population	
General hospitals					
1971	131,231	609.9	2,366,826	10,999.9	18.0
1981-82	156,171	640.8	4,458,704	18,294.4	28.6
1983-84	158,796	637.9	4,225,801	16,976.1	26.6
1985-86	156,622	622.6	4,619,079	18,362.0	29.5
1987-88	160,434	625.6	5,091,383	19,854.5	31.7
1989-90	155,991	593.7	4,884,305	18,588.3	31.3
Psychiatric hospitals					
1971	51,208	238.0	19,783,129	91,942.7	386.3
1981-82	34,755	153.5	6,866,727	30,319.5	197.5
1983-84	34,309	148.3	7,803,988	33,739.2	227.5
1985-86	34,544	147.8	7,152,070	30,590.7	207.0
1987-88	33,872	132.1	7,728,359	30,137.7	228.2
1989-90	31,634	120.4	6,907,315	26,287.3	218.4

4.10 PERCENTAGE DISTRIBUTION OF HEALTH EXPENDITURES, PUBLIC AND PRIVATE

	Hospitals	Other institutions	Physicians	Dentists	Other professional services	Drugs and appliances	All other health costs
1960	37.9	5.7	16.6	5.1	2.3	14.2	18.2
1965	42.7	6.1	16.0	4.7	1.9	13.3	15.3
1970	45.0	7.2	16.6	4.2	1.5	12.5	13.0
1975	44.4	9.7	15.7	4.9	1.1	10.7	13.5
1980	40.9	11.6	15.2	5.8	1.1	10.8	14.6
1981	41.2	11.4	15.0	5.6	1.2	11.0	14.6
1986	39.6	10.3	15.8	5.5	1.2	13.4	14.2
1987	39.2	10.3	16.0	5.4	1.4	13.9	13.8
1988[e]	38.9	10.5	15.7	5.5	1.4	. .	. .
1989[e]	38.6	10.6	15.5	5.5	1.4	. .	. .
1990[e]	38.2	10.7	15.2	5.5	1.5	. .	. .

4.11 GOVERNMENTAL HEALTH EXPENDITURES, FEDERAL, PROVINCIAL AND LOCAL

	Expenditures $'000,000	Annual percentage increase	Percentage of GNP	Per capita $	Percentage of total national health expenditures
1960	915	–	2.4	51	42.7
1965	1,779	14.2	3.1	90	52.1
1970	4,389	19.8	5.0	206	70.2
1975	9,371	16.4	5.5	412	76.4
1980	16,967	12.6	5.6	705	74.7
1981	20,139	18.7	5.8	827	75.6
1986	32,948	9.2	6.7	1,299	74.4
1987	35,567	7.9	6.6	1,387	74.2
1988[e]	38,322	7.7	6.5	1,479	73.7
1989[e]	41,249	7.6	6.6	1,572	73.1
1990[e]	44,773	8.5	6.9	1,603	72.5

4.12 TOTAL OPERATING EXPENSES FOR REPORTING PUBLIC HOSPITALS[1], 1989–90[p]
(THOUSAND DOLLARS)

	Gross salaries and wages	Medical and surgical supplies	Drugs	Employee benefits	Supplies and other expenses	Total
Newfoundland	280,655	18,470	14,460	35,437	85,228	434,249
Prince Edward Island	47,297	3,296	2,545	5,218	13,893	72,250
Nova Scotia	488,496	36,054	26,791	44,308	154,065	749,715
New Brunswick	366,611	28,484	18,791	34,184	114,547	562,618
Quebec	3,621,654	175,241	161,848	376,999	1,014,590	5,350,332
Ontario	4,786,606	318,777	251,765	516,608	1,434,469	7,308,224
Manitoba	523,657	33,229	25,430	52,669	200,107	835,093
Saskatchewan	433,944	30,554	21,780	41,031	138,066	665,375
Alberta	1,352,739	85,378	70,270	148,958	416,904	2,074,248
British Columbia	1,305,552	91,863	59,043	189,586	277,931	1,923,975
Northwest Territories	19,122	673	601	5,033	6,964	32,393
Canada	13,226,332	882,019	653,325	1,450,031	3,856,764	20,008,472

[1] Excludes data from federal and private hospitals; all four hospitals in Yukon are federal.

4.13   BEDS AND UTILIZATION OF ACUTE CARE HOSPITALS[1]

Year	Beds staffed and in operation per 1,000 population	Percent occupancy[2]	Percentage of beds for long-term and psychiatric care	Impatient admissions per 1,000 population	Outpatient visits per 1,000 population	Percentage of total surgeries performed on an outpatient basis
1980-81	5.4	80.4	17.8	148	1,272	37.5
1981-82	5.4	81.0	18.8	146	1,310	37.2
1982-83	5.3	82.1	19.3	147	1,354	39.8
1983-84	5.3	82.4	19.8	146	1,391	41.5
1984-85	5.3	83.2	20.6	146	1,448	42.0
1985-86	5.3	83.4	21.4	146	1,516	44.2
1986-87	5.2	83.6	21.7	145	1,562	44.9
1987-88	5.2	83.2	22.3	144	1,611	45.7
1988-89	5.0	82.7	22.7	139	1,603	48.5
1989-90	5.0	. .	. .	138	. .	. .

[1] Includes general and specialty hospitals (cancer, cardiology, maternity, neurology, orthopedic, etc.). Excludes extended care, rehabilitation, and psychiatric hospitals.
[2] Proportion of beds occupied by inpatients in public general hospitals, on average, during the year.

Sources
Health and Welfare Canada
Statistics Canada

THOMAS KITCHIN / *FIRST LIGHT*

EDUCATION

INTRODUCTION

Carrie Derick, Canada's first female full professor, would no doubt be astonished at the changes in Canada's educational system if she were to reappear Rip van Winkle fashion today.

A member of Montreal's McGill academic staff in 1891, she was made a full professor in 1911. By 1920, there were 302 women teaching alongside 2,696 men in the country's 22 universities.

In 1991, not only were more and more women prominent, but 7 of them were presidents of Canadian universities — out of 69 such positions.

Like other institutions in an era of rapid transitions, the field of education has evolved in the last decades of the 20th century to reflect societal concerns and changes in the composition of the population, changes in the workplace, the information explosion, the impact of new technologies and the increasing fragility of the environment.

Women's studies programs provide dynamic new interpretations of major fields of postsecondary study. As well, inclusive language — references to women as well as to men — has become a standard feature of many new study materials.

Even the traditional subject approach to learning has yielded in some areas to an issue-based, holistic emphasis on connections and relationships in an increasingly complex and interdependent world. Approaching the second millennium, students are being taught how to make choices and how to live with the consequences of their choices.

Canada has a decentralized system of education and so the delivery of formal education varies between each province and territory. Taxpayers provide most of the funding for education. Tuition fees and other private sources cover the remainder.

Depending on where they live, all Canadians from the age of 6 or 7 to 15 or 16 must attend school. Enrolments are also affected by immigration and interprovincial migration.

More people are going to school, staying there longer than ever before and emerging with higher levels of qualifications, according to statistics based on institutional surveys.

In 1990-91, more than 25% of the population — 6.2 million students — studied full time at Canadian educational and vocational institutions. Another 502,700 women and men studied part time at universities (309,200) and colleges (193,500). An additional 15% of the Canadian population — or 2.9 million adults — took part in continuing (adult) education and training activities on a mostly part-time basis.

Canadians had a median of 12.2 years of formal schooling in 1986, up from 10.6 in 1971. Most adults (82%) had at least Grade 9 education; a high proportion of the remaining 18% were more than 55 years of age. Almost half (45%) of the population aged 20 years and over had graduated from secondary school.

It cost an estimated $48.2 billion to provide a large portion of this education and training, including continuing education programs offered by government-funded institutions. The biggest expense was salaries for about 900,000 personnel (at least 359,000 of whom were full-time teachers).

The ratio of elementary and secondary students to educators continues to decrease, and the number of educators is rising. Full-time and part-time elementary and secondary teachers number 297,100, about 12,000 more than the previous peak for staff in 1976-77.

In 1990-91, Canadians on average paid 8% of their personal income to fund education. Provincial, municipal and federal governments absorbed $43.7 billion (about 90%) of the costs.

Education receives the third largest outlay of public funds, following health and social welfare. In 1989-90, Canadian governments spent 14% of their budgets on education, down slightly from the 15.5% paid out at the beginning of the decade.

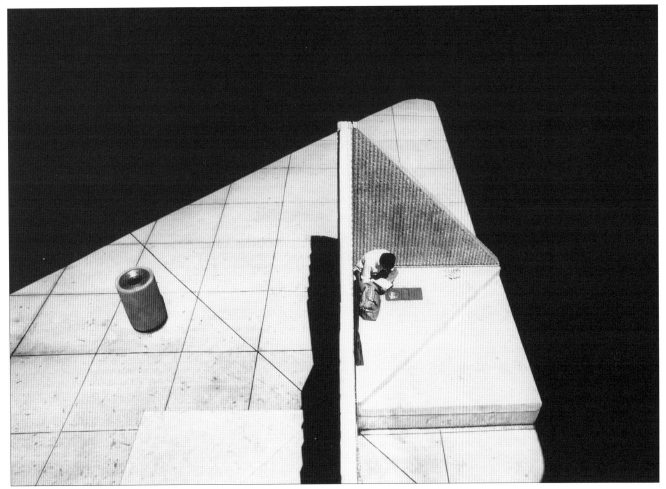

Steve Nierdorf / The Image Bank

Study time.

In 1987-88, eligible university students received nearly $1 billion in education loans and grants from federal and provincial governments. Included were $563 million in loans (an average of $1,045 for each full-time student) and $410 million in scholarships, forgiven loans, bursaries and other forms of grants (an average of $760 for each full-time student).

In our competitive society, most jobs require at least a secondary school graduation diploma. Employment opportunities for those who don't have this diploma became significantly worse during the 1980s. Unemployment in 1990 was the lowest among university degree-holders and highest among Canadians with Grade 8 or less.

The field of education has broadened so that it now includes a wide range of training possibilities which imply life-long learning offered in a variety of settings, including the workplace, and delivered by an assortment of providers, including advocacy groups.

Many new issues dominate the Canadian educational field. They range from concerns about equal educational opportunities for women and minority groups to a debate about achieving better educational results in spite of pressing budget problems.

A PERSPECTIVE ON THE ISSUES

EQUAL OPPORTUNITIES Canada's population has become increasingly diverse racially, culturally and linguistically. In major Ontario cities, it is not unusual to find classrooms composed almost entirely of visible minority children. In fact, one-half of Canada's immigrants called Ontario their home in 1991. Ontario is also home to large ethnic communities, including Canadians of African and Asian origins.

As a consequence, school boards across Canada are promoting multiculturalism, human rights, citizenship and cross-cultural understanding and, in several provinces, offering instruction in heritage languages.

Canada's educational system also faces the challenge of native needs. Native Canadians study at federal, public, separate and band schools. Some school boards now teach a native language as part of the regular school program or in after-school classes. Other important issues for native people (status and non-status Indians, Métis and Inuit people) include local control of their own schools, programs to attract northern native people into teaching, and curriculum material in various languages developed by and for native people.

Also, the arrival of a growing number of immigrants to Canada who speak neither English nor French has brought new needs for new educational services. In 1989, a total of 45,000 of the 200,000 immigrants to Canada were of school age and 72% of them settled in Ontario or Quebec. The schools they attend have had to develop and expand programs for English and French as a second language, set up learning centres, guidance programs, and, where numbers are significant, settlement counselling services.

Heritage language programs have been another response of the school system to the philosophy of multiculturalism and the linguistic and cultural diversity of much of Canadian society. The term usually refers to all modern languages other than those of aboriginal people and English or French. Many school boards in Quebec, Ontario, Manitoba, Saskatchewan and Alberta now offer heritage language programs. In British Columbia, they are in the planning stage.

Canada's Official Languages in Education Program offers minority official language communities the chance to receive education in their own language, and enables all Canadians to learn a second (official) language. Provinces provide schooling to children in the minority language (English in Quebec, French elsewhere in Canada), as well as English or French as a second language to the majority. In 1990-91, federal minority language education and second language expenditures totalled $255 million.

Children with special needs or abilities present another challenge; they make up an estimated 5% to 10% of the student population and include persons who are exceptionally gifted and those with learning disabilities. The prevailing trend is to integrate these children into the regular school system, rather than to provide special schools or classes. Trades programs are also available for people who are disabled; federal and provincial governments share the cost of these programs.

EQUALITY ISSUES The majority of elementary and secondary school teachers in Canada are women. At the primary and secondary school level in 1989-90, some 60% of educators were women, but women held only about 25% of the administrative positions. Positions of principals, vice-principals and department heads are mostly occupied by men. In the early 1980s, men occupied about 83% of all administrative positions.

Women have made substantial inroads, but remain a minority among teachers on Canadian university campuses. Women are still concentrated at the lower ranks and in traditionally 'female' fields. For example, during the last 20 years, 80% of female faculty have been concentrated in four fields: the humanities, health, education and the social sciences. By contrast, in 1989, only 1% were in engineering and applied sciences and fewer than 5% were in mathematics and physical sciences.

In 1989, only 7% of all full professors, but half of all lecturers and instructors, were women. Education faculties have the highest proportion of female staff, but even here only 15% of full professors were women versus 61% of lecturers and instructors. The concentration of women at lower ranks explains most of the gender variations in earnings, as university salaries are scaled according to rank.

Provincial and territorial education officials, working with their counterparts in status of women departments, are making it a priority to enrol and retain more girls and women in math, science and technology courses at all levels of the education system. They are also discussing other issues affecting the education of women and girls, including teen pregnancy, single parenthood, women re-entering the work force and the needs of racial minority, immigrant and native women.

Private-sector consultations, part of the federal government's Prosperity Initiative, have produced *Inventing Our Future, an Action Plan for Canada's Prosperity*. The plan was prepared by volunteers. A portion of the chapter on education concentrates on creating a culture geared to life-long learning and inclusiveness, so that everyone — regardless of gender, race or economic circumstances — can have a fair opportunity.

CANADA IN THE WORLD From the shores of the Pacific to the Atlantic coast, education authorities are debating the need to strengthen Canada's educational systems and to achieve better results with existing resources.

Throughout the 1980s and 1990s, Canada has had an eye on the increasingly tough world economy and the necessity to enhance our educational systems to compete in this economy.

Students and policy-makers alike are clamouring for new measures of the effectiveness of education. All major newspapers in Canada have full-time education reporters whose stories focus on public versus private schooling, life-long learning, labour adjustment programs and the global outlook.

LITERACY CONCERNS A major development since the early 1980s is a nation-wide awareness that many adult Canadians are undereducated. To tackle the problem, in 1988 the federal government set aside $110 million over a five-year period for

cost-sharing grants for public and private-sector literacy projects.

According to a 1990 Statistics Canada survey, an estimated 2.9 million adults (aged 16 to 69) lacked the reading skills needed to deal with much of the written material they encounter in everyday life. That is 16% of the Canadian population. An additional 4 million adults (22% of the population) can carry out only simple reading tasks.

As well, 6% of the young persons (age 16 to 24) surveyed by Statistics Canada in 1991 were functionally illiterate. The majority (71%) had sufficient reading skills for most everyday reading needs, while 23% could carry out simple reading tasks within familiar contexts. In addition, only about 56% had the math skills to do sequences of operations with numbers (such as adding and subtracting) with little help.

The mushrooming interest in educational results goes hand-in-hand with a greater emphasis on accountability. At the national level, for instance, the Council of Ministers of Education, Canada, launched its national School Achievement Indicators Program in 1992 to help provinces and territories evaluate their educational systems. One group of indicators will give information about the reading and mathematical skills of students aged 13 and 16.

NEW TEACHING TOOLS New information technologies, in particular microcomputers, are rapidly changing the way we learn and many of the jobs students prepare for. In recent years, provincial and territorial departments of education have developed programs and policies on the use of computers in education.

One example of a computer application used by students is E-STAT, Statistics Canada's new electronic data package. E-STAT was launched in schools in 1992. Using this electronic package, students can easily track a broad range of Canadian statistical data trends while learning about information retrieval and data handling. Students can map their region, zoom to their county or home town, and find and map the corresponding data. The software transforms current and historical socio-economic and demographic statistics into colourful maps and graphs.

A DEGREE OF CHANGE

The rapidly growing number of women entering Canadian universities means that a doctor, lawyer or economist is more likely to be a woman now than at any time in Canada's history.

The number of female graduates with bachelor's degrees has skyrocketed in recent years. From 1975 to 1990, their ranks increased more than 70%, from almost 36,000 to more than 61,000. In contrast, the number of male graduates with bachelor's degrees increased only 8% during this period.

Today, in fact, more bachelor's degrees are awarded to women than men. At the same time, women's shares of master's and doctoral degrees continues to rise. In 1990, 56% of bachelor's degrees, 47% of master's degrees and 32% of doctoral degrees were issued to women. These are marked increases from 1975, when women garnered only 44% of bachelor's degrees, 28% of master's degrees and 16% of doctoral degrees.

The flood of female graduates has coincided with the mass entry of women into academic fields that have been traditionally male-dominated. In fact, for several disciplines that were once overwhelmingly the domain of men — veterinary medicine, law, zoology, commerce, medicine, and political science — women now make up roughly half of all graduates with bachelor's degrees.

The largest increase in female graduates occurred in veterinary medicine. In 1975, females accounted for less than one-quarter of veterinary graduates, compared to more than 60% in 1990.

By 1990, women had increased their representation in all the undergraduate fields dominated by men, except one — computer science. In that field, the share of women graduates actually declined from 1975.

Today, women still make up only a tiny share of bachelor's degree graduates in engineering, physics and forestry. However, women's representation in these fields was so low in 1975 that even a tenfold increase in their numbers would have left them a small minority of graduates. For example, from 1975 to 1990, the share of women forestry graduates increased more than 10 times, from 1.6% to more than 16%.

While female representation rose in almost all academic disciplines, it did not always rise for the same reasons.

For some disciplines, the share of female graduates with bachelor's degrees rose because the number of women graduates grew faster than the number of men graduates. This was the case for chemistry, commerce, economics, engineering, mathematics, physics and political science. For other disciplines, the share of female graduates grew because the number of women went up, while the number of men went down. This was true for agriculture, architecture, dentistry, law, medicine and veterinary medicine.

As in 1975, education remains the most popular discipline for women. In 1990, over 18% of bachelor's degrees awarded to women were for studies in education. However, commerce had risen to second place, accounting for 10% of female graduates with bachelor's degrees, up from just 2% in 1975. Other popular disciplines for women were languages, psychology, sociology and nursing.

The inroads women are making into historically male-dominated disciplines could change the face of the labour market in Canada, as more women are now qualified to enter professions traditionally practised by men. Further, more women with bachelor's degrees can now be expected to pursue graduate work in male-dominated fields of study.

G. V. Faint / The Image Bank

School bus on a country road, British Columbia.

Today's teachers can also draw on a broader range of materials to develop course content. Environment Canada publications focus on waste management, the atmosphere, spaces and species, as well as good environmental citizenship. Five provinces have educational television services that offer curriculum-based programming for schools in addition to general educational programming for the community at large.

DISTANCE EDUCATION Distance education in the form of correspondence courses has had a long history in many parts of Canada. New technology modes of delivering independent learning have caused this section of the education industry to increase considerably in the past decade — both in numbers of students and in courses and programs offered. Universities, colleges, ministries and boards of education, business, professional associations — all are taking advantage of the capacities of communications technologies to deliver and to support learning. Computer-mediated instruction systems are a prime example.

In the 1980s, the Knowledge Network of British Columbia, a non-profit group, pioneered the use of satellites for distance education purposes. Contact North, run by the Ontario government out of Sudbury and Thunder Bay, operates a network of electronic classrooms in communities throughout northern

Ontario. Special classrooms are equipped with a variety of educational and technological devices that link remote locations to participating secondary or post-secondary institutions. In Nova Scotia, the Maritime Telegraph and Telephone Company got together with the provincial government and designed a special distance education service for College de l'Acadie and Network N.S., Nova Scotia's two distance learning networks.

EDUCATION AND THE WORK FORCE

According to the Organization for Economic Co-operation and Development (OECD), the past decade has seen an explosion of new contacts between the traditional players in education and outside individuals and groups. The main cause has been the perception that education influenced only by the state has had serious shortcomings, in particular in terms of preparing pupils for the workforce.

More and more, curriculum planners are recognizing the role of education in preparing students for employment. This has produced a variety of school-to-work transition programs, co-operative work-study arrangements, and an emphasis on work experience and career preparation. In Alberta and Ontario, two programs allow senior high school students to continue their schooling while they train as registered apprentices. The Alberta pilot project is the Registered Apprenticeship Program; its Ontario counterpart is the Secondary School Workplace Apprenticeship Program.

At the postsecondary level, Holland College in Charlottetown, Prince Edward Island, became the first educational institution in Canada to offer employers a warranty on its graduates. If the skills of its graduates don't work out on the job, the college takes them back and retrains them. In the Eastern Townships of Quebec, for instance, area school boards and businesses, with help from provincial and federal governments, set up a specialized training centre in 1986. The centre, La société de formation industrielle de l'Estrie, has the modern high-tech equipment needed to deliver up-to-date training, which had been lacking in the region's existing vocational training courses. Governments provided start-up financing. Business has provided further financial support, material resources and personnel. School boards

THE 'AFTER-SCHOOL' SHIFT

Throughout the 1980s, a growing number of young students were finding ways to juggle homework with part-time jobs. In the early 1980s, 31% of full-time students anywhere from 15 to 24 years of age worked during the school year. By the late 1980s, that figure had risen to 41%.

In 1990, the student employment rate was highest in Manitoba and Ontario, where 45% of full-time students worked, and lowest in Newfoundland, where some 14% had jobs.

Although more students are working, their hours of work have increased only slightly since the 1980s. In 1990, employed students between the ages of 15 and 24 averaged 13.9 hours a week, compared with 13.5 a week in 1980.

A number of factors may explain this rise in working students. Among them, a declining youth population seems to have reduced competition for jobs, making it easier to find one, even for the younger set.

Because of the recession, however, the percentage of students aged 15 to 24 who were employed during the school year dropped to 35% in the early 1990s.

provide equipment and free use of space. Results of a 1990 survey of student graduates showed that 90% were employed, 85% in fields related to their training. By 1993, 90% of the self-sufficient centre's work involved employee retraining.

THE MOVE BACK TO SCHOOL

School seems to be the most popular choice for young people faced with grim job prospects today. In 1992, the number of full-time students aged 15 to 24 rose 4% despite a drop in the number of young people. The trend at all levels is for students to take longer to complete their studies because they often leave for a period of time and then return to school.

Overall, the word *student* today conjures up not just young people, but also adults of all ages. 'Drop-in' rates are up, as adults head back to school in record numbers. In 1990, the majority of mature students aged 25 to 64 were studying part time while maintaining full-time jobs, and most were enrolled in universities or colleges.

THE INTERNATIONAL SCHOOL

SET Canadian colleges and universities host an increasingly large number of foreign students. In 1990-91, there were 87,000 foreign students in Canada,

Education Level[1]

[1] Of Canadians 15 years and older.

compared with 49,600 a decade earlier. An almost equal number of women (49%) came to study as men. Most of them are at university (40%), another 29% go to college and trade institutions and the balance are in elementary and secondary schools. Most foreign students come from Asia (56%) and North America (15%). Between 1977 and 1987, foreign students accounted for more than 15% of the graduate student population in Canada and about 5% of the undergraduate population.

CANADA'S EDUCATION SYSTEM

In Canada, education is primarily a provincial and territorial responsibility. Trade and vocational training and retraining might be considered an exception, where the federal government shares fiscal responsibility with the provinces and the territories.

The federal government also takes care of the educational needs of those who are outside provincial jurisdiction: native people, armed forces personnel and their families and inmates of federal prisons. As well, it is responsible for the Official Languages in Education Program and the Canada Student Loans Program.

There are two basic levels of education in Canada: elementary and secondary (including pre-elementary) and postsecondary, which includes trade and vocational programs, although these programs are offered at the elementary and secondary level in some provinces. In addition, most provinces also offer continuing education courses at each level.

ELEMENTARY AND SECONDARY

Elementary and secondary schools usually cover up to 12 grades, starting at kindergarten or Grade 1. In 1990-91, there were 12,300 elementary and 3,340 secondary schools in Canada. Most were public schools; a small portion were private or federal schools, or schools for the blind and deaf (most of which the provinces administer directly).

Most secondary schools offer a choice of purely academic courses, in preparation for university, or technical and commercial vocational training, in preparation for an occupation or for further training at a college.

Rob Allen

New computer generation.

There are also separate technical and commercial high schools. Some jurisdictions have either partially or totally eliminated age-grouped classes, and promotion is by subject rather than by grade.

Local school boards set budgets and operate public schools, including Roman Catholic and Protestant separate schools and National Defence schools in Canada. School boards obtain their revenue from two main sources: grants from provincial or territorial governments and local taxation, generally a real property tax. The relative contributions of local and provincial governments differ from province to province and from province to territory.

Private individuals or groups operate and administer private schools, including church-affiliated or non-sectarian schools. For private schools, provincial funding policies vary from direct operating grants to no support at all.

Provincial and territorial departments of education supervise elementary and secondary schools; this includes setting curriculum and approving new courses and textbooks. They usually also administer schools for the disabled, which offer special facilities and training.

POST-SECONDARY Post-secondary education is available at 69 universities and 203 colleges which are regulated by the provinces and territories.

Universities are autonomous institutions offering degree-level scholarly instruction in a number of disciplines. The usual admission requirement is

BACK TO SCHOOL

While more and more young people are dropping out of school, adults are hitting the books again in increasing numbers. In October 1990, some 705,000 Canadians between 25 and 64 years of age went back to school on either a full-time or a part-time basis. This figure has almost doubled since October 1980, when there were approximately 378,000 mature students in recognized educational institutions.

Most mature students enrol in post-secondary programs: about half take university courses and a third take college level courses. It is not nostalgia that brings them back to the classroom, but rather the demands of the labour market. In general, mature students go back to school to upgrade their skills, obtain a new job or improve their chances of promotion.

successful completion of secondary school or, in Quebec, collegial studies. There are usually special conditions for mature students who do not meet the normal entrance requirements.

Provinces and territories established college systems in the early 1960s; a few related institutions continue to operate independently. Colleges, including community colleges, are certificate or diploma-granting public or private postsecondary institutions that offer semi-professional career programs or university transfer programs. Most operate on a year-round basis and at a variety of times and places. Colleges may also offer secondary level academic upgrading, trade and vocational courses and other credit or non-credit programs oriented to community needs. College fees are lower than fees for universities. Quebec's college-level system is free to full-time students.

The colleges also include institutions of applied arts and technology or science, general and vocational education; institutes of technology; and colleges providing training in specialized fields such as nursing, art, fisheries, and marine, agricultural and para-medical technologies.

TECHNICAL AND VOCATIONAL

In the 1960s, federal funding contributed to the widespread expansion of technical and vocational education. Training is taken by those who are older than the compulsory school age and have left the regular school system; high school graduation is not usually required.

Most trade and vocational training prepares men and women to work in specific trades or occupations after a relatively short period of practical instruction. Students receive their training at public and private elementary and secondary and postsecondary institutions, including trade schools, trade divisions of community colleges and vocational centres. In addition, registered apprenticeship programs combine classroom instruction with on-the-job training.

Provincial departments of education run most public trade schools and vocational centres, which are distinct from public vocational or technical secondary schools administered by local school boards.

A primary sponsor, the federal government, channels most of its vocational training assistance through the Labour Force Development Strategy (LFDS). The LFDS, introduced in 1989, incorporates and expands on the former Canadian Job Strategy. A joint effort involving the federal government, provinces, business, labour and community groups, the LFDS promotes skills training and upgrading and the development of a training culture in Canada.

Quebec organizes trade and vocational training differently than the other provinces. Most instruction takes place in the Quebec equivalent of high schools. Local school boards administer both regular secondary schools and adult training programs, but the administration of each is separate.

CONTINUING EDUCATION Today, continuing education is defined to include all public and private education and training for adults, excluding full-time attendance in postsecondary institutions. Unlike the public school system, grant monies for adult education are not guaranteed in legislation and can be withdrawn with little notice.

School boards, provincial departments of education, colleges and universities offer a wide range of academic and vocational, credit and non-credit courses. Credit courses can lead to a high school diploma or to a university or college degree, diploma or certificate. Non-credit programs encompass adult literacy, professional development, computer technology, language studies, arts and crafts and other general interest topics. Instruction is available on campus (in classrooms) or off-campus (by correspondence, from travelling libraries, over radio and television, and different modes of distance education delivery). A vocational institute likely offers upgrading in technical areas, while accounting firms could run workshops in pre-retirement financial planning.

The business world trains new employees and retrains or upgrades experienced workers. Publicly supported in full or in part, or entirely financed by the company, training can be on-the-job, in the classroom, or a combination of the two. On-the-job training subsidies, for instance, are available through the LFDS.

Programs are also conducted or sponsored by non-profit groups, professional associations and government departments.

THE COST OF EDUCATION

Post World War II baby boomers brought tremendous growth to schools, colleges and universities until the end of the 1960s. In the years that followed, a declining birth rate and a period of economic slowdown produced restraint in education spending.

Nevertheless, education continues to be a major expenditure of Canadian governments. Spending on education has risen steadily over the past decade, growing from $22.2 billion in 1980-81 to $48.2 billion in 1990-91. The total bill, averaged over the working population, was $3,297 for every employed person, 85% higher than 10 years earlier.

The cost of education in Canada is rising faster than the rise in the Consumer Price Index (CPI), the measure of general price movements. From 1980-81 to 1990-91, spending on education increased by 117%. During the same period, the CPI rose by 78%. In 1990-91, the largest portion, an estimated $30.7 billion, was spent on the education of 5.1 million elementary and secondary students. An additional $13.7 billion supported 857,000 full-time postsecondary students and 309,200 part-time university students; $3.8 billion went to 249,000 women and men enrolled in trade and vocational training.

Provincial and territorial governments remain the principal direct source of education funding at all levels. In 1990-91, provincial and territorial governments spent $29.2 billion on education, followed by municipal governments at $9.7 billion, and the federal government (direct funding only) at $4.8 billion. Fees and other sources accounted for some $4.3 billion.

Federal spending on education includes direct and indirect contributions. Direct federal contributions go primarily to vocational training. Other direct payments finance research in universities, fund student aid programs for postsecondary education and operate federal schools. The federal government also transfers substantial amounts for the support of official languages

Robert Harris / National Gallery of Canada

A Meeting of the School Trustees.

(elementary, secondary and postsecondary levels) and postsecondary education. In addition, many federal departments provide financial support for education, offering funds for citizenship and language instruction for immigrants and human resources training programs.

Private industry also spent a substantial amount on formal training for employees. According to a 1991 survey by the Canadian Labour Market and Productivity Centre, there has been a marked increase in training, particularly in health and safety areas in recent years.

ELEMENTARY AND SECONDARY

The bill for public and private elementary and secondary schooling rose from $26.6 billion in 1988-89 to $30.7 billion in 1990-91.

In general, provinces pick up a little less than two-thirds of the costs of local school boards; local governments and school boards with powers to tax raise the remainder. As provincial purse strings tighten, local taxation authorities must raise more money. Provincial grants decreased from 64% of total school board revenues in 1985-86 to 61% in 1989-90.

P O S T · S E C O N D A R Y Canada spends 37% of its public education dollars on post-secondary education, while Belgium, France, Italy, Spain and Sweden — fellow OECD members — spend from 14% to 16%. In 1990-91, federal and provincial governments contributed 83% of the $13.7 billion spent on post-secondary education in 1990-91. This included $10.1 billion for universities and $3.5 billion for colleges.

In the early 1960s, student fees made up one-quarter of university income; with an increase in public funding, this proportion has been reduced to about one-tenth.

From 1981-82 to 1990-91, total gross university expenditures rose by 106%, representing an average annual increase of 8.4%. General operating expenditures per full-time equivalent student increased by an average 4.3% per year, reaching $10,676 in 1990-91. This compares to an average increase of 5.2% in the CPI.

The average university receives direct provincial funding (about 65%); direct federal funding, mainly for research (15%); tuition fees (11%) and monies from other sources (9%). These figures hold at the national level only. For individual institutions, government funding ranges from a nominal proportion for small, church-affiliated institutions, to more than 90% for some universities.

Tuition fees vary by province, by university and by faculty. In all provinces except Newfoundland, Saskatchewan and Manitoba, higher fees are required of foreign students. Provincial funding for general operating funds is increasing more slowly than tuition fees. From 1981-82 to 1990-91, tuition fees increased at an average annual rate of 10.8%, compared with 6.9% for provincial funding.

The federal government, through its research councils, is the principal source of funds for sponsored research in universities. The relative importance of this source of funding has declined constantly since reaching a peak share of 60.3% in 1984-85. Provincial grants, however, increased slightly over the same period, from 17.7% to 19.1% from 1981-82 to 1990-91.

T R A D E   A N D   V O C A T I O N A L The national expenditure on vocational training in 1990-91 was $3.8 billion, up from $3.5 billion in 1989-90. The federal government contributed the largest portion ($2.3 billion), followed by the provinces ($1.2 billion); $300 million was raised through fees and from other sources.

The largest expense covers LFDS programs, which pay particular attention to the plight of displaced older workers and their need for retraining. The remainder covers the cost of: training nursing assistants and aides in hospitals; government language training courses; vocational training in provincial reform schools and federal penitentiaries; private business colleges; private trade schools; and other training expenses reported by federal and provincial governments.

Participation in French Immersion[1]

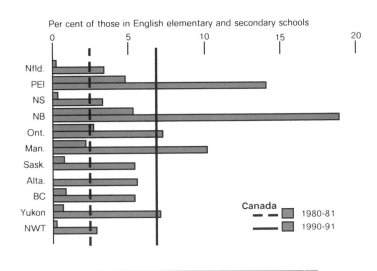

Per cent of those in English elementary and secondary schools

1 Because of the differences in French and English schooling, it is inappropriate to compare the French immersion participation rate in Quebec with those of other provinces. 17,500 Quebec students attended French immersion in 1980-81; 31,484 attended in 1990-91.

'DROP-OUT' DILEMMA

A recent study by Statistics Canada has found that nearly 24% of Canadian students leave school before graduation. According to the 1991 School Leavers Survey, nearly one in four 20-year-olds had packed in their schoolbooks at some point in the past.

Students' reasons for leaving school were varied. While the largest proportion of those who had not completed school said they preferred work to school (22%), other respondents cited boredom (20%), problems with school work (8%), or financial reasons (8%). Of female students, 9% left for pregnancy or marriage-related reasons.

Once out of school, 'non-completers' generally received a cold reception in the job market. In the sample group studied, unemployment rates were twice as high for 'drop-outs' than for those who had completed school.

Nearly half of those who had quit school regretted the decision. A similar proportion of leavers surveyed said they had returned to school to continue their educations.

CURRENT ENROLMENTS

ELEMENTARY AND SECONDARY

In Canada, pre-Grade 1 schooling is neither compulsory nor universal, but it is increasingly popular. Except in the public schools of Prince Edward Island, kindergarten is now an integral part of elementary public education. Further, because of increasing demand, school boards in some provinces are creating programs for four-year-olds. In 1990-91, 472,500 children were enrolled in pre-school programs.

Although Canada's primary and secondary school population is now less than in the 1970s, resulting in lower enrolments, students are starting school earlier and are staying in school longer. Moreover, enrolment for the 20 and over age group has tripled over the last 20 years. This trend possibly reflects the increased retention rates as well as the phenomenon of 'drop-ins', persons who return to school after being out of school for a few years.

In 1990-91, more than 5.1 million young Canadians spent their weekdays in primary or secondary schools, or were enrolled in secondary level co-op courses (courses that combine study and work) or distance education programs. The all-time high was 5.8 million in 1970-71. After 15 declining years, enrolment started to increase again in 1986-87.

In 1990-91, 61% of Canada's 15 to 19-year-olds were enrolled in elementary and secondary schools, compared to 54% a decade earlier. Most attended public schools. Another 240,968 students attended private schools, 52,285 attended federally-run native schools and schools for children of armed forces personnel, and 2,442 attended schools for persons with hearing and sight disabilities.

Since 1972-73, more students are studying privately; that is, outside of the public school system. In 1990-91, private schools accounted for 5% of the total elementary and secondary enrolment, up from 4% in 1980-81.

During the 1990 school year, almost half of all secondary school students aged 17 to 19 combined work with full-time studies.

Kryn Taconis / CMCP

Barry, a blind boy, in his home library with a Braille encyclopedia.

OFFICIAL LANGUAGES In 1989-90, schools provided minority language programs to nearly 258,000 students, representing just over 5% of the total school enrolment. New Brunswick had the largest proportion of minority language students in French public schools (33% of the total school enrolment).

French immersion programs provide regular classroom instruction in the French language to non-francophones. In 1970, except for a few experimental programs in Montreal, French immersion did not exist in Canada. By 1989-90, a total of 240,000 Canadian students were enrolled in French immersion programs outside the province of Quebec. Enrolments are reaching a plateau after years of dramatic increases. Results of a survey of 104 school boards indicate that for 54% of them, 1991-92 immersion enrolments are within 1% of what they were in 1988.

At the elementary level, a growing number of English-speaking pupils take part in second language French programs. Between 1986-87 and 1990-91, the participation rate (in nine provinces excluding Quebec) increased from 56% to 61%. At the secondary level, second language French programs started to attract more students again in 1984-85; participation increased for two years and has remained around 47% since 1985-86. (In Quebec, English is a compulsory subject for students in the French school system, from Grade 4 through graduation.)

POST-SECONDARY Universities and colleges welcomed 33% more full-time students to their campuses in 1990-91 than a decade earlier — a total of 857,000, compared to 643,400. Most of the growth occurred in the first part of the decade. Colleges claimed 38% of the students; the rest studied at universities.

Full-time university enrolment rose annually during the 1980s, reaching 532,100 in 1990-91, an increase of 39% over 1980-81 enrolment. While the majority of full-time university students in 1990-91 were in the traditional 18 to 24-year-old category, a growing number (24%) were aged 25 and over. Women, once a minority in undergraduate ranks, led the rise in full-time university enrolment in the 1980s. Since 1987-88, women have outnumbered men in full-time undergraduate programs. An important feature is women's entry into fields of study that have traditionally been the domain of men.

Part-time university enrolment grew by 26% over the decade, reaching 309,197 registered in degree programs in 1990-91.

On college campuses in 1990-91, women continued to outnumber men, both as full-time and part-time students. Women now make up 63% of the 193,544 part-time college enrolment, compared to 60% in 1988-89.

Full-time college enrolment was 324,400 in 1990-91, up 24% from a decade earlier. Nearly 70% of the students were in career/technical programs such as nursing; the remainder were in university transfer programs.

The two top fields of study for women were business/commerce (32%) and health sciences (24%); for men they were engineering and applied sciences (42%) and business/commerce (23%). The same fields of study were also the most popular 10 years ago.

TRADE AND VOCATIONAL During 1989-90, trade and vocational programs in Canada had a full-time enrolment of 249,000 trainees, about the same number as in 1985-86, but 22,800 less than in 1983-84. Trainees were enrolled in pre-employment programs (about 33%), programs for registered apprentices (23%), skills upgrading (6%) and other pre-vocational programs.

While more men (60%) than women (40%) completed trade and vocational programs in 1989-90, the proportion of female completions has increased from 35% in 1985-86. Only 4% of those completing apprenticeship

"OUI, HELLO, I'M FINE, ET VOUS..."

Canada's Official Languages Act states that both English and French — Canada's two official languages — should "enjoy quality of status and equal rights... in all institutions of the Parliament and Government of Canada." Since these aspirations were enshrined in law more than two decades ago, Canada's level of bilingualism has risen steadily.

According to the 1991 Census of Population, just over 16% of Canadians — roughly 4.5 million people — could conduct a conversation in both English and French in 1991, compared to just 13% — or about 2.8 million people — in 1971.

Of the provinces, Quebec reported the highest bilingualism rate in 1991 (35%), followed by New Brunswick (30%) and Ontario (11%). Newfoundland's was lowest at just 3%.

In recent years, Canada's bilingulism rate has risen only slightly, from 16.2% in 1986 to 16.3% in 1991. This was largely due to high levels of immigration, particularly in Ontario, where bilingualism fell by almost half of one percentage point over the same period.

For Ontario residents whose first language was English, however, the bilingualism rate actually increased, from 7.2% in 1986 to 7.5% in 1991. For Ontario residents whose mother tongue was French, the bilingualism rate also went up — from 84.6% in 1986 to 86.7% in 1991.

With the exception of Ontario, English–French bilingualism increased in every other province between 1986 and 1991.

Most Canadians speak one of Canada's official languages, although many are not bilingual. In 1991, 67% of Canadians spoke English but not French, 15% spoke French but not English, and just over 1% spoke neither language.

Kryn Taconis / CMCP

School for the Deaf, Milton, Ontario.

programs were female, compared to 80% in job readiness training programs and 73% in orientation programs.

CONTINUING EDUCATION Substantial growth in continuing education programs began in the 1960s when the federal government entered the field, and community colleges were born. Additional growth stemmed from developments in distance education and increased involvement of the business sector.

Adults enrol in continuing education courses to complete studies, to attain additional job-related or educational qualifications, or for general interest. Higher levels of education are strongly associated with the return to school. Programs include part-time and short-term courses and full-time, employer-sponsored programs.

By 1990, nearly one in five adults in Canada took part in credit or non-credit education or training activities. Most were employed and between the ages of 25 and 44. Participation rates for women and men were identical. On a provincial basis, participation rates in continuing (adult) education tend to increase from east to west.

Commerce, management and business administrations courses, which suggest upgrading, are the most popular (23%). Courses in engineering and applied science technologies and trades, which are more associated with retraining, rank second (21%). (Data processing and computer science technologies represent 54% of this category.)

Education providers include mostly tax-supported educational institutions (55%), employers (23%), and unions and non-profit groups (22%). The category of educational institutions includes: community colleges (21%), universities (14%), private and commercial schools (10%), school boards (5%) and vocational schools (5%).

In the Yukon and Northwest Territories, where there is no established tradition of continuing education, private organizations such as Frontier College and the Young Women's Christian Association of Canada (YWCA) have provided some adult basic education.

In 1990, 1.5 million of the 3.4 million adult participants took part-time education or training courses sponsored by their employers. Employees in utilities and public administration were most likely to take employer-sponsored courses.

SOURCES

The Council of Ministers of Education, Canada

Department of the Secretary of State of Canada

Employment and Immigration Canada

Statistics Canada

FOR FURTHER READING

Selected publications from Statistics Canada

▲ *Universities, Enrolment and Degrees. Annual. 81-204*

▲ *Financial Statistics of Education. Annual. 81-208*

▲ *Elementary-Secondary School Enrolment. Annual. 81-210*

▲ *Advance Statistics of Education. Annual. 81-220*

▲ *Community Colleges and Related Institutions, Postsecondary Enrolment and Graduates. Annual. 81-222*

▲ *Education in Canada, a Statistical Review. Annual. 81-229*

▲ *Teachers in Universities. Annual. 81-241*

▲ *Minority and Second Language Education, Elementary and Secondary Levels. Annual. 81-257*

▲ *University Finance Trend Analysis. Annual. 81-260*

Selected publications from Other Sources

▲ *A Statistical Portrait of Elementary and Secondary Education in Canada;* Statistics Canada, Council of Ministers of Education, Canada. 1992.

TABLES

5.1 ENROLMENT IN ELEMENTARY AND SECONDARY SCHOOLS

	Nfld.	PEI	NS	NB	Que.	Ont.	Man.
Public							
1985-86	142,332	24,996	172,614	141,332	1,041,439	1,769,074	198,937
1989-90	130,109	24,673	166,263	134,731	1,038,935	1,893,604	197,724
1990-91	127,029	24,389	165,719	132,843	1,042,894	1,932,755	197,586
Private							
1985-86	319	58	1,959	1,171	95,303	76,312	9,512
1989-90	271	76	1,850	1,013	99,696	64,116	10,161
1990-91	246	85	1,849	1,035	100,806	66,347	10,551
Federal							
1985-86	—	36	914	742	3,698	7,880	10,315
1989-90	—	40	989	783	4,080	9,044	11,223
1990-91	—	37	1,020	883	4,431	9,266	11,589
Schools for the blind and the deaf							
1985-86	106	17	591	—	718	891	140
1989-90	123	15	528	—	661	733	137
1990-91	125	12	582	—	639	722	133
Total[1]							
1985-86	142,757	25,107	176,078	143,245	1,141,158	1,854,157	218,904
1989-90	130,503	24,804	169,630	136,527	1,143,372	1,967,497	219,245
1990-91	127,400	24,523	169,170	134,761	1,148,770	2,009,090	219,859

	Sask.	Alta.	BC	YT	NWT	Canada
Public						
1985-86	202,560	448,339	486,777	4,554	13,444	4,646,398
1989-90	200,335	471,086	512,735	5,113	13,732	4,789,040
1990-91	198,933	483,857	519,958	5,266	14,079	4,845,308
Private						
1985-86	2,943	13,058	33,553	—	—	234,188
1989-90	3,048	15,084	38,438	—	—	233,753
1990-91	3,199	16,173	40,677	—	—	240,968
Federal						
1985-86	8,330	5,575	3,421	—	—	44,408
1989-90	9,242	6,643	4,394	—	—	50,160
1990-91	10,112	7,334	3,893	—	—	52,285
Schools for the blind and the deaf						
1985-86	96	123	130	—	—	2,812
1989-90	51	97	105	—	—	2,450
1990-91	34	96	99	—	—	2,442
Total[1]						
1985-86	213,929	467,095	523,881	4,554	13,444	4,927,806
1989-90	212,676	492,910	555,672	5,113	13,732	5,075,403
1990-91	212,278	507,460	564,627	5,266	14,079	5,141,003

[1] *Canada total also includes Department of National Defence schools overseas.*

5.2   FULL-TIME POSTSECONDARY ENROLMENT IN COMMUNITY COLLEGES[1]

		Career programs	University transfer programs	Total
Newfoundland	1985-86	2,967	—	2,967
	1989-90	3,490	—	3,490
	1990-91	3,666	—	3,666
Prince Edward Island	1985-86	959	—	959
	1989-90	951	—	951
	1990-91	999	—	999
Nova Scotia	1985-86	2,932	—	2,932
	1989-90	2,639	—	2,639
	1990-91	2,692	—	2,692
New Brunswick	1985-86	2,462	—	2,462
	1989-90	2,483	—	2,483
	1990-91	2,664	—	2,664
Quebec	1985-86	79,191	85,027	164,218
	1989-90	68,988	85,302	154,290
	1990-91	69,637	84,781	154,418
Ontario	1985-86	94,574	—	94,574
	1989-90	93,337	—	93,337
	1990-91	99,466	—	99,466
Manitoba	1985-86	3,743	76	3,819
	1989-90	3,780	75	3,855
	1990-91	3,880	83	3,963
Saskatchewan	1985-86	3,012	—	3,051
	1989-90	3,164	—	3,164
	1990-91	3,433	—	3,433
Alberta	1985-86	20,822	3,298	24,120
	1989-90	21,344	4,197	25,541
	1990-91	20,826	4,342	25,168
British Columbia	1985-86	13,312	9,616	22,928
	1989-90	13,218	13,445	26,663
	1990-91	13,041	14,386	27,427
Yukon	1985-86	71	17	88
	1989-90	89	87	176
	1990-91	89	87	176
Northwest Territories	1985-86	130	3	133
	1989-90	241	11	252
	1990-91	255	11	266
Canada	1985-86	224,175	98,037	322,212
	1989-90	213,724	103,117	316,841
	1990-91	220,648	103,690	324,338

[1] *Includes related institutions such as hospital schools and agricultural, arts, and other specialized colleges.*

5.3   ENROLMENT IN UNIVERSITIES

		Full-time			Part-time		
		Under-graduate	Graduate	Total	Under-graduate	Graduate	Total
Newfoundland	1985-86	9,714	638	10,352	4,092	532	4,624
	1989-90	10,887	748	11,635	3,784	564	4,348
	1990-91	11,769	765	12,561	4,057	550	4,607
Prince Edward Island	1985-86	1,768	—	1,768	781	—	781
	1989-90	2,310	22	2,332	842	8	850
	1990-91	2,502	32	2,534	894	5	899
Nova Scotia	1985-86	21,662	1,920	23,582	5,680	1,163	6,843
	1989-90	23,916	2,266	26,182	6,839	1,505	8,344
	1990-91	24,694	2,315	27,009	6,808	1,563	8,371
New Brunswick	1985-86	14,239	679	14,918	4,106	415	4,521
	1989-90	15,370	791	16,161	4,808	665	5,473
	1990-91	16,031	864	16,895	4,846	654	5,500
Quebec	1985-86	95,967	17,347	113,314	100,825	14,691	115,516
	1989-90	103,194	18,508	121,702	104,547	17,703	122,250
	1990-91	105,470	19,199	124,669	102,651	18,631	121,282
Ontario	1985-86	164,007	21,009	185,016	84,882	11,963	96,845
	1989-90	184,875	23,652	208,527	90,105	12,616	102,721
	1990-91	191,901	24,540	216,441	92,601	12,876	105,477
Manitoba	1985-86	17,950	2,389	20,339	12,464	1,591	14,055
	1989-90	17,167	2,345	19,512	14,430	1,179	15,609
	1990-91	17,474	2,224	19,698	14,900	1,262	16,162
Saskatchewan	1985-86	18,395	1,065	19,460	7,865	784	8,649
	1989-90	19,606	1,383	20,989	8,306	750	9,056
	1990-91	20,226	1,414	21,640	8,973	837	9,810
Alberta	1985-86	37,875	4,881	42,756	15,189	2,148	17,337
	1989-90	42,262	5,388	47,650	14,935	2,169	17,104
	1990-91	43,186	5,428	48,614	15,383	2,274	17,657
British Columbia	1985-86	30,835	4,964	35,799	13,879	1,848	15,727
	1989-90	33,894	6,442	40,336	17,313	1,438	18,751
	1990-91	35,043	7,053	42,096	17,834	1,599	19,433
Canada	1985-86	412,412	54,892	467,304	249,763	35,135	284,898
	1989-90	453,481	61,545	515,025	265,911	38,596	304,507
	1990-91	468,296	63,834	532,130	268,947	40,251	309,198

5.4 DIRECT SOURCES OF FUNDS FOR EDUCATION AT ALL LEVELS (MILLION DOLLARS)

	Government			Fees	Other sources	Total
	Federal[1]	Provincial	Municipal[2]			
1980-81	1,891.0	14,717.5	3,850.8	872.7	869.6	22,201.6
1985-86	3,661.5	22,375.8	5,480.5	1,545.2	1,501.1	34,564.1
1989-90	4,352.2	27,307.4	8,675.7	2,204.8	1,982.0	44,522.0
1990-91	4,854.0	29,229.2	9,746.3	2,460.4	1,893.7	48,183.7

[1] In addition to the direct funding reported here, the federal government also provides indirect support in respect of postsecondary education to provinces and territories under the Federal-Provincial Fiscal Arrangements and Federal Post-Secondary Education and Health Contributions Act, 1977 and under the Official Languages in Education Program. For futher information on the financing of these programs, please consult Financial Statistics of Education (Statistics Canada Catalogue 81–208).
[2] Includes local school taxation.

5.5 EXPENDITURES[1] ON EDUCATION (MILLION DOLLARS)

	Nfld.	PEI	NS	NB	Que.	Ont.
1989-90						
Level						
Elementary and secondary	587.3	105.0	826.8	689.5	6,516.8	11,637.1
Postsecondary	236.0	55.2	427.5	271.4	3,692.3	4,442.7
Vocational training	153.2	22.7	130.9	144.8	727.0	826.0
Direct source of funds						
Federal government[2]	136.7	22.1	157.0	133.6	943.6	1,144.9
Provincial governments	750.5	145.6	975.8	889.1	8,619.1	8,386.5
Municipal governments[3]	28.0	—	115.6	—	279.1	5,663.5
Fees and other sources	61.3	15.2	136.8	83.0	1,094.3	1,710.9
Total	976.5	182.9	1,385.2	1,105.7	10,936.1	16,905.8
1990-91[p]						
Level						
Elementary and secondary	601.7	113.2	868.9	730.7	6,941.9	12,650.3
Postsecondary	258.1	58.0	461.7	294.5	4,137.8	4,600.1
Vocational training	169.2	24.6	143.3	173.7	789.6	896.9
Direct source of funds						
Federal government[2]	152.1	24.0	180.6	159.2	1,053.9	1,288.5
Provincial governments	789.8	154.7	1,019.0	941.1	9,539.4	8,755.5
Municipal governments[3]	29.2	—	129.1	—	296.0	6,398.7
Fees and other sources	57.9	17.1	145.2	98.6	980.0	1,704.6
Total	1,029.0	195.8	1,473.9	1,198.9	11,869.3	18,147.3

5.5 EXPENDITURES[1] ON EDUCATION (MILLION DOLLARS) (concluded)

	Man.	Sask.	Alta.	BC	YT and NWT	Overseas and un-distributed	Canada
1989-90							
Level							
Elementary and secondary	1,245.4	1,043.5	2,546.5	2,808.5	182.7	65.3	28,254.2
Postsecondary	431.8	451.1	1,308.6	1,195.5	41.6	165.6	12,719.4
Vocational training	147.5	175.4	482.3	473.4	35.3	229.8	3,548.4
Direct source of funds							
Federal government[2]	237.1	225.8	405.9	516.4	8.0	421.1	4,352.2
Provincial governments	969.1	887.2	2,576.4	2,654.8	236.3	—	27,090.3
Municipal governments[3]	435.7	412.7	924.2	808.8	8.0	—	8,675.7
Fees and other sources	182.8	144.3	430.9	497.4	7.3	39.6	4,403.8
Total	1,824.7	1,670.0	4,337.4	4,477.4	259.6	460.7	44,522.0
1990-91p							
Level							
Elementary and secondary	1,345.5	1,099.8	2,763.8	3,353.8	206.9	41.6	30,718.0
Postsecondary	461.9	511.2	1,326.0	1,320.9	40.7	180.0	13,651.0
Vocational training	150.4	177.9	472.6	525.4	38.3	252.8	3,814.7
Direct source of funds							
Federal government[2]	268.3	265.2	434.3	589.5	6.0	432.4	4,854.0
Provincial governments	1,039.1	942.7	2,669.0	3,115.7	263.2	—	29,229.2
Municipal governments[3]	456.4	436.3	1,004.1	987.9	8.7	—	9,746.4
Fees and other sources	194.0	144.7	455.0	507.0	8.0	42.0	4,354.1
Total	1,957.8	1,788.9	4,562.4	5,200.1	285.9	474.4	48,183.7

[1] Includes operating, capital, student aid and all departmental expenditures.
[2] In addition to the direct funding reported here, the federal government also provides indirect support for postsecondary education to provinces and territories under the Federal-Provincial Fiscal Arrangements and Federal Post-Secondary Education and Health Contributions Act, 1977 and under the Official Languages in Education Program. For further information on the financing of these programs, please consult Financial Statistics of Education (Statistics Canada Catalogue 81–208).
[3] Includes local school taxation.

5.6 EXPENDITURES ON ELEMENTARY AND SECONDARY EDUCATION, 1990–91[P]
(MILLION DOLLARS)

	Nfld.	PEI	NS	NB	Que.	Ont.
Type of expenditure						
School boards[1]						
Teachers' salaries[2]						
including fringe benefits	366.2	67.9	510.7	343.4	3,328.2	6,926.9
Other operating expenses	119.5	27.8	189.7	182.1	2,200.2	3,514.3
Capital and debt charges	56.7	11.1	62.1	2.5	480.5	909.6
Total	542.4	106.8	762.5	528.0	6,008.9	11,350.8
Governmental expenditures						
on behalf of public schools[3]	47.7	4.4	78.1	188.4	285.8	698.8
Total	590.1	111.2	840.6	716.4	6,294.7	12,049.6
Indian and Inuit schools	0.9	0.5	9.3	7.8	69.1	89.4
Special education	[4]	[4]	[4]	2.3	16.9	85.9
Private schools	[4]	[4]	[4]	4.3	561.2	425.4
Total	601.6	113.1	868.8	730.8	6,941.9	12,650.3
Direct source of funds						
Federal government	0.9	1.2	16.6	12.5	90.6	160.4
Provincial governments	558.4	111.3	699.8	699.6	6,034.4	5,506.5
Municipal governments[5]	29.2	—	128.7	—	295.1	6,397.9
Fees and other sources	13.1	0.6	23.7	18.7	521.8	585.5
Total	601.6	113.1	868.8	730.8	6,941.9	12,650.3

	Man.	Sask.	Alta.	BC	YT and NWT	Overseas and undistributed	Canada
Type of expenditure							
School boards							
Teachers' salaries							
including fringe benefits	607.6	522.1	1,454.3	1,562.9	99.6	—	15,789.8
Other operating expenses	357.0	300.6	662.7	861.6	72.5	—	8,488.0
Capital and debt charges	94.6	82.8	300.3	240.0	12.8	—	2,253.0
Total	1,059.2	905.5	2,417.3	2,664.5	184.9	—	26,530.8
Governmental expenditures							
on behalf of public schools	140.3	83.1	146.2	448.6	18.3	−5.3	2,134.5
Total	1,199.5	988.6	2,563.5	3,113.1	203.2	−5.3	28,665.2
Indian and Inuit schools	85.2	85.4	56.3	49.5	2.9	46.9	503.2
Special education	12.1	4.6	32.9	14.6	0.8	—	192.5
Private schools	48.7	21.2	111.1	176.6	—	—	1,357.0
Total	1,345.5	1,099.8	2,763.8	3,353.8	206.9	41.6	30,718.1
Direct source of funds							
Federal government	110.3	103.5	101.0	95.9	3.6	41.6	738.1
Provincial governments	674.1	533.1	1,490.1	2,094.1	190.6	—	18,592.0
Municipal governments	456.2	435.6	1,003.4	987.7	8.7	—	9,742.5
Fees and other sources	104.9	27.6	169.3	176.1	4.0	—	1,645.3
Total	1,345.5	1,099.8	2,763.8	3,353.8	206.9	41.6	30,718.1

[1] *Expenditures of school boards cover calendar year.*
[2] *Includes principals and vice-principals.*
[3] *Includes departmental administration as well as spending by federal departments in foreign countries.*
[4] *Confidential.*
[5] *Includes local school taxation.*

5.7 EXPENDITURES ON POSTSECONDARY EDUCATION, 1990–91ᴾ (MILLION DOLLARS)

	Nfld.	PEI	NS	NB	Que.	Ont.
Type of expenditure						
Operating						
Community colleges	32.1	10.5	33.6	31.6	1216.4	934.5
Universities	181.9	37.2	374.8	210.8	2175.2	3,210.8
Total	214.0	47.7	408.4	242.4	3,391.6	4,145.3
Capital	8.4	7.0	11.9	3.7	333.8	12.7
Student aid						
Scholarships and awards	19.1	3.1	26.5	21.1	296.1	267.3
Cost of loans[1]	12.5	2.4	15.7	14.0	86.5	106.2
Total	254.0	60.2	462.5	281.2	4,108.0	4,531.5
Other direct departmental						
expenditures	4.1	−2.2	−0.9	13.3	29.8	68.6
Total	258.1	58.0	461.6	294.5	4,137.8	4,600.1
Direct source of funds						
Federal government[2]	32.7	4.8	71.2	34.6	405.2	582.9
Provincial governments	186.4	37.8	272.5	200.4	3,316.8	2,986.2
Municipal governments	—	—	0.3	—	0.8	0.9
Fees and other sources	39	15.4	117.6	59.5	415.0	1,030.1
Total	258.1	58.0	461.6	294.5	4,137.8	4,600.1

	Man.	Sask.	Alta.	BC	YT and NWT	Overseas and undistributed	Canada
Type of expenditure							
Operating							
Community colleges	42.5	39.5	257.8	254.7	29.0	—	2,882.2
Universities	333.2	303.6	767.8	716.5	—	—	8,311.8
Total	375.7	343.1	1,025.6	971.2	29.0	—	11,194.0
Capital	7.5	92.0	120.4	97.3	2.6	—	697.3
Student aid							
Scholarships and awards	27.9	47.7	80.5	71.3	6.5	49.9	917.0
Cost of loans	15.1	10.6	73.3	27.1	1.1	—	364.5
Total	426.2	493.4	1,299.8	1,166.9	39.2	49.9	13,173.0
Other direct departmental							
expenditures	35.7	17.8	26.2	153.9	1.5	130.1	478.0
Total	461.9	511.2	1,326.0	1,320.8	40.7	180.0	13,651.0
Direct source of funds							
Federal government	75.5	68.0	161.1	225.6	1.8	180.0	1,843.5
Provincial governments	305.7	347.8	935.3	846.1	35.7	—	9,470.7
Municipal governments	0.2	0.7	0.7	0.2	—	—	3.8
Fees and other sources	80.5	94.7	228.9	248.9	3.2	—	2,333.0
Total	461.9	511.2	1,326.0	1,320.8	40.7	180.0	13,651.0

[1] *Excluding the value (principal) of loans.*
[2] *In addition to the direct funding reported here, the federal government also provides indirect support for postsecondary education to provinces and territories under the Federal-Provincial Fiscal Arrangements and Federal Post-Secondary Education and Health Contributions Act, 1977 and under the Official Languages in Education Program. For further information on the financing of these programs, please consult Financial Statistics of Education (Statistics Canada Catalogue 81–208).*

5.8 EXPENDITURES ON VOCATIONAL TRAINING, 1990–91[P] (MILLION DOLLARS)

Type of training and direct source of funds	Nfld.	PEI	NS	NB	Que.	Ont.
Human resource training[1]						
Federal government	113.7	17.8	90.6	109.4	540.0	507.3
Provincial and municipal governments	36.8	4.4	28.9	40.3	180.4	208.7
Fees and other sources	5.6	1.0	1.8	19.6	31.9	66.5
Total	156.1	23.2	121.3	169.3	752.3	782.5
Other[2]	12.9	1.3	20.0	3.6	26.0	91.2
Private	0.2	0.1	2.1	0.8	11.3	23.2
Total	169.2	24.6	143.4	173.7	789.6	896.9

	Man.	Sask.	Alta.	BC	YT and NWT	Overseas and undistributed	Canada
Human resource training[1]							
Federal government	79.9	67.5	169.2	256.7	0.1	24.4	1,976.6
Provincial and municipal governments	23.2	53.5	168.2	122.5	11.4	—	878.3
Fees and other sources	5.9	19.2	54	78.6	0.9	—	285.0
Total	109.0	140.2	391.4	457.8	12.4	24.4	3,140.0
Other[2]	38.7	34.4	76.4	64.3	26.0	186.4	581.2
Private	2.7	3.2	4.8	3.3	—	42.0	93.7
Total	150.4	177.8	472.6	525.4	38.4	252.8	3,814.7

[1] *Includes training courses purchased by the federal government, capital expenditures, grant for training in industry and allowances to trainees.*
[2] *Includes nursing assistants, training, trades training in reform schools and in penitentiaries and other training programs within federal and provincial departments.*

Source
Statistics Canada

CHAPTER SIX

EMPLOYMENT AND INCOMES

INTRODUCTION

The Canadian economy produces many things, two of the most important of which are jobs and incomes. Indeed, Canadian earnings, employment opportunities and working conditions are impressive by any standards. Internationally, Canada is recognized for its dynamic workforce — among the most highly skilled, highly paid in the world.

In 1991, the average Canadian family pre-tax income was $53,131, and roughly four-fifths of this was employment income. In the same year, wages and salaries alone accounted for some $338 billion, roughly half of Canada's Gross Domestic Product (GDP) — the measurement of the value of all goods and services produced in the economy.

Despite the strong performance and growth of Canada's workforce in the past, it has not been immune to the most recent downturn in the Canadian economy, the 1990-91 recession. From 1989 to 1992 alone, unemployment rose by almost four percentage points, from 7.5% in 1989 to 11.3% in 1992. And from 1989 to 1991, family incomes actually declined in real terms.

At the same time, Canada's economy has continued to diversify, and young people prepare for careers in fields unheard of a few decades ago: from advanced robotics and computer programming to agricultural engineering and satellite communications.

Although the economy began showing signs of recovery by 1992, several trends in Canada's labour market still warrant concern. Unemployment among youths remains well above the national unemployment rate. Increasing numbers of Canadians hold down two or more jobs to make ends meet. And those who are looking for work find themselves unemployed for increasingly long periods of time.

This chapter presents an overview of Canada's labour market — where we work, what we earn and how this is changing. It also surveys several key trends in employment and unemployment, the role of education in employment, labour force growth, the length of the work week, union membership and work stoppages. It profiles income trends and the prevalence of low

income in Canada, and it features a general overview of federal and provincial regulations governing the workplace.

CANADA'S LABOUR SCENE

Canada's labour force — which includes all those Canadians aged 15 and older who are working or actively looking for work — numbered some 13.8 million people in 1992. At any given time during the year, however, roughly 1.5 million members of the labour force were unemployed.

The growth in Canada's labour force has been gradually slowing over the past two decades. Fed by the post-war baby boom, Canada's labour force increased by an average of more than 3% per year throughout the 1970s. By the 1980s, as a result of the declining proportion of youths in the general population, this growth had slowed to an average of less than 2% per year. In the early 1990s, the pattern of decreasing growth has continued to less than 1% by 1992.

LABOUR TRENDS The recession that began in 1990 left a battered labour market in its aftermath. In November 1992, amid signs of sluggish economic recovery, Canada's seasonally adjusted unemployment rate had climbed to a nine-year peak of 11.8%. The last time unemployment reached this level was in 1983, when the labour market was still reeling from the 1981-82 recession.

In the wake of the recession, thousands of Canadians found themselves without employment — in November of 1992, when joblessness peaked, some 1.6 million Canadians were unemployed. (The unemployment rate is an estimate of the percentage of the labour force not employed and seeking work. The measure does not include the so-called hidden unemployed — those who report that they would like to work, but who have quit searching because they believe no work is available. Statistics Canada does provide measures of these so-called discouraged workers, and it produces alternative measures of unemployment which include them).

Petrisse Briel / The Image Bank

Worker in coveralls.

The recession affected employment in virtually every age group and profession. From 1990 to 1992 alone, the number of employed Canadians declined by more than 330,000. Younger Canadians — particularly those with limited education — were greatly affected.

Many employers trimmed their workforces and delayed new hiring, as they were confronted with increased global competition, near record-low profitability and declining economic prospects.

In terms of the number of job losses, Ontario was hit especially hard. In 1992 alone, employment in the province fell by some 56,000 workers and job losses accounted for more than half of all the jobs lost in Canada. In terms of the proportion of jobs lost, Newfoundland was hardest hit; in 1992, employment declined 4.4% — roughly 9,000 jobs disappeared. A major blow to employment there was a two-year moratorium on cod fishing.

The decline in employment during the latest recession was reflected in regional unemployment figures. The unemployment rate more than doubled in Ontario from 5.1% in 1989 to 11.3% in September of 1992. Other provinces hit hard by job losses were, again, Newfoundland, where the unemployment rate jumped to almost 22% in November of 1992, and Prince Edward Island, where the rate peaked at more than 19% in May of that year.

Pierre Gaudard / CMCP

At work at Dominion Engineering, Montreal.

The only provinces to escape overall job losses in 1992 were British Columbia, with employment up 1.9% from the year before; New Brunswick, with employment up 1.1%; and Prince Edward Island, with the employment level remaining unchanged from a year earlier. Despite the relatively strong employment picture in these provinces in 1992, their unemployment rates still increased as overall job growth lagged behind growth in the labour force.

In early 1993, an economic recovery was underway, but the national unemployment rate remained high; while the rate showed intermittent declines, it was still above 11% in May of that year.

Although Canada's unemployment rate broadly rises and falls with the business cycle, there has been an underlying upward trend for the last three decades. During the mid to late 1960s, the unemployment rate averaged less than 5%, jumping to an average of 6.8% in the 1970s and 9.3% in the 1980s. As Canada emerges from its most recent recession, it is yet to be seen where unemployment rates will stabilize.

Average Duration of Unemployment When Canadians find them themselves out of work, their periods of joblessness are longer than in the past. The average duration of unemployment has increased in recent years, from 15.1 weeks in 1981, to 17.3 weeks in 1989, and then to 22.6 weeks in 1992. Despite recent increases in the unemployment rate, in Canada, as in the United States, unemployment still tends to be primarily short-term (less than six months).

Young Workers Facing High Unemployment Young people aged 15 to 24 have been especially hard-hit by recent changes in employment patterns. From 1989 to 1992, there was a decline of more than 400,000 full-time jobs held by youths, a drop of 26%. Unemployment for youths traditionally has been high, and this situation worsened during the recession. The number of unemployed youths jumped from 303,000 in 1989 to 431,000 in 1992. Accordingly, the unemployment rate for youths rose sharply from 11.3% in 1989 to 17.8% in 1992. In comparison, for those aged 45 and older, unemployment rates were less than half as high, averaging only 8.3% in 1992. Of those aged 15 to 24, young men experienced the highest unemployment rate, at more than 20.2% in 1992, compared to 15.2% for women in this age group.

Part-time Work Increasing Faster Than Full-time Work For the past several decades, a major trend in job growth has been the substantial increase in part-time employment compared to full-time employment.

In 1992, part-time workers accounted for close to 17% of all Canadian workers aged 15 and older. In 1975, by comparison, part-time workers accounted for less than 11% of the workforce.

In 1975, some 8.3 million Canadians held full-time jobs. Seventeen years later, in 1992, this figure stood at roughly 10.2 million Canadians — an increase of more than 20%.

From 1975 to 1992, part-time employment increased from 988,000 to more than 2 million — a rise of more than 100%. This trend became even more pronounced during the most recent recession. From 1990 to 1992, full-time employment dropped by some 458,000 workers. In comparison, during the same period, the number of part-time workers grew by 127,000.

The recent increase in part-time work is partly due to a growing preference by employers. Part-time employment gives employers more flexibility and lowers benefits costs. In 1992, some 32.5% of part-time

work was involuntary in the sense that such workers would have preferred to work full time. This is up from 20% in 1989.

Self Employed While 9 out of 10 Canadian workers work for someone else, the proportion who are self-employed has been growing steadily in recent years. According to the 1991 Census, a full 10% of the labour force, or some 1.4 million Canadians, were self-employed. Indeed, the number of self-employed Canadians grew 16% from 1986 to 1991. This compares to an 11% increase in the number of employees during the same period.

Participation Rate Prior to the recession, the labour force participation rate — the percentage of people either working or seeking work — stood at 67% in 1989, some 10 percentage points higher than in 1966.

Labour Force Participation Rate

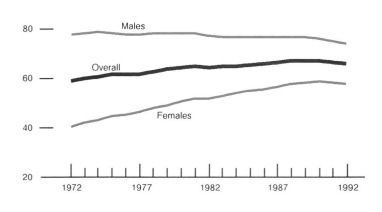

Per cent

REAL LIFE FOR LONE PARENTS

The life of the lone parent has been immortalized in film and in literature, mostly in terms of the struggle and hardship it can impose on a lone parent. In the 1970s, the American television comedy "One Day at a Time" found the humour in the situation but for many people who live the day-to-day reality of lone parenting, life can be fairly tough going.

Census data shows that in 1991, some 1 million Canadian families were headed by a single parent. These families tend to be poorer than their two-parent counterparts, with many female lone parents receiving a significant part of their incomes in the form of government transfer payments.

Lone-parent families are mostly the result of ended marriages, widowhood and births out of wedlock. But lone parenthood is often a transitional period, generally lasting about five years.

Most one-parent families are headed by women — 83% in 1991 — and most lone parents are young, anywhere from 25 to 44 years of age.

Lone-parent families tend to have slightly fewer children. In 1991, the average lone parent had 1.6 children, compared to 1.9 for two-parent families.

On the other hand, the surge in lone-parent families means more children are living with just one parent. In 1991, 17% of Canadian children — or some 1.5 million young people — lived in a lone-parent family.

The Labour Force Survey shows that employment and education play a large role in determining income level. Only 52% of female lone parents were employed outside the home in 1991. Roughly 19%, or one in five, worked part time. While half of part-time workers said they would prefer to work full time, they said they could not find full-time jobs. Fewer lone parents complete high school or university than parents in two-parent families.

Lone-parent families tend to be poorer than two-parent families, and especially those headed by women. In 1990, lone-parent families headed by women had an average income of $26,550, or about half of what two-parent families averaged. In the same year, lone-parent families headed by men had an average income of $40,792, or about 75% of what their two-parent counterparts would have earned.

However, as the recession took hold, the rate dropped to just above 65% in 1992. As difficult economic conditions continued to keep Canadians out of the labour force in 1992, the rate hovered just above 65%.

A major reason for the overall increase in the participation rate in the past few decades has been the massive entry of women into the labour force. In 1992, women comprised 45% of the labour force, compared to just 31% in 1966. Similarly, the participation rate for women increased to 57.6% in 1992 from just 35.4% in 1966. In contrast, the participation rate for men has declined marginally during the same period, from 79.8% in 1966 to 73.8% in 1992.

Length of Work Week Although the Canadian workplace is becoming increasingly competitive, full-time workers are generally spending no more time at work than they have in the past. Canada's full-time workers spent an average of 42.1 hours per week at work in 1992 — exactly the same number as in 1975. During the interim years, this figure fluctuated by less than 20 minutes in either direction.

For part-time workers, the length of the average work week has fallen in recent years, though it remains higher than in 1975. While part-time workers averaged 15.7 hours in 1992 — almost 45 minutes more than in 1975 — the part-time work week has steadily declined since 1989, when it peaked at 15.9 hours per week.

However, when the hours of full-time and part-time workers are added together, the average time spent at work per week actually declined. When looked at this way, Canadians spent an average of only 33.9 hours per week at work in 1992 — or 2.1 hours less than in 1975. This decline can be partly traced to the steady increase in the proportion of part-time workers.

Employment Linked to Education Education continued to play a key role in determining who worked in 1992 — and who didn't. Of those aged 15 to 24, unemployment rates were more than twice as high for those with incomplete high school educations than for those who had completed a university degree (27.8% versus 10.6%). While the same was true for older Canadians, the figures were much less dramatic.

Of those aged 45 and older, 8.3% of those with incomplete high school educations were unemployed in 1992, compared to just 3.9% of those with university degrees.

Calling in Sick Calling in sick for work was not an uncommon event in 1992. Full-time workers missed an average of nine days of work throughout the year for reasons such as illness and family responsibilities. Canadian women — who tend to have more family responsibilities than men — tended to take significantly more time off work. While full-time male workers missed an average of 6.7 days of work for such reasons, full-time female workers missed an average of 12.8 days of work in 1992 — almost double.

Holding Down Two or More Jobs Although unemployment remained high throughout 1992, many Canadian workers managed to find — or keep — more than one job. In 1992, some 593,000 Canadians held multiple jobs, up from 202,000 in 1976 — a three-fold increase. This rate of growth in multiple job holders was considerably greater than the growth in overall employment from 1976 to 1992.

Understandably, multiple job holders tend to work longer hours than those who hold only one job. The vast majority of multiple job holders — more than 70% — worked 40 or more hours per week in 1992. Some 45%, in fact, spent more than 50 hours per week at work.

Age Structure Predictably, Canada's labour force continues to be dominated by those aged 25 to 54. In 1992, this age group comprised some 10 million people — almost 73% of the workforce. While this age group's share of the labour force has increased in recent years, the shares of other age groups have declined.

The 15 to 24-year-old group, after growing an average of 3.4% a year from 1969 to 1981, has since declined by an average of about 2% annually. As a result of this decline, this age group's share of the labour force dropped to 17.5% in 1992, from 25.8% in 1981.

Recent years have also seen the gradual but steady decline in the proportion of workers aged 55 and over. This decline began before the 1970s, and has affected

6803579

men more than women. In 1992, this age group comprised 9.8% of the labour force, down from 15% in 1981. This decline is due in part to the post-war immigration to Canada of younger workers, and from the influx of baby-boomers into the labour market. It also reflects a long-term decline in this age group's participation rate.

The Service Sector Canada's economy can be broken down into two major sectors, the goods-producing sector and the service sector. The goods-producing sector comprises fishing and hunting, agriculture, forestry, mining, manufacturing and construction. The service sector, meanwhile, consists of sectors ranging from trade to transportation, public administration, finance, and community, business and personal services.

Persons Employed

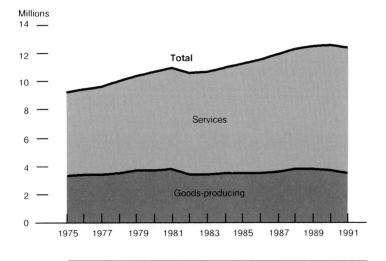

A major, ongoing development in Canada's employment landscape has been the tremendous growth in the service sector. In the early 1970s, some 37% of employment was in goods-producing industries, with the remainder of employment in service-producing industries. By 1992, goods-producing industries accounted for only 26% of employment.

From 1976 to 1992, employment in Canada increased by 29%, from 9.5 million to 12.3 million. All of this increase is accounted for by the service sector, which registered an increase in employment of 46% during the period. In 1992, some 8.9 million Canadians held jobs in the service sector, compared to 3.3 million who held jobs in the goods-producing sector. In line with the rapid expansion of the service sector, employment in white-collar occupations was up 30% in the 1980s, compared to 3% for blue-collar jobs. This trend has continued into the 1990s.

Although employment growth in the goods-producing sector remains stagnant, such employment is a vital part of the Canadian economy. Some 3.3 million Canadians still make their livelihoods in this sector, down from a peak of roughly 3.7 million reached in 1989. In addition, the goods-producing sector accounts for a significant share of Canada's international trade and is a crucial support to the burgeoning service sector; indeed, the goods-producing sector continues to be a major client of the services sector, helping to fuel its remarkable growth.

Organized Labour Union membership represented 29.7% of Canada's civilian labour force in 1992, the same as in 1991, but down from a peak of 31.2% in 1978. The number of union members stood at almost 4.1 million in 1992, up slightly from the previous year. The four largest unions — the Canadian Union of Public Employees (CUPE), the National Union of Public and General Employees (NUPGE), the United Food and Commercial Workers International Union (UFCW) and the Public Service Alliance of Canada (PSAC) — accounted for more than a quarter — or almost 26% — of all union membership.

Major Wage Settlements Historically, wage increases are more modest in tough economic times. This proved true during the recent economic downturn.

In 1990, wage increases for all collective agreements in Canada covering 500 or more employees increased by an average of 5.6% over 1989. However, as the effects of the recession became more pronounced, wage settlements declined sharply in 1991, posting a 3.6% increase over 1990, and fell further to only 2.1% in 1992, as unemployment remained high and worker concerns focused on job security.

Work Stoppages Rising unemployment and falling inflation, which restrained wage increases, also worked to curb labour disputes. In 1991, work stoppages caused a loss of 2.6 million person days (a full day of work for one person), and fell to a record low of 2.2 million in 1992. Measured as a percentage of the total working time of non-agricultural paid workers, time lost in 1991 was 0.21% — well below the average for the 1980s. Preliminary data for 1992 indicated that the number of workers involved in stoppages continued to decrease dramatically.

INCOMES

FAMILIES AND UNATTACHED INDIVIDUALS Statistics Canada produces annual statistics on income distribution for families and individuals. These statistics are essential for developing and evaluating policies and programs that ensure the economic well-being of Canadians.

Predictably, family incomes declined during the recession. Average family income before taxes in 1991 was $53,131, down 2.6% from 1990, after adjusting for inflation. This decline marked the second consecutive year of declining average income; as a result, 40% of the income gains since the 1981-82 recession were eroded. Recent declines brought 1991 average family gross income to a level only slightly above that recorded in 1980 ($52,641 in 1991 constant dollars) and well below the 1989 peak of $55,423 (1991 constant dollars).

Family income before taxes ranged from an average of $58,634 in Ontario to $41,654 in Newfoundland. Besides Ontario, only two other provinces had average family incomes above the national average in 1991: Alberta ($55,552) and British Columbia ($54,895).

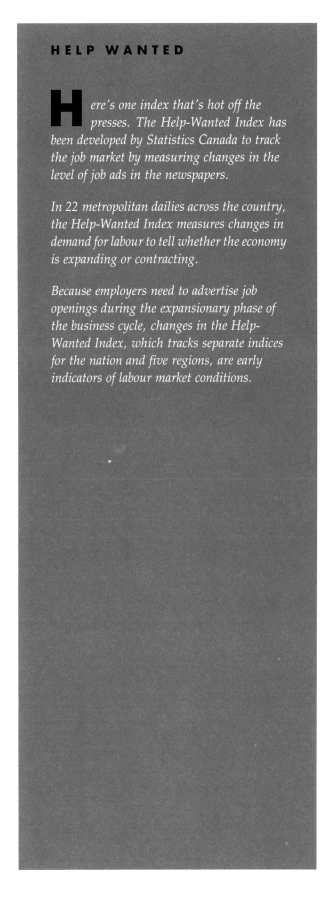

HELP WANTED

*H*ere's one index that's hot off the presses. The Help-Wanted Index has been developed by Statistics Canada to track the job market by measuring changes in the level of job ads in the newspapers.

In 22 metropolitan dailies across the country, the Help-Wanted Index measures changes in demand for labour to tell whether the economy is expanding or contracting.

Because employers need to advertise job openings during the expansionary phase of the business cycle, changes in the Help-Wanted Index, which tracks separate indices for the nation and five regions, are early indicators of labour market conditions.

Median Income,[1] 1991

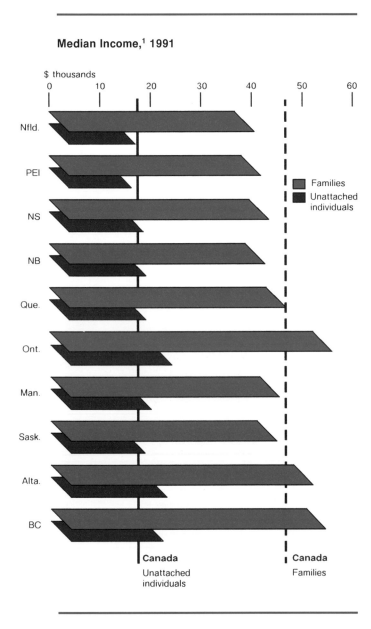

$ thousands

Nfld.
PEI
NS
NB
Que.
Ont.
Man.
Sask.
Alta.
BC

Families
Unattached individuals

Canada
Unattached individuals

Canada
Families

[1] *Median income refers to the middle value when incomes are ranged in order of magnitude. Median income is lower than average income in Canada because it is not as affected by a few large values in the distribution.*

The bulk of family income in 1991 was derived from earnings (78%), followed by government transfer payments such as Old Age Security and Unemployment Insurance (12%), investment income (5.1%) and other sources such as private pension income (4.4%).

Historically, the growth in average family pre-tax income in Canada has been extraordinary. From 1951 to 1991, average family pre-tax incomes increased one and a half times (150.9%) in real terms, from $21,172 in 1951 (1991 constant dollars) to $53,131 in 1991.

The decade of the 1960s experienced the greatest increase in family incomes, followed by the 1950s. Throughout the 1970s, real family income growth was significant, but down sharply from growth rates of the 1960s. The 1980s was a period of much reduced growth compared to the previous three decades. Much of the increase that did occur in the 1980s was offset by reductions during the recessions at the beginning and end of the decade.

Despite the overall gains in family pre-tax income during the past several decades, income inequality remains little changed in Canada. Families in the top 20% of the income range (those with incomes above $74,232) accounted for 40% of all family income in 1991, up from 39.3% in 1990. In contrast, families in the lowest 20% of the income range (those with incomes no higher than $25,234) accounted for 6.4% of all family income in 1991, the same as in 1990.

The average pre-tax income of unattached individuals was especially hard hit in 1991, averaging $22,514, a drop of 5.7% from 1990, after adjusting for inflation. In 1991, the average pre-tax income for unattached men ($25,179) continued to outstrip that of unattached women ($20,203).

INCIDENCE OF LOW INCOME

In tough economic times, the share of the population living in low-income situations tends to increase. This was true for the 1990-91 recession. Statistics Canada uses what are called 'low income cut-offs' to determine the level of low income in Canada. Generally, these limits or 'cut-offs' are selected on the basis that unattached individuals and families with incomes below

Pierre Gaudard / CMCP

Pointe Saint-Charles factory, Montreal.

these levels spend, on average, 56.2% or more of their income on food, shelter and clothing. These indicators of low income are not intended as measures of poverty.

Overall, there were an estimated 4.2 million Canadians living in low-income situations in 1991, an increase of more than 400,000 from 1990. This was the second consecutive increase in low income Canadians — in 1990, the number of such Canadians increased more than 300,000 from 1989. The percentage of Canadians living in low-income situations went from 13.6% in 1989 to 14.6% in 1990 to 16.0% in 1991.

For families, the rate of low income in 1991 was 13.1%, representing almost 950,000 families. This was up from 12.1% in 1990 and 11.1% in 1989. Female lone-parent families had the highest rate of low income, rising to almost 62% in 1991, up more than a full percentage point from 1990.

For children under age 18, some 18.3% or some 1.2 million young people were living in low-income situations in 1991, up from 16.9% in 1990 and 14.5% in 1989. The low income rate for children under age 18 has remained above 14% throughout the 1980s and 1990s.

Unattached Canadians younger than 25 years of age have the highest rate of low income of any age group — in 1991 it stood at 55.5%, up from 52.6% in 1990 and 47.8% in 1989. The rate of low income for all unattached Canadians was significantly lower — 36.5% in 1991.

INCOME EQUALITY?

To many Canadians, particularly those in the lower and middle income brackets, it often seems that "the rich get richer and the poor get poorer". However, it is difficult to determine whether this age-old adage was true in the 1980s.

A Statistics Canada study shows that while income inequality between income groups rose marginally in the early part of the 1980s, it began to decline again later in the decade. By the end of the decade, it was still unclear whether the 'haves' benefitted more than the 'have-nots'.

At first glance, it would appear that very little has changed for the average family from 1980 to 1989. Overall, average family after-tax incomes in 1989 ($40,400) were very similar to 1980 incomes ($40,200). There were, however, important off-setting trends in the interim years. From 1980 to 1983, after-tax incomes fell by an average of 6%, then rebounded back by 7% from 1984 to 1989.

Although average after-tax income is an important indicator, it does not always tell the whole story. For example, a few very large incomes can have a dramatic affect on the overall figures. A measure that is not so affected is median after-tax income — the income at which 50% of families have higher incomes and 50% have lower incomes. While median after-tax incomes followed the same general trend as mean incomes during the 1980s, the fall was steeper and the increase was smaller. As a result, the 1989 median after-tax income of $36,800 was less than the $37,300 recorded in 1980. It is difficult to conclude, however, exactly which families benefitted during the 1980s and which families, if any, lost out.

One way to determine income distribution is to rank families according to the size of their incomes, divide them into 10 equal groups (deciles) and then calculate the share of total income received by each group. In 1980, for example, the lowest decile accounted for 2.5% of total earnings, while the highest decile accounted for 21.7%.

While the share of income of the top three deciles increased between 1980 and 1983, the income shares of the lowest five deciles declined over the same period, indicating a marginal increase in income inequality. Starting in 1984, however, this pattern reversed, and income inequality declined for the rest of the decade. By 1989, income shares for both the two highest and two lowest deciles were higher than they were in 1980. Consequently, it is difficult to say whether income inequality actually grew overall.

As it stood in 1989, the lowest decile accounted for 2.9% of total income while the highest decile accounted for 22.0%. In plain dollars and cents, the average after-tax income of the top 10% of families was $88,800, compared to $11,600 for the bottom 10% (a ratio of roughly 8 to 1).

As families in the lower deciles generally tend to be taxed less and rely more on transfer payments than families in the higher decile, the government plays a large role in promoting income equality. Without these taxes and transfers, the 1989 ratio of average income between the highest and lowest deciles would have increased from 8 to 1, to a massive 65 to 1.

WE'RE EARNING LESS

*D*uring the 1950s, 60s and 70s, Canadian incomes increased with no apparent end in sight. Even after accounting for inflation, average family incomes more than doubled during these three decades alone. The 1980s and 1990s, however, have not been so generous. In fact, average family incomes have actually declined in recent years.

In 1991, Canadian families earned an average of $53,131 — $1,406 or 2.6% less than in 1990 (in 1991 dollars). This marked the second consecutive year of declining incomes.

Some families were hit harder than others — particularly those who were already on the lower rungs of the income ladder. In 1991, childless non-elderly couples with only one earner made $40,848, or 8.2% less than in 1990. Non-elderly lone-parent families saw their incomes drop by more than 4% in 1991, to $22,186. Elderly couples, meanwhile, saw their incomes fall to $35,553 in 1991 — a decrease of more than 3% from 1990.

Changing patterns of employment during the recent recession were at least partly to blame for these falling incomes. For example, 2.2% fewer people worked full time for the full year in 1991 than in 1990.

Overall, families were marginally better off in 1991 than they were 10 years earlier. In 1981, the average Canadian family made $51,756 (in 1991 dollars) — $1,375 less than in 1991.

Low-income incidence for elderly persons (those aged 65 and older) has dropped significantly since the early 1980s. In 1991, the rate for the elderly was 20%, up from 19.3% in 1990, but much lower than the 1981 rate of 33%.

AVERAGE WEEKLY EARNINGS

In 1992, the average weekly earnings of Canadians, including overtime, stood at $550, an increase of 3.4% from $532 in 1991. Average weekly earnings were highest in the Northwest Territories ($714) followed by the Yukon ($678), Ontario ($578), British Columbia ($549) and Alberta ($546). Earnings were lowest in Prince Edward Island ($444) and Saskatchewan ($472).

Average weekly earnings including overtime were highest for those working in the mining, quarries and oil wells industry ($935), followed by public administration ($723), forestry ($701) and transportation ($705). Earnings were lowest in trade ($401) and community, business and personal services ($477).

INCOME SAFETY NETS

Because most Canadian families support themselves with employment income, programs that replace earnings in the event of job loss or an injury at work are an essential part of the social safety net. This section briefly reviews the Unemployment Insurance and workers' compensation programs.

UNEMPLOYMENT INSURANCE

The Unemployment Insurance (UI) program provides income insurance to virtually all Canadians who receive a salary or an hourly wage. Financed by premiums paid by employees and employers, as well as federal government contributions, the program protects those who lose all or a significant portion of their employment incomes. In 1993, eligible recipients were entitled to benefits of up to 57% of their insurable earnings, to a maximum of $425 in weekly benefits.

Under the Unemployment Insurance Act, claimants must work a minimum number of insurable weeks within a specified period — usually the 52 weeks preceding the claim — to be eligible for benefits. The number of weeks needed to qualify varies according to regional unemployment rates, ranging from a low of 10 weeks in areas with more than 15% unemployment to a high of 20 weeks in areas with unemployment rates of less than 6%.

In addition to these 'regular'benefits, which apply to those who lose their jobs, the UI program also provides 'special' benefits to cover illness, birth and adoption. In some cases, benefits are also available for those in training and job creation programs.

In recent years, the federal government's expenditures on the program have risen dramatically. While Canadians received almost $10.5 billion in benefits in 1986, the UI program paid out close to $17.7 billion in benefits in 1991. To help reduce this cost and to help prevent potential abuse of the system, the federal government recently introduced sweeping reforms to the Unemployment Insurance Act.

Under Bill C-113, which took effect in early 1993, workers who quit their jobs without 'just cause' or who are fired for misconduct are no longer eligible to receive benefits. Under the Act, 'just cause' may include the following: sexual or other harassment, discrimination, the necessity of following a spouse to another residence, an obligation to care for a child or another member of the immediate family, an employer's refusal to pay for overtime work, a significant change in wages or salary, unsafe working conditions, or significant changes in work duties. Also included in the legislation was the reduction in the maximum benefit rate. Whereas employees are now entitled to up to 57% of their insurable earnings, they were previously eligible for up to 60% of their wages.

WORKERS' COMPENSATION

Workers' compensation legislation protects workers who are the victims of work-related accidents and illnesses. Each province has its own workers' compensation system, which replaces lost wages and pays health care expenses of affected workers. Benefits also cover rehabilitation, funeral costs and disability pensions. In some provinces, employees who are affected by work-related accidents and illnesses are guaranteed the right to be re-hired by their employer.

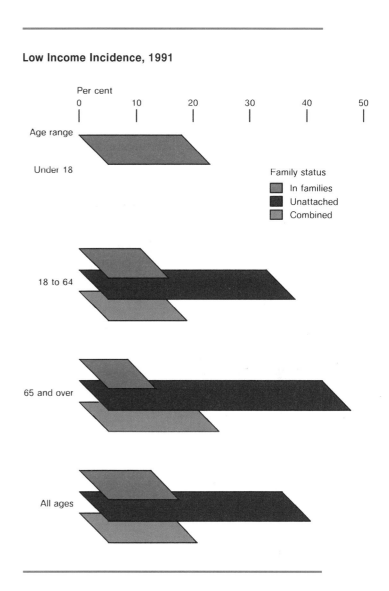

Low Income Incidence, 1991

Daryl Benson / Masterfile

Employers pay all the costs of workers' compensation by way of assessments levied by provincial workers' compensation boards. When employees submit claims, these boards determine the amount of compensation and pay the benefit to the workers.

Every year approximately 1 worker in 10 suffers an occupational injury and 1 in 18 workers suffers an injury serious enough to force them to miss work.

In 1990, workers' compensation boards received more than 1 million claims and paid more than $4.3 billion in compensation. About 46% of this total compensated for lost earnings, 31% went for pensions, 12% for medical aid, 11% for hospitalization, and less than 1% for funeral expenses.

Some work injuries result in death; in 1990, some 1,127 work-related deaths were reported; of these, 809 were awarded compensation.

INDUSTRIAL RELATIONS Part I of the Canada Labour Code regulates labour-management relations under federal jurisdiction. This includes all federal undertakings and many interprovincial projects, such as the proposed new bridge between New Brunswick and Prince Edward Island.

The Code sets out clear provisions to help settle or prevent labour relations disputes, such as lockouts or strikes. Under the Code, the Minister of Labour may appoint conciliators or mediators to assist both sides in resolving the issue.

The Canada Labour Relations Board, which deals with complaints about issues such as unfair labour practices and employees' rights, bases its decisions on Code regulations. The board has the authority to order forms of relief such as reinstatement, compensation, and cease and desist orders. The board also supervises hiring-hall rules, and requires trade unions and employer organizations to provide annual financial statements to their members.

Canada's provinces and territories also impose their own industrial regulations, and often help to settle industrial disputes. In some provinces, separate statutes regulate labour relations for essential service occupations such as civil servants, hospital workers and police.

Occupational Safety and Health Part II of the Canada Labour Code deals exclusively with occupational safety and health. Together with provincial and territorial regulations, these workplace regulations set minimum health and safety standards for virtually all aspects of the Canadian workplace. Regulations are in place for everything from fire safety and lighting requirements to protective clothing and radiation exposure. Under these laws, employers must submit to regular safety inspections, and those that break the rules face stiff penalties. These laws also give workers the right to refuse to work when their health or safety could be endangered, and authorize funding for research into preventing accidents and for safety education programs.

Labour Standards Part III of the Canada Labour Code sets minimum employment standards in areas such as holidays and overtime pay. Under the Code, the maximum work week is 40 hours, and employees who work beyond those hours must be paid a minimum of one and one-half times their regular hourly wage. The Code also dictates that employers must offer their employees a minimum of two to three weeks of paid vacation every year, depending on their tenure.

EARNING TIMES TWO

In the popular 1960s television show "Leave it to Beaver", the lifestyles of June, Ward, Wally and 'Beaver' Cleaver were similar to those of many Canadian families. While Ward went to work to earn the family's living, June stayed at home to care for the kids.

In 1967, only one spouse — usually the husband — worked in two-thirds of Canadian husband-wife families.

Today, however, Ward and June would probably both be going to work.

In 1989, both spouses worked in 62% of all husband-wife families in Canada.

Today, someone else would probably be minding the kids. In the 1980s, wives in the labour force were more likely to continue working even after they had had children. By 1991, more than two-thirds of wives with children under six years of age were in the labour force, compared to less than one-third in 1967.

Not surprisingly, the incomes of dual-earning families are higher than for families with only one earner. In 1990, dual-earning families earned an average of $62,808, compared to $47,803 for those husband-wife families in which one spouse was employed.

Husbands in dual-earner families generally earn more than their wives do. In 1990, husbands accounted for over half of total family incomes (56%), while wives accounted for less than one-third (29%). Other family members accounted for the other 15% of family earnings. In almost 20% of dual-earner families, however, the wife earned more than the husband.

CLOSING THE WAGE GAP

In workplaces all across Canada, women often still do not earn as much as men. While the notion of equal pay for equal work may be far from reality, Canadian women are making impressive gains in closing the wage gap.

Females who worked full time for the full year in 1991 earned an average of $26,842 — barely 70% of the average $38,567 earned by similarly employed men. However, this is a marked improvement from 1967, when females earned less than 60% of what males earned.

Women closed the wage gap by a full two percentage points in 1991. This is the largest single-year decrease in the wage gap since 1978, when women closed the wage gap by three percentage points.

The current wage gap may be explained partly by differences between male and female work patterns. Generally, men tend to work longer hours. Full-time male workers spent an average of 40.4 hours per week working, compared to 35.2 hours for full-time female workers.

In 1991, women's earnings varied by province, ranging from a low of 65% of men's wages in Alberta to a high of 81% in Prince Edward Island.

The highest earnings, for both men and women, were reported in Ontario. Fully employed males earned an average of $41,519 in 1991, compared to $28,969 for women. Ontario's comparable earnings ratio for women, almost 70%, was close to the national average.

The wage gap was lower for women with higher levels of education. Women with university degrees earned almost 72% of what similarly educated men earned. In contrast, women with limited secondary school educations earned only 64% of what their male counterparts earned.

Older women experience the largest wage gap. In 1991, women aged 55 and older earned only 64% of what their male counterparts did, compared to 86% for younger women, those aged 15 to 24.

While the wage gap was smaller for younger women, these women reported the lowest earnings — an average of $19,381 in 1991.

Single women's earnings are similar to those of married women; however, the wage gap is much narrower for single women than for those who are married. In 1991, single women earned an average of $26,041, or 91% of what single men earned. Married women earned a similar amount, $26,654, but this was only 65% of what married men earned. In contrast, single men earned an average of $28,570 in 1991, while those who were married earned an average of $41,048 — a full 44% more.

The wage gap also varied by occupation. Comparable earnings for women ranged from 85% in artistic and recreational occupations to 49% in medicine and health occupations. For women, the highest average earnings were reported by those in teaching occupations ($39,723). For men, average earnings were highest among those in medicine and health occupations ($65,175).

Unlike the wage gap for full-time female workers, which has been gradually shrinking, the wage gap for part-time workers has widened in recent years. Part-time workers include those who worked full time for less than 49 weeks of the year. In 1991, female part-timers earned an average of 71% of what male part-timers earned — far less than the 77% reported in 1987. Despite this decrease, however, the wage gap for part-time work remained smaller than for full-time work.

Provincial and territorial governments also impose their own employment standards, including compensation for general holidays. Currently, the number of paid general holidays under provincial/territorial jurisdiction varies between five and nine. Nine other general paid holidays — such as Christmas and Canada Day — fall under federal jurisdiction.

MINIMUM WAGE In Canada, employers cannot pay adult workers less than minimum wage, the lowest hourly wage permitted by law. There are two sets of minimum wages in Canada — the wage set by the federal government and those set by the provincial and territorial governments. The federal minimum wage, which stood at $4.00 per hour in March 1993, applies to employees in industries under federal jurisdiction such as railways, ship-loading and grain elevators. Provincial and territorial wages apply to most other workers. Farm workers, who often work on a 'piece-rate', are often exempt from such requirements.

Minimum wage requirements vary widely by province/territory. In March of 1993, the Northwest Territories had the highest minimum wage. For those in the Northwest Territories who worked in areas far away from the highway system, the minimum wage was $7.00 per hour. Those working in less remote areas, meanwhile, were guaranteed a minimum of $6.50 per hour. The next highest rates were paid in Ontario ($6.35), followed by the Yukon ($6.24) and British Columbia ($6.00). The lowest rates were paid in Newfoundland and Prince Edward Island (both $4.75). Some provinces have instituted separate rates for young workers and students.

Minimum wage requirements are reviewed frequently. Generally, those working on a 'piece-rate' basis must be paid the equivalent of minimum wage. In many cases, employers providing on-the-job training may be exempt from such requirements for all or part of the training period.

In some provinces, supplemental regulation of wages and hours apply to specific industries, occupations or classes of workers. For example, Quebec regulates wages in the retail food trade, British Columbia has special rates for domestics, farm workers and residential caretakers, and Alberta has special weekly minimums for commercial agents and salespeople. Generally, these special rates are slightly lower than 'regular' rates.

OTHER LABOUR REGULATIONS **Maternity leave** and job security before and after childbirth are guaranteed in Canada. Maternity leave is 17 or 18 weeks and is usually divided into prenatal and postnatal leave. Most jurisdictions now give full access to parental leave, which varies from 12 to 35 weeks, depending on the jurisdiction. This leave is normally available to either or both parents, whether natural or adoptive.

All jurisdictions have a **human rights code** with employment provisions that prohibit discrimination on the basis of race, religion, national origin, colour, sex, age and marital status. In some jurisdictions, discrimination is also prohibited on the basis of political beliefs, creed, ethnic origin, physical handicaps, sources of income, ancestry, social condition, criminal convictions for which pardons have been granted, or sexual orientation.

The federal government has guidelines for equal employment opportunities in the public service for Canadians with disabilities, and many federal public buildings are now accessible to persons with disabilities.

Apprenticeship laws in Canada require on-the-job training and school instruction for designated skilled trades. Certain classes of tradespeople are legally required to hold certificates of competency. The provinces are responsible for issuing qualification certificates.

Employers must give notice of **termination of employment**. Under federal jurisdiction, employees with three consecutive months of employment must be given two weeks' notice in writing or two weeks' wages. The federal Labour Code prohibits dismissal, layoff or suspension because of garnishment or notice of garnishment proceedings. Employees are protected against dismissal for absences due to sickness for up to 12 weeks, or for a longer period if the employee is undergoing treatment and rehabilitation at the expense

Gar Lunney / CMCP

Brown's Bread Plant, Toronto.

of a worker compensation authority. Employees with at least one year of continuous service, who are not covered by a collective agreement and who do not have access to a redress procedure, can lay complaints if they feel they have been dismissed unjustly. Quebec protects employees with five years' service against dismissal without just cause. Nova Scotia does the same for employees with 10 years' service.

For **group termination of employees**, special rules apply under federal jurisdiction and in six provinces.

The notice period required ranges from 4 to 18 weeks depending on the number of employees being terminated.

Under federal jurisdiction, **severance pay** is required when an employer terminates an employee who has 12 months of service. The prescribed payment is five days' wages or two days' wages for every year of employment, whichever is greater. Ontario provides for severance payments in certain circumstances, which can amount to a maximum of 26 weeks of pay.

SOURCES

Canada Employment and Immigration Commission

Labour Canada

Statistics Canada

FOR FURTHER READING

Selected publications from Statistics Canada

▲ *The Labour Force. Monthly. 71-001*

▲ *Historical Labour Force Statistics, Actual Data, Seasonal Factors, Seasonally Adjusted Data. Annual. 71-201*

▲ *Annual Report of the Minister of Industry, Science and Technology under the Corporations and Labour Unions Returns Act. Part II, Labour Unions. Annual. 71-202*

▲ *Labour Force Annual Averages. 71-220*

▲ *Women in the Workplace: Selected Data, 1987. 71-534*

▲ *Labour Force Research Series, 1982. 71-601*

▲ *Employment, Earnings and Hours, Preliminary Data. Monthly. 72-002*

▲ *Estimates of Labour Income. Quarterly. 72-005*

▲ *Work Injuries. Annual. 72-208*

▲ *Trusteed Pension Funds, Financial Statistics. Annual. 74-201*

▲ *Perspectives on Labour and Income. Quarterly. 75-001*

TABLES

6.1 LABOUR FORCE CHARACTERISTICS[1]

	Population '000	Labour Force '000	Employed '000	Unemployed '000	Not in labour force '000	Participation rate %	Unemployment rate %	Employment/ population ratio %
Both sexes								
1951	9,732	5,223	5,097	126	4,509	53.7	2.4	52.4
1961	12,053	6,521	6,055	466	5,531	54.1	7.1	50.2
1971[2]	14,872	8,639	8,104	535	6,233	58.1	6.2	54.5
1981	18,368	11,899	11,001	898	6,469	64.8	7.5	59.9
1991	20,746	13,757	12,340	1,417	6,989	66.3	10.3	59.5
Males								
1951	4,857	4,076	3,974	103	781	83.9	2.5	81.8
1961	5,991	4,782	4,381	401	1,209	79.8	8.4	73.1
1971[2]	7,329	5,667	5,329	338	1,662	77.3	6.0	72.7
1981	8,994	7,051	6,556	494	1,944	78.4	7.0	72.9
1991	10,117	7,569	6,751	817	2,548	74.8	10.8	66.7
Females								
1951	4,874	1,147	1,123	24	3,728	23.5	2.1	23.0
1961	6,061	1,739	1,674	65	4,322	28.7	3.7	27.6
1971[2]	7,543	2,972	2,775	197	4,571	38.4	6.6	36.8
1981	9,374	4,849	4,445	403	4,525	51.7	8.3	47.4
1991	10,629	6,188	5,589	599	4,441	58.2	9.7	52.6

[1] *Annual averages.*
[2] *Population aged 15 and over from 1966. Data prior to 1966 are based on population aged 14 and over.*

6.2 EMPLOYMENT BY INDUSTRY[1] (THOUSANDS)

	1951	1961	1971[2]	1981	1991
Agriculture	939	681	514	488	448
Other primary industries	224	184	221	321	280
Manufacturing	1,350	1,452	1,766	2,124	1,865
Construction	348	376	489	651	695
Transportation, communication and other utilities	449	563	707	911	916
Trade	718	1,025	1,335	1,884	2,169
Finance, insurance and real estate	154	239	399	594	760
Service	916[3]	1,178	2,128	3,262	4,376
Public administration	..	356	545	767	832

[1] *Annual averages.*
[2] *Population aged 15 and over from 1966. Data prior to 1966 are based on population aged 14 and over.*
[3] *Includes public administration.*

6.3 EMPLOYMENT AND PARTICIPATION RATE[1]

	Employed ('000)					
	1969	1974	1979	1984	1989	1991
Newfoundland	127	149	170	174	201	197
Prince Edward Island	36	41	46	49	54	53
Nova Scotia	254	292	311	335	373	371
New Brunswick	190	221	243	247	284	286
Quebec	2,126	2,401	2,619	2,692	3,031	2,987
Ontario	2,979	3,523	3,993	4,235	4,949	4,770
Manitoba	371	419	450	470	498	494
Saskatchewan	339	350	411	436	446	449
Alberta	621	754	1,007	1,104	1,214	1,246
British Columbia	788	976	1,144	1,191	1,435	1,489
	Participation rate (%)					
	1969	1974	1979	1984	1989	1991
Newfoundland	43.7	49.2	52.3	53.0	55.7	55.3
Prince Edward Island	54.4	55.4	59.0	60.5	65.0	65.1
Nova Scotia	52.8	55.8	56.6	59.4	61.2	61.3
New Brunswick	50.3	53.3	55.0	55.2	59.5	58.6
Quebec	55.9	58.0	60.2	61.5	64.0	63.4
Ontario	60.5	63.4	66.5	67.6	69.8	68.3
Manitoba	58.1	61.5	63.6	65.8	67.0	66.9
Saskatchewan	55.4	57.9	62.7	65.2	66.2	67.1
Alberta	63.4	65.6	69.7	71.9	72.4	72.5
British Columbia	58.2	60.3	63.2	64.1	66.8	66.4

[1] *Annual averages.*

6.4 PARTICIPATION AND UNEMPLOYMENT RATE[1]

	Participation rate (%)					
	1969	1974	1979	1984	1989	1991
Total	57.9	60.5	63.4	64.8	67.0	66.3
Men	78.3	78.7	78.5	76.6	76.7	74.8
Women	38.0	43.0	49.0	53.6	57.9	58.2
Age 15-24	56.4	62.5	66.2	66.8	70.2	67.1
Men	62.7	68.9	71.3	69.8	73.0	69.0
Women	50.2	56.0	61.0	63.8	67.4	65.1
Age 25-54	68.0	71.6	76.4	80.2	84.1	66.1
Men	95.6	95.4	95.1	93.4	93.8	76.1
Women	40.6	48.0	57.8	67.1	74.5	56.8
Age 55+	35.9[2]	32.5[2]	31.6	29.3	26.7	25.6
Men	56.4[2]	50.8[2]	47.1	42.9	38.1	36.0
Women	17.6[2]	16.6[2]	18.6	17.9	17.1	17.0

	Unemployment rate (%)					
	1969	1974	1979	1984	1989	1991
Total	4.4	5.3	7.4	11.2	7.5	10.3
Men	4.3	4.8	6.6	11.2	7.3	10.8
Women	4.7	6.4	8.8	11.3	7.9	9.7
Age 15-24	7.5	9.3	12.9	17.8	11.3	16.2
Men	8.3	9.6	13.2	19.3	12.4	18.8
Women	6.5	8.9	12.7	16.1	10.1	13.4
Age 25-54	3.3	3.9	5.7	9.6	6.7	9.0
Men	3.0	3.2	4.6	9.3	6.1	9.1
Women	3.9	5.3	7.4	10.1	7.5	8.8
Age 55+	4.2[2]	3.9[2]	4.2	7.1	5.7	7.6
Men	4.9[2]	4.3[2]	4.1	7.4	5.8	7.6
Women	1.9[2]	2.5[2]	4.5	6.6	5.4	7.5

[1] *Annual averages.*
[2] *As published by the old Labour Force Survey. These estimates are not entirely comparable to estimates produced after 1974 by the revised Labour Force Survey.*

6.5 UNEMPLOYMENT AND UNEMPLOYMENT RATE[1]

	Unemployed ('000)					Unemployment rate (%)				
	1974	1979	1984	1989	1991	1974	1979	1984	1989	1991
Newfoundland	22	30	44	38	44	13.0	15.1	20.2	15.8	18.4
Prince Edward Island	[2]	6	7	11	11	[2]	11.2	12.8	14.1	16.8
Nova Scotia	21	35	50	41	51	6.8	10.1	13.0	9.9	12.0
New Brunswick	18	30	43	41	42	7.5	11.1	14.8	12.5	12.7
Quebec	169	278	396	311	405	6.6	9.6	12.8	9.3	11.9
Ontario	164	278	420	264	506	4.4	6.5	9.0	5.1	9.6
Manitoba	16	25	43	41	48	3.6	5.3	8.4	7.5	8.8
Saskatchewan	10	18	38	36	36	2.8	4.2	8.0	7.4	7.4
Alberta	27	41	138	94	111	3.5	3.9	11.1	7.2	8.2
British Columbia	64	95	206	144	163	6.2	7.6	14.7	9.1	9.9

[1] *Annual averages.*
[2] *Estimates less than 4,000.*

6.6 NUMBER OF EMPLOYED, BY OCCUPATION GROUP[1,2] (THOUSANDS)

Occupation	1984	1989	1991	Percentage change 1989-1991
Managerial and administrative	1,169	1,545	1,660	7.4
Natural sciences, engineering and mathematics	388	457	488	6.8
Social sciences	181	218	263	20.6
Religion	32	32	29	−9.4
Teaching	473	528	561	6.3
Medicine and health	540	628	674	7.3
Art, literature and recreation	182	233	231	−0.9
Clerical	1,876	2,090	2,029	−2.9
Sales	1,043	1,171	1,192	1.8
Service	1,491	1,655	1,642	−0.8
Farming, horticultural and animal-husbandry	497	435	459	5.5
Fishing, hunting and trapping	32	37	40	8.1
Forestry and logging	64	55	46	−16.4
Mining and quarrying	63	61	56	−8.2
Processing	366	410	341	−16.8
Machining	220	228	183	−19.7
Product fabricating, assembling and repairing	942	1,050	930	−11.4
Construction trades	568	744	660	−11.3
Transport equipment operating	398	469	450	−4.1
Material handling	261	281	254	−9.6
Other crafts and equipment operating	144	155	151	−2.6
All occupations	10,932	12,486	12,339	−1.2

[1] Annual averages.
[2] Standard Occupational Classification 1980.

6.7 UNION MEMBERSHIP

	Union Membership '000	Non-agricultural paid workers '000	Membership as a percentage of civilian labour force	Union membership as a percentage of non-agricultural paid workers
1971	2,231	6,880	26.6	32.4
1976	3,042	8,238	30.5	36.9
1981	3,487	9,495	30.1	36.7
1986	3,730	9,888	29.8	37.7
1987	3,782	10,219	29.7	37.0
1988	3,841	10,519	29.5	36.5
1989	3,944	10,891	29.7	36.2
1990	4,031	11,147	29.9	36.2
1991	4,068	11,195	29.7	36.3
1992	4,089	10,931	29.7	37.4

6.8 MAJOR WORK STOPPAGES INVOLVING 500 OR MORE WORKERS

	Number beginning during year	Work stoppages in existence during year			Percentage of estimated working time
		Number	Workers involved	Person-days not worked	
1981	92	100	240,972	6,169,670	0.25
1982	67	67	389,985	3,859,810	0.16
1983	59	61	279,826	2,882,110	0.12
1984	64	67	130,852	2,331,350	0.10
1985	52	56	98,252	1,348,760	0.05
1986	86	89	430,086	5,673,310	0.22
1987	58	64	531,470	2,408,490	0.09
1988	53	54	158,888	3,393,880	0.12
1989	66	67	394,351	2,177,040	0.08
1990	64	66	226,263	3,520,150	0.13
1991	34	36	218,639	1,453,110	0.05
1992p	35	36	111,317	1,088,620	0.05

6.9 EFFECTIVE WAGE INCREASES[1] IN BASE RATES (PERCENT)

Sector	1989	1990	1991
All industries			
Agreements without COLA	5.3	6.1	3.4
Agreements with COLA	5.2	5.1	4.6
All agreements	5.3	5.6	3.6
Public Sector			
Agreements without COLA	5.3	6.2	3.4
Agreements with COLA	5.3	5.0	4.6
All Agreements	5.3	5.6	3.5
Private Sector			
Agreements without COLA	5.2	6.0	3.9
Agreements with COLA	5.2	5.3	4.6
All Agreements	5.2	5.7	4.2
Commercial sector			
Agreements without COLA	5.2	6.0	3.7
Agreements with COLA	4.5	5.2	4.6
All agreements	5.1	5.7	4.0
Non-commercial sector			
Agreements without COLA	5.4	6.2	3.4
Agreements with COLA	5.5	5.0	4.6
All agreements	5.4	5.6	3.5

[1] *Cost of Living Allowance (COLA) formulae are quantified using a combination of the latest relevant Consumer Price Index (CPI) data available and/or a projected CPI increase of 3%.*

6.10 HELP-WANTED INDEX[1], ANNUAL AVERAGES (1981 = 100)

	Atlantic region	Quebec	Ontario	Prairie region	British Columbia	Canada
1982	71	57	59	47	45	55
1983	73	66	59	43	43	57
1984	93	86	83	50	48	75
1985	106	97	111	61	53	91
1986	122	119	130	64	67	108
1987	157	155	167	69	80	136
1988	179	171	179	80	94	150
1989	195	171	166	89	127	151
1990	159	127	111	80	116	114
1991	110	85	69	53	80	75

[1] *The Help-wanted Index serves as an indicator of labour market conditions. It is constructed from a count of help-wanted ads published in the classified sections of 22 metropolitan area newspapers.*

6.11 NUMBER OF ACCEPTED TIME-LOSS INJURIES[1]

	1986	1987	1988	1989	1990	1991
Newfoundland	8,624	9,047	10,066	10,689	10,368	9,421
Prince Edward Island	1,935	2,068	2,435	2,450	2,551	2,250
Nova Scotia	12,620	11,732	11,219	13,897	12,870	12,730
New Brunswick	9,909	10,918	12,119	13,083	12,508	11,670
Quebec	213,366	216,724	218,057	218,708	204,734	178,689
Ontario	195,937	205,259	208,499	200,967	184,444	155,473
Manitoba	23,495	22,510	22,612	21,618	21,369	18,095
Saskatchewan	15,916	15,715	14,888	13,886	13,715	12,701
Alberta	42,249	41,236	43,349	44,782	45,869	38,724
British Columbia	61,711	66,200	73,418	79,613	84,464	79,484
Northwest Territories	956	1,122	1,335	1,286	1,060	989
Yukon	. .	. .	. .	. .	. .	321
Canada	586,718	602,531	617,997	620,979	593,952	520,547

[1] *Injuries resulting in compensation for wage loss and/or permanent disability.*

6.12 WORKERS' COMPENSATION, 1990P

	Medical aid $'000	Hospitalization/ rehabilitation $'000	Funeral $'000	Pension $'000	Compensation for lost earnings $'000	Total payments $'000	Total claims No.
Newfoundland	14,203	5,753	[1]	6,057	33,984	59,997	21,489
Prince Edward Island	1,647	1,367	5	3,750	3,643	10,412	4,843
Nova Scotia	15,459	8,357	116	46,732	38,724	109,388	37,846
New Brunswick	18,505	[2]	43	16,442	31,729	66,719	39,921
Quebec	83,188	105,238	738	348,558	649,657	1,187,379	241,391
Ontario	234,000	284,000	[3]	560,000	777,000	1,855,000	390,214
Manitoba	16,425	12,727	36	27,983	48,947	106,118	38,136
Saskatchewan	15,927	1,479	[2]	26,528	37,209	81,143	33,126
Alberta	70,043	29,700	264	115,285	144,958	360,250	54,283
British Columbia	68,508	35,798	446	164,287	192,224	461,263	165,907
Yukon	554	35	12	1,289	1,528	3,408	1,756
Northwest Territories	768	1,873	3	5,897	5,631	14,172	3,170
Canada	539,217	486,327	1,663	1,322,808	1,965,234	4,315,249	1,032,082

[1] Included in Pensions.
[2] Included in Medical aid.
[3] Included in Compensation for lost earnings.

6.13 WORK INJURIES

	Number of employees '000	Disabling	Fatal		Non-disabling	All
			Compensated	Reported		
1981	9,340	584,443	967	1,175	622,208	1,207,618
1982	9,039	518,751	861	1,201	496,437	1,016,049
1983	8,767	490,463	718	970	462,704	953,885
1984	8,902	524,948	744	889	510,652	1,036,344
1985	9,209	570,616	733	932	504,424	1,075,773
1986	9,845	598,424	762	894	474,624	1,073,810
1987	10,081	612,127	796	1,090	421,564	1,034,487
1988	10,285	614,012	835	1,151	456,265	1,071,112
1989	10,518	615,089	830	1,143	434,330	1,050,249
1990p	10,326	592,824	809	1,127	438,449	1,032,082

6.14 UNEMPLOYMENT INSURANCE CLAIMS AND AVERAGE PAYMENTS

	Persons covered by Unemployment Insurance[1] '000	Claims data ('000)		Benefit data	
		Beneficiaries[2]	Initial and renewal claims received	Number of weeks paid '000	Average weekly payment $
1986	12,191	3,137	3,353	58,063	181.07
1987	12,522	3,080	3,221	54,875	190.26
1988	12,891	3,016	3,231	53,527	202.75
1989	13,264	3,025	3,215	53,399	215.88
1990	13,434	3,261	3,695	57,053	231.18
1991	13,142	3,663	3,877	71,460	243.91

[1] *Persons who during the year, contributed toward the Unemployment Insurance program. Estimates are derived by adding to the 'employed paid workers' the strength of the Armed Forces and the number of beneficiaries.*
[2] *Unduplicated counts of all persons who, during the course of a calendar year, received unemployment insurance benefits.*

6.15 UNEMPLOYMENT INSURANCE BENEFITS (THOUSAND DOLLARS)

	Benefits paid								
	Regular	Sickness	Family related[1]	Retirement	Fishing	Training	Work sharing	Job creation	Total
1986	9,209,882	242,065	476,693	21,802	208,515	236,933	21,653	96,014	10,513,557
1987	9,076,420	278,693	510,791	23,110	223,321	223,776	16,979	87,619	10,440,709
1988	9,309,381	325,159	571,384	19,190	270,062	238,219	16,828	102,178	10,852,401
1989	9,846,725	356,501	637,109	26,046	269,648	269,041	21,138	101,829	11,528,036
1990	11,293,748	390,397	721,090	18,326	263,706	330,754	61,732	109,655	13,189,409
1991	14,783,294	409,663	1,136,831	. . .[2]	287,048	803,727	160,119	114,935	17,695,617

[1] *Family related includes persons receiving maternity, parental or adoption benefits.*
[2] *Program discontinued.*

6.16 AVERAGE FAMILY INCOME

	Current dollars				
	1981	1986	1989	1990	1991
Newfoundland	25,870	30,383	39,648	40,770	41,654
Prince Edward Island	23,455	32,029	38,726	39,701	42,779
Nova Scotia	24,862	35,352	43,123	44,385	45,130
New Brunswick	24,608	33,313	40,670	42,356	44,323
Quebec	28,568	38,110	44,860	47,158	48,634
Ontario	32,322	45,778	57,330	57,027	58,634
Manitoba	28,606	37,875	46,551	47,178	46,621
Saskatchewan	30,575	37,025	42,978	44,234	45,930
Alberta	36,279	43,729	49,734	51,985	55,552
British Columbia	33,687	40,590	49,442	54,448	54,895
Canada	30,973	41,240	50,083	51,633	53,131

6.16 AVERAGE FAMILY INCOME (concluded)

	Constant (1991) dollars				
	1981	1986	1989	1990	1991
Newfoundland	43,229	38,346	43,875	43,064	41,654
Prince Edward Island	39,193	40,423	42,855	41,934	42,779
Nova Scotia	41,544	44,617	47,721	46,882	45,130
New Brunswick	41,120	42,044	45,006	44,739	44,323
Quebec	47,737	48,098	49,643	49,811	48,634
Ontario	54,010	57,776	63,443	60,235	58,634
Manitoba	47,801	47,801	51,514	49,832	46,621
Saskatchewan	51,091	46,729	47,560	46,723	45,930
Alberta	60,622	55,190	55,037	54,910	55,552
British Columbia	56,291	51,228	54,714	57,511	54,895
Canada	51,756	52,048	54,423	54,538	53,131

6.17 FAMILY INCOME DISTRIBUTION IN CONSTANT (1991) DOLLARS

Percentage distribution	1981	1986	1989	1990	1991
Under $10,000	2.7	2.3	1.8	2.3	2.4
$10,000 - $19,999	10.5	11.1	9.6	9.5	10.4
20,000 - 29,999	11.9	13.1	12.1	12.9	13.7
30,000 - 39,999	14.2	14.3	13.5	13.4	14.0
40,000 - 49,999	14.8	14.0	14.2	13.6	13.6
50,000 - 59,999	13.5	12.9	12.8	12.7	12.1
60,000 - 74,999	14.5	14.2	14.4	14.3	14.0
75,000 and over	17.9	18.2	21.6	21.2	19.5
Total	100.0	100.0	100.0	100.0	100.0
Income ($)					
Average income	51,756	52,048	55,423	54,537	53,131
Median income[1]	47,326	46,516	49,166	48,620	46,742

[1] *Median income refers to the middle or central value when incomes are ranged in order of magnitude. Median income is lower than average income in these tables since it is not as affected by a few abnormally large values in the distribution.*

6.18 LOW INCOME[1] INCIDENCE AND DISTRIBUTION

	Families			Unattached individuals		
	Incidence of low income[2]	Percentage distribution of		Incidence of low income[2]	Percentage distribution of	
		Low income	All other		Low income	All other
All families and unattached individuals	13.1	100.0	100.0	36.5	100.0	100.0
Estimated numbers ('000)	949	949	6,317	1,258	1,258	2,185
By province of residence						
Atlantic provinces	13.4	8.9	8.6	36.9	6.2	6.1
Newfoundland	16.4	2.6	2.0	41.3	1.1	0.9
Prince Edward Island	9.9	0.4	0.5	40.5	0.5	0.4
Nova Scotia	12.9	3.3	3.4	35.6	2.7	2.8
New Brunswick	12.3	2.6	2.8	35.6	1.9	1.9
Quebec	15.9	31.6	25.2	44.2	32.0	23.3
Ontario	11.2	31.9	38.0	31.8	30.2	37.2
Prairie provinces	14.1	17.8	16.4	34.8	15.9	17.2
Manitoba	17.1	5.0	3.6	38.2	4.3	4.0
Saskatchewan	13.4	3.7	3.5	34.5	3.2	3.5
Alberta	13.1	9.2	9.2	33.4	8.4	9.7
British Columbia	11.1	9.8	11.9	35.7	15.7	16.2
By size of area of residence						
Urban areas 500,000 and over	15.8	53.7	43.0	40.4	59.1	51.0
Urban areas 100,000 - 499,999	11.9	13.0	14.5	36.5	14.6	14.6
Urban areas 30,000 - 99,999	12.0	8.4	9.3	36.6	9.1	9.0
Urban areas under 30,000	11.3	11.3	13.3	32.1	10.6	12.9
Rural areas	9.3	13.6	19.8	23.5	6.7	12.5
By tenure						
Owners	7.1	39.8	78.8	24.1	19.0	34.5
With mortgage	6.9	20.3	41.0	15.1	4.1	13.4
Without mortgage	7.2	19.5	37.7	28.9	14.9	21.1
Renters[3]	29.9	60.2	21.2	41.6	81.0	65.5
By age of head						
24 years and under	36.9	9.0	2.3	55.5	19.3	8.9
25 - 34 years	18.6	30.2	19.9	24.8	15.8	27.7
35 - 44 "	12.7	25.5	26.3	25.5	10.4	17.5
45 - 54 "	7.6	11.6	21.2	29.2	7.9	11.0
55 - 64 "	12.0	13.5	14.9	42.5	13.1	10.2
65 - 69 "	8.7	3.9	6.1	37.6	7.5	7.1
70 years and over	9.2	6.3	9.4	46.0	26.0	17.5
By sex and age of head						
Males						
Under 65 years	9.6	55.6	78.3	30.5	32.9	43.1
65 years and over	8.3	8.3	13.8	33.4	6.5	7.4
Females						
Under 65 years	45.6	34.2	6.1	37.6	33.7	32.2
65 years and over	13.8	1.9	1.8	47.4	26.9	17.2

6.18   LOW INCOME[1] INCIDENCE AND DISTRIBUTION (concluded)

	Families			Unattached individuals		
	Incidence of low income[2]	Percentage distribution of		Incidence of low income[2]	Percentage distribution of	
		Low income	All other		Low income	All other
By family characteristics						
Married couples only	9.2	21.8	32.4	. . .	100.0	100.0
Married couples with single child only	9.3	35.2	51.4	. . .	. . .	. . .
Married couples with children and/or other relatives	7.6	2.7	4.9	. . .	. . .	. . .
Lone-parent families						
Male head	16.0	1.8	1.4	. . .	. . .	. . .
Female head	47.6	32.1	5.3	. . .	. . .	. . .
All other families	17.3	6.3	4.5	. . .	. . .	. . .
By number of children under 18						
None	8.7	33.7	53.3	36.5	100.0	100.0
One child	17.7	26.7	18.7	. . .	. . .	. . .
Two children	15.6	24.2	19.7	. . .	. . .	. . .
Three or more children	21.8	15.4	8.3	. . .	. . .	. . .

[1] Estimates based on low income cutoffs, 1986 base.
[2] Percentage of families and unattached individuals with income below the low income cutoffs.
[3] Includes roomers, lodgers and families and unattached individuals who receive free lodging or who reside with employers.

6.19   LOW INCOME INCIDENCE (1986 BASE)

	Incidence of low income				
	1981	1986	1989	1990	1991
Persons - total	15.3	16.0	13.6	14.6	16.0
Children under 16	15.2	17.0	14.5	16.9	18.3
Elderly, 65 and over	33.0	24.9	21.4	19.3	20.0
All others	12.7	14.2	11.8	12.9	14.3
Persons in families - total	12.4	13.1	10.6	11.8	12.9
Children under 16	15.2	17.0	14.5	16.9	18.3
Elderly, 65 and over	18.9	13.4	9.8	7.5	8.5
All others	10.2	11.2	8.9	10.1	11.0
Unattached individuals - total	40.3	38.3	34.4	34.1	36.5
Elderly, 65 and over	62.8	50.7	45.2	43.6	43.8
All others	31.3	33.7	30.0	30.3	33.7

6.20 PATTERNS OF FAMILY EXPENDITURES, 17 METROPOLITAN AREAS[1]

| | 1969[2] | 1978[2] | 1986 | 1990[2] | 1990 | | | | | |
| | | | | | Lowest Income Quintile | Highest Income Quintile | All home-owners | All tenants | Less than 45 years old | |
									Male one-person households	Female one person households
Number of families in sample	6,296	5,178	5,899	4,856	1,100	783	2,714	1,974	260	224
Estimated number of families ('000)	2,904	3,545	4,424	4,720	944	944	2,578	2,009	275	219
Average:										
Family size	3.10	2.74	2.63	2.56	1.59	3.37	2.98	2.02	1.00	1.00
Age of head	46	45	46	47	57	46	50	44	33	33
Family income ($)	9,089	21,139	38,925	49,085	13,814	100,459	61,649	32,866	34,688	29,262
Other money receipts ($)	115	434	975	1,689	825	1,019	2,041	1,058	2,886	778
Change in assets and liablities ($)	248	1,543	1,784	3,239	−1,511	11,543	5,640	187	1,706	1,243
Percentage:										
Homeowners	47.9	52.2	51.6	56.8	26.1	87.9	100.0	. . .	22.6	14.7
Automobile owners	68.1	72.4	74.4	78.4	36.4	95.2	91.8	60.2	70.2	56.8
Total expenditure ($)	9,038	19,990	38,236	47,474	16,391	88,806	57,797	33,852	36,674	29,390
					Percentage share					
Food	17.7	16.7	13.9	12.6	18.4	10.3	12.0	14.0	11.6	11.1
Food from restaurant	3.3	3.7	4.0	3.6	3.3	3.6	3.3	4.4	6.1	4.6
Shelter	16.6	17.3	16.7	17.3	30.5	13.9	15.9	19.6	19.4	21.4
Household operation	3.6	3.7	4.1	4.0	5.9	3.6	3.8	4.3	3.0	4.0
Household furnishings	3.9	4.1	3.3	3.0	3.1	3.1	3.0	2.8	2.8	2.8
Clothing	8.8	7.2	6.3	5.5	5.5	5.6	5.3	5.8	4.5	6.3
Transportation	11.6	11.7	12.5	11.8	9.3	10.9	11.8	11.7	11.3	9.4
Operation of auto-mobiles and trucks	5.2	5.3	5.4	5.8	4.3	5.1	5.9	5.4	5.7	4.3
Health care	3.2	2.0	1.8	1.8	2.6	1.5	1.8	1.8	1.3	2.0
Personal care	2.0	1.7	1.9	1.9	2.8	1.5	1.7	2.2	1.0	2.7
Recreation	4.1	5.0	4.9	5.0	4.0	5.2	5.1	4.8	7.3	4.4
Reading materials	0.7	0.6	0.6	0.6	0.8	0.5	0.5	0.7	0.7	0.8
Education	1.0	0.8	1.0	0.9	1.0	1.0	0.9	0.8	0.7	0.5
Tobacco products and alcohol	3.7	3.2	3.1	2.7	3.7	2.0	2.3	3.6	3.5	2.5
Miscellaneous	1.4	2.2	2.4	2.7	1.9	2.4	2.7	2.9	3.2	2.2
Total current consumption	78.4	76.1	72.6	69.7	89.5	61.6	66.9	75.0	70.1	70.2
Personal taxes	14.2	16.9	19.9	22.2	4.9	29.7	24.6	17.5	22.6	22.2
Security	4.6	4.6	4.5	4.5	1.1	5.0	4.5	4.3	4.4	5.3
Gifts and contributions	2.7	2.3	3.0	3.7	4.5	3.6	3.9	3.2	2.9	2.3
Total expenditures	100.0	100.0	100.0	100.0	100.0	100.0	100.0	100.0	100.0	100.0

[1] *St. John's, Charlottetown, Summerside, Halifax, Saint John, Quebec, Montreal, Ottawa, Toronto, Thunder Bay, Winnipeg, Regina, Saskatoon, Calgary, Edmonton, Vancouver and Victoria.*
[2] *Figures changed to agree with the 1986 item definitions.*

Sources
Labour Canada
Statistics Canada

CHAPTER SEVEN HOUSING

INTRODUCTION

In 1993, Canada ranked second to Japan as the best country in the world in which to live, according to the most recent *United Nations Human Development Report*. This was due in part to a level of income that in 1991 enabled 6 of every 10 households to own their home, almost half of them outright — that is, free of a mortgage. This rate of ownership has been stable for more than a decade.

Canadians are encouraged to realize the dream of home-ownership by tax incentives such as home-ownership savings plans, the tax-exempt status of house sales and capital gains tax exemptions for principal residences. In addition, in 1992, the federal government introduced two initiatives to promote home-ownership: the First Home Loan Insurance program and the Home Buyers' Plan.

The First Home Loan Insurance program, administered by Canada Mortgage and Housing Corporation (CMHC), allows first-time buyers to purchase moderately priced homes with a down payment of only 5% instead of the minimum 10% required under regular National Housing Act (NHA) mortgage financing. The program had financed over 63,000 housing units by year end.

The Home Buyers' Plan, introduced as part of the 1992 federal budget, allows home buyers to withdraw up to $20,000 from existing Registered Retirement Savings Plans (RRSPs) for a downpayment on a new or existing residence without tax penalties. By the end of the year, 127,000 people had taken advantage of this plan.

HOMING IN...

The typical Canadian homeowner is generally around 50 years of age. According to the 1991 Census of Population, 75% of primary household maintainers (the person who pays the largest share of the expenses of the dwelling) in the 45 to 54 age group were homeowners. By contrast, only 14% of those under 25 were homeowners. For the 25 to 34 age group, the proportion increased to about 47%. For the 65 to 74 age group, the rate was 71%, and for the 75 and

over group it was 59%; these figures reflect the fact that some seniors rent apartments or move to institutions rather than maintain a household.

Having someone with whom to share the expenses makes home-ownership more likely. In 1991, almost four-fifths (77%) of households with more than one income earner owned their homes, in contrast to slightly more than one-fifth (23%) of households with only one income earner.

In 1991, Newfoundland had Canada's highest percentage of homeowners at 79%. At the other end of the scale was the Northwest Territories, at 32%.

In 1991, 49% of homeowners reported having no mortgage. Among these, the proportion was highest in Newfoundland (65%) and lowest in Alberta (43%). In metropolitan areas, the highest proportions are found in Thunder Bay (54%), Windsor, Victoria and St. Catharines (53% each), and the lowest in Quebec City and Calgary (38% and 37% respectively).

There were slightly more than 10 million occupied dwellings in Canada in 1991, up from 9 million in 1986. The census has several categories for these dwellings: single-family detached, low density, high-rise, mobile and other movable dwellings. The single-family dwellings make up 57% of all dwellings, while 32% are low density, 9% highrise and 2% mobile dwellings.

Between 1986 and 1991, the number of households increased faster than the population (11.4% versus 7.9%); this reflects a 30-year trend toward smaller households. One-person households grew by 19% over this period, while households with six or more people fell by 4%. The number of households increased fastest in the Yukon (24%), the Northwest Territories (17%) and British Columbia (14%); at the other end of the scale were Manitoba and Saskatchewan with increases of 6% and 1% respectively.

The 1991 Census found that almost half of Canada's homes had been built since 1970, while only 8.2% were built before 1921. The Northwest Territories has the highest proportion of newer homes, with 72% built

L. L. FitzGerald / National Gallery of Canada

Doc Snyder's House.

since 1970. In major urban centres, the Ottawa-Hull and Vancouver metropolitan areas topped the list with one-quarter of dwellings built between 1981 and 1991.

Not unexpectedly, therefore, most Canadians reported to the census that their homes were in good shape. In 1991, only 8.2% of homes needed major repairs such as replacement of wiring or plumbing or structural repairs. This figure was even lower for owner-occupied dwellings (7.5%), but higher for tenant-occupied buildings (9.0%).

The 1991 Census found a continuing trend to larger homes but decreasing household size. Homes averaged 6.1 rooms with an average of 2.7 people living in them, up from 5.8 rooms housing 2.8 people in the 1986 Census. Homeowners tend to own bigger homes (with an average 7.0 rooms) than renters (with 4.5 rooms).

BUYING A HOME

To the many Canadians who were priced out of the housing market in the late 1980s, the dream of buying a home is slowly becoming less daunting.

According to figures from Canada Mortgage and Housing Corporation and the Canadian Real Estate Association, while the average price of existing homes rose by more than 48% from 1986 to 1989, house prices have remained relatively stable ever since.

The average purchase price of a Canadian home was roughly $151,000 in 1992, up less than 2% from the average price of $149,000 in 1989.

Average house prices vary considerably by province. In Saskatchewan, where houses cost the least, the average purchase price of a home was $68,400 in 1992 — $2,000 less than in 1989.

In British Columbia, by contrast, average home prices continued to rise through the roof. The average purchase price of a BC home was $190,000 in 1992 — more than in any other province. Furthermore, BC led the nation in price growth. Home prices in BC rose by more than 24% from 1989 to 1992 alone.

Price growth was also well above the national average in Alberta and Newfoundland, where house prices rose by 15% and 9%, respectively, from 1989 to 1992.

In Ontario, where house prices had risen the most dramatically in the late 1980s, the cost of buying a home has steadily fallen since 1989. Whereas Ontario homes sold for an average of more than $185,000 in 1989, they fetched an average of only $163,000 each in 1992, or 12% less.

In 1991, the number of owner-occupied condominiums had increased 57% from 1986, jumping from 235,000 to over 367,000. Condominiums are found mainly in the large metropolitan areas of Quebec, Ontario and British Columbia, with Montreal, Ottawa-Hull, Toronto and Vancouver together accounting for nearly two-thirds (233,000) of the Canadian total.

According to figures reported by homeowners in the 1991 Census, Toronto and Vancouver topped the list of major urban centres in the overall value of homes. In fact, Toronto home values in 1991 were almost double what they were in 1986. In metropolitan Toronto, the average estimated home value was $280,000, up from $142,000 in 1986. Vancouver home values averaged an estimated $245,000. Hamilton was in third place at $192,000.

In 1991, those who owned their home but had mortgages spent an average of $1,056 a month on shelter costs (mortgage payments, property taxes, heat and utilities). Those who owned their home mortgage-free spent an average $284. Average costs for renters were $546.

It pays to pay off the mortgage. The 1991 Census found that Canadians are spending more on housing than they used to. Over 2.2 million households reported that housing costs accounted for upwards of 30% of their income, compared with 1.9 million in 1986. However, only 6% of these were owner households without mortgages, while 58% were renter households and 36% owner households with mortgages. Housing is proportionately more expensive for renters because they tend to have lower incomes, and are more likely to be living on their own.

Consumer Price Index In 1991, Canadians paid 3.5% more for housing than they had in 1990, whether they owned or rented their accommodation. Costs were affected by a double-digit (11.8%) increase in water, fuel and electricity prices, partly resulting from the implementation of the Goods and Services Tax. However, the increase in costs was substantially lower for both owners and renters than in the previous two years. For owners, the main cause of the slowdown was a drop in the costs of replacement (−4.3%) and home insurance (−2.9%).

Gabor Szilasi / CMCP

Canadian living room decor in Albanel, Lac Saint-Jean County, Quebec.

New House Price Index People looking to buy a new house got a break in 1991. The price of new houses declined for the first time since 1983 due to declines in the cost of both land and construction. The price of land fell by 5.1% from 1990 levels, led by sharp drops in Toronto (10.7%) and Vancouver (6.1%). Construction costs dropped 7.5%.

Buyers in southern Ontario and the Vancouver region got the biggest break, while new house prices remained stable in almost all other urban areas. In southern Ontario, Toronto led the way with a large drop of 14.9% in the value of a new home in 1991. Outside the southern Ontario region, the next largest drop

was in Vancouver, where the price fell 7.3% after solid gains in each of the previous two years.

In 1991, the drops in land and construction costs together resulted in a fall of 8.8% in the price of new houses. This followed increases of 1.4% and 13.2% in the previous two years.

MORTGAGE LENDING

For most people, the first step towards home-ownership is saving for a down payment. Most financial institutions in Canada are prohibited by governing

HOME SWEET HOME

On a hilltop in Prince Edward Island sits a two-storey family home that uses only one-quarter of the energy and less than half of the water of the average Canadian home. On frosty winter days, a special underground pump pulls heat from the earth into the house for warmth. Outside, a turbine spins wind into electricity that complements the conventional electrical supply. Solar panels, well-insulated tanks, and a waste water heat recovery system provide hot water at less than 40% of the energy cost of conventional systems. A computer monitors every change in energy consumption and feeds the information to scientists in Charlottetown.

This house, along with nine similar homes across Canada, is part of the Advanced Houses Program, a project directed by Energy, Mines and Resources' Canada Centre for Mineral and Energy Technology (CANMET). Each house is a test site for prototype technologies that are energy-efficient, cost-efficient and environmentally friendly, and each is intended to exceed the high standards already set by R-2000 standard. (The R-2000 homes were developed in the early 1980s by the federal department of Energy, Mines and Resources to consume only half as much energy as conventional houses of the same size.)

Builders, renovators, designers, suppliers and manufacturers, along with interested parties such as utilities and provincial agencies, worked together to prepare proposals for houses employing the latest improvements in energy consumption and environmental impact.

Performance criteria for these houses have been strict. Water consumption is half that of conventional houses and the building materials contain recycled or recyclable contents. Natural landscaping around the home requires minimal watering.

Each of the 10 homes selected in the Advanced Houses Program will be monitored for a minimum of one year to determine whether the homes meet the original design criteria, and to assess the commercial potential of the innovative technologies and products. Open to the public for one full year after their completion, these projects can be studied and observed by both consumers and builders.

What they will find challenges the imagination. Some houses feature electricity provided in part by wind or sunlight. In others, part of the space heating and hot water loads are supplied by the sun, collected in solar collector tubes and stored in large water tanks in the basements.

Home management systems handle everything from home temperature to home security. Lights, appliances, thermostats and security systems can be automatically controlled from one monitoring system. To walk into a comfortable house at the end of a hard day, residents can even activate their heating or air conditioning with a simple call from a touch-tone phone just before they arrive home.

While the Advanced Houses Program is still in its early stages, it has captured the imagination of Canada's building industry, attracting millions of dollars in sponsorships from industry, power utilities and provincial government departments.

Meanwhile, many Canadian families are consciously trying to keep the costs of shelter low by remembering to turn off lights and appliances, lowering their thermostats, and buying energy-efficient windows, heating systems and appliances that are now on the market.

In 1990, Canadian families spent an average of $1,200 on water, electricity and fuel, according to a Statistics Canada survey of 17 metropolitan areas.

regulations from making high-ratio mortgages (in excess of 75% of property value) unless the loans are insured under the National Housing Act (NHA) or by a private mortgage insurance company. But prospective buyers with a lower down payment can still purchase a home. CMHC's Mortgage Loan Insurance Program encourages financing for residential housing by ensuring NHA-approved lenders against borrower default. This has helped many Canadians who otherwise would not have been able to own their home. In fact, since World War II, more than a third of all mortgages have been insured under the program.

In 1991, lower interest rates helped make home-ownership more affordable. As a result, the increase in mortgage approvals was the largest since 1987, and the value of residential mortgage approvals grew by 25% to $69.3 billion. The number of approvals was up 28% to just under 1 million. In contrast, in 1990, high interest rates and falling real estate prices led to a drop of 7.3% in the dollar value of mortgage lending.

In 1991, first-time buyers, often unable to afford big down payments, were more visible in the housing market than they had been in the past. As a result, the dollar value of approvals increased more for NHA-insured loans (51.4%) than for conventional loans (19.1%). In fact, the number of NHA-insured loans set new records in 1991, reaching over 184,000 for a total value of $15.4 billion. Conventional approvals totalled 764,000 for a total value of $53.9 billion. By contrast, in 1990, high interest rates had caused a more severe drop in NHA approvals than in conventional approvals.

For first-time buyers, existing units are usually cheaper than new properties. Not surprisingly, the rise in mortgage approvals was concentrated among existing homes, as is usually the case during the first stages of an economic recovery. In 1991, mortgage lending on existing properties rose 32.8% to $58.6 billion, while approvals for new properties actually declined by 5% to $10.8 billion.

British Columbia led the rebound in mortgage lending with an increase of 62.5% during 1991, followed by Ontario (22.6%) and the Prairie region (15.1%).

Lynne Cohen / CMCP

Mobile Home Park.

HOUSING STARTS

In 1991, as the economy recovered only slowly from recession, construction of housing declined, falling to its lowest level since 1984. Housing starts had declined in 1991, for the fourth year in a row. Total housing starts fell 14% to just over 156,000 units. Single-detached starts fell faster than multiple unit starts, falling 15% to fewer than 87,000 units; multiple units fell 12% to fewer than 70,000 units.

Although 1991 as a whole showed a decline in housing starts, the quarterly picture was more favourable as major cuts in interest rates and an easing in house prices began to make home-ownership more affordable. As a result, having reached bottom in the first three months of the year, housing starts surged in the spring, and continued to climb in the summer and fall.

The recovery was dampened initially by excess supply in the housing stock. The apartment vacancy rate, 4.4% nationally in October 1991, was at its highest level since 1972. In addition, there were indications of excess supply in new housing, with the number of vacant new dwellings dropping only slowly from the high levels posted at the end of 1990.

THE PROVINCIAL PERSPECTIVE
In 1991, housing starts were down from the previous year in all provinces except New Brunswick. Manitoba fared worse than any other province as a result of a

weak provincial economy and the number of people leaving the province. Starts fell by 41% from 1990 to 1,950 units.

Saskatchewan shared the experience of an all-time low in housing starts due to net migration (people leaving the province) and weak consumer confidence. Housing starts dropped 30% to fewer than 1,000 units in 1991.

While new construction in Alberta declined 27% to slightly over 12,000 units in 1991, the trend was favourable with the year closing on a strong note.

Conversely, after modest improvements during the early part of 1991, housing starts in Prince Edward Island declined during the later part of the year. The year-end figure marked the lowest level since 1982 at 550 units started, a decline of 27% from 1990.

Less drastic drops were experienced by Ontario, British Columbia and Newfoundland. The Ontario economy began to recover in the spring of 1991, but signs of renewed weakness appeared in the fall. Total starts were down 16% to under 53,000 units, with the single-detached market dropping 19%.

In British Columbia, the sharp drop in interest rates in 1991, the solid performance of the provincial economy and the continued influx of people from other provinces and countries led to a strong recovery for the housing market after the first three months of the year. Total housing starts nonetheless dropped 13% to under 32,000 units; the decline was largely due to a 26% drop in multiple starts.

Newfoundlanders took matters into their own hands in 1991 as high levels of owner-builder activity in rural areas helped sustain construction. Despite higher unemployment and lower confidence stemming from economic uncertainty in the provincial economy, new home construction declined only 13% to 2,800 units.

Quebec and Nova Scotia shared a drop of 7% in 1991 to 45,000 and 5,000 units respectively. In Quebec, market activity was boosted, especially toward the end of the year, by the provincial government's construction and home-ownership support programs.

In 1991, New Brunswick was the only province to show a modest increase in house building. Total housing starts moved up 7% to almost 2,900 units, mainly due to a 32% increase in multiple housing construction.

CONSTRUCTION AND REPAIRS

In 1991, more building was going on in Mississauga, Ontario, than in any other municipality in Canada. Mississauga issued building permits worth a total of $910 million in 1991. Next were Sainte-Foy ($875 million), Montreal ($870 million) and Vancouver ($849 million).

The 1991 total value of permits issued for building construction was $28.5 billion, down from $32.3 billion in 1990. For residential construction, the value of permits issued was $16.6 billion, compared to $17.5 billion in 1990.

For 1992, construction expenditures in Canada were an estimated $83.9 billion. This was an increase of 3.5% from the 1991 total ($81.1 billion), but lower than the 1990 figure ($87.1 billion). Data for construction cover the estimated value of new construction and repairs performed by contractors, by government departments, by other persons or firms not primarily engaged in the construction industry, by home-owners, and by the construction units of utility, manufacturing, mining and logging companies.

Where we live, 1990

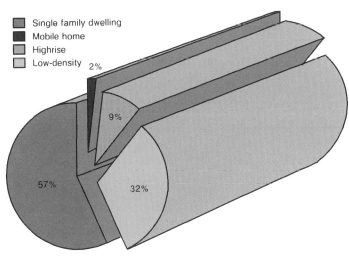

- ■ Single family dwelling
- ■ Mobile home
- ■ Highrise
- □ Low-density

2%
9%
57%
32%

REDUCING CONSTRUCTION WASTE

Canadians are among the largest generators of garbage on a per capita basis, and construction is a big contributor. An army of thrifty scavengers could probably build entire houses with the materials contractors usually throw away — keeping in mind that taking anything including scrap from a building site without the contractor's or owner's permission constitutes theft.

According to Canada Mortgage and Housing Corporation, waste from demolished buildings, renovations and new home construction fills more than 5% of the volume of Canada's already-filled landfill sites. Demolition and construction waste from non-residential buildings accounts for another 9%.

Construction waste is a big concern in this country. Environment Canada wants to halve the amount of waste going into landfills by the end of the century, so the push is on.

The construction industry is acknowledging its role in creating waste, and is finding surprisingly effective ways to reduce scrap heaps. For instance, in a pilot project in Vancouver, home builders found other uses for 70% to 90% of the material they once would have scrapped.

Reducing waste is also sound economics, because in the long run, it saves contractors money on materials and landfill fees.

Essentially, builders are using an industrial-strength version of the same 'three Rs' many Canadians already apply to household waste: reducing at the source; re-using materials that would normally go into landfills; and recycling materials that cannot be re-used in other ways.

For example, contractors might locate a building so trees don't have to be felled. Architects may set floor plans to fit standard sizes of construction materials like lumber and wall board, reducing the scrap that is sawn off. Builders may also buy materials cut to size, and better protect their material piles against weather damage and subsequent discards.

Some builders have suppliers take back packaging of anything they deliver. Fasteners, paint, caulking and drywall mud may be purchased in bulk containers instead of individual packages. Contractors may use kiln-dried lumber because it doesn't warp as easily as lower grades, and that cuts back on discards, too.

Another way to handle waste is to re-use scraps to brace frames or concrete forms. Renovators find careful demolition can yield doors, windows, decorative mouldings, sinks and bathtubs they can re-use in other projects or sell to shops specializing in architectural heritage items.

Recycling is probably the least desirable option. Whenever old materials are made into new ones, new kinds of waste may result, and new energy must be used to convert them. But it still beats throwing things away. In various parts of Canada, asphalt, wood, drywall, cardboard, masonry, metals, glass, and even plastics and paints are being recycled — and the list is growing.

Of the 1992 residential construction total of $41.1 billion, therefore, only $3.9 billion went for repair expenditures, while capital expenditures accounted for $37.2 billion. The 1992 residential construction total was up from both 1991 ($36.8 billion) and 1990 ($41.0 billion).

Housing Starts in Urban Centres[1]

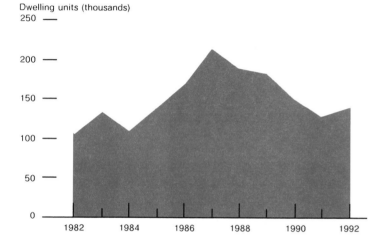

[1] Centres of 10,000 population and over.

Canada's Housing Price Index

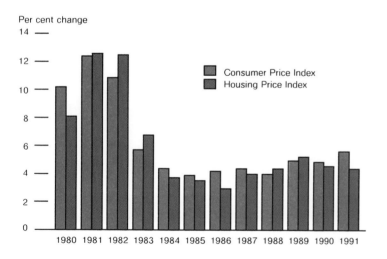

SOCIAL HOUSING

The federal, provincial and municipal governments all deliver social housing programs. The federal agency responsible for these programs is Canada Mortgage and Housing Corporation (CMHC).

CMHC was established in 1946 under the National Housing Act. The Great Depression, followed by World War II, had left a weakened construction industry. At the same time, war veterans were returning from service overseas and starting families. The result was a demand for housing that the industry was unable to meet on its own. The Corporation's mandate, therefore, was "to promote the construction of new houses, the repair and modernization of existing houses, and the improvement of housing and living conditions".

In addition to supporting the private housing market (which meets 80% of Canada's housing needs) through its mortgage lending activities, CMHC works together with most provinces and territories to deliver social housing programs and manage the nation's stock of social housing units. There are currently over 650,000 social housing units receiving federal assistance through CMHC.

Although 63% of Canadians own their homes, a significant number of the remaining 37% cannot afford to do so. Instead, they rent. But for some, even finding the rent money can be difficult. This is especially true of households headed by seniors — particularly women — or very young adults, one-person households and lone-parent families headed by women. In 1991, 35% of renters were spending more than 30% of their income on housing. CMHC offers a number of programs to ensure that Canadians have affordable, suitable and adequate shelter.

The Non-Profit Housing Program subsidizes public and private non-profit organizations and non-profit co-operatives for housing projects that rent to households in need on a rent-to-income basis. In 1991, 8,679 additional housing units became eligible for assistance.

Ursula Heller / CMCP

Home at Alma, New Brunswick.

The Rent Supplement Program subsidizes owners of private rental housing who offer their units to households in need. It also provides assistance to up to 50% of units in federal co-operative housing projects. In 1991, 2,188 additional units became available.

Several programs provide housing assistance for native Canadians. These include the Urban Native Non-Profit Housing Program, the On-Reserve Non-Profit Housing Program and the Rural and Native Housing Program. These programs combined offered an additional 4,465 units in 1991.

The Residential Rehabilitation Program offers loans to homeowners and native people on reserves to help repair sub-standard housing. In 1991, $112.6 million was provided for 27,325 dwellings.

The Emergency Repair Program assists rural households (80% of them native households) to ensure that their homes are safe. Approximately $3.1 million went to repair 1,501 units in 1991.

CMHC is working with other federal departments and agencies on the prevention of family violence. Projects Haven and Next Step, delivered in conjunction with Health and Welfare Canada, provide emergency refuge and long-term transitional housing for victims of domestic violence. Project Haven provided 453 bedroom units across Canada. In 1991, $11.3 million was committed for an additional 249 units. Under Project Next Step, $20.6 million will go to producing 250 longer-term units.

In 1990, 5% of Canadian households were receiving rent subsidies. Older women living on their own made up the largest single group. Canada's aging population and increasing numbers of marriage breakdowns and lone-parent families indicate that the need for subsidized housing will increase in coming years.

RED WIGGLERS RECYCLE

School children in Canada's North are learning about recycling from one of the planet's most energetic, productive and unflagging environmentalists — the red wiggler earthworm. Red wigglers recycle everything from apple peels to maple leaves, turning it all into rich compost, the organic portion of soil. So, to take advantage of this 'expertise', direct from nature, schoolchildren in the North have set up worm composters right in their schools.

One of many projects being run across the country, this project reflects Canadians' growing concern about the environmental impact of traditional ways of throwing away garbage. Indeed, almost one in every two Canadian households today put aside bottles, cans and newspapers for recycling.

Canadians use more energy and produce more garbage than anyone else in the world per person, and rank second only to the Americans in water consumption. Every four months, the greater Toronto area alone throws out enough garbage to fill its huge SkyDome Stadium to the roof. In 1988, Canadians generated 30 million tonnes of non-hazardous solid waste — a third of that from households.

Although about one-half of Canadian households recycle, this varies greatly across the country with accessibility to recycling services being a major factor. Ontario's households, for example, have the most recycling services available, and make better use of them than do households in other regions. Take newspaper recycling, for example. Where paper recycling was available, 72% of households in Ontario used the service in 1991, compared with 53% in the country as a whole. In fact, Ontarians were able to recycle 170 000 tonnes of newspapers in 1989, saving 510 000 cubic metres of landfill space and 3.2 million trees. In Newfoundland, on the other hand, only 11% of households had access to paper recycling and only 55% of these households used the paper recycling services.

In 1991, people living in large cities had better access to recycling than their rural counterparts. Of households in centres with more than 100,000 people, 59% had access to paper recycling and 55% to metal can and glass recycling. Only 33% of households in rural areas had access to these services.

Whether Canadians recycle or not also depends on the kind of home they live in. People living in single detached dwellings are almost twice as likely as apartment dwellers to have paper recycling services.

Since Canada's best recycling programs divert only 10% to 15% of residential waste from disposal sites, Canadians are combining 'green thinking' with business savvy to further reduce the amount of garbage they throw away. A company in Newfoundland, for example, collects and pays for plastic and metal soft drink containers, which it then recycles. The scheme is a money-generator and prevents hundreds of thousands of containers from otherwise filling up landfill sites.

Many municipalities in Canada are cutting garbage-collection costs by encouraging homeowners to compost their vegetable peelings, grass clippings and other organic waste. In fact, 17% of Canadian households either compost at home or use a municipal composting service. By selling homeowners inexpensive composters, Ontario municipalities divert thousands of tonnes of organic waste from landfill sites every year, and the homeowners get rich topsoil for their gardens. Other municipalities in Quebec and British Columbia are experimenting with curbside collection of yard waste, and with money-making composting depots.

David Nunuk / First Light

West End, Vancouver.

SPECIAL NEEDS HOUSING

The aging of the Canadian population has stimulated growing interest in housing the elderly and the disabled. CMHC carries out research and development to respond to the housing needs of these special-needs groups.

Together with provincial housing agencies and the private sector in some cases, CMHC is doing a number of things to provide older Canadians with a wider variety of housing options: holding conferences with seniors to obtain their views, demonstrating new types of accommodation such as 'granny flats' and garden suites, and providing a wide variety of information to consumers and the construction industry.

Canada's seniors are not only growing in number; they are also living longer and enjoying better health. In terms of health, income and living preference, today's seniors are a far more diverse group than they used to be. They want a wider choice of housing options than exists today — particularly options that allow them to live as independently as possible. They also require the means to choose the option they prefer. For some, this is a problem as they face the future with a reduced income. To guide seniors through this difficult decision-making process, CMHC has made available information on new financial options.

With age comes the increasing likelihood of disability. In fact, some 46% of those over 65 have difficulty with everyday activities as a result of disability, compared with 13% of the adult population under 65.

Today, people with disabilities are expressing a determination to become more independent. In response, CMHC is working with other federal departments and agencies on the National Strategy for the Integration of Persons with Disabilities. In 1992, Open House, a barrier-free house taking into account problems with mobility, impaired sight, hearing limitations and environmental

sensitivities was on display in various places across Canada. CMHC has also carried out research and provided information on how to make homes safer and more secure for people with Alzheimer's Disease and life less difficult for the people who care for them.

With the efforts being made to help Canadians buy, maintain and remain in their own homes, chances are good that Canada's record of home-ownership will be maintained or improved in the years to come.

SOURCES

Canada Mortgage and Housing Corporation

Statistics Canada

FOR FURTHER READING

Selected publications from Statistics Canada

▲ *Households and the Environment, 1991.* 11-526

▲ *Household Facilities by Income and Other Characteristics.* Annual. 13-218

▲ *Construction in Canada.* Annual. 64-201

▲ *Household Facilities and Equipment.* Annual. 64-202

▲ *Building Permits, Annual Summary.* Annual. 64-203

▲ *Mechanical Trade Contractors.* Annual. 64-204

▲ *Electrical Trade Contractors.* Annual. 64-205

▲ *Residential General Contractors and Developers.* Annual. 64-208

▲ *Dwellings and Households, 1991 Census.* 93-311

Selected publications from Other Sources

▲ *Initiatives Relating to Housing Choices for Older Canadians.* Canada Mortgage and Housing Corporation, 1991.

▲ *Housing for Older Canadians: New Financial and Tenure Options.* Canada Mortgage and Housing Corporation, 1988.

TABLES

7.1 VALUE OF BUILDING PERMITS (MILLION DOLLARS)

	Residential construction			Non-residential construction			Total
	New	Improvements	Total	Industrial	Commercial	Institutional and government	
1990							
Newfoundland	168.9	34.9	203.8	11.8	75.8	21.2	312.6
Prince Edward Island	62.9	12.8	75.7	18.5	43.5	20.9	158.5
Nova Scotia	371.9	94.8	466.7	39.9	232.9	43.6	783.1
New Brunswick	213.5	54.4	267.9	17.2	137.0	71.5	493.6
Quebec	3,132.3	581.7	3,714.0	1,008.2	1,675.6	745.0	7,142.8
Ontario	6,469.6	975.6	7,445.2	1,661.6	3,455.2	1,501.0	14,063.1
Manitoba	273.9	70.1	344.0	57.4	196.2	134.0	731.5
Saskatchewan	96.9	27.3	124.2	29.7	162.5	143.7	460.1
Alberta	1,549.6	123.1	1,672.7	364.6	717.9	261.5	3,016.8
British Columbia	2,921.9	227.8	3,149.7	179.3	1,259.4	394.7	4,983.0
Yukon	23.0	3.8	26.8	2.5	22.7	4.5	56.5
Northwest Territories	19.7	4.1	23.8	9.1	22.5	5.2	60.7
Canada	15,295.1	2,210.4	17,514.5	3,399.8	8,001.2	3,346.8	32,262.3
1991							
Newfoundland	128.8	31.2	160.0	9.8	57.6	47.6	275.0
Prince Edward Island	49.1	11.4	60.5	3.8	33.4	23.4	121.1
Nova Scotia	304.7	86.0	390.7	16.1	126.3	101.2	634.3
New Brunswick	170.6	49.1	219.7	33.3	102.4	58.4	413.9
Quebec	3,113.7	588.6	3,702.3	437.6	1,339.8	761.9	6,241.6
Ontario	6,228.2	790.7	7,018.9	1,140.1	2,271.6	1,567.1	11,997.8
Manitoba	197.3	54.3	251.6	43.5	128.7	137.3	561.1
Saskatchewan	67.9	22.9	90.8	14.9	145.3	76.4	327.5
Alberta	1,244.8	114.4	1,359.2	261.3	608.1	410.6	2,639.3
British Columbia	3,086.5	241.7	3,328.2	151.8	1,058.6	592.9	5,131.5
Yukon	21.5	5.7	27.2	4.4	11.6	30.6	73.7
Northwest Territories	20.7	1.9	22.6	3.0	22.5	3.1	51.2
Canada	14,633.8	1,997.9	16,631.7	2,119.6	5,905.9	3,810.5	28,468.0

7.2 VALUE OF BUILDING PERMITS ISSUED IN THE MOST ACTIVE MUNICIPALITIES
(MILLION DOLLARS)

	1986	1990	1991
Newfoundland			
St. John's	88.1	109.5	105.6
Prince Edward Island			
Charlottetown	17.7	23.8	481.0
Nova Scotia			
Dartmouth	80.1	91.5	80.7
Halifax	129.2	107.7	126.3
New Brunswick			
Fredericton	72.8	71.2	45.3
Moncton	51.4	47.9	33.4
Saint John	47.8	42.5	64.5
Quebec			
Gatineau	100.9	169.8	184.9
Hull	86.1	96.8	86.9
Jonquière	50.9	52.2	42.8
Laval	441.3	388.1	388.9
Longueuil	137.7	86.1	100.9
Montreal	1,022.1	1,054.7	869.6
Quebec	225.0	206.4	248.1
St. Laurent	102.0	162.9	33.4
Ste-Foy	118.0	109.3	875.0
Sherbrooke	95.9	64.8	59.9
Ontario			
Ajax	146.5	135.8	92.8
Brampton	414.7	388.3	202.7
Burlington	152.5	179.3	148.7
Cumberland	63.7	116.7	76.1
Etobicoke	180.1	396.0	168.1
Gloucester	116.8	119.7	110.9
Hamilton	381.2	384.2	147.2
Kitchener	163.4	94.9	221.0
London	327.1	444.9	289.2
Markham	295.6	347.2	308.6
Mississauga	1,095.9	966.7	910.0
Nepean	176.2	84.0	125.6
Newmarket	70.6	157.6	235.3
North York	606.9	643.7	538.8
Oakville	259.7	299.8	254.6
Oshawa	156.9	58.4	104.5
Ottawa	330.3	507.7	459.1
Pickering	184.2	103.4	100.3
Richmond Hill	313.4	326.7	479.4
St. Catharines	87.1	112.2	71.8
Scarborough	490.1	317.8	300.9
Toronto	867.2	1,290.6	727.9
Vaughan	633.0	524.8	425.2
Waterloo	158.0	89.7	93.1
Whitby	115.0	209.2	155.1
Windsor	106.3	154.0	136.2
Manitoba			
Winnipeg	600.8	467.3	345.7

7.2 VALUE OF BUILDING PERMITS ISSUED IN THE MOST ACTIVE MUNICIPALITIES
(MILLION DOLLARS) (concluded)

	1986	1990	1991
Saskatchewan			
Regina	198.7	102.0	99.2
Saskatoon	259.8	164.5	86.4
Alberta			
Calgary	569.6	946.3	759.3
Edmonton	530.8	615.4	607.5
Lethbridge	42.6	47.6	57.3
Medicine Hat	26.6	34.2	26.0
British Columbia			
Burnaby	162.8	373.8	321.2
North Vancouver	43.7	63.4	20.8
Richmond	134.9	231.2	260.9
Saanich	78.9	95.4	111.6
Surrey	310.3	607.6	586.7
Vancouver	460.2	851.4	849.0

7.3 ESTIMATED VALUE OF BUILDING PERMITS ISSUED IN CENSUS METROPOLITAN AREAS (MILLION DOLLARS)

	1986	1990	1991
Calgary	569.6	1,060.9	851.4
Chicoutimi-Jonquière	107.4	131.6	143.3
Edmonton	640.8	959.0	876.4
Halifax	384.8	380.3	299.5
Hamilton	695.3	778.1	457.3
Kitchener	451.0	376.6	454.1
London	362.6	558.0	375.0
Montreal	3,285.7	3,664.0	3,048.8
Oshawa	271.9	332.7	330.9
Ottawa-Hull	1,069.2	1,458.1	1,379.0
Quebec	662.6	758.6	851.2
Regina	198.9	112.0	105.1
St. Catharines-Niagara	250.8	408.0	256.3
Saint John	83.8	73.3	83.0
St. John's	150.5	187.7	165.1
Saskatoon	259.8	180.8	96.2
Sherbrooke	. . .	144.7	119.0
Sudbury	66.6	253.9	288.3
Thunder Bay	79.2	108.5	134.8
Toronto	5,898.7	6,391.1	5,339.8
Trois-Rivières	128.8	183.2	195.2
Vancouver	1,602.8	3,085.9	3,007.5
Victoria	229.7	387.5	337.3
Windsor	184.5	269.1	247.1
Winnipeg	611.3	480.6	361.1

7.4 VALUE OF CONSTRUCTION WORK PURCHASED (MILLION DOLLARS)

	New		Repair		Total		Total construction as percentage of Gross Domestic Expenditure	
	Current dollars	Constant 1986 dollars	Current dollars	Constant 1986 dollars	Current dollars	Constant 1986 dollars	Current dollars %	Constant 1986 dollars %
1982	46,516	51,513	9,548	11,545	56,064	63,058	15.0	14.8
1983	45,678	50,031	10,270	11,273	55,948	61,304	13.8	14.0
1984	45,770	48,383	10,804	11,555	56,574	59,938	12.7	12.8
1985	58,090	59,825	9,893	10,241	67,983	70,066	14.2	14.3
1986	61,117	61,117	10,584	10,584	71,701	71,701	14.2	14.2
1987	69,920	65,900	12,051	11,734	81,971	77,634	14.9	14.8
1988	77,353	69,004	13,518	12,610	90,871	81,614	15.0	14.8
1989	85,347	72,267	15,065	13,633	100,412	85,900	15.4	15.2
1990	87,160	72,573	15,207	13,578	102,367	86,151	15.3	15.3
1991	78,939	65,618	15,216	12,917	94,155	78,535	14.0	14.2
1992[p]	76,065	62,657	15,796	13,131	91,861	75,787	13.4	13.6
1993[e]	78,768	. . .	15,643	. . .	94,411	. . .	. . .	. . .

7.5 VALUE OF CONSTRUCTION WORK PURCHASED BY TYPE OF STRUCTURE (THOUSAND DOLLARS)

	1981	1986	1990	1991	1992[p]	1993[e]
Total construction	53,883,932	71,700,629	102,366,980	94,154,850	91,861,165	94,411,261
Total building construction	31,537,256	47,426,866	70,046,939	60,900,660	59,947,990	61,315,197
Residential	16,364,781	28,885,267	41,012,053	34,767,715	37,314,812	38,432,467
Single detached	6,100,522	9,827,291	13,408,342	10,205,943	11,129,938	12,802,046
Semi-detached including duplexes	611,443	440,084	603,049	634,133	840,453	723,108
Apartments including row housing	3,086,021	3,392,526	6,026,216	4,403,344	4,873,542	4,795,268
Other	6,566,795	15,225,366	20,974,446	19,524,295	20,470,879	20,112,045
Industrial	3,610,794	3,201,324	4,343,950	3,641,823	2,776,879	2,594,152
Commercial	6,983,185	10,119,112	16,574,178	13,436,164	11,184,899	11,146,469
Institutional	2,593,224	3,565,185	5,535,512	5,844,677	5,964,204	6,205,352
Other building construction	1,979,127	1,655,978	2,581,246	3,210,281	2,707,196	2,936,757

7.6 VALUE OF CONSTRUCTION WORK PURCHASED, NEW AND REPAIR (THOUSANDS)

1991	New	Repair	Total
Total construction	78,938,442	15,216,408	94,154,850
Total building construction	51,554,838	9,345,822	60,900,660
Residential	30,903,517	3,864,198	34,767,715
Industrial	2,550,746	1,091,077	3,641,823
Commercial	11,239,210	2,196,954	13,436,164
Institutional	4,355,341	1,489,336	5,844,677
Other building construction	2,506,024	704,257	3,210,281

1992[p]	New	Repair	Total
Total construction	76,065,359	15,795,806	91,861,165
Total building construction	50,370,621	9,577,369	59,947,990
Residential	33,246,030	4,068,782	37,314,812
Industrial	1,736,852	1,040,027	2,776,879
Commercial	9,058,242	2,126,657	11,184,899
Institutional	4,369,108	1,595,096	5,964,204
Other building construction	1,960,389	746,807	2,707,196

1993[e]	New	Repair	Total
Total construction	78,768,309	15,642,952	94,411,261
Total building construction	52,004,403	9,310,794	61,315,197
Residential	34,552,647	3,879,820	38,432,467
Industrial	1,502,051	1,092,101	2,594,152
Commercial	9,114,816	2,031,653	11,146,469
Institutional	4,640,219	1,565,133	6,205,352
Other building construction	2,194,670	742,087	2,936,757

7.7 HOUSING STOCK, 1992

	Permanent residence		Temporary residence	
	Single	Multiple	Mobile homes	Cottages
Newfoundland	138,968	43,293	2,470	..
Prince Edward Island	33,798	11,006	820	..
Nova Scotia	227,404	98,004	5,290	..
New Brunswick	186,834	64,495	2,391	..
Quebec	1,225,956	1,522,812	16,772	..
Ontario	2,170,224	1,621,215	7,854	..
Manitoba	283,146	126,933	5,860	..
Saskatchewan	286,692	88,063	5,532	..
Alberta	595,809	323,963	18,491	..
British Columbia	764,901	507,693	32,406	..
Yukon and Northwest Territories	17,035	9,400	2,369	..
Canada	5,930,767	4,416,877	100,291	570,266

7.8 NEW HOUSING PRICE INDEXES (1986 = 100)

	1988	1989	1990	1991	1992
St. John's	107.4	113.2	117.3	125.8	126.8
Halifax	107.2	109.2	109.5	109.3	110.5
Saint John-Moncton	107.8	111.6	113.2	114.2	115.3
Quebec	118.4	126.6	130.8	134.5	135.5
Montreal	126.0	130.2	133.7	134.6	134.7
Ottawa-Hull	112.7	119.1	123.8	123.3	123.4
Toronto	147.2	180.2	173.3	147.2	140.7
Hamilton	130.3	141.3	144.5	136.0	131.0
St. Catharines-Niagara	119.9	130.0	139.0	134.2	130.9
London	125.1	137.3	145.1	145.9	146.2
Kitchener-Waterloo	124.7	137.5	140.2	129.3	125.4
Windsor	112.3	122.3	127.7	127.7	127.6
Sudbury-Thunder Bay	118.1	125.8	132.9	133.4	132.8
Winnipeg	107.1	106.6	108.7	108.5	108.4
Regina	105.2	106.9	108.9	111.4	116.6
Saskatoon	106.1	106.9	107.6	106.7	107.2
Calgary	113.0	121.1	136.2	132.5	133.3
Edmonton	109.5	118.6	137.5	140.6	141.9
Vancouver	109.9	127.1	134.4	124.7	135.7
Victoria	104.8	115.2	123.3	121.5	127.5
Canada	125.6	142.2	144.3	134.3	134.3

Source
Statistics Canada

J. COCHRANE / FIRST LIGHT

CHAPTER EIGHT

INCOME SECURITY

INTRODUCTION

Canadians are on record for wanting to lend a helping hand. A goodly number translate this concern for others into doing volunteer work. It may be anything from fundraising, providing information or organizing events to fire-fighting, first aid or search and rescue; it can be for religious, sport and recreation or social service organizations; but over 5 million Canadians — 27% of the adult population — were volunteering their time and skills to help others in 1987. The 1 billion hours contributed in a 12-month period would have amounted to over half a million full-time jobs.

A significant number of volunteer jobs serve health and social service organizations. The efforts of volunteers in the past — often linked to religious organizations — laid the foundation for the array of social services available today. With the Great Depression of the 1930s, when 30% of the labour force was unemployed, Canadians came to see unemployment as a national problem, and demanded that government take a more active role in providing economic security. In 1940, the British North America Act was amended to allow the federal government to legislate on social welfare and a nationwide program of unemployment insurance was introduced.

Since this historical departure, Canada has developed a social security network for families, for the elderly, for aboriginal peoples, for veterans — for virtually anyone in Canada who may need it.

BRIGHTER FUTURES
FOR FAMILIES

Delivery of federal family benefits changed in 1993 with the introduction of the Child Tax Benefit. The Child Tax Benefit consolidated the existing programs for family allowances, the refundable Child Tax Credit and the non-refundable Dependent Child Tax Credit into a single monthly payment. A supplement provides additional benefits to low-income working families with children. Monthly payments are based on the latest tax information on family income and are updated automatically to reflect any change in family status. While the benefits paid under the Family Allowances Program were universal, they were taxable. Payments made to eligible recipients for the Child Tax Benefit are not taxable.

The Child Tax Benefit is one of a series of steps proposed by the government to improve the education, protection and nurturing of Canada's children. In September 1990, the leaders of 71 nations gathered at the United Nations World Summit for Children to commit their governments to acting on behalf of the world's children. The summit participants prepared a *World Declaration on the Survival, Protection and Development of Children and Plan of Action*. In May 1991, the Government of Canada set up a Children's Bureau to co-ordinate Canada's response to the declaration. In December 1991, the Convention on the Rights of the Child was ratified, providing a set of standards designed to ensure respect for all children.

FAMILY VIOLENCE INITIATIVE
In 1991, the federal government announced a $136 million four-year Family Violence Initiative involving seven federal departments. In that year, Statistics Canada reported that 54% of female homicide victims were killed by a family member. The initiative is directed at six areas of action: mobilizing community action; helping service providers and professionals do their jobs better; improving treatment and support for victims; sharing information and solutions; providing better national information about the extent and nature of family violence; and co-ordinating federal action on family violence.

INCOME SUPPLEMENTS All Canadian provinces offer income supplements to qualified low-income families. A few provinces have implemented initiatives specifically for low-income households not eligible to receive social assistance. In 1988, Quebec initiated its Parental Wage Assistance Program, which supplements employment income, partially reimburses day-care expenses and provides special benefits to families with high shelter costs. For families with children, this replaces the Work Income Supplement Program; there is currently no income supplementation for single persons and childless couples in Quebec.

Todd Korol / First Light

Manitoba's Child Related Income Support Program and Saskatchewan's Family Income Plan support low-income families with children.

SENIOR CITIZENS

Both the federal and provincial governments provide income support programs for Canadian seniors. In addition, all three orders of government offer supplementary social services.

INCOME SUPPORT PROGRAMS

A program of pensions for the elderly introduced in 1927 was the federal government's first major sortie into the social security arena. In 1991, the $17.1 billion spent on this program represented the largest single expenditure under social security programs.

Canada's Old Age Security pension today provides monthly benefits to individuals aged 65 and over who meet residency requirements. Since 1967, pensioners with little or no other income have also been eligible for the Guaranteed Income Supplement. In addition, Spouse's Allowances have been available since 1975 to spouses of pensioners when the couple has little or no income other than the pension. In 1979, Spouse's Allowances became available to low-income surviving spouses of pensioners. This provision was expanded in 1985 to include widows and widowers aged 60 to 64, subject to an income test.

Reciprocal international social security agreements help people qualify for benefits by letting them add periods of residence in another country to years of residence in Canada, or vice versa. As of July 1992, Canada had reciprocal agreements with 24 other countries.

WEAVING THE SOCIAL SAFETY NET

Legislative milestones in the development of the Social Security System:

YEAR	ACT
1914	Ontario Workmen's Compensation Act
1916	Manitoba Mothers' Pension Act
	Saskatchewan Union Hospital Act
1927	Federal Old Age Pensions Act
1930	Federal War Veterans' Allowances Act
1935	Federal Employment and Social Insurance Act (ruled *ultra vires* by courts)
1940	Federal Unemployment Insurance Act (major reforms in 1955 and 1971)
1944	Family Allowances Act
1946	Saskatchewan Hospitalization Act
1951	Federal Old Age Assistance Act and Old Age Security Act (replaced Old Age Pensions Act)
	Federal Blind Persons Act
1954	Federal Disabled Persons Act
1956	Federal Unemployment Assistance Act
1957	Federal Hospital Insurance and Diagnostic Services Act
1961	Quebec School Allowances Act

YEAR	ACT
1962	Saskatchewan Medical Care Insurance Act
1964	Federal Youth Allowances Act
1966	Federal Canada Pension Plan Act
	Federal Canada Assistance Plan Act (ultimately earlier assistance legislation for the blind, disabled, elderly and unemployed were repealed)
	Federal Medical Care Act
1967	Federal Guaranteed Income Supplement introduced to Old Age Security Act
1973	New federal Family Allowances Act (replaced old act of same name and Youth Allowances Act)
1977	Federal Extended Health Care Services Program implemented in Federal-Provincial Fiscal Arrangements and Established Programs Financing Act
1978	Federal Child Tax Credit introduced to Income Tax Act
1984	Federal Canada Health Act (replaced Hospital Insurance and Diagnostic Services Act and Medical Care Act)
1992	Federal Child Tax Benefit introduced to Income Tax Act (Child Tax Credit deleted and Family Allowances Act repealed)

PENSION PLANS Many Canadian seniors receive income from the Canada and Quebec Pension Plans which provide monthly benefits to retired contributors.

In the Canada Pension Plan (CPP) and the Quebec Pension Plan (QPP), both employees and employers contributed an amount equal to 2.4% of the employee's eligible earnings in 1992. Self-employed persons contributed the full 4.8%.

The CPP and QPP provide similar benefits to contributors and their families. They are reciprocal: people who have contributed to both plans apply for benefits where they live. The contributor's place of residence at the time of death determines which plan pays survivors' benefits.

Children's benefits are given to dependent children of disabled pensioners. Orphans' benefits apply to the dependent children of a deceased contributor. Benefits are paid until age 18, but may be extended to age 25 if the child is attending school full time. Dependent children are eligible for two CPP benefits if both parents' earnings have been lost through disability or death. In 1992, the monthly CPP children's benefit was $154.70 per child; that of the QPP was $29.00.

A death benefit is payable to the estate of a deceased contributor who has contributed to the plan for at least three years. In 1992, the maximum death benefit was $3,220 under both the CPP and the QPP.

Assignment of pensions On retirement, either spouse in a marriage or common-law union may apply to share pension benefits earned during the union. Both spouses must be aged at least 60 and must have applied for the retirement benefits to which they are entitled.

Division of Pension Credits Under the CPP, provisions for dividing pension credits between spouses in the event of divorce or annulment were introduced in 1978 and substantially revised in 1987. For divorce and for legal or common-law separation, spouses who have lived together for at least one year now divide equally all CPP pension credits earned while they lived together. (This does not occur if both parties have signed a spousal agreement containing a credit-splitting waiver; however, such waivers are legal only in Saskatchewan.)

Under the QPP, spouses who have divorced or received a legal annulment on or after January 1, 1977 may apply for division of pension credits provided they lived with their spouse for at least three years. There are no credit-splitting provisions for separations.

SOCIAL SERVICES Seniors Independence Program Scientists are discovering that exercise programs can increase the physical strength of elderly people and decrease their dependence on institutional care. The Seniors Independence Program, introduced in 1988, funds health, education or social welfare projects that improve the quality of life for seniors. The program emphasizes community-based projects involving seniors and promoting independent living. The program includes both extended projects and conferences and workshops at the local, regional and national level.

New Horizons Program Established in 1972 to reduce the social isolation and loneliness of the elderly, the program helps senior citizens' groups help themselves while contributing to their communities. In 1990-91, just over $15 million was spent on 1,888 New Horizons Projects.

The program marked its 20th anniversary in 1992. Special activities included a national conference, Interchange Canada, sponsored by the Alberta Council on Aging. The conference enabled 50 seniors from across Canada to share their New Horizons project experiences with a view to bringing new ideas back to their organizations.

INCOME SUPPLEMENTS All but five provincial governments provide monthly, quarterly or annual income supplements for the elderly. Two provinces and both territories also extend benefits to Spouse's Allowance recipients. Manitoba covers residents over 55 whose incomes do not exceed specific levels. Alberta covers low-income widows and widowers over 55. The Saskatchewan Income Plan covers seniors who receive the Guaranteed Income Supplement and whose incomes do not exceed specific levels. Provincial governments may also offer property-related or shelter-related tax credits, grants or rebates.

Nick Boothman / Masterfile

Tea time, Victoria, British Columbia.

VETERANS

Canada has long recognized the sacrifice, hardship and suffering of veterans and civilians in Canada's war and peacekeeping efforts. The Department of Veterans Affairs has developed programs and activities to respond to their needs.

Assistance for veterans and their dependents is administered by the Department of Veterans Affairs, the Canadian Pension Commission, the Veterans Appeal Board, and the Bureau of Pensions Advocates.

SERVICES FOR VETERANS

The Department of Veterans Affairs provides medical treatment, in-home care, housing, educational assistance, counselling and other services to veterans and their spouses, widows, widowers and children. Civilians who served in close support of the armed forces in wartime are also eligible for these programs.

Health care and treatment for veterans is available throughout Canada at veterans' hospitals and homes, in private facilities funded by the department, and in individual homes and communities. Outside Canada,

ALIMONY AND CHILD SUPPORT

In Canada, alimony and child support payments total a billion and a half dollars a year, and the bulk of this money goes toward single mothers with children.

According to a Statistics Canada study, **Alimony and Child Support**, support payments in 1990 averaged about $400 a month. The report points out, however, that families who receive support payments form only a small part of the general population.

For women, support payments totalled 14% of their average yearly family income.

Among men paying support, the financial outlay represented an average of 9% of their family income.

The average family income of women who received support payments was almost two-thirds that of the men who paid them. While women's average incomes generally are lower than those of men, this difference is greater than for men and women in the general population.

While the report focused on women, it did note that a few men are paid support: about 2% of all recipients in 1990.

In 1990, federal tax records showed that some 312,000 Canadian men reported paying support, while 265,000 women reported receiving it. The difference is due to a number of facts: some recipients may not have filed tax returns because their income was too low; some received their income solely from welfare payments, mothers' allowance and other non-taxable benefits; and some lived outside the country.

The issue of support has been the subject of much concern in Canada, partly because those ordered to make payments have not always done so. As well, there has been concern that average child support payments might be inadequate when measured against the actual costs of raising children. In recent years, all levels of government have been working to make support orders fairer, more consistent and more enforceable.

Responsibility for enforcing support payment agreements within the country falls under provincial or territorial jurisdiction. During the past 10 years, every province and territory in Canada has set up programs to enforce support payments. The federal government contributes to these programs by searching federal data banks for defaulters, and garnishing federal monies where appropriate.

In 1990, federal, provincial and territorial justice ministers set up the Child Support Guidelines Project. This project is studying different ways of setting child support payments, based on economic studies of actual costs of raising children.

In 1992, the Department of Justice also set up a $5.5 million Family Support Enforcement Fund to help provinces and territories reduce the number of people defaulting on support payments.

And in early 1993, Parliament amended the Family Orders and Agreement Assistance Act to allow the Justice Department to trace child support debtors for one year, and to garnish any federal monies payable to them for a period of five years.

Federal Income Security Expenditures

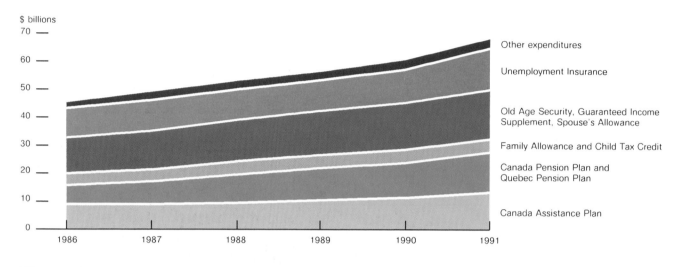

Veterans Affairs pays for health care and treatment of conditions resulting from war service. The department also pays for prosthetic devices that help minimize handicaps. The Veterans Independence Program helps aging veterans remain independent and healthy in their own homes and communities.

Special programs meet specific needs or help perpetuate the memory of deceased veterans. These programs include the Assistance Fund, the Educational Assistance Program, funeral and burial assistance, veterans' insurance, and the maintenance of veterans' cemeteries, plots and memorials in Canada and abroad.

PENSIONS AND ALLOWANCES

As might be expected, the number of recipients of war veterans' allowances and pensions is dwindling — from over 88,000 in 1984 to fewer than 57,000 in 1990. Nevertheless, expenditures on veterans' benefits amounted to $1.2 billion in 1991.

The Canadian Pension Commission administers most aspects of the Pension Act, the Compensation for Former Prisoners of War Act, and parts of the Merchant Navy Veteran and Civilian War-related Benefits Act.

Pensions for Death and Disability Under the Pension Act, Canadians affected by injuries or diseases incurred during service with Canadian forces qualify for pensions as do dependents of a disabled member of the forces or the dependents of a war veteran. Disability pension rates are set by the Pension Act and are indexed to account for inflation.

Former prisoners of war and their dependents receive regular payments under the Compensation for Former Prisoners of War Act. These payments may be in addition to a disability pension.

Under the Merchant Navy Veteran and Civilian War-related Benefits Act, benefits are available to merchant navy veterans and some groups of civilians and their widows, widowers or orphans.

Allowances War veterans who, because of age or incapacity, can no longer maintain their income at a specified level receive assistance under the War Veterans Allowance Act. Widows, widowers and orphans of qualified veterans are also eligible for benefits.

Reviews and Appeals Clients not satisfied with decisions on disability pensions, allowances or health care may appeal or ask to have their cases reviewed. The Veterans Appeal Board hears appeals against decisions of the Assessment and Entitlement Boards of the Canadian Pension Commission in disability matters, and appeals from decisions of Regional Review Committees of the department in allowance matters.

The Bureau of Pensions Advocates provides free legal aid to individuals seeking to establish claims for pensions and allowances. The bureau will initiate claims, search records, identify evidence, counsel applicants, and prepare and present claims to the Canadian Pension Commission and its Entitlement and Assessment Boards. The bureau also represents eligible allowance applicants on appeals to the Veterans Appeal Board.

ABORIGINAL PEOPLES

In September 1990, the Department of Indian Affairs and Northern Development (DIAND) launched the Native Agenda to help settle land claims, improve economic and social conditions on reserves, build a new relationship between Canada and native peoples, and address the concerns of native people in contemporary Canadian society. The department is transferring to aboriginal reserve communities the responsibility for managing their own affairs. They now control 77% of all Indian and Inuit affairs funds. Funds are used for housing, education and economic development, as well as to provide child and family services, prevent family violence and provide adult care services, social assistance and other social services.

The department provides child and family services funds for child protection services, institutional, foster and group home placements, and counselling and prevention services to maintain family unity. These services are delivered through provincial agencies or through the expanding network of Indian Child and Family Services agencies. Under the Family Violence Initiative, the department provides funds to native communities for services dealing with family violence.

Adult care helps the elderly and the physically disabled or mentally handicapped maintain their independence. Services include homemaking assistance, foster care and institutional care.

DIAND offers financial support to band councils and their staff, and funds projects such as drop-in centres, hotlines and rehabilitation counselling.

Under the Government of Canada's Brighter Futures Action Plan, an Indian and Inuit Community Action Strategy addresses three key areas of concern: promoting community mental health; establishing child development programs; and supporting affected communities in dealing with substance abuse.

Expenditures on social assistance and social services to registered natives exceeded $624 million in 1990.

SECURITY FOR ALL: THE CANADA ASSISTANCE PLAN

Through the Canada Assistance Plan (CAP), the federal government works with the provinces to help families and individuals in need, regardless of cause.

The plan is actually a consolidation of four cost-shared programs: the 1951 Old Age Assistance Act, the 1951 Blind Persons Allowance Act, the 1954 Disabled Persons Allowance Act and the 1956 Unemployment Assistance Act. CAP also extended cost-sharing to provincial mothers' allowance programs and to welfare services, including those for children.

Eligibility for programs that are cost-shared under CAP is based on a needs test that examines a family's basic requirements and the income and assets available to meet them. Assistance covers food, clothing, shelter, fuel, utilities, household and personal needs, special needs, welfare services, and specified health and social services. CAP also covers job-search and certain other employment-related needs.

CAP can also cover child welfare services and some of the costs for special-care facilities, including homes for the aged, nursing homes, child-care facilities and hostels for battered women and children.

PROVINCIAL SOCIAL SERVICES

Social services vary at the community level as well as by province, depending on needs and available resources. The federal government, through CAP, shares in the costs of many of these programs.

UNEMPLOYMENT INSURANCE CLAIMANTS COME BACK

During the 1990-91 recession, long line-ups for Unemployment Insurance (UI) benefits were common at government employment offices everywhere. However, for many of those waiting in line, the claims process had become all too familiar — chances are they'd been there before.

A recent study by the Economic Council of Canada detailing the history of UI claimants from 1971 to 1989 shows that most of recent claimants are 'repeat users'. Of the more than 1,800,000 UI claims made in 1989, roughly 80% were made by people who had received UI benefits before.

Men were more likely than women to be repeat users of UI benefits. In 1989, some 48% of claims made by men were made by those with four or more prior claims, compared to 30% of UI claims made by women.

Repeat use was far more prevalent in the Atlantic provinces than in the rest of the country. For example, over 90% of claims made in Newfoundland and Prince Edward Island in 1989 were made by those with prior claims.

According to the study, it can be expected that a male with at least one UI claim will make another one every three to four years, while a female with at least one claim will make another one every four to five years.

Some critics have argued that the availability and accessibility of UI benefits are partly to blame for the high levels of repeat users. Seasonal workers, for example, often take UI benefits for granted, relying on UI during the off-season instead of looking for employment year-round.

Some social service programs focus on alleviating immediate problems, such as crises, while others involve long-term services. All are guided by a desire to help disadvantaged individuals help themselves, and to prevent, delay or reduce the need for institutional care of the elderly and disabled. Social services also help support families affected by such things as divorce or separation or a move to a new community.

Services funded in part by CAP include: crisis intervention, referrals, and social integration services to help individuals isolated from community life; day care and protective and developmental welfare services for children; and home support to enable people to remain in their own homes. Personal, family and financial counselling are also available. A range of community and residential programs exists to reduce family violence and deal with its consequences.

Communities offer activity centres, sheltered workshops, vocational rehabilitation and day programs for the elderly. The provinces provide nursing and medical services, nutrition counselling, nursing home and intermediate care, residential care, and ambulatory health services.

Federal and provincial expenditures under the Canada Assistance Plan amounted to $12.6 billion in 1991.

INCOME SECURITY

FEDERAL Unemployment Insurance In the United States, income inequality (the rich getting richer and the poor getting poorer) increased dramatically throughout the 1980s. In Canada, income 'safety nets' such as Unemployment Insurance decrease the likelihood of this gap widening.

The Unemployment Insurance Program, funded through employer and employee contributions, was originally designed as an insurance scheme to protect workers during short periods of unemployment. By 1971, the program covered virtually the entire labour force including self-employed fishers. It has gradually been broadened to provide benefits for individuals leaving the labour force temporarily because of illness, pregnancy, care of a newborn (parental benefits) and for those participating in work sharing and job

Provincial, Territorial and Municipal Income Security Expenditures

creation projects and job training. Assistance is also provided to unemployed workers attending courses, moving to seek employment or attempting to become self-employed.

In December 1992, over 1.2 million people were receiving regular Unemployment Insurance benefits. In 1992, some $19.3 billion was disbursed, an increase of 9% over the total for 1991. Over the same period, the average weekly payment rose 4.4% to $254.72, and the number of benefit-weeks rose 3.3%. At the same time, the total number of claims received was down 1.8%.

Canadian Jobs Strategy The federal government introduced its Canadian Jobs Strategy in 1985 to provide equal opportunities for all Canadians, particularly those at a disadvantage in the labour market, by giving allowances to encourage skills upgrading. Special emphasis is given to the four groups designated in the Employment Equity Act — women, persons with disabilities, aboriginal peoples and visible minorities. In 1991, expenditures on this program were $1.5 billion.

PROVINCIAL ASSISTANCE Each province designs and administers its own social assistance program, which the federal government partly

funds. Most provincial governments cover both long- and short-term assistance. In Nova Scotia, Ontario and Manitoba, the provincial governments cover long-term assistance, while short-term and emergency assistance is the responsibility of municipalities.

Social assistance covers the cost of food, clothing, household and personal needs, shelter, fuel, items of special need and other essential items. Services such as training, counselling and health care may also be provided. Benefit levels vary by province and may also be affected by the applicant's age, health and employability.

Workers' Compensation The Ontario Workmen's Compensation Act of 1914 was Canada's first modern social security program. Other provinces soon followed this example. Provincial programs provide income compensation and medical and rehabilitative services for those injured at work. The programs are administered by boards on behalf of the province's employers, who fund the program.

Tax Credits In nearly all provinces, homeowners and renters are eligible for income tax or property tax credits or rebates, or shelter subsidies or grants. These concessions help families and the elderly meet the high costs of shelter. Rebates are administered by income tax or property tax collection authorities;

Thomas Bruckbauer / First Light

Three generations, Robson Square, Vancouver.

shelter allowances are usually paid by provincial housing authorities.

Some provinces have expanded their tax credit programs in recent years. For example, Ontario now offers a home-ownership savings plan tax credit, and Manitoba provides a cost-of-living credit. In total, the provinces offer over 40 tax credit and rebate and shelter assistance programs.

Disabled People Various types of financial support, including those mentioned above, are available to disabled people. Provincial vocational programs for the physically and mentally handicapped help

disabled people maintain their independence by getting jobs, becoming self-employed or finding sheltered employment or other paid work. In 1990-91, some $222 million was spent on these programs. This cost was shared by the federal government under the Vocational Rehabilitation of Disabled Persons Act.

Income assistance for disabled people includes needs-tested social assistance programs in all provinces, such as British Columbia's Handicapped Benefits under the Guaranteed Available Income for Need Act and Ontario's Guaranteed Annual Income System for the Disabled. In addition, Alberta offers an income-tested flat rate benefit for disabled people under the Assured

Income for the Severely Handicapped program. Most provinces offer financial assistance to families caring for a disabled child at home.

Also contributing to income security is minimum wage legislation enacted by the provinces.

CANADA'S SOCIAL SECURITY NETWORK

Social security means more than income security and social assistance programs. It also means reaching out for new ideas and approaches.

The National Welfare Grants program develops and strengthens social services by funding social welfare research carried out by provincial and municipal social service departments, non-governmental organizations or universities. The program also offers fellowships for advanced training in social welfare. In 1990-91, program expenditures were about $7.9 million.

As part of an innovative response to a serious social problem, the federal government helps the provinces expand and improve alcohol and drug treatment and rehabilitation programs, particularly for young people.

ON THE INTERNATIONAL SCENE

Canada plays an important role in the social development activities of the United Nations, particularly through the United Nations International Children's Emergency Fund (UNICEF). Canada is also active in the social programs of the Organization for Economic Co-operation and Development (OECD). Canada exchanges information on social affairs with, among others, the Council of Europe, the OECD, the Overseas Development Institute and the social affairs departments of other countries. Canada also belongs to the International Social Security Association, the International Council on Social Welfare, and the social security program of the International Labour Organization. Through these international ventures, Canada contributes its own experience while receiving valuable information on the maintenance and development of social security in other countries.

THE NEW CHILD TAX BENEFIT

*C*anada's first universal social program was the federal Family Allowances program, which was introduced in 1945 and paid a monthly allowance to families with children to help cover the costs of raising a family.

In January 1993, Canadians bid farewell to the Family Allowances program, as it was merged into a larger program targetting families with children.

Instead of the now-familiar family allowance cheques, Canadian families who qualify will now receive a monthly cheque called the Child Tax Benefit. The Child Tax Benefit consolidates Family Allowances, the refundable Child Tax Credit and the non-refundable Dependent Child Tax Credit into a single monthly payment. The new program currently pays out about $5 billion in benefits.

Under the new system, a larger proportion of benefits will be directed towards low-income and modest-income families. A single mother of two young children, for example, with an annual income of $18,000, will receive roughly $2,500 per year — over $600 more than under the old system.

THE COST OF SECURITY

In 1990-91, Canada's income security system delivered an estimated $78 billion in direct financial benefits, compared to $56.5 billion in 1986-87. Aid to the elderly accounted for more than one-fifth of total expenditures. From 1986-87 to 1990-91, the disability and retirement components of the Canada and Quebec Pensions Plans increased more than any other program: payments for disability rose 87% to $1.9 billion, and retirement payments climbed nearly 81% to $9.1 billion. The largest decrease occurred in the War Veteran's Allowance program, where expenditures dropped almost 49% in 1990-91.

Continuing to address the needs of families and the disabled is an important goal of the federal government. In its 1992 budget, the government proposed tax measures to reform the child benefit system, to treat common-law couples the same as married couples for tax purposes, and to provide additional support to the disabled. While the cost of providing social security may be high, Canadians believe — and their action as volunteers bears this out — that the cost to society of not doing so is much higher.

SOURCES

Health and Welfare Canada

Indian and Northern Affairs Canada

Statistics Canada

Veterans Affairs Canada

FOR FURTHER READING

Selected publications from Statistics Canada

▲ *Health and Social Support, 1985. 11-612E No. 1*

▲ *Giving Freely: Volunteers in Canada, Doreen Duchesne. 71-535 No. 4*

▲ *Unemployment Insurance Statistics. Monthly. 73-001*

▲ *Unemployment Insurance Statistics, Annual Supplement. Annual. 73-202S*

TABLES

8.1 CANADA ASSISTANCE PLAN[1]

	General assistance beneficiaries[2] (Including dependents)					
	1986	1987	1988	1989	1990	1991
Newfoundland	47,000	50,500	47,900	44,800	47,900	51,800
Prince Edward Island	9,200	9,300	8,900	8,300	8,600	10,300
Nova Scotia	72,100	73,000	73,800	75,600	78,900	86,200
New Brunswick	68,800	73,700	70,600	67,700	67,200	71,900
Quebec	693,900	649,600	594,000	559,300	555,900	594,900
Ontario	485,800	518,400	533,500	588,200	675,700	929,900
Manitoba	62,600	60,600	62,700	63,000	66,900	71,700
Saskatchewan	62,700	62,100	60,300	57,200	54,100	53,400
Alberta	126,600	150,500	149,800	151,700	148,800	156,600
British Columbia	255,700	247,700	241,100	230,000	216,000	244,000
Yukon	1,400	1,200	1,100	900	1,000	1,200
Northwest Territories	7,100	8,300	9,300	9,400	10,000	10,300
Canada	1,892,900	1,904,900	1,853,000	1,856,100	1,931,000	2,282,200

	General assistance expenditures (total federal-provincial[3]) ($'000,000)					
	1986	1987	1988	1989	1990	1991
Newfoundland	85.2	108.0	107.8	109.3	119.2	142.5
Prince Edward Island	22.4	23.2	24.6	24.9	27.5	33.1
Nova Scotia	143.3	165.2	178.5	204.9	219.9	249.3
New Brunswick	206.7	229.3	235.0	227.5	236.2	261.1
Quebec	2,221.9	2,146.7	2,118.1	2,121.5	2,144.0	2,408.6
Ontario	1,479.5	1,642.8	1,831.5	2,124.4	2,425.1	3,639.2
Manitoba	156.8	179.8	177.8	219.1	206.3	242.3
Saskatchewan	190.7	215.5	215.0	200.1	189.3	201.5
Alberta	481.7	543.4	593.0	655.7	683.5	710.3
British Columbia	879.0	859.7	895.1	878.4	872.3	966.6
Yukon	2.2	--	1.3	6.1	2.8	3.6
Northwest Territories	11.0	12.0	16.2	14.4	20.3	24.7
Canada	5,880.4	6,125.7	6,393.9	6,786.3	7,146.3	8,882.8

[1] Fiscal years ending March 31st.
[2] Beneficiaries as of March 31st of each fiscal year.
[3] Total federal-provincial expenditures are estimates. They have been calculated by doubling the federal amount paid for claims received each year.

8.2 SENIOR CITIZENS' BENEFITS[1]

	Old Age Security (OAS), annual average number of beneficiaries					
	1986	1987	1988	1989	1990	1991
Newfoundland	49,686	50,808	52,079	53,076	53,974	54,784
Prince Edward Island	15,835	16,029	16,199	16,347	16,545	16,718
Nova Scotia	102,166	104,402	106,671	108,412	110,104	111,669
New Brunswick	78,238	80,068	82,239	83,836	85,369	87,083
Quebec	635,335	655,714	677,648	697,799	719,400	741,380
Ontario	955,854	990,665	1,026,282	1,058,044	1,091,477	1,124,959
Manitoba	131,629	134,201	137,063	139,305	141,659	143,930
Saskatchewan	126,197	128,481	131,073	133,086	135,293	137,266
Alberta	181,436	188,579	196,006	202,528	209,585	217,489
British Columbia	331,271	344,830	358,528	370,758	383,422	395,978
Yukon	804	843	894	918	970	1,005
Northwest Territories	1,349	1,400	1,428	1,451	1,491	1,538
International operations[2]	6,961	10,657	14,265	17,477	21,111	25,232
Canada	2,616,762	2,706,676	2,800,375	2,883,037	2,970,401	3,059,029

	OAS, net benefit expenditures ($'000,000)					
	1986	1987	1988	1989	1990	1991
Newfoundland	168.4	179.7	191.6	203.2	216.7	230.3
Prince Edward Island	53.4	56.3	59.4	62.4	66.2	70.0
Nova Scotia	345.4	367.8	391.7	414.2	441.4	468.8
New Brunswick	264.5	281.8	301.4	320.1	341.3	365.2
Quebec	2,157.3	2,314.1	2,493.6	2,671.0	2,884.8	3,113.3
Ontario	3,244.5	3,495.0	3,768.0	4,041.2	4,350.1	4,689.0
Manitoba	444.4	471.3	501.7	529.9	564.4	599.8
Saskatchewan	426.4	452.3	481.1	507.8	541.5	574.9
Alberta	616.2	666.4	720.3	774.3	837.4	908.4
British Columbia	1,120.6	1,214.8	1,314.7	1,411.3	1,526.9	1,646.6
Yukon	2.8	3.0	3.3	3.6	4.0	4.3
Northwest Territories	4.7	5.1	5.3	5.7	6.2	6.6
International operations[2]	9.1	12.9	15.6	18.7	23.2	28.0
Canada	8,857.7	9,520.0	10,247.7	10,963.4	11,803.8	12,705.2

	Guaranteed Income Supplement (GIS), annual average number of beneficiaries					
	1986	1987	1988	1989	1990	1991
Newfoundland	39,652	40,196	41,325	41,640	41,770	41,431
Prince Edward Island	10,914	10,897	10,903	10,872	10,810	10,588
Nova Scotia	64,525	64,461	65,417	65,031	64,385	63,085
New Brunswick	51,172	51,562	52,547	52,672	52,555	51,624
Quebec	385,965	391,496	403,480	408,919	412,510	407,201
Ontario	386,762	393,438	402,753	400,207	393,091	376,564
Manitoba	66,343	66,881	67,913	67,747	66,725	64,205
Saskatchewan	61,985	62,982	64,049	64,362	64,277	62,321
Alberta	85,626	87,892	91,735	92,899	93,145	90,568
British Columbia	141,528	144,362	149,029	150,845	150,598	144,204
Yukon	406	433	464	455	468	456
Northwest Territories	1,092	1,135	1,179	1,172	1,193	1,168
International operations[2]	3,051	4,327	5,878	6,711	7,569	7,819
Canada	1,299,019	1,320,059	1,356,672	1,363,532	1,359,096	1,321,234

8.2   **SENIOR CITIZENS' BENEFITS**[1] (concluded)

	GIS, net benefit expenditures ($'000,000)					
	1986	1987	1988	1989	1990	1991
Newfoundland	110.0	114.8	120.5	125.1	130.4	133.9
Prince Edward Island	29.6	30.5	31.6	32.4	33.4	33.5
Nova Scotia	166.4	172.0	178.0	182.4	186.5	189.1
New Brunswick	134.5	139.5	145.5	150.4	155.2	158.6
Quebec	1,009.9	1,043.2	1,097.9	1,150.1	1,188.8	1,248.4
Ontario	944.5	978.2	1,020.0	1,050.4	1,066.6	1,081.8
Manitoba	166.4	172.0	178.5	184.8	187.4	186.0
Saskatchewan	160.1	166.7	174.0	180.9	185.7	185.0
Alberta	217.4	228.1	242.7	254.7	264.4	268.7
British Columbia	350.1	366.7	384.9	404.3	416.4	423.7
Yukon	1.3	1.4	1.5	1.5	1.5	1.6
Northwest Territories	3.7	4.0	4.2	4.3	4.5	4.8
International operations[2]	25.4	34.2	38.8	44.5	52.4	60.6
Canada	3,319.4	3,451.3	3,618.1	3,765.8	3,873.2	3,975.7

	Spouse's Allowance (SPA), annual average number of beneficiaries					
	1986	1987	1988	1989	1990	1991
Newfoundland	4,287	5,108	5,109	4,994	5,009	4,874
Prince Edward Island	961	1,090	1,086	1,010	971	920
Nova Scotia	5,967	7,016	6,991	6,609	6,399	6,123
New Brunswick	5,264	6,109	5,870	5,732	5,622	5,373
Quebec	35,591	44,202	44,744	44,099	42,709	41,082
Ontario	31,218	41,568	41,303	38,239	34,744	31,689
Manitoba	5,562	6,563	6,294	5,852	5,451	5,104
Saskatchewan	4,984	5,911	5,874	5,646	5,494	5,287
Alberta	6,813	8,689	8,862	8,706	8,336	7,854
British Columbia	11,121	13,594	13,523	12,866	12,026	10,850
Yukon	30	52	51	46	41	39
Northwest Territories	68	97	110	116	129	126
International operations[2]	118	221	342	364	377	359
Canada	111,984	140,219	140,159	134,279	127,308	119,677

	SPA, net benefit expenditures ($'000,000)					
	1986	1987	1988	1989	1990	1991
Newfoundland	17.6	22.3	22.6	22.1	22.7	22.8
Prince Edward Island	3.6	4.4	4.5	4.3	4.2	4.0
Nova Scotia	20.4	26.1	26.1	25.1	24.7	24.3
New Brunswick	18.6	23.5	23.5	22.8	23.0	23.0
Quebec	111.7	147.5	149.5	151.2	152.4	150.6
Ontario	87.5	130.3	134.7	128.1	118.8	112.1
Manitoba	17.2	22.1	21.9	21.1	20.2	19.7
Saskatchewan	16.0	20.4	20.7	20.7	20.4	20.5
Alberta	21.3	29.4	30.8	30.3	30.1	29.5
British Columbia	32.5	44.4	44.9	44.0	42.0	39.6
Yukon	0.1	0.2	0.2	0.2	0.2	0.2
Northwest Territories	0.4	0.6	0.7	0.8	0.8	0.9
International operations[2]	0.8	1.9	2.4	2.7	2.6	2.8
Canada	347.8	473.2	482.5	473.4	462.1	449.9

[1] *Fiscal years ending March 31st.*
[2] *All persons paid under international agreements, including persons outside Canada.*

8.3 CANADA PENSION PLAN AND QUEBEC PENSION PLAN[1]

	Annual average number of beneficiaries				
	Retirement pensions	Disability pensions	Survivors' pensions[2]	Children's benefits[3]	Total
1986	1,518,571	175,271	536,611	190,250	2,420,703
1987	1,651,384	187,945	582,690[r]	188,250	2,610,269[r]
1988	1,891,972	196,365	647,952	186,340	2,922,629
1989	2,078,758	219,939	704,293	198,539	3,201,529
1990	2,266,385	235,433	750,090	199,217	3,451,125
1991	2,365,516	245,573	795,387	200,349	3,606,825
	Net benefit expenditures[4] ($'000,000)				
	Retirement pensions	Disability pensions	Survivors' pensions[2]	Children's benefits[3]	Total
1986	4,325.9	879.1	1,378.6	203.3	6,786.9
1987	5,054.0	1,045.0[r]	1,547.2[r]	207.6	7,854.0[r]
1988	6,281.1	1,408.5	1,824.5	221.6	9,735.7
1989	7,234.6	1,631.9	2,008.3	233.8	11,108.6
1990	8,159.0	1,799.2	2,215.8	245.0	12,419.1
1991	9,134.1	1,955.9	2,434.3	257.9	13,782.2

[1] *Fiscal years ending March 31st.*
[2] *Survivors' pensions include one-time death benefits.*
[3] *Children's benefits include benefits to children of disabled contributors and orphans.*
[4] *Payments outside Canada are included as of 1979–80.*

8.4 FAMILY ALLOWANCE[1]

	Annual average number of children[2]			
	1988	1989	1990	1991
Newfoundland	177,417	172,552	168,200	163,749
Prince Edward Island	35,665	35,691	35,702	35,537
Nova Scotia	229,426	227,152	225,329	224,698
New Brunswick	196,401	193,523	191,166	189,373
Quebec	1,616,472	1,610,752	1,613,004	1,625,991
Ontario	2,313,690	2,334,322	2,354,698	2,395,240
Manitoba	291,169	290,182	289,008	288,782
Saskatchewan	294,011	291,193	287,437	283,979
Alberta	674,200	676,857	684,946	696,448
British Columbia	728,917	735,811	749,021	768,028
Yukon	7,460	7,605	7,663	7,778
Northwest Territories	20,365	20,485	20,753	21,077
Canada	6,585,193	6,596,125	6,626,927	6,700,683

	Annual average number of families			
	1988	1989	1990	1991
Newfoundland	95,596	94,528	93,616	92,296
Prince Edward Island	18,717	18,858	18,935	18,871
Nova Scotia	128,956	128,195	127,506	127,301
New Brunswick	109,695	108,957	108,323	107,936
Quebec	938,360	938,001	940,770	948,048
Ontario	1,293,212	1,304,454	1,313,613	1,334,875
Manitoba	153,467	153,220	152,761	152,611
Saskatchewan	146,954	145,355	143,128	141,037
Alberta	356,708	356,721	359,941	364,758
British Columbia	403,028	405,625	411,609	420,821
Yukon	4,168	4,261	4,303	4,365
Northwest Territories	9,504	9,645	9,823	10,031
Canada	3,658,365	3,667,820	3,684,328	3,722,950

	Net benefit expenditures ($'000,000)			
	1988	1989	1990	1991
Newfoundland	68.6	67.6	66.8	66.2
Prince Edward Island	13.8	14.0	14.2	14.4
Nova Scotia	88.9	89.2	89.6	91.0
New Brunswick	76.0	75.9	76.0	76.6
Quebec	627.8	635.3	646.0	664.4
Ontario	904.4	926.8	947.6	981.7
Manitoba	113.3	114.5	115.6	117.7
Saskatchewan	114.1	114.6	114.5	115.3
Alberta	263.1	266.4	272.0	283.0
British Columbia	283.5	290.3	299.6	313.8
Yukon	2.9	3.0	3.1	3.2
Northwest Territories	8.0	8.2	8.4	8.7
Canada	2,564.4	2,605.8	2,653.4	2,736.0

[1] *Fiscal years ending March 31st.*
[2] *Number of children on whose behalf Family Allowances are paid.*

8.5 WAR VETERANS' ALLOWANCES AND PENSIONS[1]

	Recipients of allowances[1]					
	1986	1987	1988	1989	1990	1991
Newfoundland	4,964	4,845	4,486	4,122	3,863	3,484
Prince Edward Island	1,387	1,303	1,155	1,024	902	795
Nova Scotia	7,504	7,100	6,239	5,460	4,708	4,143
New Brunswick	5,459	5,225	4,527	3,955	3,430	2,983
Quebec	10,258	10,292	9,495	9,049	8,678	7,833
Ontario	29,064	28,525	24,288	20,685	17,581	14,638
Manitoba	3,689	3,607	3,125	2,682	2,300	1,995
Saskatchewan	3,100	3,081	2,768	2,430	2,120	1,800
Alberta[2]	4,831	4,854	4,239	3,714	3,254	2,735
British Columbia[3]	11,917	11,822	10,435	9,044	7,586	6,273
Outside Canada	1,653	1,746	1,901	2,117	2,325	2,505
Canada	83,826	82,400	72,658	64,282	56,747	49,184

	Benefit expenditures[1] ($'000,000)					
	1986	1987	1988	1989	1990	1991
Newfoundland	24.5	23.0	20.2	17.4	15.4	13.5
Prince Edward Island	7.9	6.9	5.6	4.5	3.5	2.9
Nova Scotia	41.5	36.5	29.8	24.0	19.3	14.8
New Brunswick	31.4	27.7	22.7	17.8	13.9	10.7
Quebec	58.6	55.5	52.8	52.0	51.8	46.9
Ontario	155.7	144.9	120.4	97.7	78.3	59.6
Manitoba	18.7	17.5	14.4	11.6	9.0	6.6
Saskatchewan	16.0	14.8	12.2	9.8	7.7	5.8
Alberta[2]	25.9	24.9	20.6	17.3	13.7	10.5
British Columbia[3]	61.0	59.4	51.5	40.7	31.0	22.5
Outside Canada	12.8	14.4	15.4	17.7	20.7	24.0
Canada	454.0	425.5	365.6	310.5	264.3	217.8

	Payments, veteran disability and dependent pensioners ($'000,000)					
	1986	1987	1988	1989	1990	1991
Newfoundland	9.7	9.9	10.4	10.9	12.2	13.4
Prince Edward Island	10.1	10.8	11.0	11.8	13.2	14.6
Nova Scotia	55.3	58.5	60.1	62.5	57.9	72.2
New Brunswick	33.3	34.9	36.8	39.1	42.8	46.7
Quebec	87.4	92.4	100.2	104.0	109.4	114.9
Ontario	254.8	263.4	272.6	283.6	317.0	339.6
Manitoba	47.2	49.4	50.5	52.4	54.9	58.9
Saskatchewan	29.0	31.0	32.7	33.9	36.7	39.4
Alberta	50.6	52.3	54.3	57.5	62.4	70.0
British Columbia	122.9	128.3	132.7	139.9	152.9	170.4
Outside Canada	36.8	37.3	37.5	37.0	38.4	42.9
Canada[4]	737.1	768.2	798.8	832.6	897.8	982.0

[1] *Fiscal years ending March 31st.*
[2] *Includes data for Northwest Territories.*
[3] *Includes data for Yukon.*
[4] *Includes persons who reside in the territories and outside Canada.*

8.6 SOCIAL SECURITY EXPENDITURES[1] (MILLION DOLLARS)

	1986	1987	1988	1989	1990	1991
Federal social security						
Canada Assistance Plan						
General Assistance[2]	5,880.4	6,125.7	6,393.9	6,786.3	7,146.3	8,882.8
Homes for Special Care	788.5	634.6	729.0	854.4	846.9	931.0
Child Welfare	246.0	209.2	249.1	313.8	270.8	319.0
Work Activity and other welfare	1,345.1	1,570.0	1,691.7	1,838.0	2,253.1	2,477.3
Child Tax Credit[3]	1,537.3	1,639.4	1,967.9	2,064.0r	2,110.0r	2,270.0e
Canada and Quebec Pension Plans						
Retirement	4,325.9	5,054.0	6,281.1	7,234.6	8,159.0	9,134.1
Survivors	1,378.6	1,547.2	1,824.5	2,008.3	2,215.8	2,434.3
Disability	879.1	1,045.0	1,408.5	1,631.9	1,799.2	1,955.9
Children's	203.3	207.7	221.6	233.8	245.0	257.9
Family Allowance	2,500.6	2,534.4	2,564.4	2,605.7	2,653.5	2,736.0
National Training Program[4]	165.8	—	—	—	—	—
Canadian Jobs Strategy	643.6	1,542.8	1,528.8	1,501.9	1,550.7	1,553.5
OAS/GIS/SPA						
Old Age Security	8,857.7	9,520.0	10,247.9	10,963.4	11,803.8	12,705.2
Guaranteed Income Supplement	3,319.4	3,451.4	3,618.2	3,765.8	3,873.3	3,975.7
Spouses' Allowances	347.8	473.2	482.6	473.2	462.2	449.9
Registered Indians						
Social assistance	255.2	278.1	314.4	351.7	392.5r	459.6
Social services	82.3	93.0r	106.0r	125.5r	137.4r	164.6
Unemployment Insurance						
Unemployment	8,887.3	9,317.8	9,158.8	9,408.4	10,077.6	12,455.1
Sickness	223.5	250.3	292.3	334.1	365.0	392.1
Maternity	443.1	484.7	524.6	583.4	657.5	747.2
Retirement	21.8	22.2	23.4	22.3	22.2	12.8
Fishing	188.0	216.9	247.8	265.4	271.8	275.2
Training	234.8	233.5	226.8	242.4	293.9	171.6
Work sharing	19.5	23.7	14.3	18.4	25.7	105.7
Job creation	108.6	90.7	88.9	104.9	104.7	111.5
Veterans' benefits						
War Veterans' Allowances	453.9	425.4	365.6	310.5	264.4	217.8
Disability and dependents	696.9	729.0	798.6	832.5	897.8	982.0
Vocational Rehabilitation of Disabled Persons	148.0	175.6	185.3	193.3	213.0	222.3

8.6 **SOCIAL SECURITY EXPENDITURES[1]** (MILLION DOLLARS) (concluded)

	1986	1987	1988	1989	1990	1991
Provincial social security						
Workers' Compensation						
Permanent disability	1,019.0[r]	1,172.0	1,202.1[r]	1,242.0[r]	1,324.4[r]	1,414.1[e]
Temporary disability	1,570.0[r]	1,483.7	1,616.5[r]	1,706.6[r]	1,965.2[r]	2,078.6[e]
Medical aid	558.8[r]	750.9	828.9[r]	887.9[r]	1,025.5[r]	1,193.6[e]
Tax credits and rebates	1,690.3[r]	1,765.6	1,860.0[r]	1,785.6	1,948.0[r]	2,013.0[e]
Other welfare programs	2,296.7[r]	2,856.5	2,987.3	3,286.0[e]	3,615.0[e]	3,976.0[e]
Municipal social security[5]	608.3[r]	667.0	749.2	824.0[e]	906.0[e]	997.0[e]
Total	51,961.2[r]	56,591.4[r]	60,800.0[r]	64,804.0[r]	69,897.2[r]	78,072.0[e]

[1] *Fiscal years ending March 31st, except as noted.*
[2] *Total federal-provincial expenditures.*
[3] *Calendar year data.*
[4] *The National Training Program was phased out in 1986.*
[5] *Excluding CAP cost-sharable expenditures.*

Sources
Health and Welfare Canada
Veterans Affairs Canada

RON WATTS / FIRST LIGHT

CHAPTER NINE

●

GOVERNMENT

INTRODUCTION

DEMOCRACY IN ACTION On October 26, 1992, Canadians voted in a national referendum to accept or reject a set of proposals for constitutional reform known as the Charlottetown Accord. This was only the third national referendum in Canada's history, and the first to deal with constitutional reform, although at the provincial level both Newfoundland (in 1948) and Quebec (in 1980) have held referendums on constitutional issues.

Although Canada as a nation gained sovereignty, subject to certain limitations, with the passing of the British North America Act in 1867, it was not until 1982 that we had a constitution we could call our own. Before that, any amendments to the constitution had to be adopted by the British Parliament. This situation was eliminated by the Constitution Act of 1982, which patriated the constitution and set forth a package of reforms. Agreed upon by the federal government and nine provinces (the exception being Quebec), these reforms included a *Charter of Rights and Freedoms*, and the recognition and reaffirmation of the existing rights of Canada's aboriginal peoples, and of course a new constitutional amending formula.

But patriation of the constitution did not mean the end of constitutional debate. An aboriginal constitutional process led to the Constitution Amendment Proclamation of 1983, which included recognition of aboriginal rights arising from land claims, and a commitment to the participation of aboriginal people in constitutional conferences dealing with aboriginal rights. In response to the aspirations of Quebec, the federal government and the governments of all provinces reached agreement-in-principle at Meech Lake in 1987 on another package of amendments, including new provincial powers and the recognition of Quebec as a distinct society. The National Assembly of Quebec was the first provincial legislature to ratify the Meech Lake Accord, in 1987, but the legislatures of two other provinces (Newfoundland and Manitoba) did not approve it within the three-year deadline specified in the Constitution, and the Accord died.

In the Speech from the Throne of May 13, 1991, the federal government promised legislation "to provide for greater participation . . . in constitutional change."

Thus began a series of open and extensive public consultations on constitutional reform — the so-called Canada Round. Hundreds of thousands of Canadians participated in the process, by submitting briefs and attending public hearings, forums and conferences, and through various provincial and territorial constitutional committees and task forces. These events culminated in the Charlottetown Accord of August 28, 1992, a unanimous consensus reached by the federal government, the governments of the 10 provinces and 2 territories, and the leaders of Canada's 4 national aboriginal associations.

The key elements of the Charlottetown Accord included recognizing the aboriginal right to self-government within Canada; reforming the Senate — senators would be elected, whether by the general population or by provincial or territorial legislatures, there would be six senators for each province and one for each territory, and the Senate would have greater powers of veto and more influence over policy issues before Parliament; recognizing Quebec as a distinct society; promoting Canada's social and economic union; and rebalancing the roles and responsibilities of the federal and provincial governments.

The Canadian public participated in October 1992 by voting in the national referendum on the Charlottetown Accord. The result: a rejection of the proposals. After the referendum, the government declared the constitutional debate closed for the time being, and turned its attention to other, more immediate concerns, particularly the economy. On the positive side, both the referendum and the Canada Round discussions that preceded it gave Canadians an opportunity to participate fully in the democratic process and to reflect on the nature of their country.

CANADA'S SYSTEM OF GOVERNMENT

In many democracies, government is comprised of three separate powers — legislative, executive and judicial. In a constitutional monarchy such as Canada, all three powers flow from the same source: the Crown.

Arthur Lismer / National Archives of Canada C 119887

MacKenzie King with his dog, Pat. King was Canada's Prime Minister for a total of almost 22 years, between 1921 and 1948.

Canada's constitutional head of state is the Queen. Her representative in Canada, the Governor General, acts on her behalf on the advice of federal ministers. The role of the Governor General is, for the most part, purely ceremonial.

The government, whose ministers are members of Parliament, exercises the Crown's executive powers on its behalf, proposes legislation and presents budgets to the legislature, and implements laws. In the legislature, elected representatives adopt laws and vote on proposals for taxes and other revenues.

THE GOVERNMENT The government consists of a Ministry, led by the Prime Minister, who is normally the leader of the party which enjoys the support of a majority in the House of Commons. (In certain cases, for example when an election fails to produce a clear majority, or when the government resigns, a minority party may form a government.) As well as the Prime Minister, the Ministry comprises ministers, appointed by the Governor General on the Prime Minister's recommendation, usually from among members of the majority party in the legislature. Generally, ministers head a government department, but some may be assigned special parliamentary duties, or may act as ministers of state to assist. Together, the Prime Minister and other ministers meet in Cabinet to determine government policies.

The Prime Minister recommends to the Governor General the appointment of ministers, Privy Councillors, lieutenant-governors (the Queen's provincial representatives), speakers of the Senate, chief justices, senators and deputy ministers in the public service. The Prime Minister also recommends the appointment of the Governor General to the Queen. The Prime Minister is supported by the Prime Minister's Office, the Privy Council Office, and the Federal-Provincial Relations Office.

On February 24, 1993, the then Prime Minister of Canada, the Right Honourable Brian Mulroney, announced in a letter to the President of the governing Progressive Conservative Party of Canada his intention of resigning as Party Leader as soon as a replacement could be found. Accordingly, the Party held a leadership convention in Ottawa on June 9-13, 1993. As a result of this, the Right Honourable Kim Campbell

was on June 25, 1993 sworn in as Canada's 19th Prime Minister, becoming the first woman in Canada's history to hold that office.

THE PRIVY COUNCIL AND THE CABINET The Queen's Privy Council for Canada is a constitutional body entrusted with aiding and advising the Queen in the government of Canada. However, in fact, the business of government is handled by the Committee of Council — that is, the Cabinet.

The Privy Council comprises present and former Cabinet ministers and chief justices of Canada, former speakers of the Senate and the House of Commons and other distinguished Canadians whose appointment is conferred as an honour, notably on special State occasions such as the 100th and 125th anniversaries of Confederation. Membership in the Privy Council is for life. All Cabinet ministers, as a condition of office, must first be sworn into the Privy Council.

The Cabinet exercises formal authority through legal instruments called orders-in-council. The Cabinet submits these to the Governor General for approval, which is given in almost all circumstances. Thus the Governor General acts as the Governor in Council.

In the past, the Prime Minister acted as President of the Privy Council and Government Leader in the House of Commons; in recent years, these responsibilities have been delegated to senior colleagues who assist the Prime Minister in managing the government's agenda.

THE LEGISLATURE

THE HOUSE OF COMMONS The House of Commons is Canada's elected federal legislative body. For the purpose of electing members to the House, Canada is divided into electoral districts (also called constituencies or ridings). One member of Parliament is elected from each constituency, although any number of candidates may run. The number of seats in the House is based on representation by population, according to a formula set out in the Constitution. After each decennial census, the number of seats is adjusted and constituencies are redrawn to reflect population changes. As of the 1988 General Election, there were 295 constituencies.

Canada has a multi-party system; each party chooses a leader to speak on behalf of the party both within and outside the House of Commons. Over the years, parties representing many different viewpoints have elected members to Parliament. Following the 1988 general election, three parties were represented in the House of Commons: the Progressive Conservative Party of Canada, who formed the government; the Liberal Party of Canada, the official opposition; and the New Democratic Party. Since then, by-elections and changes in political affiliation have resulted in the representation in the House of Commons of two new parties: the Bloc Québécois and the Reform Party of Canada.

THE ELECTORAL PROCESS Before an election, the Governor General, at the request of the Prime Minister, dissolves Parliament and sets a date for the poll. This must be at least 47 days away, to allow time for candidates, parties and election officials to organize. Constitutionally, the mandate of a Parliament should not be longer than five years. However, it is unusual for a Parliament to last its full term. Federal elections are usually held some four to four-and-a-half years apart. They are sometimes held sooner, as may happen when, for example, the government is defeated on a motion on which it has explicitly staked its future or when a vote of non-confidence is passed. Barring unforseen circumstances, by the end of December 1993, Canada's 35th general election will have been called, the allotted five years having passed since the December 12, 1988 return of the election writs following the general election of November 21, 1988.

To determine election results, Canada employs the 'first-past-the-post'system: the candidate with more votes than any other single candidate in the constituency wins the seat representing that constituency. It is not necessary for the winner to poll more than 50% of the vote (an absolute majority), nor are parties assigned seats according to the percentage of votes they obtain (the 'proportional representation' system).

Federal elections are governed by the Constitution Act and the Canada Elections Act. All Canadians aged 18 and older are eligible to vote, with the exception of the chief and assistant chief electoral officers, the returning officer for each district, and people

NEW KIDS ON THE HILL

Since Confederation, a number of federal political parties have entered and left the political stage. In fact, two of Canada's newest parties with representation in Parliament — the Bloc Québécois and the Reform Party — have only been around for a few years.

The Bloc Québécois was created in the early 1990s. Most of the Bloc Members of Parliament (MPs) defected from the Conservatives to form their own party, which focuses on the sovereignty and interests of Quebec. In 1990, one MP was elected as a member of the Bloc Québécois. The Reform Party, meanwhile, was founded in 1987, and won its first federal seat in the House of Commons in a 1989 by-election. A member of the Reform Party was also appointed to the Senate following his winning a non-binding provincial vote.

In 1992, MPs from five different political parties occupied seats in the House of Commons. The bulk of Canada's 295 federal seats were held by the three major parties — the Progressive Conservatives with 157, the Liberals with 80, and the New Democratic Party with 44. Of the two recently established parties, the Bloc Québécois held eight seats, and the Reform Party held one. In addition, two seats were held by MPs who were independent of any party.

Chris Lund / CMCP

Rotunda, Centre Block, Parliament buildings.

convicted of illegal practices under the Canada Elections Act. Special voting rules apply to members of the Canadian forces and federal public servants posted abroad, as well as their spouses and dependents, and to veterans receiving care in certain institutions. Advanced polls and proxy voting accommodate those not able to vote at their local polling stations on election day.

Ballot papers identify candidates and their political affiliation, if any. A political party may be registered before the Chief Electoral Officer of Canada if, among other conditions, it has candidates officially nominated in at least 50 electoral districts for the next general election. A registered party may give its endorsement to only one candidate in each electoral district.

In recent years a process of electoral reform has begun in Canada. The Royal Commission on Electoral Reform and Party Financing, established in 1989, made a series of recommendations for changes to the way Canada votes in federal elections. In reviewing these recommendations, the Special Committee on Electoral Reform (established February 14, 1992) divided its work into three phases, the first two of which were in process as the *Year Book* was being

prepared. The first phase was to be implemented before the next general election; it proposed changes in regulations to make it easier for Canadians to be put on the list of voters, and to make the act of voting more accessible. The second phase dealt with broadcasting, disclosure of information in public opinion polls, third party advertising, campaign financing at both the local and the national level, decriminalizing of certain election offences, and enforcement. The third phase was to be implemented after the next election; it deals with the assignment of seats to provinces, the drawing of constituency boundaries, measures to increase the number of female candidates, and the establishment of aboriginal constituencies, among other matters.

THE SENATE Reform of the Senate was a major issue in the constitutional debate of 1991-92, and the Charlottetown Accord contained a number of proposals on Senate reform. By voting no in the referendum of October 1992, Canadians ruled out any immediate implementation of these proposals. Thus the Senate continues in its present form, which has remained largely unchanged (except for expansion to accommodate members from newly created provinces) since the time of Confederation.

One of the reasons the Senate was established is to protect the interests of the less populous regions of Canada. Accordingly, Senate membership is based on regional representation rather than representation by population. Senators are appointed in the Queen's name by the Governor General on the advice of the Prime Minister. Until 1965, senators were appointed for life; now the retirement age is 75, the same as for federal judges.

Ordinarily, the Senate has 104 seats, distributed as follows: Newfoundland, 6; Maritime Provinces Division, 24 (10 each from Nova Scotia and New Brunswick and 4 from Prince Edward Island); Quebec Division, 24; Ontario Division, 24; the Western Provinces Division, 24 (6 each from Manitoba, Saskatchewan, Alberta and British Columbia); and the Yukon and Northwest Territories, 1 each. Senators are usually affiliated with a political party.

On September 27, 1990, the Governor General, acting on the advice of ministers under the authority of Section 26 of the Constitution Act, 1867, and upon direction of the Queen, summoned eight additional senators. This was the only time in Canadian history that this measure has been taken. It was invoked to assure a Conservative majority in the Senate, to allow the government to secure the passage in the Senate of such government measures as the Goods and Services Tax. Without further recourse to Section 26, no more senators can be named for any division except to restore that division to its ordinary complement of 24. Although all of these Section 26 senators were still sitting as of June 8, 1993, other vacancies had reduced membership from 112 to 104. Representation by party was: Progressive Conservatives, 58; Liberals, 41; Independents, 5.

The Senate performs three basic functions. In its legislative role, its major work is the detailed consideration and revision of government bills. Committees of senators with experience in law, business or administration study bills, hear witnesses and recommend amendments. In its deliberative role, the Senate is a national forum for debating public issues and airing regional concerns. On two days' notice, a senator can start a debate, with no time limits, on any subject. In its investigative role, the Senate looks into major social and economic issues. Its standing and special committees produce reports that can lead to corrective legislation or changes in government policy.

THE JUDICIARY The judiciary interprets the laws enacted by Parliament and, notably, determines whether these are unconstitutional (for example, if they are contrary to the Charter of Rights and Freedoms or if they fall outside the jurisdiction of Parliament or provincial legislatures). Canada's judiciary is independent of government, in that appointments to the courts cannot be revoked by government.

LAYING DOWN THE LAW

Legislation can originate in the House of Commons or the Senate. However, bills to appropriate public revenue or to impose taxes (money bills) must originate in the House of Commons.

THE CABINET COMMITTEE SYSTEM The Cabinet is the collective decision-making forum where ministers determine the policy underlying proposed legislation. This is done through cabinet policy committees that are determined by the Prime Minister. With the support of public servants in their department, the minister prepares a policy proposal for new or amended legislation. This proposal is first considered by the relevant policy committee. If recommended, it then goes to full Cabinet or to the Priorities and Planning Committee for approval.

If the Cabinet confirms the proposal, the Justice Department prepares a draft bill expressing the intent of the proposal in legal terms. This draft bill is first approved by the minister, then submitted to the Cabinet committee on Legislation and House Planning, where it is examined from a technical and legal rather than a policy point of view. Once this committee finds the bill acceptable (sometimes with modifications), it is referred back to Cabinet for confirmation, then initialled by the Government House Leader on the Prime Minister's behalf and introduced in the House of Commons or the Senate.

The order and manner in which bills are considered in Parliament is the responsibility of the Government

CUT, COMBINED, CONDENSED

The current buzzwords — 'streamlining', 'downsizing', and 'rationalizing' — all mean the same thing: cutting an organization's duplications, costs and size to save money. They're bland words to describe a sometimes-traumatic process undertaken by many businesses during the recession in the early 1990s.

But it wasn't just business that did the cutting. In its budget of February, 1992, the federal government announced it wanted to eliminate, merge, or consider turning over to the private sector 46 different government boards, commissions, Crown corporations and advisory bodies. Some changes were still in progress at publication.

ELIMINATED

▲ *Science Council of Canada:* created in 1966 to advise the federal government, stimulate research and debate on science policy.

▲ *Economic Council of Canada:* created in 1963 to give independent economic advice to the federal government.

▲ *Canadian Institute for International Peace and Security:* advised government on foreign policy and international events.

▲ *Law Reform Commission:* created in 1971 to research legal issues, give independent advice to the Minister of Justice.

▲ *International Centre for Ocean Development:* created in 1983 to work with developing countries to manage ocean resources. Residual functions absorbed by the Canadian International Development Agency.

▲ *Veterans Land Administration:* set up after World War II to provide loans and other assistance to veterans.*

▲ *Agricultural Products Board:* created in 1951 to stabilize agricultural commodity markets.*

▲ *Demographic Review Secretariat:* researched population trends for Health and Welfare Canada.

▲ *Canadian National (West Indies) Steamships Ltd:* a Crown corporation which held assets of Canadian National's former ocean freighter fleet.

▲ *Pay Research Bureau:* set up in 1957 to survey pay rates, benefits and employment conditions in the public and private sectors, to assist collective bargaining.

▲ *International Aviation Advisory Task Force and Committee:* set up to review and report on international rights of Canadian air carriers.

▲ *National Advisory Committee on Development Education:* formed in 1988 to advise the Minister of External Relations on educating Canadians about international development issues.

▲ *Canadian Environmental Advisory Council: formed in 1972 to advise the Minister of the Environment on sustainable development.*

▲ *Canada Employment and Immigration Advisory Council: formed in 1977 to advise the Minister of Employment and Immigration on departmental policies.*

▲ *Advisory Committee on Lay Members of the Competition Tribunal: established in 1986 as part of the establishment of the Competition Tribunal.*

▲ *Advisory Committee on La Francophonie: **created in 1990 to advise the former Minister of Communications on his responsibilities regarding La Francophonie.***

▲ *Advisory Committee on Le Musée de la Nouvelle France: created in 1990 to advise the Minister of Communications on issues relating to a possible museum in Quebec City.*

▲ *Montreal Science and Technology Museum Advisory Committee: created in 1990 to advise the Minister of Communications on issues relating to a proposed museum in Montreal.*

▲ *Advisory Committee for Le Musée des arts du spectacle vivant (de la scène): created in 1990 to advise the Minister of Communications on issues relating to a proposed museum in Montreal.*

▲ *Marine Advisory Board on Research and Development: formed in the mid-1980s to advise the Coast Guard on marine research and development projects.*

MERGED

▲ *Enterprise Cape Breton Corporation: created in 1987 to broaden industrial development on Cape Breton. Merged into the Atlantic Canada Opportunities Agency.**

▲ *Canadian Commercial Corporation: started in 1946 to develop trade with other countries, merged into the Department of Supply and Services.**

▲ *Emergency Preparedness Canada: created in 1988 to plan and co-ordinate civil emergency response, returned to the Department of National Defense.**

▲ *Trade Marks Opposition Board and Copyright Board: rolled into a single Intellectual Property Tribunal.**

▲ *RCMP External Review Committee and RCMP Public Complaints Commission: reviewed internal and external complaints respectively (combined).**

▲ *Petroleum Monitoring Agency: formed in 1982 to analyze petroleum supplies and prices. Merged into Energy, Mines and Resources Canada.**

▲ *Privacy Commissioner and Information Commissioner: created in 1983 to monitor public rights to access and privacy (requires new legislation).*

▲ *Procurement Review Board: created in 1988 for the Canada-US free trade agreement, to review government procurement decisions, folded into the Canadian International Trade Tribunal.**

▲ *Social Sciences and Humanities Research Council and the International Cultural Programs: folded into the Canada Council.**

▲ *Communications Research Centre Advisory Committees: three separate committees dealing with communications technology, components and devices, and broadcast technology, (combined).*

CONSIDERED FOR PRIVATIZATION

▲ *Dosimetry Services Unit: Health and Welfare Canada unit monitored radiation for workers across the country.*

▲ *Cape Breton Development Corporation (DEVCO): operates coal mines and a railway in Nova Scotia (in progress).*

▲ *Royal Canadian Mint: strikes coins for the Bank of Canada (idea dropped after study).*

▲ *Blainville Motor Vehicle Test Centre: tests vehicle fuel efficiency for Transport Canada (in process).*

OTHERWISE CHANGED

▲ *International Development Research Centre: created in 1970 to research problems of developing regions. Changed to a departmental corporation (cancelled).*

▲ *Canadian Race Relations Foundation: proposed as part of the government's Japanese-Canadian redress legislation. (On hold for fiscal reasons).*

▲ *Canadian Heritage Languages Institute: proposed to preserve use of heritage languages — those other than French and English. (On hold for fiscal reasons).*

▲ *Sentencing and Conditional Release Commission: proposed, to promote understanding of the link between sentencing and conditional release. (On hold for fiscal reasons).*

▲ *Co-operative Energy Corporation: a publicly traded corporation in which the government owned 32.5% interest. Shares to be sold on the open market (completed).*

* Senate voted June 10, 1993 to reject enabling legislation.

House Leader, who negotiates these matters with counterparts in the opposition parties. If a bill is to be introduced in the Senate, the Government House Leader will discuss timing and tactics with the Leader of the government in the Senate, who will negotiate with the Senate opposition leader.

There are two main types of bills: public and private. Public bills can be introduced under the sponsorship of a minister (government public bills) or a member of Parliament (private members' public bills). Public bills deal with matters of public policy, whereas private bills are specific to a particular individual or group. Government bills are allotted more time for debate (about 21 hours per week) than members' bills (one hour per day). All bills must be considered in principle and in detail by both houses before they are passed. Government bills are normally introduced by the sponsoring minister; a private bill is introduced by means of a petition signed by the interested parties and presented in the House by a member who has agreed to sponsor it. In either case, the bill is automatically given first reading, after which it is printed and distributed to members of the House of Commons.

At a later sitting, the minister moves that the bill be given second reading and referred to an appropriate House of Commons committee. There is often extensive debate at this stage, because a favourable vote at second reading implies approval of the bill in principle. If the vote is indeed favourable, the designated House committee considers the bill clause by clause. These House committees, which include members of both the government and the opposition who have a particular interest in legislation, fall under four envelopes of responsibility: departmental, economic, human resources, and natural resources.

At the committee stage, which often lasts several weeks, expert witnesses may be invited to give their views on the bill. After the study is completed, the committee submits to the House of Commons a report that may include amendments to the bill.

When the House considers the committee report, any member may, with 24 hours' notice, suggest an amendment to the bill. After a debate, such amendments are put to a vote, and the report is agreed upon, with or without amendments.

After the report stage, the minister moves that the bill be given third reading and passage. Debate on this motion is limited to whether or not the bill should be given third reading; amendments at this stage are very restricted. If the vote is favourable, the bill is introduced in the Senate, where it goes through a similar process. Except for money bills and constitutional amendments, the Senate has the same legislative and veto power as the House of Commons. However, the House of Commons may readopt constitutional amendments not agreed to by the Senate after 180 days; the Senate's legislative authority in this respect is therefore called a 'suspensive veto'.

Before becoming law, a bill must pass both houses and must also receive royal assent from the Governor General (or more usually, the Governor General's deputy). This procedure is generally a formality: never in Canadian history has royal assent to any federal legislation been denied. The bill then comes into force, unless it includes a provision for coming into force at a later date (either set out in the Act or to be determined by the Governor in Council). Money bills making changes to taxes usually take effect retroactively to the day they were announced in the House of Commons.

Government[1] Balance

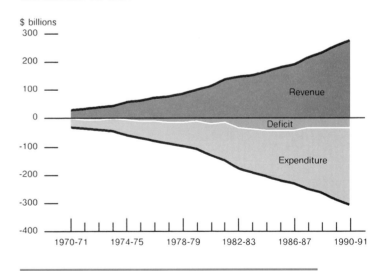

$ billions

‡ Consolidated federal, provincial, territorial and municipal governments.

Government[1] Revenue

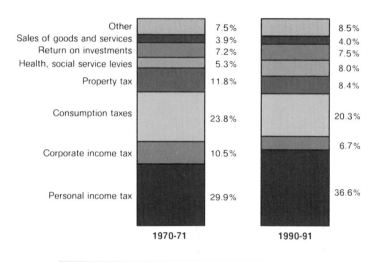

	1970-71	1990-91
Other	7.5%	8.5%
Sales of goods and services	3.9%	4.0%
Return on investments	7.2%	7.5%
Health, social service levies	5.3%	8.0%
Property tax	11.8%	8.4%
Consumption taxes	23.8%	20.3%
Corporate income tax	10.5%	6.7%
Personal income tax	29.9%	36.6%

[1] Consolidated federal, provincial, territorial and municipal governments.

Government[1] Expenditures

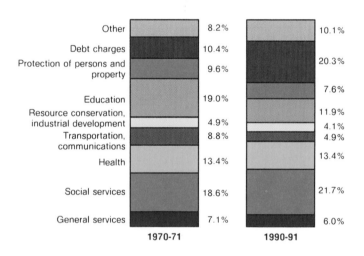

	1970-71	1990-91
Other	8.2%	10.1%
Debt charges	10.4%	20.3%
Protection of persons and property	9.6%	7.6%
Education	19.0%	11.9%
Resource conservation, industrial development	4.9%	4.1%
Transportation, communications	8.8%	4.9%
Health	13.4%	13.4%
Social services	18.6%	21.7%
General services	7.1%	6.0%

[1] Consolidated federal, provincial, territorial and municipal governments.

PROVINCIAL, TERRITORIAL AND LOCAL GOVERNMENTS

Canada has three levels of government: the federal, the provincial and the local, although only the federal and provincial have constitutional standing. The Territories are under federal administration. Whereas defence and external relations, criminal law, money and banking, trade, transportation, citizenship and native affairs are federal concerns, the provinces are responsible for education, health and welfare, civil law, natural resources and local government. Joint jurisdiction exists in areas such as agriculture and immigration.

In each of the provinces, the Queen is represented by a lieutenant-governor appointed by the Governor General. The lieutenant-governor acts on the advice of a ministry or executive council responsible to the provincial legislature.

Originally, the provinces of Quebec, New Brunswick, Nova Scotia, Manitoba and Prince Edward Island all had bicameral legislatures consisting of an elected assembly and an appointed legislative council. Today, however, all the provincial legislatures are unicameral; they consist of the lieutenant-governor and a provincial assembly. Paralleling the federal system, the provincial assembly is elected for a term of up to five years and may be dissolved by the lieutenant-governor on the advice of the premier of the province. Provincial assemblies function much like the federal House of Commons.

The territorial governments have no constitutional standing, but are structures of the federal governments. They comprise legislative assemblies and commissioners who perform duties similar to those of lieutenant-governors, but report to the Minister of Indian Affairs and Northern Development, who has jurisdiction over renewable and non-renewable natural resources.

Local governments in Canada are also without constitutional standing. They include municipalities, metropolitan and regional governments and other entities created by provincial and territorial governments to provide local services. The roles of local governments vary considerably across Canada. They may provide services such as police and fire, transportation, health and welfare and recreation. Education is normally administered separately from other local functions. Local governments may also supply electricity and gas.

The unit of local government is usually the municipality. The powers and responsibilities of municipalities are delegated through statutes passed by provincial and territorial legislatures. In 1991, Canada counted about 5,000 municipalities: some 120 cities, nearly 800 towns, over 1,000 villages and close to 3,000 rural municipalities.

Special agencies or joint boards and commissions are often created to provide certain services, such as public transit, for groups of municipalities. Another recent trend is for provinces to assume certain functions traditionally assigned to local government (for example, social services in New Brunswick). The provinces have also established new levels of government to provide services regionally.

ABORIGINAL PEOPLES

Canada's aboriginal peoples have long aspired to a greater degree of self-government within or alongside the Canadian political system. Since 1986, the Canadian government has pursued community self-government negotiations with individual aboriginal communities. As of March 1993, two native communities in Canada (the Cree-Naskapi of Quebec and the Sechelt Band of British Columbia) were self-governing in the sense that they have their own local governments which are legal and political entities of municipal status, accountable to an aboriginal electorate. Negotiations were continuing on 15 other community government projects involving 45 First Nations. In addition, negotiations regarding comprehensive land claims were under way with four groups: the Council for Yukon Indians (in the Yukon), the Nisga'a First Nation (in British Columbia), and the Gwich'in and Sahtu First Nations (both in the Northwest Territories).

In September 1990, the government launched a Native Agenda addressing four main areas: settling land claims, improving economic and social conditions on reserves, building a new relationship between Canada and its native peoples, and addressing the needs of

native peoples in contemporary society. An indication of this new relationship was the important role played by aboriginal leaders in the Canada Round of constitutional talks; the Charlottetown Accord included concrete proposals on aboriginal self-government.

Furthermore, in April 1991, the Royal Commission on Aboriginal Peoples was launched, with a broad mandate to review the fundamental place and role of aboriginal peoples in contemporary Canada, and to work towards building a new relationship between aboriginal and non-aboriginal people in Canada. The Commission is expected to present its recommendations to the federal government in late 1994.

Canada's aboriginal population includes Status Indians, Inuit, Métis and non-Status Indians. The Charter of Rights and Freedoms recognizes and affirms the rights of Canada's aboriginal peoples.

Indian and Northern Affairs Canada administers the Indian Act and other legislation relating to Status Indians (those registered as Indians under the Act). The department fulfils the federal government's treaty obligations, supports Indian and Inuit economic development and self-sufficiency, negotiates for increased autonomy for Status Indian communities; and negotiates for settlement of aboriginal land claims.

STATUS INDIANS Canada's total registered Status Indian population is 533,461 (Indian Register figures as of December 31, 1992); they belong to 604 Indian bands. About 295,000 live on Indian reserves, 217,800 outside reserves and 20,600 on Crown-leased land. In northern and outlying regions, hunting, fishing and trapping are still important means of livelihood for many bands.

INUIT Most of Canada's 33,400 Inuit live in the Northwest Territories, northern Quebec or Labrador. While some Inuit still follow a traditional lifestyle, continuing political and economic development in the North has wrought many changes in the life of the Inuit population. One of the most significant changes in recent years has been the increased control the Inuit have gained in governing their own affairs. This trend is expected to accelerate with the settling of land claims and the creation of Nunavut, a new northern territory in the eastern Arctic.

VOTER TURNOUT

In every federal election over the past century, roughly three-quarters of eligible Canadian voters have cast ballots. While Canada's voter turnout is high compared to that of the United States, we still lag far behind many other democratic nations.

A recent study by Canada's Royal Commission on Electoral Reform and Party Financing found that Canada ranked 28th out of 33 democracies in voter turnout rates in the 1980s.

Voter turnout was highest in Australia and Belgium, where 94% of eligible voters cast ballots. In these and many other countries, however, voting is a legal requirement. Nonetheless, voter turnout topped 90% in Austria, the Bahamas and New Zealand — where voting is not compulsory.

Canada's turnout rate in the 1980s (73%) was higher than that of Japan (71%), India (62%), Trinidad and Tobago (59%), the United States (54%) and Switzerland (48%).

While Canada's voter turnout has remained relatively stable over the last century, the proportion of Canadians who have been allowed to vote has changed dramatically. With the right to vote extended to women in 1918, and other groups more recently, 97% of Canadian adult electors have been included on federal voters lists since 1972, compared to less than 40% before 1918.

In 1992, prisoners, judges and the mentally disabled were enfranchised in time for the federal referendum on the Charlottetown Accord, following several court decisions.

SOCIAL SUPPORT FOR ABORIGINAL PEOPLES The Canadian government, through the Department of Indian Affairs and Northern Development (DIAND), works closely with aboriginal governments to meet the needs of native Canadians living on reserves.

The department is transferring to aboriginal reserve communities the responsibility of managing their own affairs. These communities now control 77% of all funding from Indian and Inuit Affairs, one of four programs within DIAND. These funds are used to provide housing, education, economic development, child, family and adult care services, and other social services including initiatives to prevent family violence and substance abuse. Funds may be used for special needs like therapeutic diets or household appliances, as well as for basic requirements like food and clothing.

GOVERNMENT FINANCES

Federal government revenues have increased seven-fold over the last 20 years, with similar increases being recorded at provincial and local levels of government. However, expenditures at all three levels have increased at a faster pace, resulting in deficits that in 1991-92 were among the highest ever recorded.

The causes of these large deficits, their effects on the Canadian economy, and suggestions for reducing them are the subject of extensive public policy debate. They result from a complex interaction of the ways in which government expenditures, especially social program expenditures, and government revenues have evolved. High interest rates and fluctuating economic conditions over the last 15 years have made the problem of controlling deficits even more difficult.

Comparisons of today's figures for revenues and expenditures with those of 20 years ago are risky because many factors not contained within the data come into play. For example, the indexing of income tax to inflation, the maturation of social programs over time, and the transfer of federal and provincial responsibilities in taxation all stand outside, but have an effect on, the cold hard figures. Nevertheless, comparison of consolidated data (all three levels of government taken together) between 1990-91 (the latest year for which consolidated data are available) and 1970-71 do reveal some interesting trends.

There have been noticeable changes in the structure of government revenues in the last two decades. Personal income tax, the largest single source of revenue, generated a still larger proportion of total revenue in 1990-91 than 20 years previously: an estimated 36.6%, compared with 29.9% in 1970-71. The shares contributed by consumption taxes, corporation income tax, and property and related taxes have all declined, while the share contributed by returns on investments has risen slightly over the 20-year period.

Similarly, there have been noticeable shifts in the distribution of government expenses. In 1990-91, the biggest single expenditure was on social services: 21.7% of the total, compared to 18.6% in 1970-71. The share of health expenditures remained roughly unchanged over this period, at around 13.4%. The biggest changes have been in debt charges (20.6% in 1990-91, compared to 10.4% in 1970-71) and in education (11.9% in 1990-91, compared to 19.0% 20 years previously). Burgeoning public debt due to persistent deficits, combined with historically high interest rates, underlie the growing share of debt service charges in spending by Canadian governments.

FEDERAL REVENUES AND EXPENDITURES

The federal deficit increased again in 1992-93. Revised estimates for that fiscal year put total revenues at $133.7 billion and total expenditures at $170.4 billion, resulting in a deficit of $36.7 billion, up from an estimated $33.5 billion the previous year.

Personal income tax generated an estimated 47% of total federal revenues in 1992-93. Corporation income taxes accounted for an estimated 6.3% and unemployment insurance contributions for 13.1%. The rest was raised by a variety of taxes and other revenues.

GOODS AND SERVICES TAX

The Goods and Services Tax (GST) introduced in January, 1991, replaced the old Manufacturers Sales Tax, which applied to manufactured and selected other goods. The GST is more comprehensive, imposing a 7% levy on all goods and services sold in Canada, with some exceptions such as certain health, legal aid, educational and financial services. Some goods are considered taxable but rated at 0%; these include basic groceries, agricultural and most fishery products, prescription drugs and medical devices, and exports. In 1992-93, the GST contributed an estimated 13.3% of total federal revenue.

The three largest federal expenditures are for social services, debt charges and protection of persons and property. In 1992-93, social services represented roughly 34.6% of total expenditures, debt charges accounted for 23.1%, and protection of persons and property, 8.9%. As of March 31, 1992 the federal net debt was $419.9 billion, an increase of $34.9 billion or 9.1% over the March 31, 1991 figure. The estimated figure for March 31, 1993, was $456.6 billion.

FEDERAL-PROVINCIAL FISCAL RELATIONS

Fiscal relations between the federal government and the provinces and territories are dictated either by acts of Parliament or by formal agreements. These financial arrangements, many of which have existed since Confederation, include tax collection agreements and federal-provincial transfers, which are either general or for specific purposes.

Today, general purpose transfers are essentially equalization payments that reduce disparity in fiscal capacity between the 'have' and 'have-not' provinces. Equalization payments are intended to ensure that all Canadians have access to reasonably comparable public services at reasonably comparable levels of taxation. The Equalization Program is based on a formula which is usually reviewed at five-year intervals. From its general revenue, the federal government compensates provinces having per capita revenue below the representative average standard, which is based on revenue from five representative provinces. Seven provinces currently receive equalization payments: Newfoundland, Prince Edward Island, Nova Scotia, New Brunswick, Quebec, Manitoba and Saskatchewan.

Specific purpose transfers are now mainly for large-scale social programs such as health care, social welfare and postsecondary education.

''OUR LAND''

For generations, the Inuit of Canada's North have regarded the vast expanse of land inhabited by their ancestors as an extension of their being. Rather than saying "this land belongs to us," the Inuit would say "we have all belonged to this land." According to the federal government, however, the land belonged to the Crown.

These differences were resolved recently, as the Inuit people in the eastern Arctic approved a historic land claim package that will change the face of Canada. The agreement is also responsible for the Nunavut Political Accord, which was signed in October 1992. The accord sets out guidelines establishing a new region to be carved out of the Northwest Territories by 1999.

*The new region, to be called Nunavut, covers roughly 2.2 million square kilometres — an area twice the size of British Columbia. **Nunavut** is the Inuktitut word for 'our land'. Essentially, the formation of the new region cuts the present Northwest Territories in half.*

In a vote held from November 3-5, 1992, some 69% of the almost 10,000 Inuit eligible to vote agreed to the settlement, which gives them clear title to 350 000 square kilometres of the new territory. The Inuit are guaranteed hunting, fishing and trapping rights throughout Nunavut. In addition, the deal will provide the Inuit with approximately $1.15 billion over 14 years.

The Nunavut political accord provides for a phase-in period to allow the Inuit time to set up a new government.

Nunavut's government is expected to operate much the same as the present territorial governments in the Northwest Territories and the Yukon. It will have its own legislative assembly, Cabinet, territorial court and civil service.

Because the Inuit make up about 80% of Nunavut's population, they are expected to dominate its legislature and although it is public government and not self-government, the Inuit will control their own lives. Bill C-132, an act to create the Nunavut Territory, and Bill C-133, the Land Claim Agreement Act received Royal Assent on June 10, 1993. The Nunavut territory and government will officially be established in 1999.

Support for the division of the Northwest Territories has already been established among the region's residents. In a 1982 plebescite, 56.5% of residents in the Northwest Territories voted in favour of the concept of dividing the region. Furthermore, in May of 1992, residents of the Northwest Territories voted 54% in favour of the proposed new boundary.

Nunavut is expected to face many challenges in its early years. Those people living in the eastern Arctic already face high unemployment, low income and education levels, and high costs for goods and services.

The creation of their own government, however, will give the residents of Nunavut greater control in meeting these challenges. In addition, new public sector jobs will be created and the monetary settlement of the Inuit land claim should help stimulate the region's economy.

Dividing existing territories is not a new practice in Canada. The current Northwest Territories was once a much larger territory known as ''Rupert's Land and the North-western Territory''. The province of Manitoba was separated from the Northwest Territories in 1870, the Yukon Territory in 1898, and the provinces of Alberta and Saskatchewan in 1905.

The present boundaries of the Northwest Territories were finally established in 1912, following the northward extension of Manitoba, Ontario and Quebec.

TAX COLLECTION The federal government collects provincial personal income taxes in all provinces except Quebec and corporation income tax in all provinces except Quebec and Ontario. This collection is made at no cost to the provinces except for a small administration fee for special tax rebates. Since July 1992, Quebec has administered the GST for registrants in that province. Elsewhere, the GST is administered by the federal government. Tax collection agreements are renegotiated every five years and are usually accompanied by revenue guarantees.

PROVINCIAL REVENUES AND EXPENDITURES Total provincial and territorial revenue is estimated at $150.0 billion for 1992-93. Expenditures are estimated at $171.2 billion, for a deficit of $21.2 billion.

Provincial and territorial governments rely chiefly on income taxes, general sales taxes and transfers from other levels of government as sources of revenue. Personal income taxes raised an estimated 26.4% of total revenue in 1992-93, while general sales taxes accounted for 12.9%. Specific purpose transfers from the federal government, chiefly for health and education, amounted to 11.9% of total revenues.

Health remains the largest provincial and territorial expense: an estimated 26.9% of total expenditures in 1992-93. Education, the second-largest expense, represented 18.7%, while social service expenditures were expected to account for 18.3%. The rest went towards general services and other programs.

The estimated net debt of provincial and territorial governments as of March 31, 1993 was $126.8 billion, an increase of 51.9% over the figure for March 31, 1991.

LOCAL GOVERNMENT REVENUES AND EXPENDITURES Local government revenue was $62.8 billion in 1991. The major revenue source for local government is property and related taxes, which accounted for 36.9% of the total. Sales of goods and services, licenses and permits, concessions and franchises, fines and surplus funds from local enterprises also provide revenue, as do transfers from other levels of government, particularly from provincial governments for education (25.7% of total revenue in 1991).

Local government expenditures stood at $64.8 billion in 1991. Education is by far the largest expense, representing 39.0% of total expenditures in 1991. The most significant other expenditures are transportation and communications, environmental, person and property protection, and social services expenditures.

FEDERAL GOVERNMENT STRUCTURE

The federal government administers legislation and government policies through departments, departmental corporations, corporations (including Crown corporations) owned or controlled by the Government of Canada and special boards, commissions, agencies and advisory bodies. Departments and departmental corporations generally perform administrative, research, supervisory, advisory or regulatory functions. Departments also play a fundamental role in policy development; it is this function that sets them apart from departmental corporations. Crown corporations often operate in a competitive or commercial environment.

Each department and departmental corporation is accountable to Parliament through a minister. Crown corporations are wholly owned by the Crown and are also accountable to Parliament through a minister. Some Crown corporations operate with special autonomy. These include the Bank of Canada, the Canada Council, the Canadian Broadcasting Corporation, Telefilm Canada, the Canadian Wheat Board, the International Development Research Centre and the National Arts Centre Corporation.

The federal government owns share capital in various business enterprises, including Canarctic Shipping Company Limited and Petro-Canada. Its scope for directing and influencing the activities of these corporations is limited as it is not the sole owner.

The federal government can appoint a minority of members to the board of directors of certain other entities which do not have a share capital structure — for example, Harbour Commissions, the Medical Council of Canada and the Canada Grains Council. The government has varying scope for directing these entities.

Chris Lund / CMCP

Looking up at the dome of the Parliamentary Library, Centre Block, Parliament buildings.

FINANCIAL ADMINISTRATION

The basic principles guiding the government's financial affairs were set in the Constitution Act, 1867: no tax shall be imposed and no money spent without the authority of Parliament; and expenditures must be in accordance with the conditions authorized by Parliament.

The government introduces all money bills and exercises financial control through a budgetary system that fixes the financial needs of the government annually, making the current and prospective condition of the public treasury apparent. The government's fiscal year ends March 31.

THE BUDGET The Minister of Finance presents a budget speech near the end of the fiscal year. The speech reviews the state of the national economy and the financial operations of the government in the

REFERENDUM # 3

There have been only three national referendums in Canadian history. In 1898, Canadians were asked to vote on prohibition. Forty-four years later, in 1942, Canadians were asked to vote on conscription. In the third referendum, in 1992, Canadians were asked to give their opinion on proposed changes to the Constitution.

The results of the prohibition vote were so close that the Prime Minister at the time, Sir Wilfred Laurier, took no further action on the issue. In the conscription vote, however, roughly 65% of Canadians voted in favour of the proposition, and the federal government subsequently passed a law authorizing conscription if it were deemed necessary. In Canada's most recent referendum, held October 26, 1992, 54.3% of Canadian voters rejected the Charlottetown Accord, the federal government's most recent attempt at constitutional reform.

The accord — negotiated and endorsed by all 10 premiers, leaders from the two territorial governments, representatives from Canada's four national aboriginal associations, and the federal government — called for senate reform, the recognition of Quebec as a distinct society, and the acceptance of aboriginals' rights to self-government.

The official referendum campaign for the Charlottetown Accord began September 18, 1992, and lasted five weeks. The question Canadians were asked on referendum day was ''Do you agree that the Constitution of Canada should be renewed on the basis of the agreement reached on August 28, 1992?''

In Quebec, where debate had been particularly fierce, 55.4% of voters said ''no''. In Canada's two territories, results were divided: the accord was approved in the Northwest Territories, and rejected in the Yukon.

The Accord had the least support in the West, where all four western provinces soundly rejected the pact. In both the West and in Canada as a whole, opposition was highest in British Columbia, where 68.3% of voters — more than two in three — said "no".

Support for the agreement was highest in the East. Newfoundland, New Brunswick and Prince Edward Island residents approved the accord by healthy margins. Nova Scotia — where 51.2% voted no — was the exception.

Voters in Ontario, meanwhile, approved the accord by a narrow margin — 50.1% voted yes while 49.9% voted no.

There were no major differences between the voting patterns of men and women. Overall, the accord was rejected by 55% of males and 57% of females.

Despite the Charlottetown Accord's failure to gain widespread acceptance, a nationwide poll on the day of the referendum showed that roughly 50% of Canadians wanted new constitutional talks to begin within a year.

The federal government's previous attempt at constitutional reform was the Meech Lake Accord, but it died in 1990 after failing to pass the provincial legislatures of Manitoba and Newfoundland by the ratification deadline.

previous fiscal year, and forecasts probable financial requirements for the coming year. At the end of the budget speech, the Minister introduces bills for proposed changes to taxes and duties. Proposed changes to sales taxes or excise duties are usually effective immediately.

The budget speech supports a motion that the House give general approval to the government's budgetary policy. The debate on this may take six or more sitting days. Once the motion is passed, the way is clear to consider specific budget resolutions and tax bills.

ESTIMATES AND APPROPRIA-TIONS Treasury Board, a statutory committee of the Privy Council, reviews and assigns priorities to government expenditure plans and programs. The board does this by reviewing multi-year operational plans submitted by individual departments, agencies and (in some cases) Crown corporations, and by preparing an overall Fiscal Plan. The expenditure component of the Fiscal Plan comprises estimates on the cost of existing government programs, major statutory payments, public debt charges, and reserves for new initiatives and contingencies. The expenditure forecasts for the first year of the plan form the basis of the Main Estimates. These estimates give details by ministerial portfolio, department or agency, program and activity.

The Main Estimates are tabled in the House of Commons by the President of the Treasury Board before March 1 each year; they are then referred to House committees for study. The committees must report back to the House of Commons by May 31; in the meantime Parliament approves an interim supply bill to provide for forecast expenditures until June 30.

The expenditure plan also includes reserves for funding new initiatives and for meeting contingencies that arise during the course of the year. Access to reserves for new policy initiatives can only be authorized by the Cabinet's Priorities and Planning Committee. The Treasury Board authorizes access to reserves for emergencies, minor program enhancements, or continuation (or renewal) of existing initiatives. In cases where social or demographic changes in the country necessitate the use of additional funds for the

government's major statutory programs, the Department of Finance authorizes access to the reserves for those programs.

Once such authorization is obtained, Parliament then authorizes the spending of these monies through the Supplementary Estimates, which are normally tabled twice a year by the President of the Treasury Board. The Supplementary Estimates are immediately referred to Parliamentary committees, and are approved by means of an Appropriation Act, usually three to four weeks after their introduction in the House of Commons.

PUBLIC MONIES The Financial Administration Act outlines procedures for controlling and accounting for revenues and expenditures.

All public money must be paid into the consolidated revenue fund in the name of the Receiver General for Canada, who is also the Minister of Supply and Services. The fund is held on deposit with the Bank of Canada and with chartered banks and other financial institutions. If the cash balance of the fund exceeds immediate requirements, the surplus may be invested to earn interest. In recent years, a special fund has been established to assist in reducing the cumulative public debt.

Treasury Board controls government department budgets and financial administration in general. The board makes annual budgetary allotments to each department after analysis of the multi-year operational plans submitted by the departments for the Main Estimates.

In addition to collecting and disbursing public money, the government receives and pays out substantial sums in connection with the public debt. To cover interest payments and to redeem securities as they mature, the government issues and sells securities. The Bank of Canada acts as the government's agent in the management of public debt.

Under the Financial Administration Act, the President of the Treasury Board and the Minister of Finance decide how the accounts of Canada and of individual departments will be kept. The Public Accounts are prepared by the Receiver General and laid before

Parliament by the President of the Treasury Board each year on or before December 31, or within 15 days of the resumption of Parliament after December 31.

The Public Accounts include the audited financial statements of the Government of Canada. These comprise statements of transactions, revenue and expenditure, assets and liabilities, accumulated deficit, and changes in financial position. In addition, the accounts include departmental financial reports and other financial information on the government's operations. The government also issues a consolidated report on Crown corporations and other corporate interests of Canada, which contains audited financial statements of Crown corporations and related financial information. Monthly financial statements are also published in the *Canada Gazette*.

Independent of the government and reporting directly to Parliament, the Auditor General audits government departments, agencies and some government-owned corporations. These audits assess authorization procedures, accounting policies and the accuracy of financial statements, and identify inefficiencies and mismanagement of resources.

FEDERAL GOVERNMENT EMPLOYMENT

TREASURY BOARD Responsible for the management framework for human resources in the federal public service, the Treasury Board develops, applies and evaluates personnel policies, systems and methods to ensure that qualified personnel are hired at competitive wages and are deployed efficiently.

The board has authority over employee classification and pay, conditions of employment, collective bargaining and staff relations, training and development, employee benefits, and incentives and recognition. The Board also implements employment equity, equal pay for work of equal value, and health and safety standards.

Under the Official Languages Act, Treasury Board is responsible for ensuring the public has access to federal government services in both official languages. The board is also responsible for administrative

management in the federal government, including information and information technology management, contracting, regulatory affairs, and material and property management.

THE PUBLIC SERVICE COMMISSION A politically independent agency accountable to Parliament, the Public Service Commission of Canada (PSC) administers the Public Service Employment Act, which requires that public service staffing be based on merit. The Act gives the PSC exclusive authority for making public service appointments. The PSC sets standards for selecting candidates, audits staffing actions, operates an appeals system, and investigates alleged improprieties in lateral transfers and in non-appealable staffing matters. It also deals with allegations of unlawful political activity by public servants and approves employees' requests for leave to be candidates in elections.

Some of the PSC's activities are shared with or delegated from Treasury Board. These include training programs, auditing of personnel management, investigating complaints of personal harassment, human resource planning, counselling and career development for the executive group, and promoting the participation of underrepresented groups.

WORKING FOR THE GOVERNMENT About one in five working Canadians is employed by the public sector, whether at the federal, provincial, territorial or local level — some 2.7 million people in 1991. Of these, less than half (around 44%) are actually involved in the administrative business of government; 5% are RCMP and military personnel, some 18% work in hospitals and other health or social welfare institutions, 19% are teachers or administrators in schools and other educational institutions, and the remainder (about 14%) work in government business corporations, including Crown Corporations.

In December 1990, the Canadian government published a White Paper announcing a major overhaul of the federal public service. The Public Service 2000 initiative (or PS 2000) comprises a large number of reforms aimed at cutting internal red tape, empowering employees, and reorienting the federal public service towards providing better service to Canadians.

The Public Service Reform Act, passed December 17, 1992, was a key element of the implementation of PS 2000. It streamlined internal administration by providing for quick deployment of employees, with their consent, to where they are most needed; quick recruitment of employees for short-term requirements; less red tape in staffing; consolidated processes by which employees are released from public service, and clearer authority to contract out work.

The issue of contracting out work has been perceived in some quarters, notably the Public Service Alliance of Canada (PSAC), as a potential threat to job security. On September 9, 1991, PSAC members in the federal public service went on strike over the issues of job security, wage curbs and pay equity. While support for the strike was widespread, it was not universal, either within or outside of the public service. The strike lasted, with a brief interruption, until October 2; it finally ended when the government passed legislation forcing the strikers back to work. As part of the collective agreement between Treasury Board and all 17 public service unions, federal public servants continue to have employment security; in some 95% of job terminations, alternative employment has been offered.

In 1990, only 22% of Canada's public servants were federally employed; local governments accounted for 37%, while the largest proportion of public servants (41% of all government employees) worked for the provinces. Indeed, the federal government has over the years shrunk in proportion to Canada's total working population. Only 5.2% of paid workers in Canada were working for the federal government in 1991, down from 6.8% in 1974 (the first year for which reliable figures are currently available). In contrast, provincial governments employed 10.1% of Canadian paid workers in 1991, a significant increase over the 1974 figure of 9.3%. Local governments employed 9.7% in 1974; by 1981 their share had fallen to 8.5%, but it rose again to reach 9.1% in 1991.

Public sector employees do not make significantly more money than the average Canadian; in 1991 the public sector represented 24% of all paid workers in Canada and accounted for 27% of all salaries and wages paid — the same figures as for the previous year. Public servants earned a total of $92.7 billion in 1991, of which 39% was paid to provincial and territorial employees, 37% to local government workers and 24% to federal public servants.

More than one-third of all government employees worked in Ontario, which accounted for 22% of federal employees, 34% of provincial employees and 44% of local government employees. Only Quebec, British Columbia and Newfoundland had substantially smaller proportions of public sector workers than their shares of total population.

Federal, provincial, territorial and local government business enterprises, which are included in the public sector, accounted for 365,000 employees in 1991, 3.3% of paid workers in Canada. Of these, almost half (44%) were employed by federal government business enterprises.

SOURCES

Department of Finance Canada

Department of Justice Canada

Elections Canada

Federal-Provincial Relations Office

Indian and Northern Affairs Canada

Office of the Auditor General of Canada

Privy Council Office

Public Service Commission of Canada

Revenue Canada, Customs and Excise

Revenue Canada, Taxation

Statistics Canada

The Senate

Treasury Board of Canada

FOR FURTHER READING

Selected publications from Statistics Canada

▲ *Federal Government Enterprise Finance, Income and Expenditure, Assets, Liabilities and Net Worth. Annual.* 61-203

▲ *Provincial Government Enterprise Finance. Annual.* 61-204

▲ *Public Finance Historical Data 1965/66-1991/92.* 68-512

▲ *Public Sector Employment and Remuneration. Annual.* 72-209

▲ *Government Expenditures on Culture in Canada. Annual.* 87-206

▲ *Federal Scientific Activities. Annual.* 88-204

▲ *Directory of Federal Government Scientific & Technological Establishments. Annual.* 88-206E

Selected publications from Other Sources

▲ *Canada's Electoral System: How It Evolved and How It Works,* Elections Canada, 1988.

TABLES

9.1 REPRESENTATION IN THE HOUSE OF COMMONS, FOLLOWING FEDERAL GENERAL ELECTIONS

	1867	1872 1878	1874	1882	1887 1891	1896 1900	1904	1908 1911	1917 1921	1925 1926 1930	1935 1940 1945	1949	1953 1957 1958 1962 1963 1965	1968 1972 1974	1979 1980 1984	1988
Ontario	82	88	88	91	92	92	86	86	82	82	82	83	85	88	95	99
Quebec	65	65	65	65	65	65	65	65	65	65	65	73	75	74	75	75
Nova Scotia	19	21	21	21	21	20	18	18	16	14	12	13	12	11	11	11
New Brunswick	15	16	16	16	16	14	13	13	11	11	10	10	10	10	10	10
Manitoba	...	4	4	5	5	7	10	10	15	17	17	16	14	13	14	14
British Columbia	...	6	6	6	6	6	7	7	13	14	16	18	22	23	28	32
Prince Edward Island	...	...	6	6	6	5	4	4	4	4	4	4	4	4	4	4
Saskatchewan	...	...	...	...	4	4	10	10	16	21	21	20	17	13	14	14
Alberta								7	12	16	17	17	17	19	21	26
Yukon													1	1	1	1
Mackenzie River / Northwest Territories[1]	...	...	...	...	...	...	1	1	1	1	1	1				
Northwest Territories[1]													1	1	2	2
Newfoundland	...	...	...	...	...	...	...	...	...	...	...	...	7	7	7	7
Canada	181	200	206	210	215	213	214	221	235	245	245	262	265	264	2 82	295

[1] Electoral district of Northwest Territories in 1963, 1965, 1968, 1972 and 1974. Northwest Territories has been divided into two electoral districts since 1976.

9.2 VOTERS REGISTERED AND VOTES POLLED AT FEDERAL GENERAL ELECTIONS

	Voters on the lists[1]			
	1979	1980	1984	1988
Newfoundland	338,730	346,281	370,219	384,236
Prince Edward Island	80,332	83,976	87,215	89,546
Nova Scotia	567,648	592,992	613,964	644,353
New Brunswick	456,707	473,972	491,169	508,741
Quebec	4,281,669	4,395,389	4,575,493	4,740,091
Ontario	5,328,123	5,597,683	5,882,320	6,309,375
Manitoba	670,098	687,702	704,585	729,281
Saskatchewan	619,144	639,649	673,289	675,160
Alberta	1,249,688	1,315,770	1,479,675	1,557,669
British Columbia	1,604,890	1,718,562	1,853,110	1,954,040
Yukon[2]	13,785	14,046	15,056	16,396
Northwest Territories	24,183	24,394	28,916	30,113
Canada	15,234,997	15,890,416	16,775,011	17,639,001

9.2 VOTERS REGISTERED AND VOTES POLLED AT FEDERAL GENERAL ELECTIONS (concluded)

	Votes polled			
	1979	1980	1984	1988
Newfoundland	205,080	206,130	242,491	257,793
Prince Edward Island	65,964	67,507	73,801	75,986
Nova Scotia	434,625	431,061	462,885	481,682
New Brunswick	342,919	341,212	379,850	386,201
Quebec	3,270,827	3,018,501	3,485,815	3,562,777
Ontario	4,191,809	4,054,194	4,461,416	4,706,214
Manitoba	518,572	481,546	516,053	544,756
Saskatchewan	493,706	461,359	524,566	525,219
Alberta	860,701	803,904	1,022,274	1,167,770
British Columbia	1,208,398	1,223,821	1,437,904	1,538,628
Yukon[2]	10,403	9,912	11,731	12,849
Northwest Territories	16,933	16,398	19,638	21,316
Canada	11,619,937	11,115,545	12,638,424	13,281,191

[1] *For every province the number of voters on the lists includes Canadian Forces and Public Service electors, but does not include dependant electors nor veteran electors.*
[2] *Electoral district of Yukon.*

9.3 CONSOLIDATED FEDERAL, PROVINCIAL, TERRITORIAL AND LOCAL[1] GOVERNMENT REVENUE (MILLION DOLLARS)

	1970-71	1980-81	1989-90[r]	1990-91[e]
Own source revenue	30,442	114,621	254,192	273,612
Income taxes	12,568	47,165	110,706	120,270
Personal income taxes	9,120	34,566	89,670	100,414
Corporation income taxes	3,189	11,733	19,675	18,306
Taxes on payments to non-residents	258	867	1,361	1,550
Property and related taxes	3,610	9,855	21,156	23,051
Real property taxes	3,138	8,297	17,586	19,142
Other property and related taxes	471	1,558	3,570	3,909
Consumption taxes	7,260	20,169	54,630	55,813
General sales taxes	4,073	11,655	35,752	35,817
Motive fuel taxes	1,094	2,317	6,579	7,585
Alcoholic beverages and tobacco taxes	1,081	2,286	5,478	6,045
Customs duties	815	3,188	4,592	4,150
Other	198	723	2,230	2,215
Health and social insurance levies	1,606	6,988	20,396	22,068
Petroleum and natural gas taxes	—	2,241	56	—
Miscellaneous taxes	536	1,381	5,139	7,701
Natural resource revenues	610	7,416	5,610	6,061
Privileges, licenses and permits	589	1,799	3,856	4,368
Sales of goods and services	1,203	5,366	10,358	11,110
Return on investments[2]	2,202	10,435	19,160	20,468
Other revenues from own sources	259	1,627	3,275	2,701
Transfers	48	317	870	927
Transfers from other levels of government	—	—	—	—
Transfers from government enterprises	48	317	870	927
Total revenue	30,490	114,939	255,210	274,539

[1] *Local government data are on a calendar year basis; federal, provincial and territorial government data are for fiscal years ending March 31st.*
[2] *Includes interest from provincial government enterprises related to direct borrowings of provincial governments made on their behalf.*

9.4 CONSOLIDATED FEDERAL, PROVINCIAL, TERRITORIAL AND LOCAL[1] GOVERNMENT EXPENDITURE (MILLION DOLLARS)

	1970-71	1980-81	1989-90[r]	1990-91[e]
General services	2,284	8,564	16,739	18,668
Protection of persons and property	3,068	10,267	22,344	23,557
Transportation and communications	2,797	9,222	14,430	15,136
Health	4,272	15,962	39,228	41,570
Social services	5,944	26,720	59,664	67,128
Education	6,089	18,096	35,091	36,768
Resource conservation and industrial development	1,564	10,775	13,219	12,787
Environment	557	3,157	6,311	6,884
Recreation and culture	584	3,103	6,006	6,617
Labour, employment and immigration	179	658	2,469	2,620
Housing	78	1,521	2,885	3,115
Foreign affairs and international assistance	289	1,076	4,120	3,495
Regional planning and development	197	808	1,584	1,601
Research establishments	395	1,137	1,549	1,780
Transfer to own enterprises	338	2,823	4,880	4,682
Debt charges[2]	3,327	17,395	57,982	62,682
Other expenditures	3	173	413	410
Total expenditure	31,965	131,758	288,914	309,501
Surplus	−1,474	−16,819	−33,704	−34,962

[1] *Local government data are on a calendar year basis; federal, provincial and territorial data are for fiscal years ending March 31st.*
[2] *Includes interest related to direct borrowings of provincial governments on behalf of their government enterprises.*

9.5 FEDERAL GOVERNMENT REVENUE[1] (MILLION DOLLARS)

	1988-89	1989-90	1990-91	1991-92	1992-93
Own source revenue	109,420	120,572	126,986	131,190	140,981
Income taxes	61,386	69,766	73,903	75,131	76,536
Personal income tax	48,078	55,384	60,805	65,153	65,876
Corporation income tax	11,730	13,021	11,726	9,069	9,500
Taxes on payments to non-residents	1,578	1,361	1,372	909	1,160
Consumption taxes	26,334	28,759	27,551	28,645	33,241
Sales tax/goods and tobacco taxes[2]	15,744	17,768	17,061	17,055	21,020
Motive fuel tax	2,542	2,414	2,472	2,972	3,260
Alcoholic beverages and tobacco taxes	2,706	3,032	3,173	3,900	4,705
Air transportation tax	499	494	488	480	429
Custom duties	4,527	4,592	4,005	4,032	3,650
Other consumption taxes	317	460	353	206	177
Health and social insurance levies	11,252	10,646	12,682	15,462	18,575
Unemployment Insurance contributions	11,252	10,646	12,682	15,462	18,575
Petroleum and natural gas taxes	112	56	−1	—	—
Miscellaneous taxes	683	642	642	586	651
Natural resource revenues	56	67	64	100	100
Privileges licences and permits	216	249	276	282	295
Sales of goods and services	2,854	3,070	3,315	3,501	4,212
Intergovernment	450	506	573	526	596
Other	2,404	2,564	2,742	2,975	3,615
Return on investments	5,577	5,843	7,554	6,556	6,238
Own enterprises	4,978	5,244	6,887	6,196	5,665
Profits remitted	3,662	3,932	5,614	4,902	4,635
Interest	1,316	1,312	1,273	1,294	1,030
Other return on investments	600	599	664	360	573
Interest	535	580	605	360	573
Other	64	19	62	—	—
Other revenue from own sources	949	1,511	999	928	1,133
Contributions to government operated benefit plans	69	73	77	75	79
Bullion and coinage	108	355	111	150	195
Fines and penalties	57	182	58	200	220
Miscellaneous revenues	715	901	752	503	639
Transfer revenue	86	137	126	137	137
Transfers from other levels of government	45	94	81	92	92
Transfers from government enterprises	41	43	45	45	45
Gross revenue	109,506	120,748	127,112	131,327	141,118

[1] *Fiscal years ending March 31st.*
[2] *Revenue from the Goods and Services Tax (effective January 1, 1991) in 1990-91 was $3,366,726, in 1991-92 was $18,465,000.*

9.6 FEDERAL GOVERNMENT EXPENDITURE[1] (MILLION DOLLARS)

	1988-89	1989-90	1990-91	1991-92	1992-93
General services	6,012	6,350	7,383	7,933	8,156
Executive and legislative	381	328	382	365	381
Administrative	3,161	3,397	4,115	4,407	4,488
Contributions to employee benefit plans	1,714	1,798	1,955	2,189	2,348
Other general services	755	827	930	971	939
Protection of persons and property	13,440	14,441	15,175	14,788	15,706
National defence	10,416	11,070	11,557	11,297	11,817
Courts of law	159	181	199	216	237
Correctional services	889	996	1,039	991	1,108
Police services	1,479	1,664	1,781	1,616	1,879
Regulatory services	89	93	106	145	116
Other protection of persons and property	407	436	493	523	549
Transportation and communications	3,727	3,610	3,640	3,364	3,577
Air	1,337	1,464	1,511	1,281	1,521
Road	242	265	357	249	261
Rail	1,015	690	759	812	859
Water	766	792	623	643	539
Telecommunications	213	232	249	256	264
Other transportation and communications	154	167	141	123	133
Health	7,685	7,780	7,354	7,674	7,599
Hospital care	5,435	5,344	4,739	5,001	4,776
Medical care	1,342	1,435	1,434	1,609	1,610
Preventive services	222	279	322	259	301
Other health	686	722	858	806	912
Social services	39,280	43,210	48,592	55,216	57,065
Social security	30,557	32,543	31,796	36,992	38,777
Canada Pension Plan	156	208	187	180	190
Quebec Pension Plan	26	28	32	35	40
Old Age Security	15,202	16,154	17,131	18,381	19,520
Unemployment Insurance	10,933	11,772	14,407	18,350	18,975
Workers' Compensation	41	38	41	46	52
Family Allowance	2,606	2,654	2,736	2,819	2,159
Veterans benefits	1,594	1,689	1,802	1,885	2,016
Social welfare	6,999	7,520	8,840	9,080	9,294
Social welfare assistance	5,296	5,613	6,672	6,825	6,886
Other social welfare	1,703	1,907	2,167	2,255	2,408
Tax credits and rebates	1,723	3,147	3,419	4,440	4,820

9.6 FEDERAL GOVERNMENT EXPENDITURE[1] (MILLION DOLLARS) (concluded)

	1988-89	1989-90	1990-91	1991-92	1992-93
Education	4,251	4,441	4,194	4,445	4,468
Elementary and secondary	609	524	549	645	791
Post-secondary	2,708	2,924	2,606	2,656	2,640
Special retraining services	549	550	576	621	522
Other education	384	442	464	523	516
Resource conservation and industrial development	7,440	6,486	6,145	6,917	6,911
Agriculture	3,614	3,011	2,593	3,633	3,281
Fish and game	393	402	470	431	449
Forest	312	284	215	230	237
Mines	76	96	94	83	64
Oil and gas	691	269	289	356	423
Tourism	43	37	33	34	40
Trade and industry	1,597	1,618	1,713	1,511	1,720
Water	5	8	11	9	4
Other resource conservation and industrial development	708	760	726	630	693
Environment	530	610	690	598	670
Recreation and culture	1,044	1,123	1,275	1,276	1,445
Recreation facilities	234	252	278	248	270
Cultural facilities	575	657	765	805	905
Other recreation and culture	235	214	233	224	270
Labour employment and immigration	1,790	2,000	2,150	2,080	2,442
Labour and employment	1,429	1,524	1,772	1,624	1,905
Immigration	206	303	364	438	516
Other labour employment and immigration	155	173	14	18	21
Housing	1,598	1,736	1,979	1,911	2,090
Foreign affairs and international assistance	3,632	4,120	3,514	3,434	3,747
Regional planning and development	443	482	468	327	401
Research establishments	1,059	1,276	1,497	1,408	1,820
General purpose transfers to other government	9,104	10,040	10,248	9,915	10,010
Statutory subsidies	36	36	36	36	37
Income tax on privately-owned public utilities	301	280	236	280	280
Payments in respect of reciprocal taxation	285	319	247	49	.3
Equalization	7,290	8,155	8,409	8,122	8,258
Grants in lieu of taxes	341	330	353	386	389
Other general purpose transfers	851	921	966	1,042	1,045
Transfer to own enterprises	2,125	2,250	2,159	2,141	2,071
Debt charges	33,167	38,771	42,484	41,366	39,928
Interest	32,826	38,437	42,239	40,991	39,566
Other debt charges	341	334	245	375	362
Other expenditures	8	20	22	12	1,912
Total gross expenditure	136,334	148,748	158,971	164,807	170,019
Surplus	−26,828	−28,000	−31,859	−33,480	−28,900

[1] *Fiscal years ending March 31st.*

9.7   FEDERAL GOVERNMENT BALANCE SHEET[1] (MILLION DOLLARS)

	1986-87	1987-88	1988-89	1989-90	1990-91	1991-92
Financial assets						
Cash on hand and on deposit	6,599	6,196	3,973	3,928	3,491	4,727
Receivables	2,000	2,103	2,137	2,148	2,475	3,174
Advances	23,372	27,494	35,172	36,257	32,787	35,996
Securities	10,827	10,910	8,893	9,113	9,612	9,755
Other financial assets	2,404	1,952	2,404	3,535	4,429	4,579
Total financial assets	45,202	48,655	52,580	54,980	52,794	58,230
Liabilities						
Bank overdrafts	2,934	2,895	2,735	2,381	2,563	4031
Payables	18,292	19,263	21,413	22,817	24,129	24405
Advances	1,568	1,861	1,899	1,932	1,905	2097
Treasury bills	61,950	76,950	81,050	102,700	118,550	139150
Canada bills	—	1,045	1,045	1,131	1,446	1008
Savings bonds	44,245	44,310	53,323	47,756	40,929	34444
Bonds and debentures	87,402	102,090	112,713	124,127	134,883	150596
Other securities	11,833	9,370	8,407	5,895	4,036	3868
Deposits	3,642	3,702	3,982	3,709	5,219	5837
Other liabilities	51,873	56,732	63,263	68,372	73,424	77842
Total liabilities	283,739	318,218	349,830	380,820	407,083	443,277
Excess of financial assets over liabilities or (excess of liabilities over financial assets)	−238,537	−269,563	−297,250	−325,839	−354,289	−385,047

[1] *Fiscal years ending March 31st.*

9.8   FEDERAL GOVERNMENT DEBT[1] (MILLION DOLLARS)

	Net federal debt	Gross federal debt	Components of the gross debt					
			Marketable bonds	Treasury bills	Savings bonds	Other securities	Pension plans	Other liabilities
1866-67	76	93	69	—	—	—	—	24
1917-18	1,192	1,863	1,428	75	—	—	5	355
1949-50	11,645	16,723	12,882	450	891	850	175	1,475
1974-75	23,958	55,289	14,490	5,630	12,915	51	12,378	9,825
1982-83	125,625	173,660	51,714	29,125	32,641	1,996	34,126	24,058
1983-84	162,250	210,841	58,994	41,700	38,204	3,228	37,988	30,727
1984-85	202,424	249,052	71,373	52,300	41,959	7,165	42,290	32,965
1985-86	238,537	283,739	86,957	61,950	44,245	8,366	46,970	35,251
1986-87	269,563	318,218	100,294	76,950	44,310	7,938	51,969	36,757
1987-88	297,250	349,830	110,222	81,050	53,323	7,463	57,388	40,384
1988-89	325,839	380,820	121,121	102,700	47,756	6,048	63,213	39,982
1989-90	354,289	407,084	131,810	118,550	40,929	4,696	69,597	41,502
1990-91	385,047	443,278	147,104	139,150	34,444	4,514	74,807	43,259

[1] *Fiscal years ending March 31st.*

9.9 PROVINCIAL AND TERRITORIAL GOVERNMENT REVENUE[1,2] (MILLION DOLLARS)

	1988-89	1989-90	1990-91[r]	1991-92[e]	1992-93[e]
Income taxes	37,176	41,293	44,827	43,481	44,845
Personal income taxes	31,156	34,639	39,406	38,556	39,623
Corporation income taxes	6,020	6,654	5,422	4,924	5,223
Real property taxes	1,158	1,260	2,254	2,217	2,320
Consumption taxes	23,873	25,809	26,109	27,012	28,400
General sales tax	16,521	17,952	17,966	18,547	19,291
Motive fuel taxes	4,189	4,165	4,307	4,707	5,236
Alcoholic beverages and tobacco taxes	2,316	2,446	2,673	2,936	3,072
Other consumption taxes	847	1,246	1,163	822	799
Health and social insurance levies	9,478	9,750	9,144	9,230	9,872
Health insurance premiums	4,684	4,775	3,638	3,978	4,245
Workers compensation contributions	4,794	4,975	5,506	5,252	5,628
Miscellaneous taxes	3,665	4,384	6,658	6,680	7,458
Natural resource revenues	5,274	5,543	5,449	4,594	4,664
Privileges, licences and permits	2,967	3,234	3,661	3,877	4,232
Sales of goods and services	2,467	2,317	2,390	2,749	3,831
Return on investments	12,209	13,034	13,837	14,094	13,814
Liquor board profits	2,252	2,430	2,440	2,424	2,527
Other return on investment	9,958	10,604	11,397	11,670	11,287
Other revenue from own sources	688	844	900	1,015	1,063
General purpose transfers from other levels of government	8,648	9,525	9,813	8,881	11,443
Specific purpose transfers from other levels of government	15,492	15,993	16,727	17,738	18,109
Specific purpose transfers from federal government	15,219	15,680	16,460	17,470	17,822
Specific purpose transfers from local governments	123	159	67	53	56
Specific purpose transfers from government enterprises	150	154	200	214	231
Total, gross revenue	123,092	132,986	141,768	141,567	150,050

[1] *Financial Management Systems basis.*
[2] *Fiscal years ending March 31st.*

9.10 PROVINCIAL AND TERRITORIAL GOVERNMENT EXPENDITURE[1,2] (MILLION DOLLARS)

	1988-89	1989-90	1990-91	1991-92[e]	1992-93[e]
General services	6,932	7,467	7,555	8,118	8,228
Protection of persons and property	4,063	4,214	5,125	5,476	5,602
Transportation and communications	5,913	6,759	7,223	7,312	7,077
Health	33,603	37,139	40,515	43,945	45,995
Hospital care	20,230	22,205	24,282	26,087	27,048
Medical care	11,090	12,125	13,301	14,850	15,481
Preventive care	1,271	1,622	1,488	1,655	1,779
Other health	1,012	1,187	1,445	1,353	1,687
Social services	19,552	21,043	23,985	28,574	31,342
Education	24,878	26,037	28,458	30,770	31,963
Elementary and secondary	15,568	16,444	18,128	19,562	20,297
Postsecondary	8,154	8,499	9,199	10,083	10,183
Special retraining services	914	867	897	951	1,138
Other education	243	226	235	175	346
Resource conservation and industrial development	7,581	6,844	7,760	9,069	8,405
Environment	1,702	1,644	1,768	1,922	1,906
Recreation and culture	1,451	1,645	1,680	1,838	1,761
Regional planning and development	838	1,005	817	811	835
General purpose transfers to local government	2,528	1,636	2,240	2,295	2,432
Debt charges	15,855	16,832	17,957	19,546	21,297
Other expenditures	3,106	3,380	4,496	4,108	4,342
Total, gross expenditure	128,002	135,643	149,577	163,784	171,184
Surplus or deficit	−4,910	−2,658	−7,809	−22,217	−21,134

[1] *Financial Management System Basis.*
[2] *Fiscal years ending March 31st.*

9.11   PROVINCIAL AND TERRITORIAL GOVERNMENT BALANCE SHEET[1] (MILLION DOLLARS)

	1986-87	1987-88	1988-89	1989-90	1990-91	1991-92
Financial assets						
Cash on hand and on deposit	7,930	9,822	11,214	12,348	13,377	18,425
Receivables	7,182	7,149	6,974	7,927	8,715	9,802
Advances	11,321	12,707	13,885	15,824	17,278	18,945
Securities	60,662	62,617	66,001	72,245	77,406	78,276
Other financial assets	816	1,149	1,098	1,043	1,289	1,445
Total, financial assets	87,911	93,444	99,172	109,387	118,065	126,893
Liabilities						
Bank overdrafts	2,424	3,075	3,127	3,991	4,728	4,634
Payables	8,179	8,711	8,724	9,352	10,252	10,546
Advances	3,432	3,462	3,423	3,624	4,129	3,953
Treasury bills	4,339	4,638	5,240	5,388	4,937	5,647
Savings bonds	2,733	2,808	3,489	3,267	3,192	3,010
Bonds and debentures	89,308	98,459	103,901	108,850	121,395	133,981
Other securities	8,431	13,078	13,321	15,494	18,673	18,604
Deposits	1,687	2,140	5,773	7,248	8,543	10,197
Other liabilities	16,313	18,937	22,181	24,984	18,066	19,822
Total, liabilities	136,846	155,308	169,179	182,198	193,915	210,394
Excess of financial assets over liabilities	−48,935	−61,864	−70,007	−72,811	−75,850	−83,501

[1] *Fiscal years ending March 31st.*

9.12   LOCAL GOVERNMENT REVENUE[1,2] (MILLION DOLLARS)

	1986	1987	1988	1989	1990[r]	1991[e]
Property and related taxes	15,721	17,009	18,599	20,307	21,401	23,147
Miscellaneous taxes	156	193	189	189	196	207
Amusement taxes	28	31	32	30	29	31
Other taxes	128	162	157	159	167	176
Privileges, licences and permits	282	341	366	412	428	459
Sales of goods and services	4,925	5,511	6,079	6,501	6,946	7,436
Return on investments	1,284	1,338	1,430	1,571	1,589	1,663
Other revenue from own sources	780	881	916	920	963	1,021
General purpose transfers from other levels of government	2,454	2,593	2,752	2,923	3,061	3,250
General purpose transfers from federal government	272	292	308	319	337	342
General purpose transfers from provincial governments	1,711	1,821	1,897	2,006	2,082	2,236
General purpose transfers from government enterprises	471	480	547	598	642	673
Specific purpose transfers from other levels of government	17,961	19,165	20,371	21,384	23,454	25,585
Specific purpose transfers from federal government	164	182	187	175	185	205
Specific purpose transfers from provincial governments	17,708	18,897	20,079	21,108	23,164	25,257
Specific purpose transfers from government enterprises	87	86	104	100	106	123
Total, gross revenue	43,562	47,032	50,702	54,206	58,038	62,768

[1] *Financial Management System basis.*
[2] *As of December 31st.*

9.13 LOCAL GOVERNMENT EXPENDITURE[1,2] (MILLION DOLLARS)

	1986	1987	1988	1989	1990[r]	1991[e]
General services	2,263	2,498	2,712	2,874	3,130	3,486
Protection of persons and property	3,621	3,816	4,165	4,470	4,822	5,131
Transportation and communications	4,523	4,905	5,119	5,766	6,318	6,635
Health	2,644	2,816	3,015	3,104	3,461	3,608
Social services and social welfare	1,680	1,905	2,120	2,348	2,657	3,459
Education	17,859	19,155	20,601	21,876	23,218	25,301
Resource conservation and industrial development	538	570	622	607	614	693
Environment	3,361	3,689	3,952	4,973	5,765	6,306
Recreation and culture	2,708	3,019	3,145	3,385	3,804	3,985
Housing	239	219	245	213	268	329
Regional planning and development	391	464	414	512	532	562
Transfer to own enterprises	897	933	922	1,013	1,072	1,149
Debt charges	3,298	3,322	3,401	3,533	3,696	3,862
Other expenditure	327	391	341	316	333	328
Total, gross expenditure	44,348	47,703	50,775	54,990	59,688	64,836
Surplus or deficit	−786	−671	−72	−784	−1,650	−2,067

[1] *Financial Management System basis.*
[2] *As of December 31st.*

9.14 LOCAL GOVERNMENT[1] BALANCE SHEET[2] (MILLION DOLLARS)

	1986	1987	1988	1989[e]	1990[e]
Financial assets					
Cash on hand and on deposit	3,868	4,109	4,152	4,304	4,308
Receivables	4,513	4,732	4,752	4,978	5,020
Advances	1,905	1,997	2,052	2,316	2,239
Securities	4,587	4,956	5,404	5,619	5,914
Other financial assets	1,637	1,600	1,605	1,706	1,760
Total financial assets	16,510	17,394	17,965	18,923	19,241
Excess of financial assets over liabilities	−19,286	−20,221	−20,407	−21,157	−22,035
Total financial assets per capita ($)	651	679	693	721	723
Total liabilities per capita ($)	1,412	1,468	1,481	1,527	1,551

[1] *Local governments include municipalities (towns, villages, etc.), elementary and secondary schools (except in Newfoundland, New Brunswick and Yukon), municipal hospitals and other special authorities which carry out municipal functions.*
[2] *As of December 31st.*

9.15 **PUBLIC SECTOR EMPLOYMENT, 1991** (AVERAGE NUMBER OF EMPLOYEES)

	Public sector	Government				Government business enterprises			
		Federal	Provincial	Local	Total	Federal	Provincial	Local	Total
Newfoundland	45,191	9,786	25,346	3,109	38,241	4,192	2,758	[1]	6,950
Prince Edward Island	14,897	3,103	7,544	2,891	13,538	1,016	343	[1]	1,359
Nova Scotia	106,169	33,442	31,789	31,268	96,499	4,365	4,829	476	9,670
New Brunswick	77,819	14,930	45,614	5,077	65,621	6,840	5,058	300	12,198
Quebec	660,594	78,052	294,741	200,153	572,946	37,759	37,857	12,032	87,648
Ontario	984,540	159,494	298,336	397,719	855,549	55,716	45,110	28,165	128,991
Manitoba	123,809	19,288	36,533	41,634	97,455	11,311	12,812	2,231	26,354
Saskatchewan	100,975	11,140	27,028	44,564	82,732	5,092	12,505	646	18,243
Alberta	263,229	28,624	78,191	125,917	232,732	15,937	6,488	8,072	30,497
British Columbia	278,789	40,489	111,123	90,917	242,529	13,218	22,745	297	36,260
Yukon	4,887	1,172	2,943	322	4,437	342	108	[1]	450
Northwest Territories	10,238	1,563	6,530	1,398	9,491	229	518	. . .	747
Outside Canada	21,253	16,213	. .	. . .	16,213	5,040	. .	. . .	5,040
Total	2,692,573	417,294	965,718	944,969	2,327,981	161,056	151,130	52,406	364,592

[1] *Confidential, included in national total.*

9.16 **PUBLIC SECTOR REMUNERATION, 1991** (MILLION DOLLARS)

	Public sector	Government				Government business enterprises			
		Federal	Provincial	Local	Total	Federal	Provincial	Local	Total
Newfoundland	1,372	363	702	80	1,145	132	95	[1]	227
Prince Edward Island	448	118	196	95	409	31	8	[1]	39
Nova Scotia	3,498	1,238	962	956	3,156	151	178	13	342
New Brunswick	2,422	531	1,294	147	1,972	258	182	10	450
Quebec	22,038	2,928	8,560	6,908	18,396	1,379	1,741	522	3,642
Ontario	36,254	6,457	9,896	14,415	30,768	2,071	2,207	1,208	5,486
Manitoba	4,017	718	1,062	1,289	3,069	410	462	76	948
Saskatchewan	3,103	428	785	1,211	2,424	176	480	23	679
Alberta	8,545	1,068	2,504	3,841	7,413	633	185	314	1,132
British Columbia	9,492	1,588	3,463	3,099	8,150	464	868	10	1,342
Yukon	207	56	127	12	195	8	4	[1]	12
Northwest Territories	445	78	285	42	405	11	29	. . .	40
Outside Canada	832	646	. .	. . .	646	186	. .	. . .	186
Total	92,671	16,217	29,836	32,093	78,146	5,908	6,441	2,176	14,525

[1] *Confidential.*

Sources
Elections Canada
Statistics Canada

RON WATTS / FIRST LIGHT

THE LEGAL SYSTEM

INTRODUCTION

Canada is often cited as one of the safest countries in the world. But, as with many other western countries, it faces growing crime rates, and a growing series of related problems.

In the late 1980s, a crime victimization survey carried out by Statistics Canada revealed that 4 out of 10 Canadians live in fear of violent crime. Another one out of four Canadians said they felt unsafe walking alone at night, in their own neighbourhoods.

The statistics tend to support this concern. From 1990 to 1991, the rate of violent crime per 100,000 people increased overall by 9%: homicide was up 13%, sexual assault 8% and robbery 16%.

Alarming at first glance, these statistics may actually indicate improved policing methods, or growing public co-operation with the authorities. For example, new legislation dealing with sexual assault has made it easier for victims to come forward. Increasingly, women are demanding that violence in the family and towards women be addressed by the police, the courts and legislation.

Yet, if Canada has its fair share of problems and challenges, compared with other industrialized

Bob Anderson / Masterfile.

In Canada, there is one police officer for every 476 people.

countries, it is still a relatively safe place to live. A 1992 United Nations report states that Canada's 1987 homicide rate was 2.1 per 100,000 people, half the industrialized world's average and well under the high set by the United States at 9.0 per 100,000.

To deal with these problems, Canada has a complex criminal law system concerned with protecting society from violent crimes as well as crimes against property, public peace, morality and the state.

To deal with private disputes between individuals, Canada has in place a civil law system based on two of the finest legal systems in the world: common law and *le droit civil*. These legal systems are rich in tradition; common law tracing its roots to medieval England and *le droit civil* drawing its legacy from early Roman principles of law.

In support of this legal system, Canada also maintains several police forces, federal and provincial parole boards and adult and youth correctional services across the country.

Canada's Legal System

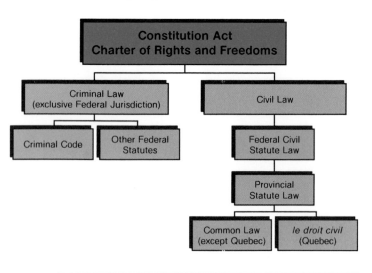

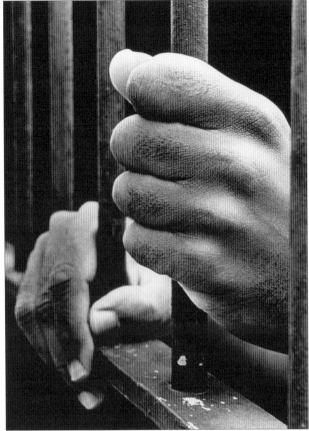

G. and V. Chapman / The Image Bank.

Parliament or provincial or territorial legislatures can make or change laws within their jurisdictions by enacting written statutes. All laws are subject to the provisions of the Constitution Act, 1982 and the Canadian Charter of Rights and Freedoms. The Act holds that any law that is inconsistent with the "provisions of the Constitution is, to the extent of the inconsistency, of no force and effect". In other words, such laws become invalid.

In Canada, human rights come with certain responsibilities. Section 1 of the Charter states that rights and freedoms are subject to limits prescribed by law that can be justified in a free and democratic society.

Criminal law is a federal body of law that prohibits certain kinds of conduct and actions. Most criminal offences are set out in the Criminal Code, but some are also contained in other federal statutes such as the Narcotic Control Act and the Young Offenders Act (YOA). Generally, criminal law is concerned with protecting the public at large and the social values of society — it includes offences such as homicide and assault, theft and fraud, obscenity and prostitution, and treason.

This chapter presents a review of Canada's legal system, along with descriptions of its supporting infrastructure and a brief overview of crime trends and rates.

CANADIAN LAW

Canada's Constitution Act, 1982 forms the basis of the country's legal system, by listing the jurisdictions over which federal and provincial governments have exclusive lawmaking authority. Under the constitution, the federal government maintains the "peace, order and good government of Canada" through legislation affecting all of the country — for instance, criminal law, immigration and unemployment insurance, trade and commerce, national defence, and native affairs.

Provincial governments handle laws of a private, or local nature, such as those relating to education, property rights, administration of justice and municipalities.

There are three types of criminal offences: indictable, summary conviction and hybrid. Indictable offences include serious crimes such as murder, robbery and aggravated assault. They provide for the possibility of imprisonment for a period of 2 to 14 years, or a life term. Summary conviction offences are usually less serious and include, for example, parking violations or disturbing the peace. They carry a maximum penalty of a $2,000 fine and six months' imprisonment. A hybrid offence allows the prosecutor to decide whether the crime should be prosecuted as a summary conviction or an indictable offence.

Criminal cases are prosecuted according to procedure set out in the Criminal Code. Provincial court judges have exclusive jurisdiction over summary conviction offences and certain indictable offences. Other indictable offences often require the accused to choose among trial by a provincial court judge, a judge without jury or a judge and jury. More serious offences, such as murder or treason, fall under the authority of a superior court of criminal jurisdiction.

CANADA ON THE WORLD BEAT

A Canadian perspective is currently shaping one of the world's most legendary police agencies. Interpol, also known as the International Criminal Police Organization (ICPO), is a mysterious and glamorous presence in films, literary thrillers and newspapers around the world. As the commissioner of the Royal Canadian Mounted Police (RCMP) — legendary in its own right — Norman Inkster is Canada's top policeman. In his parallel role as elected president of the organization that combats the shadowy connections of international crime, he is also the world's. He'll serve from 1992 until 1996.

Canadians have played a solid role in Interpol since this country joined in 1949. Two Canadian RCMP officers are permanently assigned to work at Interpol headquarters in Lyon, France, as part of a working group of about 75 police officers coming from the nations of the globe. As well, a previous RCMP commissioner, L. Higgitt, was president from 1971 to 1975.

Policing the world is a big job, and the story of Interpol is rife with exotic locales. Fourteen European nations met to lay the foundations for Interpol in Monaco in 1914, but it didn't really get off the ground until the year after the end of World War II, in Paris, France. It had 169 member nations by the end of 1992. While the role of the elected president is not day-to-day, the work of the organization is tied closely to street-level police work in member nations.

Interpol aims to promote "mutual assistance between all criminal police authorities within the limits of the laws existing in the different countries and the spirit of the Universal Declaration of Human Rights". It is also dedicated to helping set up and develop any institutions that effectively help prevent or suppress ordinary-law crimes. Member police agencies in each country use Interpol as a confidential clearing house to exchange information about groups and individuals involved in international crime; particularly narcotics, counterfeiting and smuggling. Interpol also routinely circulates information on wanted criminals, missing property, and unidentified bodies.

Interpol's constitution forbids it to act in, or intervene in, any activities of a political, military, religious or racial nature. These policies mean Interpol does not become involved in cases of espionage or violent political activity, for example. However, through Interpol, people who commit criminal acts in one country can be found in another and extradited.

The RCMP is Canada's liaison with Interpol, and a special office at RCMP headquarters in Ottawa co-ordinates Interpol-related activities in this country, either by passing on enquiries from police departments in Canada to similar Interpol offices in other countries, or vice-versa. Although it's officially labelled the National Central Bureau, it's usually known as Interpol Ottawa.

Because the vagaries of modern crime wait for no one, Interpol Ottawa, like most of the national offices world wide, is a highly sophisticated communications centre. Links include an international crime computer system, facilities to send photos by wire, photophones and fax machines to Interpol headquarters in France.

Over the years, criminal laws have been amended in response to technological advances or changing public values. For example, in 1859, eight years before Confederation, death was punishment for some 230 offences including theft of turnips. Six years later, only murder, treason and rape were capital offences. One hundred years later, in 1967, the government eliminated the death penalty in all cases except when the murder victim was an on-duty law officer or prison guard. By 1976, the death penalty had been abolished altogether.

Civil law in Quebec is governed by *le droit civil*, a written code of principles that can be traced back through France to the ancient Roman Empire. In 1763, the sovereign territory — now known as Canada — was transferred from the French to the English. Eleven years later, the Quebec Act of 1774 guaranteed the place of *le droit civil* alongside English public law and parlimentary institutions. Under *le droit civil*, a judge first consults the written code for guidance, then considers precedents set by earlier decisions. A new *Code Civil du Québec* will come into effect in January 1994.

Canada's Court System

Federally Constituted

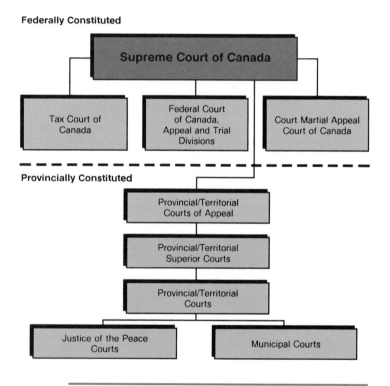

Provincially Constituted

Civil law governs conflict between individuals and other private parties. Civil cases include matters such as contract disputes, property, wills, certain areas of family law and civil rights. In most of Canada, civil law is based on common law, which originated in medieval England. This law is built upon tradition: a legally binding judicial decision sets a precedent, which then guides future decisions made in similar cases.

COURTS OF LAW

STRUCTURE Canada's Constitution provides for federally and provincially appointed judges. The provinces are charged with administration of justice within their boundaries. They set up, maintain and organize the court system to deal with all Canadian laws.

The Yukon and Northwest Territories Acts, 1971, allows territorial governments to assume responsibility for administration of justice, except for criminal prosecutions. Both territories have supreme courts, courts of appeal and territorial courts.

Federal Judiciary The **Supreme Court of Canada** represents the highest court of appeal for all cases including constitutional, criminal and civil cases. Some cases are heard as a matter of right. In the majority of cases, leave or permission must be obtained for hearings in the Supreme Court. Leave may be granted when a case raises an important question of law, such as the constitutional validity of a statute, or the application of the Charter of Rights and Freedoms.

The Supreme Court consists of a chief justice and eight associate puisne judges, three of whom must be appointed from Quebec. Supreme Court judges are appointed by the Governor-in-council upon the recommendation of the government of the day. The composition of this court can only be amended by resolutions of Parliament and each province. In all cases, decisions by the Supreme Court are final and binding.

National Archives of Canada PA 31188.

Justices of the peace, Montreal, 1904.

The **Federal Court of Canada**, established by Parliament in 1971, deals with claims against the government and handles other matters such as patents, copyright and maritime law. The Federal Court's appeal division consists of the chief justice and 10 other judges. The trial division consists of the associate chief justice and 13 other judges.

Other federal courts include the Tax Court, which rules on tax matters, and the Court Martial Appeal Court, which hears appeals from decisions of the service tribunals of the Canadian Armed Forces.

Canada also has a number of federal boards and tribunals to deal with administrative rules and regulations in areas such as broadcasting licences, safety standards and labour relations. Decisions of these boards are subject to review by the Federal Court.

NEW CHALLENGES The Constitution Act of 1982 has expanded the role of the courts, particularly the Supreme Court of Canada. Although Canadian courts have always had the power to declare laws or other government activities invalid, this power was previously limited. Legislation could only be struck down if the government introducing it had exceeded its legislative authority as defined in the earlier Constitution Act of 1867 (the former British North America Act).

Since 1982, courts have had the power to strike down legislation or invalidate other government actions if they infringe or deny any of the fundamental privileges recognized in the Charter of Rights and Freedoms. Essentially, this new power has made the Supreme Court judges the guardians of Canada's constitutionally guaranteed rights.

Criminal Code Offence Rate, 1991

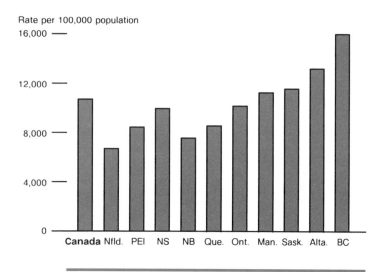

Rate per 100,000 population

Canada Nfld. PEI NS NB Que. Ont. Man. Sask. Alta. BC

Criminal Code Offence Rate by Category

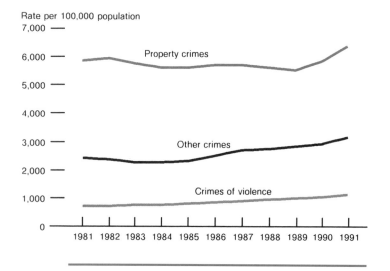

Rate per 100,000 population

Property crimes

Other crimes

Crimes of violence

1981 1982 1983 1984 1985 1986 1987 1988 1989 1990 1991

PATH TO JUSTICE In Canada, anyone accused of a crime has the right to a fair and speedy trial. In some courts, a backlog of cases has meant that alleged offenders have had to wait months for their hearings. Rising caseloads and increased demographic pressures have prompted many fundamental changes in the court system. To reduce court backlog, jurisdictions have created mediation and arbitration programs aimed at resolving disputes that could be settled out of court.

Courts have also attempted to reduce the 'mystique' of the legal system by using plain language to simplify legal documents for the general public.

Legal Advice Lawyers in Canada must comply with standards for practice set by provincial law societies. All provinces operate publicly funded legal aid programs that provide legal advice or representation at limited or no cost. Legal aid originated as a charitable service provided by the legal profession. Since the mid-1970s, publicly funded legal aid plans have been established in all provinces and both territories. Though criteria for qualifying for legal aid vary among the provinces, the common goal is to ensure that those in need are not denied professional legal assistance because they may not have the money.

CRIME AND LAW ENFORCEMENT

Whether they are 'keeping the peace' or 'fighting the war against crime', Canadian police officers have the challenging role of ensuring law and order throughout the nation. Combined, the Criminal Code, other federal statutes and provincial laws contain over 40,000 offences for which Canadian citizens can be prosecuted. The Criminal Code is amended to keep up with new offences that arise as a result of new technologies or changing attitudes toward existing offences. Advances in technology have created new crimes such as telecommunications theft. Attitudes toward offences such as sexual assault or impaired driving have led to stiffer penalties and tougher sentences.

When examining criminal statistics, it is important to consider that some crimes, even violent ones, are never reported. This also makes it difficult to establish whether crime is actually on the rise, or whether it is more frequently detected, reported or prosecuted. This section offers a brief look at reported crime in Canada.

CRIMES OF ASSAULT In 1990-91, violent crimes accounted for only 10% of the 2.9 million Criminal Code offences reported to police. A 1991 crime victimization survey revealed that 75% of both male and female violent crime victims had been assaulted. Women were far more likely to know or to be related to their assailants. Of the assault victims, 52% of females were assaulted by husbands or estranged husbands. About 44% of male assault victims did not know their assailants. About 8% of all female violent crime victims were sexually assaulted, compared with only 1% of male violent crime victims. Yet, of all violent crime victims, more males (18%) than females (12%) were robbed.

HOMICIDES In 1991, 753 homicides were reported by law enforcement agencies, representing a rate of 2.8 homicides per 100,000 population, or 8% above the average for the previous 10 years. That year, 45% of homicide victims had a record for Criminal Code or other federal statute offences themselves.

For the 582 homicides where an accused was identified, 34% were related to the victim, 53% were acquainted with the victim, and 13% were strangers. As with assault offences, women homicide victims were more likely to know their murderers; 54% of female victims were killed by family members, 38% by acquaintances, and 8% by strangers. By contrast, about 22% of male victims were killed by family, 62% by acquaintances and 16% by strangers.

In 1991, men were accused in homicide incidents almost 10 times more frequently than women, accounting for 90% of all accused. Of all individuals (male and female) accused of homicide, 47% were aged 18 to 29, and approximately one-half of all accused had consumed alcohol, drugs, or both at the time of the offence. Over half of men accused were single, compared with 30% of women, and 55% of women accused were married. Of individuals accused of homicide, 14% of males and 15% of females were divorced or separated from their spouses at the time of the event — well over four times the proportion of estranged spouses in the general Canadian population.

CHANGING OF THE GUARD

Cops and robbers has traditionally been the little boys' game of choice. Armed with toy guns and stick rifles, the play cops track down their evil adversaries and bring them to justice, risking life, limb and grass-stains. Nowadays, being a police officer, pretend or for real, is no longer a role played only by men.

Today, the constable on patrol is more likely to be a woman.

The number of female police officers has increased steadily in recent years.

Throughout the 1960s, less than 1% of Canada's municipal, provincial and federal police officers were women. By 1980, the proportion of female officers had doubled, to 2%.

From 1980 to 1985, their proportion doubled yet again, to 4% of all officers. By 1991, women accounted for roughly 7% of Canada's police officers — about 4,000 of more than 56,000 officers.

The trend is expected to continue as police forces strive to more accurately reflect the communities they serve.

Despite their under-representation as police officers, women continue to be over-represented in police support positions. The representation of women in civilian support roles, such as dispatchers and secretaries, has remained at roughly 60% since the early 1960s.

CANADA'S HOMICIDE RATE

In 1991, more Canadians were victims of homicide than in any of the 32 years since Statistics Canada began compiling homicide data.

Compared with other nations, however, Canada's homicide rate is relatively low. It's half the industrial world average and three and a half times lower than the US rate, the world's highest. In 1991, there were 753 homicides in Canada. That's a national homicide rate of 2.8 per 100,000 people, up 8% from Canada's average for the past 10 years.

FROM WEST TO EAST...

As with other violent offences, homicide rates in Canada are generally highest in the Western provinces and lowest in the Atlantic region. British Columbia and Manitoba had the highest provincial homicide rates in 1991, each with 3.9 per 100,000 people. Prince Edward Island, on the other hand, with two homicides in 1991, recorded the lowest rate in the country, at 1.5. Except for Quebec and Saskatchewan, every province in 1991 exceeded both its homicide rate for the previous year and its average rate for the past 10 years.

This west-east picture doesn't hold true for sheer numbers of homicides, however. Ontario had the most homicides in 1991, with 244, followed by Quebec with 180 and British Columbia with 127.

IN THE BIG CITIES...

Despite the popular notion that homicide is mainly a big-city crime, Canadians in 1991 were just as likely to be murdered in a small town as in a large city. This is because Canada's rural communities and large cities have homicide rates that mirror their shares of the total population. Canada's 25 Census Metropolitan Areas (CMAs), for example, contained 61% of the country's total population — and witnessed 61% of its homicides.

The CMAs with the highest homicide rates in 1991 were Oshawa and Sudbury. Each had a homicide rate of about 4.5 per 100,000 people — considerably higher than that of Toronto, at 2.6, and of Montreal at 3.3. London, Ontario, had the lowest CMA homicide rate in the country, at 0.5.

VICTIMS AND ACCUSED

The majority of homicides in Canada are not anonymous attacks in dark alleys but fatal confrontations at home. More than half of 1991's female homicide victims were killed in their own homes, compared with one-third of males. And just over half of all female victims were killed by a current or estranged intimate partner, compared with only 9% of male victims.

Regardless of where the victim was killed, the accused was almost 10 times more likely to be male than female. As in past years, two-thirds of all victims were male.

MODUS OPERANDI

The highest percentage of homicide victims in 1991 were shot (36%), followed by stabbings and beatings. Shooting homicides jumped 40% during the year, and those involving handguns doubled.

Sharon Uno / RCMP Photo Library.

FIREARMS LEGISLATION

I*n 1993, new federal legislation came into force to stiffen the screening process for Firearms Acquisition Certificates (FACs) and change the ways Canadians may legally handle firearms.*

Media reports linked the bill's passage to the tragic 1989 Montreal Massacre, in which 14 women students at a Montreal engineering school were murdered. The murder weapon was a rapid-fire semi-automatic rifle with a large-capacity ammunition clip.

The new legislation restricts ammunition magazine sizes on all semi-automatic weapons, limiting rifles, shotguns and assault pistols to 5 shots and handguns to 10.

During a firearms amnesty declared in the days before the legislation took effect, many Canadians chose to dispose of weapons they already owned. Some 19,561 firearms were surrendered to police forces across the country, and another 8,553 registered. Explosives, grenades and military shells were also turned in, together with some 700,000 rounds of ammunition.

CRIMES OF PROPERTY Property crimes, which account for approximately 60% of Criminal Code offences, also increased in all categories in 1991: 23% in theft of motor vehicles, 13% in break and enter, 13% in possession of stolen goods, 9% in theft over and theft under $1,000 and 3% in fraud.

CRIMES OF SUBSTANCE ABUSE
A 1992 United Nations report ranked Canada the country with the highest rate of drug crimes out of 60 industrialized countries. Between 1980 and 1985, Canada reported an average of 308 drug offences per 100,000 people — well above New Zealand with 276 and the United States with 234. At first glance, these figures are cause for great concern. In fact, they are based on charges laid by police and may very well indicate that Canada's war against drugs is well under way.

Yet Canadians have cause for concern. Police and educators alike have seen the average age of substance abusers decline, while the drugs of choice have become harder. In 1991, cocaine offences rose 25% from the previous year, and heroin offences remained the same. Yet overall, 1991 offences under the Narcotic Control Act decreased 9% from the previous year because cannabis (marijuana and hashish) offences, which account for the majority of all narcotic offences, declined by 18%.

DRINKING AND DRIVING These days, before heading out with friends for a few drinks, most adult Canadians are choosing 'designated drivers'. Increasingly, Canadians are realizing that the combination of alcohol and automobiles makes a lethal cocktail. Regardless of whether it is heightened awareness of the inherent danger, or the fear of getting caught, fewer and fewer Canadians are taking to the road while under the influence. Public awareness, increased policing and stiffer penalties have all contributed to a 31% decline in the number of impaired driving charges between 1981 and 1991. The proportion of fatally injured drivers found to have a blood alcohol concentration above the legal limit has decreased from a high of 52% in 1981 to 35% in 1990.

CRIMES OF YOUTH Violent youth crime in Canada appears to have increased in recent years. While violent offences still account for a small proportion of all youth crime, increasing numbers of young people are being charged and tried for violent crimes, including homicide, sexual and non-sexual assault, and robbery.

Under the Young Offenders Act (YOA), 1984, offenders appearing in youth court are guaranteed all the legal rights of the adult court system. However, youth courts acknowledge that young people have special needs and should be held accountable in a manner appropriate to their age and maturity.

The three-year maximum sentence under the YOA best illustrates this limited accountability approach. Although two years is the normal maximum sentence allowed in youth courts, a young offender can be given three years for a combination of offences, or for murder. A 1992 amendment to the YOA raised the maximum sentence for convicted murderers to five years. The amendment also limits the length of sentences given to youth who have been transferred and convicted of murder in adult court.

In some cases, young offenders may be tried in adult courts, provided the accused was at least 14 years of age at the time of the offence. Under the YOA, judges must consider several factors when deciding whether to transfer a case to adult court: the seriousness of the alleged offence; the young person's maturity, character and offence history; and the availability of treatment and correctional resources. Transfer orders are subject to review by a higher court. In practice, few violent offence cases are moved to adult courts. In 1990-91, only 23 violent youth court cases were transferred to adult court.

In 1991, youths aged 12 to 17 represented 22% of all persons charged with Criminal Code offences. A total of 116,397 cases were heard in youth courts in 1991-92, with an average of two charges per case. Over 80% of the young persons who appeared before youth courts were male, and 52% of the total young offenders were 16 and 17 years of age. About 62% of offenders faced property offences as their most serious charge and 21% were charged with a violent offence. Young persons charged with other Criminal Code offences accounted for about 10% of the total, Young Offenders

Act offences (failure to comply with a youth court disposition) for 4%, and drug-related charges for 2%.

In 1991-92, 42% of the young offenders received a term of probation as their most serious penalty; open custody was ordered in 17% of cases, secure custody in 13% and fines in 8% of cases. Community service orders were assigned to about 13% and the remaining

Homicide Victims and Accused, by Age, 1991

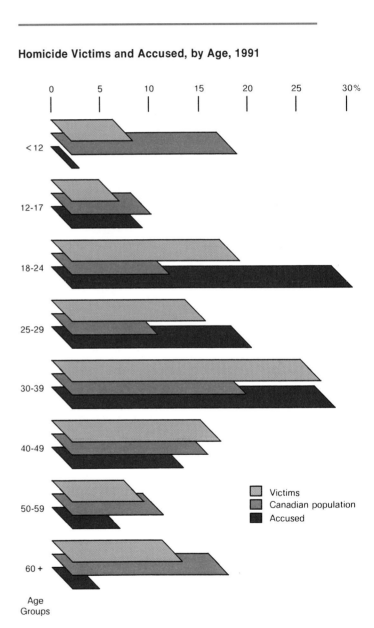

Francis Sanagan / CMCP.

Prison Cells, The Don, Toronto.

8% of offenders received an absolute discharge or another type of disposition ordered by the youth court judge. Such dispositions may include: compensation, detainment for treatment, apology, essay, jail tour, curfew or an order to obtain treatment for alcohol or drug abuse.

FIGHTING CRIME To keep Canada safe, taxpayers spent some $5 billion to sustain police forces in 1991. That year, Canada's police numbered almost 57,000 — that's one officer for every 476 Canadians.

More women are fighting crime. While still a small percentage of all peace officers, women comprised 7% of total police officers in 1991, compared with 5% in 1988, and less than 1% in the early 1970s.

CANADA'S FORCES Royal Newfoundland Constabulary (RNC) Created in 1872, the Royal Newfoundland Constabulary polices the urban centres of St. John's, Labrador City and Corner Brook. The Royal Canadian Mounted Police patrol the remainder of the province. In 1991, there were 368 RNC officers.

Sûreté du Québec (SQ) The Quebec police force has jurisdiction throughout the province in areas not required to maintain municipal police departments. The SQ force reports to Quebec's Ministère de la Justice and has a mandate to maintain peace, order and public safety throughout the province. It enforces criminal and provincial laws. In 1991, there were 4,431 SQ officers.

Ontario Provincial Police (OPP) The Ontario police force falls under the jurisdiction of the provincial government. It enforces the Criminal Code and provincial statutes in those parts of Ontario where provincial law does not require municipal police forces (areas with populations under 500). The OPP force also maintains a traffic patrol on many provincial highways, enforces the Liquor Licence Act, and provides municipal policing services under contract. In 1991, there were 4,630 OPP officers.

Royal Canadian Mounted Police (RCMP) The Royal Canadian Mounted Police was founded as the North-West Mounted Police in 1873. Maintained by the federal government, the 'mounties' fall under the jurisdiction of the federal solicitor general. The RCMP provides provincial policing services under contract to all provinces (except Ontario and Quebec) to enforce all federal, provincial and municipal laws in communities that do not maintain their own police forces. It is also solely responsible for patrolling the Yukon and Northwest Territories. In 1991, there were 15,555 RCMP officers.

Municipal Police Provincial law requires each city and town to have enough police to maintain law and order. Municipalities either operate their own forces or contract with the RCMP or provincial police for necessary police services.

VICTIMS OF CRIME Criminal injuries compensation is a recent effort to improve the criminal justice system. It ensures that innocent victims of crime have income security and necessary social services, regardless of socio-economic status. Each province and territory has a program to compensate victims or their families for injury or death resulting from specified crimes or from efforts to prevent crimes.

Administration of these programs varies among jurisdictions. Although all programs cover compensation for offences specified in the federal-provincial cost-sharing agreement (such as homicide, assault and robbery), a jurisdiction may also compensate for other offences, such as abduction and impaired or dangerous driving. Compensation may be in lump-sum, a periodic award, or a combination of both. Maximum amounts payable vary and, as a general rule, no compensation is given for property damage.

FAMILY VIOLENCE In recent years, much public attention has been paid to the issue of domestic, or family violence. Yet data on these types of crimes are difficult to collect for a number of reasons. Family violence is often considered a private matter; victims tend to keep to themselves and not ask for formalized help.

To gain a better understanding of the nature of family violence, seven federal government departments began working on the four-year, $136 million Initiative on Family Violence in 1991 to gather information, examine existing laws, implement social programs and increase awareness of the issue of family violence. In 1993, at the time of research for this *Year Book*, the Canadian Centre for Justice Statistics, under contract to Health and Welfare Canada, began a special survey on violence against women. About 15,000 women were randomly selected and interviewed about their experiences as victims of violence and about their fear of victimization. Highlights of this survey will be published in autumn of 1993. Two additional surveys on family violence — one on childhood injuries and one on transition houses — will be available in autumn of 1993.

Suspect–Victim Relationship in Solved Homicides, 1991

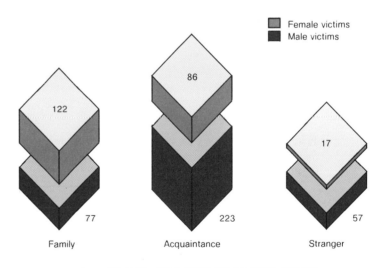

Female victims
Male victims

122   86   17

77   223   57

Family   Acquaintance   Stranger

CRIME AGAINST WOMEN

It's a disturbing kind of equality, but a new study has found that adult women are reported the victims of violent crime as often as adult men. —

Before 1992, when Statistics Canada published **Gender Differences Among Violent Crime Victims***, women were likely to worry more than men about being victims of violent crime, but they were less likely to be reported as victims.*

Researchers now believe the apparent new equality among victims of violent crimes may be occuring because women are becoming more likely to report sexual assaults or assaults by people close to them.

IT'S CLOSE TO HOME...

By far the largest proportion of adult female violent crime victims (80%) covered in the study were harmed by people they knew, particularly their husbands or ex-spouses. Male victims were more likely to be assaulted by strangers.

As well, men and women tend to fall victim to different types of offenders in different proportions. For instance, although three-quarters of all adult victims of violent crime were assaulted, women victims tended to be assaulted by their husbands or ex-husbands (52%) and men victims tended to be assaulted by strangers (44%). And the largest proportion of women homicide victims were killed by their husbands or ex-husbands (48%), while the largest proportion of men were killed by acquaintances (53%).

THE SCENE OF THE CRIME...

Where violent crimes took place was related to the gender of the victim, too. Women were most likely to be assaulted in a residence, while men were most likely to be assaulted outdoors.

The largest proportions of violent crimes against both sexes were most likely to involve physical force alone. However where weapons were involved, men were more likely to be the victims than women — 31% of all adult male victims were assaulted with weapons, compared with 19% of all adult female victims.

The new gender equality in violent crime does not apply, however, to the accused. In all violent crimes against both men and women, 91% of all accused were male. In sexual assault cases, 98% of all accused were male.

WHO GETS HURT...

Relying on police reports, the study determined physical injury rates for victims of violent crime. Similar proportions of men and women (60% and 56% respectively) received physical injuries during violent crimes.

During assaults, there were no gender differences for injuries. But larger proportions of men were injured during robberies and other violent offences, while larger proportions of women were injured during sexual assaults. Over four-fifths of the physical injuries recorded during crimes were minor, and required no professional medical treatment and only small amounts of first aid.

However, that does not cover the whole picture: an important aspect of violent crime, emotional injury, is not assessed in police reports.

MISSING

Losing a child is every parent's nightmare.

In Canada, about 1,800 children, most between 12 and 17 years old, are missing from their parents' or legal guardians' homes at any given time, more often girls than boys. In three-quarters of these cases, the child was a runaway. The rest range from children who have been abducted by strangers — or other parents — to those who have wandered and become lost. In 1991, some 59,135 missing children were reported to Canadian police departments.

The national focal point for missing children is the Royal Canadian Mounted Police Missing Children's Registry. The registry works with Canadian police departments, Canada Customs, External Affairs, International Social Services, Child Find, the Missing Children's Society of Canada, the Missing Children's Network Canada, and law enforcement and search agencies around the world.

CORRECTIONAL SERVICES

Correctional services are the third major component in Canada's legal system, after police and the courts. Federal and provincial governments share the responsibility for adult prisons, or correctional institutions. Criminal offenders sentenced to two years or more serve those sentences in federal correctional institutions. Offenders sentenced to less than two years are placed in provincial custody. An average of 24,470 inmates were serving custodial sentences in 1990-91, some 54% in provincial institutions, and 46% under federal custody.

In 1991-92, Canadian taxpayers spent almost $2 billion on adult correctional services, an increase of 4% over the previous year. The federal government spent $876 million and the provinces spent $1 billion of this amount. These figures translate into a housing cost of $136 per day for each federal inmate, and $115 per day for each provincial inmate.

In 1991-92, there were 135,270 offenders in the Canadian corrections caseload, an increase of 10% from the previous year. About 23% of these offenders were held in custody, with the majority (77%) under some form of community supervision. Even for 'lifers', those offenders who have been given life sentences, prison is not necessarily the last stop. Many offenders are eligible for parole after serving a certain portion of their sentences.

PROTECTION OF THE PUBLIC

Recent legislative changes are aimed at reducing violence in society. The Corrections and Conditional Release Act, proclaimed in November 1992, considers protection of the public the most important factor in all decisions relating to the release of prison inmates. Replacing the Parole Act of 1959 and the Penitentiary Act (parts of which date back to the 1860s), the new legislation empowers judges to lengthen the period that offenders are kept in prison.

Under the old law, offenders convicted of violent crimes became eligible for full parole after serving one-third of their sentence. Judges may now delay eligibility for full parole until offenders have served one-half of their sentence. The earlier law decreed that violent offenders could be kept in prison for their entire

Pierre Gaudard / CMCP.

A maximum security prison, Ste. Anne des Plaines, Quebec.

sentence if authorities considered them likely to commit new crimes. The new legislation has extended this rule to include offenders convicted of serious drug crimes or sexual assault against children.

However, non-violent and first-time offenders who are considered low-risk may be eligible for parole after serving only one-third of their sentences.

The new act also allows, for the first time, victims of violent crime to be formally recognized in the parole process: information they provide can be considered at parole hearings, and victims (or their families) may

attend such hearings at the discretion of the Parole Board, rather than at the discretion of the offender.

The National Parole Board bears the ultimate responsibility for releasing inmates back into the community. An integral part of Canada's criminal justice system, the board falls under the authority of the solicitor general. It may grant full parole or day parole to both federal and provincial inmates. It also grants federal inmates temporary absences that cannot be authorized at the institutional level, terminates or revokes day paroles, and revokes parole and statutory supervision releases.

NO MEANS NO

In Canada, more than 35,000 cases of sexual assault were reported in 1991 alone. The vast majority of these victims were women. Under new provisions included in Bill C-49, otherwise known as the "No-means-no" rape law, the meaning of consent is defined. The new law, which came into effect in 1992, marks the first time in Canadian history that sexual consent has been clearly defined by the law.

Sexual consent is now defined as "the voluntary agreement... to engage in the sexual activity in question," and when consent cannot be given (such as when a woman is unconscious), the answer is still assumed to be no.

The new law sets strict guidelines for judges on the admission of evidence about a complainant's sexual history. These guidelines, which judges must use when determining whether or not to allow such evidence, are designed to balance the rights of the accused to a fair trial with the complainant's rights to dignity and privacy. In any case, past sexual history cannot be used to suggest that the complainant is more likely to have given consent, or that she is in any way less credible.

These changes come as a result of a Supreme Court of Canada decision that struck down Canada's old 'rape shield' provision. (The old provision, Section 276 of the Criminal Code, protected victims from having to disclose their sexual histories during sexual assault trials, except for a few specific circumstances).

The federal government, through extensive consultations with women's groups across Canada, designed the new law to more accurately reflect the concerns of Canadian women.

While many women's groups have hailed the law as a bold step forward, others insist that the new law still doesn't go far enough. Many women's groups would have liked to see those most vulnerable to sexual abuse — aboriginal and disabled women, lesbians, prostitutes and members of visible minorities — mentioned specifically in the Bill's preamble. As well, many wanted tougher provisions for determining sexual consent.

The Canadian Bar Association, which worked with the federal government on the wording of the new law, has strongly endorsed it.

In determining whether an inmate should be paroled, the board considers all relevant information provided by the courts, prison authorities, case workers, and other professionals, depending on the case. Information provided by the victim or the victim's family might typically include the extent of physical or psychological suffering they have endured over the long term, and how their lives have been affected by the crime.

ALTERNATIVE SERVICES Rising custodial costs and questions regarding the benefit of custodial services for certain types of offenders have led to an increase in alternative, or community-supervised sentences. Probation is the primary community-based alternative to imprisonment, but in recent years, other non-custodial correctional programs have emerged.

Most alternative programs are aimed at specific groups such as women, natives and impaired driving offenders. For example, in some cases, native communities can petition the courts to release non-violent native offenders into their custody. Community leaders and family members rally to rehabilitate the offender through a healing process using traditional spiritual practices.

Until recently, the country's only federal women's prison was located in Ontario, which meant that inmates were frequently isolated from their children and other family members. Recognizing that contact with family members can enhance rehabilitation, the federal government set up regional correctional centres for women. Now women can serve their sentences closer to home.

Compensatory sentences, community service orders, fine options and restitution have also increased. The involvement of probation and parole officers in supervising temporary absence cases varies by province; as a result, reported caseloads are not definitive counts of community supervision. Volunteer programs have been established in most jurisdictions to help with increasing community supervision in caseloads.

SOURCES
National Parole Board
Statistics Canada

FOR FURTHER READING
Selected publications from Statistics Canada

▲ *Juristat.* 85-002
▲ *Canadian Crime Statistics. Annual.* 85-205
▲ *Adult Correctional Services in Canada. Annual.* 85-211
▲ *Policing in Canada, 1990.* 85-523

TABLES

10.1   JUDGES OF THE SUPREME COURT OF CANADA

	Date appointed
Chief justice	
The Rt. Hon. Antonio Lamer, PC	July 1, 1990
Puisne judges	
The Hon. Mr. Justice Gérard V. La Forest	January 16, 1985
The Hon. Madam Justice Claire L'Heureux-Dubé	April 15, 1987
The Hon. Mr. Justice John Sopinka	May 24, 1988
The Hon. Mr. Justice Charles Doherty Gonthier	February 1, 1989
The Hon. Mr. Justice Peter deCarteret Cory	February 1, 1989
The Hon. Madam Justice Beverley McLachlin	March 30, 1989
The Hon. Mr. Justice Frank Iacobucci	January 7, 1991
The Hon. Mr. Justice John Charles Major	November 13, 1992

10.2   ACTUAL OFFENCES BY TYPE[1]

Type of offence	1987	1988[r]	1989[r]	1990	1991	Percentage change in rate per 100,000 1987-91
Violent offences						
Homicide[2]	642	575	657	656	753	50.0
Attempted murder	916	835	830	905	1,041	—
Sexual assault	22,369	24,898	26,795	27,800	30,314	28.7
Other assault	169,325	177,917	190,004	207,178	226,340	28.1
Other sexual offences	2,639	3,150	3,569	3,611	3,928	50.0
Abduction	967	1,059	1,002	1,054	1,095	—
Robbery	22,523	24,172	25,722	28,177	33,209	41.4
Violent offences — total	219,381	232,606	248,579	269,381	296,680	29.8

10.2   ACTUAL OFFENCES BY TYPE[1] (concluded)

Type of offence	1987	1988[r]	1989[r]	1990	1991	Percentage change in rate per 100,000 1987-91
Property offences						
Breaking and entering	364,144	359,198	348,430	379,009	434,307	14.4
Theft — motor vehicle	87,061	89,454	100,208	112,364	139,479	53.9
Theft over $1,000	71,608	80,074	86,995	102,479	117,584	57.6
Theft under $1,000	792,623	776,356	757,119	797,635	864,275	4.6
Have stolen goods	27,013	27,507	27,663	29,713	33,980	21.1
Frauds	126,142	124,772	122,633	130,078	136,601	3.9
Property offences — total	1,468,591	1,457,361	1,443,048	1,551,278	1,726,226	12.8
Other criminal code offences	680,984	700,040	734,309	801,257	874,584	21.9
Total criminal code offences	2,368,956	2,390,007	2,425,936	2,621,916	2,897,490	17.3
Federal statute offences						
Drug offences	61,658	59,430	66,961	60,026	55,385	−14.9
Other federal statutes	40,344	37,042	39,940	31,545	36,194	−14.1
Total federal statutes	102,002	96,472	106,901	91,571	91,579	−14.8
Total provincial statutes	380,692	367,798	360,852	349,170	349,061	−12.0
Total municipal bylaws	109,258	101,551	98,943	101,399	102,541	−10.0
Total offences	2,960,908	2,955,828	2,992,632	3,164,056	3,440,671	11.5

[1] *Based on uniform crime reporting.*
[2] *Updates to the homicide data occur within the homicide project but are not conducted in the uniform crime reporting project; therefore, totals for homicide may vary between these two projects. Homicide includes murder, manslaughter and infanticide.*

10.3 YOUNG PERSONS APPEARING IN YOUTH COURTS FOR FEDERAL STATUTE CHARGES, BY MOST SERIOUS DECISIONS[1] AND MOST SERIOUS CHARGE[2], 1991–92

Most serious charge	Most serious decision												
	Total young persons	Transfer to adult court		Guilty		Not guilty/ dismissed		Stay of proceedings/ withdrawn		Other[3]	
	No.	No.	%	No.	%	No.	%	No.	%	No.	%
Violent	15,226	27	0.2	10,944	71.9	916	6.0	3,334	21.9	5	..
Property	44,885	21	0.1	29,211	65.1	2,267	5.1	13,320	29.7	66	0.1
Other criminal code	7,102	4	0.1	4,669	65.7	360	5.1	2,066	29.1	3	..
Drug related	1,720	1	0.1	1,290	75.0	82	4.8	346	20.1	1	0.1
YOA[4]	3,225	1	..	2,136	66.2	78	2.4	1,006	31.2	4	0.1
Other	277	—	—	216	78.0	10	3.6	51	18.4	—	—
Total	72,435	54	0.1	48,466	66.9	3,713	5.1	20,123	27.8	79	0.1

[1] *Refers to the most significant decision rendered during the fiscal year. Decisions are ordered from most to least serious as follows: transfer to adult court; guilty; other decisions (e.g. not fit to stand trial); stay of proceedings; charges withdrawn; transfer to other jurisdiction; not guilty; or charges dismissed.*

[2] *Refers to the most significant charge; that is, the most serious from the perspective of the final outcome of the case upon adjudication or disposition. Where a person has only one charge, it is defined as the most significant. Where more than one charge is linked to a person, two criteria are used to select one charge as the most significant: (1) decision of the court; and (2) the nature of the offence.*

[3] *Includes those transferred to other jurisdictions and all other types of decisions.*

[4] *Young Offenders Act (YOA).*

10.4 AVERAGE OFFENDER CASELOAD IN CANADIAN CORRECTIONS[1]

Average actual caseload	Year	Provincial corrections	Federal corrections	Canada total
Custodial[2]	1986-87[r]	15,787	11,106	26,593
	1987-88[r]	16,077	10,557	26,634
	1988-89[r]	16,436	11,030	27,466
	1989-90[r]	18,116	11,415	29,531
	1990-91	17,944	11,289	29,233
	1991-92	18,944	11,783	30,727
Non-custodial[3]	1986-87[r]	69,775	8,465	78,240
	1987-88[r]	68,904	8,962	77,866
	1988-89[r]	71,133	8,713	79,846
	1989-90[r]	75,518	8,941	84,459
	1990-91	85,340	8,804	94,144
	1991-92	95,726	8,817	104,543
Total	1986-87[r]	85,562	19,571	105,133
	1987-88[r]	84,981	19,519	104,500
	1988-89[r]	87,568	19,743	107,312
	1989-90[r]	93,634	20,356	113,990
	1990-91	103,284	20,093	123,377
	1991-92	114,670	20,600	135,270

[1] *Includes the offender caseload handled by both the federal and provincial governments combined but excludes offenders by municipal governments.*

[2] *Refers to actual count and therefore excludes inmates temporarily not in custody at the time of count. In 1991–92, approximately 2,414 provincial and 1,465 federal inmates fell into this category.*

[3] *Figures for the federal non-custodial population include full parole, day parole and mandatory supervision counts.*

10.5 CASELOAD CHARACTERISTICS, PROVINCIAL AND FEDERAL CORRECTIONS, FISCAL YEAR 1990–91

Jurisdiction	Sentenced admissions				
	Total number	Female %	Male %	Median age[1]	Median sentence
Provincial corrections					
Custodial	114,834	8	92	28 yrs	20 days
Probation	65,881	17	83	28 yrs	12 months
Federal corrections[2]	4,296	6	99	31 yrs	44.9 months

[1] *The age reported here for federal corrections is mean age.*
[2] *Excludes releases to parole and mandatory supervision.*

10.6 NUMBER OF POLICE OFFICERS[1], 1991

	Independent municipal	Independent provincial	RCMP					Total police	Population per police officer
			Municipal	Provincial[2]	Federal	Other[3]	Total		
Nfld.[4]	...	368	...	423	89	37	549	917	625
P.E.I.	64	...	13	83	17	11	124	188	695
N.S.	754	...	61	531	144	52	788	1,542	584
N.B.	670	...	80	426	82	40	628	1,298	560
Que.[5]	9,025	4,431	...	...	996	123	1,119	14,575	470
Ont.[6]	14,920	4,415	...	...	1,770	105	1,875	21,210	467
Man.	1,245	...	165	544	192	47	948	2,193	498
Sask.	868	...	213	711	152	52	1,128	1,996	498
Alta.	2,549	...	598	912	383	84	1,977	4,526	557
B.C.	1,910	...	2,051	1,328	738	122	4,239	6,149	523
Yukon	...	...	...	86	20	11	117	117	230
N.W.T.	...	...	...	202	15	21	238	238	230
RCMP[7]	...	...	...	...	...	1,825	1,825	1,825	...
Canada	32,005	9,214	3,181	5,246	4,598	2,530	15,555	56,774	476

[1] *Represents actual number of police officers as of September 30, 1991.*
[2] *Provincial RCMP police officer totals will not match the RCMP provincial contract strengths which may include special constables and civilians.*
[3] *Includes Canadian Police Services and departmental and Divisional Administration.*
[4] *The Royal Newfoundland Constabulary shares provincial policing duties with the RCMP.*
[5] *The Quebec Provincial Police provides all provincial policing services in Quebec.*
[6] *Excludes personnel from RCMP ''HQ''.*
[7] *''HQ'' and training Academy.*

Source
Statistics Canada

JOHN SYLVESTER / FIRST LIGHT

CHAPTER ELEVEN COMMUNICATIONS

INTRODUCTION

NEW MEDIA, NEW MESSAGES

"The new electronic independence recreates the world in the image of a global village," wrote Canadian media philosopher Marshall McLuhan in 1962; since then, his revolutionary insights have proved prophetic as more and more people participate, via radio and television, telephones, fax machines, modems and an increasing diversity of other devices, in the electronic global village. Were he alive today, McLuhan himself would likely be astonished at the new media that are proliferating, both in Canada and around the world, in the information society of the 1990s.

New media combine technology, networks, software, content and traditional media to create new information applications, products and services. New media provide better-adapted means to create, organize, share and store information; they cut across traditional boundaries, appearing in every sector and affecting every aspect of our lives. New media are found in business offices, in medical and educational institutions, and in the home. In 1990, the new media market in Canada was estimated to be one-fifth of the domestic communications and information market, which totalled approximately $46 billion.

Business applications are likely to drive the future development of new media. Multimedia software, digital video conferencing systems, geographic information systems, desk-top publishing systems — all these new media are increasingly available, not only to large corporations, but also, as prices decrease, to medium-sized and small businesses.

New media are just as likely to be based in the home as in the workplace. Television cameras, computers, electronic games, online databases and a wide range of communications and information services have all found new markets. In Canada, the estimated total spending on electronic communication products and services in the home in 1990 was in the order of $11 billion. Over $7 billion of this amount was spent in telephone services, computers and cable television subscriptions.

The technological advance that has spurred the tremendous advances in communications of recent years is digitization, the encoding of information of whatever kind into a uniform system based on the binary code, which combines the digits 0 and 1 in an infinity of ways.

Digitization has improved the quality of information that is copied or transmitted over distances, and has also increased the compatibility of different sorts of information. Text, music and moving images can all be recorded in digital form and transmitted via digital communications carriers. For this reason, the boundaries between telecommunications, broadcasting, computing and recording are beginning to dissolve. For example, telephone companies will soon be in a position to transmit video that could compete with the cable television industry, while cable TV networks will be able to provide new data and voice services that could compete with telephone companies. Cable companies already offer services that traditionally have been supplied by telephone, such as leased data channels and security alarm systems.

Not only are new business, educational and leisure opportunities emerging for consumers, but also new industry patterns and structures are developing as lawmakers, computer software and hardware companies, broadcasters, communications carriers, the cultural industries and other players reposition themselves in the changing marketplace.

TELECOMMUNICATIONS

The telecommunications industry is one of the fastest-growing sectors of our economy; in 1989, the total economy grew by 2.2%, while the telecommunications industry grew by 13.4%. And in both 1990 and 1991, while the recession-hit economy as a whole actually shrank, the telecommunications industry recorded growth rates of 8.4% and 5.8% respectively.

In 1991, Canada's telecommunications industry was larger than the electric power industry and 10 times the size of the forestry industry. Telecommunications services represented 2.9% of Canada's Gross Domestic Product; the industry had a growth rate of 8% and revenues of $23 billion ($7 billion for telecommunications equipment and $16 billion for services).

Pete Ryan / GeoStock

Television camera . . . dressed for the weather.

THE MESSAGE IS NEW MEDIA

They're here and more are coming: new electronic media. Our lives are changing as existing media and information technologies combine with new products and services.

New media are really about new ways to create and share information. Some enhance existing ways of exchanging information, some combine previously-separate media and some create entirely new ones.

Among them:

▲ *Digital audio broadcasting offers clearer radio broadcasts, for instance, by reducing static and fading problems associated with interference or distance.*

▲ *CD-ROM (Compact Discs) provides a way of digitally storing text, data, audio and still or moving video images on silvery 12 centimetre discs. Variations include CDs, which store music or voice, CD-ROM (the ROM means 'Read Only Memory') and CD-I (the I stands for 'Interactive'). The latter two are usable on specialized computers.*

▲ *High Definition Television (HDTV) offers a sharper TV picture.*

▲ *Touch-tone telephones, now a fixture, have opened up new services like telephone university registrations that allow students to call up and choose courses by pressing numbers on a phone keypad, and electronic call management features such as call-forwarding, caller identification and voice messaging.*

▲ *Computer Aided Design/Computer Aided Manufacturing (CAD CAM) speeds development of new products and gets them to customers faster by using computers to do formerly labour-intensive jobs like drafting plans and running production equipment.*

▲ *Digital audio and video production* make traditional music recording and film-making more precise and less costly, with more efficient recording and editing equipment.

▲ *Multimedia* kiosks or computer workstations can combine media that until now have been paper based — such as maps — with online text and graphics in one package on a monitor screen.

▲ *Digital video conferencing* combines features of telephone and television to allow people scattered across the country, for instance at different branch offices of a company, to meet face-to-face in an updated version of the telephone conference call.

▲ *Computer-based art* allows artists to link traditional graphic and creative art skills with computers to create or change whole images, or some of their colours and details.

▲ *Virtual Reality* creates the sensory experience of moving through an electronic 'reality' of three-dimensional space by using computer programs and equipment. A user sees the environment on a screen or through television goggles, and using devices such as a computer mouse, a 'data-glove' which digitizes finger movements and spatial positions, or even a computer-wired body suit can 'feel' the experience.

On a per capita basis, Canada has the most extensive telecommunications system in the world. In 1991, over 98% of Canadian homes had telephones. The assets of the telephone industry in 1991 were more than $32 billion, while operating revenues were $14 billion.

Regulatory power over the Canadian telecommunications industry is primarily federal with a number of small companies coming under provincial governments. Federal regulatory control is vested in the Canadian Radio-television and Telecommunications Commission (CRTC), which ensures that rates charged for telecommunications services are fair. In recent years, technological and economic pressures have prompted the CRTC and the federal government to deregulate many segments of the industry, such as the manufacture of telephone sets and computer terminals.

In February 1992, the Canadian government tabled a comprehensive bill designed to consolidate and modernize the statutes that govern telecommunications services and ensure that Canada's telecommunications system can respond to rapid technological change and the demands of the marketplace. As the Year Book was going to press, the bill was still before Parliament.

STRUCTURE OF THE INDUSTRY

There are two major telecommunications carriers operating nationally: Stentor and Unitel. In addition, there are about 50 independent telephone companies and hundreds of cable companies.

The Stentor Alliance is a consortium linking Canada's regional networks. It comprises seven privately-owned telephone companies and two provincially owned companies in Saskatchewan and Manitoba. Formed in January 1992, the Stentor Alliance involves the incorporation of two jointly held companies — the Stentor Resource Centre Inc. and Stentor Telecom Policy Inc. — as well as a revised mandate for Telecom Canada, which has been renamed Stentor Canadian Network Management (SCNM). Telesat, Canada's satellite communications company, is also a member of SCNM, and Québec-Téléphone is an associate member.

In January 1992, SCNM completed installation of the longest fibre optic transmission system in the world, a 7 000 kilometre network stretching from Newfoundland to Canada's West Coast. A second cross-Canada route, combining fibre and digital radio, was completed in early 1993. Overall, the Stentor network comprises some 211 million kilometres of wire and cable. With its 73 000 route kilometres of microwave system and more than 75 000 route kilometres of fibre, the network would wrap around the earth's equator more than 450 times.

Almost all of the SCNM national long-distance network is supported by digital transmission and switching systems, and the use of digital technology is also growing rapidly at the local level. By 1995, virtually all Canadian subscribers will have access to digital facilities. In 1993, SCNM also had two digital microwave systems in Western Canada, and one in Eastern Canada. By the end of 1992, switched and private line traffic between Canada and the US was 100% digital. Traffic was 98% digital on the Canada West network, 95% digital on the Canada East network. By the end of 1993, all networks were scheduled to be 100% digital.

Unitel (formerly CNCP Telecommunications) was formed in May 1990 by a merger of Canadian Pacific Limited and Rogers Communications Inc. Shortly thereafter, Unitel filed a request with the CRTC for permission to provide competitive long-distance telephone services in Canada, and in June 1992, that permission was granted. Also in 1992, the American communications company AT & T became a minority shareholder in Unitel. As a facilities-based carrier with a national digital microwave and fibre-optic network, Unitel now competes with Stentor in every area except local telephone services.

Citing eroded revenues due to this competition in long-distance services, the entry into the market of cellular service providers and other equipment retailers, and a generally weakened economy, Bell Canada, the largest of the telephone companies in the Stentor Alliance, applied in 1993 to the CRTC for permission to increase local rates for telephone service. If approved, the increases would be the first in 10 years, and would be introduced in stages through 1993.

Teleglobe Canada, established as a Crown corporation but privatized in 1988, is the country's international carrier, connecting domestic and overseas networks. Teleglobe is one of only a few telecommunications companies in the world that focuses particularly on intercontinental communications.

INNOVATIONS Bell Canada and other telephone companies have in recent years introduced a number of new services, including answering services, call forwarding, three-way calling, call tracing, and a service that displays on a Liquid Crystal Display (LCD) screen the number from which an incoming call is placed. This allows subscribers to choose how — and whether — to answer incoming calls. To protect user privacy, a complementary service allows subscribers to block the display of their number when making a call.

Mobile cellular telephones — or more properly, radiotelephones — have been available in Canada since 1985. In a cellular telephone system the service area is divided into a number of small districts, called cells, which vary from 1.5 kilometres to 15 kilometres in diameter. Inside each cell, a low-powered radio base station sends and receives signals to and from the mobile cellular phones in the cell. A master computer connected with all of the base stations automatically gives a caller an available radio channel in the proper cell, and automatically ''hands over'' a mobile call to another cell if callers travel between cells as they speak. This way, calls are not interrupted when a cellular phone moves out of range of a single base station. In earlier radiotelephone systems, a single powerful radio base station blanketed a large area, and mobile users lost their link with the base when they travelled to the area's edge. The low power of the base stations means different callers can use the same radio channels at the same time in different districts, so more callers can use the system at once than in an old-style radiotelephone system. In April 1993, Communications Canada estimated that there were about 1.1 million cellular phones in use in this country.

In 1994, Canada will introduce an affordable two-way public access cordless telephone service which will link pocket-sized telephones to nearby base stations having access to the public switched telephone network. As long as they are within 50 metres of one of

ELECTRONIC HIGHWAYS

Imagine being able to plug all of your home electronic equipment — television, telephone, fax, computer, central fire and burglar alarms, and more — into a single wall outlet.

This 'everything connection', known as the 'electronic highway system', may be coming closer to reality in Canada, since planners at Communications Canada envisioned a 'Trans-Canada highway' for information in late 1992.

Like our road system, the electronic version would include major highways, secondary roads and urban streets. The 'cars' and 'trucks' would be bundles of information that can travel along all the roads with all kinds of cargo.

Once completed, it would be a 'network of networks', joining telecommunications, broadcasting cable, wireless and satellite systems, all seamlessly and transparently interconnected so that hooking up to any one of them would give you, in effect, access to all of them.

This is possible because as more kinds of information are digitized, old technological boundaries between these services are blurring, although some regulatory boundaries remain.

Precedents for this type of seamless transparent connection already exist. Canadians who telephone Europe don't know or care if their voices are routed through land and undersea cable or satellite links, as long as they connect.

Similarly, television could come to you by cable, telephone, satellite, or a blend of all three in the very near future.

TALKING BACK TO TV

In the heat of the moment many of us have blurted something at our TV sets — and perhaps felt foolish when we've remembered there's no way the box can hear us.

After all, television has traditionally been one-way: networks or cable companies pour in programs at one end of the system, and their choices spill out of your TV.

But now a Canadian cable company is marketing television technology that hears and answers watchers through a converter box, remote control and onscreen menu not unlike those on some computers. The remote resembles an ordinary TV clicker, but it goes far beyond changing channels and volume.

At the beginning of 1993, the company had about 200,000 subscribers world wide: most in Canada but some in test markets in England and Denmark.

In part, the system makes every viewer their own program director, capable of picking the camera angles they like best.

Watching a hockey game, viewers might opt for the regular network feed, order camera angles that track either team's star player, or call up an instant replay . . . at any time.

During a rock concert, viewers can switch between close-ups of band members, and the sound of their instrument will dominate the stereo musical mix. Or they can pick a view of the whole stage, with lyrics scrolling across the bottom of the screen.

There are other capabilities: a few button clicks and viewers are playing against on-air game show contestants, using the remote to pick answers as the score is displayed in the corner of the screen.

Viewers can also choose from the cable company's library of videotex services: weather forecasts, road, ski and water conditions, news and stock market quotations, lottery results, TV listings and daily horoscopes. The system also offers several dozen arcade-style interactive video games.

Cable subscribers in Montreal have had interactive television since 1990, where a private Canadian company, Videoway, spent about a decade developing the system. The company began a similar service in Edmonton in May, 1993.

The service offers options that have becoming usual for cable — pay television, closed captioning for the hearing impaired, pay TV channels and pay-per-view selections.

Because of the amount of information the system can carry, the company plans more in the near future.

It has the capability of providing interactive video catalogues, home shopping and banking. For instance, users could call up theatre listings, check which seats are for sale, then use an accessory credit card reader to buy their tickets by cable.

There's also the promise of home automation, which would allow subscribers to manage energy and water use by programming the cable system to turn lamps or appliances on or off through their house's electrical wiring. The converter could also provide central fire and burglar alarms or home medical monitoring.

Still other capabilities to come include a modem connection that would allow users to read computer bulletin boards and download software into their computers over the cable system.

Bob Anderson / CMCP

Pierre Elliott Trudeau, Canada's 15th Prime Minister, arrives in style at Government House, Ottawa, 1979.

these base stations, users will be able to place and receive calls with other users and with subscribers to the regular telephone service.

But telecommunications carriers now offer much more than telephone voice transmissions: with the advent of new technology such as digital communications, fibre-optic cables and satellite transmission, new data and video services are now available.

For example, video conferencing facilities are becoming increasingly accessible. For the price of a few phone calls, you could organize a video conference with colleagues in Great Britain, Australia or Hong Kong via Teleglobe Canada's Globeaccess-64 international switched data service. Employing digital switching so that any phone lines may be used, rather than a specially dedicated network, this service adheres to the Integrated Services Digital Network (ISDN) standards for voice, data, and video communications. Similar services are offered domestically through Stentor's Digital Switched Network and services such as Bell's Microlink and Megalink. Unitel offers video conferencing services through specially dedicated lines.

In 1992, Teleglobe Canada announced the inauguration of TAT-9, a large-capacity transatlantic fibre-optic cable connecting Canada and the United States with England, France and Spain. Teleglobe is the third-largest investor among an international consortium of 38 telecommunications firms holding interests in the TAT-9 cable, which can carry over 75,000 phone conversations simultaneously.

Also in 1992, Teleglobe announced the formation of another international consortium to lay another fibre-optic cable between North America and Europe. The CANTAT-3 cable will have four times the capacity of TAT-9 and will connect North America with Germany, the United Kingdom and Scandinavia. Through linking cables in Denmark and Germany, the cable will also have access to the potentially growing markets of Eastern Europe and the Confederation of Independent States.

In March 1993, the Stentor Alliance and Newbridge Networks Corporation (a telecommunications equipment firm based in the Ottawa region) reached agreement with the Financial Network Association (an alliance of 12 of the world's biggest telecommunications companies) to set up a financial data network based in Ottawa and linking banks, investment firms, insurance companies and other financial institutions around the world. The network, the first of its kind in the world, was scheduled to go into commercial service as early as September 1993.

Making use of these advances in the telecommunications infrastructure, and of others to come, are several initiatives to provide data network services linking schools, universities, research establishments, health facilities, businesses of all kinds and other users with personal computers. For example, in Ottawa, the National Capital FreeNet service plans, by the end of 1993, to offer free access to a network of communities, databases, and information providers for anyone who has a personal computer and a modem. FreeNet will also provide electronic mail services and will serve as a forum for public debate.

Such networks as these have the potential to revolutionize the way we work, study, do business and research, communicate about topics that interest us, and even vote. Indeed, the Canadian government has envisaged an 'electronic highway system' with the potential to reach each and every Canadian over all kinds of networks, offering us access to all kinds of information, government or business services, health care, police protection, educational resources, entertainment and more. Funds are to be set aside for the development of a Canadian Network for the Advancement of Research, Industry and Education (CANARIE) to provide access to advanced information, perhaps by the end of this decade.

BROADCASTING

The technologies of television, computers, and digital telecommunications are converging, and may well merge together over the next few years. Instead of each using its particular medium or mode of delivery, the telephone, broadcasting and cable industries may all deliver their services via the same plug in the wall.

Already, however, digitization is having a profound effect on broadcasting. The digital processing of television data streams makes possible an explosive growth in the number of channels delivered to the home TV, and paves the way for the delivery of high definition television (HDTV), a system offering higher resolution (picture quality) and other improvements over the current National Television System Committee standard. The images transmitted by HDTV will be of the same quality as 35 mm photographs. HDTV broadcasting might begin as early as 1994; experts predict that by 1997 it will be available over-the-air, on cable, and by satellite.

Digital radio broadcasting is also getting closer. Under a joint initiative of the Department of Communications and Canadian broadcasters, the successful testing of new experimental transmitters in 1992-1993 has brought the implementation of consumer-level digital radio services in Canada, projected for 1995, a step closer. Under the auspices of the Task Force on the Introduction of Digital Radio, created by the Minister of Communications in 1992, experiments will continue using the European EUREKA technology and making use of the new radio L-band frequency. Digital radio broadcasts will be of a sound quality comparable to that of the Compact Disc, or CD.

With the introduction of fibre-optic cables, cable technology has also advanced considerably. As well as an increase in the number of channels available to subscribers, recent years have seen the introduction of new services, including interactive TV. In 1991, Canada's 1,800 licensed cable operators provided up to 60 channels, and some were preparing to expand to as many as 80 channels. Of the 92% of Canadian homes with access to cable services, four out of five are subscribers. Canadian cable systems offer a basic service which usually includes local broadcasters' signals, a community channel, the parliamentary channel and some American signals. In addition, most offer a range of specialty, pay and non-programming services.

THE CANADIAN BROADCASTING CORPORATION

The Canadian Broadcasting Corporation (CBC) is the major broadcaster in Canada. In 1991-92, the CBC's budget was around $1.4 billion. The major part of this budget is paid for by the government; in 1991-92, the Corporation's parliamentary appropriation was $1.03 billion. The rest of the budget (about $377 million) was covered by advertising and other revenues. The CBC costs each Canadian about nine cents a day.

In 1991-92, the CBC operated several national services: a French television network; an English television network; CBC North, serving Canada's North by providing radio and television programs in English, French and seven native languages; Newsworld (a 24-hour, satellite-to-cable English-language news and information service funded entirely by cable subscription and commercial advertising revenues); and Radio Canada International, a shortwave radio service which broadcasts in seven languages, managed by the CBC and financed by External Affairs and International Trade Canada.

The English and French CBC television services are available to more than 99% of Canadians (or at least, of those owning television sets — which, according to Statistics Canada, means virtually every household in the country). These services present Canadian-produced news, current affairs, drama, sports, religion, science, children's programs, consumer information and light entertainment. In 1991, the CBC owned and operated 29 television stations and 605 television network relays and broadcast transmitters. CBC television programming was also carried by 29 affiliated stations and 169 rebroadcast transmitters.

In 1990-91, CBC radio, in English or French, was available to more than 99% of Canadians owning radio receivers (which, Statistics Canada reports, were to be found in 98.9% of Canadian households in 1991). To provide this service, the CBC owned and operated 65 radio stations, as well as 615 rebroadcasters and low-power relay transmitters. CBC programming was also carried by 19 private affiliate radio stations and 28 rebroadcast transmitters.

The CBC offers a wide range of radio programming on AM and FM frequencies, including popular and classical music, serious drama and light comedy, talk shows, analyses of politics and the arts, local news, current affairs, sports, weather and traffic reports, and regional and network programming.

The CBC was created in 1936 with a dual mandate: to provide a national radio service, and to regulate all broadcasting in Canada. The first television service was added in 1952. In 1958, the CBC's regulatory function was reassigned to the Board of Broadcast Governors. Under the 1968 Broadcasting Act, the Board was succeeded by the CRTC, which became responsible for all broadcasting regulation.

On June 4, 1991, a new Broadcasting Act was proclaimed. It reaffirms the general principles of earlier legislation, notably that the broadcasting system must be Canadian, offer services in English and French that should be widely available throughout Canada and provide a wide range of programming that informs, enlightens and entertains.

The new act also takes into account the many social and technological changes that have occurred since 1968. It recasts the statutory definitions in a technology-neutral way that focuses on programming and distribution activities rather than the technology used. Also, it reflects the diversity of Canadian society and the need to ensure fair representation and freedom of expression for all Canadians.

The broadcasting Act recognizes that French-language and English-language broadcasting operate under different circumstances and may have different needs. It gives the CRTC more flexibility to tailor its regulatory approach to changing circumstances and changes the CRTC's decision-making process to provide for greater regional sensitivity. In addition, the new Act grants the Governor in Council (that is, the Governor General acting on the advice of ministers) the power to issue policy directions to the CRTC. Finally, it confirms explicitly the CBC's journalistic and creative independence, restructures its senior management and clarifies its accountability to Parliament in financial and management matters.

LONG-DISTANCE DOLLARS

As new competitors stake their claims on Canada's public long distance voice telephone services market, Canadians can expect to pay lower rates for "that long-distance feeling".

In 1992, the Canadian Radio-Television and Telecommunications Commission (CRTC) — the federal body that regulates Canada's broadcasting and major telecommunications companies — opened the door to new competition for Canada's long distance dollars, estimated at $7.5 billion annually. It also opened the door for more competition in the telecommunications resale market.

It began in May, 1990, when Unitel Communications, a Toronto-based company owned by Canadian Pacific and Rogers Communications, applied to the CRTC for permission to provide Canadians with a competitive long distance service. The CRTC received another joint application from Rail Telecommunications and Lightel Incorporated (BCRL) for similar rights just two months later.

To provide such competitive telecommunications services, the applicants required access to the local telephone networks of telephone companies: the British Columbia Telephone Company (B.C. Tel), Bell Canada (Bell), Maritime Telegraph and Telephone Company, Limited (MT&T), The New Brunswick Telephone Company Limited (NBTel), The Island Telephone Company Limited (Island Tel), and Newfoundland Telephone Company Limited (Newfoundland Tel).

The CRTC's decision to open the public long distance and resale markets followed the most extensive series of hearings in telecommunications history — over 90 days of hearings, more than 50,000 pages of oral and written evidence were submitted.

Unitel, which plans to compete nationally, promises, on average, to cut public long distance voice charges by about 15%. BCRL, meanwhile, plans to also provide cheaper long distance services, mainly in selected markets in Ontario, Quebec and British Columbia.

These new competitors, in turn, will be required to contribute part of their earnings to help maintain local telephone services. Their contributions, based on the amount of business taken away from the traditional telephone companies, may help to keep local telephone rates down.

In 1992, the CBC launched the 'Repositioning' initiative, an overhaul and reorientation of its programming, operations and relationship with the Canadian public. This initiative, a response to new technologies, budget cuts, falling revenues and a market increasingly fragmented by competition from pay TV and other specialty services, aimed to maintain the CBC's competitiveness by providing Canadians with distinctive radio and television not available from any other source.

PRIVATE BROADCASTING   In addition to private stations affiliated with the CBC, Canada's non-public television includes the Canada-wide CTV English-language network; Global Television, based in Ontario; Le Réseau de Télévision Quatre Saisons, based in Quebec; the TVA network, with originating stations and several rebroadcast facilities in Quebec and one facility in the Atlantic provinces; the Atlantic Satellite Network, a regional satellite-to-cable service; and a number of independent stations generally located in large cities. Several independent stations broadcast in languages of Canada's ethnic minorities.

For private television, profits were $95 million (before taxes) in 1989, but dropped to $14 million in 1990. In 1991, private television as an industry lost money — $70 million — for the first time ever.

There are four provincial educational television networks: Radio-Québec, TVOntario, Access Alberta and British Columbia's Knowledge Network. TVOntario began a French-language network in 1987.

Discretionary or Pay-TV services were first licensed by the CRTC in 1982, and specialty services in 1984. Examples of discretionary and specialty services are MuchMusic, The Sports Network, The Movie Channel and Superchannel; some of these services may be offered by cable companies as part of a basic package, while others are available at the viewer's 'discretion' (and expense). Recent CRTC hearings on the structure of the broadcasting and cable industries are expected to lead to major changes in the viewing options offered to consumers.

By 1991, Canada had 498 privately owned radio stations. Some private radio stations feature a particular musical style, such as rock, country, adult contemporary or 'oldies.' Others focus on news programming. In 1991, private radio revenues were at $756 million, down from $780 million in 1990. The radio industry lost a total of $34 million (before taxes) in 1991, compared with a profit (before taxes) of $184 million in 1986.

CANADIAN CONTENT   Recognizing the economic realities Canadian producers and broadcasters face competing with larger US networks, the federal government has taken a number of measures to maintain and protect Canada's cultural identity in its television and radio broadcasting. The 1968 Broadcasting Act requires broadcasters to provide high-quality programming using predominantly Canadian resources; the 1991 Broadcasting Act reaffirmed this principle.

Established in 1983, the Canadian Broadcast Program Development Fund encourages the production and broadcast of quality television programs by private Canadian producers. From 1983 to 1992, the Fund invested approximately $522 million in the production of 913 projects whose total budgets exceeded $1,553 million. The Fund is administered by Telefilm Canada, a Crown Corporation set up in 1967 and dedicated to the development of the Canadian Television and feature film industry. Providing financial support to the private sector Canadian film and television industry, Telefilm Canada gives precedence to the high-quality productions that are original reflections of Canada's identity and culture and that have wide audience appeal, both at home and abroad. For example, the *Road to Avonlea* series, based on the famous *Anne of Green Gables* novels of Lucy Maud Montgomery, has been sold in some 120 countries around the world; the series *Les filles de Caleb*, from the novel by Quebec writer Arlette Cousture, has won audiences of more than 4 million in France alone.

In 1991-1992, the CBC's English-language television programming consisted of about 89% Canadian content in prime time; for French-language programming, the figure was about 88%. Overall, some 71% of CBC television (English and French combined) was Canadian produced, although not necessarily all by the CBC. Most of the remainder was imported from the US, France, England and Belgium.

FRENCH-LANGUAGE BROAD-CASTING

French-language television viewers in Canada are offered a wide variety of programming. French television services include the national public network (Société Radio-Canada — the French name for the CBC), two private networks (Télé-Métropole and Télévision Quatre Saisons), two educational broadcasters (Radio-Québec and TVOntario's La Chaîne), one international satellite- to-cable broadcaster (TV5), four specialty channels, a Pay-TV network and a variety of community television stations.

French-language broadcasting is monitored by a joint federal government–Quebec committee set up in 1985 to address the challenges facing the future of French-language radio and television in Canada.

NORTHERN SERVICE

Television Northern Canada (TVNC) is the country's newest national television network and the only undertaking of its kind for indigenous people in the world. Licenced as a network by the CRTC in October 1991, it began broadcasting in January 1992. TVNC delivers a unique programming service to an audience of approximately 100,000 people, over half of whom are of aboriginal ancestry. These people live in 95 communities from the Yukon/Alaska border to the Atlantic coast of Labrador, an area spanning over one-third of Canada's land mass.

By May 1993, TVNC was broadcasting over 100 hours per week of aboriginal language, cultural, information and educational programming. There are broadcasts in 15 aboriginal languages as well as English and French.

Core funding for TVNC comes from the Department of Communications. Other revenues are raised via commercial advertising sales and rental of facilities to southern broadcasters. TVNC is governed by a consortium of broadcasting, educational and other organizations that also produce its programming. To deliver that programming, TVNC makes use of three presentation centres, the Anik E-1 satellite, and receive-and-rebroadcast facilities located in the communities it serves.

SATELLITE SYSTEMS

Communications satellites are used both for broadcasting and for telecommunications purposes. A communication satellite can be thought of as an elevated microwave tower locked into geostationary orbit about 35 900 kilometres above the equator. Hundreds of strategically located earth stations transmit and receive satellite broadcasting signals and relay them to Canadian viewers and listeners. Portable earth stations developed by the Department of Communications (DOC) have allowed on-the-spot television coverage of news stories, elections, sports and special events.

The domestic satellite system supplementing Canada's terrestrial network is owned and operated by Telesat Canada. Formed in September 1969, Telesat became wholly private when the government sold its shares in the company in 1992, with the guarantee that Telesat would have a 10-year monopoly on communications satellites in this country. In 1991, Telesat launched the Anik E1 and E2 communications satellites, which, together with the Anik C and D series, provide television, radio, data and message services.

Television signals from major companies are distributed via satellite 'in the clear' — that is, without the use of encryption or 'scrambling'. However, to counteract revenue losses due to the theft or piracy of satellite signals, programmers who supply services on a pay-per-view or pay-per-month basis are making use of encrypted or scrambled images. In 1991, the Radiocommunication Act was amended to deal with the unauthorized decoding of scrambled satellite signals and a number of distributors of various kinds of illegal decoding devices have been prosecuted. As the technology advances, life will become harder for the pirates; the new Digital Video Compression system (DVC), expected to come into use in 1994-95, will, because of the way it breaks down images into discrete parts, constitute a de facto scrambling device.

A new development in satellite broadcasting is Direct Broadcasting Satellites (DBS). Using the DVC

Gary Wilson / CMCP

Sandy Cove, Digby County, Nova Scotia.

technology, DBS will be able to offer up to 250 more channels of programming to small and user-friendly home-owner receiver systems. As the Year Book was going to press, Telesat was involved in the promotion of the Select Canada Package, a Canadian response to U.S. DBS services expected to commence in 1994.

As with terrestrial systems, satellite telecommunications services are becoming increasingly sophisticated. The Very Small Aperture Transmitter (VSAT) network is a two-way, point-to-multipoint interactive data service network. It consists of a master-hub earth station linked via satellite to a large number of small and relatively inexpensive earth stations located at customer sites. The network can be used for a host of applications, including electronic funds transfer,

point-of-sale credit card transactions, on-line transaction processing, down-line software loading, inventory control, videoconferencing, training and information sessions. Canada's VSAT network began with the Telesat Anikom 200 service, which was followed by CANCOM Satlink service. Unitel has also introduced a VSAT system.

Within the next few years, mobile satellite (MSAT) communications services are expected to revolutionize mobile communications in North America. Telesat Mobile Incorporated (TMI) will launch a specially developed high-power satellite in 1994; once this satellite is operational, MSAT users will be able to communicate directly by satellite to and from virtually any point in North America, regardless of speed, direction or geographical location, and using only a small and inexpensive radio terminal. The system will also provide a direct link for Canadians in rural and remote areas to radio and public telephone systems. The MSAT service is expected to be of particular usefulness in transportation, law enforcement, resource exploration, coastal and in-land shipping, general aviation, and the monitoring and control of utilities such as pipelines and remote weather stations. By the year 2000, TMI projects 120,000 to 160,000 MSAT users will be on the air.

COMMUNICATIONS CANADA

The federal government's communications policies and programs are administered by Communications Canada. The full legal name of Communications Canada is the Department of Communications; its primary goals are to ensure that Canadians have access to a broad range of communications services at reasonable cost, and that new information technologies are developed and introduced in ways that benefit all Canadians. Communications Canada provides technical certification for broadcasting and regulates the use of the radio frequency spectrum.

As part of its research efforts, Communications Canada operates two laboratories: the Communications Research Centre (CRC) and the Canadian Workplace Automation Research Centre (CWARC). The CRC researches communication devices and components, and broadcast, communication and space technologies. CWARC performs applied research in computerized office systems (including integrated work stations, open systems interconnection, computer-assisted translation, expert systems and knowledge management), and in the organizational aspects of office automation.

TRADITIONAL MEDIA

IT'S IN THE MAIL . . . Regardless of the technological advances taking place with ever-increasing speed around us, Canadians still make good use of perhaps the most traditional means of communication over long distances: the post. In the

1991-92 fiscal year, Canada Post delivered 10 billion pieces of mail, a 50% increase since its first full year of incorporation a decade previously.

With one of the country's largest corporate workforces (about 57,000 full- and part-time employees), Canada Post delivers mail to over 11 million addresses in urban and rural Canada. To move the mail, the Corporation operates a network of 25 major mail processing plants and a fleet of 5,300 vehicles. Its products and services are sold at over 18,200 points of sale, more than 75% of which are privately operated. Many of its postal outlets also distribute government forms such as income tax returns and application forms for passports.

Following three successive years of profitability, Canada Post suffered a temporary financial setback in 1991/92 due to a major labour disruption and a weaker-than-expected economy. The Corporation expects to return to profitability in 1992/93.

The Canada Post Corporation came into being in 1981, when the federal government, faced with rising deficits and increasing competition from the private sector, turned the Post Office into a Crown corporation. Since then, Canada Post has made mail delivery faster and more reliable, and has introduced new products and services for a rapidly changing marketplace. Recent innovations include bar-code technology that allows the movement of mail to be tracked, and, in September 1992, our first ever hologram stamp, commemorating the achievements of Canadians in space and showing a three-dimensional image of a space shuttle orbiting over Canada.

Another innovation has been hybrid mail — a marriage of telecommunications and traditional mail delivery. Hybrid mail is mail that changes its form between creation and delivery. One example of this is volume electronic mail, in which a large-volume mailing company sends in electronic form a message, a corporate logo and a mailing list to Canada Post, which communicates it, also electronically, to one of seven print sites in Canada, nearest the mailing's final destination. There the message is printed, put into envelopes, addressed and inserted into the regular mail system. Other examples of hybrid mail are Telepost and Envoypost, in which various kinds of

. . . BEAM ME UP

First it was cellular phones. At the end of the last decade, their stubby antennas suddenly began sprouting up beside ears everywhere from the board room to the street corner. Now it's 'public cordless telephones', lighter, lower-cost roving telephones designed for use in major cities.

In December, 1992, Canada became the first country in the world to license private companies to sell these new lightweights. They are expected to cost as little as half the price of a conventional cellular phone, and should make calls sound clearer under less-than perfect conditions.

Anyone owning these handsets can pack them into a pocket, purse or briefcase to make or take calls at home, at work, or in most public places.

Public cordless telephones can be roughly compared to the cordless telephones which have been common in many homes for years. However, anyone who dials on a public cordless telephone can link up to any of thousands of radio base stations, not just a single one plugged into a home phone jack. Public cordless base stations will be set up in high-traffic locations like shopping malls, subway stations and airports, in most mid-size to large municipalities beginning in late 1994.

The handset forms a low-powered digital radio bridge with the base station. The base station takes the radio signal from the handset and plugs it into the regular public telephone system. This means the handset can link with any other phone number the caller dials.

All cellular, private and public cordless telephones use radio to form a bridge between the handset and the regular telephone network. However, public cordless telephone handsets use much lower-powered radio signals than cellular telephones. Public cordless phone users must be within 50 metres of a base station to make a call, whereas cellular phones work some kilometres away from their bases. The trade-off is that public cordless phones will probably be lighter and cheaper than cellulars, and will use relatively new digital radio signals, which can be clearer to listen to than the conventional analogue ones on which present cellular and private cordless phones rely.

As well, the expectation is that public cordless base stations will eventually almost completely blanket urban areas, meaning users should be able to call from anywhere in a city. And, while allowing the people at each end of a conversation to hear each other with more clarity, the digital technology will protect callers' privacy... somewhat. Currently-available radio scanners cannot listen to digital signals, although that could change. Anybody trying to eavesdrop electronically would need to be within 50 metres of a caller, in any case.

In Canada, four private companies have been licensed to offer the service on a competitive basis. However, they will build all personal cordless phones to the same technical standard, and agreements between these companies will mean any customer can gain access to every company's base stations.

Al Harvey / Masterfile

Canada Post delivers 10 billion parcels and messages annually.

messages sent electronically are converted to hard copy before being delivered by traditional means. Omnipost, a new service scheduled for launch in 1993-94, will allow subscribers to prepare messages on their personal computers for delivery by Lettermail, Fax and E-Mail (electronic mail).

THE PRINTED WORD Although listening to music and watching TV rank as Canada's favourite leisure activities, the printed word still commands a good deal of attention in this country. In a 1991 survey conducted on behalf of several federal government departments, Canadians reported spending an average of 4.4 hours over the preceding week reading books, 3.6 hours reading newspapers and 2.1 hours reading magazines.

Newspapers In 1991, Canada had 106 daily newspapers with a combined daily circulation of 5.8 million, down from 6.3 million in 1989. Of these papers, 11 were published in French and 95 in English.

Canada also has a large number of non-daily newspapers, including community newspapers, specialized newspapers, armed forces newspapers, supplements, ethnic non-dailies and 'shoppers' (free-distribution papers consisting almost entirely of advertising).

In 1989, Canada's 1,215 community papers had a combined circulation of 117.2 million, with an average circulation of 14,196. The 60 'shoppers' in Canada had a combined distribution of 1.6 million and an average circulation of 27,050 — almost twice the average for community papers.

As well as using their own news-gathering staff and facilities, Canadian newspapers subscribe to a number of syndicates and news services. The largest Canadian news service is The Canadian Press (CP), a co-operative agency jointly owned by the majority of Canadian dailies. CP delivers Canadian and world news in English and French to about 100 member newspapers via satellite. Subscribers to the CP photo service also receive about 1,000 photos a week. A CP affiliate, Broadcast News Ltd., distributes print and audio news by satellite to hundreds of radio and television stations. Another CP subsidiary, Press News Ltd., distributes news services to the Canadian Broadcasting Corporation (CBC), weekly newspapers, magazines and corporate and government clients.

CP has news-gathering staff in 13 Canadian cities as well as in Washington, London and Moscow. Member newspapers provide local news and photographs that can be used by other members. CP's international report includes material from The Associated Press, Reuters, and Agence France-Presse.

Periodicals Whether in the dentist's waiting room, at the local library, or on a plane, the majority of Canadians enjoy reading magazines and other periodicals. In the 1991 survey, some 78% of respondents had read a magazine some time in the last week. The 1978 figure was only 58%.

In 1990-91, nearly 1,100 publishers produced some 1,500 Canadian periodicals of consumer, business, farm, religious or scholarly interest. Consumer periodicals accounted for 71% of total circulation, business periodicals for 15%, religious periodicals for 3%, and scholarly periodicals for the remaining 2%.

Weekly Reading

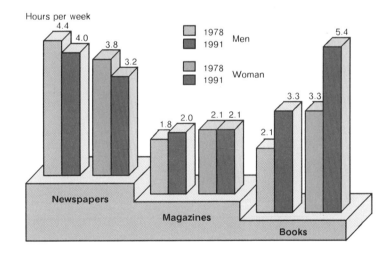

Hours per week

1978 / 1991 Men
1978 / 1991 Woman

Newspapers: 4.4, 4.0, 3.8, 3.2
Magazines: 1.8, 2.0, 2.1, 2.1
Books: 2.1, 3.3, 3.3, 5.4

With an annual circulation of more than 521 million copies in 1990-91, Canadian periodicals had estimated revenues of $884 million, down 2% from the previous year. Advertising sales generated 65% of this total, followed by subscription sales with 21%. Single-copy sales generated 7%, while the remaining 7% came from other sources such as grants, donations and membership fees.

Canada has, since 1965, set up a number of regulatory and legislative measures to foster and support the growth of a Canadian-owned magazine industry. In March 1993, the government confirmed its commitment to this policy, and announced the setting up of a task force to review the instruments by which the policy is implemented to take into account the rapidly evolving technologies that have transformed the industry over the last decade. For example, the electronic transmission of page proofs across the border for printing and distributing in Canada, now a common practice, was not envisaged when the original policy instruments were set up in 1965.

Cover to cover Books have gained in popularity over the last decade or so. The survey reports that in 1978, men spent an average of only 2.1 hours reading books in the week preceding the survey; by 1991, the figure had climbed to 3.3 hours. For women, the increase has been even more marked: in 1991, they reported spending an average of 5.4 hours in the preceding week reading books, compared with 3.3 hours in 1978.

Overall, some 70% of respondents had read at least 1 non-fiction book over the last year (the average number of titles read was actually about nine); around 64% had read at least 1 fiction title and the average number of fiction titles read was about 15. The most popular forms of fiction were romance and mysteries, and of non-fiction, self-help and 'how-to' books.

SOURCES

Canada Post Corporation

Communications Canada

Statistics Canada

The Canadian Press

FOR FURTHER READING

Selected publications from Statistics Canada

▲ *Telecommunications Statistics. Annual. 56-201*

▲ *Telephone Statistics. Annual. 56-203*

▲ *Radio and Television Broadcasting. Annual. 56-204*

▲ *Cable Television. Annual. 56-205*

Selected publications from Other Sources

▲ *New Media...New Choices. Communications Canada, 1992.*

▲ *Reading in Canada 1991. Ekos Research Associates Inc., Ottawa.*

TABLES

11.1 DAILY NEWSPAPERS

	English language		French language		Other		Total	
	Number	Average daily circulation '000	Number	Average daily circulation '000	Number	Average daily circulation '000	Number	Average daily circulation '000
1981	106	4,608	11	980	3	38	120	5,62
1986	100	4,719	11	1,001	5	28	116	5,747
1989	96	5,312	11	1,035	—	—	107	6,347
1990	96	4,778	11	1,022	—	—	107	5,800
1991	95	4,828	11	987	—	—	106	5,815

11.2 NON-DAILY NEWSPAPERS

	Number			Circulation ('000)			Average circulation per issue		
	1986	1988	1989	1986	1988	1989	1986	1988	1989
Community newspapers	942	1,207	1,215	9,749	16,394	17,248	10,349	13,582	14,196
University and school newspapers	169	178	189	2,079	1,559	1,718	12,302	..	9,090
Ethnic newspapers	81	123	131	1,082	467	566	13,358	3,797	4,321
Shoppers	57	66	60	1,686	2,291	1,623	29,579	34,712	27,050
Weekend tabloids	10	3	3	620	231	235	62,000	..	78,333
Armed Forces newspapers	13	12	12	50	21	36	3,846	1,750	3,000
Specialized newspapers	8	6	6	367	165	199	45,875	27,500	36,167
Supplements	15	11	11	621	381	417	41,400	34,630	37,909
All non-daily newspapers	1,295	1,606	1,627	16,255	21,509	22,042	12,552	13,838	13,548

11.3 PERIODICAL CIRCULATION TRENDS

	Number			Circulation ('000)			Average circulation per issue		
	1986	1989	1990	1986	1989	1990	1986	1989	1990
Consumer	599	680	618	26,271	28,838	27,970	43,858	42,409	45,259
Business or trade	321	362	398	4,556	5,380	5,944	14,193	14,862	14,935
Farm	65	63	66	1,401	1,298	1,241	21,554	20,603	18,803
Religious	181	171	184	3,646	3,139	3,514	20,144	18,357	18,554
Scholarly	163	217	237	492	695	842	3,018	3,203	3,553
All periodicals	1,329	1,493	1,503	36,366	39,350	39,510	27,740	26,356	26,287

11.4 FINANCIAL STATISTICS OF TELEPHONE SYSTEMS (THOUSAND DOLLARS)

	Capital stock[1]	Long-term debt	Cost of plant	Revenue	Expenses	Construction expenditures
1981	4,119,997	8,015,933	22,297,545	7,379,725	6,715,815	2,853,237
1986	5,339,718	9,047,073	29,986,087	11,029,738	9,949,213	2,860,062
1989	7,052,114	10,667,486	37,693,601	12,898,292	11,448,267	4,166,257
1990	8,860,338	10,295,722	40,347,751	13,555,365	12,036,431	4,276,653

[1] *Includes premium on capital stock.*

11.5   TRENDS IN THE CANADIAN TELEPHONE INDUSTRY

	Number of systems reporting	Number of employees[1]	Salary and wage payments[2] $'000,000	Telephones in use (company owned)/Access lines[3]			
				Business '000	Residential '000	Total '000	Per 100 population
1981	153	102,625	2,563.5	5,193	11,751	16,944	70
1986	95	91,671	3,387.4	3,247	9,701	12,948	50
1989	66	98,625	4,166.7	4,070	10,578	14,648	55
1990	62	98,166	4,365.37	4,430	10,866	15,296	57

[1] *Full-time employees only.*
[2] *Full-time and part-time employees.*
[3] *Telephones in use: 1981, 1986; Access lines: 1989, 1990.*

11.6   LOCAL AND LONG-DISTANCE CALLS

	Local calls '000	Long distance calls '000	Total calls '000	Long distance calls per capita	Long distance calls per access line
1986	34,672,867	1,959,151	36,632,018	77	151
1989	. .	2,846,597	. .	108	194
1990	. .	3,094,080	. .	115	202

11.7 OPERATING AND FINANCIAL SUMMARY OF THE RADIO AND TELEVISION BROADCASTING INDUSTRY (MILLION DOLLARS)

	1986			1990			1991		
	Private stations		CBC	Private stations		CBC	Private stations		CBC
	Radio	Television		Radio	Television		Radio	Television	
Operating revenue									
Revenue from sale of air time	611	924	171	764	1,248	307	741	1,263	283
Local time sales	466	232	15	586	340	33	573	325	32
National time sales	144	533	77	177	734	124	165	751	109
Network time sales	1	159	79	2	174	150	3	187	143
Production and other revenue									
Syndication revenue	--	19	—	1	39	—	1	37	—
Production revenue	8	47	—	6	56	—	5	52	—
Other revenue	3	19	19	9	21	27	9	26	40
Total, operating revenue	623	1,008	190	780	1,365	334	756	1,378	323
Departmental expenses									
Program	194	489	392	249	774	501	254	790	515
Technical	26	54	291	32	74	384	33	70	429
Sales and promotion	146	93	31	200	150	37	195	147	41
Administration and general	179	149	310	232	226	365	234	223	289
Total, departmental expenses	545	785	1,025	712	1,224	1,287	715	1,230	1,273
Depreciation	22	35	47	31	55	68	32	54	72
Interest expense	31	29	—	68	96	—	69	110	—
Other adjustments — income (expense)	1	25	11	12	23	31	26	−54	16
Net profit (loss) before income taxes	25	184	. . .	−20	14	. . .	−34	−70	. . .
Net cost of CBC operations	. . .	. . .	871	. . .	. . .	989	. . .	. . .	1,007
Salaries and other staff benefits	292	287	573	375	406	683	387	421	720
Average number of employees	10,094	7,554	11,612	10,417	8,673	10,733	10,213	8,524	9,814

11.8 OPERATING AND FINANCIAL SUMMARY OF THE CABLE TELEVISION INDUSTRY

	1986	1990	1991
Revenue ($'000)			
Subscriptions (direct and indirect)	727,003	1,294,698	1,413,764
Installation (including reconnect)	36,340	51,928	54,510
Advertising	—	1,480	1,522
Other revenue	3,697	8,516	7,813
Total, revenue	767,040	1,356,622	1,477,609
Expenses ($'000)			
Affiliation Payments	—	137,089	141,845
Program origination	44,346	61,369	63,269
Technical	205,245	311,520	363,150
Sales and promotion	28,155	45,287	42,511
Administrative and general	180,523	296,914	298,574
Depreciation	110,148	197,815	232,908
Interest expense	69,005	123,573	156,166
Total, expenses	637,422	1,173,567	1,298,423
Other adjustments — (income) expense	−11,229	−8,743	−7,701
Net profit (loss) before income taxes	140,847	191,798	186,887
Provision for income taxes	65,686	56,846	60,250
Net profit (loss) after income taxes	75,161	134,952	126,637
Number ('000)			
Direct subscribers	5,309	6,466	6,620
Indirect subscribers	696	657	666
Total, subscribers	6,005	7,123	7,286
Total, households served by cable	7,686	9,097	9,241
Total, households in licensed area	7,988	9,383	9,533

11.9 PAY TELEVISION, FINANCIAL SUMMARY FOR DISCRETIONARY SERVICES[1]

	1986	1990	1991
Revenue ($'000)			
Subscriptions	149,592	226,597	249,948
Installations	6,649	3,667	3,957
Converters	37,969	41,092	38,553
Other revenue	7,630	13,151	19,393
Total, revenue	201,840	284,507	311,851
Expenses ($'000)			
Affiliation payments	93,176	141,079	148,632
Program origination	. . .	. . .	. . .
Technical	13,753	17,364	18,326
Sales and promotion	9,718	14,026	14,831
Administration and general	18,332	28,695	27,499
Depreciation	30,201	21,719	17,220
Interest expense	3,603	3,020	5,007
Total, expenses	168,783	225,903	231,515
Other adjustments — (income) expense	−1,863	−816	262
Net profit (loss) before income taxes	34,920	59,420	80,074
Provision for income taxes	10,330	12,936	17,883
Net profit (loss) after income taxes	24,590	46,484	62,191
Salaries and other staff benefits	. .	26,736	24,751
Number of employees (weekly average)	. .	848	715
Historical cost of fixed assets ($'000)	. .	172,130	219,565
Accumulated depreciation (recorded in accounts)	. .	115,126	124,258
Net book value	. .	57,004	95,307
Number of subscribers (unduplicated) ('000)	939	2,035	2,279

[1] *Discretionary services are services provided by cable systems in addition to basic cable television services.*

Source
Statistics Canada

CHAPTER TWELVE

DAVE REEDE / FIRST LIGHT

▲

TRANSPORTATION

INTRODUCTION

Canadians may be the most mobile people on earth, and with good reason. As Prime Minister Mackenzie King put it: ''...if some countries have too much history, we have too much geography...''. Canada is the second largest country in the world next to the Commonwealth of Independent States. It stretches 5 514 kilometres from east to west, and 4 634 from north to south. Canada's population of 27.3 million compares with 249 million in the United States, and gives us a population density of fewer than three people per square kilometre compared to the United States' 26.

This fact of life has led Canadians to demand safe, reliable and efficient transportation systems. And, not surprisingly, transportation has played an important role in building the nation we know today. In fact, Canada has witnessed some of the world's most impressive feats of transportation engineering.

Canadians have access to four main modes of transportation: air, rail, road and water. Today, an increasingly mobile population and intensifying international competition are placing new demands on Canada's transportation systems.

TURBULENCE IN AIR TRANSPORT

Canada has two major transcontinental airlines: Air Canada and Canadian Airlines International (CAIL). The 1990s have been difficult for the Canadian airline industry. Air Canada and Pacific Western Airlines (the parent of CAIL) have experienced significant losses — almost $1.5 billion from 1990 to 1992. High debt loads, sluggish traffic breeding capacity exceeding demand, and vigorous price competition have all contributed to the poor financial performance.

This situation, however, is not unique to Canada. World-wide the airline industry lost some $10 billion in the first three years of the decade. This financial crisis is largely due to the Gulf War and the associated threat to security; fuel price increases; and the global recession.

On the heels of deregulation in the United States during the 1970s, the airline industry has undergone considerable change. Globalization and consolidation through airline mergers and alliances are prevalent trends.

In Canada, the era of airline deregulation began in 1984. In the following year, the Minister of Transport's white paper *Freedom to Move* was circulated. Since then, many changes have taken place in the structure of the Canadian air transport industry.

In April 1987, Pacific Western Airlines obtained control of Canadian Pacific, which had already purchased control of Eastern Provincial, Nordair and, indirectly, Québecair. The result was a new airline, Canadian Airlines International, large enough to compete domestically with Air Canada, and internationally with the world's major airlines. In 1989, Canadian Airlines International acquired Wardair, originally a bush charter operation based in Yellowknife, Northwest Territories, which by the mid-1970s had become Canada's largest international charter carrier.

Air Canada realigned its operations into a mainline and regional carrier configuration. In August 1988, Air Canada made 45% of its shares available for purchase by employees and the general public. Until this point, the company had been entirely Crown-owned. Air Canada was fully privatized in July 1989.

International routes are split between the two carriers. They compete directly in only the largest international markets in Europe.

Both airlines have entered into commercial alliances with foreign carriers to extend their market reach internationally.

To compete effectively in the domestic sector, both Air Canada and CAIL have dropped a number of shorter routes that were difficult to service profitably with large jet aircraft. Instead, both airlines have entered into agreements with affiliated 'feeder' airlines, which schedule flights between smaller airports and the main airports.

Lumber train, Horseshoe Bay, British Columbia.

CARS, COACHES AND CARBON MONOXIDE

What produces more air pollution — 43 cars and their drivers, or a bus carrying 43 people? That's what Environment Canada asked when it compared the exhaust emissions of a 43-seater diesel bus with those of 43 new cars. Their findings? The cars together produced about 8 times more pollution than the bus — 54 times the carbon monoxide, 8.4 times the hydrocarbons and 2.4 times the nitrogen oxides — all known to contribute to the greenhouse effect. The bus, however, because it used diesel, produced more 'particulate matter' (tiny particles of pollution) than the cars.

Today these two carriers and their affiliates serve over 95% of the domestic market. Feeder agreements enable Air Canada and Canadian Airlines to compete more effectively on longer-haul domestic and international routes. At the same time, the regional feeders offer more request services to smaller urban centres using smaller, state-of-the-art, turbine-driven propeller (turbo-prop) aircraft. At airports with air traffic control towers, turbo-prop aircraft have almost tripled their share of total landings and take-offs from 10% in 1980 to 28% in 1991.

The vast majority of the smaller non-affiliated airlines operate independently of the major carriers. In 1992, there were more than 800 smaller carriers providing scheduled services, up from 77 in 1984.

In 1955, Canadian carriers took on just under 3 million passengers; in 1989, the total increased to over 37 million, but fell to 32 million in 1992. The only other decline occurred from 1981 to 1983, also during a time of economic slowdown. There have been many years when the industry reported a net loss. However, the loss of $997 million in 1992 represents by far the worst financial performance ever reported by the two air carriers.

In November 1992, to put itself on a better financial footing, CAIL undertook to restructure and reduce its debt load. As part of its revitalization effort, the corporation also sought an alliance with American Airlines involving a $246 million equity infusion. In support of the deal, CAIL employees agreed to wage concessions. To enable the corporation to explore with all interested parties the actions necessary to improve its financial position, the federal government agreed to provide $50 million in loan guarantees. The provinces of Alberta and British Columbia subsequently offered $70 million in loan guarantees.

NEW AIRPORT MANAGEMENT
In 1991, there were 512 certified aerodromes in Canada, of which Transport Canada operated 85, and another 658 non-certified aerodromes. During 1992, Transport Canada divested itself of five airports, leasing them to local airport authorities, with an option to buy. These international airports were Vancouver, Calgary, Edmonton International and the two Montreal

National Archives of Canada C 110428

The note that launched a transportation trademark...

airports, Dorval International and Mirabel International. The policy of transferring management to local authorities allows airports to serve their communities better and fosters regional economic development. Transport Canada retains responsibility for air traffic control and air navigation aids, and regulatory authority for airport security. In response to the Gulf War situation, Transport Canada stepped up security measures for both airports and air carriers; some of these measures have become permanent.

In 1991, Lester B. Pearson International Airport in Toronto increased its capacity by 40% or 10 million enplaning/deplaning passengers annually with the opening of Terminal 3. The $550 million project was financed, designed and constructed by the private sector, which is also operating the terminal. Pearson International ranked as Canada's busiest airport in 1991 with itinerant aircraft movements (landings or take-offs leaving or entering the tower control zone) at 322,278. The airports at Vancouver and Calgary ranked second and third with 288,106 and 205,086 itinerant movements respectively.

In 1991, Pearson International handled 18.5 million enplaning/deplaning passengers, Vancouver handled 9 million and Montreal's Dorval 5.6 million. Calgary ranked fourth with 4.6 million passengers, followed by Ottawa with 2.4 million.

From 1964 to 1980, the number of itinerant movements increased an annual average of 8.8% at Transport Canada airports, rising from just under 1 million to 3.7 million. The recession of the early 1980s had a strong effect: itinerant movements dropped from 3.7 million in 1980 to 3 million in 1985. However, this total had increased to 3.5 million in 1991.

Growth in local movements (flights remaining within the control zone) has suffered a number of setbacks. In the 1960s, the federal government eliminated the subsidy it had paid for students of flying clubs, and in the early 1970s fuel scarcities and consequent hikes in fuel prices led to further declines.

UP, UP AND AWAY Canadians love to travel — particularly if it means a rendez-vous with the sun! The most popular city-pair for all charter regions in 1991 was Montreal–Fort Lauderdale with 236,000 passengers. In the Canada–US region, Florida appeared in seven of the top ten city-pairs.

In international charter passenger traffic, Montreal–Paris retained its position in 1991 as the top Canada–Europe city-pair with 198,000 passengers. Toronto–London was a distant second with 66,000 passengers.

Cancun, in conjunction first with Toronto (95,000 passengers) and then with Montreal (87,000 passengers), retained its top position as Canadians' preferred city in the South.

RAIL TRANSPORT

Canada's railways — a major factor in bringing this country together — also face hard times today. In March 1993, Canadian National announced that it would cut 10,000 jobs (about one-third of its workforce) over a three-year period to get the Crown corporation back to a profitable position. This follows the 1989 announcement that the federal subsidy of Via Rail, the Crown corporation responsible for passenger transportation, would be reduced by more than 40% over five years. The Via cutbacks, including the cancellation of the historic daily Transcontinental,

WHAT IF . . .

In 1979, a 106-car train jumped the tracks in the middle of Mississauga, Ontario. A leaked chemical witches' brew fed a fire and explosion that destroyed buildings, shattered windows, and released a choking green cloud that turned Canada's ninth-largest city into a virtual ghost town for three days.

Environmental incidents like this pose Canadian society a very serious challenge. In fact, every year, about 15,000 spills of hazardous materials take place on Canadian soil, and the Canadian Coast Guard estimates that 3,500 more happen in Canada's territorial waters. Whether they involve a quiet leak of a few litres of oil or a spectacular accident like that in Mississauga, they're labelled 'environmental emergencies'.

Canada has legislation covering the transportation of dangerous goods, and an information bank on hazardous materials. But unlike many industrialized countries, it does not have unified national legislation requiring industries to have emergency plans for all hazardous chemicals. What it does have is a network of regional emergency teams, response centres, a national research centre and Environment Canada's Atmospheric Environment Service, all of which can be called in to assist, and to give advice about monitoring the polluting impact, and cleanup.

A lot of planning concerns the 'what-ifs'. One 'what-if' watchdog is the Major Industrial Accidents Council of Canada (MIACC), formed of federal and provincial governments, industry associations and first-response groups that exchange information with a view to preventing as many accidents as they can. MIACC uses information on past emergencies and practices to analyze what's needed to prevent or cope with future accidents. For example, in 1992, when a train carrying toxic chemicals jumped the tracks at Oakville, Manitoba, ways of dealing with it were already planned and ready.

Since 1991, Environment Canada and MIACC have been assembling a national list of all industrial sites where the potential for major accidents may exist. It also grades their ability to prevent spills, and to deal with them when they do occur. As well as assembling information on locations of critical quantities of industrial toxic chemicals, it encourages industry to follow environmental guidelines.

However, most spills fall under municipal or provincial jurisdiction. Polluters themselves are responsible for damages and cleanup, and they may be supported by municipal or provincial emergency organizations.

The chemical most frequently spilled in Canada is ammonia, followed by chlorine and acids. Alberta and Ontario, each of which has legislation requiring such spills to be reported, account for 30% of all land-based hazardous spills reported in the country. Of the other provinces, Quebec accounts for 14%, Saskatchewan accounts for 10%, and the rest of Canada's provinces combined account for the remaining 15%.

The ideal is to prevent as many such incidents as possible, by encouraging precautions before they occur. Fortunately, most are comparatively small and can be cleaned up within hours. While a 'Mississauga' only takes place every decade or two, every day many Canadians handle common substances that can be hazardous when they break loose, and even with proper precautions and good intentions, accidents happen.

Under **Canada's Green Plan**, $165 million is being invested to reduce the number and impact of domestic oil and chemical spills, and also environmental emergencies caused by severe weather. The Government of Canada also works with its counterparts in other countries, and with international organizations, to design ways to prevent and cope with cross-border spills.

sparked an emotional national debate reflecting the vital nature of transportation in Canada. In April 1993, further reductions to the VIA Rail subsidy were announced as part of the deficit reduction measures contained in the federal budget. The full impact of these cuts on passenger services had not been determined by the corporation when the *Year Book* went to print.

In 1917, Canada had the highest per capita railway mileage in the world. However, by the mid-1950s the trucking and aircraft industries had taken a significant bite out of the monopoly of the railways. In 1990, the total length of track operated was down 5% from 91 365 kilometres in 1988. In the same period, freight car equipment in use decreased 8%, and passenger car equipment decreased 12%.

Between 1988 and 1990, freight revenue was down 9%, passenger revenue 21%, and total revenue 12%. A reduction of 11% in the number of railway employees was recorded.

Railway carriers used 4% less electric energy in 1990 than in 1988 and 13.6% less diesel oil. On the other hand, the consumption of crude oil increased 44%, approaching the level in 1986.

Traffic Fatalities

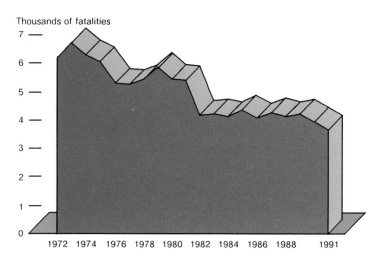

Thousands of fatalities

CANADIANS...A DRIVEN PEOPLE

While once considered a luxury, the automobile has become a virtual necessity for most Canadians. Car ownership is now within the reach of most families — in fact, Canada has more cars than households. In 1990, there were 12.6 million passenger cars in Canada, compared with 10.3 million a decade ago. Moreover, it is estimated that the average car travelled 17 380 kilometres in 1988 — 2.7 times across Canada. This compares with average mileage of 15 820 kilometres in 1980.

Total motor vehicle registrations reached nearly 17 million in 1990, up 4% from 1988. Ontario, with 6 million, registered 35% of the national total, with Quebec second at 21% or 3.5 million vehicles, and British Columbia third at 15% or 2.5 million vehicles. Passenger cars represent the single largest category of motor vehicle registrations at 74% of the total. At 12.6 million, this figure is up 4% from 1988. The second largest category is trucks, truck tractors and buses.

In 1989, 86% of those old enough to drive (17.6 million Canadians) held a driver's licence. This figure represents 67% of the population. A decade earlier, 58% of the population was licensed, representing 78% of those eligible. This increase is partially due to the aging of the Canadian population.

The ever-increasing number of vehicles puts a growing demand on the nation's highways. Canada's Constitution gives jurisdiction over highways to the provinces. The federal government contributes to the building and improving of roads, particularly the Trans-Canada Highway. At 7 821 kilometres, the Trans-Canada Highway, completed in 1970 at a cost of over $1 billion, is the longest national highway in the world.

In 1992, expenditures on highways in Canada totalled over $7 billion. To ease the burden on taxpayers, governments are turning to private developers who, in turn, are expected to collect tolls, thus returning to the user-pay principle of the stagecoach era of the early 19th century. This approach will be used in the construction of a nine-kilometre bypass for Highway 401 in Toronto; tolls will be in effect in 1996.

Dave Pritchard / First Light

Even with the increase in the number of drivers and vehicles, today's highways are a lot safer than they were. With minor exceptions, annual fatalities have decreased steadily over the years. In 1991, the number stood at 3,685, a level not seen since 1961 when there were only 5 million drivers in Canada, as opposed to the over 17 million today.

A 1% increase in seatbelt wearing rates will reduce driver fatalities by 150 over 10 years. In 1992, some 87% of Canadian drivers were using seat belts. The federal and provincial governments are working to achieve a level of 95% restraint use by 1995.

Canadians' dependence on the automobile also takes a toll on the nation's health, posing a threat to people with asthma or lung disease. Motor vehicles not only emit carbon monoxide but also contribute to nitrogen oxide and volatile organic compound emissions. Passenger car emissions of hydrocarbons and carbon monoxide have been reduced by 96% and those of nitrogen oxides by 76% since the introduction of emission controls. The introduction in 1971 of the catalytic converter and the move to more fuel-efficient cars have led to decreasing concentrations of carbon monoxide in our towns and cities. As part of Canada's *Green Plan*, the Canadian Council of Ministers of the Environment has developed a 10-year national plan to manage emissions of nitrogen oxides and volatile organic compounds.

Due to the popularity of smaller, lighter cars and the introduction of more stringent emission standards, cars consumed less fuel on average in 1988 (2 090 litres) than in 1980 (2 620 litres). Sales of gasoline remained fairly constant from 1988 to 1990, while diesel oil sales jumped 50% over the same period. Sales of liquified petroleum gases experienced a decline in 1989 and a recovery in 1990, with the 1990 figure representing an increase of 8% over that for 1988.

PUBLIC TRANSIT   Most Canadians have access to public transit systems and, despite the fact that there are more cars than ever on the road, substantial numbers of Canadians are making use of them. In 1991, Canada's major urban transit systems carried 1.4 billion passengers, 5% more than a decade earlier, but 6% less than the peak year of 1988. This translates into 96 rides per capita. The total number of transit vehicles increased slightly from 1990 to 13,542, with 10,390 in service in peak hours. The urban transit industry employed a total of 39,578 people in 1991.

ACCESSIBLE TRANSPORTATION

In 1992, Statistics Canada released the results of the 1991 Health and Activity Limitation Survey which reported an increase of persons with disabilities in Canada from 3.5 to 4.2 million.

Transport Canada has gained world-wide recognition for achievements in the area of research, development and demonstration of accessible transportation over the last 10 years. For example, the department contributed funding towards the development of a new world class 13.5 metre accessible intercity bus with a self-contained wheelchair lift and a wheelchair-accessible lavatory. The production model is now available on the market. The main thrust for accessible transportation over the next five years will be in moving such technologies into the market place.

In 1991, Transport Minister Jean Corbeil announced Transport Canada's involvement in the five-year interdepartmental National Strategy for the Integration of Persons with Disabilities. The strategy seeks to remove barriers in transportation, communications, housing, education and recreation for persons with disabilities. Transport Canada's financial incentive programs help the industry acquire accessible vehicles or equipment for intercity coaches; small aircraft boarding devices; airport ground transportation; airport rental vehicles; and accessible vehicles and community buses in small urban and rural areas.

Response to the programs has been good. In the area of rental vehicles at airports, some 23 accessible vehicles and 103 hand controls will be placed in service at 36 airports across Canada. Sixty-four taxis/limousines and 19 airport shuttle buses for use at 20 airports across Canada have been approved for contributions under the program. Also, accessible intercity coaches are now operating in 6 of the 10 provinces.

TRUCKING

During 1990, truckers mounted blockades in several parts of the country to draw attention to the position in which they found themselves compared with that of their American counterparts. In 1992 the federal government provided seed money for the creation of the Canadian Trucking Research Institute and two owner-operator buyers' co-operatives to help the trucking industry stay competitive in difficult economic times.

In 1990, Canada's for-hire trucking industry represented by carriers with annual revenues greater than $1 million reported a gross operating revenue of $8.4 billion, down 5% from the 1989 total of $8.8 billion. Operating expenses in 1990 were $8.2 billion, down 4% from 1989. Total equipment in use increased from 1989 levels and the average fleet size increased 6% over 1989.

WATER TRANSPORT

THE ST. LAWRENCE SEAWAY

The St. Lawrence Seaway is an example of the extraordinary engineering feats that are part of Canada's history. Completed and opened to commercial traffic in 1959, it can accommodate vessels up to 222.5 metres long and 23.1 metres wide and with a draft of up to 7.9 metres. The system of locks lifts vessels some 170 metres between Montreal and Lake Superior.

The Seaway has had an enormous impact on Canada's economy and has made it possible for Canada to become a world leader in the export of grain. Grain remains the largest single commodity handled, followed by iron ore, coal and processed iron and steel products.

FROM SEA TO SEA TO SEA

As a country bounded on three sides by oceans, Canada inevitably has a long history of ocean shipping and shipbuilding. Canada can lay claim to the famous Cunard Shipping Company, founded by Samuel Cunard of Halifax in 1840. Following World War I, our merchant fleet and shipbuilding capacity were among the largest in the world. Canada has also distinguished itself in the design and construction of ice capable vessels and vessels for ocean and fisheries research, and the development of self-dumping log barges. Today, however, Canada's shipbuilding industry is in decline.

Ron Watts / First Light

Lion's Gate Bridge, Vancouver.

BRIDGE OVER TROUBLED WATER

The construction of a controversial new bridge that would link Prince Edward Island and New Brunswick was stalled in early 1993, but as the **Year Book** was going to print, the Government of Canada was still negotiating with the province of Prince Edward Island.

The proposed bridge — an $850 million, 13-kilometre span of concrete and steel — would connect Cape Tormentine, NB, to Borden, PEI, eventually replacing the ferry service which now operates between the two points.

A small but determined group of PEI residents have been fighting the idea; they see it as a major assault on their largely rural way of life. Citing the eventual loss of over 500 ferry jobs and potential damage to the island's fishing industry, the Friends of the Island, as they have called themselves, recently took their case to the federal courts — and won.

In April of 1993, Public Works Canada released an evaluation summarizing all of the environmental issues that had been raised regarding the bridge. The primary concern had been the bridge's design, which has now been refined to discourage ice jams. Initial studies had sparked concern about the effects of ice scour on marine biota.

In the same ruling, the Federal Court also ruled that eliminating the ferry service between the two provinces would be unconstitutional. Indeed, in 1873, when PEI joined Confederation, the federal government of the time promised — and entrenched in the Constitution — an efficient steam service to and from the island. The federal government is negotiating with the province for a change in constitutional wording that would guarantee general — not just steam — transportation service in the future.

To proponents of the bridge, the current furor is much ado about nothing. The federal government believes that its environmental review was adequate, and that the proposed bridge meets constitutional requirements by providing a continuous passageway to the island.

Proponents of the bridge also point out that the costly structure would provide the area with badly-needed jobs. The Calgary-based company contracted to build the bridge, Strait Crossing Inc., estimates that almost 2,000 person-years of employment will be created over its five-year construction period. The federal government anticipates that another 640 spinoff jobs will be created over the time frame. If completed, operations and maintenance would be conducted from Borden, creating permanent employment for about 60 people.

The federal subsidy received by the ferry service — about $42.5 million a year — would be put into trust to help finance the construction of the bridge. Strait Crossing's profits would be determined by the amount of traffic using the bridge, as they would be charging tolls.

By taking the bridge, commuters are expected to save an average of 85 minutes per trip. Furthermore, vehicles crossing the bridge would use five times less fuel than it would take for the ferry to carry them.

The past few years have seen an alarming number of marine spills around the world. As a result, Transport Canada is taking steps to protect Canada's marine environment by phasing in double-hulled tankers and undertaking a complete assessment of Canada's marine spill response capability.

PORTS OF CALL The federal Minister of Transport is responsible for three Canadian port groups, all of which are primarily involved in commercial transportation: the Canada Ports Corporation (Ports Canada); the Harbour Commissions; and the Public Harbours and Ports Group. These, together with private and other ports, collectively handled 351 million tonnes of cargo in 1991.

The objectives of the national ports policy include efficiency, equatability, accessibility, and effective support for national trade, and regional and local socio-economic needs.

To serve Canada's international trade needs, Ports Canada administers 15 ports located on three coasts and inland waterways.

With total cargo in 1991 of over 180 million tonnes, Ports Canada handles over half of Canada's waterborne exports and imports. Goods handled include general cargo; forest products such as newsprint, lumber and pulp; mineral products made up largely of coal, iron ore, potash, sulphur and concentrates; and agricultural products including grain.

In 1991, Ports Canada registered over 20,000 vessel arrivals. By far the busiest port was Vancouver, with 9,614 arrivals and nearly 71 million tonnes of cargo handled — over three times as much as the next busiest, Sept-Îles. During the same year, the number of vessels entered at all Canadian ports was 29,532 in international shipping and 23,108 in domestic shipping for a total of 52,640 vessels.

ON GUARD AT SEA The Canadian Coast Guard provides marine navigational systems, ice breaking and Arctic support; administers a number of regulations related to ship safety and pollution prevention; co-ordinates marine pollution counter-measures and the clean-up of spills; and maintains a system of ports and public harbours. It also saves lives.

The Canadian Coast Guard Marine Search and Rescue Program co-ordinates marine search and rescue response in collaboration with the Department of National Defence, provides primary vessels to maintain effective search and rescue coverage, promotes safety to the marine public and co-ordinates the Canadian Marine Rescue Auxiliary, whose volunteers share the Coast Guard's objective of preventing loss of life at sea.

In 1991-92, the Coast Guard saved 1,968 lives in the course of 7,242 marine search and rescue operations. Its search and rescue prevention program serves and benefits many mariners. Even with a steady increase in pleasure craft operators, the number of marine incidents remained fairly steady from 7,080 in 1987-88 to 7,242 in 1991-92.

The Coast Guard Radio Station (CGRS) system handles distress and search and rescue communications and provides the following maritime mobile radiocommunications services: weather, navigational hazard and ice information broadcasts. These services are provided by a network of 30 Coast Guard radio stations controlling 141 remote communications facilities. In 1992-93, the CGRS handled 6,251 maritime distress incidents and nearly 1.3 million messages and radiotelephone calls.

The safety of ships in Canadian waters is the prime concern of the Coast Guard. In 1990-91, the Coast Guard's vessel traffic services helped 663,000 vessels move safely through Canadian waters.

In 1990-91, in excess of 1,200 vessels received support from Coast Guard icebreakers, 42 000 kilometres of channel were broken out, and 82 fishing harbours and 232 commercial harbours opened. During the summer months, icebreakers take part in the annual Eastern Arctic Sealift resupply operations. In 1992, some 54 510 tonnes of food, materials, fuel and equipment were supplied to 35 remote settlements and defence sites, proving yet again just how essential transportation is to the well-being of Canada and its people. In addition, the Coast Guard fleet provides support to other government departments, such as Environment Canada, Fisheries and Oceans Canada and Energy, Mines and Resources Canada in meeting their program objectives, including marine research and development.

MOVING TRENDS

Following the passage of the National Transportation Act of 1967, Canada's transportation system matured but transportation regulation did not keep pace with the times, and slowed progress in services and technology. In response, the government passed a new National Transportation Act, which took effect in 1988. The new act retained many of the principles from 1967 but introduced new concepts as well. It was designed to lessen economic regulation while making safety of paramount importance, to improve operating efficiency, and to increase the range of services available by promoting competition within modes as well as between them. Prices went down as a new balance was struck between the needs of users and carriers.

Canada's transportation policy will need to continue to respond to changing needs. This will mean ensuring that transportation, by achieving world standards of operational efficiency and service, fully supports Canadian shippers in meeting global competition. Governments will focus more on removing barriers — on being facilitators of transportation improvement, rather than being operators of facilities.

SOURCES

Canada Ports Corporation

The St. Lawrence Seaway

Transport Canada

Statistics Canada

FOR FURTHER READING

Selected publications from Statistics Canada

▲ *Air Carrier Operations in Canada*. Quarterly. 51-002

▲ *Air Carrier Traffic at Canadian Airports*. Quarterly. 51-005

▲ *Air Passenger Origin and Destination, Domestic Report*. Annual. 51-204

▲ *Air Passenger Origin and Destination, Canada-United States Report*. Annual. 51-205

▲ *Canadian Civil Aviation*. Annual. 51-206

▲ *Air Charter Statistics*. Annual. 51-207

▲ *Aviation in Canada: Historical and Statistical Perspectives on Civil Aviation*. 51-501E

▲ *Railway Carloadings*. Monthly. 52-001

▲ *Railway Operating Statistics*. Monthly. 52-003

▲ *Rail in Canada*. Annual. 52-216

▲ *Passenger Bus and Urban Transit Statistics*. Annual. 53-215

▲ *Road Motor Vehicles, Fuel Sales*. Annual. 53-218

▲ *Road Motor Vehicles, Registrations*. Annual. 53-219

▲ *Trucking in Canada*. Annual. 53-222

▲ *Shipping in Canada*. Annual. 54-205

TABLES

12.1 CANADIAN AIR CARRIERS[1], OPERATIONAL STATISTICS

	Passengers '000	Passenger kilometres '000 000	Cargo kilograms '000	Mail kilograms '000	Hours flown '000
1955	2,763	1 983	105 163	11 008	623
1960	4,830	4 507	95 401	15 709	879
1965	6,832	8 729	128 618	22 879	1,128
1970	12,031	18 605	256 420	30 068	1,669
1975	20,493	31 539	362 711	45 032	2,466
1980	28,554	46 996	399 418	59 978	3,091
1985	29,056	49 580	498 706	81 457	2,273
1990	36,813	66,791	654,483	..	2,267
1991	32,302	57,873	639,778	..	2,083

[1] *Levels I–V 1955–85, levels I–IV 1990–91. Level V air carriers are those which realized less than $250,000 in gross revenues in one of the two years preceding the report year and are not licensed for the sole purpose of serving the needs of a lodge operation. Level I–IV air carriers realized $250,000 or more in gross revenues, transported 5,000 or more revenue passengers, or transported 1,000 or more tonnes of revenue goods in each of the two years preceding the report year.*

12.2 CANADIAN AIR CARRIERS[1], FINANCIAL STATEMENTS, SELECTED COMPONENTS
(MILLION DOLLARS)

	Operating revenues	Operating expenses	Total net non-operating income	Net income	Total assets	Interest expenses
1955	153	147	—	4	123	2
1960	243	245	−4	−7	335	9
1965	408	383	−10	13	397	15
1970	842	811	−31	−2	1,166	48
1975	1,891	1,823	−90	−7	2,261	108
1980	3,985	3,798	−1	112	3,963	139
1985	5,621	5,520	−123	4	5,942	236
1990	8,240	8,238	−163	−122	9,116	345
1991	7,601	7,855	−339	−427	8,750	382

[1] *Levels I–V 1955–85, levels I–IV 1990–91. Level V air carriers are those which realized less than $250,000 in gross revenues in one of the two years preceding the report year and are not licensed for the sole purpose of serving the needs of a lodge operation. Level I–IV air carriers realized $250,000 or more in gross revenues, transported 5,000 or more revenue passengers, or transported 1,000 or more tonnes of revenue goods in each of the two years preceding the report year.*

12.3 AIRCRAFT MOVEMENTS AT AIRPORTS WITH AIR TRAFFIC CONTROL TOWERS

	Number of airports	Number of movements by type of operation ('000)		
		Itinerant[1]	Local[2]	Total movements
1975	60	2,994	3,404	6,398
1980	61	3,697	3,368	7,065
1985	61	3,031	1,907	4,938
1990	60	3,759	2,299	6,058
1991	56	3,488	2,052	5,540

[1] *Landings or take-offs that enter or leave the tower control zone.*
[2] *Landings or take-offs that remain at all times within the tower control zone.*

12.4 LENGTH OF RAILWAY TRACK OPERATED[1] (KILOMETRES)

	1986	1989	1990
Class I			
Canadian National	50 708	47 243	46 205
Canadian Pacific	33 458	31 720	30 367
Sub-total	84 166	78 963	76 572
Class II and III	9 378	10 141	10 308
Total	93 544	89 104	86 880

[1] *As of December 31st.*

12.5   RAILWAY EQUIPMENT IN SERVICE[1]

	1986	1989	1990
Locomotives			
Road freight	3,019	2,908	2,833
Road passenger	226	221	211
Yard	518	561	577
Associated equipment	134	119	98
Total	3,897	3,809	3,719
Freight cars			
Box	43,746	36,037	33,221
Hopper	28,989	40,037	40,306
Gondola	19,310	15,201	15,136
Refrigerator	974	572	486
Flat	27,692	28,825	27,538
Stock	710	259	162
Caboose	1,808	1,662	1,275
All other freight cars	6,280	5,947	5,013
Total	129,509	128,540	123,137
Passenger cars			
Head-end	148	82	60
Meal service and lounge	120	111	93
Sleeping	159	157	96
Conventional coach	315	288	207
Tempo coach	25	4	—
LRC coach	100	110	110
Rail diesel	85	6	6
Commuter	343	523	516
Total	1,295	1,281	1,088

[1] *As of December 31st.*

12.6 RAILWAY CARRIERS, SUMMARY STATISTICS

	1989	1990
Revenues ($'000)		
Freight revenue	6,084,497	5,993,115
Passenger revenue	317,552	219,130
Miscellaneous rail reven	262,035	256,114
Revenue from services fo	129,174	84,976
Government payments	653,387	515,043
Total revenue	7,446,645	7,068,378
Expenses ($'000)		
Ways and structures	1,258,855	1,237,998
Equipment	1,826,355	1,672,911
Rail operation	2,315,022	2,288,248
General	1,680,059	1,517,736
Total expenses	7,080,291	6,716,893
Number of employees		
General	12,298	11,332
Road maintenance	17,118	15,712
Equipment maintenance	20,118	18,477
Transportation	25,428	23,598
Total	74,962	69,119
Fuel and power consummed		
Electric energy ('000 kwh)	30 715	33 043
Diesel oil ('000 litres)	2 050 148	1 937 852
Crude oil ('000 litres)	116 771	126 482

12.7 HIGHWAY, ROAD, STREET AND BRIDGE CONSTRUCTION EXPENDITURES, 1992[1]
(MILLION DOLLARS)

	Federal and provincial governments		Municipal governments		All other sectors		Total
	New	Repair	New	Repair	New	Repair	
Newfoundland	127.9	31.9	31.6	1.2	9.5	3.0	205.1
Prince Edward Island	49.3	13.0	0.6	0.1	0.9	0.2	64.1
Nova Scotia	160.4	79.1	28.2	11.4	4.7	2.6	286.4
New Brunswick	173.0	7.5	26.5	9.3	3.5	5.0	224.8
Quebec	453.0	226.3	458.1	87.3	61.6	50.9	1,337.2
Ontario	668.0	327.6	911.5	299.9	80.7	41.4	2,329.1
Manitoba	124.6	49.8	69.0	27.7	7.8	6.1	285.0
Saskatchewan	86.3	78.8	46.7	17.0	6.2	8.3	243.3
Alberta	360.1	132.1	231.4	68.7	19.3	28.2	839.8
British Columbia	529.7	262.3	193.9	47.6	69.7	59.7	1,162.9
Yukon and Northwest Territories	27.7	58.3	11.4	0.9	1.6	0.3	100.2
Canada	2,760.0	1,266.7	2,008.9	571.1	265.5	205.7	7,077.9

[1] 1992 forecast data.

12.8 MOTOR VEHICLES REGISTERED FOR ROAD USE

	1986	1989	1990
Newfoundland	273,192	301,152	305,851
Prince Edward Island	78,619	88,377	84,716
Nova Scotia	505,116	566,902	603,615
New Brunswick	426,482	455,252	475,671
Quebec	3,145,116	3,527,732	3,580,765
Ontario	5,367,277	5,943,747	6,000,322
Manitoba	758,947	775,267	779,069
Saskatchewan	669,256	736,638	735,964
Alberta	1,739,472	1,850,771	1,861,662
British Columbia	2,222,717	2,420,890	2,499,485
Yukon	20,886	27,072	30,952
Northwest Territories	20,231	25,729	23,058
Canada	15,227,311	16,719,529	16,981,130

12.9 MOTOR VEHICLES REGISTERED BY TYPE, 1990

	Passenger cars	Trucks, truck tractors and buses	Motorcycles and mopeds	Other	Total
Newfoundland	200,374	90,394	9,134	5,949	305,851
Prince Edward Island	59,970	23,176	1,512	58	84,716
Nova Scotia	418,135	170,351	14,689	440	603,615
New Brunswick	312,948	145,915	10,521	6,287	475,671
Quebec	2,917,255	529,677	84,823	49,010	3,580,765
Ontario	4,756,855	1,118,629	124,838	—	6,000,322
Manitoba	543,095	224,273	11,680	21	779,069
Saskatchewan	448,518	276,117	4,456	6,873	735,964
Alberta	1,187,948	635,958	37,756	—	1,861,662
British Columbia	1,753,372	687,918	58,195	—	2,499,485
Yukon	12,770	17,348	791	—	30,909
Northwest Territories	10,798	11,548	620	92	23,058
Canada	12,622,038	3,931,304	359,015	68,730	16,981,087

12.10 MOTIVE FUEL SALES (THOUSAND LITRES)

	1986	1989	1990
Gasoline			
Newfoundland	521 886	583 386	572 472
Prince Edward Island	165 107	175 896	177 133
Nova Scotia	1 039 829	1 105 209	1 039 206
New Brunswick	914 122	970 293	956 257
Quebec	6 578 395	7 051 184	6 982 566
Ontario	11 715 600	12 660 325	12 129 200
Manitoba	1 296 202	1 341 072	1 298 488
Saskatchewan	. . [1]	683 659	1 191 433
Alberta	. . [1]	3 774 250	3 788 294
British Columbia	3 551 813	3 599 180	3 539 953
Yukon	54 591	60 155	57 932
Northwest Territories	21 679	33 807	33 253
Total, net sales	25 859 224	32 038 416	31 766 187
Total, gross sales	32 830 267	34 375 144	33 646 741
Diesel oil			
Total, net sales	3 304 689	5 935 529	8 646 337
Liquefied petroleum gases			
Total, net sales	40 043	68 982	90 851

[1] *Road tax removed (Alberta, April 1, 1978; Saskatchewan, April 1982).*

12.11 URBAN TRANSIT INDUSTRY (MILLION DOLLARS)

	1989	1990	1991
Operating expenses	2,622.9	2,840.5	2,976.1
Revenue	1,268.9	1,334.0	1,421.6
Capital expenditures	599.5	504.0	477.8
Capital subsidies	580.3	504.3	485.7

12.12 URBAN TRANSIT INDUSTRY, OPERATING STATISTICS, 1991

	Service population '000	Revenue passengers '000	Revenue kilometres '000	Rides per capita	Revenue kilometres per capita	Rides per kilometres
Newfoundland	125	3,626	2 601	29.01	20.81	1.39
Nova Scotia	398	15,683	9 731	39.41	24.45	1.61
New Brunswick	120	3,532	2 863	29.43	23.86	1.23
Quebec	2,918	430,915	186 889	147.66	64.04	2.31
Ontario	7,241	685,475	352 295	94.66	48.65	1.95
Manitoba	657	52,160	26 981	79.41	41.07	1.93
Saskatchewan	356	19,179	9 987	53.92	28.08	1.92
Alberta	1,628	97,261	73 969	59.76	45.45	1.31
British Columbia	1,597	141,800	84 275	88.77	52.76	1.68
Yukon Territory	15	416	518	28.59	35.61	0.80
Canada	15,055	1,450,047	750 109	96.32	49.83	1.93

12.13 URBAN TRANSIT INDUSTRY, VEHICLES AND EMPLOYEES, 1991

	Active revenue vehicles							Employees (full and part time)
	Motor bus	Articulated bus	Trolley coach	Light rail vehicle	Heavy rail vehicle	Other	Total	
Newfoundland	74	—	—	—	—	—	74	159
Nova Scotia	218	—	—	—	—	—	218	515
New Brunswick	62	—	—	—	—	—	62	128
Quebec	2,682	22	—	—	759	58	3,521	10,882
Ontario	4,439	192	269	291	620	309	6,120	18,466
Manitoba	578	—	—	—	—	—	578	1,458
Saskatchewan	240	—	—	—	—	—	240	499
Alberta	1,376	60	3	122	—	3	1,564	3,557
British Columbia	796	244		114	—	2	1,156	3,892
Yukon Territory	9	—	—	—	—	—	9	23
Canada	10,474	518	272	527	1,379	372	13,542	39,579

12.14   CANADIAN FOR-HIRE TRUCKING[1], 1990

	Number of establishments reporting	Operating revenues $'000	Operating expenses $'000	Net operating revenues $'000	Number of employees
Newfoundland	13	54,906	53,099	1,807	496
Prince Edward Island	2	2	2	2	2
Nova Scotia	34	141,760	136,791	4,969	1,209
New Brunswick	52	443,227	424,849	18,378	3,146
Quebec	319	1,352,292	1,278,183	74,109	12,363
Ontario	441	3,634,475	3,571,277	63,198	34,327
Manitoba	49	588,711	582,497	6,214	5,039
Saskatchewan	55	214,565	203,438	11,127	1,837
Alberta	175	1,116,988	1,080,130	36,857	9,214
British Columbia	199	770,205	744,095	26,110	5,390
Yukon	2	2	2	2	2
Northwest Territories	6	34,031	33,898	133	302
Canada	1,350	8,423,600	8,177,455	246,155	73,716

	Equipment				
	Straight trucks	Road tractors	Semi & full trailers	Other equipment	Total
Newfoundland	102	139	382	19	642
Prince Edward Island	2	2	2	2	2
Nova Scotia	388	423	1,327	280	2,418
New Brunswick	394	844	4,128	129	5,495
Quebec	1,553	5,592	14,971	2,068	24,184
Ontario	3,769	13,565	44,704	3,485	65,523
Manitoba	240	1,746	7,174	150	9,310
Saskatchewan	209	703	2,032	74	3,018
Alberta	1,106	3,621	12,011	644	17,382
British Columbia	775	1,959	6,400	584	9,718
Yukon	2	2	2	2	2
Northwest Territories	44	70	125	0	239
Canada	8,609	28,740	93,526	7,458	138,333

[1] *Carriers $1 million and over including household goods movers.*
[2] *Confidential, included in Canada total*

12.15   PRIVATE TRUCKING[1], 1990

	Total[1]	General freight	Bulk liquids	Dry bulk materials	Forest products	Other commodities
Carriers reporting (Number)	505	279	39	114	28	45
Operating expenses ($'000)	2,330,656	1,283,120	398,010	399,589	91,145	158,792
Transportation expenses	1,669,937	915,281	312,973	270,612	62,093	108,978
Maintenance and garage expenses	316,548	164,327	36,407	73,188	18,931	23,695
Terminal expenses	114,704	80,587	16,996	8,812	3,948	4,361
Administrative and general office expenses	229,467	122,925	31,634	46,977	6,173	21,758
Number of employees (Number)	32,778	19,375	2,706	7,292	883	2,522
Salaries and wages ($'000)	937,609	567,139	108,161	167,256	25,153	69,900
Equipment operated (Number)	32,802	21,464	2,060	5,144	1,023	3,111
Straight trucks	12,538	7,333	447	3,277	52	1,429
Road tractors	5,850	3,940	632	561	367	350
Semi-trailers	12,572	9,225	849	914	526	1,058
Other	1,842	966	132	392	78	274

[1] Carriers with annual expenses over $1 million.

12.16   VESSELS ENTERED AT CANADIAN PORTS

	In international shipping		In domestic shipping		Total	
	Vessels	Net register tons[1]	Vessels	Net register tons[1]	Vessels	Net register tons[1]
1980	28,754	168,477,033	38,015	87,846,321	66,769	256,323,354
1985	26,555	167,701,297	27,228	79,243,728	53,783	246,945,025
1990	28,999	177,051,537	25,004	72,223,019	54,003	249,274,556
1991	29,532	180,012,770	23,108	69,626,946	52,640	249,639,716

[1] The capacity of the spaces within the hull, and the enclosed spaces above the deck, available for cargo and passengers; excluding spaces used for the accommodation of officers and crew, navigation, propelling machinery and fuel. A register ton is equivalent to 100 cubic feet.

12.17 CARGOES LOADED AND UNLOADED AT PRINCIPAL CANADIAN PORTS
(THOUSAND TONNES)

	International		Coastwise		Total		
	loaded	unloaded	loaded	unloaded	1991	1990	1989
Newfoundland	4 166	3 910	160	2 077	10 313	12 711	12 137
Prince Edward Island	147	58	1	622	828	721	782
Nova Scotia	10 279	6 597	3 242	1 371	21 489	23 583	24 480
New Brunswick	7 249	9 075	1 890	639	18 853	16 273	16 627
Quebec	51 318	19 346	13 540	21 506	105 710	107 363	105 405
Ontario	9 757	20 064	22 718	15 301	67 840	69 693	76 194
Manitoba	220	—	—	—	220	415	277
British Columbia	84 894	6 814	16 807	16 797	125 312	122 040	128 059
Northwest Territories	1	—	12	116	129	155	151
Total, all Canadian ports[1]	168 030	65 863	58 430	58 430	350 753	353 049	363 419

[1] *Totals may not add due to rounding.*

12.18 VESSELS AND TONNAGE HANDLED BY CANADA PORTS CORPORATION, 1991

Port	Vessel arrivals		Cargo handled '000 t	Grain elevator shipments '000 t
	Number	Gross register tonnage[1] '000 t		
St. John's	875	2,959	947	—
Halifax	2,054	35,816	14 892	380
Saint John	1,472	20,549	17 094	—
Belledune	34	318	329	—
Sept-Îles	640	14,772	21 919	—
Saguenay	112	948	513	—
Baie-des-Ha! Ha!	193	3,229	4 133	—
Quebec	1,099	16,902	18 536	4 480
Trois-Rivières	270	2,424	1 397	340
Montreal	2,247	26,220	17 470	1 425
Prescott	31	482	472	226
Port Colborne	2	33	21	70
Churchill	44	213	265	233
Vancouver	9,614	79,590	70 714	13 665
Prince Rupert	1,597	16,110	13 256	5 088
Total	20,284	220,565	181 958	25 907

[1] *The capacity of the spaces within the hull, and the enclosed spaces above the deck. A register ton is equivalent to 100 cubic feet.*

12.19 ST. LAWRENCE SEAWAY TRAFFIC, 1991

	Montreal — Lake Ontario section			Welland Canal section		
	Tonnes, revenues and transits	% of total	Percentage change from 1988	Tonnes, revenues and transits	% of total	Percentage change from 1988
Cargo tonnes by toll classification						
Bulk	15 771 687	45.2	−23.3	18 326 722	49.6	−23.0
Grains	15 444 845	44.2	26.3	15 851 375	43.0	25.2
Government aid	159 449	0.4	81.7	121 628	0.3	80.9
Containers	20 472	0.1	−14.4	10 274	0.0	−14.6
General cargo	3 513 990	10.1	−6.4	2 608 973	7.1	−9.2
Total, cargo tonnes	34 910 443	100.0	−4.8	36 918 972	100.0	−6.3
Traffic revenue ($) by toll classification						
Bulk	15 077 580	41.6	−18.7	8 749 779	26.8	−17.0
Grains	9 260 708	25.5	33.0	7 739 819	23.7	34.1
Government aid	-	0.0	−100.0	-	0.0	−100.0
Containers	20 063	0.1	−8.0	5 034	0.0	−9.0
General cargo	8 358 403	23.1	−0.7	2 034 769	6.2	−4.3
Gross registered tonnage	3 487 729	9.6	17.2	5 341 273	16.4	11.6
Other	44 123	0.1	11.4	36 728	0.1	36.1
Lockage fees	-	0.0	0.0	8 738 160	26.8	2.9
Total traffic revenue	36 248 606	100.0	2.0	32 645 562	100.0	2.8
Gross registered tonnage[1]						
Cargo vessels	35,287,176	99.7	4.6	45,299,074	99.7	1.9
Non-cargo vessels	108,025	0.3	−26.0	140,893	0.3	0.7
Total, gross registered tonnage	35,395,201	100.0	4.4	45,439,967	100.0	1.9
Vessel transits						
Loaded cargo vessels	1 911	66.8	−5.0	1 963	55.0	−9.0
Ballast cargo vessels	689	24.1	46.9	1 209	33.9	12.8
Non-cargo	259	9.1	−9.8	398	11.1	14.4
Total, vessel transits	2 859	100.0	3.3	3 570	100.0	−0.2
Agricultural products						
Wheat	12 216 891	35.0	31.7	12 432 804	33.7	32.7
Corn	1 503 622	4.3	24.7	1 557 323	4.2	11.8
Rye	1 403	0.0	−75.3	1 403	0.0	−75.3
Oats	1 050	0.0	−81.3	1 050	0.0	−81.3
Barley	664 207	1.9	−41.0	664 207	1.8	−41.0
Soybeans	469 412	1.4	72.0	469 412	1.3	28.7
Flaxseed	171 718	0.5	3.6	171 718	0.5	3.6
Other grains	465 341	1.3	43.5	565 626	1.5	50.8
Total, grains	15 493 644	44.4	25.1	15 863 543	43.0	23.9
Other agricultural products	39 060	0.1	587.9	64 807	0.2	648
Total, agricultural products	15 532 704	44.5	25.4	15 928 350	43.2	24.4
Mine products						
Iron ore	8 455 027	24.2	−26.7	5 698 201	15.4	−23.9
Coal	591 980	1.7	21.0	5 276 522	14.3	−15.8
Coke	503 410	1.4	−46.8	459 181	1.2	−55.7
Stone, ground, crushed, or rough	598 944	1.7	−46.8	1 179 384	3.2	−55.7
Salt	1 029 814	3.0	−13.0	1 355 831	3.7	−10.4
Other mine products	1 183 369	3.4	−29.6	1 214 195	3.3	−19.6
Total, mine products	12 362 544	35.4	−25.3	15 183 314	41.1	−22.5

12.19 ST. LAWRENCE SEAWAY TRAFFIC, 1991 (concluded)

	Montreal — Lake Ontario section			Welland Canal section		
	Tonnes, revenues and transits	% of total	Percentage change from 1988	Tonnes, revenues and transits	% of total	Percentage change from 1988
Processed products						
Iron and steel	3 438 134	9.9	−4.7	2 549 540	6.9	−7.8
Fuel oil	866 101	2.5	−2.8	655 024	1.8	−30.2
Other petroleum products	415 327	1.2	−27.2	177 699	0.5	−39.2
Chemicals	568 383	1.6	−30.4	529 638	1.4	−22.7
Other processed products	1 648 361	4.7	−4.7	1 856 261	5.0	17.8
Total, processed products	6 936 306	19.9	−8.9	5 768 162	15.6	−16.9
Miscellaneous cargo						
Forest products	27 619	0.1	−57.3	21 501	0.1	−63.9
Animal products	51 270	0.1	11.5	17 645	0.0	92.3
Total, miscellaneous cargo	78 889	0.2	−28.7	39 146	0.1	−43.0
Total, all commodities	34 910 443	100.0	−4.8	36 918 972	100.0	−6.3

[1] *The capacity of the spaces within the hull and the enclosed spaces above the deck. A register ton is equivalent to 100 cubic feet.*

Sources
Canada Ports Corporation
Canadian Urban Transit Association
St.Lawrence Seaway Authority
Statistics Canada

G. KRASICHYNSKI / FIRST LIGHT

CHAPTER THIRTEEN

▲

SCIENCE AND TECHNOLOGY

INTRODUCTION

The late 20th century turns on an axis of science and technology spun from the ingenuity and determination of the researcher and the imagination and often poetry of the inventor. Canadians have a tradition of contributing to this breadth of inspiration. Our early pathfinders found themselves scattered across a daunting new land with little more than their wits to match an often cold-blooded climate. Not surprisingly, much of our cleverness has been spent on problems of distance and communications.

When the Canadian Science and Engineering Hall of Fame announced its inaugural induction in 1992, the list featured a who's who of Canadian inventors: Alexander Graham Bell, for the telephone and the first powered flight in Canada; Sir Frederick Banting, the discoverer of insulin; J. Armand Bombardier, inventor of the snowmobile; Wilder Penfield, the developer of surgical treatments for epilepsy; Sir Sandford Fleming, the architect of the transcontinental railway; and Wallace Turnbull, the inventor of the variable pitch propeller. And there were many more.

These celebrated Canadians have been true scientists who learned their rare knowledge through observation, experimentation, commitment and vision. Almost all of them then used or produced technology which solved a problem or met a need.

Today, science and technology (S&T) refers to a range of innovative projects designed to introduce and apply new scientific knowledge. S&T not only makes our lives easier and more pleasant, but also encourages the development of natural resources and industrial processes which in turn stimulate national and regional economies.

The federal and provincial governments, industry, universities, and private non-profit organizations, all fund and perform S&T ventures. These ventures fall into two broad categories: research and development (R&D), the creative arm of S&T that increases the store of scientific knowledge, and related scientific activities (RSA) which complement and extend R&D by the generation, dissemination and application of scientific and technological knowledge.

S&T also encompasses two major fields of endeavour: natural sciences and engineering, and social sciences and humanities. Natural sciences and engineering are areas of study concerned with understanding, exploring, developing or utilizing the natural world. This includes engineering, mathematical, life and physical sciences. Social sciences and humanities embrace the study of human actions and the social, economic and institutional mechanisms affecting humans. This includes anthropology, demography, economics, geography, sociology, history, and law.

The federal government still plays a significant role in Canada's R&D endeavours but its rank as the primary source of R&D funding has gradually been eclipsed by the private sector. Over the past two decades, the private sector's share of R&D investment has climbed by 12% and by 1992 had reached 41% of the nation's total R&D expenditures. At the same time the federal government's funding of R&D dropped by 13% to 30%. But the federal government remains an active participant with 75 departments and agencies involved in S&T to various degrees. The most active of these are the Canadian Space Agency, the National Research Council (NRC), Statistics Canada, the Canadian International Development Agency (CIDA), Environment Canada, Energy, Mines and Resources Canada (EMR), Agriculture Canada, the Natural Sciences and Engineering Council (NSERC) and the Medical Research Council.

Canada's provincial governments make a smaller contribution to the R&D funded and performed in Canada than the federal government or the private sector. Ontario and Quebec lead the provinces in this area, with Alberta third. In 1992, provincial governments funded $729 million and performed $345 million of Canada's total of over $10 billion in R&D.

NATIONAL DEVELOPMENTS

S&T is a dynamic force in the creation of employment, solving environmental, health and safety problems, and keeping resource industries competitive in the global market for new products. This is why the federal government invests billions of dollars in S&T every

Hans Blohm / Masterfile

Silicon highway — a magnified computer chip.

year — some $5.9 billion in 1992-93, up 2.5% from the previous fiscal year. The funds support both the private sector (extramural funding) and the mandates of government departments and agencies which help industrial development through in-house (intramural funding) activities. The federal government directly employs some 34,900 people in S&T activities, mostly in the departments of Environment, Agriculture, Statistics Canada and the National Research Council.

The federal government invests in both major fields of S&T but leans heavily toward the natural sciences (such as biology, chemistry and physics) and engineering. Since 1984, the government's funding in this area has jumped 42%. In 1992, this amounted to approximately $4.6 billion. Of this, $3.5 billion (71%) went to R&D and $1.3 billion (29%) to RSA. Almost half the R&D expenditures were spent intramurally,

23% went to industry, 22% to universities and the remainder to private non-profit groups, provincial and municipal governments, other Canadian organizations and foreign entities. Most of the RSA expenditures ($666 million) were devoted to collecting data, on everything from monitoring acid rain to conducting wildlife surveys.

Federal expenditures for the social sciences and humanities mainly involve the routine gathering, analysis and publishing of data needed for government policy and research. This includes Gross Domestic Product estimates, employment estimates and demographic statistics. In 1992, the social sciences and humanities accounted for about $1.3 billion in federal funding, with 17% for R&D and 83% for RSA. About 30% of the R&D expenditures were intramural and 38% went to universities through the Social Sciences and Humanities Research Council. The remainder was distributed to the private sector, non-profit groups, provincial organizations and others. Approximately 76% of RSA expenditures were spent intramurally, mostly by Statistics Canada for data collection.

R&D Funding

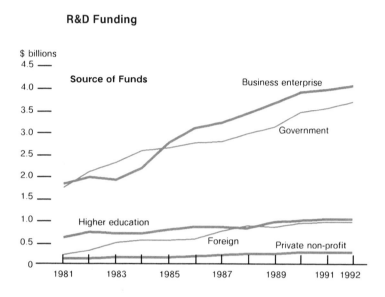

CREATING NEW FRONTIERS

In 1992, some $10 billion in R&D took place in Canada, up about 3% from the previous year. These expenditures are referred to as the Gross Domestic Expenditure on R&D (GERD). The GERD is calculated by totalling the intramural expenditures of all institutions performing R&D in Canada, even if it is funded from abroad. R&D funded by Canada, but performed abroad, is not part of the GERD.

The amount of money spent on R&D activities is an important indicator of the degree of creative activity taking place in a country's S&T sector. Many major industrialized countries spend a higher proportion of their Gross Domestic Product on R&D than Canada. Much of their R&D involves a greater emphasis on military activities which often results in products with commercial or industrial uses.

R&D is the first step in developing the new products and processes that help generate economic and industrial growth, particularly in the business enterprise sector. Its preeminence also indicates the extent to which a nation contributes to world science, and the level of its intellectual activity in solving its own problems and challenges.

THE NEW R&D TREND A notable trend over the past two decades has been the business enterprise sector's emerging role as the dominant performer of R&D in Canada, a position it has gradually taken over from the federal government. In natural sciences and engineering, for example, the business enterprise sector's share of the GERD has jumped by 18% since 1971, and now accounts for more than half of the R&D performed in Canada. Over the same period, the federal proportion has dropped from 29% to 17% and universities' share fell from 31% to 26%.

Industrial R&D is the sector most clearly linked to technological innovation and therefore to economic growth. R&D generally does not produce quick profits. In fact, sometimes it produces no profits. However, for daring companies with the financial resources and vision to embark upon R&D, it can result in successful and innovative products which catch the imagination of the marketplace.

Total expenditures on industrial R&D were expected to reach their highest levels ever in 1992 — almost $5.3 billion or 53% of the GERD. It includes private enterprises such as Northern Telecom, public ones such as the Canadian National Railways and industrial research institutes.

Today, Canadian R&D often involves the adaption or imitation of work completed in other countries, rather than retracing every step in the long creative journey. For example, much information comes from abroad in the form of new machinery and equipment, scientific and technical journals, designs, drawings, tooling and manufacturing specifications. It is more efficient to acquire the results of R&D performed elsewhere than to duplicate the research. In some cases the Commissioner of Patents can order that a compulsory licence be granted, allowing one or more companies to import or produce a patented invention, subject to payment of royalties.

Some indigenous R&D is necessary however, not only to ensure that inventions fit Canadian manufacturing and marketing conditions, but also to confirm that foreign R&D can be properly assimilated into our production processes.

Although the business enterprise sector is supporting more R&D, less than 1% of all Canadian firms actually perform R&D. Of the 3,500 Canadian firms conducting R&D, about 1% accounted for almost half the total of industrial R&D performed in 1992-93. In terms of geographic concentrations, some 56% of all R&D activity, and more than 89% of telecommunications R&D, takes place in Ontario. This concentration means that the decisions of a few companies can significantly alter the nation's overall R&D expenditures, particularly in specific industry sectors.

From 1988 to 1992, 53% of all R&D expenditures were concentrated in seven major industries: telecommunications equipment; aircraft and parts; engineering and scientific services; business machines; other electronic equipment; pharmaceutical and medicinal products; and computer and related services. As a result, business enterprise sector R&D decisions are affected by government policy on defence, transportation and communications, as well as by national and international economic trends.

For example, amendments to the Patent Act in early 1993 were designed to increase pharmaceutical R&D in Canada. Companies which develop new drugs now have patent protection from generic drug producers for 20 years instead of 17. This gives successful drug R&D a monopoly until the patent expires.

With this legislation, Canada also did away with compulsory licensing of new drug products — a system which had spawned a generic drug industry. Similar legislation in 1987 afforded drug producers some patent protection while maintaining the policy of mandatory licensing. Companies which produce generic brand drugs can still produce drugs licensed prior to 1992, but must now wait for new patents to expire.

Critics of the policy of removing mandatory licensing have expressed concern that drug prices will rise as a result.

Changes to the Patent Act now bring patent protection for medicines into line with the protection afforded new products in all other sectors of the Canadian economy. Through a patent, the government gives inventors the right to exclude others from making, using, or selling a patented invention from the day a patent is granted up to a maximum of 20 years. A patent can be used to make a profit by being sold, licensed, or used as an asset to negotiate funding. Patents apply to new technologies, processes, structures or functions. Canada is a signatory to a number of international patent organizations and treaties including the Paris Convention for the Protection of Industrial Property and the World Intellectual Property Organization (WIPO). WIPO administers the Patent Co-operation Treaty which allows Canadian companies to file patents in as many as 43 member countries, including most of our major trading partners, through a single application filed in Canada.

Some companies specialize in specific forms of R&D. For example, 8% of Canadian firms reported doing energy R&D in 1990. Their $602 million contribution accounted for 12% of the industrial R&D. In addition, these companies spent $810 million on non-energy R&D, for a total of $1.41 billion. Although governments only funded 6% of intramural energy R&D, they funded 20% of all the R&D on renewable energy resources.

In 1990, the business enterprise sector employed 53,240 individuals in R&D. More than half (55%) were professionals, about 30% were technicians, and the remainder served other functions. Almost half of the industrial R&D workforce is concentrated in two areas of industry: electrical and electronic products employs 30% of all industrial R&D personnel; the service sector (mostly engineering and scientific services) employs another 18%.

Software R&D activities have become an important part of Canadian R&D. In 1990, software R&D accounted for 21% of all R&D in Canada's manufacturing sector and for 28% of the services sector. In 1990, the computer services software industry undertook $256 million in software R&D. The 11,023 firms in this industry employed 65,417 people and declared earnings of almost $6 billion.

CHANGING OF THE KILOGRAM

In 1993, Canada's national kilogram was replaced after serving Canadians faithfully for more than 40 years.

The kilogram is the only base unit of the International System of Units (SI) still defined by an actual physical object. The old official kilogram, about the size of a baby-food jar, and made of solid platinum-iridium, had served as the benchmark for all weight measurements in Canada since 1950.

However, with weather changes, the old kilogram had become...well...moody. Its weight fluctuated, often by as much as 35 micrograms. Its 'dependability' was in question.

Ideally, a kilogram that acts as a national standard should vary in weight by no more than 12 micrograms... the equivalent mass of half a square millimetre of aluminum foil, a piece smaller than a flea.

Canada's new official kilogram, which looks similar to the old kilogram, arrived in early 1993 from the International Bureau of Weights and Measures in Sèvres, near Paris.

The new kilogram, is expected to be much less moody. Also a shiny silver colour and made of platinum-iridium, it is less porous than the old kilogram, and less susceptible to weight changes caused by humid or dry air.

With a purchase price of $45,000, it is literally more valuable than its weight in gold.

To those who rely on accurate mass measurements, it's worth every penny. Every product sold by weight in Canada will be traceable to the new official kilogram. The Ministry of Consumer and Corporate Affairs, for example, relies on weights traceable to Canada's official kilogram to test everything from grocer scales to grain elevator scales. Accurate measurements ensure that Canadian consumers get exactly what they pay for.

Because of its importance to the Canadian marketplace, extraordinary precautions were taken to ensure that the kilogram arrived from France in perfect condition. Its handlers could not touch the kilogram with bare hands for fear that any oils or acidity would affect its mass.

Encased in an armoured cylinder, the kilogram, in the custody of Canadian Military Police, was escorted to the airport in France by a diplomatic courier. Once there, the courier and a scientist from Canada's National Research Council (NRC) accompanied the precious cargo aboard the flight home.

The courier, who was charged with the kilogram's in-flight care, rode with the kilogram in first class, jealously guarding it from unforeseen dangers. (The NRC scientist, meanwhile, scoped the scene from the economy seats).

Once the kilogram had arrived safely in Canada, it was driven (slowly) to the vaults of the Department of External Affairs and International Trade. It was then escorted by the Royal Canadian Mounted Police to its new home in an NRC vault in Ottawa, Ontario. Safe from harm, Canada's new official kilogram now rests on a bed of quartz, under two protective layers of glass.

In Canada, other official units do not require the same royal treatment. That's because other SI units exist only as equations. For example, the length of a metre is the distance light travels in 1/299 792 458ths of a second.

Originally, the kilogram was defined as the mass of 1 000 cubic centimetres of water at 4°C. This was not considered precise enough, however, because water does not have a reproducible density. As a result, this standard was made from platinum-iridium — a dependable and stable metal. Following this change, the kilogram was defined as the mass of that artifact.

THE FEDERAL FACTOR The federal government supports private sector S&T through a varied industrial development program. This initiative assists industry through direct payments in the form of government contracts, contributions to specific projects, and the provision of testing facilities on a cost-recovery basis. A favourable financial climate is aided with supportive tax, tariff, trade and procurement policies.

In 1992-93, the federal government gave industry about $311 million in grants and contributions, mostly (58%) through Industry, Science and Technology Canada. The National Research Council (NRC) is also a strong industry supporter, largely through its Industrial Research Program (IRAP).

KEY PLAYERS

Although the federal government's S&T activities are spread across many federal departments and agencies, there are key areas which direct most of the government's efforts. About half of the federal funding of S&T activities in natural sciences and engineering comes from five departments and agencies. Similarly, about half of the government's funding of S&T activities in the social sciences and humanities also comes from five departments and agencies. These departments and agencies fund activities ranging from industrial development to researching global social problems.

Environment Canada Environment Canada supports both major fields of S&T endeavour, but leans heavily toward the natural sciences and engineering. With a 1992-93 expenditure of $645 million, it is the largest federal S&T spender. Most of this amount (91%) is spent in the department's own laboratories, with 82% devoted to RSA (primarily data collection) and 18% to R&D. The department operates a network of laboratories across the country that deal with regional and national environmental concerns.

The largest chunk of Environment Canada's S&T resources (49% in 1992-93) went to the Atmospheric Environment Service which provides historical, current and predictive meteorological, sea-state and ice information. The next largest portion (37%) was allotted to environmental conservation and protection,

which includes water resources development, water quantity and quality research, hydrometric data collection, and development of inventories of land capability and use. The remainder of the S&T budget went to Parks Canada.

National Research Council The National Research Council (NRC) is the federal government's second largest S&T spender. Its 1992-93 expenditure of $505.6 million represents only a 4.4% increase since 1984-85, due to major budget cutbacks by the federal government in the mid-1980s and general restraint in subsequent years. Most of the NRC's budget (77% in 1992-93) was spent intramurally, 14% went to the industrial sector and 6% to universities.

Through its Industrial Research Assistance Program (IRAP), the NRC contributed $86 million to industry in 1992-93. Its work with the private sector helps industry to increase its technical competence, improve productivity, develop new products and solve technical problems in areas such as transportation, construction, biotechnology, manufacturing systems and industrial materials. It also provides technical advice which has helped thousands of firms develop world-class technology.

The NRC operates facilities that are available to scientists and engineers in industry, universities and government. By joining forces with these experts, the NRC makes important advances in countless areas ranging from new techniques for identifying the early stages of cancer to creating the world's most reliable bomb sniffer. The NRC is also the largest scientific and technical information service in the country. Its Canada Institute for Scientific and Technical Information answers close to half a million requests for information every year.

Canadian Space Agency In 1990, the Canadian Space Agency (CSA) was created by Parliament to further the development of advanced Canadian technology for space applications. In 1992-93, it funded more than half of the $463 million in R&D contracts awarded to industry by the government. The CSA is responsible for 29% of the government's funding of scientific activities in the industry sector, the largest of any government department or agency.

Roger Lloyd / Nova Scotia Department of Education Media Services

Nova Scotia museum staffer touches forehead of the East Milford Mastodon's skull, atop five vertebrae.

The CSA's total S&T expenditures have grown from $138 million in 1989-90 to $417 million in 1992-93. All of this has been spent in natural sciences and engineering, with $411 million allocated for R&D and $6 million for RSA.

In 1992-93, the business enterprises sector received 70% of these S&T resources ($291 million), while another 22% ($91 million) was spent intramurally and 7% ($32 million) was spent abroad.

One of the CSA's major projects is the design, production and operation of the Mobile Servicing System (MSS), which will be the next generation of the Space Shuttle's Canadarm. The MSS will be used on the international space station Freedom, a joint effort of Canada, the United States, Japan and the European Space Agency.

Statistics Canada Statistics Canada collects and disseminates the data needed to help understand Canada's economy and institutions, and develop economic and social policies and programs. It is the government's major user of social sciences and humanities funds — $347 million in 1992-93.

Canadian International Development Agency The Canadian International Development Agency (CIDA) provides Official Development Assistance (ODA) to developing countries to help them achieve

MARVIN THE MASTODON

Its official name is the East Milford Mastodon, but the 80,000-year-old skeleton found in a gypsum quarry near Halifax in 1991 was quickly dubbed "Marvin" by the paleontological crew that worked for eight months to dig him out.

While the odd mastodon tooth or bone had been found elsewhere in Nova Scotia, it was the first time such a complete find had been made in the province — the Nova Scotia Museum's geology staff, helped by local volunteers and researchers from Australia, the United States, and across Canada, recovered about 60% of the bones. They will go on display at the museum in Halifax late in the decade. The research will continue for many years and will involve scientists from Australia, the US and across Canada.

The state of Marvin's teeth and tusks tell experts he was a male of about 10, a relative teenager among animals that may have lived as long as 50 years.

Speculation is that he was one of a herd of mastodons lured to a boggy area by exposed gypsum deposits that may have formed natural salt licks. He died when he fell into a sinkhole, and became too mired to escape. In the following months, as his body fell apart, it was engulfed in wet clay as the sinkhole filled with sediment.

Marvin stayed damp after he was buried. The speed with which the skeleton was sealed in clay protected his bones from oxygen, preserving them as actual bone rather than fossils. Over thousands of years, the moisture dissolved the natural glues which hold bone together. When they were exposed again, their texture in places resembled that of a bran muffin, and they would have fallen apart if picked up as they were found.

Because of the condition of the bone, the dig was unusual: what is known as a 'wet bone site'. As they uncovered bones, one of the scientists stabilized them by spraying syringes full of a plastic solution resembling white glue over the most badly damaged areas. Then they layered on plastic cling wrap to keep the bones from drying out and sprayed rigid foam insulation around them to keep them from breaking during the move to the museum's lab.

Museum staff now face a huge job getting Marvin ready to show. First they will remove the wrappings and wash off all traces of clay and contamination. The interior of the bones resembles porous sponge toffee, light brown and full of tiny bubble-like holes.

Workers will then place the clean bones in stainless steel tanks full of more plastic stabilizing solution until they are soaked through. Next they'll dry them for about three years in a series of special drying chambers. If they dry them any faster, the bones may split and crack badly, as staff found during a test on one of Marvin's small toe bones.

After Marvin is dry, museum staff will begin to reassemble his skeleton. It's a little like putting together a huge three-dimensional jigsaw puzzle, and will take up to two years. Since they recovered most of one side of the mastodon, they can fill in the missing pieces by copying existing bones. Once together, Marvin the East Milford Mastodon will go on display, not many miles from where he once roamed.

self-sustainable development. In 1992-93 this included S&T investments of $225 million in natural sciences and engineering, representing 59% of CIDA's science expenditures, and $156 million on social sciences and humanities, representing 41% of expenditures.

Energy, Mines and Resources Energy, Mines and Resources Canada (EMR) spent about $367 million on S&T in 1992-93 — 87% intramurally and 8% going to the industrial sector. With its series of laboratories across the country, EMR is responsible for geological surveys, mapping, developing R&D policies to support national energy options, and the management and technical evaluation of the government's energy R&D program.

Agriculture Canada Agriculture Canada spent approximately $373 million on S&T in 1992-93, with 90% devoted to R&D. Almost all of Agriculture Canada's S&T budget is spent intramurally; only 3% is split among the industrial sector, universities and other recipients. The Research Branch conducts most of the department's S&T activities through research units across the country that specialize in local problems. The department also operates six national research centres that study soil properties, forestry, water use and management, energy, environmental quality, production development including animal crossbreeding, feed lot systems, genetics, processing, distribution, retailing and consumer concerns.

University Grants The federal government provides R&D grants to universities primarily through three councils: the Natural Sciences and Engineering Research Council (NSERC), the Medical Research Council, and the Social Sciences and Humanities Research Council (SSHRC). Altogether, these councils distributed $863 million in 1992-93, some 88% to the natural sciences and engineering and 12% to the social sciences and humanities.

In 1992-93, NSERC provided an estimated $503 million in grants for natural sciences and engineering, a 61% increase since 1984-85. About 92% of NSERC's budget goes to Canadian universities, 3% to foreign research organizations and the remainder to cover administrative costs. The Medical Research Council provided another $257 million for the health sciences. The SSHRC, the granting council for the social sciences and

humanities, granted about $103 million in 1992-93 for social science research which includes scholarly publications and major editorial projects, career scholars and international scholar exchanges.

PROVINCIAL RESEARCH ORGANIZATIONS

Canada's provincial research organizations are relatively small compared with their federal counterparts. Although they only accounted for 1% of the total scientific activities in Canada in 1991, they have a substantial impact on industry in their respective areas because of the significant role they play in the transfer of technology from laboratory to production. Their primary objective is to provide technical support to local firms and they help develop provincial natural resources. In 1991, 36% of all scientific activities were related to development, making it the focus of provincial S&T. Such organizations exist in Quebec, Ontario, Nova Scotia, New Brunswick and the four western provinces. They research and test everything from nuclear reactors and pest control to wood stoves, and apply new technology to provincial industries.

Combined, these organizations spent approximately $174 million in 1991 and employed some 2,100 people. About 37% of the funding comes from provincial government grants and 32% from research contracts from the private sector.

The Alberta Research Council is the largest provincial research organization, with a 1991 budget of $52 million, spending 60% of this on development.

The Centre de recherche industrielle du Québec is the second largest such organization with 1991 expenditures of $33 million. Ontario's ORTECH International and the Saskatchewan Research Council have the third and fourth largest expenditures respectively.

Some provincial foundations, such as Ontario's research council, ORTECH International, also run centres to apply the research they conduct. For example, ORTECH International researches energy conservation and also runs a centre for alternate fuel use.

PRIVATE NON-PROFIT ORGANIZATIONS

In 1991, the total intramural expenditures of private non-profit organizations were $110 million, an increase of 8% over 1990, accounting for about 1% of all R&D performed in Canada. More than two-thirds of this R&D was performed in Ontario, followed by Quebec, with 16%.

The private non-profit sector is made up of four types of organizations which include private philanthropic foundations, voluntary health organizations, associations and societies, and research institutes. Private philanthropic foundations are mainly concerned with charitable and educational work and allocate all their R&D funds extramurally. Large voluntary health organizations are generally concerned with a specific topic, for example cancer research. In 1991, research institutes conducted about 97%, or $107 million of the intramural R&D in this group, while associations and societies conducted none.

In 1991, $101 million, or 92% of expenditures, was spent on R&D in medical sciences. Most of this R&D involved research into drugs, immunology, cellular biology, cancer, endocrinology, and nutrition and metabolism.

The private non-profit sector employed slightly more than 1,900 people in 1991, mostly technicians, technologists, scientists and engineers.

R&D IS HIGHER EDUCATION

The higher education sector is one of the components of the national R&D system. It includes universities, colleges of technology and other institutes of post-secondary educations, regardless of their source of funding or legal status. R&D in this sector is not necessarily an organized institutional activity, but something conducted as a personal activity by members of the institutions.

In 1990-91, R&D expenditures for this sector were almost $2.5 billion, up from $920 million in 1979-80. Social sciences accounted for $686 million, health sciences for $776 million, and other natural sciences and engineering used $991 million. Most of this activity occurred in Ontario, where $958 million was spent on R&D, followed by Quebec with $690 million, and Alberta with $250 million. By contrast, R&D in Prince Edward Island amounted to only $3.4 million. Almost $13 million was funded by foreign sources.

SOURCES

Statistics Canada

FOR FURTHER READING

Selected publications from Statistics Canada

▲ *Science Statistics. Irregular. 88-001*

▲ *Industrial Research and Development, ... Intentions. Annual. 88-202*

▲ *Federal Scientific Activities. Annual. 88-204*

▲ *Directory of Federal Government Scientific & Technological Establishments. Annual. 88-206E*

▲ *Human Resources for Science and Technology. 88-508E*

▲ *Price Indexes for Canadian Industrial Research and Development Expenditures, Jeffrey I. Bernstein. 88-509*

▲ *The Individual Canadian Inventor, Louise Séguin-Dulude and Claude Desranleau. 88-510*

TABLES

13.1 FEDERAL GOVERNMENT EXPENDITURES ON ACTIVITIES IN THE NATURAL SCIENCES AND ENGINEERING (MILLION DOLLARS)

Department or Agency	1986-87	1989-90	1990-91	1991-92^p	1992-93^e
Agriculture	405.2	341.0	371.8	364.5	365.3
Atomic Energy of Canada Ltd.	170.8	136.0	157.1	162.1	170.1
Canadian Space Agency	. . .	138.4	128.0	339.9	416.9
Communications	70.0	59.8	55.9	48.0	66.3
Energy, Mines and Resources	397.4	351.1	365.5	361.2	366.6
Environment	362.2	431.1	503.7	489.1	551.4
Fisheries and Oceans	212.4	225.7	247.9	242.8	248.4
Forestry	. . .	78.3	83.6	88.4	92.9
Health and Welfare Canada	90.7	128.1	140.2	134.1	134.1
Medical Research Council	168.3	202.9	242.3	247.8	256.5
National Defence	221.4	276.0	277.9	266.9	270.1
National Research Council	468.2	471.6	501.8	497.5	505.7
Natural Sciences and Engineering Research Council	320.9	393.5	467.9	485.2	502.5
Industry, Science and Technology	188.1	223.7	226.8	212.6	227.1
Transport	30.0	31.6	33.0	30.0	35.0
Other	314.6^r	513.5	578.3	414.5	414.7
Total	3,420.3	3,884.4	4,217.1	4,384.6	4,623.6

13.2 FEDERAL GOVERNMENT EXPENDITURES ON ACTIVITIES IN THE SOCIAL SCIENCES AND HUMANITIES (MILLION DOLLARS)

Department or Agency	1986-87	1989-90	1990-91	1991-92^p	1992-93^e
Canadian International Development Agency	124.7	133.0	143.7	145.3	156.4
Employment and Immigration	39.3	60.4	45.9	43.4	60.3
Finance	18.6	21.5	22.5	22.8	27.1
Health and Welfare Canada	32.7	50.7	50.2	48.4	42.2
International Development Research Centre	36.3	45.8	41.3	44.5	43.9
National Library	45.2	49.6	51.5	52.7	57.4
National Museums	75.2	109.1	96.0	97.3	94.4
Public Archives	22.2	32.7	33.5	38.5	40.8
Secretary of State	6.7	4.0	5.9	6.3	5.6
Social Sciences and Humanities Research Council	70.6	82.4	91.2	98.7	103.2
Statistics Canada	360.7	308.7	369.3	478.3	346.6
Treasury Board	21.0	23.3	23.8	26.6	29.3
Other	180.1	257.0	279.3	287.8	291.2
Total	1,033.3	1,178.2	1,254.1	1,390.4	1,298.4

13.3 INDUSTRY'S INTRAMURAL R&D[1] EXPENDITURES (MILLION DOLLARS)

	1983	1984	1985	1986	1987	1988	1989	1990	1991	1992
Agriculture, fishing and logging										
Agriculture	5	7	9	9	12	14	11	11	11	11
Fishing and trapping	--	--	2	8	2	1	1	2	2	2
Logging and forestry	4	5	5	5	6	7	8	11	8	9
Total agriculture, fishing and logging	9	12	16	23	19	22	20	24	21	22
Mining and oil wells										
Metal mines	28	30	34	32	32	34	35	49	55	60
Other mines	12	14	13	17	10	9	10	9	5	6
Services incidental to mining	3	4	4	2	4	4	4	4	5	5
Crude petroleum and natural gas	49	67	69	38	47	52	49	48	55	50
Total mining and oil wells	92	115	119	90	93	99	99	110	119	121
Manufacturing										
Food	52	52	57	63	63	65	60	62	63	69
Beverages and tobacco	12	12	11	9	10	9	9	11	10	10
Rubber products	10	10	11	8	7	7	5	5	6	6
Plastic products	8	9	10	15	15	17	14	14	15	16
Textiles	25	29	34	36	41	43	46	43	45	46
Wood	11	13	15	17	19	20	18	42	21	22
Furniture and fixtures	1	1	4	6	4	6	3	3	3	3
Paper and allied products	56	64	75	89	87	145	151	112	112	113
Printing and publishing	3	5	5	5	4	5	8	6	6	6
Primary metals (ferrous)	21	26	27	27	31	30	24	22	21	22
Primary metals (non-ferrous)	82	95	93	88	111	130	138	165	169	172
Fabricated metal products	27	24	30	34	35	39	41	37	35	39
Machinery	78	71	77	90	81	87	96	89	95	92
Aircraft and parts	279	282	337	369	467	421	421	455	437	429
Motor vehicle, parts and accessories	66	70	79	91	104	102	86	80	79	81
Other transportation equipment	19	15	20	20	22	97	90	155	114	123
Telecommunication equipment	457	528	611	621	686	720	705	712	819	764
Electronic parts and components	25	31	34	31	33	37	39	41	39	41
Other electronic equipment	148	188	256	282	289	299	329	362	343	343
Business machines	140	171	191	238	268	295	299	302	315	326
Other electrical products	78	73	78	75	68	65	63	58	54	61
Non-metallic mineral products	10	17	19	16	15	20	20	16	15	14
Refined petroleum and coal products	184	218	205	147	101	130	131	152	158	144
Pharmaceutical and medicine	66	63	81	103	107	134	177	237	249	286
Other chemical products	115	132	164	164	181	201	199	194	201	213
Scientific and professional equipment	25	33	42	51	54	52	62	66	66	70
Other manufacturing industries	12	13	21	30	29	26	25	27	24	26
Total manufacturing	2,012	2,244	2,586	2,726	2,930	3,199	3,260	3,470	3,515	3,536

13.3 INDUSTRY'S INTRAMURAL R&D[1] EXPENDITURES (MILLION DOLLARS) (concluded)

	1983	1984	1985	1986	1987	1988	1989	1990	1991	1992
Construction	4	4	7	5	4	7	8	14	14	15
Utilities										
Transportation and storage	17	18	26	27	21	21	20	19	21	21
Communication	76	78	96	121	116	100	118	140	140	139
Electrical power	119	149	180	211	213	231	233	238	263	267
Other utilities	1	1	2	1	5	3	5	6	7	7
Total utilities	213	246	30	361	356	355	376	403	430	434
Trade										
Wholesale trade	13	32	76	88	120	130	164	158	152	149
Retail trade	9	5	6	7	8	18	19	21	17	18
Total trade	22	37	82	95	127	148	183	179	170	167
Finance and insurance	10	18	32	98	145	125	149	186	181	189
Services										
Computer and related services	58	94	146	195	219	222	254	255	262	280
Engineering and scientific services	143	206	281	360	357	359	355	385	385	404
Management consulting services	3	4	11	15	22	24	25	32	34	42
Other services	18	14	27	34	36	49	48	48	53	55
Total services	222	318	464	605	633	654	682	720	734	781
Total all industries	2,585	2,994	3,610	4,001	4,307	4,610	4,777	5,105	5,184	5,265

[1] R&D (research and development).

13.4 GROSS DOMESTIC EXPENDITURES ON R&D (MILLION DOLLARS)

	Federal government	Provincial government	Business enterprise	Higher education	Private non-profit	Foreign	Total
Performing sector							
1971	368	43	430	436	10	. . .	1,287
1976r	565	82	755	624	17	. . .	2,043
1981r	859	162	2,124	1,177	36	. . .	4,358
1986r	1,319	217	4,001	1,753	65	. . .	7,355
1987r	1,292	228	4,307	1,849	67	. . .	7,743
1988r	1,322	234	4,610	1,998	85	. . .	8,249
1989r	1,428	269	4,777	2,213	90	. . .	8,777
1990r	1,547	303	5,105	2,453	103	. . .	9,511
1991p	1,593	322	5,184	2,527	111	. . .	9,737
1992p	1,682	345	5,265	2,603	120	. . .	10,015
Funding sector							
1971	574	76	348	226	38	25	1,287
1976r	827	149	625	332	60	50	2,043
1981r	1,416	303	1,800	573	97	169	4,358
1986r	2,281	462	3,077	828	143	564	7,355
1987r	2,321	476	3,203	824	172	747	7,743
1988r	2,430	530	3,415	811	209	854	8,249
1989r	2,545	591	3,666	941	204	830	8,777
1990r	2,782	664	3,929	965	239	932	9,511
1991p	2,855	696	995	995	250	947	9,737
1992p	2,979	729	1,025	1,025	260	961	10,015

13.5 GROSS EXPENDITURES ON R&D, 1990

Province	Gross expenditures on research and development	Ratio of gross expenditures on R&D to provincial gross domestic product	Gross expenditures on R&D per capita
	$'000,000	%	$
Newfoundland	86	1.0	150
Prince Edward Island	15	0.7	115
Nova Scotia	208	1.2	231
New Brunswick	116	0.9	160
Quebec	2,353	1.5	345
Ontario	4,893	1.8	497
Manitoba	249	1.0	228
Saskatchewan	193	1.0	194
Alberta	710	1.0	284
British Columbia	684	0.8	214
Canada[1]	9,511	1.4	354

[1] *Includes the Yukon and Northwest Territories.*

13.6 PERSONS ENGAGED IN R&D, 1990 (PERSON-YEARS[1])

Industries	Professionals	Technicians	Other	Total
Agriculture, fishing and logging				
Agriculture	55	65	75	195
Fishing and trapping	15	10	10	35
Logging and forestry	65	15	25	105
Total agriculture, fishing and logging	140	90	110	340
Mining and oil wells				
Metal mines	150	165	30	345
Other mines	30	35	10	75
Services incidental to mining	20	20	5	45
Crude petroleum and natural gas	165	85	55	300
Total mining and oil wells	365	305	95	765

13.6 PERSONS ENGAGED IN R&D, 1990 (PERSON-YEARS[1]) (concluded)

Industries	Professionals	Technicians	Other	Total
Manufacturing				
Food	415	250	90	755
Beverages and tobacco	55	50	20	125
Rubber products	40	25	20	85
Plastic products	65	65	45	175
Textiles	255	205	100	565
Wood	110	85	55	250
Furniture and fixtures	25	20	10	50
Paper and allied products	395	425	255	1,075
Printing and publishing	75	30	10	115
Primary metals (ferrous)	135	100	20	255
Primary metals (non-ferrous)	425	475	205	1,105
Fabricated metal products	225	255	85	565
Machinery	540	355	275	1,170
Aircraft and parts	1,805	1,050	870	3,725
Motor vehicle, parts and accessories	500	400	245	1,145
Other transportation equipment	455	225	380	1,060
Telecommunication equipment	4,645	970	1,140	6,755
Electronic parts and components	290	185	50	525
Other electronic equipment	2,895	1,255	410	4,565
Business machines	2,365	605	250	3,220
Other electrical products	410	270	75	755
Non-metallic mineral products	75	55	25	150
Refined petroleum and coal products	445	475	105	1,025
Pharmaceutical and medicine	905	370	305	1,580
Other chemical products	1,195	615	205	2,020
Scientific and professional equipment	540	290	80	910
Other manufacturing industries	160	170	45	380
Total manufacturing	19,465	9,265	5,360	34,090
Construction	80	71	15	165
Utilities				
Transportation and storage	100	85	50	230
Communication	890	380	160	1,435
Electrical power	910	615	315	1,840
Other utilities	35	10	10	55
Total utilities	1,935	1,085	535	3,560
Trade				
Wholesale trade	1,065	590	305	1,955
Retail trade	295	115	40	455
Total trade	1,355	710	345	2,410
Finance and insurance	610	1,275	225	2,110
Services				
Computer and related services	2,230	1,280	325	3,840
Engineering and scientific services	2,520	1,465	790	4,775
Management consulting services	290	160	65	515
Other services	335	270	65	665
Total services	5,375	3,175	1,245	9,795
Total all industries	29,330	15,970	7,935	53,240

[1] *Person years are rounded to the nearest 5.*

Source
Statistics Canada

ERIC ALDWINCKLE / NATIONAL ARCHIVES OF CANADA C 87430

CHAPTER FOURTEEN INTERNATIONAL RELATIONS

INTRODUCTION

CANADA ON THE WORLD STAGE
In a world that has seen dramatic changes — political, social and economic — in recent years, Canada has a number of important roles to play: promoter of peace, democracy and the rule of law; major donor of food and economic aid; and trading nation with one of the most prosperous and fastest-growing economies in the world.

Canada has much to offer a world in need of stability, development and prosperity. Canadian expertise, whether in telecommunications, nuclear power technology, prospecting and mining, medicine, bio-engineering or other areas, has made its mark in every corner of the globe. In the wake of the Gulf War, 732 oil wells were left burning or otherwise out of control in Kuwait; a Canadian firm, Safety Boss of Calgary, received international attention by capping more wells (180 in all) than any other company.

External Affairs and International Trade Canada is the government department responsible for handling Canada's international relations. Over the years, the department's role has changed; it now includes foreign policy, trade policy and promotion, consular services and aid. Created in 1909, the Department of External Affairs first initiated independent diplomatic relations between Canada and other countries in the late 1920s; our first foreign embassy was established in Washington in 1927. By 1993, Canada had more than 100 diplomatic and consular missions around the world.

In 1982, Canada's trade commission service became part of the Department of External Affairs. Since then, External Affairs and International Trade Canada has been Canada's primary contact with foreign governments and international organizations that influence trade. With more than 80 trade offices around the world, the department promotes Canada's export trade and protects the nation's international commercial interests.

Each of Canada's provinces has particular needs and interests; in recognition of this, a federal-provincial co-ordination office at External Affairs and International Trade Canada helps meet provincial objectives in international activities, provides assistance for certain provincial activities abroad, and keeps provinces informed of foreign developments and policy changes.

Canada has permanent delegations at the United Nations (UN) in New York and Geneva. Canada also has permanent missions to various UN agencies including the United Nations Educational, Scientific and Cultural Organization (UNESCO), the Organization for Economic Co-operation and Development (OECD), the International Energy Agency, the North Atlantic Council, the Conference on Security and Co-operation in Europe (CSCE) Forum for Security Co-operation, the European communities, and the Organization of American States.

Today, Canada's status as a key player on the world stage is reflected in its participation in international negotiations on such vital issues as human rights, the environment, disarmament, the law of the sea, energy management and nuclear non-proliferation.

INTERNATIONAL ACTIVITIES

THE COMMONWEALTH Canada has been a leader in the evolution of the Commonwealth, a unique 50-member association of states with one-quarter of the earth's population. Evolving out of the relationship between Great Britain and its former colonies (the 50th member, Namibia, joined upon independence in March 1990), the Commonwealth brings together developed and developing nations that share numerous traditions, political and social values, attitudes and institutions. Without binding rules or uniformity of outlook, the Commonwealth continues to be an active forum for diplomacy.

The Commonwealth provides funding for technical co-operation, a youth program, a scholarship and fellowship plan, and a science council. Membership in the Commonwealth and pursuit of its goals are important to Canadian foreign policy. In recent years, Canada supported the Commonwealth's heightened commitment to human rights, democratic values and women's equality.

David Nunuk / First Light

Canada's 1991 exports were led by automotive products, machinery and equipment, and industrial goods and materials.

John McQuarrie / GeoStock

Canadian-manned UN post, Middle East.

LA FRANCOPHONIE *La Francophonie* is a community of countries sharing to varying degrees the French language and culture. These countries have formed an assembly of heads of state and government, and work together through intergovernmental institutions and various private organizations.

Unlike the Commonwealth, *la Francophonie* is not an institutional arrangement, but it has, like the Commonwealth, become a forum for international problem-solving. It offers Canada an excellent framework for co-operation and dialogue with industrialized countries and with some of the poorest developing countries.

La Francophonie also promotes French culture in Canada by giving it an international dimension, and strengthens Canadian unity by involving provinces that have recognized French as an official language in international concerns. With the governments of Quebec and New Brunswick, Canada participates in

the Agency for Cultural and Technical Co-operation (the main international francophone organization) and in major francophone ministerial conferences. Quebec and New Brunswick are also represented by their premiers at *la Francophonie* summits and meetings of heads of state and government.

ECONOMIC SUMMITS Every year, the leaders of the seven major industrialized democracies and the European Community hold an Economic Summit. The first of these summits took place in 1975 between France, the Federal Republic of Germany, the United Kingdom, the United States, Italy and Japan. Canada began participating in 1976; the European Community followed suit in 1977.

Economic summits foster personal contact among leaders, helping to bring about progress on world issues. Powerful enough to have a bearing on world economic and political developments and yet small enough for open and direct discussions, the summit groups develop economic policies to help balance global economic growth. Summits emphasize the inter-relationship of economic concerns — growth, employment, inflation, energy, debt and trade. This approach recognizes the close connection between the industrialized countries and the developing world.

THE OECD Established in 1961, the Organization for Economic Co-operation and Development (OECD) brought Canada and the United States together with Western European countries in a major forum for consultation and co-operation among industrialized nations. Japan, Australia and New Zealand later joined the organization.

The OECD works to achieve stability, balanced economic growth and social progress. Over the years, the OECD has broadened its scope to include almost every aspect of economic and social policy in modern society.

THE UNITED NATIONS Canada was one of the 50 original signatory nations of the United Nations (UN) Charter in 1945, and has been a strong supporter of the UN ever since. On January 1, 1991, Canada completed a two-year term on the UN Security Council. Canada has also played a significant role in the General Assembly and in a number of special committees.

When military forces have been dispatched under the UN flag to counter threats to peace and security, Canada has provided personnel and equipment. To date, Canada has contributed to every UN peacekeeping mission.

Canada has also served at regular intervals on the Economic and Social Council. The Council discusses social, humanitarian and economic issues such as food shortages and international co-operation.

Canada has been prominent in UN efforts to promote and protect human rights and currently serves on the UN Commission on Human Rights. Canada is also active in international efforts to end illicit drug trafficking, and is a major donor to the UN Fund for Drug Abuse Control.

PEACE DIVIDENDS

*C*anada's defense priorities have been altering over the last few years as world events have modified defense needs. Specifically, the cold war between the East and West has ended, and the federal government has begun to reap the dividends of this new peace.

It is estimated that between 1992-93 and 1996-97, Canada's defense budget will drop by more than $2 billion. The reduction is largely due to the decision to close Canadian military bases in Europe. The two slated for closure are the Canadian Forces Bases in Lahr and Baden Soellingen, both in Germany. This will reduce Canada's forces in Europe under the North Atlantic Treaty Organization (NATO) command by some 7,000 troops once plans are complete in 1995.

From 1991-92 to 1993-94, Canada's defense budget has dropped about $400 million, from $12.8 billion to $12.4 billion.

KEEPING THE PEACE

Peace, wrote Canadian novelist Margaret Laurence, is "a word reverberating with meanings, achievable meanings." From their bed in a Montreal hotel room in 1969, John Lennon and Yoko Ono told the world: "All we are saying is, give peace a chance."

Achieving the meanings of peace has long been a goal of Canadian foreign policy. Indeed, Canada is the only country in the world to have participated in every United Nations (UN) peacekeeping operation ever undertaken.

Peacekeeping aims to halt conflict and to encourage negotiation. However, Canada acknowledges that international peacekeeping has its limits and should not be viewed as an end in itself or as a substitute for such things as political leadership and compromise.

The Canadian Forces provide personnel, equipment and resources to support UN and other peacekeeping forces around the world. Since 1947, some 88 Canadians have lost their lives while serving in peacekeeping forces.

By the end of 1992, Canada was involved in the largest number of peacekeeping missions ever undertaken at one time. These include:

▲ the European Community Monitoring Mission (ECMM). Since 1991, Canadians have been monitoring and reporting on the implementation of ceasefires.

▲ the United Nations Protection Force (UNPROFOR). This mission involves establishing UN-protected areas in the former Yugoslavia, and delivering humanitarian relief aid. Canada's contribution is twofold: Operation Harmony, begun in March 1992 and headquartered in Daruvar, Croatia; Operation Cavalier, begun in October 1992 and based in the Banja Luka-Doboj region of Bosnia-Hercegovina.

▲ security operations in Somalia (UNOSOM). Some 1,300 Canadian personnel, as part of a multinational UN sanctioned force, and the supply ship HMCS Preserver, were committed in December 1992 to the objectives of securing ports, airfields and convoy routes, and distributing relief supplies in strife-torn and famine-stricken Somalia.

▲ the United Nations Transitional Authority in Cambodia (UNTAC). This mission is a 1992 expansion of the UN Advance Mission in Cambodia, begun in 1991. Canadians are providing mine awareness training, transportation, communications assistance and logistical support in Cambodia.

▲ the United Nations Angola Verification Mission (UNAVEM). Since June 1991, Canadian Forces personnel have been monitoring the ceasefire between the Government of Angola and the forces of Angolan resistance (National Union for the Total Independence of Angola (UNITA) rebels).

▲ the United Nations Mission for the Referendum in the Western Sahara (MINURSO). Established in April 1991, Canadians are serving as observers, movement control and support personnel.

▲ the United Nations Iraq/Kuwait Observer Mission (UNIKOM). Established in April 1991, this mission monitors the demilitarized zone between Iraq and Kuwait and helps clear the area of undetonated explosives.

▲ several missions in the Middle East. These include: the United Nations Truce Supervisor Organization (UNTSO), for the supervision of General Armistice Agreements between Egypt, Israel, Jordan, Lebanon, and Syria (since 1954); the United Nations Disengagement Observer Force (UNDOF), which supervises the redeployment of Israeli and Syrian forces in the Golan Heights (since 1974); and the Multinational Force and Observers (MFO) based in the Sinai peninsula, to prevent violation of the Camp David Accord (since 1986).

▲ other peacekeeping activities in various parts of the world, including the United Nations Military Armistice Commission, supervising the 1953 Armistice Agreement in Korea (since 1953); Office of the Secretary General in Afghanistan and Pakistan (since 1990); and the United Nations Observer Mission in El Salvador (since 1991).

For many years, Canadians assisted in maintaining law and order between the Greek and Turkish communities in Cyprus, as part of the United Nations Force in Cyprus (UNFICYP), created in 1964. In December 1992, Canada announced its intention to withdraw its troops from Cyprus, beginning in mid-1993. This decision, taken after discussions with the UN, the United States, and other countries that contribute troops to UNFICYP, reflects Canada's desire to see a permanent, negotiated solution to the conflict.

In 1993, Canada contributed about $40 million to the UN organization. In addition to assessed contributions, Canada makes voluntary contributions to the UN's development program, the High Commission for Refugees, the Children's Fund, the Relief and Works Agency for Palestine Refugees, the World Food Program, the Educational and Training Program for Southern Africa, the Fund for Population Activities, the Committee on Racial Discrimination, the Trust Fund for South Africa and the Fund for Drug Abuse Control.

Canada is a member of numerous specialized UN agencies that focus either on broad issues such as world health, nutrition and education, or on particular areas of global interest such as aviation, telecommunications and the environment.

DISARMAMENT Canada has a number of priorities in the area of disarmament, including: a radical reduction in nuclear forces, encouraging compliance with existing treaties, strengthening nuclear non-proliferation, banning chemical weapons, and developing co-operative arms control verification activities.

To help meet these goals, Canada participates in the principal multilateral forums on disarmament, including the United Nations First Committee and Disarmament Commission, and the Conference on Security and Co-operation in Europe (CSCE) Forum for Security Co-operation. Canada also pursues arms control through bilateral consultations with countries from the East and West, and with neutral and non-aligned states active in arms control and disarmament. In February 1990, Canada hosted the first Open Skies Conference, attended by the foreign ministers of the 23 North Atlantic Treaty Organization and Warsaw Pact nations and resulting in the Open Skies Treaty.

THE ENVIRONMENT Canada is taking a leadership role in international efforts to protect and preserve the global environment.

The most important environmental event of 1992 was the United Nations Conference on Environment and Development (UNCED), which was held in Rio de Janeiro, Brazil. Canadians from all sectors of society participated in this event, known as the Earth Summit, and Canada was the first industrialized country to ratify both of the conventions issuing from UNCED: the Convention on Biological Diversity and the Framework Convention on Climate Change. Canada has moved quickly to implement UNCED's Agenda 21, a blueprint for sustainable development, and is a member of the United Nations Commission on Sustainable Development (UNCSD). Canada is working with the United Nations Development Program (UNDP) to assist developing nations in formulating national plans for sustainability.

Canada is also furthering the goals of UNCED through financial commitments toward forest management in developing countries, through increasing access for developing countries to Canada's markets, through the conversion of $145 million of debt in Latin American countries to local currency so that it may be used to finance sustainable development projects in those countries, and through other programs. Canada continues to work toward the development of an Earth Charter by 1995.

Canada is active in various international environmental organizations, a number of which are specialized UN agencies. Canada is also a signatory to several international environmental conventions, including the Montreal protocol on ozone-depleting substances, the protocol to reduce sulphur emissions (or their transboundary fluxes) by 30% by 1993, and an agreement to control nitrogen oxide emissions.

Canada has signed international agreements on environmental co-operation with several countries, including Russia, China and Mexico. Canada also participates in a wide range of international environmental efforts, including global environmental monitoring and assessment; weather, climate and atmospheric research; scientific and technical commissions; registries of hazardous materials; waste management; natural resource management; and protection of endangered species.

TOURISM AND CONSULAR SERVICES

Through diplomatic and consular missions, External Affairs and International Trade Canada provides passports, citizenship documents and notarial services. The department also offers advice and assistance to

Canadians who lose money and travel documents, are arrested and imprisoned, become ill, or are affected by civil disturbances or natural disasters.

External Affairs and International Trade Canada issues passports to Canadian citizens through offices in Canada and at Canadian diplomatic and consular missions abroad. In 1992, the Passport Office issued over 1.2 million passports.

INTERNATIONAL TRADE AND THE BALANCE OF PAYMENTS

Canada's history and development have been shaped by international trade. Initially, trade helped to open up the new frontier as trappers ventured further afield to obtain furs and skins to be sent back to markets in Europe. The colonies' trading relationships with the mercantilist British Empire helped them to prosper and grow, while ensuring that the military aid required to maintain our sovereignty from the United States was provided. Since Confederation, constant growth and change in the raw materials, goods and commodities Canada buys and sells has led to a system that plans, monitors, and regulates international trade. Trade issues have also played a pivotal role in Canadian politics, be it the abrogation of the reciprocity treaty of 1854 by the United States in 1866, the protective tariffs of Sir John A. Macdonald's National Policy in 1879, the defeat of Sir Wilfrid Laurier's Liberal government and its platform of free trade in the infamous election of 1911, or the election of Brian Mulroney's Conservative government in 1988, also on a platform of free trade.

Maintaining healthy trade relations involves meeting the needs of Canada's trading partners while at the same time safeguarding national interests. The emergence of trading blocs and supra-national political bodies (for example, the General Agreement on Tariffs and Trade, the Free Trade Agreement, the North American Free Trade Agreement, and the European Economic Community) has made it clear that Canada must have a sophisticated approach to trade negotiations. This requires a good understanding of who our trading partners are, how these relationships are changing, and what our comparative advantages are.

As the developed world moves from production-based prosperity to a mixed economy dominated by service industries, Canada's natural wealth, maturing exporting capacity and industrious and educated population place the nation in a strong position to compete successfully in the world's markets.

BALANCE OF PAYMENTS Canada's Balance of Payments — the record of all our economic transactions with other countries — is divided into two parts: the Current Account and the Capital Account. The Current Account records international transactions in merchandise trade and non-merchandise trade (services, investment incomes and transfers). The Capital Account records financial claims on and liabilities to the rest of the world (investments, stocks, bonds and other capital flows).

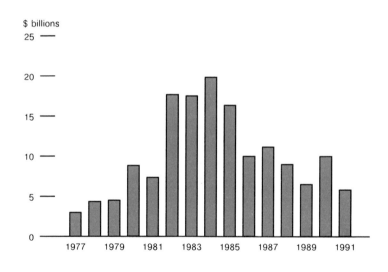

Canada's Trade Balance

INTERNATIONAL MERCHANDISE TRADE Over the last 20 years, Canada has consistently sold more than it has bought in terms of merchandise trade with other countries. The merchandise trade surplus — the amount by which exports exceed imports — reached an all-time high of nearly $20 billion in 1984. Since then, the trade surplus has tended to decline somewhat, mostly because of a slower growth in exports than in imports; between 1988 and 1991, imports increased by 5.5% while exports increased by only 2.9%.

In 1991, Canada's merchandise trade surplus was $5.8 billion, compared to $9.9 billion the previous year. Imports were at $135.9 billion, and exports at $141.7 billion. We achieved this surplus entirely thanks to exports to our largest trading partner, the United States; in trade with the rest of the world, dollar for dollar, we bought more than we sold.

What We Buy and Sell... Overall, the commodities in which Canada does the most business with other countries are machinery and equipment, industrial goods and materials, and automotive products. The key factor in Canada's international automotive trade is the Canada-United States Auto Pact, which allows the duty-free movement between the United States and Canada of automobiles, trucks, buses, and parts for the manufacture of such vehicles (except for tires and rubber tubes). Except for some modifications made with the Free Trade Agreement of 1989, the pact has remained largely unchanged since it came into force in 1965, and provides the essential underpinning for Canada's auto trade.

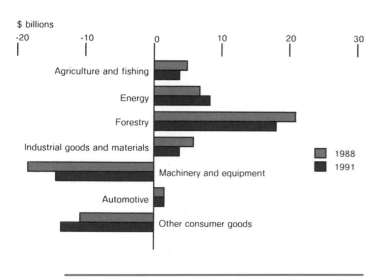

Canada's Trade Balance by Sector

Indeed, Canada's exports in 1991 were led by automotive products; these were followed by machinery and equipment, industrial goods and materials, forestry products, energy products, and agricultural and fishing products. Between 1988 and 1991, exports of machinery and equipment, energy products, other consumer goods, and agricultural and fishing products all went up.

In 1991, machinery and equipment accounted for the largest share of total imports by value, followed by automotive products, industrial goods and materials, other consumer goods, agricultural and fishing products, and energy products. Between 1988 and 1991, imports dropped in three areas: automotive products, forestry products, and industrial goods.

Overall, the major contributor to the 1991 trade surplus was forestry products, with energy products, industrial goods and materials, agricultural and fisheries products, and automotive products all playing a role. On the other hand, other consumer goods and machinery and equipment brought the surplus down; we imported more than we exported of these items.

... and With Which Countries Imports and exports also vary among Canada's principal trading areas. The European Economic Community (EEC) group comprises Belgium, Denmark, France, the Federal Republic of Germany, Ireland, Italy, Luxembourg, the Netherlands, Greece, Portugal, Spain and the United Kingdom. The 'other OECD countries' grouping comprises Austria, Finland, Iceland, Norway, Sweden, Switzerland, Turkey, Australia and New Zealand (the EEC countries, the United States, Japan and Canada are also members of the OECD).

Between 1988 and 1991, Canada's imports from the 'other OECD countries' increased by 22%, those from 'other countries' by 15%, those from Japan by 9%, and those from the United States by 6%. Imports from the EEC declined by 9% over the same period. Japan, the 'other OECD countries,' and the 'other countries' all increased their share of the Canadian import market between 1988 and 1991. The United States' share remained unchanged, while the EEC's share declined.

Between 1988 and 1991, Canada's exports to the United States increased by 4.6%, those to the EEC by 4.9%, and those to 'other countries' by 4.4%. Exports to Japan decreased by 18%, and those to the 'other OECD countries' declined by 19%.

Trade Agreements Trade relations between Canada and a number of countries are governed by trade agreements, by exchanges of most-favoured-nation treatment, and by less formal arrangements.

The cornerstone of Canada's involvement in the world trading system is the General Agreement on Tariffs and Trade (GATT). This agreement, to which Canada became a signatory in January 1948, grants tariff concessions and an exchange of most-favoured-nation treatment among participating countries, and also prescribes rules and regulations for international trade. Under the auspices of the GATT, seven rounds of multilateral trade negotiations have taken place since the inception of the GATT in 1947, all aimed at lowering barriers to trade. As of March 1993, negotiations were continuing for the completion of the eighth round, called the Uruguay Round because it was launched in Punta del Este, Uruguay, in 1986.

The North American Free Trade Agreement (NAFTA) was signed by Canada, the United States and Mexico in December of 1992, to extend the free trade area created by the Canada-United States Free Trade Agreement (FTA) of 1987 to include Mexico. As the *Year Book* was going to press, a bill to implement the NAFTA was before the Canadian House of Commons, and implementation processes were also under way in the United States and Mexico. NAFTA is expected to come into force on January 1, 1994.

The United States Tariff (UST) rates were established under the FTA, and have been incorporated into NAFTA. All goods qualifying for the UST will be completely free of duty by January 1, 1998. For a transition period of 15 years commencing January 1, 1994, two additional tariff treatments will be established for goods that originate under NAFTA.

As well as these agreements, a number of other measures affect Canada's international trade. The Special Import Measures Act protects against dumping (the exporting of goods at lower prices than apply in

John McQuarrie / GeoStock

Canadian soldier.

THE BIGGEST TRADING BLOC IN THE WORLD

If all goes according to plan, Canada will, on January 1, 1994, become part of the largest trading area in the world. The North American Free Trade Agreement (NAFTA), reached by Canada, the United States and Mexico in August 1992, needs to be ratified by the Parliament of Canada and the Congresses of Mexico and the United States before taking effect. The Canadian senate was debating NAFTA as the **Year Book** *was going to press. If ratified it will eliminate most restrictions on trade and investment between the three countries by the year 2003.*

The North American free trade area will include some 363 million consumers (20 million more than the European Community), and have a combined Gross Domestic Product of nearly $7 trillion. Incorporating and building upon the current Canada-United States Free Trade Agreement (FTA), NAFTA also includes provisions for more countries to be included, subject to the approval of the three original signatories.

NAFTA will provide for the phase-out of all tariffs on goods qualifying as North American under its rules of origin. Special rules will apply in certain key sectors, such as energy, agriculture, textiles and apparel. The Canada-United States Auto Pact remains, while the restrictive Mexican Auto Decree will be phased out. Trade in services including transportation, financial and some telecommunications services will also be facilitated, as will investments in each country by investors from another NAFTA country. Other provisions include measures governing temporary relief or protection for sensitive industries, technical and environmental standards, and dispute settlement. Not affected by the agreement are Canada's cultural industries, or its health and social services programs. Canadian government policy prohibiting the large-scale export of water is unaffected.

The agreement should provide Canadian goods, services and capital with increased access to the Mexican market, consisting of some 87 million consumers. With the elimination of Mexican tariffs and restrictive import licensing requirements, Canadian firms will be able to participate in most areas of the Mexican economy — one of the fastest-growing in the world.

Currently, trade between Canada and Mexico is quite small, and heavily tilted in Mexico's favour. In 1991, Mexico exported $2.6 billion worth of goods and services to Canada, while Canada exported only $543 million worth to Mexico. Indeed, Canada exported less to Mexico in the whole of 1991 than it did to the United States in an average period of two days the same year.

The elimination of tariffs and other barriers to free trade will have an impact on a number of sectors, including the auto industry, agriculture, forestry and fisheries, textiles and apparel, metals and minerals, machinery and equipment, services such as transportation, business and professional services, certain enhanced telecommunications services, and financial services. While Canada can expect to reap immediate benefits from many of these provisions, others may, as with the FTA, require readjustments on the part of Canadian industry to meet changing conditions.

Canada's largest export sector is the auto industry; in 1991, Canada's total exports of automotive products to all countries were valued at $35 billion dollars. The Canada-United States Auto Pact remains in place under NAFTA; in addition, Mexican and Canadian tariffs on auto parts will be phased out over the next five to ten years. While critics of the deal have suggested that new rules of origin may discourage European and Asian investment in the Canadian auto industry, increased access for Canadian auto products to the Mexican market could more than offset this.

Canada will gain increased access to the Mexican services market, including financial services. However, NAFTA does not substantially improve Canadian access to the American financial services market.

Mexico will lower barriers to foreign investment in various sectors including the auto industry, mining, agriculture, fishing, transportation and most manufacturing. This will undoubtedly attract foreign investment to that country, and may even cause some Canadian and American companies to consider relocating to Mexico where labour is cheaper and health, environmental and safety standards less rigorously enforced. However, NAFTA does contain a number of positive environmental measures designed to protect human, animal, or plant life or health.

NAFTA also affirms workers' rights and improved working conditions in each country. And Canada's stability, modern infrastructure, good access to resources and skilled and productive workforce mean that this country remains an attractive place to invest.

a country's domestic market), instituting countervailing duties that offset these lower prices when Canada determines that foreign governments are unfairly subsidizing imports. Drawback legislation helps manufacturers to compete abroad and at home by providing relief from customs duty on imported parts or materials that are used to manufacture exportable goods. Drawback also applies to imports used in the manufacture of certain goods for the domestic market. This relief is essential for key industries, such as automobile manufacturing, that import large quantities of parts and materials.

Export Development Corporation   The Export Development Corporation (EDC) is a unique financial institution that specializes in helping Canadian exporters compete internationally. EDC facilitates export trade and foreign investment through the provision of risk management services, including insurance and financing, to Canadian companies and their global customers.

EDC's programs fall into four major categories: export credits insurance, covering short-term and medium-term credits; performance insurance, extending cover for risks inherent in performance and bid guarantees including consortium risks; foreign investment insurance, providing political risk protection for equity and other investments abroad; and finance, providing medium-term and long-term export financing.

The Role of Revenue Canada   Revenue Canada administers Canada's trade policy by verifying the origin, value and description of goods, investigating (and where necessary taking action against) unfair trade practices (such as dumping) and imposing and collecting trade protection revenue. In administering our border policy, Revenue Canada protects Canadian society from the entry of illegal goods (such as drugs), unsafe products, and dangerous individuals (such as terrorists), and controls the entry of goods subject to import restrictions.

NON-MERCHANDISE TRADE

Although merchandise trade is by far the largest component of the Current Account, non-merchandise receipts and payments also play an important part. Non-merchandise items include: services such as

those rendered to and by businesses and governments, freight and shipping, travel and other services; income from investments; and transfers, such as those for international development assistance.

The Current Account has been in an uninterrupted deficit since 1985, growing steadily from $3.1 billion in that year to $29.2 billion in 1991. In 1992 it dropped slightly to $28.6 billion. These deficits are partly due to a net deficit in services. For example, in each year since as far back as 1968, Canadians have paid out more on travel services than they have received; in 1992 the travel deficit was $8.3 billion. Business services, such as consulting and professional services and insurance services, have regularly registered a net deficit; in 1992 the net payments were $4.5 billion. But the largest net deficits have almost always been in investment income; in 1992 investment income payments exceeded receipts by $24.9 billion, representing 87% of the Current Account deficit (65% of the non-merchandise deficit).

Capital Flows   In principle, any deficit in the Current Account is matched by an inflow of capital (an increase in liability or decreased asset), usually in the form of foreign investment in Canada. Similarly, Current Account surpluses correspond to increased assets or decreased liabilities, such as Canadian investments abroad. These flows of capital are recorded in the Capital Account. Normally, owing to the different methods used to calculate the two figures and to possible omissions or errors in each, there is a statistical discrepancy between the 'bottom line' of the Current Account and that of the Capital Account.

A major component of these capital flows is foreign direct investment in Canada. In the past, there was concern about foreign investment, and particularly, in the 1960s, direct investment from the United States. The focus of the Foreign Investment Review Agency (FIRA) was to control foreign investment, which was seen by some as a potential threat to Canada's economic autonomy. Over the years, however, the sources of foreign direct investment diversified, and such investment came to be seen as healthy for Canadian prosperity. Reflecting this new view, FIRA was renamed Investment Canada with the proclamation of the Investment Canada Act of June 1985. Investment Canada continues to review major foreign investments to determine if they are likely to be of net benefit for Canada, but it also actively promotes investment in Canada by Canadians and non-Canadians, undertakes research and provides policy advice on matters related to investment. Between June 1985 and April 1992, Investment Canada recorded a total of 6,278 new foreign investments in Canada. About 70% of these were acquisitions and the remainder new businesses; more than half came from the United States, nearly a quarter came from the European community, and less than one in twenty came from Japan. (These figures comprise foreign investments as defined by the Investment Canada Act, including certain investment proposals that may not have come to fruition; they do not include expansions of facilities by established investors, or portfolio investments that do not involve the acquisition of control of a Canadian business. Thus they represent only a partial measure of the foreign direct investment activity recorded in the Capital Account of the Balance of Payments.)

Canada's International Investment Position Canada's international investment position is the balance sheet of Canada's external assets and external liabilities. These data reveal the extent to which Canada has been both a receiver from and a supplier to the rest of the world of real and financial resources.

While the international investment position is closely related to the capital flows shown in the Balance of Payments, it is a more comprehensive statement in that it also reflects many other influences, including exchange rate fluctuations, effects of migrations and inheritances, undistributed earnings and other factors. The investment position is also a representation of the cumulative Current Account balance (including retained earnings and other adjustments), although here again the statistical discrepancy must be taken into account.

By the end of 1992, Canada's liabilities to non-residents were at $541 billion, while external assets amounted to $240 billion. Thus the net international liability position stood at $301 billion, an increase of $25 billion over the previous year; the $41 billion increase in liabilities was more than double the increase in assets ($16 billion). Canada's net liability with non-residents represented 44% of the Gross Domestic Product in

1992. This proportion has been steadily increasing in recent years.

Canada's assets were led by direct investment abroad, which amounted to $99 billion or 41% of all external assets at the end of 1992. There was a sharp increase (16%) in Canadian portfolio investment in foreign stocks, which climbed to $37 billion.

Among the liabilities, the largest was in non-resident holdings of Canadian bonds (at $231 billion, up from $204 billion the previous year), and the second largest was in the form of foreign direct investment in Canada, at $137 billion. The United States continued to be the largest foreign net investor in Canada ($128 billion), followed by Japan ($59 billion) and the United Kingdom ($40 billion).

Part of these liabilities takes the form of short-term and long-term borrowings (whether by governments, government business enterprises or corporations) from non-residents, resulting in what is commonly known as the foreign debt. At the end of 1992, the foreign debt amounted to $385 billion, of which $231 was in the form of bonds.

Canada's International Investment Position

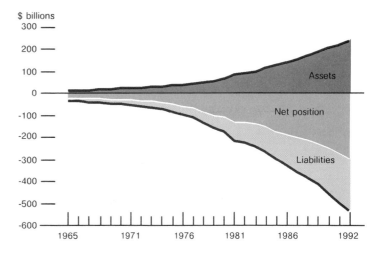

CANADA AND THE GATT

In early 1993, Canada and 110 other nations were still locked in negotiations for a new world trade deal aimed at reducing tariffs and subsidies, and liberalizing trade practices. These negotiations were part of the General Agreement on Tariffs and Trade (GATT) — the only contract governing world trade.

Essentially, GATT's ongoing role is to provide a process for securing a predictable international trading environment. Its purpose is to strengthen an open, rules-based system to govern trade around the world.

The first GATT agreement came into force in 1948, when 23 countries agreed to sharply reduce tariffs to energize international trade and stimulate the world economy. Since then, many more countries have joined the 'GATT club', and there have been several rounds of negotiations to further liberalize international trade.

The latest GATT negotiations, the Uruguay Round, began in 1986 and were to have been completed in 1991. However, the negotiations between the member countries got bogged down, primarily in a dispute between the United States and the European Economic Community over the contentious issue of reducing farm subsidies. These subsidies are huge, totalling some $320 billion in 1991 for the developed countries alone. It is generally recognized that these subsidies are harmful to world trade as they promote inefficient farm industries, skew world trade patterns in agricultural products, and discourage efficient low-cost farm operators in developing countries. A significant milestone was reached in November 1992 when the United States and European Community reached agreement on several key elements of the Multilateral Trade Negotiative (MTN) agricultural agreement. The resulting Blair House Accord continued to be opposed by France in early 1993, leaving the issue unresolved.

In Canada, the federal government was fighting to keep a clause permitting supply management, a system of quotas it uses to manage the supply of products such as milk, eggs and poultry. However, there was little international support for Canada's position. Canada was also fighting to remove trade-distorting export subsidies.

As the Uruguay Round remained unresolved in early 1993, fears were being raised that the failure of this round could lead to a more protectionist world trading environment.

For Canada, a successful round will provide important export opportunities for agriculture, wood and paper products, non-ferrous metals, chemicals, farm equipment, financial and other commercial and professional services, and many other goods and services. As well, it will provide more security to Canadian exporters through improved provisions governing subsidies and countervailing measures, anti-dumping and safeguard provisions, better dispute settlement mechanisms and other institutional arrangements.

To date, seven completed rounds of GATT negotiations have led to a steep decline in the tariff levels of developed countries since World War II. Shortly after the war, tariffs on industrial goods in developed countries averaged about 40%, whereas today they have declined to an average of about 5%. At the same time, the value of world merchandise trade has soared from $57 billion to more than $3.7 trillion per year.

Since the first GATT agreement, rounds focusing on specific areas of trade have taken place. For example, the Kennedy Round, which was negotiated from 1964 through to 1967, resulted in tariff reductions and an anti-dumping agreement preventing companies from selling goods abroad for less than they are sold for domestically. The Tokyo Round, negotiated from 1973 through to 1979, reduced tariffs on thousands of industrial and agricultural products.

The GATT secretariat, based in Geneva, Switzerland, oversees trade negotiations such as the Uruguay Round, helps resolve trade disputes, and interprets GATT rules and precedents.

Together, GATT members account for some 90% of world trade. More than two-thirds of GATT membership is from developing countries. As of June 1993, the addition of several countries including the Czech Republic, the Slovak Republic, Dominica, Mali, St. Lucia and Swaziland brought GATT membership to 111.

Robert Semeniuk / First Light

Canadian aid helps counter starvation in Somalia.

CANADIAN DEVELOPMENT ASSISTANCE PROGRAMS

C I D A   Assistance to developing countries has been forthcoming from the Canadian government since 1946. The Canadian International Development Agency (CIDA), established in 1968, manages most of Canada's international development assistance programs.

In 1990-91, Canadian aid totalled $3 billion. From 1981-82 to 1990-91, Canada spent $23 billion on international aid.

Canada's aid to developing countries can be grouped broadly into two programs: the National Initiatives Program and the Partnership Program.

Under the National Initiatives Program, Canada contributes to development projects in Asia, Africa and the Americas, often by providing various forms of technical assistance, and funds scholarships for Third World students and trainees. Through the partnership program, Canada supports development initiatives beyond the scope of any single donor country.

Before 1988, about half of Canada's aid was tied to recipient countries procuring Canadian goods and services. In recent years, Canada has eased this policy to allow developing countries to use their own resources for development projects. This new aid strategy is based on six development priorities: alleviating poverty, achieving economic stability, increasing women's participation, fostering environmentally sound development, securing food supplies and ensuring access to energy resources.

Since 1986, Canada's Development Assistance Program has been financed completely by grants rather than by development loans. At the same time, Canada has periodically forgiven loans to help developing countries cope with their growing debt problems.

Canada has long been one of the world's major suppliers of food aid — mostly through shipments of wheat, flour and canola oil. In 1990-91, Canada contributed $382.3 million in food aid, making Canadians the most generous per capita donors of food aid in the world. This aid is disbursed through multilateral agencies, through country-to-country agreements with recipients such as Bangladesh, Jamaica and Ethiopia, and through Canadian non-governmental organizations.

I D R C The International Development Research Centre (IDRC) is an independent international corporation financed mainly by an annual grant from the Government of Canada. Through support for research, IDRC helps developing countries find their own long-term solutions to pressing development problems. Support is given directly to Third World institutions whose research focuses on meeting the basic needs of the population and overcoming the problems of poverty.

To meet the needs of its Third World partners, IDRC has a wide variety of interests, including: agriculture; forestry; fisheries; animal sciences; food storage, processing, and distribution; health systems; education; population studies; economics; urban policies; environmental strategies; science and technology policy; information systems; earth sciences; communication processes; and the dissemination and utilization of research results. Since its creation in 1970, IDRC has supported some 4,000 projects in more than 100 countries.

In June 1992, the Prime Minister of Canada announced at the United Nations Conference on Environment and Development (UNCED) that IDRC's mandate was to be broadened to emphasize issues of sustainable development. In assisting the implementation of UNCED's Agenda 21 Global Action Plan, IDRC will become one of the world's key organizations for making sustainable development a reality.

C U S O Founded in 1961, the Canadian University Service Overseas is an independent Canadian voluntary organization working with communities and groups committed to development and social change in Canada and the Third World. CUSO recruits Canadians skilled in trades, business, agriculture and renewable resources, health, education, technology and community development for two-year postings in the Third World. CUSO also provides funding and other support to self-help and community development projects. Within Canada, CUSO promotes international co-operation by building links between its overseas partners and Canadian groups having similar goals, such as women, labour unions and aboriginal peoples.

Core funding for CUSO comes from CIDA, with other contributions coming from provincial governments, businesses, and Canadian organizations and individuals.

C E S O Created in 1967, the Canadian Executive Service Organization (CESO) is an independent, non-governmental organization which provides Canadians experienced in business and technology as short-term volunteer consultants to Canadian aboriginal peoples and to businesses and organizations in the developing world and in former Eastern Bloc countries of Central and Eastern Europe.

CESO receives core funding from CIDA, External Affairs and International Trade Canada and Indian and Northern Affairs Canada. Contributions also come from provincial and territorial governments, from businesses, from other organizations and from overseas clients.

DEFENCE

Canada's international defence policy rests on three major elements: the peaceful resolution of disputes; defence and collective security; and arms control and disarmament. The core military capabilities of the Canadian Forces may be used to protect Canada and Canadian sovereignty and carry out civil responsibilities in Canada, to contribute to collective defence through the North Atlantic Treaty Organization (NATO) including our continental relationship with the United States, and to contribute to peacekeeping and stability operations, arms control verification, and the provision of humanitarian assistance.

Because of the collapse of the Soviet Union and the other dramatic changes that have occurred in Central and Eastern Europe in recent years, many of the assumptions underpinning Canada's security policy are no longer valid. To deal with the uncertainties of the new international environment, Canada's armed forces emphasize combat-readiness, multi-purpose resources and flexibility.

EXTERNAL AFFAIRS AND INTERNATIONAL TRADE CANADA

Canada's official representation abroad began in 1840 with the posting of migration agents in the United Kingdom to help arrange passage to British North America. In 1895, Canada's first trade commissioner outpost was established in Sydney, Australia. The Department of External Affairs was created in 1909, initially to deal with Canada's relations with countries outside the British Empire.

Canada now has missions in over 120 countries. In most countries, Canada's official quarters are known as embassies and headed by an ambassador, the senior Canadian representative. Other Canadian missions in the same country are known as consulates general. In the United States for example, the Canadian Embassy is in Washington and Canadian consulates general are found in major cities such as Boston, Chicago, Los Angeles and New York. A consulate general is under the direction of a consul general.

In Commonwealth countries, Canada's missions are known as high commissions, with a high commissioner occupying the position of Head of Mission, which is equivalent to that of Ambassador.

Ambassador or High Commissioner is the highest rank a Canadian diplomat can hold, serving as the eyes and ears for our country by observing and reporting economic, political, military, social and cultural developments. These heads of mission represent Canada both formally and informally as the official agents of communication and, in their personal conduct, as an example of the Canadian people.

Heads of missions and all Canadian diplomats working abroad are members of the federal government department called External Affairs and International Trade Canada. Its main functions are: promoting Canada's economic, political, security and other interests abroad; supporting the export marketing efforts of Canadian business through the Trade Commissioner Service; providing development assistance and emergency aid relief in co-operation with the Canadian International Development Agency (CIDA); and helping Canadians travelling and living abroad through consular services.

MISSIONS ABROAD

EMBASSIES:

- Abidjan
- Addis Ababa
- Algiers
- Amman
- Ankara
- Athens
- Baghdad
- Bangkok
- Beijing
- Belgrade
- Berne
- Bogota
- Bonn
- Brasilia
- Brussels
- Bucharest
- Budapest
- Buenos Aires
- Cairo
- Caracas
- Copenhagen
- Dakar
- Damascus
- Dublin
- Guatemala
- The Hague
- Hanoi
- Havana
- Helsinki
- Holy See
- Jakarta
- Kiev
- Kinshasa
- Kuwait
- Libreville
- Lima
- Lisbon
- Madrid
- Manila
- Mexico City
- Moscow
- Oslo
- Paris
- Port-au-Prince
- Prague
- Pretoria
- Rabat
- Riyadh
- Rome
- San José
- Santiago
- Seoul
- Stockholm
- Tehran
- Tel Aviv
- Tokyo
- Tunis
- Vienna
- Warsaw
- Washington
- Yaoundé

CANADIAN HIGH COMMISSION LIAISON OFFICES:

- Abuja
- Accra
- Bridgetown
- Canberra
- Colombo
- Dar-es-Salaam
- Dhaka
- Georgetown
- Harare
- Islamabad
- Kingston
- Kuala Lumpur
- Lagos
- London
- Lusaka
- Nairobi
- New Delhi
- Port of Spain
- Singapore
- Wellington
- Windhoek

CONSULATES GENERAL:

- Atlanta
- Berlin
- Boston
- Buffalo
- Chicago
- Cleveland
- Dallas
- Detroit
- Dusseldorf
- Los Angeles
- Milan
- Minneapolis
- Munich
- New York
- Osaka
- San Francisco
- Sao Paulo
- Seattle
- Shanghai
- Sydney

CONSULATES:

- Auckland
- Bombay
- Fukuoka
- Lyon
- Melbourne
- Nagoya
- Santo Domingo
- Tegucigalpa

NATO COMMITMENTS Canada was one of the 12 original signatories of NATO in 1949. Subsequent Canadian governments have re-affirmed the view that Canada's security is linked to that of Europe and the United States. However, with the end of the East-West confrontation in Europe, NATO is adapting its purpose, strategy and force structure to the changing circumstances. While the threat of simultaneous full-scale attack on all of NATO's fronts has effectively disappeared, some risks do remain. The new NATO strategy emphasizes the mobility, flexibility and sufficient size of standing forces, the availability and sufficient numbers of well-trained, well-equipped reserves, and the timely flow of supplies and reinforcement in a crisis. While NATO is an alliance for defence through deterrence, it is also a major forum for political consultation among members. Canada's NATO membership fosters political, economic and scientific/technological relations with Europe, helping to balance Canada's relations with the United States.

North American Air Defence Canada's geographic size, its strategic location, and the limited resources it has available for defence mean that it will maintain its long-standing relationship with its closest neighbour, the United States. The North American

Air Defence (NORAD) agreement, in effect since 1959, provides for the joint monitoring and controlling of Canadian and American airspace. NORAD is undergoing modernization to improve its ability to identify and intercept aircraft and cruise missiles. New radar systems will detect and track intruders so that our tactical aircraft can identify and, if necessary, engage them.

Canadian Forces Europe Canadian Forces Europe (CFE) has provided the basis for Canada's NATO commitment over the last 40 years. A defence policy update announced in April 1992 that by 1995 CFE will cease to exist, as Canada proceeds with the withdrawal of troops from the European continent. The Canadian Forces will maintain the links forged with Canada's NATO allies through the continuation of regular joint training and operations, and the presence of Canadian staff in NATO command organizations.

KEEPING THE PEACE Over the years, Canada's commitment to promoting international peace and security has been an ongoing feature of its foreign and defence policy. Canada has participated in all of the UN's peacekeeping missions, of which the first was undertaken in 1947. That mission's purpose was to bring an end to the war between India and Pakistan that broke out when the countries gained independence from Britain; Canadian military observers served there until 1976. Canada still assists in that mission by providing CC-130 Hercules aircraft for the biannual move of the mission's headquarters between Srinigar, India, and Rawalpindi, Pakistan.

Since 1948, more than 85,000 Canadian service personnel have participated in more than 20 different UN peacekeeping, peace-restoring or truce supervisory operations, as well as several non-UN missions. The effective involvement of the Canadian Forces in peacekeeping operations has contributed directly to the easing of tensions in trouble spots around the world. Canada will continue to emphasize peace-making and peacekeeping efforts in the process of international conflict resolution.

THE CANADIAN ARMED FORCES The Canadian Forces is a combined service comprising five major commands and National Defence Headquarters, all reporting to the chief of defence staff.

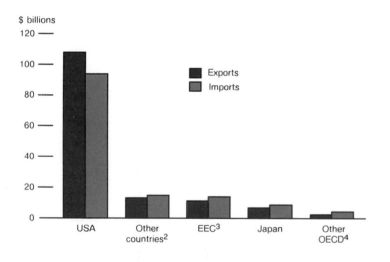

Canada's Merchandise Trade[1] with Other Countries, 1991

$ billions

[1] Balance of payments basis.
[2] Countries not in the Organization for Economic and Cultural Development (OECD).
[3] European Economic Community (EEC).
[4] OECD countries not in the EEC.

John McQuarrie / GeoStock

CF18 takes off, Operation Desert Storm.

In peacetime, the Canadian Forces consist of a regular, full-time force and a reserve force with several components. In September 1992, the regular force numbered 81,000 and the primary reserve force 30,500. The primary reserve comprises personnel who perform part-time military duty and training. The supplementary reserve is not required to perform military duty or training unless placed on active service. The Canadian Rangers perform military duty or training as required but do not undergo annual training. Rangers generally patrol remote or isolated areas of Canada.

The Canadian Forces also staff rescue co-ordination centres, with Canadian Coast Guard officers performing liaison duties. Aircraft specially equipped and staffed for search and rescue are periodically augmented by other aircraft and resources.

Maritime Command Maritime Command maintains combat-ready, general-purpose maritime forces to meet Canada's defence commitments. As well as supporting Canadian military operations, the command also conducts search and rescue operations in the Atlantic provinces, in British Columbia and in surrounding ocean areas.

The command's increased surface and air resources have been used for surveillance, for countering illicit drug traffickers, for detecting fishing violations in Canadian waters and for identifying vessels that pollute Canadian coastal waters.

Maritime Command includes the naval reserve, which has units across Canada. The reserve's major role is maritime coastal defence — mine countermeasures and naval control of shipping. To improve overall readiness, the naval reserve is integrated with regular forces.

Land Force Command Formerly called the Mobile Command, Land Force Command has combat-ready land forces trained and equipped to protect Canadian territory, to meet Canada's overseas commitments, and to support UN or other peacekeeping operations.

In addition, Land Force Command contributes to the joint defence of North America and to NATO collective security. This is achieved through a total force structure combining both manoeuvre and deployment troops organized into four Land Force Areas (Atlantic, Quebec, Central and Western).

Air Command Air Command's combat-ready regular and reserve air forces meet Canada's national, continental and international commitments, as well as supplying air support to both Maritime and Land Force Commands. Air Command consists of six functional air groups.

The Fighter Group's air defences enforce Canadian sovereignty in national airspace. The group's forces are also required to meet Canada's commitments to continental defence under the NORAD agreement, and to Central European defence through NATO. The group provides fighter support to Maritime Command and Mobile Command, and trains fighter pilots.

The Air Transport Group supplies the Canadian Forces with worldwide air transport, including strategic airlifts, tactical airlifts, and general air transport. The group commands all primary air search and rescue forces in Canada.

The Maritime Air Group manages anti-submarine air resources as part of Canada's contribution to NATO, patrols Canada's coastal waters and the Arctic Archipelago, and conducts pollution-monitoring flights and fisheries patrols.

The 10 Tactical Air Group supports the army with fire support and reconnaissance and tactical transport over battle areas.

The Air Reserve Group comprises two wings, each with two tactical helicopter squadrons and three other squadrons. As part of recent efforts to revitalize reserves, air reservists are increasingly involved in air force operations.

Communication Command This command provides strategic communications for the Canadian Forces and, in emergencies, for the federal and provincial governments. It encompasses message handling and data transfer; telephone systems; high frequency radio direction finding; and communications research. The communication reserve comprises 6 communication regiments, 12 communication squadrons and 3 independent communication troops. The reserve enhances the communications capability of regular force communications units.

Headquarters Northern Area This command co-ordinates forces employed in Canada's northern region, including the Yukon and Northwest Territories and all islands in Hudson Bay, James Bay and the Arctic Archipelago. This region extends to the geographic North Pole, and comprises about 4 million square kilometres, or 40% of Canada's area.

Canadian Forces Training System In addition to the five operational commands, a sixth formation provides all basic recruit and officer training as well as training for occupations required by more than one operational command. As such, the Canadian Forces Training System is jointly staffed by personnel from all three environments (land, sea and air).

SOURCES

Canadian Executive Service Organization

Canadian International Development Agency

CUSO

Environment Canada

Export Development Corporation

External Affairs and International Trade Canada

International Development Research Centre

Investment Canada

National Defence

Revenue Canada, Customs and Excise

Statistics Canada

FOR FURTHER READING

Selected publications from Statistics Canada

▲ *Exports, Merchandise Trade. Annual. 65-202*

▲ *Imports, Merchandise Trade. Annual. 65-203*

▲ *Canadian International Trading Patterns. 65-503*

▲ *Canada's Balance of International Payments. Quarterly. 67-001*

▲ *Canada's International Investment Position. Annual. 67-202*

▲ *Canada's International Transactions in Services. Annual. 67-203*

▲ *Canada's Balance of International Payments, Historical Statistics 1926 to 1990. 67-508*

TABLES

14.1   TOTAL IMPORTS, EXPORTS AND TRADE BALANCE ON A BALANCE-OF-PAYMENTS BASIS

	Imports		Exports[1]		Trade balance $'000,000	Ratio of exports to imports %
	Value $'000,000	Change from previous year %	Value $'000,000	Change from previous year %		
1976	36,608	7.8	38,167	13.5	1,559	104.3
1981	77,140	13.6	84,432	10.1	7,292	109.5
1986	110,374	7.5	120,318	1.1	9,944	109.0
1987	115,119	4.3	126,340	5.0	11,222	109.7
1988	128,862	11.9	137,779	9.1	8,917	106.9
1989	135,347	5.0	141,767	2.9	6,420	104.7
1990	136,600	0.9	146,520	3.4	9,920	107.3
1991	135,948	−0.5	141,728	−3.3	5,780	104.3

[1] *Exports include domestic exports and re-exports.*

14.2 IMPORTS INTO CANADA ON A BALANCE-OF-PAYMENT BASIS (MILLION DOLLARS)

	1988	1989	1990	1991	Percentage of 1991 Total
Agricultural and fishing products					
Fruits and vegetables	2,576	2,729	2,912	3,078	2.3
Other agricultural and fishing products	4,981	5,527	5,827	5,926	4.4
Sub-total, agricultural and fishing products	7,558	8,256	8,739	9,005	6.6
Energy products					
Crude petroleum	2,977	3,705	5,444	4,508	3.3
Other energy products	2,199	2,515	2,754	2,121	1.6
Sub-total, energy products	5,176	6,221	8,198	6,629	4.9
Forestry products	1,293	1,358	1,324	1,218	0.9
Industrial goods and materials					
Metals and metal ores	7,801	7,571	7,052	5,915	4.4
Chemical and plastics	7,423	8,125	8,273	8,293	6.1
Other industrial goods and materials	9,947	10,776	10,767	10,145	7.5
Sub-total, industrial goods and materials	25,172	26,472	26,092	24,353	17.9
Machinery and equipment					
Industrial and agricultural machinery	12,876	13,528	12,579	11,142	8.2
Aircraft and other transportation equipment	5,966	5,505	4,826	5,302	3.9
Office machines and equipment	5,851	6,285	6,280	6,911	5.1
Other machinery and equipment	15,773	17,960	18,959	19,347	14.2
Sub-total, machinery and equipment	40,466	43,279	42,644	42,703	31.4
Automotive products					
Passenger autos and chassis	12,164	11,834	10,718	11,666	8.6
Trucks and other motor vehicles	3,656	3,458	3,449	3,689	2.7
Motor vehicle parts	17,580	16,835	16,458	15,782	11.6
Sub-total, automotive products	33,400	32,127	30,624	31,137	22.9
Other consumer goods					
Apparel and footwear	3,107	3,474	3,746	3,462	2.5
Miscellaneous consumer goods	10,461	11,549	12,107	13,153	9.7
Sub-total, other consumer goods	13,568	15,023	15,853	16,615	12.2
Special transactions trade	2,610	2,884	2,966	3,650	2.7
Unallocated adjustments	−381	−273	159	639	0.5
Total, imports	128,862	135,347	136,600	135,948	100.0

14.3   TOTAL EXPORTS FROM CANADA ON A BALANCE-OF-PAYMENT BASIS
(MILLION DOLLARS)

	1988	1989	1990	1991	Percentage of 1991 Total
Agricultural and fishing products					
Wheat	3,559	2,508	3,209	3,452	2.4
Other agricultural and fishing products	8,841	9,197	9,498	9,333	6.6
Sub-total, agricultural and fishing products	12,400	11,705	12,707	12,785	9.0
Energy products					
Crude petroleum	4,043	4,475	5,687	5,882	4.2
Natural Gas	2,954	3,025	3,574	3,581	2.5
Other energy products	4,884	4,786	5,478	5,483	3.9
Sub-total, energy products	11,881	12,286	14,739	14,947	10.5
Forestry products					
Lumber and sawmill products	6,896	7,081	6,587	6,178	4.4
Woodpulp and other wood products	6,370	6,881	5,928	4,744	3.3
Newsprint and other paper and paperboard	8,892	8,520	8,355	8,365	5.9
Sub-total, forestry products	22,158	22,482	20,871	19,287	13.6
Industrial goods and materials					
Metals and metal ores	5,249	5,578	5,290	4,432	3.1
Chemicals, plastics and fertilizers	7,260	6,900	7,161	6,918	4.9
Metals and alloys	12,820	13,918	12,006	11,491	8.1
Other industrial goods and materials	5,765	5,528	5,629	5,292	3.7
Sub-total, industrial goods and materials	31,094	31,923	30,087	28,133	19.8
Machinery and equipment					
Industrial and agricultural machinery	4,907	5,494	6,041	5,743	4.1
Aircraft and other transportation equipment	4,218	5,517	6,471	6,536	4.6
Other machinery and equipment	12,808	13,831	15,867	16,121	11.4
Sub-total, machinery and equipment	21,933	24,842	28,378	28,401	20.0
Automotive products					
Passenger autos and chassis	15,725	15,549	16,196	16,367	11.5
Trucks and other motor vehicles	8,204	8,389	8,168	7,792	5.5
Motor vehicle parts	10,890	11,100	9,977	8,431	5.9
Sub-total, automotive products	34,819	35,038	34,341	32,591	23.0
Other consumer goods	2,745	2,617	2,814	3,024	2.1
Special transactions trade	1,433	1,546	3,076	2,987	2.1
Unallocated adjustments	−685	−673	−493	−425	−0.3
Total, exports	137,779	141,767	146,520	141,728	100.0

14.4 CANADA'S TRADE ON A BALANCE-OF-PAYMENT BASIS

	United States		Japan		EEC[1]		Other OECD[2]		Other Countries[3]	
	Value $'000,000	%	Value $'000,000	%	Value $'000,000	%	Value $'000,000	%	Value $'000,000	%
Imports										
1988	88,794	68.9	7,960	6.2	15,349	11.9	3,632	2.8	13,128	10.2
1989	94,025	69.5	8,297	6.1	14,574	10.8	4,055	3.0	14,396	10.6
1990	93,726	68.6	8,255	6.0	15,114	11.1	4,903	3.6	14,601	10.7
1991	93,733	68.9	8,686	6.4	13,963	10.3	4,448	3.3	15,118	11.1
Exports										
1988	102,642	74.5	8,339	6.1	10,903	7.9	3,077	2.2	12,817	9.3
1989	105,657	74.5	8,526	6.0	11,870	8.4	3,452	2.4	12,261	8.6
1990	110,475	75.4	7,654	5.2	12,020	8.2	3,494	2.4	12,877	8.8
1991	107,617	75.9	6,813	4.8	11,435	8.1	2,483	1.8	13,380	9.4

[1] European Economic Community (EEC) countries are Belgium, Denmark, France, the Federal Republic of Germany, Ireland, Italy, Luxembourg, the Netherlands, Greece, Portugal, Spain and the United Kingdom.
[2] Organization for Economic Cooperation and Development (OECD) countries include EEC countries, (referred to above) Austria, Finland, Iceland, Norway, Sweden, Switzerland, Turkey, Australia, New Zealand, the United States, Japan and Canada.
[3] This group includes all countries other than the EEC countries and other OECD countries.

14.5 CANADA'S BALANCE OF INTERNATIONAL PAYMENTS (MILLION DOLLARS)

	1990	1991	1992
Current account			
Receipts			
Merchandise exports	146,520	141,728	157,549
Non-merchandise services:			
Travel	7,748	7,802	8,072
Freight and shipping	5,291	5,443	5,812
Business services	8,252	8,303	8,924
Government transactions	886	854	883
Other services	868	903	960
Total services	23,045	23,305	24,651
Investment income[1]	9,764	9,714	7,723
Transfers	4,143	3,575	4,203
Total non-merchandise receipts	36,953	36,594	36,576
Total receipts	183,473	178,322	194,125
Payments			
Merchandise	136,600	135,948	148,063
Non-merchandise services:			
Travel	14,507	15,365	16,364
Freight and shipping	5,443	5,403	5,844
Business services	12,295	12,507	13,401
Government transactions	1,437	1,633	1,708
Other services	644	680	728
Total services	34,326	35,588	38,045

14.5 CANADA'S BALANCE OF INTERNATIONAL PAYMENTS (MILLION DOLLARS) (concluded)

	1990	1991	1992
Investment income[1]	34,020	32,099	32,614
Transfers	4,235	3,937	3,967
Total non-merchandise payments	72,581	71,623	74,626
Total payments	209,182	207,571	222,689
Balances			
Merchandise	+9,920	+5,780	+9,487
Non-merchandise	−35,629	−35,030	−38,050
Total current account	−25,709	−29,249	−28,563
Capital Account[2]			
Canadian claims on non-residents, net flows			
Canadian direct investment abroad[1]	−5,100	−4,400	−3,336
Portfolio securities:			
Foreign bonds	−31	−1,128	−537
Foreign stocks	−2,269	−5,710	−4,887
Government of Canada assets:			
Official international reserves	−649	+2,830	+6,978
Loans and subscriptions	−1,450	−1,781	−1,725
Non-bank deposits abroad	−481	−439	+1,527
Other claims	+715	+2,610	+693
Total Canadian claims, net flow	−9,266	−8,018	−1,286
Canadian liabilities to non-residents, net flows			
Foreign direct investment in Canada[1]	+6,820	+5,890	+4,717
Portfolio securities:			
Canadian bonds	+13,296	+25,829	+18,224
Canadian stocks	−1,735	−990	+1,034
Canadian banks' net foreign currency			
transactions with non-residents[3]	+3,155	+4,957	−3,553
Money market instruments:			
Government of Canada paper	+2,666	+2,288	+1,915
Other paper	+2,223	+2,140	+3,071
Allocation of special drawing rights	—	—	—
Other liabilities	+8,288	+2,948	+3,188
Total Canadian liabilities, net flow	+34,712	+43,062	+28,595
Total capital account, net flow	+25,446	+35,044	+27,309
Statistical discrepancy	+262	−5,795	+1,254

[1] *Excludes retained earnings.*

[2] *A minus sign denotes an outflow of capital resulting from an increase in claims on non-residents or a decrease in liabilities to non-residents.*

[3] *When the banks' foreign currency position (booked in Canada) with non-residents is a net asset, this series is classified as part of Canadian claims on non-residents.*

14.6 BILATERAL ACCOUNT WITH THE UNITED STATES[1] (MILLION DOLLARS)

	1990	1991	1992
Current account			
Receipts			
Merchandise exports	110,475	107,617	122,288
Non-merchandise services:			
Travel	4,407	4,519	4,637
Freight and shipping	3,140	3,388	3,893
Business services	4,998	5,028	5,390
Government transactions	307	267	275
Other services	396	407	440
Total services	13,248	13,608	14,634
Investment income[2]	4,339	4,898	3,768
Transfers	1,987	1,659	1,728
Total non-merchandise receipts	19,574	20,166	20,130
Total receipts	130,049	127,783	142,418
Payments			
Merchandise	93,727	93,733	104,610
Non-merchandise services:			
Travel	9,289	10,804	11,250
Freight and shipping	3,367	3,350	3,784
Business services	8,835	8,775	9,563
Government transactions	566	723	757
Other services	494	522	538
Total services	22,550	24,174	25,892
Investment income[2]	15,872	14,052	13,891
Transfers	627	658	665
Total non-merchandise payments	39,049	38,884	40,447
Total payments	132,776	132,618	145,057
Balances			
Merchandise	+16,748	+13,884	+17,678
Non-merchandise	−19,476	−18,718	−20,137
Total current account	−2,727	−4,835	−2,639
Capital Account[3]			
Canadian claims on non-residents, net flows			
Canadian direct investment abroad[2]	−2,761	−1,748	−1,513
Portfolio securities:			
Foreign bonds	+344	−1,508	−1,424
Foreign stocks	−1,271	−3,926	−3,229
Government of Canada assets:			
Official international reserves	+602	+401	. .
Loans and subscriptions	−158	−267	+52
Non-bank deposits abroad	−154	+891	+1,818
Other claims	−945	+251	−1,812
Total Canadian claims, net flow	−4,343	−5,905	−6,108

14.6   BILATERAL ACCOUNT WITH THE UNITED STATES[1] (MILLION DOLLARS) (concluded)

	1990	1991	1992
Canadian liabilities to non-residents, net flows			
Foreign direct investment in Canada[2]	+1,979	+3,205	+2,932
Portfolio securities:			
Canadian bonds	+9,345	+8,905	+17,457
Canadian stocks	−1,476	−1,463	+1,096
Canadian banks' net foreign currency			
transactions with non-residents[4]	+854	−6,204	−3,200
Money market instruments:			
Government of Canada paper	+264	−2,126	+3,454
Other paper	+1,499	+3,122	+3,772
Other liabilities	+3,540	+1,024	+681
Total Canadian liabilities, net flow	+16,005	+6,465	+26,191
Total capital account, net flow	+11,661	+559	+20,083
Statistical discrepancy and interarea transfers	−8,934	+4,275	..

[1] *Official international reserves are excluded from the current year as the geographical details are not yet available.*
[2] *Excludes retained earnings.*
[3] *A minus sign denotes an outflow of capital resulting from an increase in claims on non-residents or a decrease in liabilities to non-residents.*
[4] *When the banks' foreign currency position (booked in Canada) with non-residents is a net asset, series is classified as part of Canadian claims on non-residents.*

14.7 OVERSEAS DEVELOPMENT ASSISTANCE DISBURSEMENTS[1] (MILLION DOLLARS)

	1986-87	1987-88	1988-89	1989-90	1990-91
Government-to-government					
Anglophone Africa	218.12	293.70	309.49	267.45	290.25
Francophone Africa	198.99	200.67	242.31	228.67	251.58
Americas	153.03	165.53	178.16	160.87	181.19
Asia/Europe/Oceania	376.57	414.81	444.80	367.79	368.92
Miscellaneous	20.30	26.49	2.23	1.51	0.59
Sub-total, government-to-government	967.01	1,101.20	1,176.99	1,026.29	1,092.53
Other country-to-country					
Canadian non-governmental organizations	224.72	250.38	280.57	303.28	307.93
International non-governmental organizations	24.04	24.55	23.98	24.75	26.17
International Development Research Centre	90.69	93.93	101.89	110.55	101.35
Humanitarian assistance	37.73	47.53	56.43	42.56	90.84
Industrial co-operation	32.38	38.53	60.55	58.92	62.31
Petro-Canada International Assistance Corp.	55.32	65.77	59.81	47.90	38.44
International Centre for Ocean Development	2.33	4.01	5.16	6.52	8.51
Scholarship programs	8.55	11.57	16.28	19.82	20.90
Miscellaneous programs	0.50	13.40	62.07	86.28	103.03
Administrative costs	124.85	134.85	174.06	210.53	197.19
Sub-total, other country-to-country	601.11	684.52	840.80	911.10	956.17
Multilateral assistance					
General funds	78.50	84.20	90.00	81.68	83.25
Renewable natural resources	22.57	32.37	17.74	30.34	31.13
Population and health	17.75	16.05	16.70	15.10	16.75
Commonwealth and francophone programs	19.97	22.83	22.66	22.65	22.31
Other programs	12.45	21.62	15.90	16.86	19.16
International humanitarian assistance	14.75	15.15	17.25	17.25	18.94
World Food Program	166.38	172.77	188.40	173.57	182.10
Contributions to regular budgets and voluntary funds by External Affairs and other departments	30.96	36.25	35.19	41.72	38.68
International financial institutions	590.82	437.10	524.95	513.30	559.92
Sub-total, multilateral assistance	954.15	838.34	928.78	912.47	972.22
Total assistance (ODA)	2,522.27	2,624.06	2,946.59	2,849.87	3,021.42

[1] *Fiscal years ending March 31st.*

Sources
Canadian International Development Agency
Statistics Canada

SECTION FOUR THE ECONOMY

CHAPTER FIFTEEN

DAVID REEDE / FIRST LIGHT

RON WATTS / FIRST LIGHT

AL HARVEY / MASTERFILE

AGRICULTURE

INTRODUCTION

Fewer and fewer Canadians make their living from farming, yet much of Canada's wealth still lies in its cultivated soil. Grainfields, pastures, orchards, and other kinds of farms encompass about 45 million hectares of Canada, an area roughly twice the land mass of Britain. The goods and products from this land account for some 10% of Canada's economy. More than half of these agricultural products go to export and make an important contribution to Canada's balance of trade.

Farming in Canada has come a long way from the small, subsistence endeavour it once was. Improvements in, among other things, equipment, management practices, seeds and breeding techniques have made production soar. Compared with 50 years ago, today's farms are larger, but there are fewer of them. This has been the trend since 1941, when farms peaked at well over 732,000. In 1991, the Census of Agriculture recorded 280,000 census farms (those that produce agricultural products intended for sale), down 4.5% from the 1986 figure.

Against this drop-off, however, is the growth in the number of larger farms (those with gross receipts of $50,000 or more in constant 1990 dollars). These numbered about 111,000 in 1986, but some 118,000 in 1991. They call for major investments in buildings and machinery and demand sophisticated know-how. Today's farmer may have one hand on a computer and one on the wheel of 100-or-more horsepower's worth of tractor.

Big changes have also occurred in food processing and distribution. Most of what consumers pay for food goes toward the cost of processing, packaging, transportation and retailing. As a result, farmers receive an ever-smaller slice of the food-dollar pie.

As a contributor to the Gross Domestic Product, however, agriculture and related services continue to play an important role. In terms of Canada's primary industries, in fact, agriculture places second only to the mining and oil well industries, outpacing both the logging and forestry and fishing and trapping industries.

Despite modern technology, farming is still a risky business. Not only do farmers have to contend with natural disasters — droughts, hail, floods, livestock diseases, to name a few — but also with an increasingly competitive and interdependent world market, and changes in prices and consumer preferences. The price Canadian goods can fetch has much to do with what happens abroad. Bumper crops in other producing countries, protectionist policies and trade barriers — these greatly affect how Canadian agriculture fares.

To help producers face these challenges and to support this key industry, Canadian governments, both federal and provincial, have set up a number of programs over the years. There are programs for research, regulation, inspection, credit and financial assistance, and community development. Universities and colleges across Canada also contribute to agricultural education and research, in partnership with farmers.

Over the years, Canadian farmers have also formed a number of their own associations to meet economic, social and professional needs. Their main voice is the Canadian Federation of Agriculture, a coalition of provincial farm organizations, commodity associations and national marketing boards.

Today's agricultural sector in Canada provides quality food at good prices for consumers. It also means jobs, not just for farmers, but for the many people involved in spin-off industries, from the trucker to the factory worker. And it means valuable export dollars. The industry's ongoing success is vital to Canada. Its future rests largely in the hands of the individual producers and their continued imagination, co-operation and hard work.

BOUNTIFUL LANDS

Great rolling wheatfields, fruit-laden orchards, cattle ranches, dairy farms, purple concords, prize Leghorns, sweet maple sap. From sea to sea and even in places 'north of 60' (the 60th parallel), the vast Canadian land yields its bounties. Each region has its specialties, together forming the proverbial horn of plenty.

There are four main types of farms in Canada. Livestock farms specialize in beef cattle and hogs,

Dave Reede / First Light

Grain field at dusk.

Roth and Ramberg

Midway attraction, country fair.

poultry or dairy cattle. Grain and oilseed farms produce wheat, canola, barley, rye, corn, soybeans, oats and flax. Mixed farms produce both grain and livestock. Special crop farms produce vegetables, fruits, root crops, tobacco or forest products. In each region of the country, one of these farm types predominates.

THE ATLANTIC PROVINCES This region includes Newfoundland, Prince Edward Island, Nova Scotia, New Brunswick and the Gaspé district of Quebec. The land is hilly, with fairly rich soil developed under forest cover. The climate can be tempered by the all-embracing sea, but it is also affected by cold currents from the coast of Labrador and by northern winds. Mixed farming is most common, with forage crops supporting the livestock industry. Small farm operators often have other sources of income, such as lumbering or fishing.

The major Atlantic production areas include Prince Edward Island, potato capital of Canada, the St. John River Valley, New Brunswick, and Nova Scotia's Annapolis Valley, famous for fruit, especially apples.

THE CENTRAL LOWLANDS The lowlands hug the St. Lawrence River, stretch out through the Ottawa Valley and parts of Quebec, and extend through Southern Ontario to Lake Huron's shores. Fertile soils — mostly formed by glacial deposits and lake sediment — and a mild climate, modified by the Great Lakes and the St. Lawrence River, allow for many kinds of farms. Densely populated by Canadian standards, the region offers large, concentrated markets for farm produce.

Ontario's agricultural sector is Canada's largest and most diverse. Forage crops are the most common use of cultivated land in Ontario, and the lush Niagara Peninsula produces most of Canada's fruit and grapes.

In Quebec, more than half the commercial farms are dairy farms. This province is also the world's largest producer of maple syrup.

PRAIRIE SEAS Manitoba, Saskatchewan and Alberta contain 82% of the farmland in Canada: the prairie grain seas. Long sunny summer days and generally reliable precipitation produce quality grains — hard red spring wheat (the largest single cereal crop), barley, canola and other grains and oilseeds. Native grasslands and cultivated forage crops and feed grains support a large beef cattle industry.

Saskatchewan produces more than half of the Canadian wheat crop and large quantities of other grains. Alberta is Canada's chief producer of feed grains and beef cattle, and is second only to Saskatchewan in wheat production. Manitoba, with the highest Prairie rainfall and over 100 frost-free days, supports more varied farming.

THE PACIFIC Concentrated in river valleys, the southwestern mainland and southern Vancouver Island, British Columbia farms are mostly small and highly productive. Only 2% of BC land is used for agriculture. Of this, most is taken up with thriving dairy and livestock farms. But the province is also home to the Okanagan Valley, Canada's largest producer of apples, and is noted for its peaches, plums, apricots, cherries and grapes.

THE NORTH Some farmers brave the land north of latitude 57°, tilling soil or tending livestock in parts of northern British Columbia, the Yukon Territory and the Mackenzie River Valley in the Northwest Territories. But the cold climate and long distances to markets limit commercial agriculture. The North has an estimated 1.3 million hectares of potentially arable land and large expanses of grazing land. However, only 140 farms were enumerated in the 1991 Census. Precipitation varies from light in the northern Yukon to heavy on the mountainous coast of British Columbia. Frosts can occur year round, but some crops grown on well-drained, south-facing slopes can overcome this problem.

WHO'S DOWN ON THE FARM?

The family-operated farm still accounts for the vast majority of Canada's farms. The 1991 Census of Agriculture found that this category accounted for 98% of all census farms; the remainder was made up of non-family corporations (1%) and institutional farms, community pastures and Hutterite colonies. Canada's farm population is steadily declining. Between 1986 and 1991, the number of people living in farm households dropped from 930,000 to 867,000, a 7% reduction. Farm people now account for 3.2% of Canada's total population, while a decade ago they made up roughly 5%. The trend has been downward since World War II.

The province with the most farmers is Saskatchewan, with the proportion of farm to total population at 16%, but even here, the number is declining.

It is not only the farm population, but rural and small town population in general that is declining. Between 1986 and 1990, one-half of Canadian census divisions lost population.

Percentage of Canadians on Farms

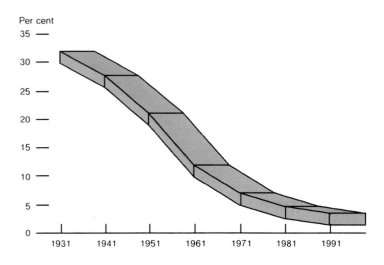

George Hunter

Harvest rows, Saskatchewan.

*The 1991 Census of Agriculture has uncovered a rather interesting new statistic about women in Canada —
26% of those who farm in Canada are women.*

*The news is interesting but not exactly new. While large numbers of women have always farmed in Canada,
they haven't shown up in canada's national farm statistics. That changed, however, in 1991 when — for the
first time ever — the Census of Agriculture asked that respondents report more than one operator per farm.*

With that simple question, the story was formally out. The 1991 Census tells us that more than 100,000 of Canada's 391,000 farmers are women.

Women farmers were most common in British Columbia where they made up 35%, or more than one-third, of all operators. In Prince Edward Island, where female representation was lowest, only 15% of farmers were women.

The majority of Canadian farms (63%) reported having one principal operator in 1991. Of Canada's 177,000 one-operator farms, 6%, or about 10,000, were headed by women.

The share of female farmers was far greater for farms with two operators. On the more than 90,000 such farms in Canada, women accounted for 44% of all operators. On the overwhelming majority of two-operator farms, management was shared by both a man and a woman.

Farms with three or more operators were relatively rare in 1991 (5%). Of these farms, however, more than three-quarters had one or more female operators. In total, 30% of all operators on such farms were women.

Female farmers were generally younger than their male counterparts. In 1991, the average age for female operators was 46 compared to 48 for males.

In total, 20% of all farm operators were under 35. On average the youngest farmers were in Quebec, while the oldest were in British Columbia.

Women farm operators were more likely to be married than male operators. In 1991, 87% of female farm operators were married, compared to 81% of male operators. This trend was reversed, however, on one-operator farms where only 42% of women sole operators were married, compared to 79% of men.

Of Canada's farmers, 37% supplemented their incomes in 1991 by working off the farm. Men reported an average of 72 days at their off-farm work, while women reported an average of 63 days. In Saskatchewan and Prince Edward Island the opposite was true — women spent more time at their off-farm jobs than men.

FARMS EARNING MORE

Fewer farms now appear on the Canadian landscape than at any time in recent history. However, as the number of farms continues to decline, those farms that remain are earning more than ever before.

In 1991, the Census of Agriculture recorded 280,000 Canadian farms, 4.5% fewer than in 1986. This continued the 50-year downward trend that began in 1941, when the number of farms peaked at more than 730,000.

From 1986 to 1991, the number of farms increased in only two provinces — British Columbia (1%) and Newfoundland (11%). The number of farms fell in all other provinces. Prince Edward Island reported the greatest reduction in farm numbers (17%), followed by New Brunswick and Quebec with reductions of about 8% each.

Those farms that remain, however, tend to earn more. The number of farms with gross receipts of $50,000 or more (in constant 1990 dollars) increased by 6% between 1986 and 1991. That's 111,414 farms in 1986 and 118,365 farms in 1991.

Newfoundland reported the greatest increase in these high-earner farms (21%), followed by Alberta (14%) and British Columbia (13%). In three provinces, however, the proportion of farms with gross receipts of $50,000 or more actually decreased — by 4% in both Prince Edward Island and New Brunswick and by 1% in Ontario.

The linkages between the farm business and the non-farm sector are therefore assuming increased importance. Many farmers supplement their incomes with part-time jobs elsewhere: about a third of operators reported off-farm work in 1990. Canadian farm families receive over one-half of their income from off-farm sources, and even for families on the largest farms, over 40% have at least one member working off-farm.

Trends in rural employment show that agriculture and agriculturally-related employment make up only a small share of rural jobs. They are surpassed by the service sector, which employs the most rural residents, and the trade and manufacturing sectors.

FARMING WOMEN For the first time, in 1991, people responding to the Census of Agriculture could name more than one farm operator. This census better depicted women's contribution to Canadian agriculture, revealing that women represent more than a quarter, or 26%, of all farm operators. Indeed, 100,000 of the country's 391,000 farmers are women.

British Columbia reported the highest percentage of female operators in 1991, at 35%. Prince Edward Island had the lowest, at 15%. Women were best represented on two-operator farms, where they accounted for close to half the operators.

Today's farm operators tend to be in their forties. In 1991, the average farm operator was aged 47.5. Male operators, on average, are about two years older than female operators. While both male and female operators are likely to be married, this is somewhat more true for women. In 1991, 87% of female farm operators were married compared with 81% of males.

Farms are increasingly going high-tech, with 11% using computers to manage the business in 1991, according to the Census of Agriculture. This number had quadrupled in the five-year period between 1986 and 1991. Most likely to use a computer were farms with receipts of $500,000 or more.

The old standbys are changing too: the 1991 Census of Agriculture found that, since 1986, the number of four-wheel drive tractors had increased by one-third, and that half of these fell in the 100 horsepower or over category. Newfoundlanders seem particularly keen to embrace new technology: the province with the fewest census farms, it had the largest proportion (31%) of four-wheel drive tractors to total tractors.

Environmental awareness may be having an impact on farming. The 1991 Census of Agriculture showed a reversal in the previously steady upward trend in the use of commercial fertilizer and herbicides. In 1990, 59% of census farms were using commercial fertilizer, compared with 66% in 1985; the percentage using herbicides had dropped significantly to 49% in 1990 from 59% in 1985. As well, in 1991, one-quarter of Canadian land seeded was prepared using conservation tillage; 'no till' seeding was used on an additional 7% of land.

canola oil and canola meal, there was agreement to reduce tariffs more quickly. CUSTA has been a contributing factor in the significant increase in exports of some of these commodities.

The North American Free Trade Agreement (NAFTA) may, with time, further improve Canada's export position. This deal will not affect Amerian-Canadian trade all that much, but it may improve the standing of Canadian exporters in the Mexican market. Over the next decade Canada is expected to see a gain in exports to Mexico, particularly in wheat, barley, pork and specialty products. This will still represent only a small portion of Canada's overall trade activities, however.

RECENT AGRICULTURAL TRENDS

GLOBAL TRADE WINDS Like many other industrialized nations, Canada is a net exporter of agricultural products; that is, it exports more than it imports. A little more than half of the total Canadian agricultural production ($13 billion worth in 1991 representing 9% of all exports) goes to the international market. In the five years between 1987 and 1991, Canada's agricultural exports rose 5.5%. However, global trade has presented tough challenges. The major exporting countries, including Canada, are keen to shore up their own producers and protect domestic markets while gaining access to consumers abroad. These countries have subsidized their farmers, causing a glut of certain foodstuffs on the global market and a lowering of prices. They have also shielded home markets from international market forces, which has led to trade disputes, particularly between the European Community and the United States. The protectionist climate and oversupply of goods has made it harder for Canadian producers to get what they perceive to be fair prices for their exports.

The two crop years since the signing of the Canada-United States Trade Agreement (CUSTA) have seen substantial growth in Canadian grain and oilseed exports: 7% in 1990-91 and 43% in 1991-92. Under CUSTA, agricultural tariffs between Canada and the United States are being gradually eliminated over 10 years. For many commodities, however, such as

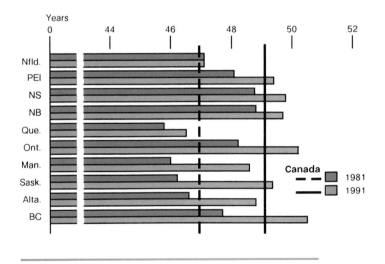

Average Age of Farm Operators[1]

[1] First operator only

Lionel Stevenson / Camera Art

Harvest time, Prince Edward Island.

PRODUCTION AND CONSUMPTION TRENDS

G R A I N S G A L O R E The types and quantity of farm goods Canadians produce depend very much on consumer demand, both at home and abroad. Grains and oilseeds continue to be key products, particularly for the export market. Canadian wheat growers, however, faced some difficult times during the past decade. From year to year, growing conditions fluctuated widely, causing dramatic ups and downs in production. At the same time, the 1980s saw a significant rise in wheat production worldwide, making it harder to sell Canadian wheat. The result was large annual variations in wheat exports, which ranged from 12 to 23 million tonnes. Still, Canada supplied about 16% of the world market.

Production of canola, Canada's major oilseed, rose significantly in the 1980s. The global market for this high quality edible oil will likely continue to expand. This is due to the fact that European farmers are producing less canola for the edible oil market, and interest in the United States and Japan in Canadian canola remains high. In the United States in particular, canola is viewed as a very health-conscious food.

In Eastern Canada, varieties of soybeans developed in the 1980s are becoming increasingly popular crops.

Barley continues to be the major feed grain in Western Canada; in the East, corn is most important. Exports of feed grains are relatively small compared to wheat exports.

L E A N T I M E S More and more Canadians are heeding warnings to cut fat and improve their diets. Increasingly, we are replacing red meat with poultry and fish, while cutting down on eggs and butter in favour of low-fat milk, cheese and yogurt.

Fresh vegetables are also in higher demand, a sign of rising concerns over nutrition and the linkages made between certain foods and heart disease, cancer and other illnesses.

In 1991, domestic consumption of red meat slipped to 68 kg per capita. The record high was in 1976 at 82 kg. (That translates to roughly 360 hamburgers and 360 porkchops per person over the year.) The downward shift in red meat-eating reflects beef-reduced diets. In 1991, Canadians made do with only 35 kg of beef per capita — at least two kilograms less than during the 1980s. Pork consumption, however, has gone up — 28 kg per person in 1991, a rise of more than half a kilogram since 1990.

F A R M · T E C H It would appear that there is more chicken for dinner these days, too. The trend toward more poultry consumption, set in the 1980s, has continued. In 1991, Canadians consumed a record 29 kg of poultry per person. On the other hand, fewer eggs were cracked. From 1981 to 1991, per capita egg consumption decreased 16% to 16 dozen.

Low-fat milk is in higher demand than ever, but overall, milk consumption is down. Cheese consumption, which rose during the 1980s, has levelled off to 3 kg per capita in 1991, while "variety" cheeses dipped to 5 kg. The hot item in the dairy market nowadays is yogurt; consumption has skyrocketed 95% over the last 10 years. But Canadians are more restrained about butter. Consumption of this product decreased steadily from 1983 to 1991.

C A S H F L O W S It is expensive to run a farm these days, and it's getting harder to make it pay. The main sources of cash for farmers are from sales of their goods (crops and livestock products) or from direct government payments to farmers. The total cash receipts for all Canadian farms during the five-year period from 1987 to 1991 rose only 2%, but operating expenses, including depreciation of equipment and buildings, soared 10%.

The net cash income — that is, the income derived after subtracting expenses from receipts — fell 19% during this period. A major cause for the drop in cash receipts was the decline in government payments. In 1987, farmers received $3.3 billion through various assistance programs. In 1990, these payments fell by about a third, to $1.9 billion. They rose again the next year but not to previous levels. In 1991, program payments and rebates were $2.3 billion.

Statistics Canada uses two other measures to determine farm earnings, and both show a similar picture.

IT'S A LIVING...

Canadian farmers have often found ways to make a little extra cash away from their farms ever since colonists began to till the soil in this country — it's known that Louis Hébert, the first European farmer in New France in the early 1600s, combined an apothecary practice with his farm work.

Today, mid-size farms are the backbone of Canada's agriculture industry, but more and more, the families running them are taking second jobs outside agriculture to help support their farms and subsidize their standards of living.

Indeed, while four-fifths of all Canadian families running mid-size farms report adequate total incomes, they earn more than half their money off the farm. A tenth of all farm family income in Canada comes from off-farm investments, and another third from working at jobs outside farming.

Realized net income takes into account depreciation of equipment and property and income-in-kind (the value of agricultural goods produced and consumed on the farm). From 1987 to 1991, realized net income fell 30%.

Total net income measures the value of production by adjusting realized net income to account for changes in unsold farm inventory during the year. Total net income fell 22% from 1987 to 1991.

When these measures are expressed in constant dollars — that is, in terms of actual purchasing power — all three declined to an even greater extent between 1987 and 1991. Net cash income fell 31%, realized net income plunged 40% and total net income dropped 34%.

Looking at the Canadian agricultural balance sheet, the picture is a little rosier. Total farm assets increased from $107 billion in 1988 to $128 billion in 1990, falling off slightly to $125 billion in 1992. Over the same period, total farm liabilities remained fairly constant with the result that net farm worth grew from $85 billion in 1988 to $103 billion in 1992.

On the other hand, farmers have been bringing in more cash from off-farm work. This means that farm family incomes have remained constant, in constant dollars, between 1987 and 1991. However, the gap between the incomes of farm and non-farm families is widening.

AGRICULTURAL MARKETING AND PRODUCT CONTROLS

MAKING THE GRADE The high standard of Canadian farm goods is due at least in part to government efforts to guarantee that only the best reaches market.

Early government attention to agriculture in this country focused on boosting production and controlling pests and diseases. At the same time, policymakers brought in grading procedures and standards to ensure quality. Today, federal and provincial departments of agriculture work together to keep quality high.

Dave Reede / First Light

Stockpiling wheat, Manitoba.

Agriculture Canada has some control over the sizes and types of containers used for food products, while Consumer and Corporate Affairs Canada enforces regulations on weights and measures. Health and sanitation standards for food handling include provincial and municipal laws that require milk pasteurization, regular inspections of slaughter houses, and maintenance of sanitary conditions in restaurants. Agriculture Canada is mandated to inspect meat carcasses traded interprovincially but, as it turns out, most beef and pork is slaughtered in federally inspected plants. Health and Welfare Canada oversees food composition standards, and Consumer and Corporate Affairs Canada ensures that advertising of food products is fair.

MARKETING CONTROLS Farmers market their products through private trading, public sales and auctions, sales under contract, and through co-operatives and marketing boards. These activities may be regulated by marketing control legislation which covers several agricultural products.

Marketing controls were introduced in response to problems that emerged in Canada as farm production rose and became more specialized. At the same time, buyers dwindled and producers lost bargaining power. To attempt to rebalance the scales, some farmers formed voluntary marketing co-operatives. Over time, the provinces passed legislation allowing co-operatives to incorporate; most provinces also provided financial

Roth and Ramberg

On the range.

assistance. Federally, the 1939 Agricultural Products Co-operative Marketing Act guaranteed prices for producers willing to market their crops on a pooling-of-returns basis.

Co-operatives were successful at first, but their voluntary nature became a problem. In good times many members dropped out to make their own deals. To eliminate this weakness, marketing control legislation created marketing boards, agencies and commissions for a number of key agricultural products. This approach was introduced in 1935, when the Canadian Wheat Board became the sole marketing agency for Prairie wheat.

MILK CONTROLS The Canadian Dairy Commission was established in 1966. At that time, it stabilized the market by offering fixed prices for butter, skim milk powder and other major dairy products. Today, it stabilizes the market by restricting the quantity

of milk that producers may deliver. The commission also pays subsidies to producers of milk and cream to keep consumer prices at reasonable levels.

Since 1971, the Canadian Dairy Commission and the milk marketing agencies of Ontario and Quebec have agreed to a comprehensive plan for balancing supply and demand and for generating funds to help increase exports. The plan established a market-sharing quota system for milk and cream producers; in the following three years the other provinces joined the program. Prices for deliveries that exceed a producer's quota are based on world prices for surplus dairy products.

PRODUCER MARKETING BOARDS Introduced during the 1930s, provincial boards give agricultural producers legal authority under certain conditions to control the marketing of their produce. Participation in these boards is compulsory.

Usually, a new board must be approved by a majority of producers of the product. If this occurs, every producer must then market under authority of the board. The board may negotiate prices, may set production or marketing quotas, and may designate times and places for marketing.

Provincial marketing boards have jurisdiction only within the province. Under the 1949 Agricultural Products Marketing Act, the federal government can delegate powers to a marketing board for interprovincial and export trade.

MARKETING AGENCIES Not all agricultural goods can be effectively marketed by individual provincial boards. Some require a national approach. The 1972 Farm Products Marketing Agencies Act allows the federal government to establish national marketing agencies at the request of producers and provincial authorities. The four national agencies created so far cover table eggs, turkey and chicken meat and broiler hatching eggs. The National Farm Products Marketing Council — comprising representatives from producer, consumer and labour groups — works with marketing agencies and provincial governments to improve interprovincial and international marketing of regulated products.

PROMOTING GRAINS

In 1991, grains and oilseeds represented about 50% of Canada's $13 billion in food and agricultural exports, making the grain industry once again Canada's premier agricultural sector.

The federal government's involvement in the grains industry predates Confederation, going back at least as far as the early 1800s, when wheat was the dominant crop in what is now Ontario.

Today's federal policies and programs cover land use and settlement, transportation, grain storage, handling, forwarding, marketing and income security. The government also helps grain producers deal with the many ramifications of international competition — Canada has been a leading participant in the search for international co-operation in grain sales.

The key government agencies in the grains industry are the Grains and Oilseeds Branch of Agriculture Canada, (which now includes the National Grains Bureau), the Canadian Grain Commission, and the Canadian Wheat Board. The grain commission and the wheat board are semi-autonomous, reporting to Parliament through the Minister of Agriculture.

The grains industry supports two important agencies. The Canadian International Grains Institute helps expand markets for Canadian grains and oilseeds through research and education. The Canada Grains Council identifies issues in the grains sector, offers an industry perspective on government policy, and co-ordinates efforts to increase efficiency and Canada's share of world markets.

Established in 1986, the Grains and Oilseeds Branch of Agriculture Canada develops, analyzes and manages domestic and international grains and oilseeds policies, programs and issues. The branch also oversees some income stabilization programs.

Key branch activities include: incorporating industry input into policy development for the sector; providing industry with timely information and analysis on key issues; and playing an active role in trade matters. In the latter area, the branch supports trade policy and marketing interests of the industry and co-operates with the public and private sectors to promote and facilitate the export of grains, oilseeds and their products.

The Net Income Stabilization Administration (NISA) is part of the branch as is the Livestock Feed Bureau (LFB), which joined in 1991. The bureau administers the Feed Freight Assistance Act, providing support to livestock producers in grain-deficient regions.

CANADIAN GRAIN COMMISSION Established in 1912 by the Canada Grain Act, the Canadian Grain Commission regulates grain handling in Canada, and establishes and maintains standards of quality for Canadian grains. In 1992, the Commission became a Special Operating Agency, which gave it more financial independence and flexibility to operate.

Commissioners develop policies, deal with enquiries from grain producers and supervise the operations of licensed elevators. The commission also supervises grain futures trading and examines appeals on official grading of grain.

Quality control of grains moving through the handling system is maintained by the commission's Inspection Division. The Weighing Division supervises the weighing of grain at elevators, and audits grain stocks to ensure that all grain is accounted for during shipment. The Grain Research Laboratory assesses the quality of new crops, conducts basic and applied research, and supplies technical assistance to marketers. The Economics and Statistics Division issues dealer and elevator licences, monitors security, allocates producer rail cars, conducts economic studies and publishes statistics.

CANADIAN WHEAT BOARD

The Canadian Wheat Board (CWB) is a Crown agency responsible for marketing wheat and barley grown in Manitoba, Saskatchewan, Alberta and the Peace River region of British Columbia. Established by an act of Parliament in 1935, the CWB has exclusive marketing authority for wheat and barley sold for export or to domestic processors for human consumption. The CWB also sells feed-quality wheat and barley into the domestic feed grain market in competition with grain companies.

Producers receive an initial payment when delivering their grain to the CWB. The grain is then sold for the best price possible, given market circumstances, and the proceeds pooled in four separate accounts. After deducting operating costs, the board distributes the proceeds remaining in the pool accounts at the end of the marketing year to producers in a final payment.

The Government of Canada guarantees initial payments which, once established for the crop year, cannot be lowered. The federal government bears the deficit in the pool account if market returns do not cover initial payments. However, if market prices rise substantially during the crop year, initial payments can be increased. Farmers who delivered prior to the increase would then receive an adjustment payment called an 'interim payment'.

The CWB is also involved in organizing grain transportation. It authorizes quotas for delivery of grain into railcars and country elevators as needed to meet sales commitments. As well, the board works with railway and grain companies to ensure that transportation is available to meet sales requirements.

OTHER GOVERNMENT INVOLVEMENT

Under Canada's Constitution, agriculture is a shared federal/provincial responsibility. The federal government focuses on research, policy, standards, quality assurance and regional development. The provinces focus on research, policy and extension work.

AGRICULTURE CANADA

Agriculture Canada helps maximize agriculture's contribution to Canada's economy by promoting growth, stability and competitiveness. The department's responsibilities cover three broad areas: development and regulatory services, research, and assistance programs.

Development and regulatory services improve crops and livestock and their products, inspect and grade agricultural products, help control insect pests and diseases, register pesticides and fertilizers, and develop markets.

The department's Research Branch works in four principle areas: resource conservation research, crop research, animal research, and food research.

Assistance programs serve to cushion producers from the impact of low commodity prices and high input costs as well as natural disasters such as drought.

To help keep up the high demand for Canadian farm goods both at home and abroad, Agriculture Canada has done a thorough review of its policies on farm products and processing. New strategies for the industry are attempting to accommodate regional diversity, to stimulate self-reliance and to make the industry responsive to market demands and environmentally sustainable.

Jay Maisel / The Image Bank

In addition to departmental activities, the Minister of Agriculture is responsible for three Crown corporations: the Farm Credit Corporation, the Canadian Dairy Commission and the Canadian Wheat Board. The Farm Credit Corporation helps farmers establish and develop viable farm enterprises by providing long-term credit and other financial services.

ASSISTANCE PROGRAMS The assistance programs administered by Agriculture Canada and by the agencies reporting to the Minister of

Agriculture attempt to contribute to a stable agricultural industry and food supply.

Revenue support and production management programs are available to stabilize farm incomes. Other income support programs help farmers cover expenses during periods of depressed prices. The federal government contributes to provincial crop insurance programs that protect farmers against losses caused by natural forces such as hail, drought and insects. Other programs help finance farm improvements and expansions, offer marketing assistance, and help producers purchase feed grain.

The provinces also support agriculture. Through regional offices and extension programs in rural areas, provincial agriculture departments provide advice on farm management (including crops, livestock, finances and animal health), farm labour, and home design and household budgeting. The departments also support 4-H and other youth groups.

Provincial engineering sections consult on soil and water management, farm machinery and equipment,

and structures. Provincial research programs help to develop and apply new technologies to increase farm productivity and conservation of resources.

In partnership with the federal government, the provinces also work to expand markets and develop the food processing industry.

In several provinces, loans, grants and financial services help farmers upgrade or expand operations, and shield them from income fluctuations.

SOURCES

Agriculture Canada

Canadian Dairy Commission

Canadian Federation of Agriculture

Canadian Grain Commission

Statistics Canada

FOR FURTHER READING

Selected publications from Statistics Canada

▲ *Agricultural Financial Statistics*. Annual. 21-205

▲ *Farming Facts*. Annual. 21-522E.

▲ *Fruit and Vegetable Production*. Quarterly. 22-003

▲ *Cereals and Oilseeds Review*. Monthly. 22-007

▲ *Grain Trade of Canada*. Annual. 22-201

▲ *Greenhouse Industry*. Annual. 22-202

▲ *The Dairy Review*. Monthly. 23-001

▲ *Livestock Report*. Quarterly. 23-008

▲ *Production of Poultry and Eggs*. Annual. 23-202

▲ *Livestock and Animal Products Statistics*. Annual. 23-203

▲ *1991 Census of Agriculture products*.

Selected publications from Other Sources

▲ *Rural and Small Town Canada*, Ray. D. Bollman, ed. Thompson Educational Publishing C15E.SRC - 2 - June 23, 1993 Inc. in co-operation with Statistics Canada and Supply and Services Canada, 1992.

TABLES

15.1   USE OF FARM LAND (HECTARES)

		Improved land			All other land	Total area of farms
		Under crops	Improved pasture	Summer fallow		
Newfoundland	1981	4 744	4 148	358	24 207	33 457
	1986	4 876	3 822	385	27 479	36 562
	1991	6 274	4 606	145	36 327	47 352
Prince Edward Island	1981	158 280	36 228	3 027	85 489	283 024
	1986	156 498	22 622	2 647	90 666	272 433
	1991	154 103	19 278	997	84 497	258 875
Nova Scotia	1981	112 782	46 106	5 154	301 997	466 039
	1986	109 512	36 236	3 910	266 848	416 506
	1991	106 231	30 723	1 186	258 892	397 032
New Brunswick	1981	130 526	41 479	5 183	260 714	437 902
	1986	129 475	27 204	4 289	247 925	408 893
	1991	122 247	25 048	1 551	226 785	375 631
Quebec	1981	1 756 038	443 559	53 077	1 526 526	3 779 280
	1986	1 744 396	301 133	31 802	1 561 470	3 638 801
	1991	1 638 453	270 924	14 712	1 505 520	3 429 609
Ontario	1981	3 632 727	657 009	63 309	1 686 286	6 039 331
	1986	3 457 966	431 286	80 337	1 676 993	5 646 582
	1991	3 411 667	390 212	63 657	1 585 843	5 451 379
Manitoba	1981	4 420 369	352 507	598 338	2 363 766	7 734 980
	1986	4 519 335	274 944	509 213	2 436 733	7 740 225
	1991	4 761 050	341 291	296 998	2 325 650	7 724 989
Saskatchewan	1981	11 740 864	975 364	6 704 464	7 112 163	26 532 855
	1986	13 325 811	878 726	5 658 251	6 736 567	26 599 355
	1991	13 458 915	1 075 655	5 712 830	6 618 088	26 865 488
Alberta	1981	8 441 242	1 581 443	2 205 468	7 978 329	20 206 482
	1986	9 162 524	1 376 814	2 127 013	7 988 989	20 655 340
	1991	9 292 044	1 742 479	1 771 395	8 005 085	20 811 003
British Columbia	1981	568 241	266 884	63 528	1 568 677	2 467 330
	1986	570 843	206 428	81 167	1 552 622	2 411 060
	1991	556 796	241 004	57 476	1 537 065	2 392 341
Canada	1981	30 965 813	4 404 727	9 701 906	22 908 234	67 980 680
	1986	33 181 235	3 559 215	8 499 016	22 586 292	67 825 758
	1991	33 507 780	4 141 221	7 920 948	22 183 752	67 753 701

15.2 SEEDED AREA AND PRODUCTION OF FIELD CROPS

	Area ('000 ha)				Production ('000 t)			
	1987	1990	1991	1992	1987	1990	1991	1992
Wheat								
Prince Edward Island	5.2	4.4	4.6	4.6	18.5	14.0	15.4	17.8
Nova Scotia	2.8	1.6	1.5	1.1	11.5	5.1	3.3	3.0
New Brunswick	3.0	2.4	2.2	0.8	9.9	7.7	6.9	2.3
Quebec	61.8	48.6	37.5	38.6	173.5	152.0	107.8	122.0
Ontario	200.3	335.9	180.5	301.5	672.3	1 418.4	623.1	1 257.5
Manitoba	1 962.7	2 205.5	2 173.1	2 092.1	3 946.0	5 884.4	4 806.3	5 241.7
Saskatchewan	8 235.4	8 308.2	8 595.1	8 555.2	15 211.0	17 485.9	18 501.2	16 114.2
Alberta	2 942.0	3 140.3	3 122.1	3 255.8	5 796.6	6 994.8	7 772.7	7 242.0
British Columbia	44.5	50.6	43.1	48.5	106.0	136.0	106.2	49.6
Canada	13 457.7	14 097.5	14 159.7	14 298.2	25 945.3	32 098.3	31 942.9	30 050.1
Oats								
Prince Edward Island	9.7	7.3	6.5	8.1	23.0	17.2	14.0	21.0
Nova Scotia	6.7	4.5	2.4	4.5	13.3	9.3	3.9	8.3
New Brunswick	12.1	9.3	7.2	12.1	25.9	19.5	13.7	24.9
Quebec	101.0	87.0	79.0	109.0	227.0	238.0	178.0	295.0
Ontario	93.1	89.0	64.7	80.9	215.9	211.3	137.3	183.5
Manitoba	190.2	145.7	109.3	230.7	431.8	339.3	222.1	493.5
Saskatchewan	323.7	323.7	206.4	485.6	709.4	694.0	385.6	709.4
Alberta	485.6	465.4	344.0	688.0	1 249.2	1 110.4	786.5	1 210.6
British Columbia	26.3	22.3	22.3	44.5	61.7	53.2	52.8	52.4
Canada	1 248.4	1 154.2	841.8	1 663.4	2 957.2	2 692.2	1 793.9	2 998.6
Barley								
Prince Edward Island	26.7	32.4	33.2	35.2	84.9	88.1	97.0	125.0
Nova Scotia	5.3	5.7	4.0	4.5	16.3	14.4	10.1	12.0
New Brunswick	11.3	12.5	12.1	14.2	37.5	38.0	32.7	43.9
Quebec	174.0	146.0	153.0	164.0	457.0	490.0	454.0	555.0
Ontario	226.6	178.1	190.2	178.1	740.3	581.3	548.7	609.6
Manitoba	688.0	607.0	505.9	455.3	1 937.1	1 959.5	1 426.1	1 393.4
Saskatchewan	1 537.8	1 436.6	1 254.5	1 254.5	3 919.0	3 897.3	3 069.9	2 819.5
Alberta	2 266.2	2 063.9	2 023.4	1 942.5	6 586.2	6 248.7	5 878.6	5 181.8
British Columbia	56.7	46.5	40.5	38.4	137.2	124.1	100.2	56.6
Canada	4 992.6	4 528.7	4 216.8	4 086.7	13 915.5	13 441.4	11 617.3	10 796.8
Rye								
Ontario	18.2	20.2	20.2	24.7	35.6	43.2	43.2	25.4
Manitoba	26.3	72.8	32.0	30.4	45.7	157.5	61.0	57.2
Saskatchewan	137.6	188.2	91.0	76.9	198.1	299.7	147.3	82.5
Alberta	70.8	56.7	32.4	58.7	121.9	91.4	76.2	67.3
British Columbia	4.0	3.2	2.0	2.6	7.6	7.6	4.4	1.5
Canada	256.9	341.1	177.6	193.3	408.9	599.4	332.1	233.9
Peas								
Manitoba	72.8	36.4	51.6	..	144.2	73.5	84.4	..
Saskatchewan	137.6	52.6	79.3	..	223.2	103.4	160.6	..
Alberta	26.3	34.4	67.6	..	47.6	87.1	164.7	..
Canada	236.7	123.4	198.5	..	415.0	264.0	409.7	..
Beans (dry white)								
Ontario	54.6	54.6	50.1	40.5	66.1	59.9	68.0	43.5
Canada	54.6	54.6	50.1	40.5	66.1	59.9	68.0	43.5

15.2 SEEDED AREA AND PRODUCTION OF FIELD CROPS (continued)

	Area ('000 ha)				Production ('000 t)			
	1987	1990	1991	1992	1987	1990	1991	1992
Soybeans								
Quebec	8.0	18.2	25.3	33.0	17.8	51.0	66.0	87.0
Ontario	453.2	465.4	570.2	607.0	1 251.9	1 211.1	1 388.0	1 456.0
Canada	461.2	483.6	595.5	640.0	1 269.7	1 262.1	1 454.0	1 543.0
Buckwheat								
Quebec	5.3	4.3	3.2	..	7.0	5.9	3.2	..
Ontario	6.2	2.8	3.0	..	8.9	3.0	2.7	..
Manitoba	16.2	20.2	15.7	..	20.2	21.8	17.4	..
Canada	27.7	27.3	21.9	..	36.1	30.7	23.3	..
Mixed grains								
Prince Edward Island	25.9	17.8	16.5	16.6	75.8	49.0	40.8	51.0
Quebec	29.0	26.0	25.7	29.0	78.0	80.0	73.0	90.0
Ontario	210.4	157.8	153.8	125.5	611.4	453.6	393.7	381.0
Manitoba	14.2	10.9	12.1	14.2	36.7	26.5	30.6	22.5
Saskatchewan	10.1	12.1	12.1	20.2	24.5	30.6	26.5	16.3
Alberta	20.2	20.2	20.2	80.9	53.1	51.0	40.8	40.8
British Columbia	1.6	2.4	3.4	4.0	4.1	7.6	8.2	4.1
Canada	311.4	247.2	243.8	290.4	883.6	698.3	613.6	605.7
Flaxseed								
Manitoba	315.7	295.4	250.1	149.7	398.8	381.0	330.2	208.3
Saskatchewan	226.6	344.0	220.4	137.6	271.8	431.8	266.7	165.1
Alberta	22.3	54.6	28.5	26.3	30.5	76.2	38.1	35.6
Canada	564.6	694.0	499.0	313.6	701.1	889.0	635.0	409.0
Canola/rapeseed								
Ontario	16.2	20.2	26.0	14.2	29.5	43.1	45.4	29.5
Manitoba	392.5	352.1	507.8	627.3	567.0	460.4	796.1	986.6
Saskatchewan	1 396.2	1 133.1	1 359.4	1 375.9	1 406.1	1 451.5	1 723.7	1 746.3
Alberta	1 173.6	991.5	1 206.8	1 133.1	1 667.0	1 281.4	1 621.6	1 383.5
British Columbia	40.5	32.4	40.5	44.5	49.9	29.5	37.4	22.7
Canada	3 019.0	2 529.3	3 140.5	3 195.0	3 719.5	3 265.9	4 224.2	4 168.6
Sunflower seed								
Manitoba	28.3	56.7	73.8	..	44.5	100.7	124.3	..
Saskatchewan	4.0	6.9	7.1	..	5.3	7.3	8.2	..
Canada	32.3	63.6	80.9	..	49.8	108.0	132.5	..
Mustard seed								
Manitoba	6.1	10.1	6.6	..	7.7	13.2	8.9	..
Saskatchewan	85.0	188.2	82.0	..	100.2	201.8	81.7	..
Alberta	22.3	32.4	24.2	..	24.5	34.5	30.5	..
Canada	113.4	230.7	112.8	..	132.4	249.5	121.1	..

15.2 SEEDED AREA AND PRODUCTION OF FIELD CROPS (concluded)

	Area ('000 ha)				Production ('000 t)			
	1987	1990	1991	1992	1987	1990	1991	1992
Grain corn								
Nova Scotia	1.2	1.4	1.5	..	6.4	6.4	7.7	..
Quebec	237.0	283.0	293.8	308.0	1 470.0	1 900.0	1 870.0	2 000.0
Ontario	744.6	740.6	765.5	720.3	5 461.3	5 258.0	5 308.8	4 775.4
Manitoba	20.2	34.4	40.5	..	109.2	165.1	205.7	..
Alberta	3.2	2.8	3.5	..	17.8	16.5	20.3	..
Canada	1 006.2	1 062.2	1 104.8	..	7 064.7	7 346.0	7 412.5	..
Potatoes								
Newfoundland	0.2	0.2	0.7	..	3.4	3.8	3.8	..
Prince Edward Island	27.1	30.4	77.8	..	724.5	850.5	851.6	..
Nova Scotia	1.7	1.8	4.4	..	40.0	34.7	37.1	..
New Brunswick	20.4	21.0	50.6	..	662.4	589.7	488.6	..
Quebec	17.9	17.4	43.3	..	407.7	377.6	361.0	..
Ontario	14.8	13.8	35.1	..	326.1	339.3	286.6	..
Manitoba	18.8	20.0	49.5	..	431.1	385.0	418.0	..
Saskatchewan	1.5	1.7	4.5	..	34.4	38.7	36.7	..
Alberta	9.9	12.1	28.3	..	302.3	310.3	271.4	..
British Columbia	3.4	3.2	8.3	..	109.5	74.8	104.7	..
Canada	115.7	121.6	302.5	..	3 041.4	3 004.4	2 859.5	..
Tame hay								
Newfoundland	3.8	5.1	4.9	..	13.0	23.6	25.2	..
Prince Edward Island	54.2	52.2	50.9	..	281.2	269.4	192.3	..
Nova Scotia	69.2	68.0	67.5	..	353.8	430.0	323.9	..
New Brunswick	68.4	64.7	64.6	..	363.8	379.2	257.6	..
Quebec	951.0	890.0	869.3	..	6 280.0	6 300.0	3 990.0	..
Ontario	1 031.9	1 052.2	1 041.0	..	7 711.1	7 438.9	7 257.5	..
Manitoba	627.3	716.3	697.9	..	2 903.0	3 628.7	3 538.0	..
Saskatchewan	809.4	910.5	945.6	..	2 540.1	2 857.6	3 719.5	..
Alberta	1 760.4	1 800.9	1 754.9	..	8 164.7	9 162.6	8 164.7	..
British Columbia	339.9	344.0	350.1	..	1 995.8	2 131.9	1 723.7	..
Canada	5 715.5	5 903.9	5 846.7	..	30 606.5	32 621.9	29 192.4	..
Fodder corn								
Nova Scotia	2.1	1.7	1.6	..	59.0	38.1	37.2	..
Quebec	54.5	36.5	31.8	34.0	1 880.0	1 220.0	880.0	1 060.0
Ontario	161.9	141.6	132.3	139.6	5 806.0	4 989.5	3 628.7	3 964.4
Manitoba	10.1	8.1	11.7	..	208.7	181.4	317.5	..
Alberta	7.3	6.1	6.1	..	226.8	181.4	199.6	..
British Columbia	10.9	9.3	9.7	13.4	390.1	408.2	453.6	471.7
Canada	246.8	203.3	193.2	..	8 570.6	7 018.6	5 516.6	..
Sugar beets								
Manitoba	10.5	10.9	10.7	..	441.8	352.0	453.6	..
Alberta	12.1	13.4	14.2	..	565.2	598.7	631.4	..
Canada	22.6	24.3	24.9	..	1 007.0	950.7	1 085.0	..

15.3 LIVESTOCK, 1991

	Nfld.	PEI	NS	NB	Que.	Ont.	Man.	Sask.	Alta	BC	Canada
Cattle ('000 head)	9	95	129	106	1,368	2,210	1,100	2,200	4,403	749	1,088
Pigs ('000 head)	16	108	130	79	2,994	3,112	1,256	828	1,702	229	10,454
Sheep and lambs ('000 head)	7	6	35	10	124	209	24	59	247	59	780
Poultry (tonnes)	7 062	2 311	20 581	16 425	176 596	207 124	27 765	17 873	50 591	75 676	602 004
Turkey (tonnes)	—	25	3 597	2 444	28 330	56 174	9 759	5 064	11 805	13 972	131 170
Eggs ('000 doz.)	7,138	2,764	19,508	11,067	82,701	17,9217	54,538	19,797	37,255	58,223	472,208
Milk and cream ('000 kilolitres)	[1]	96	170	127	2 793	2 463	286	213	581	511	7 240

[1] *Confidential.*

15.4 CENSUS-FARMS CLASSIFIED BY SALES CLASS

		\$100,000 and over	\$50,000- \$99,999	\$25,000- \$49,999	\$10,000- \$24,999	\$5,000- \$9,999	\$2,500- \$4,999	Under \$2,500	Total
Newfoundland	1981	78	35	35	68	64	104	295	679
	1986	110	43	41	77	67	77	236	651
	1991	150	45	47	94	103	88	200	725
Prince Edward Island	1981	381	414	473	569	386	362	569	3,154
	1986	553	433	422	496	292	262	375	2,833
	1991	717	355	261	383	244	184	217	2,361
Nova Scotia	1981	515	388	342	601	634	689	1,876	5,045
	1986	735	333	316	641	578	567	1,113	4,283
	1991	807	365	404	726	586	412	680	3,980
New Brunswick	1981	383	423	382	477	501	536	1,361	4,063
	1986	644	369	296	511	466	490	778	3,554
	1991	780	272	288	542	445	359	566	3,252
Quebec	1981	4,145	8,500	8,825	7,509	4,562	4,643	9,960	48,144
	1986	9,121	8,378	5,638	5,590	4,016	4,417	4,288	41,448
	1991	12,467	6,541	4,240	5,231	3,680	3,441	2,476	38,076
Ontario	1981	12,559	12,510	10,963	13,952	10,158	8,818	13,488	82,448
	1986	16,436	10,453	9,034	12,620	8,842	5,868	9,460	72,713
	1991	18,628	8,368	8,670	12,669	8,258	4,839	7,201	68,633
Manitoba	1981	3,191	5,530	6,394	6,308	3,053	2,041	2,925	29,442
	1986	5,878	5,905	4,839	4,807	2,310	1,523	2,074	27,336
	1991	6,318	5,358	4,548	4,287	2,007	1,365	1,823	25,706
Saskatchewan	1981	5,813	15,453	18,961	15,392	5,773	2,950	2,976	67,318
	1986	10,947	16,998	14,670	11,649	4,304	2,241	2,622	63,431
	1991	12,041	16,468	13,699	10,508	3,882	2,053	2,189	60,840

15.4 CENSUS-FARMS CLASSIFIED BY SALES CLASS (concluded)

		\$100,000 and over	\$50,000– \$99,999	\$25,000– \$49,999	\$10,000– \$24,999	\$5,000– \$9,999	\$2,500– \$4,999	Under \$2,500	Total
Alberta	1981	7,327	9,873	11,049	12,003	6,387	4,525	6,892	58,056
	1986	11,364	10,549	9,842	10,244	5,697	4,047	6,034	57,777
	1991	13,588	10,681	9,950	11,255	4,810	3,159	3,802	57,245
British Columbia	1981	2,154	1,346	1,748	2,802	2,487	3,060	6,415	20,012
	1986	2,616	1,231	1,757	2,832	2,456	2,807	5,364	19,063
	1991	3,002	1,416	1,818	2,965	2,624	2,693	4,707	19,225
Canada	1981	36,546	54,472	59,172	59,681	34,005	27,728	46,757	318,361
	1986	58,404	54,692	46,855	49,467	29,028	22,299	32,344	293,089
	1991	68,498	49,869	43,925	48,660	26,639	18,593	23,861	280,043

15.5 CENSUS-FARMS WITH SALES OF \$25,000 OR MORE, 1991

Product type	Nfld.	PEI	NS	NB	Que.	Ont.
Dairy	72	498	633	512	12,952	9,757
Cattle	48	488	1,011	822	6,583	16,853
Hogs	14	203	99	71	2,308	3,830
Poultry	47	27	117	78	912	1,583
Wheat	—	3	—	—	94	529
Small grains (excl. wheat farms)	2	60	13	23	2,423	11,432
Field crops, other than small grains	32	530	82	376	1,903	3,535
Fruits and vegetables	112	80	652	269	2,091	3,746
Miscellaneous specialty	126	144	543	404	5,355	7,312
Mixed farms						
Livestock combination	19	83	92	69	405	1,921
Other combinations	53	28	58	62	574	934
Total	525	2,144	3,300	2,686	35,600	61,432

	Man.	Sask.	Alta.	BC	Canada
Dairy	1,195	754	1,379	1,158	28,910
Cattle	5,071	9,037	22,143	4,224	66,280
Hogs	1,242	790	1,653	254	10,464
Poultry	311	140	412	584	4,211
Wheat	6,479	29,777	6,015	91	42,988
Small grains (excl. wheat farms)	6,303	14,183	12,659	361	47,459
Field crops, other than small grains	1,032	945	2,540	886	11,861
Fruits and vegetables	142	46	142	2,750	10,030
Miscellaneous specialty	1,041	914	3,730	3,364	22,933
Mixed farms					
Livestock combination	727	1,423	1,775	520	7,034
Other combinations	340	642	995	326	4,012
Total	23,883	58,651	53,443	14,518	256,182

15.6 NUMBER AND PERCENTAGE OF FIRST FARM OPERATORS

	1971	1981	1986	1991
Number of operators	367,195	318,360	293,090	277,330
Male	352,880	307,125	279,785	260,790
Percentage	96.1	96.5	95.5	94.0
Female	14,315	11,235	13,300	16,540
Percentage	3.9	3.5	4.5	6.0

15.7 NUMBER OF FARM OPERATORS

	Total	Operators of farms with one operator	Operators of farms with two operator	Operators of farms with three or more operators
Canada	390,870	175,495	179,245	36,135
Males	290,550	165,010	100,130	25,415
Females	100,320	10,485	79,115	10,720
Newfoundland	900	560	275	60
Males	730	520	170	40
Females	170	40	105	20
Prince Edward Island	3,130	1,675	1,115	335
Males	2,655	1,610	770	265
Females	475	65	345	70
Nova Scotia	5,165	2,895	1,875	400
Males	4,080	2,655	1,125	300
Females	1,090	240	750	100
New Brunswick	4,235	2,375	1,480	375
Males	3,465	2,250	935	280
Females	770	125	545	95
Quebec	53,350	24,425	22,880	6,045
Males	40,150	22,820	13,065	4,265
Females	13,200	1,605	9,815	1,780
Ontario	100,910	38,750	51,355	10,805
Males	71,980	36,040	28,510	7,430
Females	28,930	2,710	22,845	3,375
Manitoba	34,780	17,050	14,700	3,030
Males	27,010	16,390	8,400	2,210
Females	7,775	660	6,300	815
Saskatchewan	78,025	43,350	29,355	5,320
Males	61,840	41,415	16,575	3,850
Females	16,185	1,935	12,780	1,470
Alberta	81,415	34,290	39,850	7,280
Males	59,710	32,540	21,985	5,185
Females	21,710	1,750	17,865	2,095
British Columbia	28,955	10,125	16,365	2,470
Males	18,935	8,765	8,590	1,580
Females	10,025	1,360	7,775	895

15.8 SUPPLY AND DISPOSITION OF CANADIAN GRAIN (THOUSANDS TONNES)

	Wheat	Oats	Barley	Rye	Flaxseed	Canola/rapeseed
Crop year 1990-91[1]						
Carryover, Aug. 1, 1990	6 442	936	2 056	378	54	749
Production	32 098	2 692	13 441	599	889	3 266
Imports	- -	3	1	—	—	19
Total supply	38 541	3 631	15 498	977	943	4 034
Exports	22 106	383	4 823	342	497	1 888
Domestic use	6 150	2 303	8 029	311	89	1 748
Carryover, July 31, 1991	10 285	945	2 646	324	358	399
Crop year 1991-92[1]						
yover, Aug. 1, 1991	10 285	945	2 646	324	358	399
Production	31 945	1 794	11 617	339	635	4 224
Imports	22	2	2	—	- -	42
Total supply	42 253	2 741	14 265	663	993	4 664
Exports	25 376	351	3 659	226	458	1 894
Domestic use	7 073	1 846	8 121	249	115	2 137
Carryover, July 31, 1992	9 803	945	2 485	188	420	633

[1] *Year ending July 31st.*

15.9 EXPORTS OF WHEAT AND WHEAT FLOUR[1] (THOUSANDS TONNES)

Destination	1987-88	1988-89[r]	1989-90[r]	1990-91	1991-92
Western Europe	1 469.8	1 271.5	1 088.3	939.1	919.9
United Kingdom	413.2	410.2	272.0	281.7	291.9
Italy	439.5	409.5	356.6	319.6	309.4
Eastern Europe	4 649.5	2 728.5	3 598.0	7 228.0	4 969.1
Poland	—	—	32.9	—	—
CIS (formerly USSR)	4 500.2	2 666.0	3 497.0	7 228.0	4 968.8
Middle East	2 564.2	1 074.7	2 679.5	1 785.1	1 585.2
Africa	1 089.6	622.4	1 034.4	1 896.8	703.8
Algeria	764.4	337.2	610.7	872.7	369.3
Asia	10 617.4	5 216.3	7 501.4	7 357.8	11 793.9
People's Republic of China	7 663.9	2 830.2	4 580.8	2 923.5	7 184.4
South America	1 305.2	531.0	603.6	1 496.5	3 355.2
Brazil	448.8	14.3	220.1	382.9	1 824.4
Central America and Antilles	1 421.3	685.4	539.8	720.6	1 009.5
Cuba	952.7	605.5	434.4	499.3	192.1
North America	397.3	280.0	372.1	679.6	1 002.6
Total	23 514.3	12 409.9	17 417.1	22 104.8	25 371.4

[1] *Years ending July 31st.*

15.10 SUPPLIES OF FOOD MOVING INTO CONSUMPTION (KILOGRAMMES PER CAPITA PER ANNUM)

Kind of food	Weight base	1986	1990	1991
Cereals	retail weight	72.60	76.51	73.59
Wheat flour	"	59.55	62.07	60.18
Rye flour	"	0.34	0.34	0.33
Oatmedqal and rolled oats	"	1.59	1.70	1.42
Pot and pearl barley	"	[1]	[1]	[1]
Corn flour and meal	"	[1]	[1]	[1]
Rice	"	4.48	4.63	4.98
Breakfast food	"	4.46	5.06	4.11
Sugar and syrups	sugar content	42.65	42.69	42.87
Sugar	retail weight	42.55	41.55	41.50
Maple sugar	"	0.10	0.21	0.16
Honey	"	. .	. .	. .
Other	"	. .	. .	. .
Pulses and nuts	retail weight	7.22	5.94	6.88
Dry beans	"	0.62	0.33	1.66
Dry peas	"	2.65	1.88	2.64
Peanuts	"	3.03	3.06	3.13
Tree nuts	"	1.55	1.01	1.11
Oils and fats	retail weight			
Margarine	"	6.13	5.66	5.76
Shortening and shortening oils	"	7.86	8.14	9.42
Salad oils	"	5.49	[1]	. .
Butter	"	3.16	3.41	3.10
Tomatoes				
Fresh	retail weight	7.53	5.59	5.77
Canned	net wt. canned	3.04	3.20	3.15
Juice	"	2.55	2.16	[1]
Pulp, paste and purée	"	2.04	3.15	2.42
Apples				
Fresh	retail weight	11.01	15.64	. .
Juice	net wt. canned	7.13	7.14	. .
Sauce	"	0.47	0.47	. .
Pie filling	"	0.05	0.28	. .
Apricots, fresh	retail weight	0.12	0.15	0.12
Bananas, fresh	"	11.85	12.79	13.15
Blueberries				
Fresh	"	0.23	0.36	0.41
Frozen	"	0.18	0.20	0.22
Cherries, fresh	"	0.30	0.36	0.37
Melons, fresh	"	5.83	3.73	. .
Pineapples				
Fresh	"	0.50	0.61	0.61
Canned	net wt. canned	1.10	. .	. .
Juice	"	0.31	0.27	0.27
Raspberries				
Fresh	retail weight	0.01	0.07	0.01
Canned	net wt. canned	[1]	[1]	[1]
Juice	retail weight	0.23	0.43	0.31
Strawberries				
Fresh	"	1.69	[1]	[1]
Canned	net wt. canned	[1]	[1]	[1]
Frozen	retail weight	0.36	0.41	0.36

15.10 SUPPLIES OF FOOD MOVING INTO CONSUMPTION (KILOGRAMMES PER CAPITA PER ANNUM) (continued)

Kind of food	Weight base	1986	1990	1991
Grapes, fresh	retail weight	5.72	6.41	6.22
Vegetables[2]	fresh equiv.	67.40	. .	. .
Fresh	retail weight	56.68	. .	. .
Canned	net wt. canned	4.66	. .	. .
Frozen	retail weight	3.74	. .	. .
Cabbage, fresh	"	5.49	5.10	4.70
Lettuce	"	10.19	9.08	10.73
Spinach, fresh	"	. .	. .	. .
Carrots				
Fresh	"	8.33	10.48	8.59
Canned	net wt. canned	0.21	0.13	0.09
Frozen	retail weight	1.03	0.91	1.08
Beans				
Fresh	"	0.74	0.72	0.85
Canned	net wt. canned	1.01	1.09	0.91
Frozen	retail weight	0.45	0.56	0.54
Peas				
Fresh	"	0.09	0.11	0.07
Canned	net wt. canned	1.26	1.07	0.75
Frozen	retail weight	0.98	1.16	1.35
Beets				
Fresh	"	0.31	0.31	0.47
Canned	net wt. canned	0.21	0.11	0.32
Cauliflower, fresh	retail weight	3.01	2.82	2.46
Celery, fresh	"	4.35	4.30	4.78
Corn				
Fresh	"	3.16	5.44	[1]
Canned	net wt. canned	[1]	[1]	[1]
Frozen	retail weight	0.80	[1]	[1]
Cucumbers, fresh	"	3.03	3.15	2.91
Onions, not processed	"	7.62	6.62	7.07
Asparagus				
Fresh	"	0.16	[1]	0.21
Canned	net wt. canned	0.15	0.13	0.13
Frozen	retail weight	0.01	[1]	0.03
Rutabagas, fresh	"	2.18	2.88	2.09
Broccoli				
Fresh	"	2.32	2.83	2.85
Frozen	"	0.16	0.28	0.32
Brussels sprouts				
Fresh	"	0.20	0.16	0.16
Frozen	"	0.18	0.19	0.09
Unspecified				
Fresh	"	1.10	. .	. .
Canned	net wt. canned	0.32	. .	. .
Mushrooms	fresh equiv.	2.77	[1]	[1]
Fresh	retail weight	1.53	1.69	1.69
Canned	net wt. canned	1.50	[1]	[1]
Potatoes	fresh equiv.	78.90	59.25	65.60
White	"	77.99	58.98	65.48
Sweet	"	0.41	0.27	0.12
Meat	carcass weight	72.73	68.13	67.84
Pork	"	28.82	27.47	28.05
Beef	"	39.51	36.09	35.29
Veal	"	1.76	1.81	1.76
Mutton and lamb	"	0.92	0.84	0.86
Offal	"	1.73	1.92	1.88

15.10 SUPPLIES OF FOOD MOVING INTO CONSUMPTION (KILOGRAMMES PER CAPITA PER ANNUM) (concluded)

Kind of food	Weight base	1986	1990	1991
Eggs	fresh equiv.	11.55	10.80	10.72
Poultry[3]	eviscerated wt.	25.80	29.31	29.41
Chicken	"	20.48	23.04	23.10
Fowl	"	1.08	1.58	1.60
Turkey	"	4.24	4.69	4.71
Fish	edible weight			
Fish and shellfish			..	..
Fresh and frozen[4]	"	5.24	..	..
Canned	"	2.17	..	..
Fish, cured (smoked, salted, pickled)	"	..	..	..
Beverages				
Coffee	green been equiv.	4.38	4.64	4.85
Cocoa	"	0.28	..	0.19

[1] *Confidential.*
[2] *Includes pickles, relishes and vegetables used in soups.*
[3] *Excludes Newfoundland.*
[4] *Excludes herring (fresh and frozen) and all fish used for bait.*

15.11 INDEX OF APPARENT DOMESTIC CONSUMPTION OF MAJOR DAIRY PRODUCTS

	Base year	Total consumption			
	1979	1982	1986	1990	1991
Butter (t)	105 794	100	94	86	79
Cheddar cheese (t)	93 115	97	115	113	114
Variety cheese (t)	85 548	118	158	182	185
Skim milk powder (t)	51 877	118	86	90	58
Concentrated whole milk ('000 l)	58 680	105	71	70	68
Ice cream ('000 l)	307 669	99	103	103	174
Yogurt (t)	39 070	109	180	233	225

15.12 **PRODUCTION AND UTILIZATION OF MILK** (THOUSAND KILOLITRES)

	1979				1991			
	Total milk shipped	Fluid	Industrial delivered as		Total milk shipped	Fluid	Industrial delivered as	
			Milk	Cream			Milk	Cream
Newfoundland	8	8	—	—	1	1	1	1
Prince Edward Island	90	17	62	11	96	15	77	4
Nova Scotia	168	106	56	6	169	108	60	1
New Brunswick	110	69	31	10	126	65	59	2
Quebec	2 719	591	2 125	3	2 793	710	2 083	—
Ontario	2 387	999	1 297	91	2 463	1 019	1 366	78
Manitoba	280	111	132	37	287	113	146	28
Saskatchewan	192	109	46	37	214	94	112	8
Alberta	508	239	203	66	581	270	303	8
British Columbia	438	295	141	2	511	321	190	—
Canada	6 899	2 543	4 093	263	7 240	2 716	4 395	129

[1] *Confidential*

Source
Statistics Canada

CHAPTER SIXTEEN ENERGY

INTRODUCTION

Canadians thrive on energy. In this sprawling country of extreme temperatures, Canadians consume enormous amounts of energy for industry, transportation and heat. In fact, Canadians consume more energy per capita than any other industrialized country. Our way of life depends upon steady and inexpensive supplies of energy in many forms such as falling water, burning coal or liquid fuels.

Energy has distinct effects on Canadian lifestyles: it runs our cars, heats our ovens and furnaces, and lights our homes. It is also used in most leisure activities — travel, electronic games and television, to name a few.

FUELING THE ECONOMY Energy is also an important element in Canada's economy. In 1990, the energy supply sector accounted for about 7% of real Gross Domestic Product (GDP) and 17% of total investment. That year, the sector provided about 2% of total employment. Energy exports generated 11% of export income.

Canadian consumers also spend a lot of money on energy: in 1990, Canadian households spent an average

of $644 on electricity and $409 on fuels and piped gas for heating. They also spent an average of $1,144 on automotive fuels. Canadians also purchase 'hidden' energy: a Torontonian buying a bag of potatoes from Prince Edward Island is also paying for the diesel fuel that ran the tractors, trains and trucks used to harvest the vegetables and bring them to local supermarkets. Canada is indeed one of the world's most energy-intensive countries.

BRIGHT LIGHTS AND BIG CARS Canada was built upon its wealth of natural energy resources. At the turn of the century, domestic coal fuelled a growing country: furnace coal was delivered to city homes in horse-drawn carts. By the end of World War II, seemingly endless supplies of inexpensive oil created a thriving petroleum industry. Trains, trucks and eventually pipelines carried the 'black gold' from the oil basins to the buyers.

Technological advances in machinery and automation further increased demand for energy. Between the mid-1950s and 1960s, Canada's annual energy use increased by up to 5% each year — roughly 2% to 3% higher than the annual population growth for that period. By the time the first baby boomers reached their teen years, energy consumption was conspicuous: bright lights, big cars and convenient modern appliances were symbols of a civilized society. On frosty winter days thermostats were simply cranked up a few more degrees. Little attention was paid to energy-efficient technologies.

CAPPING THE WELL When world oil prices skyrocketed in 1973, Canadians learned about non-renewable resources and rising energy costs. In its response to the energy crisis, the federal government launched a number of incentive programs aimed at reducing fuel consumption and conserving energy in general.

An entire generation of Canadians has grown up since then in better insulated homes with more energy-efficient appliances and fuel-efficient vehicles. Between 1985 and 1991, Canada's average yearly increase in energy consumption was between 1% and 2%, just

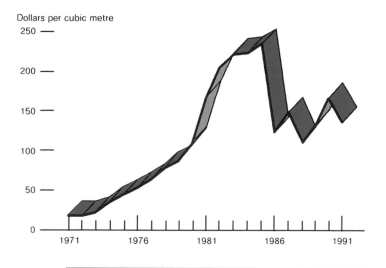

Crude Oil Cost[1]

Dollars per cubic metre

[1] At Edmonton.

Henry Glyde / The National Gallery of Canada

Wildcat #3, Excelsior Field near Edmonton.

slightly higher than the average annual population growth for the same period.

Industry has also become more energy-efficient. For example, in 1973, the federal government began an incentive program to get older industrial plants to save 31% of their fuel use by 1993, with usage in 1973 as a base line. As of 1990, industry had achieved a 26% saving.

In the past 20 years, Canadian researchers have found ways to use energy more efficiently. In fact, Canada has become a world leader in constructing energy-efficient buildings: in 1973, a typical office building used about 600 kilowatt hours per square metre of space. In 1992, an experimental office building using underground heat storage and solar panels used only 20 kilowatt hours.

Robert Semeniuk / First Light

Petroleum pipeline, Alberta.

CANADIAN ENERGY SUPPLY AND DEMAND

CROWN JOULES In 1991, Canada produced nearly 12 000 petajoules of energy. That's an increase of almost 4% from 1990 and almost 6% from 1988. Natural gas, including natural gas liquids (NGLs), accounted for about 42% of total production, crude oil for 32%, coal for 15% and hydro and nuclear energy, including nuclear steam, for 12%. After adjustments for exports, imports and inventory changes, about 8 500 petajoules were available for consumption in Canada. Crude oil accounted for about 38% of the total primary energy consumption, natural gas and NGLs for 34%, hydro and nuclear for 15% and coal for 13%. One petajoule contains enough energy to run 13,800 average-sized cars for a year.

Roughly 75% of primary energy — energy that has been recovered from natural resources such as crude oil, coal or natural gas — is used in final consumption such as gasoline for cars, or fuels for heating. Industry is the largest single energy user, followed by transportation, residential and farm, commercial and institutional and public administration. Most of the remaining 25% of primary energy is used to convert energy from one form to another — such as burning coal to create electricity — and in refineries.

SHARING THE WEALTH Canada produces more energy than it uses. We are, therefore, major exporters of energy commodities. We export electricity,

oil and natural gas to the United States, and coal and uranium around the world. In 1991, Canada earned about $16 billion in energy exports, and spent about $7 billion on imports, netting a trade balance of $9 billion. Natural gas exports accounted for $3.5 billion, crude oil and equivalent for $1.6 billion, coal for $1.6 billion, natural gas liquids for $600 million and electricity for $500 million. Other energy products accounted for the remaining $1.6 billion.

DOMESTIC SUPPLY Even though oil and gas met over 70% of Canada's energy needs in 1991, experts predict that crude oil production will ease over the next few years. Accessible conventional oil fields are near depletion. While Alberta's tar sands offer potential for new sources of crude, this oil is expensive to recover and upgrade. Because foreign crude oils are less expensive, Canada will likely become a net importer of this resource in the next few decades.

In 1991, Canada had roughly 1% of the world's proven conventional crude oil reserves, produced 3% of the world's crude oil and had 2.5% of global petroleum refining capacity. Its coal reserves accounted for slightly less than 1% of the world's total, while production (in heat equivalents) was just under 2% and usage was about 1%. Natural gas proven reserves accounted for about 2.2% of world reserves, while production equalled 5.2%. Nuclear energy consumption was 4.3% of the world total.

Most of Canada's oil, natural gas, coal and uranium are found in the western provinces. Nuclear and hydro power are produced mainly in Ontario and Quebec respectively. The balance of these latter provinces' energy needs are met through supplies of oil, natural gas and coal from Western Canada or through imports.

THE POWER OF RESEARCH Compared with other countries, Canada, with its legacy of energy resources, makes limited use of renewable energy forms such as solar and wind energy which are in developmental stages. Alternative, or renewable energy accounts for only 7% of Canada's energy needs. Most of this is biomass energy — energy that comes from non-fossil organic materials such as liquid waste from pulp and paper processing, wood, straw, vegetable oils and agricultural and municipal wastes. The industrial sector uses over 95% of renewable energy — mainly for producing process steam and space heating, with a small amount used to generate electricity.

Researchers are looking for ways to make Canada's non-renewable energy reserves last longer. The federal Department of Energy, Mines and Resources (EMR) has a number of ongoing research projects aimed at finding cleaner and more efficient ways of using non-renewable energy resources and reducing overall consumption. EMR projects such as the R-2000 Homes and the Advanced Houses programs are aimed at improving energy efficiency in homes in various climatic regions of the country. The department also researches ways of using solar, wind and biomass energy.

U N D E R G R O U N D   A L T E R N A T I V E S

Geothermal energy — a procedure to tap into underground natural heat sources for space heating or electricity — has potential in Canada. Surface water that has seeped into deep cracks of sedimentary rocks eventually becomes trapped in large reservoirs where it warms to the temperature of the rock. The deeper the reservoir, the hotter the rocks. Some experts believe that the usable heat contained in the prairie sediments can theoretically provide thousands of times more energy than Canada needs each year. Yet, they admit, current technology and energy prices allow for only a small fraction of this energy to be exploited. In volcanic areas, water becomes extremely hot at a shallow depth. British Columbia's mountains contain many volcanic centres that have enough potential energy for production of electricity.

In Eastern Canada, two experimental projects using groundwater as a source for heat pumps have shown considerable savings over other forms of space heating. Carleton University in Ottawa is pumping groundwater from shallow limestone aquifers. A similar project in Springhill, Nova Scotia, is drawing water from abandoned coal mine workings. Both projects indicate that geothermal energy has excellent potential in Canada.

Canada's Primary Energy Production

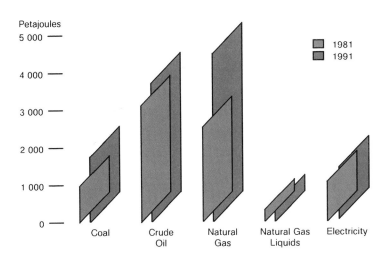

Canada's Final Energy Use

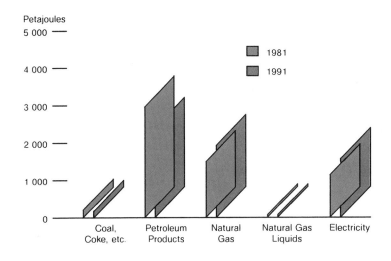

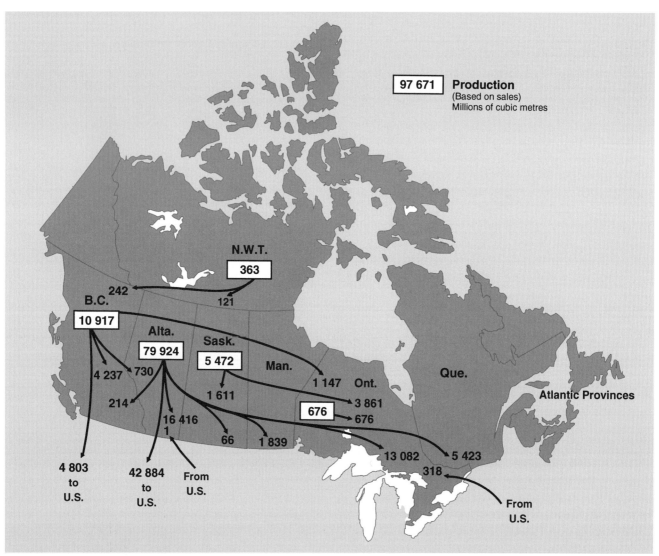

Natural Gas Production and Movements, by Source, 1991.

OIL AND GAS

SLICK BUSINESS Domestic oil and gas prices are closely tied to international supply and demand. In 1973, international prices skyrocketed with the oil embargo imposed by members of the Organization of Petroleum Exporting Countries (OPEC). World prices fluctuated in subsequent years because of a continuing imbalance between international supply and demand. In 1979, they took off again during the Iranian revolution. Since 1986, except for a brief surge caused by Iraq's 1990 invasion of Kuwait, world oil prices have fluctuated between $112 and $148 per cubic metre. Crude oil prices in Canada peaked in 1985 at almost $234, but plunged to $129 early in 1986 because of a collapse in world prices. In 1990, the Kuwait invasion sent Edmonton prices up from a low of $116 in June, to a new peak of $282 in October, resulting in an average price for 1990 of $166. The average price of oil in Canada in 1991 was $137.

PRODUCTION AND SUPPLY Crude Oil and Equivalent After six years of increasing production levels, Canada's crude oil production fell about 5 million cubic metres, from a high of 75 million cubic metres in 1988, to 70 million in 1991. Exports equalled almost 46% of production in 1991, compared to 41% in 1988.

GREENING THE ARCTIC

From Tuktoyaktuk in the west to Pangnirtung in the east, Canada's Arctic is in trouble. Much of the land is littered with garbage, and many of its rivers and lakes have been polluted by heavy industry in the south. Chemical contaminants, such as PCBs and DDT, have been found in the air, water, plants and wildlife — even mothers' milk.

But Canadians north of the 60th parallel are facing these environmental problems head on. Everyone — from school kids to dog teams — is involved in a six-year, $100 million strategy to help northerners understand and manage their environment. Launched in April 1991 as part of Canada's **Green Plan**, the Arctic Environmental Strategy (AES) is getting territorial and federal governments, indigenous peoples, environmental groups, industry, business, and others working together to clean up waste, improve water quality, reduce chemical contaminants, and combine economic growth with protection of the environment.

Paid workers and volunteers across the North started by cleaning up their own backyards of discarded barrels, car wrecks and household waste. They then led major clean-ups of dump sites, fuel stations and abandoned mines. And in Yellowknife, government workers even took an afternoon off and swung picks to help build an experimental botanical garden.

Some of the keenest environmentalists in the North are children. In Pangnirtung, students are shredding old paper to make packing material for the Inuit carvings being shipped to markets in the south. In Igloolik, children are composting kitchen scraps into potting soil for their Adopt a Plant Program. Cub Scouts in Yellowknife have painted the covers of storm sewers with neon-blue fish symbols. The symbols tell residents not to dump hazardous household products into drains that discharge untreated water into local lakes and streams.

One of the most innovative ways of combining economic growth with protection of the environment is taking place in Cambridge Bay, Northwest Territories. Students at Ilihakvik School are working with the local Hunters' and Trappers' Association to study the environmental and financial costs of the traditional and modern ways of gathering food — dog team versus snowmobile. Funded by the AES, students have purchased and are looking after a team of Husky sled dogs. Hunters are using the dog team to hunt for food for a single-parent family in the community.

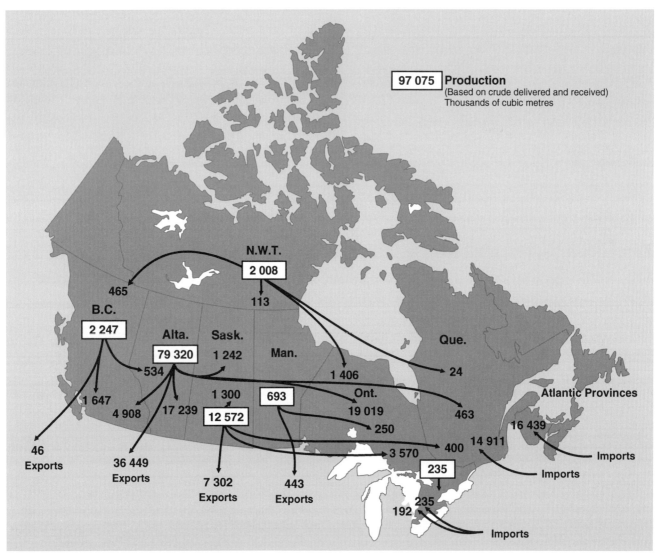

Crude Oil Production and Movements, by Source, 1991.

Over the past few years, a decline in the productive capacity of Alberta's older established oilfields has signalled a decrease in light crude oil production. This was temporarily reversed in 1987 and 1988 through increased developmental drilling. There are two full-scale oil sands plants in Alberta producing synthetic crude oil, and in 1990 and 1991 these plants have had an average production of 13 million cubic metres per year. In 1991, they accounted for about 14% of Canada's total crude oil and equivalent production. In 1989, a new upgrader in Regina, Saskatchewan began operation. The plant changes heavy oils into lighter, more usable components. In 1992, a second upgrader began operations in Lloydminster, Saskatchewan.

Natural Gas Production and export of natural gas has increased steadily since 1986. That year, 110 492 million cubic metres were produced. By 1991, production reached 147 108 million cubic metres. Exports have also risen steadily since 1986, reaching 47 688 million cubic metres in 1991, giving Canada a share of almost 10% of the United States' natural gas market.

In 1989, the National Energy Board granted 20-year licences, beginning in 1997, for the export of natural gas to the United States from the Beaufort Sea and the Mackenzie Delta. Exporting will not begin until specific conditions with regard to native land claims, environmental requirements and facility construction are met.

The majority of Canada's natural gas is produced in Alberta, although British Columbia and Saskatchewan also produce significant amounts. Almost 80% of Alberta's gas leaves the province for other parts of Canada, or for export to the United States. Ontario is responsible for about 38% of Canada's total natural gas consumption. Although Ontario produces small quantities of natural gas, it imports most of it from Alberta and Saskatchewan.

Natural Gas Liquids Production of the liquids propane, butane and ethane from natural gas has increased steadily since 1985. That year, 13 886 million cubic metres were produced. By 1991, production reached 18 020 million cubic metres. Some 97% of this was produced in Alberta.

Of the 18 020 million, 37% was propane, 21% was butane, and 42% was ethane. The primary energy uses of natural gas liquids are in heating and transportation. The primary non-energy use is the production of a wide range of petrochemical products from plastics to fertilizers. Less than 1% of Canada's natural gas liquids are imported, while Canada exported 36% of its available natural gas liquids in 1991.

OIL REFINING Rationalization and declining domestic demand caused the Canadian refining industry to close 12 refineries between 1974 and 1985. In 1987, a Newfoundland refinery that had closed in 1976 was reopened to supply products from imported crude oil to the export market.

Domestic demand for all petroleum products has declined every year since 1989, with the demand for motor gasoline, heavy fuel oil, diesel and light fuel oil reporting the largest declines in absolute terms.

EXPLORATION AND DEVELOPMENT
The 1985 collapse of world crude oil prices resulted in a dramatic decline in drilling activity. After a record 12,171 wells were completed in 1985, an annual average of only 6,750 wells were drilled in the following four years. By 1989, activity was further slowed by unstable oil and gas prices, the effects of mergers and takeovers, ongoing rationalization and the termination of government incentive programs. After 1988, improved market opportunities for natural gas caused a shift from oil to gas exploration and development.

Prior to 1985, oil exploration flourished — wells were drilled in Canadian frontier regions such as the Arctic Islands, the Beaufort Sea and the east coast offshore — but activity has been curtailed because of enormous costs. The cost of drilling a single well in a frontier area can exceed $50 million. Current plans are focusing on the development of oil reserves at Hibernia, off the coast of Newfoundland.

Based on revenues, Canadian ownership of the crude oil and natural gas exploration and development industries (including related service industries) increased from 42% in 1988 to 45% in 1991. During the same period, Canadian control increased from 38% to 43%.

Energy Use per Capita in G7 Countries, 1990

FISHING FOR OIL

Newfoundland's Hibernia oil project, which was seriously floundering in 1992 and part of 1993, is now back on firm footing, readying to begin production before the end of the century.

In early 1993, with the future of the giant off-shore oil project precarious at best, the federal government announced a bold new plan to keep the project from sinking.

Until recently, Hibernia's treasure of 'black gold' had seemed elusively out of reach, destined to remain far below the iceberg-laden waters of the North Atlantic, 300 kilometres to the east of St. John's.

All told, the underwater field contains an estimated 615 million barrels of recoverable oil, about the same amount consumed by Canadians in an average year.

The latest troubles began early in 1992, when Gulf Oil — one of the largest investors in Hibernia — withdrew its 25% stake in the $5.2 billion project. After almost a year of searching for a new partner, the remaining consortium members had come up empty-handed.

Finally, in January 1993, the Murphy Oil Corporation — a worldwide player in offshore development — agreed to assume a 6.5% stake in the project. In addition, the federal government agreed to assume an 8.5% stake, while two other consortium members — Chevron Canada Resources Ltd. and Mobile Oil Ltd. — took on the remainder of Gulf's 25% share.

The federal government's commitment to become an active partner in Hibernia comes in addition to the $1 billion it had previously committed in federal grants. As well, the government has provided a $1.6 billion loan guarantee to the project sponsors.

While Gulf's withdrawal from the Hibernia project was a major setback, the new arrangement appears to have put the project back on a firm footing. For the roughly 2,500 employees presently working on the project, it's business as usual.

If everything goes according to plan, Newfoundlanders can expect to pump the first barrels of Hibernia crude sometime in 1997.

R E S E R V E S   Canada's crude oil and gas reserves both dropped in 1991. Proven conventional crude oil and pentane reserves stood at 981 million cubic metres at the end of 1991, down 127 million cubic metres, or about 12%, from the 1988 year-end volume. These crude reserves include fields in the North and off the east coast of Canada. It is estimated that conventional crude oil and pentane reserves will last 13 years at the 1991 rate of Canadian usage and export.

Alberta Athabascan oil sands deposits are one of the world's largest known store of hydrocarbons. Canada's largest reserves of conventional hydrocarbons are also found in Alberta.

Natural gas established reserves were 2 700 billion cubic metres at the end of 1991, a decline of roughly 4%, or 123 billion cubic metres, from the 1988 level. Based on production, these reserves should last 24 years at the 1991 rate of usage and exports (including shrinkage at all plants that extract natural gas liquids).

P I P E L I N E S   Where long winding trains of tank cars once chugged across the country carrying oil and gas to their markets, pipelines now deliver these products to the east, west and south. It's hard to imagine, but a gas-heated house in a Montreal suburb is physically connected to a gas field in Saskatchewan by a complex system of pipelines. Indeed, as the early trans-Canada railway contributed to the country's development, pipelines have been an integral part of Canada's industrial growth since the late 1950s.

In 1989, some 65 058 kilometres of pipeline moved natural gas across the country. Since then, pipelines have been spreading east through Manitoba and Ontario and south into the Midwestern and Eastern United States to meet increased demands for natural gas.

COAL

In 1991, Canadian coal production reached a new high of 71.1 million tonnes, almost 1% above the previous high set in 1989. Domestic consumption of Canadian-produced coal increased almost 3% from the previous year, and exports were up 10% for the same period. This additional demand reduced coal inventories by

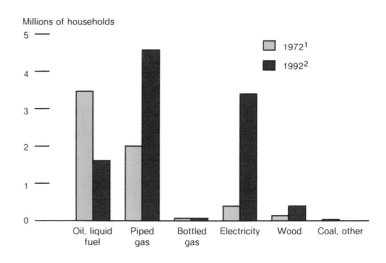

Principal Home Heating Fuel

[1] Households in private dwellings excluding the Yukon, NWT, Indian reserves, Crown lands, institutions, military camps, collective-type households and mobile homes.
[2] Includes mobile homes.

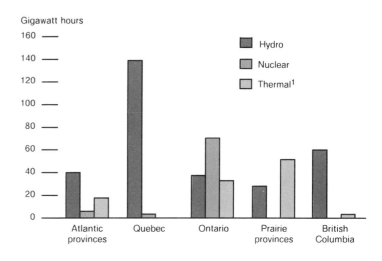

Electric Generation, 1991

[1] Includes coal, natural gas, petroleum and other.

NUCLEAR POWER

Canada is a leader in the development of nuclear reactors for civil use, with 22 in service as of 1993.

Most of them are located in Ontario — eight at the Pickering Nuclear Generating Station near Toronto, eight at the Bruce Nuclear Power Development near Kincardine and four at the Darlington Nuclear Generating Station near Bowmanville. The other two are located at Gentilly near Trois-Rivières, Quebec and Point Lepreau near Saint John, New Brunswick. All are CANDU reactors, designed and built in Canada.

CANDU stands for CANada Deuterium Uranium; unlike most other reactors in the world, a CANDU can be refuelled without shutting down. Also, its use of natural uranium instead of enriched uranium yields better fuel efficiency. (CANDUs have been exported to several countries, including India, South Korea, Pakistan, Argentina and Romania.)

In Canada, nuclear reactors supply a substantial amount of electricity: about 60% of Ontario's total production, 3% of Quebec's and 45% of New Brunswick's. In Ontario, nuclear power stations are owned and operated by Ontario Hydro; in Quebec by Hydro-Quebec and in New Brunswick by NB Power. Canada's Atomic Energy Control Board (AECB) sets safety standards and grants licenses for all reactors. No new reactors are currently planned.

The CANDU reactors used in Canada have safety systems based on an approach called 'defence-in-depth'. This means each nuclear station has at least two computerized systems to shut down the reactor — the device that breaks down uranium fuel to make energy — in case of emergency. If one system fails, a back-up takes over.

Safety systems and precautions ensure that Canadians living at the boundary of a nuclear plant are exposed to no more than about 1% of the AECB annual limit for radiation.

Nonetheless, debate over the safety of these reactors is vigorous in Canada. Those against argue that accidents would be catastrophic to people and to the environment. The 1986 nuclear disaster at Chernobyl sent radioactive clouds across Europe and the former Soviet Union and the impact of it has still not been fully assessed. Of chief concern in Canada is the safe and permanent disposal of nuclear wastes, which may stay toxic for thousands of years; and the potential for other countries to use nuclear power plant byproducts to build weapons.

Those for nuclear power argue it is superior to coal or gas fired generators because it does not produce sulphur dioxide, which causes acid rain; or carbon dioxide, which contributes to global warming. They also argue nuclear stations cause less environmental damage than hydroelectric stations, which may flood large areas for reservoirs, and which may need miles of power lines to deliver electricity from remote locations.

In recent years the AECB has looked into hundreds of unusual events at nuclear stations, but to date, the most serious accident at a CANDU reactor has been a 1983 incident at the Pickering Nuclear Generating Station, in which a pressure tube burst. While coolant was lost, no radiation was released into the environment.

Multiple spillway, hydroelectric dam.

1 million tonnes. Of current production, 34.1 million tonnes, or 48%, was exported from British Columbia and Alberta mines, with smaller quantities being shipped from Nova Scotia. Approximately 85% of Canada's coal exports are coking coal, used for producing steel, and 15% are thermal coal, used for heating.

Canada has 6 billion tonnes of proven reserves, equivalent to approximately 83 years' supply at current production rates. In addition, some 30 billion tonnes of coal contained in known deposits have not yet been fully delineated. Almost 95% of Canadian coal production takes place in surface mines in Western Canada. The remainder comes from mines in Atlantic Canada, most of which are underground.

In 1991, coal exports grew to a record level of 34.1 million tonnes in response to the buoyant steel industry and increased demand for energy from our trading partners of the Pacific Rim. US imports totalled 12.4 million tonnes. Overall, Canada was a net exporter of coal, with a trade surplus of $1.6 billion in 1991.

COAL USE In 1991, Canada consumed most of its coal to generate electricity — some 87% of the total domestic requirement of 50.4 million tonnes was used for this purpose. Alberta obtained about 82% of its electricity from coal, Saskatchewan 65%, Nova Scotia 64%, Ontario 21%, and New Brunswick 8%.

Imported coal from the United States goes mainly to Ontario for use in generating electricity and steelmaking. While this coal is less expensive, imports have declined over the past few years for two reasons: environmental considerations and diminishing demand.

Coal produced in the United States contains eight times more sulphur than domestic coal. Sulphur emissions contribute to the problem of acid rain. In the past few years, Ontario hydro has begun to burn low-sulphur thermal coal from Western Canada for electricity. For the longer term, Canadian utilities are examining more efficient generating systems that produce less carbon and sulphur dioxide emissions per unit of electricity.

The steel industry, concentrated in Ontario, is the second largest consumer of coal for the production of coke. Domestic coal has not been used for this purpose since 1988 and, as the steel industry has declined in the past few years, so has the demand for imported coal.

ELECTRIC POWER

GENERATION AND CONSUMPTION
In Canada, our trade balance can rise or fall depending on the level of rain. This is because rain fuels our generation of hydro electricity. In 1989 and 1990, low rainfall levels across Canada resulted in lower hydro generation levels. During that period, non-hydro sources, such as coal, were used to keep up with electricity demands. Because of these shortages, imports of electricity from the United States were higher than normal. Canadian exports of electricity likewise suffered, falling in 1989 and again in 1990, to the lowest level since 1976. Greater rainfalls in 1991 brought generation capacity and trade in electricity back to 1988 levels.

In 1991, hydro production reached a high of 305 444 gigawatt hours, the highest level since 1988, and the second highest ever reached in Canada.

Ontario, Quebec and New Brunswick are the only provinces that use nuclear energy to generate electricity. In 1991, nuclear generation accounted for about 16% of Canada's electrical energy, 50% of Ontario's, 34% of New Brunswick's and 3% of Quebec's.

Energy sources of electricity generation changed only slightly in 1991, with 62% of the total supply coming from hydro generation, 22% from thermal plants and 16% from nuclear plants. Coal usage was 43.9 million tonnes in 1991, down from 46.0 million in 1988. This was partly due to an increase in hydro and nuclear resources for generation of electricity. Petroleum, mainly heavy fuel oil, declined to 3.2 million cubic metres in 1991 from 4.2 million cubic metres in 1989.

Other sources of electricity, such as wind power, in Canada are limited. One full-scale demonstration tidal electric power station in Nova Scotia has a generating capacity of 4.6 megawatts — enough to supply power to more than 3,500 homes each year.

Jeffrey Spalding / National Gallery of Canada

Nightfall (Niagara Falls, Ontario).

In 1991, the industrial sector accounted for roughly 42% of Canada's electricity consumption; residential sector, 30%; government and commercial sectors, 25%; and 4% in transportation and agriculture.

URANIUM   Canada is the world's leading producer and exporter of uranium. In 1991, production for Canada's five primary uranium producers was approximately 8 800 tonnes valued at $472 million. The Canada-United States Free Trade Agreement, signed late in 1987, ensured access to the American market, which has the largest uncommitted uranium demand. In the near to medium term, this market is crucial to Canada's uranium producers.

SOURCES

BP Statistical Review of World Energy

Energy, Mines and Resources Canada

International Energy Agency

National Energy Board

Statistics Canada

FOR FURTHER READING

Selected publications from Statistics Canada

▲ *Coal Mines*. *Annual. 26-206*

▲ *The Crude Petroleum and Natural Gas Industry*. *Annual. 26-213*

▲ *Refined Petroleum and Coal Products Industries*. *Annual. 45-250*

▲ *Road Motor Vehicles, Fuel Sales*. *Annual. 53-218*

▲ *Gas Utilities*. *Monthly. 55-002*

▲ *Energy Statistics Handbook*, *monthly (a joint publication of Statistics Canada and Energy, Mines and Resources Canada). 57-601*

TABLES

16.1   CANADA'S ENERGY SUMMARY[1]

	1981 PJ	1990 PJ	1991 PJ	1989-90 % change	1990-91 % change
Primary production	8 020	11 393	11 789	0.4	3.5
Gross availability[2]	7 069	8 616	8 516	−3.7	−1.2
Net domestic consumption[3]	6 845	7 866	7 765	−2.7	−1.3
Producers' consumption	364	906	878	−0.5	−3.1
Non-energy use	532	638	666	−5.8	4.4
Energy use	5 949	6 321	6 221	−2.7	−1.6
Industrial	1 903	2 044	2 022	−3.9	−1.1
Transportation	1 794	1 821	1 785	−2.7	−2.0
Agriculture	188	205	195	2.5	−4.9
Residential	1 101	1 197	1 166	−2.2	−2.6
Public administration	138	144	137	−0.7	−4.9
Commercial and institutional	825	911	916	−2.0	0.5
Degree days below 18° C[4]	4 214	3 908	3 933	−10.1	0.6

[1] *Measured in petajoules(PJ).*
  1 Petajoule is equivalent to:
      33.3 kilotonnes imported bituminous coal,
      42.0 kilotonnes Canadian bituminous coal,
      39.2 thousand cubic metres propane,
      34.9 thousand cubic metres butane,
      54.5 thousand cubic metres ethane,
      26.0 thousand cubic metres crude oil,
      28.9 thousand cubic metres motor gasoline,
      26.3 million cubic metres natural gas, or
   277.8 gigawatt hours electricity.

[2] *Availability of each energy form (excluding crude oil) less production of coke, coke oven gas, thermal electricity and liquified petroleum gases used in the production of refined petroleum products.*
[3] *Net production of primary and secondary sources.*
[4] *Relative temperature index for space heating purposes. Data are calculated by Environment Canada to measure the extent to which the outdoor mean temperature falls below 18° C for each calendar day. The provincial and national figures have been developed using data for major population centres.*

16.2 CANADA'S PRIMARY ENERGY PRODUCTION[1] (PETAJOULES)

	Coal	Crude oil[2]	Natural gas[3]	NGLs[4]	Electricity[5]	Steam[6]	Total primary sources
1981							
Production	969.5	3 093.4	2 526.3	316.3	1 084.3	30.3	8 020.3
Exports	464.2	363.2	803.6	200.0	127.3	—	1 958.3
Imports	448.7	1 137.8	0.1	—	5.4	—	1 592.1
Stock variation	1.3	−18.7	13.0	8.0	—	—	3.7
Other adjustments[7]	−4.8	—	0.3	−20.5	—	—	−25.0
Available	947.9	3 886.8	1 710.1	87.7	962.3	30.3	7 625.3
Transformed to other energy forms[8]	900.2	3 898.6	68.6	25.9	. . .	. . .	4 893.3
1990							
Production	1 669.3	3 734.8	4 261.6	404.9	1 306.0	16.0	11 392.6
Exports	943.0	1 462.5	1 537.2	179.8	65.7	—	4 188.2
Imports	408.7	1 198.1	24.2	3.6	64.0	—	1 698.6
Stock variation	63.4	23.4	61.0	11.9	—	—	159.7
Other adjustments[7]	5.7	15.9	14.3	—	—	—	35.9
Available	1 077.2	3 463.0	2 701.9	216.7	1 304.3	16.0	8 779.2
Transformed to other energy forms[8]	1 020.1	3 463.1	93.0	43.9	. . .	. . .	4 620.1
1991							
Production	1 748.0	3 729.4	4 486.3	416.7	1 388.1	20.6	11 789.0
Exports	1 036.1	1 703.7	1 804.0	169.9	88.3	—	4 802.0
Imports	359.2	1 214.7	12.1	2.7	21.9	—	1 610.5
Stock variation	−34.8	−18.6	−17.0	17.4	—	—	−53.0
Other adjustments[7]	−1.4	−10.5	−5.9	—	—	—	−17.7
Available	1 104.4	3 248.5	2 705.4	232.1	1 321.7	20.6	8 632.8
Transformed to other energy forms[8]	1 056.1	3 248.5	87.3	54.7	. . .	. . .	4 446.7

[1] *The quantities of crude oil and natural gas shown here include an estimate of producers' own consumption in the synthetic crude and heavy sectors. Data in this table may not agree with data presented in other tables due to method of computation.*
[2] *The general terms ''crude oil'' or ''crude oil and equivalent'' comprise conventional crude, condensate, pentanes, synthetic crude oil and experimental crude oil.*
[3] *Modified gross production of natural gas; that is, gross production less reinjection and shrinkage.*
[4] *Gas plant NGLs (natural gas liquids), butane, propane and ethane.*
[5] *Hydro and nuclear only.*
[6] *Steam produced from nuclear sources.*
[7] *Includes interproduct transfers as well as other adjustments.*
[8] *For electricity and steam generation, coal coke production and for refined petroleum products.*

16.3 CANADA'S ENERGY USE[1] (PETAJOULES)

	Coal, coke and coke oven gas	Crude Oil and petroleum products	Natural gas	NGLs[2]	Electricity	Steam	Primary and secondary energy
1981							
Producers' own consumption	0.1	261.2	—	1.0	102.1	—	364.4
Non-energy use	4.7	380.2	102.3	44.5	—	—	531.7
Energy use — final demand	226.6	2 958.4	1 513.0	60.5	1 144.4	45.7	5 948.6
Industrial	221.6	452.5	646.6	12.9	523.9	45.2	1 902.8
Transportation	—	1 704.9	79.6	1.7	7.6	—	1 793.9
Agricultural	—	139.2	13.8	6.3	28.2	—	187.6
Residential	4.0	341.7	416.9	24.0	314.1	—	1 100.6
Public administration	0.3	87.7	17.2	0.5	32.8	—	138.4
Commercial and institutional	0.7	232.4	338.8	15.2	237.6	0.5	825.3
Unaccounted for[3]	—	−11.8	26.2	1.8	..	—	16.2
1990							
Producers' own consumption	4.4	238.9	530.0	2.5	130.1	—	906.0
Non-energy use	15.0	335.2	148.9	139.2	—	—	638.4
Energy use — final demand	177.6	2 550.4	1 929.9	90.7	1 551.6	21.0	6 321.2
Industrial	174.9	314.6	854.8	23.8	654.7	20.8	2 043.6
Transportation	—	1 647.8	135.7	25.9	11.8	—	1 821.3
Agricultural	—	139.8	23.2	7.1	34.7	..	204.7
Residential	2.5	185.4	528.4	12.5	468.3	..	1 197.1
Public administration	0.2	79.8	19.0	—	45.0	0.1	144.0
Commercial and institutional	—	183.0	368.8	21.3	337.3	0.1	910.5
Unaccounted for	—	..	..	0.2	..	—	0.1
1991							
Producers' own consumption	5.0	230.6	505.8	0.7	136.2	—	878.4
Non-energy use	10.0	338.6	168.7	148.5	—	—	665.8
Energy use — final demand	185.3	2 408.3	1 943.7	88.3	1 570.7	24.8	6 221.0
Industrial	183.1	284.0	834.6	28.2	667.4	24.6	2 021.7
Transportation	—	1 594.7	150.5	28.9	11.0	—	1 785.0
Agricultural	—	132.5	23.2	5.2	34.3	0.2	195.3
Residential	2.1	161.9	531.9	9.1	461.2	—	1 166.2
Public administration	0.1	71.9	17.9	—	47.0	—	136.8
Commercial and institutional	—	163.4	385.6	16.9	350.0	0.1	915.9
Unaccounted for	—	..	—	−0.6	..	—	−0.6

[1] *Net primary and secondary energy.*
[2] *NGL (natural gas liquids).*
[3] *Cyclical billing accounts for much of the natural gas number reported.*

16.4 TRADE IN ENERGY (MILLION DOLLARS)[1]

	1990	1991
Crude oil and equivalent		
Exports	5,529	6,042
Imports	5,405	4,492
Balance	124	1,550
Petroleum products[2]		
Exports	2,806	2,794
Imports	1,867	1,400
Balance	939	1,394
Natural gas		
Exports	3,267	3,511
Imports	—	32
Balance	3,267	3,479
Liquefied petroleum products[3]		
Exports	668	730
Imports	121	108
Balance	547	622
Coal		
Exports	2,110	2,051
Imports	612	478
Balance	1,498	1,573
Coal products		
Exports	26	14
Imports	74	50
Balance	−48	−36
Electric energy		
Exports	538	557
Imports	557	50
Balance	−19	507
Radioactive ores, concentrates, elements and isotopes		
Exports	421	415
Imports	111	68
Balance	310	347
Total		
Exports	15,365	16,114
Imports	8,747	6,678
Balance	6,618	9,436

[1] *Quantities and/or values may not agree with those appearing in other tables of this section due to differences in method of measurement. The introduction of the Harmonized System of commodity classification in 1988 may have caused some slight change in the grouping of commodities.*
[2] *Contains values of selected petroleum products including products destined for non-energy consumption such as asphalt and lubricating oils and grease.*
[3] *Includes petroleum refinery and natural gas processing plant propane and butane.*

16.5   CRUDE OIL AND EQUIVALENT PRODUCTION AND VALUE

	Production[1] ('000 m³)		Value ($'000 000)	
	1990	1991	1990	1991
Crude oil and condensate				
Atlantic provinces[2]	- -	- -	- -	- -
Ontario	247	235	44	36
Manitoba	738	713	115	90
Saskatchewan	12 249	12 390	1,535	1,186
Alberta	53 101	52 246	8,023	6,421
British Columbia	1 936	2 046	314	266
Northwest Territories	1 929	1 927	256	202
Canada, crude oil	70 200	69 557	10,287	8,201
Pentanes[3]				
Manitoba	2	1	- -	- -
Saskatchewan	29	30	4	3
Alberta	6 306	6 620	1,062	926
British Columbia	229	217	31	26
Northwest Territories	29	29	4	3
Canada, pentanes	6 595	6 897	1,101	958
Synthetic crude oil[4]				
Alberta	19 947	20 232	2,799	2,255
Canada, synthetic	19 947	20 232	2,799	2,255
Atlantic provinces[2]	- -	- -	- -	- -
Ontario	247	235	44	36
Manitoba	740	714	115	90
Saskatchewan	12 278	12 420	1,539	1,189
Alberta	79 354	79 098	11,884	9,602
British Columbia	2 165	2 263	345	292
Northwest Territories	1 958	1 956	260	205
Canada, total	96 742	96 686	14,187	11,414

[1] *Marketable production.*
[2] *Includes offshore production.*
[3] *A product of gas plants.*
[4] *Includes experimental crude oil.*

16.6 PETROLEUM SUPPLY AND DEMAND (THOUSAND CUBIC METRES)

	1990	1991
Supply		
Production of crude oil and equivalent[1]	97 369	97 337
Imports		
Crude oil and equivalent	31 112	31 542
Products	8 299	8 623
Sub-total, imports	39 411	40 165
Interproduct transfers		
LPG's[2] received by refineries for blending	1 577	1 963
Propane and butane to natural gas liquids stream	−2 251	−2 220
Sub-total, interproduct transfers	−674	−257
Total supply	136 106	137 245
Demand[3]		
Domestic demand		
Motor gasoline	33 945	32 832
Diesel fuel	17 005	16 074
Kerosene, stove oil	689	653
Light fuel oil	6 391	5 740
Heavy fuel oil	10 135	9 147
Aviation fuels	5 167	4 615
Non-energy products	8 160	7 892
Other[4]	6 006	5 949
Sub-total, domestic demand	87 498	82 902
Exports		
Crude oil and equivalent	37 976	44 240
Products	13 975	15 763
Sub-total, exports	51 951	60 003
Total, demand	139 449	142 905
Inventory changes and other adjustments	−3 343	−5 660

[1] Includes estimated production to cover own production used in the oil sands plants.
[2] LPG (Liquified Petroleum Gas).
[3] Includes producers' consumption as well as an estimate of consumption of producers' own production in the synthetic crude and heavy oil sectors.
[4] Includes still gas, petroleum coke and own consumption of refinery produced propane and butane.

16.7 MARKETABLE NATURAL GAS PRODUCTION AND VALUE

	Production ('000 000 m³)		Value ($'000 000)	
	1990	1991	1990	1991
Ontario	449	428	47	45
Saskatchewan	5 648	6 042	306	332
Alberta	82 214	85 477	4,842	4,435
British Columbia	10 335	12 934	491	564
Yukon	—	173	—	8
Northwest Territories	124	189	7	9
Canada	98 770	105 243	5,693	5,393

16.8 NATURAL GAS SUPPLY AND DEMAND (MILLION CUBIC METRES)

	1990	1991
Supply		
Gross new production[1]	140 666	147 108
Reinjection and storage	13 059	12 840
Process shrinkage	14 337	14 760
Other losses and adjustments	21 976	21 367
Available natural gas	91 294	98 141
Imports	641	319
Interproduct transfers[2]	380	−156
Total, supply	92 315	98 304
Demand		
Domestic demand		
Industrial[3]	22 681	20 635
Transportation	3 593	3 977
Residential and farm	14 600	14 674
Public administration	502	472
Commercial and institutional	9 763	10 193
Electrical generation	2 223	2 018
Non-energy use	3 941	4 459
Sub-total, domestic demand	57 303	56 428
Exports	40 689	47 688
Total, demand	97 992	104 116
Inventory change and other adjustments	−5 677	−5 812

[1] Includes an estimate of producers' own consumption in the synthetic crude and heavy oil sectors.
[2] Transfer of one product to another product stream which has similar characteristics.
[3] Includes any natural gas used to produce steam for sale.

16.9   NATURAL GAS LIQUIDS PRODUCTION AND VALUE

	Gas plant production ('000 m^3)		Value ($'000)	
	1990	1991	1990	1991
Propane				
Manitoba	5	3	—	—
Saskatchewan	52	49	4	4
Alberta	6 404	6 414	554	489
British Columbia	268	275	14	21
Canada, propane	6 729	6 741	572	514
Butane				
Manitoba	2	1	—	—
Saskatchewan	45	42	5	4
Alberta	3 231	3 536	330	347
British Columbia	152	162	9	16
Canada, butane	3 430	3 741	344	367
Ethane				
Alberta	7 106	7 538	352	341
Canada, ethane	7 106	7 538	352	341
Canada				
Manitoba	7	4	—	—
Saskatchewan	97	91	9	8
Alberta	16 741	17 488	1,236	1,177
British Columbia	420	437	23	37
Canada	17 265	18 020	1,268	1,222

16.10 NATURAL GAS LIQUIDS[1], SUPPLY & DEMAND (THOUSAND CUBIC METRES)

	1990	1991
Supply		
Gas plant production	17 265	18 020
Imports	155	97
Interproduct transfers		
LPGs[2] to refineries for blending	−1 577	−1 963
LPGs received from refineries[3]	2 251	2 220
Sub-total, interproduct transfers	674	257
Total supply	18 094	18 374
Demand		
Domestic energy use	2 976	3 474
Non-energy use[4]	7 141	7 474
Exports	6 964	6 546
Total demand	17 081	17 494
Inventory change & other adjustments	1 013	880

[1] Includes propane, butane and ethane.
[2] LPG (Liquified Petroleum Gas).
[3] Petroleum refinery produced LPG (propane and butane) for domestic sale or export
[4] Excludes any LPG which becomes part of the petrochemical feedstock in petroleum refineries.

16.11 COAL PRODUCTION AND VALUE

	Production ('000 t)		Value ($'000,000)	
	1990	1991	1990	1991
Bituminous				
Nova Scotia	3 415	4 138	204	245
New Brunswick	548	498	37	34
Alberta	9 153	10 312	310	358
British Columbia	24 556	24 963	1,001	990
Canada, bituminous	37 672	39 911	1,552	1,627
Sub bituminous				
Alberta	21 252	22 242	171	178
Lignite				
Saskatchewan	9 407	8 981	100	94
Total	68 331	71 134	1,823	1,899

16.12   COAL, SUPPLY AND DEMAND (THOUSAND TONNES)

	1990	1991
Supply		
Production	68 331	71 134
Imports	14 111	12 396
Total, supply	82 442	83 530
Demand		
Domestic demand		
Electric generation	42 155	43 892
Coke plants	5 001	4 906
Steam generation	29	—
Industrial	1 642	1 326
Residential	109	94
Public administration	7	5
Commercial and institutional	—	—
Non-energy use	202	176
Sub-total, domestic demand	49 145	50 399
Exports	31 009	34 113
Total, demand	80 154	84 512
Inventory change & other adjustments	2 288	−982

16.13   ELECTRICITY GENERATED AND CONSUMED[1] (GIGAWATT HOURS)

	Generation		Domestic demand	
	1990	1991	1990	1991
Newfoundland	36 689	36 943	9 388	9 491
Prince Edward Island	81	71	671	682
Nova Scotia	9 432	9 394	8 996	8 978
New Brunswick	16 751	15 808	12 277	12 635
Quebec	135 882	142 992	147 675	149 424
Ontario	129 770	142 443	134 261	134 074
Manitoba	20 242	22 891	15 319	15 520
Saskatchewan	13 542	13 598	12 215	12 419
Alberta	43 162	44 479	38 934	41 052
British Columbia	60 990	63 374	52 213	2 730
Yukon	485	461	429	409
Northwest Territories	567	572	530	532
Canada	467 593	493 026	432 908	437 946

[1] *Net generation*

16.14 ELECTRICITY SUPPLY AND DEMAND (GIGAWATT HOURS)

	1990	1991
Supply		
Production[1]		
Hydro[2]	294 005	305 456
Nuclear	68 760	80 122
Thermal	104 854	106 934
Sub-total, production	467 619	492 512
Imports	17 781	6 094
Total, supply	485 400	498 606
Demand[3]		
Domestic demand		
Manufacturing	152 848	156 270
Other industrial	29 008	29 107
Transportation	3 274	3 055
Agriculture	9 625	9 516
Residential	130 084	128 102
Public administration	12 494	13 046
Commerical & institutional	93 680	97 209
Sub-total, domestic demand	431 013	436 305
Exports	18 236	24 522
Total, demand	449 249	460 827
Own use, transmission losses and other adjustments	36 151	37 779

[1] *Net generation.*
[2] *Includes wind and tidal generation.*
[3] *Demand may not equal demand shown elsewhere due to methods of calculation and revisions.*

Source
Statistics Canada

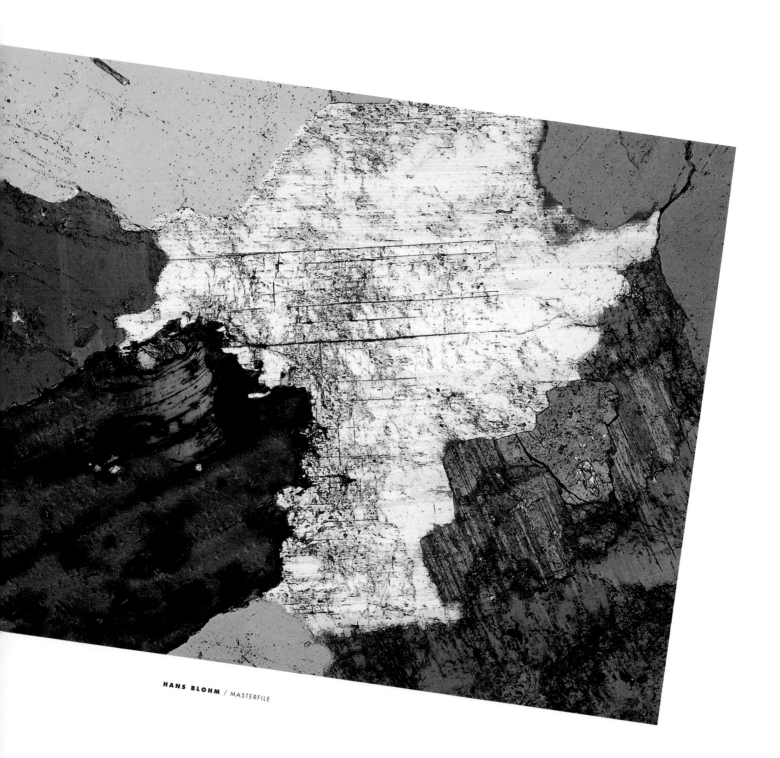

THE MINERAL INDUSTRY

INTRODUCTION

In a country that encompasses a territory of some 10 million square kilometres, the search for ores could be like finding a needle in a haystack. Not so in Canada.

Canada is one of the world's leading producers and exporters of non-fuel minerals and its mineral industry plays a strong role in the nation's economy. In 1992, the non-fuel minerals industry accounted for about 4% of the nation's Gross Domestic Product (GDP) and almost 3% of total national employment.

Five of the country's major physiographic regions contribute to and benefit from this industry. The Quebec portion of the Appalachian region contains the world's largest reserves of asbestos along with deposits of copper and zinc. The Canadian Shield is a rich source of metallic minerals such as nickel, copper, gold, uranium and zinc. The Interior Plains region produces fossil fuels such as petroleum and natural gas, and non-fuels such as potash, gypsum and salt. From the Western Cordilleran region comes a variety of minerals, principally copper, lead, zinc, molybdenum and asbestos and from the Arctic region, zinc and lead. Increasingly important to the mining industry, the Arctic region features the world's most northerly base metal mine, Polaris, on Little Cornwallis Island.

In all, Canada produces more than 60 mineral commodities. Canada meets most of its domestic mineral needs, with the exception of bauxite, chromium, manganese and phosphate.

In Canada, the mineral commodities are generally divided into four groups: metallic minerals, non-metallic minerals, structural materials, and mineral fuels. In 1992, non-fuel mineral production totalled $14.6 billion, accounting for just over 41% of the total value of Canada's mineral production. Exports of non-fuel minerals totalled $23.0 billion, accounting for over 15% of Canada's total domestic exports. Almost 63% of Canada's non-fuel mineral exports were destined for the United States, about 13% went to the European Community and about 6% went to Japan. The remaining 18% was distributed among nearly 90 other countries.

In 1992, imports of non-fuel minerals were $13.2 billion resulting in a trade surplus of more than $9.8 billion.

FROM ROCKS TO RICHES In the past, much Canadian mineral exploration was carried out by prospectors, many of whom were rugged individualists equipped only with a pick, a pan, a canoe or a horse, and a lot of optimism. Most of today's explorers are a new breed of professionals who hold one or more university degrees in geology, geophysics or geochemistry and work for mining and exploration companies. Modern exploration involves the use of fixed-wing aircraft, helicopters, 4-wheel drive vehicles and air and ground operated geophysical instruments such as magnetometers, gravimeters and various electromagnetic instruments that are essential for detecting buried orebodies. Scintillometers and gamma-ray spectrometers are used both from aircraft and on the ground to discover deposits of uranium.

Mining companies search for geophysical and geochemical anomalies and for geological clues that may indicate orebodies. They use geophysical and geological surveys and maps and various other advanced methods of mineral exploration. For example, geochemical surveys are used to locate anomalous concentrations of elements of economic interest in stream sediments in soils, lake and stream waters and plants. Such concentrations may indicate the presence of an orebody. In special cases, geobotanists may search for indicators such as species of vegetation specific to elements of possible economic interest.

In 1991, Canadian exploration expenditures totalled $532 million, down from $775 million in 1990. Senior companies spent about $416 million. Junior companies (companies that do not produce or receive significant income from mining or other activities) spent roughly $116 million. In 1991, 732 companies reported exploration projects in Canada, down from 936 in 1990. Of the total expenditures on exploration, $67 million was spent on 'on-property' exploration — the search for new mines on the properties of existing mines.

Preliminary data for 1992 show a decline in total Canadian exploration expenditures to about $420 million.

Lindeman June 6th 1898

OUR CAMP LINDEMAN

EVENGELINE   TORONTO

LINDERMAN Boats on the beach

Frederick Gardiner / National Archives of Canada C 84632

Yukon goldrush sketch book, 1898.

REGIONAL TREASURES Ontario had the largest share of non-fuel mineral output, accounting for 32.2% of the total value of mineral production in 1992, followed by Quebec with 18.0%, British Columbia with 12.7%, Saskatchewan with 8.6% and Manitoba with 7.2%. The remaining 21.3% was spread among the other five provinces and the two territories.

In 1992, commodities with the highest production value were gold and copper, each at $2.1 billion; zinc, $1.7 billion; nickel, $1.7 billion; iron ore, $1.1 billion; and potash at $1.0 billion.

METALS

COPPER Canada is rich in copper, a reddish, non-magnetic metal: we rank fourth in the world in its production. In 1992, Canadian producers benefitted from the continuing strength of international copper markets. Canadian copper mine shipments (recoverable copper) were roughly 745 000 tonnes, valued at $2.06 billion in 1992 — a decrease of almost 5% from 780 000 tonnes valued at $2.11 billion the previous year. Refined production increased slightly to 545 000 tonnes from 538 000 tonnes in 1992.

Production of Leading Metals

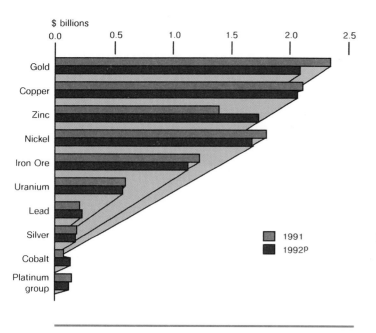

Copper has a dazzling array of uses. Its beauty and endurance have made it a distinctive ingredient of architecture, statuary and hardware of all kinds. Indeed, the copper roofs turned dusty green through oxidization on Canada's parliament buildings, are perhaps the country's best known example of architectural uses of the metal. Copper tubing, which has long been used for distributing hot and cold water, is increasingly used in natural gas distribution and fire suppression systems. In Canada, more than half of the refined copper consumed annually is used for electrical applications — mostly wire. Other important uses are in castings and heat exchanges.

As Canada heads towards the year 2000, copper consumption is expected to grow at an annual average rate of 2.0% to 2.5%.

ZINC Canada is the world's largest producer of zinc in concentrate and ranks second in zinc metal production. It ranks second in the export of zinc concentrates and first in the export of zinc metal. This bluish-white metal is used mainly as a rust-resistant coating for iron and steel products. Galvanizing, or coating, accounts for about 48% of the world's zinc consumption.

Geologically, zinc is usually found with copper or lead deposits. Mining operations generally recover these metals as co-products.

In 1992, Canadian zinc mine production rose by about 10% to 1.2 million tonnes, from 1.1 million tonnes the previous year. Its production value rose by almost 25% to $1.7 billion. The average price for zinc in 1992 was US 56 cents per pound, an increase from US 51 cents per pound in 1991.

Apart from use as protection against corrosion, particularly in the automotive and construction industries, zinc is used in the manufacture of brass and bronze in the die-casting industry and in other uses.

NICKEL Seventeenth-century German miners discovered a reddish ore that they thought contained copper. Upon processing it, they found the ore yielded a useless material and a foul odour. Thinking the ore was bewitched, they named it *Kupfer Nickel* — literally, Old Nick's Copper, meaning false or bad copper. In 1751, a Swedish scientist isolated and identified a new metallic element from an ore similar to Germany's 'kupfer nickel'. He called the new metal nickel in recognition of the traditional name of the ore.

Since then, nickel has become one of the world's most important metals. Its greatest use is an alloy, adding strength, hardness and corrosion resistance to other metals.

Canada is the world's second largest producer of nickel, topped only by Russia. In 1992, Canada's nickel mine production was 191 200 tonnes valued at $1.7 billion — a slight decrease from almost 192 300 tonnes in 1991.

In 1992, western demand for nickel declined by about 8%. Lower demand, high production levels and increased exports from Russia resulted in weaker prices. Nickel was trading on the London Metal Exchange (LME) at an average spot price of US$2.65 per pound at the close of 1992, compared with about $3.40 per pound at the beginning of the year. Nickel inventories on the LME increased to record levels during 1992 — at year's end, stocks surpassed 70 000 tonnes.

Over 60% of nickel is used in stainless steel production, which declined in Europe and Japan in 1992. However, the decline of more mature markets is expected to be offset by emerging markets such as China, Brazil and South Korea.

There are about 3,000 nickel alloys, each developed to serve a particular purpose, but the greatest demand is in the production of stainless steels used in chemical and food-processing equipment, transportation equipment, architectural construction and an array of consumer items. Currently, Canada's dime and quarter coins are made of pure nickel, and the five-cent piece is made of cupro-nickel, a mix of copper (75%) and nickel (25%).

LEAD Lead is a silver-grey metal commonly found with zinc and copper sulphides. Its high density and malleability, corrosion resistance and its ability to diminish gamma radiation have led to a wide variety of uses.

Canada ranks fifth in the world's production of lead. In 1992, preliminary estimates of shipments of recoverable lead in ores and concentrates increased by about 28% to 319 000 tonnes, from 248 000 tonnes the previous year. Value of shipments increased by almost 10% to $231 million.

In 1992, lead inventories rose as world demand weakened and as supplies increased from other countries. The average price in 1992 was US 24.5 cents per pound, only slightly lower than the 1991 price of US 25.3 cents per pound.

The largest single use of lead is in the manufacture of the lead-acid storage battery and accounts for over 60% of the market. Lead's corrosion resistant nature also lends it to be used as sheeting for roofing purposes, while its radiation attenuation properties can prevent radiation emissions from television, video and computer monitors.

Until the mid-1970s, lead additives for gasoline were one of the most important markets for the metal. However, use of lead in gasoline has been restricted in Canada and is being phased out in other countries. In spite of tighter environmental regulations, the demand for lead has increased with growth taking place in applications where lead is not dispersive or readily available in nature.

GOLD Gold has been the ultimate symbol of wealth from earliest civilizations to present day. It has been sought after and fought over more than any other metal. While it is too soft for weapons or tools, it has been treasured for its decorative and monetary value for at least 8,000 years.

Because it is the least chemically active of all metals, gold usually occurs in a free, or uncombined state. It is sometimes found as nuggets, flakes or dust in gravel or sand along creeks and streams. Such deposits are called 'placers'. More frequently, gold is found in veins or dispersed in bedrock. This bright, shiny yellow metal is noted for its great density — 19.3 times the weight of an equal volume of water — its high resistance to corrosion, its lustrous beauty and its scarcity.

George Hunter

Gold miners, Yellowknife, Northwest Territories.

Canada ranks fifth in the world production of gold. Yet, in 1992, gold production decreased by about 10% to an estimated 158 tonnes from the 1991 record level of 176 tonnes. Dwindling reserves combined with low prices resulted in a number of mine closures and reduced output at several other operations. Gold prices remained low and traded within a relatively narrow range — between US$330 and US$359 per troy ounce in 1992. The average price for the year was US$344, down from US$362 in 1991 — its lowest level since 1985. With total output valued at about $2.1 billion in 1992, gold tied with copper as Canada's leading metal in terms of overall value of production.

The most familiar use of gold is in the manufacture of jewellery, coins and other ornaments. About 85% of the total western world supply ends up in these forms. In Canada, the largest use of gold is in the Gold Maple Leaf bullion coin family produced by the Royal Canadian Mint. The manufacture of these coins has required some 470 tonnes of gold, or 31.8% of total Canadian production, since they were introduced in 1979.

SILVER Silver is a brilliant, grey-white, soft metal that takes a finish and is resistant to corrosion. Of all the metals, silver is the best conductor of electricity. Because of these qualities, and its relative scarcity, silver is classed with gold and platinum as a precious metal.

Canada is the world's fourth largest producer of silver. In 1992, shipments of silver fell to 1 147 tonnes based on preliminary estimates, and were valued at $173 million, a decrease of 9% from the 1991 level of 1 261 tonnes. Over the past decade, the price of silver has been declining as a result of relatively weak demand and increased world production. Silver prices averaged US$3.95 per ounce in 1992, down slightly from US$4.06 in 1991.

In Canada, silver was once used for coinage. However, since 1968, all coins for circulation that formerly contained silver — dimes, quarters, half-dollars and dollars — have been minted with 100% nickel content. Today, the minting of silver in Canada includes collectible coins and commemorative pieces. The use of silver in collectible coinage has been one of the fastest-growing markets for the metal in recent years. The major industrial uses for silver are in photographic materials, electrical and electronic products, sterling and electroplated ware, jewellery, and brazing alloys and solders.

IRON ORE Iron is commonly found in the earth's crust, where it occurs in combination with other elements. These combinations constitute the iron minerals, such as hematite and magnetite. The term 'iron ore' is used when the rock is sufficiently rich in the iron minerals to be mined economically.

In 1992, Canada ranked seventh in world production of iron ore, although Canadian iron ore shipments dropped 7.5% to 32.8 million tonnes. This was the lowest level of shipments recorded since 1983. Use of iron ore in Canadian blast furnaces remained low for the third year in a row, although the use of domestic ores increased by 11% since 1991.

Iron is the main element in steel — the foundation of industrial society. The most spectacular use of iron, and then steel, was in the construction of bridges and buildings. With further applications in automobiles, appliances and a host of other products, steel is the most widely used metal today.

PLATINUM METALS The platinum group elements refer to six closely related metals: the three major platinum metals — platinum (Pt), palladium (Pd) and rhodium (Rh); and the three minor platinum metals — ruthenium (Ru), iridium (Ir) and osmium (Os). These metals possess unusual qualities such as high melting points and chemical inertness, and, most importantly, exceptional catalytic properties, even under conditions of severe temperature and corrosion. These scarce metals occur together in nature.

Canada ranks third in world production of platinum-group metals (PGMs). Primary PGM output in Canada

declined almost 6% from 11.1 tonnes in 1991 to 10.5 tonnes in 1992. Total value of shipments dropped 22% from $150 million in 1991 to $117 million in 1992.

PGMs have many applications in pure form, and as alloys of various PGMs or with other metals. The largest uses of PGMs are in the production of automobile catalytic converters, jewellery, and in electrical applications.

NON-METALS

ASBESTOS Asbestos is the commercial name for fibrous varieties of several minerals. In Canada, asbestos occurs as veins within deposits of igneous rocks rich in iron and magnesium. Asbestos veins may vary from hairline size to 10 centimetres in width. In 1992, Canadian asbestos mines operated at close to 100% of capacity. That year, estimated total shipments exceeded 601 000 tonnes valued at $235.8 million, compared with 686 000 tonnes valued at $271.0 million in 1991. The drop in shipments was due to the closure of the Cassiar mine in British Columbia. Export volumes for 1992 also decreased 15% from the previous year to 580 000 tonnes. The United States Bureau of Mines estimates that 1992 Canadian asbestos imports were about 32 000 tonnes — a 7% drop from 34 525 tonnes in 1991. This decrease is a result of a 1989 ban on

Production of Leading Non-Metals

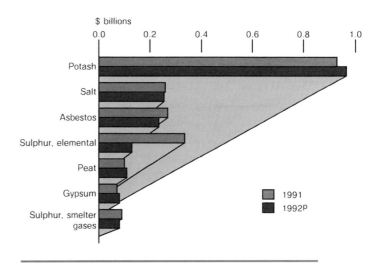

DIAMONDS IN THE ROUGH

In 1541, explorer Jacques Cartier thought, over-optimistically, that a handful of quartz crystals he had found in Canada were diamonds. The disappointment when he was proved wrong gave rise to the early French-Canadian saying, ''as false as Canadian diamonds.''

Some 450 years later, the saying itself may well be false. In the Northwest Territories, diamonds are being hunted with great zeal following the discovery of tiny diamonds called 'microdiamonds' in a rock sample drilled at Lac de Gras. (Lac de Gras is about 300 kilometres northeast of Yellowknife.) A subsequent larger sample yielded diamonds as large as three carats, or about 10 times the size of a stone on a normal engagement ring.

Since November 1991, when the first discoveries in the Northwest Territories became public, the Department of Indian Affairs and Northern Development has issued permits to explore about 110 000 square kilometres — an area larger than Iceland.

In 1993 alone, 150 permits covering 28 000 square kilometres were issued to 14 companies or individuals ranging from Canadian newcomers to long-established international diamond-mining companies. In an average year, exploration permits cover less than a tenth of that area.

The reason is simple: few minerals are more rare, treasured, or profitable, than diamonds.

Diamonds have never been mined in Canada. Geologists have known of potentially diamond-bearing rock formations since the 1940s, and diamond prospectors in Alberta, Saskatchewan, Ontario and Quebec have been quietly staking and exploring large claims since the mid-1980s. But at present, the major diamond mines of the world are in South Africa, Zaire, Botswana, Australia and Russia.

Natural diamonds can only be found in geological formations called kimberlite pipes. Of 2,500 such formations in the world, only about 25 are worth mining commercially. This rarity means a single good mine could be worth billions of dollars.

In the Northwest Territories, about 20 diamond-bearing kimberlite pipes have been found in four widely separated places: at Lac de Gras, near Dubawnt Lake, at Mountain Diatrime near the Alaska border; and on Somerset Island. The latter two were discovered before the Lac de Gras find.

Although the early results are encouraging, only a handful of diamonds have come out of Canada's North so far. At publication time, there had been no decision to start mining.

The reality is that even large quantities of diamonds may not make commercial mining worthwhile. The average size, colour and quality also have a bearing on whether or not to dig. It could take another five years to decide whether or not commercial diamond mining is worthwhile, and half a billion dollars to actually start a mine in the Northwest Territories.

The early French-Canadian saying ''as false as Canadian diamonds'' might have to be updated to : ''as expensive as Canadian diamonds.''

asbestos by the American Environmental Protection Agency. This ruling was overturned by American courts in 1991, stabilizing a negative trend in Canadian exports to the United States.

In the 1990s, demand for asbestos/cement building products such as roofing tiles, siding and sheets, and asbestos/cement pipe, is expected to remain strong in response to worldwide housing needs.

POTASH Growing plants need potassium. Where agricultural soil has been depleted by successive plantings, or where it is naturally deficient, it must be replenished through fertilization. Potassium-bearing ores such as sylvanite are processed to make potash. Canada is the world's second largest producer and leading exporter of potash. Shipments of potash (K_2O) remained at 7 million tonnes in 1992, with a total value of about $960 million. Saskatchewan produced about 85% of Canadian potash in 1992; the remainder came from New Brunswick.

On the world scale, production of potash dropped 7% to just over 24 million tonnes in 1992. About 95% of the potash produced worldwide is used for fertilizers.

SALT On a per capita basis, Canada is the world's largest consumer of salt — using about 360 kilograms of salt per person per year. Our high consumption is due to severe winter road conditions in many parts of the country. Canadians salt the roads to improve winter driving. The city of Montreal alone uses about 125 000 tonnes of salt each winter.

In 1992, Canadian salt production decreased by 7% at slightly over 11 million tonnes, compared with about 12 million tonnes in 1991. Economic recession and a relatively mild winter contributed to this decrease. In 1992, shipments from Ontario accounted for 60% of all Canadian shipments. The average unit value of salt was estimated at $22.86 per tonne, an increase of almost 5% over 1991.

The chemical industry is one of Canada's largest salt consumers. It uses salt to manufacture chemicals used to produce soap and detergents, pulp and paper, fibres and plastics, glass, petro chemicals, solvents and other chemicals. Food industries also use salt in many forms — for curing meats, packing fish, canning, pickling and flavouring. In agriculture, salt is given to livestock in the form of salt licks or food additives.

SULPHUR Sulphur is a non-metallic, highly reactive element that makes up more than half of 1% of the earth's crust. As sulphuric acid, it is the most widely used raw material in the chemical industry and it enters one way or another into the manufacture of almost everything we use. In fact, sulphur is so basic to our way of life that its rate of consumption can be taken as a reliable measure of the country's industrial activity.

In 1992, Canada accounted for about 18% of world sulphur production. That year Canadian production was about 6.4 million tonnes. Shipments dropped by 15% to almost 6 million tonnes. This decrease resulted mainly from a decline in offshore exports, which decreased by almost 1 million tonnes to 3.7 million tonnes. Sales to the United States rose slightly; domestic sales were stable in 1992.

About 60% of the sulphur consumed in the world is used as a process agent to produce fertilizers. The second largest user is the chemical industry, in products ranging from pharmaceuticals to synthetic fibres in plastics.

STRUCTURAL MATERIALS In 1992, Canadian shipments of primary construction materials, including clay products, sand and gravel, cement and lime, fell slightly over 9% to $2.2 billion from $2.4 billion the previous year. One indicator of demand for structural materials is housing starts, which increased by 8% in 1992. However, declines in non-residential building construction and in engineering construction delayed a recovery in demand for primary structural materials.

MINERAL AGGREGATES Demand for mineral aggregates including crushed stone, sand and gravel generally reflects trends in domestic construction. In 1992, total shipments of mineral aggregates decreased about 7% to 280 million tonnes — the lowest level in 10 years.

C E M E N T In 1992, total Canadian cement shipments were 8.5 million tonnes valued at nearly $740 million, a decrease of about 9% by volume and by value over the previous year.

G Y P S U M Shipments of crude gypsum were almost 6.9 million tonnes, up slightly from 6.7 million tonnes in 1991. The value of shipments was $79.2 million. Demand for gypsum by manufacturers of wallboard products in the United States and Canada was about the same as in 1991.

MANUFACTURED METALS

A L U M I N U M Aluminum is known as the 'wonder' metal of the twentieth century. Pure aluminum is a relatively soft, silvery white metal with a dull lustre that is caused by a thin coating of aluminum oxide. This coating, which forms when the metal is exposed to air, accounts for the metal's corrosion resistance. It is also exceptionally light weight — one-third the weight of an equal volume of steel. Aluminum possesses a high degree of workability and conductivity, has great strength when alloyed and is impervious to rust.

Canadian production of primary aluminum in 1992 was 1.9 million tonnes, a slight increase from 1.8 million tonnes the previous year. Canadian aluminum smelter production capacity increased by 430 000 tonnes in 1992 to 2.2 million tonnes. In the first nine months of 1992, aluminum exports were 1.17 million tonnes, compared to 1.11 million tonnes for the same period in 1991. Exports to the United States also increased in the first nine months of 1992, to a total of 791 264 tonnes from 723 900 tonnes the previous year.

Alloyed and unalloyed aluminum is used in a wide range of consumer and capital goods. The most important uses are for transportation equipment, building and construction, packaging, electrical, consumer durables, and machinery and equipment.

Aluminum prices on the London Metal Exchange averaged US 57 cents per pound in 1992, compared with an average of US 59 cents per pound the previous year.

With significant growth expected in transportation and packaging (beverage cans in particular), aluminum consumption is expected to increase between 3% and 4% per year for the remainder of the decade.

I R O N   A N D   S T E E L There are two technologies used to produce steel: basic oxygen furnaces, which are charged with blast furnace iron and ferrous scrap at integrated steel mills; and electric furnaces, which are charged with ferrous scrap and/or direct reduced iron at mini-mill plants. Primary iron includes blast furnace iron, direct reduced iron (made by reducing iron ore with a mixture of gases) and, in Canada, electric smelted iron. Ferrous scrap is a very important factor in steel production — in 1992, some 56% of the raw ferrous material used to make steel in Canada was ferrous scrap.

Canadian steel production in 1992 increased to 13.8 million tonnes from 12.9 million tonnes in 1991. The production of blast furnace and foundry iron increased to 8.6 million tonnes in 1992 from 8.2 million tonnes the year before, reflecting a higher level of steel production by integrated producers. The increase in steel output was attributed partly to an improvement in the economy, but the most significant factor was a

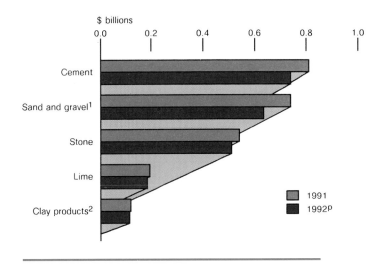

Production of Structural Materials

$ billions

Cement
Sand and gravel[1]
Stone
Lime
Clay products[2]

☐ 1991
■ 1992p

[1] Includes quartz.
[2] Includes bentonite and diatomite.

reduction in steel imports. Although the economy showed signs of gradually improving, the steel industry continued to face a very competitive and difficult pricing environment.

Although overall exports of steel products decreased by 228 000 tonnes in 1992, Canadian exports to the United States increased by 790 000 tonnes. Total imports of steel decreased by over 350 000 tonnes, including a decline of 130 000 tonnes from the United States. Nevertheless, steel imports from the United States totalled almost 1.2 million tonnes, a level which was still high by historical standards. These figures emphasize the importance of bilateral steel trade to the industries of both Canada and the United States.

Over the next 5 to 10 years, Canadian primary iron and steel production should remain constant, with the possibility of a slight increase at the end of the decade. The United States imports over 25% of its steel requirements, and Canadian steel producers are well placed to capture some of this market from overseas suppliers, especially since North America has effectively become a single market for steel.

ENERGY, MINES AND RESOURCES CANADA

Energy, Mines and Resources Canada (EMR) is responsible for federal mineral and energy policies, the management of technical surveys, and the management of research on mineral and energy resources. The Mineral Policy Sector develops specific policies, strategies and incentive programs that foster development of minerals and metals. The sector works in close co-operation with the provinces, territories, industry and labour.

EMR conducts quality surveys and research in three sectors: Mineral and Energy Technology; Surveys, Mapping and Remote Sensing; and the Geological Survey of Canada.

The Mineral and Energy Technology Sector The Mineral and Energy Technology Sector (METS) is comprised of the Office of Energy Research and Development (OERD) and the Canada Centre for Mineral and Energy Technology (CANMET).

Through its laboratories across Canada, CANMET works to find cleaner, safer and more efficient methods to develop and use Canada's mineral and energy resources. CANMET also administers the Canada Explosives Act.

Working in partnership with the minerals, metals and energy industries, CANMET sponsors and performs commercial and cost-shared research and development. The CANMET's mining R&D program focuses on design, automation and safety. It includes research on rock mechanics, mining methods, equipment certification, fire and explosive hazards, tailings control, and uranium and coal reserves assessment.

OERD is responsible for administering the Energy Research and Development Program. This program provides financial support to CANMET, and encourages the development of science and technology that diversifies and sustains the sources, production and application of energy in Canada.

Surveys, Mapping and Remote Sensing Sector The sector collects, processes and distributes topographical, remote sensing and other satellite-based data which are useful in the development of minerals and other natural resources.

Geological Survey of Canada (GSC) Since it was founded in 1842, the GSC's mandate has been to provide comprehensive geological knowledge about Canada's mineral resources and to assess resource potential. Now, at a time when the mining industry is facing declining reserves, strong competition in global markets and a need for more sophisticated techniques to find new reserves, the GSC is helping Canadian companies to achieve a sharper competitive edge by applying its expertise and vast data bases to their specific problems. It is also playing a trailblazing role in developing innovative technologies for mineral exploration.

The industry's current priorities include exploring below current reserves in existing mineral camps, and locating world class deposits in new and developed mineral areas. The GSC is working in collaboration with mining companies and provincial departments across Canada to gain a better understanding of giant deposits such as the Kidd Creek Mine near Timmins, Ontario; the Brunswick No. 12 Mines near Bathurst, New Brunswick; the Ruttan deposit near Leaf Rapids,

Charles Comfort / The National Gallery of Canada

Smelter Stacks, Copper Cliff, Ontario.

Manitoba; and the Sullivan deposit near Kimberly, British Columbia.

GSC research in less well-known and frontier areas is also providing explorationists with exciting new target areas. For instance, British Columbia's Hazelton Group in the Canadian Cordillera, which hosts a number of mineral deposits and important porphyry copper deposits, and the Ungava Peninsula in Northern Quebec where the GSC recently discovered a new greenstone belt.

The GSC's research in conjuction with the international Ocean Drilling Program at active volcanic ridges on the ocean floor off Canada's west coast is giving Canadian mining companies new approaches to understanding geological formations and finding new reserves. Three kilometres beneath the surface of the ocean, scientists are able to watch and study massive sulphide deposits as they are being formed. The knowledge gained through this study will deepen their understanding of terrestrial deposits and improve exploration strategies.

Diamonds are the focus of intense exploration in the Northwest Territories. Because this area was glaciated, explorationists require data on ice flow directions to help trace kimberlite indicator minerals back to their sources. In response to this demand, the GSC has just published maps of ice flow information for the heart of the diamond play in the Lac de Gras-Aylmer Lake area. Other GSC programs throughout the Prairies and Canadian Shield are supporting the diamond exploration boom with new surveys, detailed studies of kimberlites and re-analysis of archival samples of diamond indicator minerals.

ENVIRONMENT

Because of the importance of the environment, Canadians are turning to the idea of sustainable development, which integrates the need for both a prosperous economy and a clean, healthy environment. Sustainable development is the underlying principle of *Canada's Green Plan* (1990).

Because most minerals and metals are re-usable or recyclable by their very nature, they lend themselves to sustainable development, even though they are considered to be a non-renewable resource.

The development of new technologies and the ongoing commitment to improving the environment has led to several positive steps by both industry and government. The *Green Plan* commitment to review regulations and to expand the priority substance list is well under way. Other initiatives aimed at improving the industry's environmental performance while ensuring that it remains prosperous and competitive are also being undertaken. These include the multi-stakeholder Whitehorse Mining Initiative and sustainable development policy work at Energy, Mines and Resources Canada. The industry is working to improve its environmental performance by developing codes of practice and conducting environmental audits.

As stated in Environment Canada's 1991 *State of Canada's Environment* report, the mineral and metal sector has achieved measurable success in addressing some of the more pressing environmental problems. However, problems and concerns about the industry's impact on the environment are ongoing. Acid mine drainage and water quality are still the main environmental concerns. Other concerns involve the efficiency of the federal-provincial regulatory regime, the Canadian Environmental Assessment Act, and land access. Ongoing work will help address many of these issues, and will require the co-operation and commitment of all stakeholders.

SOURCES

Energy, Mines and Resources Canada

Statistics Canada

FOR FURTHER READING

Selected publications from Statistics Canada

▲ *General Review of the Mineral Industries: Mines, Quarries and Oil Wells*. Annual. 26-201

▲ *Canada's Mineral Production: Preliminary Estimates*. Annual. 26-202

▲ *Metal Mines*. Annual. 26-223

▲ *Non-metal Mines*. Annual. 26-224

▲ *Quarries and Sand Pits*. Annual. 26-225

Selected publications from Other Sources

▲ *Canadian Minerals Yearbook: Review and Outlook*. Annual. Energy, Mines and Resources Canada.

The Mineral Policy Sector of Energy, Mines and Resources Canada prepares a number of information products, including regular and special publications, posters and other material. These can be obtained from:

Publications Distribution Office
Mineral Policy Sector
Energy, Mines and Resources Canada
460 O'Connor Street
Ottawa, Ontario
K1A 0E4
Telephone : (613) 992-1108

TABLES

17.1   VALUE OF MINERAL PRODUCTION[1] (THOUSAND DOLLARS)

	Metallics	Non-metallics	Structural materials	Coal	Total
1970	3,073,344	480,538	450,446	86,067	4,090,395
1980	9,696,956	2,532,361	1,668,577	932,000	14,829,894
1989	13,982,451	2,663,406	2,902,965	1,907,080	21,455,902
1990					
Newfoundland	789,661	37,150	39,175	—	865,987
Prince Edward Island	—	—	3,271	—	3,271
Nova Scotia	51,790	99,812	103,421	204,465	459,488
New Brunswick	584,492	208,785	47,449	37,200	877,926
Quebec	1,923,115	576,714	537,177	—	3,037,007
Ontario	4,883,529	219,571	1,251,567	—	6,354,667
Manitoba	1,094,610	9,391	91,591	—	1,195,592
Saskatchewan	310,941	856,633	38,735	99,420	1,305,729
Alberta	3,498	350,997	312,686	482,000	1,149,180
British Columbia	1,622,514	130,198	338,585	1,000,615	3,091,913
Yukon	531,981	—	9,833	—	541,814
Northwest Territories	703,833	2,917	22,936	—	729,685
Canada	12,499,965	2,492,168	2,796,426r	1,823,700	19,612,259
1991					
Newfoundland	734,397	7,357	30,430	—	772,184
Prince Edward Island	—	—	3,261	—	3,261
Nova Scotia	32,425	94,150	87,721	245,240	459,535
New Brunswick	375,427	220,199	41,585	34,185	671,397
Quebec	1,887,985	553,540	488,486	—	2,930,011
Ontario	3,783,916	233,718	1,002,858	—	5,020,491
Manitoba	947,610	12,564	73,690	—	1,033,864
Saskatchewan	373,026	811,199	55,295	93,865	1,333,385
Alberta	3,010	337,238	264,054	553,980	1,158,282
British Columbia	1,522,200	111,737	337,325	989,510	2,960,773
Yukon	335,486	3	5,214	—	340,703
Northwest Territories	477,572	—	11,527	—	489,100
Canada	10,473,055	2,381,705	2,401,445	1,916,780	17,172,985
1992					
Newfoundland	697,565	8,365	29,372	—	735,302
Prince Edward Island	—	—	3,414	—	3,414
Nova Scotia	402	91,705	80,476	265,000	437,583
New Brunswick	568,207	248,629	36,987	32,000	885,822
Quebec	1,629,749	573,026	427,666	—	2,630,441
Ontario	3,562,432	233,449	910,044	—	4,705,925
Manitoba	956,456	15,295	77,201	—	1,048,951
Saskatchewan	407,985	818,849	30,390	94,200	1,351,425
Alberta	464	147,734	239,022	572,100	959,319
British Columbia	1,447,125	62,327	337,500	700,000	2,546,952
Yukon	462,648	—	5,223	—	467,871
Northwest Territories	476,160	—	6,758	—	482,918
Canada	10,209,192	2,199,379	2,184,052	1,663,300	16,255,923

[1] *Excludes oil and gas.*

17.2 PRINCIPAL MINING INDUSTRIES, GROSS DOMESTIC PRODUCT AT FACTOR COST
(MILLION DOLLARS[1])

Mining industry	1986	1987	1988	1989	1990	1991p
Metal mines						
Placer gold and gold quartz	881	987	1,214	1,500	1,554	1,619
Iron	453	505	569	610	513	497
Other metal mines	2,347	2,734	2,709	2,413	2,332	2,287
Non-metal mines (except coal)	723	813	850	802	790	803
Quarrying	644	688	721	727	683	635
Coal	755	850	1,013	1,005	995	1,050
Services related to mineral extraction	1,938	1,676	1,898	1,457	1,473	1,296
Total	7,740	8,252	8,973	8,513	8,341	8,187

[1] In 1986 dollars.

17.3   QUANTITY OF MINERAL PRODUCTION[1]

		1988	1989	1990	1991	1992[p]
Metals						
Antimony	t	3 171	2 818	565	429	276
Bismuth	t	181	157	74	60	89
Cadmium	t	1 664	1 711	1 334	1 549	1 328
Cobalt	t	2 398	2 344	2 184	2 171	2 219
Copper	t	758 478	704 432	771 433	780 362	744 687
Gold	kg	134 813	159 494	167 373	176 126	157 554
Iron Ore	'000 t	39 934	39 445	35 670	35 421	32 772
Lead	t	351 148	268 887	233 372	248 102	318 515
Molybdenum	t	13 535	13 543	12 188	11 437	9 602
Nickel	t	198 744	195 554	195 004	188 098	189 051
Platinum group	kg	12 541	9 870	11 123	11 123	10 505
Selenium	t	321	213	369	227	286
Silver	t	1 443	1 312	1 381	1 261	1 147
Tantalum	t	18	97	100	114	65
Tellurium	t	19	8	12	16	26
Uranium	t	12 066	10 995	9 720	8 162	9 057
Zinc	'000 t	1 370	1 273	1 179	1 083	1 194
Non-metals						
Asbestos trioxide	'000 t	710	714	686	686	601
Barite	'000 t	51	39	44	47	32
Gemstones	t	488	901	452	542	515
Gypsum	'000 t	8 814	8 180	7 978	6 727	6 892
Nepheline syenite	'000 t	540	551	533	486	566
Peat	'000 t	736	821	775	833	856
Potash (K$_2$O)	'000 t	8 154	7 014	7 345	7 087	7 324
Salt	'000 t	10 687	11 158	11 191	11 871	11 100
Soapstone, talc	'000 t	146	145	131	115	122
Sodium sulphate	'000 t	331	327	347	335	280
Sulphur in smelter gases	'000 t	856	809	790	749	774
Sulphur elemental	'000 t	5 981	5 750	5 822	6 180	6 350
Structural materials						
Clay products[2],[3]		. .	. .	. .	. .	. .
Cement	'000 t	12 350	12 591	11 745	9 372	8 484
Lime	'000 t	2 518	2	2 341	2 375	2 383
Sand and gravel[4]	'000 t	287 653	244	244 316	215 576[r]	201 082
Stone	'000 t	120 126	119 335	111 355[r]	87 807[r]	81 639
Coal	'000 t	70 644	70 527	68 332	71 133	64 550

[1] *Excludes petroleum and natural gas.*
[2] *Confidential.*
[3] *Bentonite and diatomite are included in clay products.*
[4] *Quartz is included in sand and gravel.*

17.4 VALUE OF MINERAL PRODUCTION[1] (THOUSAND DOLLARS)

	1988	1989	1990	1991	1992ᵖ
Metals					
Antimony	8,094	6,957	1,188	897	574
Bismuth	2,811	2,315	664	446	589
Cadmium	31,747	28,027	11,588	7,724	3,240
Cobalt	45,090	45,781	49,563	77,549	136,886
Copper	2,393,568	2,388,748	2,428,935	2,112,152	2,062,873
Gold	2,331,989	2,315,860	2,407,654	2,349,872	2,086,803
Iron Ore	1,323,249	1,369,193	1,258,792	1,228,188	1,129,371
Lead	356,064	279,643	279,346	210,886	230,923
Molybdenum	121,105	111,728	84,721	65,928	62,866
Nickel	2,790,417	3,042,278	2,027,917	1,807,619	1,679,853
Platinum group	190,914	141,730	189,423	150,155	117,099
Selenium	8,790	4,138	6,867	3,937	4,715
Silver	386,271	274,737	249,746	187,676	173,219
Tantalum	1,695	10,540	8,762	10,254	5,222
Tellurium	1,007	591	994	1,128	1,982
Uranium	1,018,665	912,684	887,975	595,467	575,587
Zinc	2,264,611	2,739,182	2,272,649	1,385,167	1,727,150
Non-metals					
Asbestos	251,088	289,153	272,102	271,030	235,760
Barite	4,014	3,069	3,130	3,013	2,854
Gemstones	2,143	3,238	918	663	582
Gypsum	85,650	85,713	80,080	71,654	79,206
Nepheline syenite	21,775	23,077	23,651	25,105	28,711
Peat	82,832	99,666	89,735	100,133	108,199
Potash (K_2O)	1,167,747	1,017,525	964,920	931,932	963,260
Salt	246,722	275,618	240,890	259,166	253,802
Soapstone, talc	16,023	15,108	13,895	13,278	13,481
Sodium sulphate	25,016	26,344	27,088	25,457	21,038
Sulphur in smelter gases	85,179	86,909	81,229	89,187	79,155
Sulphur elemental	444,007	419,541	368,864	335,381	131,385
Structural materials					
Clay products[2]	196,724	200,138	136,029	119,838	117,326
Cement	971,293	960,000	991,442	810,769	739,211
Lime	191,672	201,571	188,283	193,541	182,834
Sand and gravel[3]	865,900	874,078	817,317	737,728	637,035
Stone	637,993	667,178	663,354ʳ	539,569	507,645
Coal	1,804,330	1,907,080	1,823,700	1,916,780	1,663,300
Total, all minerals[4]	20,986,106	21,455,902	19,612,259ʳ	17,172,985	16,255,923

[1] *Excludes petroleum and natural gas.*
[2] *Bentonite and diatomite are included in clay products.*
[3] *Quartz is included in sand and gravel.*
[4] *Confidential data excluded at commodity level, but included in totals.*

17.5 COPPER, PRODUCERS' SHIPMENTS (TONNES)

	1986	1987	1988	1989	1990	1991	1992
Newfoundland	—	—	—	—	—	—	—
Nova Scotia	—	[1]	[1]	[1]	[1]	[1]	—
New Brunswick	6 298	7 233	7 966	7 802	8 620	28 356	15 597
Quebec	51 622	66 848	47 633	65 135	99 198	308 370	92 114
Ontario	264 870	287 354	286 536	271 914	273 448	708 862	258 547
Manitoba	65 369	66 121	53 072	50 484	55 506	148 525	60 581
Saskatchewan	3 506	2 335	2 168	[1]	[1]	[1]	120
Alberta	—	—	—	—	—	—	—
British Columbia	306 855	364 134	360 570	308 348	333 883	1 055	317 729
Yukon	6	[1]	[1]	—	—	—	—
Northwest Territories	1	2	1	—	—	—	—
Canada	698 527	794 149	758 478	704 432	771 433	780 362	744 687

[1] *Confidential.*

17.6 NICKEL, PRODUCERS' SHIPMENTS (TONNES)

	1986	1987	1988	1989	1990	1991	1992
Ontario	121 851	130 171	128 558	130 632	128 828	125 790	124 181
Manitoba	41 788	58 915	70 186	64 922	66 176	62 309	64 871
Canada	163 639	189 086	198 744	195 554	195 004	188 098	189 051

17.7 IRON ORE SHIPMENTS AND PRODUCTION OF PIG IRON AND STEEL INGOTS AND CASTINGS (THOUSAND TONNES)

	1986	1987	1988	1989	1990	1991	1992[p]
Iron ore shipments							
Newfoundland	19 184	18 423	20 507	20 662	18 969	19 799	18 399
Quebec	13 471	15 988	16 433	15 363	15 306	14 905	13 861
Ontario	3 461	3 229	2 934	3 347	1 294	650	450
British Columbia	51	61	59	73	100	67	62
Canada	36 167	37 702	39 934	39 445	35 670	35 421	32 772
Production							
Pig iron	9 249	9 719	9 498	10 139	7 346	8 268	8 621
Steel ingots and castings	14 081	14 737	14 866	15 332[1]	12 281	12 987	13 933

[1] *Steel castings excluded due to confidentiality.*

17.8 LEAD, PRODUCERS' SHIPMENTS (TONNES)

	1986	1987	1988	1989	1990	1991	1992p
Newfoundland	—	—	—	—	—	—	—
Prince Edward Island	—	—	—	—	—	—	—
Nova Scotia	—	1	—	—	1	1	1
New Brunswick	66 590	66 485	74 543	65 180	56 244	51 957	77 374
Quebec	—	—	—	—	—	—	—
Ontario	6 288	6 092	2 485	1 074	1	1	1
Manitoba	590	1	457	1 365	1 755	2 286	1 722
Saskatchewan	—	—	—	—	—	—	—
Alberta	—	—	—	—	—	—	—
British Columbia	91 947	57 078	105 103	67 006	19 312	63 385	73 991
Yukon	35 091	1	117 058	94 529	104 181	93 912	125 924
Northwest Territories	133 836	131 744	51 502	39 734	46 588	35 388	39 140
Canada	334 342	373 215	351 148	268 887	233 372	248 102	318 515

[1] *Confidential.*

17.9 ZINC, PRODUCERS' SHIPMENTS (TONNES)

	1986	1987	1988	1989	1990	1991	1992p
Newfoundland	5 712	7 643	31 817	27 362	16 463	—	—
Prince Edward Island	—	—	—	—	—	—	—
Nova Scotia	—	—	1	1	1	1	1
New Brunswick	161 807	180 298	261 089	201 550	233 933	209 790	294 978
Quebec	37 126	91 139	82 031	100 638	120 599	117 404	101 832
Ontario	265 248	294 309	326 698	266 158	276 110	213 599	190 822
Manitoba	61 463	63 551	53 746	72 096	77 507	88 486	85 263
Saskatchewan	3 527	1 764	1	1	1	1	1
Alberta	—	—	—	—	—	—	—
British Columbia	137 583	114 117	142 833	119 376	59346	125 980	130 088
Yukon	50 634	147 045	143 939	154 709	168 846	149 487	209 263
Northwest Territories	265 073	258 070	325 321	329 001	218 241	173 154	180 708
Canada	988 173	1 157 936	1 370 000	1 272 854	1 179 372	1 083 008	1 193 607

[1] *Confidential.*

17.10 GOLD, PRODUCERS' SHIPMENTS (KILOGRAMS)

	1986	1987	1988	1989	1990	1991	1992[p]
Newfoundland	—	[1]	[1]	[1]	[1]	[1]	[1]
Prince Edward Island	—	—	—	—	—	—	—
Nova Scotia	—	[1]	[1]	[1]	—	—	—
New Brunswick	374	[1]	393	359	[1]	[1]	[1]
Quebec	28 342	29 543	33 538	36 966	40 675	51 923	44 544
Ontario	46 279	52 917	62 463	78 675	79 968	77 170	73 928
Manitoba	2 555	3 697	4 469	4 056	2 680	2 921	2 629
Saskatchewan	14	1 048	1 480	2 829	3 374	2 899	1 834
Alberta	36	43	27	25	32	34	35
British Columbia	9 249	11 224	13 067	15 635	16 105	18 331	15 261
Yukon	3 547	4 674	5 052	5 652	4 639	3 865	3 831
Northwest Territories	12 503	11 740	11 880	12 208	15 557	16 752	13 799
Canada	102 899	115 818	134 813	159 494	167 373	176 126	157 554

[1] *Confidential.*

17.11 SILVER, PRODUCERS' SHIPMENTS (KILOGRAMS)

	1986	1987	1988	1989	1990	1991	1992[p]
Newfoundland	—	—	[1]	[1]	[1]	[1]	[1]
Prince Edward Island	—	—	—	—	—	—	—
Nova Scotia	—	[1]	[1]	[1]	[1]	[1]	[1]
New Brunswick	163 000	182 139	202 635	191 381	144 513	158 366	238 823
Quebec	62 000	162 596	139 665	147 804	163 509	164 032	137 574
Ontario	348 000	440 819	434 325	348 528	329 777	293 861	212 681
Manitoba	37 000	40 992	32 257	36 205	40 643	42 956	43 682
Saskatchewan	3 000	1 762	[1]	[1]	[1]	[1]	[1]
Alberta	—	[1]	—	—	—	—	—
British Columbia	380 000	400 650	446 864	498 013	597 930	497 417	373 006
Yukon	73 000	132 822	159 135	70 944	83 938	86 631	117 904
Northwest Territories	22 000	12 988	25 867	18 246	19 119	16 966	23 357
Canada	1 088 000	1 374 946	1 443 166	1 312 433	1 381 257	1 261 359	1 147 383

[1] *Confidential.*

17.12 URANIUM(U³O⁸), PRODUCERS' SHIPMENTS (TONNES)

	1986	1987	1988	1989	1990	1991	1992ᵖ
Ontario	4 752	4 901	3 872	4 099	4 598	1 251	988
Saskatchewan	6 750	8 711	8 194	6 896	5 123	6 911	8 069
Canada	11 502	13 612	12 066	10 995	9 720	8 162	9 057

17.13 SALT, PRODUCERS' SHIPMENTS (THOUSAND TONNES)

	1986	1987	1988	1989	1990	1991	1992ᵖ
Nova Scotia	1	1	1	1	1	1	1
New Brunswick	1	1	1	1	1	1	1
Quebec	1	1	1	1	1	1	1
Ontario	6 240	5 690	6 599	7 282	6 143	7 182	6 648
Saskatchewan	473	460	410	312	603	566	544
Alberta	1 304	1 191	1 256	1 426	1 326	1 245	1 245
Canada	10 332	10 129	10 687	11 057	11 191	11 871	11 100

¹ *Confidential.*

Sources
Energy, Mines and Resources Canada

DARWIN WIGGETT / FIRST LIGHT

CHAPTER EIGHTEEN INDUSTRY AND BUSINESS

INTRODUCTION

Canada's business firms are as diverse as its geography and people, ranging from multi-national enterprises whose activities span the globe to the local shoe repair shop. Almost all, however, have faced an increasingly difficult business climate in recent years as the headwinds of recession gathered force. Different industries were affected differently. Many traditional industries in manufacturing felt the recession's grip late in the 1980s, while smaller firms in the services sector were especially hard-hit in 1991.

Interestingly, it was the non-traditional approaches to business that fared relatively well in this recession. For example, co-operatives have flourished, non-traditional retailing (such as direct mail and telephone orders and vending machines) have gained market shares, while large chain stores have tumbled.

The need to adapt and adopt new techniques in the increasingly competitive environment that businesses face is also reflected in the growing demand for business services, such as computer services, advertising, accounting, lawyers and consultants. This industry has grown rapidly in recent years, despite the fall of corporate profits to their lowest levels since the 1930s. This growth also may reflect a determination by firms to improve productivity, through the better use of computer technology and more flexible use of labour. The willingness of Canadian firms to innovate and change augurs well for their prospects in the coming decade.

MANUFACTURING SLUMPS

The recession that ushered in the 1990s dealt a serious blow to Canada's manufacturing sector. This sector includes 22 industry groups that produce goods for both industrial and consumer use. In 1990, it registered its first decline since the 1982 recession with the value of shipments slipping to $298.9 billion. This was a drop of 3.2% from the 1989 total of $308.8 billion. In contrast, the last three years of the 1980s all saw increases in the value of shipments, the high point being 1988 with a jump of 9.5%.

MAJOR INDUSTRY GROUPS

The primary metals group (mostly steel and smelting) suffered the greatest setback. The value of shipments for this group slumped 15.9% to $19.2 billion. Primary textiles was the next hardest hit group with an 11.7% drop to $2.8 billion. Other groups with important losses were: leather and allied products (down 9.9% to $1.2 billion); non-metallic mineral products (down 7.4% to $7.4 billion); paper and allied products (down 7% to $24 billion); and fabricated metal products (down 6.7% to $17.9 billion).

The big winner in 1990, among manufacturing groups, was refined petroleum and coal products. This group posted a whopping increase in shipments of 24.1% to $18.6 billion. The growth was temporary, however, since it was largely due to the sharp rise in the world price of oil following the Iraqi invasion of Kuwait in August 1990. The only other groups to record gains were tobacco products (up 3.6% to $1.9 billion), food industries (up 1.5% to $38.6 billion) and printing, publishing and allied industries (up 1.3% to $13.7 billion), all industries which are largely immune to recession — people have to eat, for example.

PROVINCIAL HIGHLIGHTS

Newfoundland took the worst recessionary beating with a 6.2% drop in manufactured shipments to $1.6 billion in 1990. Prince Edward Island was second with a 5% tumble to $0.4 billion. Ontario and British Columbia each suffered drops of 4.7% to $156 billion and $25.3 billion respectively. They were followed by Manitoba (down 3.5% to $6.7 billion) and Quebec (down 2% to $74 billion).

The strongest performers in 1990, in percentage terms, were the two northern territories. Yukon enjoyed shipment increases of 16.4% to $19 million, while the Northwest Territories experienced a 12.9% rise to $56 million. Only two provinces, both in the West, posted gains. Alberta shipments climbed 4.9% to $20 billion and Saskatchewan's went up slightly (1%) to $3.8 billion.

Roth & Ramberg

Pop cans.

CORPORATE OFFICE

Lynne Cohen / CMCP

Not surprisingly, the biggest losses in primary metals occurred in Ontario and Quebec, the main producers of these goods. Ontario's shipments were down 18.1%, Quebec's by 15.4%. The decrease in primary textiles was also concentrated in Ontario (22.2%) and Quebec (12.4%). Losses in leather and allied goods were also most severe in the two central provinces, with Ontario falling by 16.5%, and Quebec by 2.6%. In the non-metallic minerals group, Ontario accounted for the bulk of the national decline with a drop of 11.5%. As well, almost all losses in fabricated metals occurred in Ontario (declining 10.3%).

British Columbia and Ontario produce half of Canada's paper and allied products. These two provinces therefore had the heaviest losses in shipments of these goods; British Columbia (15%) and Ontario (6.7%).

Ontario, Quebec, British Columbia and Alberta continue to dominate the Canadian manufacturing scene. Ontario accounts for slightly over half of all manufacturing (52.2%), while Quebec accounts for just less than 25%. The only other provinces with significant manufacturing are British Columbia (8.7%) and Alberta (6.7%).

Lawrence Weissmann / CMCP

From the photographic series *Any Old Thing.*

SERVICES — THE EMERGING GIANT

The service sector encompasses everything from ad agencies to auto repairs, computer programming to cat grooming. In 1990, a record 71.2% of all jobs were in services, compared to just under 16% in manufacturing. The trend toward a bigger service sector seems ongoing.

Despite the diversity of service businesses in Canada, they can be grouped broadly into leisure and personal services; food and beverage services; accommodation services; and business services. Statistics Canada tracks a wide range of services offered to businesses and households.

LEISURE AND PERSONAL There are two main groups in this category: amusement and recreation, and personal and household services. Activities can therefore range from hiring a cleaner to renting a video. In some cases, such as linen supply, business use can be significant.

In 1990, these two groups lost some growth momentum, compared with the previous year, but still moved forward, as total revenues increased by 9% to $12.4 billion. The year before, growth stood at 11%. The slowdown was evident throughout the two groups.

In 1990, the amusement and recreation group, with over 18,000 firms, earned $7.5 billion, with close to a third from the motion picture production, distribution and exhibition industries.

Small businesses (those earning less than $2 million annually) were again the main generators of wealth in this industry group, contributing nearly 55% of total revenues. A few large firms (those with revenues of over $5 million) dominated some industries, for example motion picture distributing, while a host of small firms such as barber and beauty shops were the main force of other industries.

FOOD AND BEVERAGE When it came to wining and dining, there is no doubt that the recession slowed things down, as consumers reined in their appetites for fine food and drink. In 1991, total receipts for the restaurant industry were $17.9 billion, a decrease of 7.5% over the previous year. Of this total, licensed restaurants accounted for $8 billion, unlicensed restaurants $4.9 billion, take-out food services $2.2 billion, caterers $1.6 billion, and taverns $1.2 billion. Licensed and unlicensed restaurants reported the largest drops in business — declines of 8.9% and 6.1% respectively.

ACCOMMODATION Accommodating people away from home depends mostly on tourism, which is slow to respond to changes in the economy. In 1990, the estimated revenues for the entire accommodation service industry reached $8.6 billion in 1990, up 6% from the previous year and down only 2% from 1989.

The increase was mainly in the hotels and motels industry, which accounted for 75% of the accommodation group. Over 50% of these revenues were earned by large firms earning more than $5 million. Smaller businesses dominated all the other accommodation industries.

BUSINESS Business services refer to those industries which primarily provide services to the business community, rather than to the general public. They include computer services, employment agencies, engineering and architectural firms, ad agencies, consulting firms, and so on.

BORDERLINE BARGAINS

Clara Gutsche / MCPC

S & B Grocery and Fruit Market, Montreal. Most cross-border shoppers are after the staples: groceries and gasoline.

Cross-border shopping, which has risen relentlessly in recent years, is estimated to drain billions of dollars a year from the Canadian economy. In 1993, the trend appeared to be reversing.

A weakened Canadian dollar has partly stemmed the flow of southbound shoppers. In late 1991, the Canadian dollar stood at 89 cents US and by late 1992, it had dropped to less than 79 cents. With this kind of drop, shoppers are finding they don't have the same purchasing power they once did.

This is good news for Canadian retailers, especially those in border communities. Already battered by the recession, retailers had been watching from the sidelines as more Canadians took their business south.

But now they're optimistic that some of the business may be returning. In 1992, the number of same-day automobile visits to the United States declined by almost 4% — the first decline since 1984. But despite the decline, the number of same-day automobile trips to the United States remains high — over 55 million trips were made by Canadians in 1992, more than twice as many as in 1986.

Stepped-up border measures — including the collection of some provincial sales taxes — have also been credited with keeping more Canadians at home.

And Canadian businesses are getting tougher. With sales declining, many stores have lowered profit margins, focussing promotional efforts on luring back shoppers.

Most cross-border shoppers, especially those from border communities, are after the staples: groceries and gasoline. Those who travel from afar make less frequent, but more expensive trips to the United States.

Despite the downturn in the number of cross-border shoppers in 1992, Canadian retailers are still far from claiming victory. Canadians still spend more while in the United States than in the past. In 1992, the average spend per trip was $30, well up from the 1986 average of $10.

Ron Watts / First Light

In 1989, total revenues for this industry were $42 billion. These are based on preliminary estimates. The business services group comprises about 110,000 firms. The big growth industry was computer services. Spurred by the advent of powerful, inexpensive computers and flexible, user-friendly software, computer service revenues tripled and employment doubled between 1983 and 1989.

Small businesses (those with revenues under $2 million) accounted for nearly half of total earnings for the whole industry. A few large firms tend to dominate portions of the sector, for instance computer services and consulting engineering. A large number of smaller firms provide building and dwelling services, photography services, advertising services, and a wide range of repair services.

MERCHANDISING

Merchandising extends from the shop floor of a major retail business to the corner store. The merchandising industry also covers the principal links in the marketing chain: the wholesalers and the retailers who bring goods from shop floor to corner store. It is the wholesalers who buy in bulk for resale to the retailers, manufacturers, farmers (for use in farm production) and other wholesale merchants. Wholesalers may also act as agents or brokers between individuals or companies on a commission basis.

Retailers, on the other hand, deal directly with the consumer, buying commodities for resale to the general public for personal or household consumption. They market their wares through traditional retail stores (anything from department store chains to the corner kiosk) or through channels such as catalogue sales and machine vending.

WHOLESALE TRADE

From 1986 to 1989, wholesale trade volume climbed by about 27%, reaching $298.8 billion. The value of goods passing through the wholesale sector is not the same as the total volume of wholesale trade; wholesale businesses sometimes sell to each other, which means that the value of the merchandise could be recorded more than once.

WHOLESALE MERCHANTS Wholesale merchants accounted for about 87% (some $261.4 billion) of wholesale trade in 1989. Within this group, the shares of certain sectors have been fairly stable in recent years. Sales of all types of machinery accounted for 21% of total volume in 1989. Food followed at 17.1%. The next most important sectors were petroleum products and other wholesalers.

Quebec and Ontario merchants had the lion's share of business — 67.2% of total volume in 1989, virtually the same as in 1988. All provinces except Saskatchewan had increases. Yukon and the Northwest Territories declined after a sharp increase in 1988.

AGENTS AND BROKERS The volume of trade for agents and brokers inched up by nearly 4% from 1986 to 1989, while gross commissions leapt by 18%. In 1989, the 3,544 establishments classified as agents and brokers reported a total volume of $37.4 billion. Gross commissions for the year were $1.2 billion, or 3.5% of the value of goods bought or sold on commission — up from 3.1% in 1988. The farm products group ranked first with commissions of $225.5 million, up 43% from 1988. The coal, coke and petroleum products group ranked second with $188.4 million in commissions, up 22% from 1988.

Ontario and Quebec together accounted for 56.1% of commissions in 1989, with Quebec increasing very slightly and Ontario decreasing significantly from 1988. Several other provinces reported increased commissions in 1989.

RETAIL TRADE The upward trend in retail sales that lasted through most of the 1980s came to a halt in 1990 and 1991. By 1991, total retail sales had plunged to $181.2 billion.

Just about everyone suffered losses, with a few exceptions. Supermarkets and grocery stores as well as drugs and patent medicine stores managed to emerge unscathed, but other trade groups saw sales plummet, with declines ranging from 22.2% for household furnishings stores to 3.1% for merchandise stores (which include department stores). Car dealerships, including sellers of motor and recreational vehicles, were the most recession-battered of all, registering a staggering $4 billion decrease in sales.

Every province showed a retail sales slump in 1991. Ontario, which has the largest retail market in Canada, was the biggest loser with a $5.4 billion, or 7.5%, decrease in sales. Quebec, Canada's second largest retailing province, saw sales fall by $2.7 billion, or 5.7%.

In 1991, Alberta led in retail sales per capita ($7,513), followed by British Columbia ($7,313), and Ontario ($6,774). The national average was $6,711.

New Motor Vehicles Sold in Canada

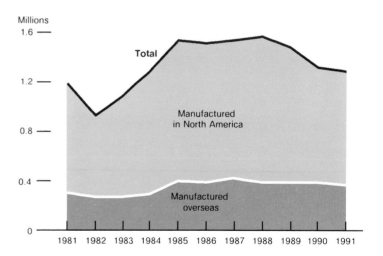

National Archives of Canada C 97797

Thrift stamp poster, circa 1914 — 1918.

TRADITIONAL RETAILING In recent years, supermarkets and grocery stores have pulled ahead of car dealerships in the race for consumer dollars. From 1988 to 1991, the supermarket and grocery store trade group gradually grew stronger to claim one-quarter of the retail trade market. The motor vehicle and recreational vehicle dealer trade group, on the other hand, slipped several percentage points to one-fifth of the market share. The third largest group continued to be merchandise stores.

Retail sales of new cars tell much about the state of Canada's economy. As major consumer goods, they are a large chunk of Gross Domestic Product (GDP) and an important indicator of economic performance. After a strong recovery from the 1982 recession, the demand for new cars shifted into reverse, starting in 1988. From 1988 to 1991, annual new motor vehicle sales fell by 278,000 to 1.3 million units, a decrease of 17.7%. Over this period, new passenger car sales dropped by 183,000 units (a 17.3% decrease) and sales of trucks and buses (including mini-vans) declined by 95,000 units (an 18.6% decrease).

Of the vehicles that Canadians have been buying since 1988, fewer are made in North America. Between 1988 and 1991 the Canadian market share for new cars manufactured in North America dropped from 75.7% to 71.5%. By 1991, sales of overseas vehicles accounted for 28.5% of the Canadian market, up from 24.3% in 1988.

Department stores are the dominant force among merchandise stores, the third biggest retail group. Between 1987 and 1990, 'junior' or discount department stores grew in strength, bringing in 43.6% of department store sales in 1990. Meanwhile, the major department stores lost market share.

NON-STORE RETAILING The traditional storefront is just one of many ways to reach consumers. Others include telephone and mail orders, pre-arranged home delivery, sales from outdoor markets and vending machines. In all these cases, the producer, manufacturer, importer wholesaler or specialized direct seller brings goods directly to consumers. Compared with traditional stores, this retail sector fared well in recession-rocked 1990.

In 1990, sales made through vending machines totalled $480 million, an increase of 8.7% from 1989.

Direct selling accounted for $3.2 billion in purchases by Canadian householders in 1990, a 4.6% increase from 1989. Two-thirds of this retail pie was shared about evenly between personal sales (individual canvassing or group demonstrations) and mail and telephone orders. The remainder was divided among other direct selling methods such as sales from manufacturing premises, home delivery and outdoor markets.

CO-OPERATIVES "Practice self-help." This was the maxim of Father James Tompkins, a pioneering educator and co-operatives founder in Nova Scotia in the 1920s. The terse slogan aptly sums up what the co-operative movement is all about. A more official definition for today's co-op is "an incorporated, non-profit business organized to meet the economic, social or cultural needs of its members". All members share control over and responsibility for the enterprise, as well as benefits and risks.

Co-operatives were started in Canada in the mid-1800s by farmers banding together in shared enterprises for mutual benefit. Early co-ops were involved in processing cream, grading eggs and marketing grain. Over the decades, co-operative principles have been applied to many economic and social activities — credit, insurance, marketing, energy supply, housing, health and day care, to name a few. The co-operative movement is now an important force in the Canadian economy and includes some 10,000 organizations.

Co-operatives fall into three main categories: marketing co-operatives that help members sell their output; consumer and supply co-operatives that provide goods to members; and associations that offer members services such as transportation, power, housing, and child care.

In 1990, business volume of Canada's non-financial co-operatives rose by 3.6% to $15.9 billion. It was the fourth year of moderate growth.

Production and services groups had the most successful year with revenue gains of $61 million and $133 million respectively — a 15% increase for both groups. The business volume of consumer co-ops climbed 7% to $214 million, while the marketing group rose 3% to $273 million. The supply and fishing groups both suffered revenue setbacks of 5%. This was due to a lower volume of agricultural supplies and farm machinery for the supply group and fewer fish products harvested by the fishing group.

The number of co-operatives reporting rose by almost 300, or better than 6% in 1990. Reported membership of non-financial co-operatives rose by 185,000, or almost 6%, for the year.

While non-financial co-operative assets rose by 6.5% to $8.9 billion, the asset increase for the overall co-operative sector including credit unions, caisse populaires, insurance and other financial co-ops rose by $15.6 billion or 14.7%.

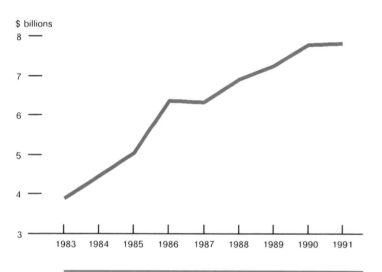

Receipts on Travel Between Canada and Other Countries

$ billions

FAMILY CO-OPERATIVES Two types of co-operatives — housing and day care — have a big impact on the quality of family life in Canada. Housing co-ops began in the 1930s when individuals created 'sweat equity' — working together to build one another's homes and share costs, but assuming individual ownership on completion.

By December 1990, Canada had 1,387 housing co-operatives which provided more than 57,000 occupied housing units. Another 183 incorporated co-operatives had 6,970 units under construction or renovation and more than 7,500 units in various stages of planning. The total value of these co-ops was estimated at $2.2 billion. They have created 500 permanent full-time jobs, while the building of housing co-ops generated 60,000 person years of employment.

But these units provide much more than shelter and jobs. Social benefits include creating supportive environments for single parents, women with housing problems, persons with disabilities and new immigrants. Co-ops that include a mix of people with different income levels can help in the integration and community acceptance of social housing.

Housing co-operative revenues in 1990 were up by $76 million, making this sector the biggest contributor to the overall gain in business volume by service co-operatives.

Child care co-ops went through a growth spurt during the past decade. In 1990, there were 339 day care/nursery school co-ops reporting with over 25,500 members and revenues of $29.2 million. Most of this amount — $20.8 million — was for salaries and wages.

The two major types of child care co-ops in Canada are day care centres and nursery schools. The day care co-op provides day-time care for children of parents who have jobs. The nursery school emphasizes education and social interaction, as well as providing parents some time for other pursuits.

WELCOME INVADERS Tourists are the welcome invaders, and together they contribute almost $25 billion to our economy, making tourism one of Canada's key industries.

The tourist dollar goes to many hands — from hotel manager to bellhop, airline company to wilderness outfitter. In fact, some 60,000 Canadian businesses cater to tourists offering accommodation, meals, transportation, entertainment, travel arrangements and other services. Not only do such businesses create employment — 554,000 jobs in 1991 — but also valuable foreign exchange. Tourism was Canada's third biggest earner of foreign exchange in 1991, preceded only by motor vehicles and automobile parts.

The bulk of tourist revenues — more than two thirds — comes from Canadians themselves, travelling on business, visiting friends and relatives, or exploring their own country. In 1991, Canadians spent an estimated $16.8 billion on domestic trips, while foreign visitors brought an additional $7.8 billion to the country. Americans were the most frequent foreign tourists, spending about $3.6 billion during some 12 million trips of one night or more to Canada. Most of these were business travellers, coming generally by car. About 3 million visitors drawn to Canada in 1991 came from overseas. A growing number of overseas travellers are from Asia, and this is likely to be the best potential source of new tourism to Canada in the future.

Tourism is significant for all provincial and territorial economies. For example, in 1990 tourism accounted for between 3% of gross provincial product in Quebec and 6.8% in Prince Edward Island. In 1991, tourism generated $16.5 billion in direct income and $11.1 billion in revenue for all levels of government.

Nonetheless, the recession did make a dent in the tourism industry. For example, in 1989, Canadian and foreign tourists together spent a full $25 billion; in 1991, they spent $24.6 billion. The decline, while slight, was entirely due to belt tightening by Canadians who spent $1 billion less in Canada in 1991 ($16.8 billion) than in 1989. Fortunately, foreign spending rose by $0.6 billion in the same period. Although the overall drop in travel receipts seems fairly low, this does not tell the whole story of the recession's effect on tourism. One must keep in mind that the tourism industry is usually slow to show the impact of economic turnarounds, both upward and downward. This is because people often plan their trips far in advance and do not necessarily cancel at the first sign of an economic slump. But they do shelve or trim down plans for future vacations, and may not upgrade them even when economic recovery is underway. Therefore the full effects of the recession on tourism may not yet have been felt.

Ron Watts / First Light

Office building, Toronto.

FEDERAL GOVERNMENT SERVICES

BUSINESS PROTECTION

The Government of Canada considers certain kinds of innovative products 'intellectual property' and offers their creators legal recognition and protection. Legislation covers patents, trade marks, copyrights, industrial designs and integrated circuit topographies. This legislation is administered through Consumer and Corporate Affairs Canada which also offers information programs on the various forms of intellectual property.

Patents valid for 20 years protect inventions; that is, new kinds of technology. Trade marks are words, symbols, pictures or combinations of these used to distinguish the goods or services of one individual or organization from those of another. Trade mark registrations last for 15 years, with the option to renew for subsequent 15-year periods. Copyrights, issued for literary, artistic, dramatic or musical works and for computer software, generally last for the lifetime of the creator plus an additional 50 years. Industrial designs are for the shape, pattern or ornamentation of an industrially-produced object. Registrations last for five years, and are renewable for a further five years. Integrated circuit topographies refer to the three-dimensional configurations of the electronic circuits used in microchips and semiconductor chips. Registration offers exclusive rights on the design for 10 years.

ENCOURAGING UNIFORMITY

The Standards Council of Canada, a Crown corporation, is a national co-ordinating body that promotes voluntary standardization in Canada. The Council encourages the use of standards to: advance the economy; benefit the health, safety and welfare of the public; facilitate domestic and international trade; and further international co-operation on standards.

To carry out its mandate, the Council created the National Standards System, a federation of organizations with expertise in standards writing, certification and testing. The Council also co-ordinates the work of Canadians in international standards-writing organizations.

INDUSTRY, SCIENCE AND TECHNOLOGY CANADA

Established on February 23, 1990, this department works with the private sector, the science community and other levels of government. Its mandate is to promote international competitiveness and industrial excellence in Canada; to build Canada's scientific, technological, managerial and production base; and to bring together the talents required to safeguard Canada's place in the first rank of industrial nations. The department is also the chief advocate within government for Canada's business and scientific communities in areas such as taxation and regulation.

The department achieves its goals by supporting strategic technologies, helping increase sector competitiveness and providing business information and development services.

FEDERAL BUSINESS DEVELOPMENT BANK

The Federal Business Development Bank (FBDB) promotes the establishment and development of business in Canada, especially small and medium-sized businesses, by providing loans, guarantees and venture capital. It also offers extensive management counselling, training and planning services.

PROVINCIAL GOVERNMENT SERVICES

While federal government efforts to encourage and assist business have a national focus, each province has its own policies and programs. Common objectives of these programs are regional development and job creation. In most provinces, several agencies work in partnership with business to accomplish these aims.

Some provincial programs focus on market development within the province, in Canada or internationally. Many programs encourage the introduction of new technology, while others focus on helping businesses create innovative products. Some provinces offer businesses tax incentives or reduced rent in industrial malls, industrial parks and incubator malls. Financial assistance, accompanied by services

Larry Goldstein / Image Finders

Granite quarry.

such as consultation and market information, is available in all provinces. Other provinces have special agencies or banks willing to take an equity position in new ventures or expansions.

REGULATIONS

Consumer and Corporate Affairs Canada (CCAC) administers broad legislation affecting the marketplace through four bureaus: Strategic and Corporate Services; Corporate Affairs and Legislative Policy; Competition Policy; and Consumer Affairs. The department's policies and programs benefit both consumers and the business community by helping to create a fair and competitive marketplace.

TRADE The Hazardous Products Act regulates household, garden and personal-use products, as well as those used by children, or in sports and recreational activities. The Act also covers poisonous, toxic, flammable, explosive and corrosive products. The Minister of Consumer and Corporate Affairs is empowered to establish mandatory standards. These have included a ban on the use of small parts in infants' toys, flammability standards for children's sleepwear and mandatory warning labels on dangerous chemicals. Rigid specifications cover such products as strollers, playpens, rattles and cribs, as well as hockey helmets, glazed ceramics and cellulose insulation.

The Consumer Packaging and Labelling Act is designed to give uniformity to packaging and labelling practices in Canada, to reduce the possibilities of fraud and deception in packaging and labelling, and to limit the number of package sizes. This Act is just one of several pieces of legislation that regulate the quality, quantity, composition, packaging, labelling and advertising of food products in Canada.

The Textile Labelling Act requires all consumer textiles to have labels identifying the dealer and the percentages of all fibres used in the product. It also covers misrepresentation in labelling and advertising. Other systems have been adopted voluntarily for textiles, including a textile care labelling system and a standard size system for children's garments. The latter is administered under the National Trade Mark and True Labelling Act.

The marking of articles made from precious metals is covered by the Precious Metals Marking Act.

COMPETITION The 1986 Competition Act was designed to encourage competition in Canada. Strong competition promotes economic efficiency and adaptability, expands opportunities for Canadian firms in world markets, ensures that small and medium-sized businesses have an equitable opportunity to participate in the Canadian economy, and ensures competitive prices and product choices for consumers. This Act prohibits price maintenance, bid-rigging, predatory pricing, misleading advertising and conspiracy to unduly lessen competition. It also covers tied selling, delivered pricing, abuses of a dominant position, mergers and specialization agreements.

MEASUREMENT Supported by a number of pieces of legislation, CCAC's Legal Metrology Branch minimizes inaccurate measurement and ensures equity in the trade of commodities and services. Measurement control is accomplished by defining units of measure, calibrating and certifying standards, inspecting and approving new trade devices for compliance with regulations, and verifying approved devices before they are used.

SOURCES

Agriculture Canada

Consumer and Corporate Affairs Canada

Federal Business Development Bank

Industry, Science and Technology — Tourism

Standards Council of Canada

Statistics Canada

FOR FURTHER READING

Selected publications from Statistics Canada

▲ *Manufacturing Industries of Canada, National and Provincial Areas. Annual. 31-203*

▲ *Manufacturing Industries of Canada, Sub-provincial Areas. Annual. 31-209*

▲ *Industrial Organization and Concentration in the Manufacturing, Mining and Logging Industries. Biennial, 31-402*

▲ *Retail Chain and Department Stores. Annual. 63-210*

▲ *Direct Selling in Canada. Annual. 63-218*

▲ *Computer Service Industry. Annual. 63-222*

▲ *Market Research Handbook. Annual. 63-224*

▲ *Wholesale Trade Statistics, Wholesale Merchants, Agents and Brokers. Annual. 63-226*

TABLES

18.1   VALUE OF SHIPMENTS OF GOODS OF OWN MANUFACTURE (MILLION DOLLARS)

	1986	1987	1988	1989	1990
Newfoundland	1,423.7	1,655.1	1,726.0	1,653.6	1,551.8
Prince Edward Island	325.8	362.5	391.7	417.3	396.4
Nova Scotia	4,650.0	4,745.6	4,790.6	5,181.4	5,150.1
New Brunswick	4,909.3	5,634.7	5,627.7	5,884.6	5,865.5
Quebec	61,101.3	66,454.1	73,631.4	75,465.1	73,973.6
Ontario	136,847.6	143,394.9	157,675.5	163,713.1	155,995.2
Manitoba	5,649.4	6,248.1	6,671.0	6,984.1	6,739.5
Saskatchewan	3,058.9	3,285.9	3,380.1	3,748.7	3,786.0
Alberta	15,175.4	16,421.8	18,078.8	19,111.0	20,048.8
British Columbia	20,224.3	23,368.9	25,510.1	26,580.2	25,335.9
Yukon and Northwest Territories	45.1	55.5	57.0	66.3	75.4
Canada	253,410.6	271,627.0	297,539.8	308,805.4	298,918.2

18.2   VALUE OF SHIPMENTS OF GOODS OF OWN MANUFACTURE (MILLION DOLLARS)

Industry group	1986	1988	1989	1990
Food	34,143.6	37,116.1	38,015.7	38,582.5
Beverage	5,045.1	5,865.4	5,779.6	5,620.6
Tobacco products	1,623.2	1,778.6	1,817.9	1,883.3
Rubber products	2,643.6	2,694.7	2,675.8	2,557.9
Plastic products	4,384.7	5,893.1	6,289.3	5,996.8
Leather and allied products	1,324.8	1,293.3	1,289.5	1,162.3
Primary textile	2,957.5	3,173.3	3,146.2	2,779.6
Textile products	2,893.0	3,411.0	3,478.1	3,363.6
Clothing	6,015.6	6,656.7	6,948.1	6,831.3
Wood	12,432.6	15,322.2	15,843.2	14,805.9
Furniture and fixture	4,012.0	4,619.7	4,902.8	4,661.9
Paper and allied products	20,066.7	25,661.1	25,847.5	24,026.3
Printing, publishing and allied	10,370.8	12,525.7	13,531.1	13,703.9
Primary metal	17,109.0	22,715.4	22,884.5	19,243.8
Fabricated metal products	15,024.3	17,946.3	19,154.3	17,876.9
Machinery	8,099.0	10,012.3	10,995.5	10,396.1
Transportation equipment	44,399.8	51,718.1	53,783.3	51,654.9
Electrical and electronic products	14,304.0	18,191.7	19,488.8	18,474.8
Non-metallic mineral products	6,632.0	7,803.6	7,983.7	7,391.6
Refined petroleum and coal products	15,756.4	14,273.8	14,958.7	18,569.5
Chemical and chemical products	18,639.2	22,775.3	23,667.7	23,117.9
Other manufacturing	5,533.5	6,092.3	6,324.0	6,217.2
All manufacturing	253,410.6	297,539.8	308,805.3	298,918.5

18.3 VALUE OF SHIPMENTS OF GOODS OF OWN MANUFACTURE, 1990 (MILLION DOLLARS)

Industry group	Nfld.	PEI	NS	NB	Que.	Ont.
Food	696.6	288.5	1,247.2	1,174.3	9,593.2	15,359.5
Beverage	[1]	[1]	139.3	137.8	1,579.3	2,507.6
Tobacco products	—	—	—	—	[1]	[1]
Rubber products	—	—	[1]	[1]	[1]	1,352.3
Plastic products	7.5	—	63.0	49.7	1,452.5	3,454.8
Leather and allied products	[1]	—	[1]	[1]	527.0	520.9
Primary textile	—	[1]	[1]	[1]	1,426.5	1,166.9
Textile products	1.6	[1]	96.7	[1]	1,641.6	1,376.3
Clothing	1.2	1.1	51.2	21.1	4,270.5	1,731.6
Wood	32.1	13.5	147.5	449.3	3,404.4	2,729.8
Furniture and fixture	2.4	—	28.1	22.2	1,458.5	2,532.0
Paper and allied products	[1]	[1]	629.8	1,514.2	7,549.9	7,606.4
Printing, publishing and allied	53.7	17.6	162.1	107.6	3,623.0	7,286.1
Primary metal	[1]	—	[1]	[1]	6,236.1	10,139.7
Fabricated metal products	40.2	8.9	122.6	206.5	4,072.7	10,370.3
Machinery	[1]	[1]	31.9	65.9	2,045.3	5,913.5
Transportation equipment	[1]	5.5	[1]	[1]	6,319.0	41,825.0
Electrical and electronic products	[1]	[1]	136.0	25.7	4,837.1	11,576.8
Non-metallic mineral products	50.6	4.1	115.1	106.7	1,632.9	3,786.2
Refined petroleum and coal products	[1]	—	[1]	[1]	3,514.8	7,198.0
Chemical and chemical products	15.4	24.6	65.1	95.8	5,630.6	12,813.1
Other manufacturing	9.2	7.6	[1]	58.3	[1]	[1]
All manufacturing	1,551.8	396.4	5,150.5	5,865.5	73,973.6	155,995.2

Industry group	Man.	Sask.	Alta.	BC	YT and NWT	Canada
Food	1,488.7	1,076.7	4,490.5	3,167.3	. .	38,582.5
Beverage	152.6	84.6	398.2	492.8	—	5,620.6
Tobacco products	—	—	—	[1]	—	1,883.3
Rubber products	[1]	[1]	[1]	38.1	—	2,557.9
Plastic products	203.1	31.3	299.6	435.3	—	5,996.8
Leather and allied products	40.7	5.8	24.0	21.2	—	1,162.3
Primary textile	[1]	—	[1]	22.2	—	2,779.6
Textile products	54.1	13.7	66.2	108.8	—	3,363.6
Clothing	323.8	16.8	157.3	256.8	—	6,831.3
Wood	209.5	124.8	933.4	6,161.7	. .	14,805.9
Furniture and fixture	149.1	8.1	240.9	220.8	—	4,661.9
Paper and allied products	305.8	[1]	795.5	4,912.1	—	24,026.3
Printing, publishing and allied	482.3	213.5	771.3	986.6	. .	13,703.9
Primary metal	559.5	[1]	873.8	909.6	—	19,243.8
Fabricated metal products	411.1	176.9	117.6	1,350.1	—	17,876.9
Machinery	523.9	221.2	798.3	782.1	—	10,396.1
Transportation equipment	763.8	95.4	296.2	922.4	—	51,654.9
Electrical and electronic products	562.8	236.2	608.6	472.2	—	18,474.8
Non-metallic mineral products	152.8	85.3	665.2	792.8	. .	7,391.6
Refined petroleum and coal products	[1]	[1]	3,749.2	1,709.6	—	18,569.5
Chemical and chemical products	240.9	203.4	3,311.1	717.7	[1]	23,117.9
Other manufacturing	84.2	33.1	298.0	255.9	[1]	6,217.2
All manufacturing	6,739.5	3,786.0	20,048.8	25,355.9	75.4	298,918.5

[1] *Confidential.*

18.4 ANNUAL CENSUS OF MANUFACTURERS[1]

	Establishments no.	Production and related workers			Cost of fuel and electricity[2,3] $'000	Cost of materials and supplies used $'000	Value of shipments of goods and of own manufacture $'000	Value added $'000
		Number	Person-hours paid '000	Wages $'000				
					Manufacturing activity			
1980	35,495	1,346,187	2,780,203	22,162,309	4,448,859	99,897,576	168,058,662	65,851,774
1981	35,780	1,337,433	2,755,669	24,539,352	5,468,509	114,283,081	191,029,704	74,050,661
1982	35,834	1,212,424	2,473,214	24,261,593	6,028,226	111,971,399	187,932,882	69,052,759
1982[4]	34,121	1,205,859	2,460,189	24,180,897	6,020,309	111,834,089	187,710,349	68,988,161
1983	35,287	1,193,912	2,455,229	25,763,545	6,637,059	119,759,106	203,366,412	76,895,569
1984	36,464	1,240,816	2,583,486	28,294,557	7,256,843	136,122,271	230,228,931	88,732,913
1985	36,854	1,305,159	2,734,519	31,072,594	7,408,353	145,790,922r	248,717,511r	95,880,165r
1986	38,380	1,351,563	2,852,525	33,081,693	6,999,645	146,336,148	253,410,556	102,459,302
1987	36,790	..	..	..	7,052,909	152,487,615	271,701,852	112,641,123
1988	40,262	1,473,102	3,086,436	38,849,955	7,363,310	166,496,490	297,539,750	124,541,854
1989	39,150	1,495,937	3,124,874	41,374,136	7,717,419	174,775,257	308,805,314	124,406,618
1990	39,864	1,393,324	2,893,337	40,406,450	7,936,055	168,664,306	298,918,513	122,972,463

	Establishments no.	Working owners and partners		Total employees[5]		Cost of materials and supplies used and goods purchased for resale[6] $'000	Value of shipments and other revenue[7] $'000	Value added[8] $'000
		Number	Withdrawals '000	Number	Salaries and wages $'000			
					Total activity			
1980	35,495	6,385	..	1,850,436	33,133,061	121,105,853	193,310,632	69,895,467
1981	35,780	5,930	..	1,853,968	37,106,195	137,410,611	218,550,416	78,443,843
1982[4]	35,834	5,405	..	1,709,418	37,712,333	134,108,948	214,429,419	73,411,747
1982	34,121	4,342	..	1,702,303	37,624,733	133,965,324	214,201,297	73,347,874
1983	35,287	4,539	..	1,671,140	39,609,111	143,453,528	231,884,329	81,719,064
1984	36,464	4,711	..	1,722,045	43,076,019	164,912,102	264,395,795	94,109,946
1985	36,854	..	..	1,766,763	46,208,030	179,244,505r	287,654,289r	101,363,360r
1986	38,380	..	..	1,808,716	48,749,085	178,740,310	293,937,278	107,581,862
1987	36,790	..	..	1,863,507	51,819,089	189,145,595	314,074,337	118,355,628
1988	40,262	..	..	1,946,702	56,792,397	205,706,663	344,125,984	131,917,915
1989	39,150	..	..	1,970,259	60,250,138	214,376,709	356,662,144	135,661,996
1990	39,864	..	..	1,868,983	59,992,094	205,818,935	344,033,336	130,932,657

[1] *Statistics for the years 1970–82 were compiled on the basis of the 1970 edition of the Standard Industrial Classification (SIC), while data for the 1982 (restated) and subsequent years have been compiled on the basis of the 1980 revision of the Standard Industrial Classification. Thus 1982 is a link year to which the reader may refer to measure the impact of the change in classification on the various manufacturing statistics.*

[2] *Cannot be reported separately for manufacturing and non-manufacturing activities but related substantially to manufacturing activity.*

[3] *From 1970–81 inclusive, the cost of fuel and electricity was not collected separately for small firms and was included in the cost of materials and supplies used.*

[4] *Data for 1982 restated to the 1980 revision of the Standard Industrial Classification.*

[5] *Includes production and related workers, administrative and office employees, sales, distribution and other employees; excludes working owners and partners.*

[6] *Includes supplies used in both manufacturing and non-manufacturing activity.*

[7] *Includes shipments of goods of own manufacture, value of shipments of goods purchased for resale and other operational revenue.*

[8] *Value of total operational revenue less total costs of materials, supplies, fuel and electricity used and goods purchased for resale in the same condition; all adjusted for inventory changes where required.*

18.5   ESTABLISHMENTS IN MANUFACTURING, 1990

Industry group	Establishments with total employment of									
	Under 5	5 to 9	10 to 19	20 to 49	50 to 99	100 to 199	200 to 499	500 to 999	1,000 or over	Total
Food	581	581	636	732	427	241	162	29	8	3,397
Beverage	43	34	32	69	33	29	15	3	2	260
Tobacco products	4	1	1	2	2	3	2	3	—	18
Rubber products	20	26	34	40	21	12	11	7	7	178
Plastic products	195	185	262	322	208	93	27	2	—	1,294
Leather and allied products	81	54	46	67	43	30	15	1	1	338
Primary textile	31	31	22	48	34	28	24	4	1	223
Textile products	230	196	169	178	100	54	31	2	—	960
Clothing	614	481	482	658	313	156	75	5	1	2,785
Wood	842	636	639	677	326	199	84	6	—	3,409
Furniture and fixture	564	359	304	372	220	84	30	6	—	1,939
Paper and allied products	58	56	97	155	118	98	82	53	14	731
Printing, publishing and allied	1861	1312	949	830	310	172	63	17	8	5,522
Primary metal	59	53	64	89	72	46	57	15	19	474
Fabricated metal products	1425	1266	1221	1265	564	211	65	12	1	6,030
Machinery	402	354	457	552	241	121	51	10	1	2,189
Transportation equipment	331	215	212	313	185	143	122	45	33	1,599
Electrical and electronic products	304	246	245	344	192	144	98	30	15	1,618
Non-metallic mineral products	358	359	329	378	157	75	29	6	—	1,691
Refined petroleum and coal products	38	17	25	22	8	12	13	2	1	138
Chemical and chemical products	273	263	253	295	165	91	87	19	4	1,450
Other manufacturing	1408	766	589	525	203	91	36	1	2	3,621

18.6   NUMBER OF EMPLOYEES, 1990

Industry group	Nfld.	PEI	NS	NB	Que.	Ont.
Food	9,998	2,257	10,479	9,251	45,445	76,927
Beverage	[1]	[1]	656	640	8,502	9,069
Tobacco products	—	—	—	—	[1]	[1]
Rubber products	—	—	[1]	[1]	[1]	13,356
Plastic products	74	—	610	384	13,184	29,693
Leather and allied products	[1]	—	[1]	[1]	7,186	8,327
Primary textile	—	[1]	[1]	[1]	11,250	8,469
Textile products	24	[1]	1,156	[1]	15,921	14,698
Clothing	34	36	997	847	58,794	29,555
Wood	438	211	1,859	4,084	30,320	27,353
Furniture and fixture	46	—	354	296	18,678	32,179
Paper and allied products	[1]	[1]	3,252	6,582	40,227	39,708
Printing, publishing and allied	733	249	2,291	1,532	34,683	73,563
Primary metal	[1]	[1]	[1]	[1]	27,579	54,055
Fabricated metal products	466	123	1,571	1,674	37,954	97,317
Machinery	[1]	[1]	566	723	16,304	47,280
Transportation equipment	[1]	71	[1]	[1]	41,044	158,227
Electrical and electronic products	[1]	[1]	1,329	281	35,687	89,837
Non-metallic mineral products	468	49	916	925	13,021	28,358
Refined petroleum and coal products	[1]	[1]	[1]	[1]	1,801	7,305
Chemical and chemical products	77	128	425	399	27,206	55,291
Other manufacturing	207	126	[1]	881	[1]	[1]
All manufacturing	16,343	3,486	37,264	34,007	512 541	945,930

18.6 **NUMBER OF EMPLOYEES, 1990** (concluded)

Industry group	Man.	Sask.	Alta.	BC	Yukon and NWT	Canada
Food	7,804	4,195	13,910	17,579	. .	197,845
Beverage	517	424	1,356	2,213	—	23,859
Tobacco products	—	—	—	116	—	4,928
Rubber products	1	1	1	583	—	24,826
Plastic products	1,828	261	2,051	3,797	—	51,882
Leather and allied products	388	47	237	216	—	16,709
Primary textile	1	—	1	258	—	20,762
Textile products	697	126	1,012	1,563	—	35,278
Clothing	5,835	300	1,955	5,075	—	103,431
Wood	2,303	1,248	7,362	40,312	. .	115,490
Furniture and fixture	1,907	121	2,888	2,641	—	59,110
Paper and allied products	1,666	1	2,536	18,427	—	115,176
Printing, publishing and allied	5,504	2,863	9,396	11,156	. .	141,970
Primary metal	2,093	1	3,632	6,887	—	96,667
Fabricated metal products	4,392	1,655	10,660	11,010	—	166,822
Machinery	3,919	2,317	7,088	6,940	—	85,300
Transportation equipment	7,216	854	3,648	7,329	—	226,712
Electrical and electronic products	2,780	1,474	4,647	5,241	—	141,418
Non-metallic mineral products	1,230	776	4,213	4,649	. .	54,605
Refined petroleum and coal products	1	1	3,945	984	—	15,868
Chemical and chemical products	1,173	609	6,229	3,351	1	94,888
Other manufacturing	1,298	563	3,983	4,141	1	75,437
All manufacturing	52,863	20,234	91,404	154,468	443	1,868,983

[1] *Confidential.*

18.7 **BUSINESSES AND REVENUES FOR LEISURE AND PERSONAL SERVICE INDUSTRIES**

	1986		1989		1990	
	No.	$'000,000	No.	$'000,000	No.	$'000,000
Motion picture, audio and video production and distribution	930	1,129.5	904	1,951.4	1,035	2,188.5
Motion picture exhibition	897	403.4	773	563.9	742	581.8
Theatrical and other staged entertainment services	2,420	420.3	6,365	760.6	6,697	855.2
Commercial spectator sports	979	529.8	1,170	730.3	1,407	789.9
Sports and recreation clubs and services	2,879	962.6	3,529	1,570.5	3,774	1,743.5
Other amusement and recreational services	4,337	799.3	4,629	1,269.6	4,797	1,356.2
Barber and beauty shops	12,334	1,174.9	15,601	1,536.4	16,161	1,612.1
Laundries and cleaners	5,240	1,192.3	5,608	1,487.7	5,921	1,572.2
Funeral services	1,389	588.3	1,243	737.9	1,187	806.4
Other personal and household services	3,813	485.4	6,110	747.0	6,361	844.7

18.8 **RECEIPTS OF FOOD AND BEVERAGE SERVICE INDUSTRIES, 1991** (MILLION DOLLARS)

Province	Restaurants, licensed	Restaurants, unlicensed	Take-out food services	Caterers	Taverns, bars and night clubs	Total
Newfoundland	41,312.9	45,519.8	43,780.7	27,154.9	37,221.6	194,989.9
Prince Edward Island	22,033.9	22,183.3	10,735.7	3,636.0	4,545.4	63,134.3
Nova Scotia	123,636.0	127,145.0	85,325.9	35,474.6	41,063.8	412,645.3
New Brunswick	68,383.3	103,651.4	82,946.5	36,482.3	34,064.7	325,528.2
Quebec	1,866,051.0	1,227,431.8	381,051.0	274,807.3	475,987.2	4,225,328.3
Ontario	3,240,185.5	1,841,293.9	1,123,303.2	743,335.3	310,001.1	7,258,119.0
Manitoba	163,225.4	216,632.2	59,641.2	49,389.6	18,035.9	506,924.3
Saskatchewan	174,125.2	206,172.6	53,112.0	26,749.8	14,278.0	474,437.6
Alberta	1,023,809.4	480,014.7	177,523.6	143,221.0	33,612.2	1,858,180.9
British Columbia	1,236,677.6	626,139.4	228,426.5	207,655.6	191,496.8	2,490,395.9
Yukon and Northwest Territories	18,577.7	7,645.4	2,689.2	9,692.1	3,336.8	41,941.2
Canada	7,978,017.9	4,903,829.5	2,248,535.5	1,557,598.5	1,163,643.5	17,851,624.9

18.9 **REVENUES OF ACCOMMODATION SERVICE INDUSTRIES, 1990** (MILLION DOLLARS)

	Hotels and motor hotels	Motels	Camping grounds and travel trailer parks	Recreation and vacation camps	Tourist courts, cabins, guest houses, tourist homes, lodging houses and residential clubs	Total
Newfoundland	73.1	29.7	[1]	[1]	6.2	113.5
Prince Edward Island	21.8	13.2	4.1	[1]	[1]	42.2
Nova Scotia	133.9	47.5	9.0	[1]	[1]	197.1
New Brunswick	78.9	50.1	5.8	[1]	[1]	144.1
Quebec	1,186.0	220.9	41.6	68.1	41.4	1,558.0
Ontario	1,967.3	355.1	133.8	141.9	106.9	2,704.9
Manitoba	417.1	26.5	11.6	19.9	8.7	483.8
Saskatchewan	335.6	32.7	9.3	15.0	3.9	396.5
Alberta	1,056.1	106.9	36.9	13.0	11.1	1,224.2
British Columbia	1,250.7	214.9	55.9	66.3	26.5	1,614.4
Yukon	47.5	[1]	6.5	5.6	[1]	73.7
Northwest Territories	46.3	[1]	[1]	12.6	[1]	70.4
Canada	6,614.4	118.1	317.6	349.9	222.8	8,622.8

[1] *Confidential.*

18.10 BUSINESSES AND REVENUES FOR BUSINESS SERVICE INDUSTRIES

	1986		1988		1989	
	No.	$'000,000	No.	$'000,000	No.	$'000,000
Employment agencies and personnel suppliers	1,637	1,186.0	2,145	1,784	2,094	2,177
Computer and related services	5,276	3,467.3	9,381	4,679	9,694	5,514
Advertising services	4,712	1,871.6	7,598	2,679	8,202	9,186
Architectural, engineering and other scientific and technical services	11,706	. .	. .	. .	. .	. .
Other business services	24,052	4,873.3	31,117	6,462	34,149	7,623
Machinery and equipment rental and leasing services	6,565	1,850.7	6,802	2,541	6,793	2,914
Automobile and truck rental and leasing services	2,480	2,061.1	2,707	2,683	2,684	3,065
Photographers	2,359	375.1	2,816	462	3,160	507
Other repair services	6,235	963.9	7,528	1,291	8,234	1,469
Services to buildings and dwellings	8,839	1,534.1	12,051	2,006	12,707	2,211
Travel services	3,714	2,899.9	4,072	3,695	4,208	4,207

18.11 WHOLESALE MERCHANT ESTABLISHMENTS, VOLUME OF TRADE[1]
(MILLION DOLLARS)

	1986	1987	1988	1989
Newfoundland	1,531	1,682	2,112	2,275
Prince Edward Island	322	337	409	516
Nova Scotia	2,363	2,992	3,893	4,206
New Brunswick	3,572	3,885	3,821	4,052
Quebec	42,405	47,648	53,460	55,271
Ontario	87,946	98,424	108,743	120,455
Manitoba	16,709	15,435	15,080	17,154
Saskatchewan	6,974	7,242	8,019	7,706
Alberta	17,248	19,206	18,406	22,750
British Columbia	20,403	23,050	26,116	26,772
Yukon and Northwest Territories	151	138	249	193
Farm products	15,855	16,427	16,478	17,119
Coal,coke and petroleum products	23,192	25,317	25,137	28,849
Paper and paper products	4,075	4,670	5,587	4,742
General merchandise	2	2	2	2
Food	33,291	36,140	40,835	44,739
Tobacco products, drugs and toilet preparations	6,598	7,085	7,738	8,299
Apparel and dry goods	4,658	5,072	5,300	5,764
Household furniture and house furnishings	2,356	2,625	3,014	3,472
Motor vehicle and accessories	17,836	19,407	21,350	23,361
Electrical machinery, equipment and supplies	15,716	17,850	21,151	23,281
Farm machinery	5,467	5,313	5,233	5,522
Machinery and equipment	19,438	22,228	24,278	26,196
Hardware, plumbing and heating equipment	6,390	7,565	8,826	9,590
Metals and metal products	2	2	2	2
Lumber and building materials	15,748	18,518	19,249	19,692
Scrap and waste materials	2	2	2	2
Other wholesalers	19,105	21,858	23,801	26,328
Canada	199,622	220,038	240,307	261,349

[1] *Sales and trading receipts, and the value of goods bought or sold on commission.*
[2] *Confidential.*

18.12 AGENTS AND BROKERS, VOLUME OF TRADE[1] (MILLION DOLLARS)

	1986	1987	1988	1989
Newfoundland	294.2	262.9	290.2	306.8
Prince Edward Island	60.8	54.6	77.7	49.6
Nova Scotia	659.7	640.0	701.9	750.8
New Brunswick	277.5	211.9	210.4	250.6
Quebec	7,636.5	7,788.1	7,759.5	7,511.5
Ontario	15,195.2	17,241.7	19,594.7	17,313.5
Manitoba	1,813.9	1,835.2	1,959.9	2,547.3
Saskatchewan	1,281.5	1,307.5	1,216.8	1,315.7
Alberta	4,652.6	3,991.7	4,403.5	3,005.9
British Columbia	4,071.3	4,386.9	4,675.3	4,283.2
Yukon and Northwest Territories	59.4	69.6	132.5	55.5
Farm products	8,360.5	8,251.5	8,526.8	8,869.1
Coal, coke and petroleum products	3,902.4	5,958.8	4,768.7	2,841.8
Paper and paper products	667.4	729.9	540.4	545.9
General merchandise	2	2	2	2
Food	7,431.2	6,970.1	7,812.9	5,796.2
Tobacco products, drugs and toilet preparations	215.9	220.6	245.3	626.1
Apparel and dry goods	2,315.1	2,047.1	2,090.1	2,128.6
Household furniture and house furnishings	934.1	959.2	1,165.4	1,307.5
Motor vehicle and accessories	1,189.4	1,000.9	923.7	1,260.9
Electrical machinery, equipment and supplies	2,184.9	1,901.8	1,956.1	2,022.5
Farm machinery	43.7	55.4	69.6	93.7
Machinery and equipment	544.3	674.4	1,371.1	1,627.3
Hardware, plumbing and heating equipment	2,073.8	2,309.6	2,428.4	2,728.7
Metals and metal products	2	2	2	2
Lumber and building materials	1,332.1	1,657.1	1,699.2	1,778.8
Scrap and waste materials	2	2	2	2
Other wholesalers	2,131.4	2,252.7	3,627.9	1,902.2
Canada	36,002.5	37,790.2	41,022.7	37,390.5

[1] *Sales and trading receipts including value of goods or sold on commission.*
[2] *Confidential.*

18.13 AGENTS AND BROKERS, GROSS COMMISSIONS EARNED (MIILION DOLLARS)

	1986	1987	1988	1989
Newfoundland	16.1	18.2	23.0	18.8
Prince Edward Island	1	1	1	1
Nova Scotia	25.8	24.0	23.8	30.0
New Brunswick	14.2	11.4	8.0	11.6
Quebec	215.7	215.3	234.3	235.5
Ontario	390.5	396.2	546.6	456.6
Manitoba	73.2	72.8	67.1	148.9
Saskatchewan	43.3	40.6	33.2	49.3
Alberta	103.6	96.1	102.4	118.2
British Columbia	158.4	161.9	160.3	159.8
Yukon and Northwest Territories	1	1	1	1
Farm products	165.8	155.6	159.1	225.5
Coal,coke and petroleum products	212.1	184.7	154.3	188.4
Paper and paper products	23.2	24.9	18.1	17.8
General merchandise	1	1	1	1
Food	136.0	139.1	150.7	157.6
Tobacco products, drugs and toilet preparations	13.4	13.5	15.0	15.9
Apparel and dry goods	112.9	102.5	103.5	106.7
Household furniture and house furnishings	39.8	40.9	48.0	45.6
Motor vehicle and accessories	31.3	34.3	36.3	42.6
Electrical machinery, equipment and supplies	63.9	60.6	84.7	94.4
Farm machinery	2.7	3.2	3.9	5.3
Machinery and equipment	38.8	47.6	72.2	74.5
Hardware, plumbing and heating equipment	54.2	55.2	58.3	63.8
Metals and metal products	1	1	1	1
Lumber and building materials	38.1	50.8	58.1	54.6
Scrap and waste materials	1	1	1	1
Other wholesalers	95.3	104.3	208.6	108.9
Canada	1,045.6	1,041.1	1,203.8	1,234.7

[1] *Confidential.*

18.14 RETAIL TRADE (MILLION DOLLARS)

	1988	1989	1990	1991
Supermarkets and grocery stores	39,709	40,741	42,475	43,512
All other food stores	3,318	3,739	3,946	3,579
Drugs and patent medicine stores	8,311	8,965	9,476	9,795
Shoe stores	1,738	1,819	1,826	1,590
Men's clothing stores	1,975	2,046	2,076	1,713
Women's clothing stores	3,926	4,003	4,000	3,691
Other clothing stores	3,738	3,956	4,017	3,756
Household furniture and appliance stores	8,401	8,838	8,597	7,412
Household furnishings stores	2,441	2,538	2,612	2,033
Motor vehicle and recreational vehicle dealers	41,978	42,894	41,695	37,689
Gasoline service stations	13,588	14,362	15,355	14,288
Automotive parts, accessories and services	10,923	11,811	12,321	10,610
General merchandise stores	19,871	20,533	21,354	20,683
Other semi-durable goods stores	6,496	7,006	6,951	5,977
Other durable goods stores	5,238	5,572	5,475	4,876
Other retail stores	10,002	10,480	10,384	10,003
Total	181,652	189,302	192,558	181,208

18.15 RETAIL TRADE (MILLION DOLLARS)

	1988	1989	1990	1991
Newfoundland	3,168	3,356	3,527	3,394
Prince Edward Island	760	788	818	759
Nova Scotia	6,034	6,210	6,215	5,851
New Brunswick	4,418	4,621	4,777	4,595
Quebec	46,583	47,192	47,578	44,850
Ontario	69,791	72,568	72,568	67,160
Manitoba	6,337	6,599	6,596	6,277
Saskatchewan	5,677	5,758	5,689	5,308
Alberta	17,563	18,875	20,023	18,950
British Columbia	20,802	22,791	24,200	23,537
Yukon and Northwest Territories	518	545	567	527
Canada	181,652	189,302	192,558	181,208

18.16 RETAIL SALES OF NEW MOTOR VEHICLES IN CANADA BY ORIGIN OF MANUFACTURE

	Passenger cars		Trucks and buses		Total	
	North America	Overseas	North America	Overseas	North America	Overseas
Vehicles (no.)						
1981	646,942	257,253	250,775	35,912	897,717	293,165
1982	489,435	224,046	166,986	40,435	656,421	264,481
1983	625,088	218,230	192,609	45,161	817,697	263,391
1984	724,932	246,278	273,604	38,688	998,536	284,966
1985	794,965	342,251	344,871	48,323	1,139,836	390,574
1986	761,169	334,144	368,423	52,184	1,129,592	386,328
1987	700,930	364,163	417,189	51,355	1,118,119	415,518
1988	724,733	331,577	459,777	49,414	1,184,510	380,991
1989	675,340	312,794	422,398	73,343	1,097,738	386,137
1990	580,397	304,167	361,403	71,902	941,800	376,069
1991	573,297	299,887	347,671	66,935	920,968	366,822
Sales ($'000)						
1981	6,033,437	2,239,092	3,334,406	311,460	9,367,843	2,550,552
1982	4,856,340	2,181,224	2,423,014	363,393	7,279,354	2,544,617
1983	6,700,490	2,340,886	2,728,842	426,108	9,429,332	2,766,994
1984	8,176,591	2,962,340	4,136,482	404,347	12,313,073	3,366,687
1985	9,545,156	4,162,481	5,641,518	540,964	15,186,674	4,703,445
1986	9,856,682	4,813,044	6,441,811	729,994	16,298,493	5,543,038
1987	10,031,339	5,717,071	7,930,141	793,211	17,961,480	6,510,282
1988	11,080,866	5,628,616	9,369,531	786,323	20,450,397	6,414,939
1989	11,034,685	5,507,114	9,059,489	1,358,096	20,094,174	6,865,210
1990	9,784,294	5,461,544	8,210,503	1,432,412	17,994,797	6,893,956
1991	9,038,584	5,064,965	7,492,699	1,248,423	16,531,283	6,313,388

18.17 DEPARTMENT STORE SALES (MILLION DOLLARS)

	1987	1988	1989	1990
Women's, misses' and children's clothing				
Women's and misses' dresses, housedresses, aprons and uniforms	198.4	192.9	195.8	154.7
Women's and misses' coats and suits	211.1	200.5	194.2	200.9
Women's and misses' sportswear	869.0	862.4	951.5	1,009.8
Furs	32.6	32.6	26.0	18.3
Infants' and children's wear and nursery equipment	389.7	421.3	516.9	580.3
Girls' and teenage girls' wear	229.7	236.2	226.4	223.2
Lingerie and women's sleepwear	257.7	267.0	256.6	264.1
Intimate apparel	177.0	183.7	194.0	212.2
Millinery	17.2	18.1	22.7	22.5
Women's and girls' hosiery	150.0	165.6	169.9	174.5
Women's and girls' gloves, mitts and accessories	233.6	229.8	229.1	231.0
Women's, misses' and children's footwear	382.2	376.9	341.4	356.3
Total, women's, misses' and children's clothing	3,148.2	3,187.0	3,324.5	3,447.8
Men's and boys' clothing				
Men's clothing	418.9	413.1	306.5	283.1
Men's furnishings	871.6	892.4	955.8	974.4
Boys' clothing and furnishings	228.2	229.1	259.0	250.9
Men's and boys' footwear	223.5	232.2	200.7	197.7
Total men's and boys' clothing	1,742.2	1,766.8	1,722.0	1,706.1
Food and kindred products	441.8	311.2	339.0	374.4
Toiletries, cosmetics and drugs	780.5	836.9	891.6	955.9
Photographic equipment and supplies	131.2	128.6	133.7	134.9
Piece goods	47.3	44.3	41.1	35.4
Linens and domestics	439.1	464.5	521.6	563.2
Smallwares and notions	113.2	113.6	126.9	124.6
China and glassware	175.4	185.7	224.9	223.4
Floor coverings	158.1	167.6	173.1	161.7
Draperies, curtains and furniture covers	190.0	190.8	184.4	177.9
Lamps, pictures, mirrors and all other home furnishings	124.4	129.0	119.7	128.2
Furniture	612.8	668.0	698.1	676.3
Major appliances	563.3	599.6	624.3	589.6
Television, radio and music	549.0	602.1	657.0	681.5
Housewares and small electrical appliances	519.0	548.8	501.3	524.7
Hardware, paints and wallpaper	372.4	382.0	439.9	427.9
Plumbing, heating and building materials	155.9	162.4	146.9	130.9
Jewellery	326.1	314.5	310.2	305.8
Toys and games	410.8	391.9	381.7	408.7
Sporting goods and luggage	356.4	392.7	522.0	527.2
Stationery, books and magazines	403.9	419.7	414.2	422.9
Gasoline, oil, auto accessories, repairs and supplies	155.6	159.5	155.9	163.5
Receipts from meals and lunches	258.1	258.0	259.4	258.2
Receipts from repairs and services	237.2	280.9	337.5	343.1
All other departments	494.0	564.8	663.2	699.1
Total, all departments	12,905.9	13,270.9	13,914.1	14,192.9

18.18   SALES THROUGH VENDING MACHINES

Commodity	1989		1990		Percent change 1989–90
	$'000	%	$'000	%	
Cigarettes	90,586	20.5	91,197	19.0	0.7
Beverages					
Coffee	128,546	29.1	137,230	28.6	6.8
Soft drinks					
Canned or bottled	85,519	19.4	110,442	23.0	29.1
Disposable cups	12,913	2.9	10,922	2.3	−15.4
Packaged milk	5,023	1.1	4,469	0.9	−11.0
Other beverages	7,878	1.8	9,856	2.1	25.1
Confectionery and food					
Bulk confectionery	10,521	2.4	10,042	2.1	−4.6
Packaged confectionery combinations	59,876	13.6	66,466	13.9	11.0
Pastries	4,406	1.0	3,372	0.7	−23.5
Snack foods	3,967	0.9	5,137	1.1	29.5
Hot canned foods and soups	1,350	0.3	1,175	0.2	−13.0
Ice cream	771	0.2	848	0.2	10.0
Fresh foods	28,292	6.4	26,471	5.5	−6.4
All other commodities	1,653	0.4	2,010	0.4	21.6
Total	441,301	100.0	479,637	100.0	8.7

18.19   DIRECT SALES

Commodity	1989		1990		Percent change 1989–90
	$'000	%	$'000	%	
Food and beverages	502,202	16.2	482,274	14.9	−4.0
Clothing, shoes, fur goods	86,715	2.8	142,620	4.4	64.5
Books and encyclopedias	313,685	10.1	321,942	9.9	2.6
Newspapers	428,270	13.8	450,723	13.9	5.2
Magazines	163,389	5.3	189,993	5.9	16.3
Home improvement products, building supplies	126,505	4.1	106,376	3.3	−15.9
Household cleaners, soaps, brushes, etc.	23,077	0.7	28,825	0.9	24.9
Dinnerware, kitchenware and utensils	127,166	4.1	119,080	3.7	−6.4
Furniture, home furnishings and repairs	43,465	1.4	39,481	1.2	−9.2
Electrical appliances	177,452	5.7	148,795	4.6	−16.1
Audio tapes, records and equipment	106,841	3.5	122,765	3.8	14.9
Vidoe tapes, games and equipment	34,040	1.1	44,503	1.4	30.7
Cosmetics	249,687	8.1	264,183	8.2	5.8
Jewellery	55,246	1.8	62,606	1.9	13.3
Canvas products: tents, awnings, sails, etc	20,994	0.7	18,174	0.6	−13.4
Greenhouse and nursery products	150,054	4.8	166,252	5.1	10.8
Orthopedic supplies, artifical limbs, etc.	10,636	0.3	9,221	0.3	−13.3
Monuments and tombstones	21,095	0.7	22,009	0.7	4.3
Toys, games, crafts, cards	90,062	2.9	106,675	3.3	18.4
All other merchandise	365,750	11.8	391,419	12.1	7.0
Total	3,096,331	100.0	3,237,916	100.0	4.6

18.20 CO-OPERATIVES, 1990

	Associations reporting	Membership reported '000	Volume of business $'000,000	Assets $'000,000
Marketing	149	301	8,981.6	2,998.2
Consumer	604	1,846	3,208.5	1,053.3
Supply	220	429	2,072.3	761.5
Fishing	58	9	184.7	90.3
Production	380	21	461.5	216.9
Services	3,069	811	1,023.8	3,736.2
Credit unions/caisses populaires	2,737	9,280	9,012.0	72,246.0
Insurance and other financial co-ops	8	. .	. .	40,444.6
Total	7,225	12,697	24,944.4	121,547.0

18.21 VALUE AND VOLUME OF SALES OF ALCOHOLIC BEVERAGES[1]

Values ($'000)	Spirits			Wines		
	1986-87	1989-90	1990-91	1986-87	1989-90	1990-91
Newfoundland	69,602	79,702	81,338	11,777	13,073	13,245
Prince Edward Island	18,147	19,806	19,223	3,674	4,060	4,118
Nova Scotia	123,365	134,257	131,261	33,780	34,083	33,323
New Brunswick	68,838	70,517	70,319	19,378	22,073	22,547
Quebec	449,200	436,963	402,073	495,248	598,340	603,338
Ontario	1,189,772	1,250,328	1,191,458	516,748	584,822	596,958
Manitoba	152,923	149,090	144,526	43,770	41,698	41,955
Saskatchewan	143,104	140,402	137,677	28,440	24,770	25,840
Alberta	392,876	418,401	423,164	134,854	134,589	138,348
British Columbia	442,909	455,993	467,125	249,921	278,423	290,599
Yukon	6,587	7,099r	7,206	2,386	2,607r	2,743
Northwest Territories	10,654	12,352	12,884	2,416	2,578	2,622
Canada	3,067,977	3,174,910r	3,088,254	1,542,392	1,741,116r	1,775,636

	Beer			Total		
	1986-87	1989-90	1990-91	1986-87	1989-90	1990-91
Newfoundland	144,391	164,373	167,102	225,770	257,148	261,685
Prince Edward Island	20,535	24,828	25,566	42,356	48,694	48,907
Nova Scotia	128,033r	161,898	164,485	285,178	330,238	329,069
New Brunswick	106,554	127,478	131,407	194,770	220,068	224,273
Quebec	1,076,301	1,317,451r	1,420,654	2,020,749	2,352,754r	2,426,065
Ontario	1,512,180	1,919,825	1,957,983	3,218,700	3,754,975	3,746,399
Manitoba	153,185	170,621	166,180	349,878	361,409	352,661
Saskatchewan	131,170	138,346	131,234	302,714	303,518	294,751
Alberta	348,857	418,447	449,781	876,587	971,437	1,011,293
British Columbia	495,433	548,713	592,351	1,188,263	1,283,129	1,350,075
Yukon	7,393	9,254r	9,545	16,366	18,960r	19,494
Northwest Territories	11,022	13,673	14,239	24,092	28,603	29,745
Canada	4,135,054	5,014,907r	5,230,527	8,745,423	9,930,933r	10,094,417

18.21 VALUE AND VOLUME OF SALES OF ALCOHOLIC BEVERAGES[1] (concluded)

Volume ('000 l)	Spirits			Wines		
	1986-87	1989-90	1990-91	1986-87	1989-90	1990-91
Newfoundland	3,706	3,983	3,936	1,691	1,586	1,543
Prince Edward Island	782	771	732	594	596	561
Nova Scotia	6,182	6,233	5,762	5,592	5,119	4,667
New Brunswick	3,379	3,039	2,943	3,267	3,480	3,422
Quebec	21,711	19,749	17,759	72,565	78,589	72,764
Ontario	63,886	63,866	59,700	85,383	80,051	79,166
Manitoba	7,577	7,250	6,908	7,456	5,761	5,586
Saskatchewan	7,553	6,641	6,461	5,102	4,089	3,896
Alberta	21,401	18,875	18,209	22,470	20,080	19,452
British Columbia	23,676	21,163	20,640	48,074	46,143	45,880
Yukon	284	268	261	356	336	335
Northwest Territories	482	533	493	270	257	251
Canada	160,619	152,371	143,804	252,820	246,087	237,523

	Beer			Total		
	1986-87	1989-90	1990-91	1986-87	1989-90	1990-91
Newfoundland	49,528[r]	49,834	48,904	54,925[r]	55,403[r]	54,383
Prince Edward Island	8,694	8,461	8,310	10,070	9,828	9,603
Nova Scotia	62,214	62,313	59,492	73,988	73,665	69,921
New Brunswick	48,701	47,708	46,473	55,347	54,227	52,838
Quebec	538,082	553,539	540,195	632,358	651,877	630,718
Ontario	805,620	829,824	813,304	954,889	973,741	952,170
Manitoba	81,621	74,476	70,946	96,654	87,487	83,440
Saskatchewan	63,248	57,955	54,766	75,903	68,685	65,123
Alberta	175,023	172,837	177,230	218,894	211,792	214,891
British Columbia	233,549	246,930	254,756	305,299	314,236	321,276
Yukon	3,304	3,617	3,581	3,944	4,221	4,177
Northwest Territories	4,187	4087	3,968	4,939	4,877	4,712
Canada	2,073,771[r]	2,111,581	2,081,925	2,487,210[r]	2,510,039	2,463,252

[1] *Fiscal year ending March 31st except for Alberta which ends December 31st.*

18.22 REVENUE OF PROVINCIAL AND TERRITORIAL GOVERNMENTS[1] DERIVED FROM THE CONTROL AND SALE OF ALCOHOLIC BEVERAGES (THOUSAND DOLLARS)

	1981-82	1986-87	1989-90	1990-91
Newfoundland	53,401	74,360	82,110	82,206
Prince Edward Island	13,759	17,436	19,065	18,781
Nova Scotia	80,028	113,612	121,868	116,491
New Brunswick	54,816	78,609	87,628	85,676
Quebec	289,292	435,198	445,913	453,711
Ontario	677,631	958,194	1,110,439	1,089,807
Manitoba	92,052	142,891	146,994	136,713
Saskatchewan	85,025	123,407	121,777	110,516
Alberta	239,131	324,020	386,247	407,240
British Columbia	334,680	445,296	420,409	450,299
Yukon	6,343	6,671	7,957	8,095
Northwest Territories	7,604	10,180	12,689	14,186
Canada	1,933,762	2,729,874	2,963,096	2,973,721

[1] *Excludes the general sales taxes levied by most provinces.*

Source
Statistics Canada

ROBIN
MERLE D'AMÉRIQUE

W. CODY / FIRST LIGHT

CHAPTER NINETEEN

BANKING AND FINANCING

INTRODUCTION

Canada has one of the most efficient and sound banking and financial sectors in the world. The industry is governed by federal and provincial regulations designed to protect the investments of Canadians, to enable financial institutions to deliver the services Canadians demand and to compete in global markets.

Canada has three major groups of financial institutions. These institutions serve Canadians by providing savings accounts, pensions, insurance, mortgages, consumer loans, and several other kinds of financial services.

The first group consists of institutions that take deposits or make loans: banks, trust and loan companies, *caisses populaires* and credit unions, and some government savings institutions (such as the Ontario Savings Office and Alberta Treasury Branches). It is this group that Canadians are most likely to encounter on an everyday basis. The second group consists of insurance companies and pension funds, while the third group includes investment dealers and investment funds. In addition to these major groups, there are a number of specialized institutions involved in various types of financial services.

The federal government regulates and supervises banks, federally incorporated trust and mortgage loan companies, the Credit Union Central of Canada and some aspects of provincial centrals, and most insurance companies and pension funds. The provincial governments regulate trust and mortgage loan companies and insurance companies incorporated in their jurisdictions, and individual credit unions and provincial centrals. Investment dealers operate mostly under a provincial legislative framework and self-regulation.

In June 1992, the federal government implemented a major overhaul of the legislative framework governing federal financial institutions. These reforms narrow the differences between types of financial institutions, particularly between banks and trust companies, and allow federal institutions to offer most types of financial services, either directly, through a financial institution subsidiary, or as an agent through a networking agreement.

Liberalized cross-ownership rules in the 1992 legislation allow federal financial institutions to own other types of financial institutions. Put simply, a trust company can now own an insurance company, or an insurance company can own a trust company, and so on. Since 1987, federal financial institutions have been allowed to own securities dealers. All the large Canadian banks subsequently acquired or established securities dealers.

The new legislation keeps in place a number of specific ownership regulations, including some governing foreign ownership. Most importantly, Schedule I banks, which include the six largest domestic banks, must still be widely held; that is, no single entity or associated group can own more than 10% of any class of shares.

The 1992 legislation will be reviewed in 1997 and every 10 years afterwards.

THE BANK OF CANADA

THE INSTITUTION Canada's central bank, the Bank of Canada, is at the heart of the Canadian financial system. The Bank of Canada was established in 1934 and was given responsibility for regulating ''credit and currency in the best interests of the economic life of the nation'' (preamble to the Bank of Canada Act). The bank does not carry out ordinary banking business, nor does it accept deposits from the general public. But its actions influence the economic circumstances of businesses and individuals across the country.

Through its responsibility for monetary policy, the Bank of Canada promotes overall economic performance in the best way it can — by seeking to preserve confidence in the value of money. But the Bank of Canada's functions involve a good deal more than monetary policy. The bank acts as the federal government's banker and fiscal agent and is the sole issuer of Canadian bank notes.

The Bank of Canada's Board of Directors plays a central role in the governance of the Bank of Canada. The board is composed of the Governor, the Senior

Benjamin Rondel / First Light

Canadian Imperial Bank of Commerce, Toronto.

National Currency Museum

In 1882, you couldn't say, "phoney as a four-dollar bill" — they existed.

Deputy Governor, 12 directors and the Deputy Minister of Finance (who has no vote). The 12 directors are appointed for three-year terms by the Minister of Finance. Coming from every province and with experience in fields as diverse as farming, business and law, they are an important link between the Bank of Canada and their respective regions. The major role of the directors is to ensure that the bank is being managed competently. They are responsible for appointing or reappointing the Governor and Senior Deputy Governor (with the approval of Cabinet), and for appointing other Deputy Governors. The board approves the corporate objectives, plans and annual budget of the bank.

Directors are not expected to be experts in economics. It is the senior management of the Bank of Canada that formulates and implements monetary policy and reports to the board at regular meetings.

In the Bank of Canada Act, Parliament has defined the relationship between the bank and the government and has placed the bank in a position to carry out its responsibilities independently. For most purposes the bank's accountability as a public institution is through its Board of Directors, but there are special arrangements for monetary policy.

The Minister of Finance and the Governor are expected to meet regularly to discuss monetary policy. If a profound disagreement were to occur over the course of monetary policy that the bank planned to follow, the government could issue a public, written directive to change policy. This provision makes it clear both that the government must take the ultimate responsibility for monetary policy and that the Bank of Canada must accept immediate responsibility so long as a government directive is not in effect.

MONETARY POLICY Monetary policy is about money. The Bank of Canada is concerned with how much money circulates in our economy and how much that money is worth. The bank seeks to protect the value of our currency and provide money that can be used with confidence — money whose value is not eroded by inflation — by influencing the pace of monetary expansion. Inflation creates uncertainty, distorts economic decision-making, and imposes costs unequally on society's members, such as individuals on fixed incomes. (For example, with inflation at 4.5% per year, money loses half of its value in about 15 years.) By fostering price stability, the bank's monetary policy goal is to promote, in the best way it can, good overall economic performance and hence enhance the standard of living of Canadians.

The bank is able to exert influence on the pace of monetary expansion in the economy because it is the source of the ultimate means of payment in the economy, that is, bank notes and the settlement balances of financial institutions. Because the bank can control the supply of settlement balances, the central bank can influence the willingness of banks and other financial institutions in turn to expand the supply of money and credit. This is the fundamental leverage, or monetary policy instrument, that the Bank of Canada has at its disposal to influence developments in the Canadian economy.

The bank affects the amount of liquidity in the financial system in a variety of ways. Its primary method involves the transfer of Government of Canada deposits between the government's account at the Bank of Canada and its accounts at financial institutions. Typically, a transfer of deposits from the government's account at the bank to the financial institutions will provide more liquidity than desired by the financial institutions. This will tend to put downward pressure on very short-term interest rates. The bank can also exert a direct influence on short-term interest rates by its purchase or sale of Government of Canada securities.

Changes in short-term interest rates lead to changes in a broad range of interest rates and in the exchange rate. Movements in these various rates influence the rate of expansion of money and credit and the growth of spending in the economy. The pressure from spending in turn determines the ease with which prices can be increased. Movements in the exchange rate also directly affect the cost of imported and exported goods and the incentive for Canadian producers competing against foreign firms to contain their costs. Over time, too-rapid growth in spending will result in increased inflation, while growth in spending which does not put pressure on prices is much more likely to be sustainable.

BANKING SERVICES The Bank of Canada is at the centre of the nation's financial system. Each day masses of cheques are written by the general public and governments on accounts with Canadian financial institutions and at the end of each day those claims must be settled. The total claim of one institution on another is calculated and a transfer of funds takes place to settle accounts — a transfer that occurs on the books of the Bank of Canada. This is called the payments clearing and settlement process. The Canadian Payments Association, established by an act of Parliament in 1980, manages Canada's payment system.

The Bank of Canada provides very short-term, secured loans to financial institutions to cover overnight shortfalls in liquidity in their settlement accounts at the Bank of Canada arising from the clearing and settlement of payment items. Shortfalls in these accounts may come about because of the need to maintain a certain level of reserves with the Bank of Canada (in the case of banks) or to maintain a non-negative balance in a settlement account at the Bank of Canada (in the case of all financial institutions with accounts at the Bank of Canada).

In addition, the bank may make 'extraordinary' loans to institutions which are solvent but experiencing persistent cash flow difficulties. In this way the Bank of Canada ensures that liquidity problems at individual financial institutions do not threaten their viability or undermine public confidence in the entire financial system.

FISCAL AGENT The Bank of Canada assists the Government of Canada in managing its debt. The government's debt includes treasury bills, which are auctioned weekly, Canada Savings Bonds and other marketable bonds. The bank also acts as an advisor and agent for the Government of Canada in the management of the nation's foreign reserves, including gold reserves, held in the Government's Exchange Fund Account.

Currency Canada's paper currency is the Bank of Canada's best known product. In fact, the signatures of the Governor and Senior Deputy Governor appear on every note. The bank has sole responsibility for issuing bank notes, including their design, production and distribution.

Before the Bank of Canada was established, paper money was issued by a number of banks, other institutions and the Government of Canada. When the bank began operations, it assumed responsibility for all government (Dominion) notes and started issuing

BANK AROUND THE CLOCK

Just 15 years ago, it would have seemed unimaginable that anyone could bank at midnight. After all, banks traditionally closed in the early afternoon. In the last few years, however, Automated Banking Machines (ABMs) have changed all that — Canadians can now bank around the clock.

In fact, in 1991 alone, Canadians made more than 700 million transactions on these little money machines, or almost 30 transactions per person. These transactions included everything from cash withdrawals and deposits to transferring funds and balance inquiries — even paying the utility bills.

Since ABMs were first introduced in Canada in the late 1970s, their numbers have grown substantially. While fewer than 300 such machines were in operation by the end of 1978, more than 14,000 had been installed by January, 1993.

As the number of ABMs has increased, so too have the number of services many ABMs provide. Recent innovations include drive-through ABMs, passbook updates, and the sale of postage stamps and bus passes.

its own notes. A little more than a decade later, on January 1, 1945, the right of chartered banks to issue paper money was revoked. The banks paid the Bank of Canada an amount corresponding to their outstanding note liabilities, and the Bank of Canada assumed responsibility for these notes as of January 1, 1950.

Although both these chartered bank notes and Dominion notes remain legal tender, they are taken out of circulation when they are returned to any financial institution. Gradually, the Bank of Canada has replaced the confusing kaleidoscope of notes which once circulated in Canada with Bank of Canada notes. As of November 1992, bank notes held by the public amounted to $20.2 billion.

The bank stays in close contact with law enforcement agencies to keep more than a few steps ahead of counterfeiters. Paper bills are designed to be difficult to forge and, in recent years, the bank has pioneered the use of an optical security device, which changes colour when tilted, starting on high denomination bills but now to be applied to $20 notes.

THE ROYAL CANADIAN MINT

Canadian coins are issued by the Royal Canadian Mint, a Crown corporation. (A Crown corporation is a legal agency or company through which a federal or provincial government conducts certain activities). The dimensions, designs and denominations of these coins are determined by the Governor-in-Council or by the Royal Canadian Mint Act.

The mint's Winnipeg plant produces the circulating coins while the Ottawa plant does the gold, platinum, and silver bullion investment coins and collectors' products and medals. The Ottawa facility also refines Canadian gold (3.9 million Troy ounces in 1991 and .6 million Troy ounces of refined silver byproduct). The mint reports to Parliament through the Minister of Supply and Services.

The mint produced 809.5 million circulation coins in 1991, compared with 423.4 million in 1990. Significant fluctuation in the demand for any of the denominations can occur each year. For instance, the number of pennies produced to meet demand jumped to

Barbara K. Deans / Canapress

The coin of the realm...

709.3 million in 1991 from 216 million in 1990 and 17 billion in 1989. The 1991 figure, in fact, represents close to the five-year average.

CHARTERED BANKS

In 1992, Canada's chartered banks earned a net income of $1.8 billion. Chartered banks are privately owned institutions chartered by Parliament. They operate under the Bank Act, which sets their powers and regulates their operations. The Bank Act is revised about every 10 years. Canada's chartered bank system consists of 8 Canadian-owned banks with almost 8,000 branch offices, and 54 foreign banks with 271 branches. Some of these banks rank among the largest in the world.

Chartered banks generally accept various kinds of deposits from the public, including accounts payable on demand, chequing and non-chequing notice deposits (notice must be given by the customer a specified amount of time before withdrawal), and fixed-term deposits (repayable after a predetermined date). In addition to holding a portfolio of securities such as bonds and treasury bills, these institutions lend money for commercial, industrial, agricultural and consumer purposes, and may conduct certain kinds of leasing and factoring through subsidiaries.

Factoring refers to the purchase of debts owed to other companies at a discount to make a profit by collecting them. Other services include dealing in foreign exchange, receiving and paying out bank notes, and providing safekeeping facilities. Chartered banks may also own trust and insurance companies.

Alan Marsh / First Light

Toronto Dominion Bank, Yonge Street.

THE FEDERAL BUSINESS DEVELOPMENT BANK

The Federal Business Development Bank (FBDB) is a Crown corporation created in 1974 to lend money or provide equity capital to Canadian companies that have been unable to obtain financing on reasonable terms and conditions from other sources. It also provides consulting and training services to small firms that want to improve their management methods.

TRUST AND MORTGAGE LOAN COMPANIES

Trust and mortgage loan companies hold about two-thirds of Canada's private mortgages. They operate under the Federal Loan Companies Act and the Trust Companies Act or corresponding provincial legislation. They must be licensed by each province in which they operate.

Trust companies do two distinct types of business: financial intermediation and fiduciary (holding assets in trust).

As financial intermediaries, they operate much like chartered banks, accepting funds in exchange for credit instruments such as trust deposits and guaranteed investment certificates. Federal and provincial legislation sets investment restrictions and maximum ratios of funds in guaranteed accounts to shareholders' equity.

Trust companies are the only corporations in Canada with the power to conduct fiduciary business. In this capacity they act as trustees for pension funds and corporate debt issues, and as registrars and transfer agents for corporate share issues.

Trust companies offer a variety of services, but their main business is channelling savings into mortgages. A few have also developed a substantial short-term business, issuing certificates for terms as short as 30 days and operating as lenders in the money market. In addition, trust companies administered estate, trust and agency accounts worth $380.5 billion at the end of 1992.

Trust companies had total assets at the end of 1992 of $122.1 billion, a 3% decrease from 1991. They held 66.0% of their total assets as mortgages, compared to 65.3% in 1991. They held $86.5 billion in term deposits and $24.4 billion in demand and notice deposits, accounting for 90.9% of total funds.

Mortgage loan companies borrow money, usually for terms of one to five years, and re-lend it in the form of mortgage loans. Most such firms either own trust companies as subsidiaries or are affiliated with the chartered banks, giving them ready access to money sources from which to borrow funds.

Mortgage loan companies may also accept deposits and issue short-term and long-term debentures. A debenture is the same as a bond except that it is issued by a corporation instead of a government and is backed by the corporation's general assets. Legislation regulates how these funds may be invested; most go into real estate mortgages.

Mortgage loan companies (including subsidiaries of banks) had total assets of $143.9 billion at the end of 1992, a 1.9% increase over 1991. Their holdings of mortgages were $121.8 billion, or 84.6% of total assets. These companies held $86.1 billion in term deposits and $36.3 billion in demand deposits.

Complete, up-to-date financial information is published quarterly in condensed form by Statistics Canada, in more detail on request by the Bank of Canada, and in the reports of the superintendent of financial institutions and of provincial supervisory authorities.

OUT OF CASH...

Imagining what the future will bring has been the preoccupation of psychics, novelists, philosophers and thinkers since time immemorial. In the 1990s, while inter-planetary cities and floating cars have not yet arrived, a new feature is here that many futurists might have had a tough time imagining: cashless cash.

Through a new service called Interac Direct Payment, many Canadians can now go shopping without cash, cheques or credit cards. All they need is a banking card. The service was developed by the Interac Association, whose members include banks, credit unions and trust companies from all across Canada.

Using the banking card is a lot like using cards to access money from automated tellers. As purchases are made, the retailer scans the card, and the customer verifies the amount, selects the account from which they wish to draw, and enters their Personal Identification Number (PIN).

This new cashless system was first introduced as a pilot project in the Ottawa area in 1990. Within two years of the pilot, more than 5 million transactions had been carried out, representing some $265 million.

The service was launched in British Columbia and Quebec in September 1992 and in Alberta in May 1993 and should be in Manitoba, Saskatchewan and northwestern Ontario by September 1993. Once the system is in place throughout the country, it is estimated that Canadians will hold more than 20 million banking cards that could be used to make cashless purchases.

At the same time, Canada is not yet a completely cashless society. More than 90% of all retail transactions still involve... cold, hard cash.

OTHER BANKING INSTITUTIONS

Two other types of institutions also offer savings and loans services — credit unions which are provincially regulated co-operative associations serving particular memberships (for example, the Civil Service Co-operative Society Limited serves federal public servants), and financial institutions that are operated by the provinces themselves (these exist in Ontario and Alberta).

Credit unions (or *caisses populaires* in Quebec) operate almost entirely under provincial jurisdiction. However, the Credit Union Central of Canada (CUCC), a national organization that provides technical and financial support services to credit, and some aspects of its provincial counterpart (those that belong to the CUCC) are governed by federal legislation. Traditionally, credit unions have invested in residential mortgages and personal loans but have more recently moved into commercial loans.

Canada's 2,613 chartered local credit unions had total assets at the end of 1992 of $85.9 billion, up 7.5% from 1991. More than half of these assets were held by *caisses populaires*. Outstanding loans (including mortgages) totalled almost $68 billion, a 9.7% increase from 1991. There were 13 central credit unions in 1992, with total assets of $24.1 billion.

INSURANCE

Canadians spend billions of dollars on various types of insurance. Although many kinds of coverage exist, they fall for the most part into life and health insurance, and property and casualty insurance.

About 900 companies and societies transact this business. Of these, 395 are federally registered and are governed by the Insurance Companies Act. The remainder are provincial or local firms. All companies are regulated federally and provincially to ensure solvency and to protect consumers from unfair practices.

Also in the insurance field but in a different capacity is the Canada Deposit Insurance Corporation which protects deposits in member financial institutions. As well, four provinces are involved in automobile insurance.

LIFE AND HEALTH INSURANCE

Canadians buy more life and health insurance on a per capita basis than any other group except the Japanese (the United States is third). In life insurance alone, Canadians owned almost $1,122 billion with federally registered companies in 1991 or about $81,300 per insured individual and $123,500 per insured household.

Canada's life and health insurance industry includes 82 federal and provincially incorporated companies, 73 branches of foreign companies and about 60 federally and provincially registered fraternal benefit societies. They have worldwide assets of $200 billion, or 13.5% of all assets held by Canadian financial institutions. These companies are rapidly expanding from traditional life insurance products into annuities and other pension services, as well as into health, accident and sickness insurance which complements public health care and disability insurance programs.

Earnings on investments account for about one-third of industry revenues, with premiums accounting for most of the rest. At the end of 1991, these companies had 39% of their assets invested in bonds, 35% in mortgage loans, 12% in stocks, 6% in real estate, and 8% elsewhere, including policy loans.

In 1990, the Canadian life and health insurance industry established a consumer protection plan to protect policyholders. All life and health insurance companies conducting business in Canada are now required by law to be members of the Canadian Life and Health Insurance Compensation Corporation (CompCorp), a non-profit organization. Within published limits, CompCorp protects Canadian policyholders against loss of benefits or unpaid claims under their life, annuity, and accident and sickness contracts, should a member of CompCorp become insolvent. As of September 1992, CompCorp had 218 member companies representing 99% of the life and health industry in Canada.

Thomas Kitchin / First Light

Royal Bank building, Toronto.

PROPERTY AND CASUALTY IN-SURANCE

Property and casualty insurers wrote $14.6 billion worth of premiums in 1992. About half ($7.7 billion) were for automobile insurance. The remainder were for personal property ($2.9 billion), commercial property ($1.7 billion) and liability insurance ($1.3 billion). The industry also covers surety (security against damage, loss and failure to do something); boiler and machinery (covers damage to machinery and surrounding buildings), and marine and aircraft risks.

These companies have smaller total assets than the life insurance or banking industries, but the comparison is somewhat misleading in that the industries have different liability structures. Property and casualty liabilities are relatively short term — more than half the premiums earned in a given year are paid in claims that same year. In terms of revenues, the property and casualty insurance industry is about one-third the size of the bank sector and about three-fifths the size of the life insurance sector.

Canada had 252 federally registered companies in 1991, some 104 of which were Canadian and 148 non-Canadian. They earn their money on investments rather than on premiums. In fact, premiums have not covered claims and operating expenses for more than a decade. From 1978 to 1991, the deficit jumped from $12.3 million to $1.4 billion.

The property and casualty insurance industry has identified key issues for the 1990s: reducing fraud (which costs the industry more than $1 billion a year);

looking into the insurance implications of environmental liability; assessing the impact of the 1992 amendments to federal financial legislation; ensuring the industry can deal with natural disasters; new technologies; and improved customer service.

GOVERNMENT INSURANCE

DEPOSIT INSURANCE The Canada Deposit Insurance Corporation (CDIC) is a federal Crown corporation created in 1967 to protect eligible deposits made in member banks, trust and loan companies.

CDIC protects up to $60,000 per individual in each member institution. It also provides separate protection for joint and trust deposits and those held in registered retirement savings plans and registered retirement income funds. Insurable deposits include savings and chequing accounts, term deposits of five years or less and debentures issued by loan companies. To be eligible for insurance protection, a deposit must be payable in Canada, in Canadian funds.

AUTOMOBILE INSURANCE Manitoba, Saskatchewan and British Columbia operate their own automobile insurance systems. Quebec operates a complementary public/private system, with each sector handling different aspects. These provincial plans provide basic universal coverage for automobiles. Government insurance companies may also offer extended coverage in competition with private insurers.

INSOLVENCY

Insolvency occurs when a person or business can no longer pay debts as they become due.

Bankruptcy is a legal process by which a financially overburdened company or person stays all legal actions pertaining to their debts. A trustee seizes the debtor's property and distributes it among creditors. The debtor is then no longer liable for most of the money owed at the time of bankruptcy.

Proceedings are regulated by the Bankruptcy and Insolvency Act and are supervised by the Superintendent of Bankruptcy, who is appointed by the Governor-in-Council. The Superintendent acts as Director of the Bankruptcy Branch of Consumer and Corporate Affairs Canada; he or she licenses and supervises all bankruptcy trustees, examines bankrupt estates for possible offences under the Bankruptcy Act or the Criminal Code and, maintains a record of bankruptcies and related statistical information.

Receiverships are the other major consequence of commercial insolvency. They occur when a creditor who has loaned money to a business under a security agreement asks that a receiver be appointed to take possession or control of all or part of the property of the business. In both bankruptcies and receiverships, secured creditors (those who have tangible assets such as office equipment) are the first to collect.

SOURCES

Bank of Canada

Canada Deposit Insurance Corporation

Canadian Life and Health Insurance Inc.

Consumer and Corporate Affairs Canada

Federal Business Development Bank

Royal Canadian Mint

Office of the Superintendent of Financial Institutions Canada

Statistics Canada

FOR FURTHER READING

Selected publications from Statistics Canada

▲ *Corporation Financial Statistics. Annual. 61-207*

▲ *Annual Report of the Minister of Industry, Science and Technology under the Corporations and Labour Unions Returns Act. Part I, Corporations. Annual. 61-210*

▲ *Capital and Repair Expenditures, Manufacturing Sub-Industries, Intentions. Annual. 61-214*

▲ *Exploration, Development and Capital Expenditures for Mining and Petroleum and Natural Gas Wells, Intentions. Annual. 61-216*

▲ *Financial and Taxation Statistics for Enterprises, Preliminary. Annual. 61-219P*

TABLES

19.1   ASSETS AND LIABILITIES OF THE BANK OF CANADA[1] (MILLION DOLLARS)

	1986	1990	1991
Assets			
Government of Canada direct and guaranteed securities			
Treasury bills	7,804	10,248	12,819
Other securities three years and under	2,969	3,997	3,920
Other securities over three years	7,438	5,753	5,356
Advances to members of the Canadian Payments Association	868	471	1,174
Other investments	1,024	3,864	3,003
Foreign currency deposits	323	368	237
All other assets	518	574	535
Total assets	20,944	25,275	27,045
Liabilities			
Notes in circulation			
Held by chartered banks	3,693	4,972	5,389
All other	14,218	17,998	19,092
Canadian dollar deposits			
Government of Canada	49	11	21
Chartered banks	2,446	1,458	1,618
Other members of the Canadian Payments Association	241	134	134
Other	159	406	559
Foreign currency liabilities	87	210	96
All other liabilities	51	86	136
Total liabilities	20,944	25,275	27,045

[1] *As of December 31st.*

19.2   **CANADIAN DOLLAR CURRENCY AND CHARTERED BANK DEPOSITS**[1]
(MILLION DOLLARS)

	Currency outside banks			Chartered bank deposits				Total currency and chartered bank deposits[2]		
	Notes	Coin	Total	Personal savings deposits	Government of Canada deposits	Other deposits[2]	Total[2]	Total including government deposits	Held by general public	
									Including personal savings deposits	Excluding personal savings deposits
1980	9,377	1,024	10,401	74,945	4,093	52,838	131,876	142,277	138,184	63,239
1981[3]	9,638	1,081	10,719	92,513	7,138	67,355	167,006	177,725	170,587	78,074
1986	14,218	1,383	15,601	129,855	2,045	67,531	199,431	215,032	212,987	83,132
1987	15,443	1,531	16,974	138,224	1,817	76,837	216,878	233,852	235,035ʳ	93,811ʳ
1988	16,604	1,654	18,258	157,333	1,844	81,593	240,770	259,028	257,184	99,851
1989	17,740	1,963	19,703	184,228	2,078	88,075	274,381	294,084	292,006	107,778
1990	17,998	2,091	20,089	202,597	3,225	91,613	297,435	332,532	314,299	111,702
1991	19,092	2,139	21,231	216,515	2,077	92,709	311,301	332,532	330,455	113,940

[1] *As of December 31st.*
[2] *Less total float (cheques and other items in transit).*
[3] *Effective November 1981, chartered bank data are reported on a consolidated basis.*

19.3   **MONETARY AGGREGATES AND THEIR COMPONENTS** (MILLION DOLLARS)

	Total[1]	M1			M2+					
		Total	Currency outside banks	Net demand deposits at chartered banks	Personal savings deposits and non-personal notice deposits at banks	Total deposits at trust and mortgage companies	Total deposits at credit unions and caisses populaires	Life insurance companies' individual annuities	Personal deposits at government savings institutions	Money market mutual funds
1981	209,440	26,878	10,596	16,282	95,189	44,458	26,644	9,689	2,107	298
1986	323,071	34,640	15,455	19,185	142,452	73,958	42,318	22,001	3,864	547
1989	453,905	41,215	19,108	22,107	203,333	110,873	57,703	32,759	6,405	2,680
1990	496,622	40,431	19,777	20,654	223,810	120,090	62,671	38,018	6,868	5,313
1991	532,694	42,180	21,051	21,129	239,289	120,881	68,263	44,543	7,342	11,460
1992	557,947	45,374	22,770	22,604	253,122	115,201	74,299	49,189	7,474	15,341

[1] *Components do not add to total because of various technical adjustments.*

19.4 BANK RATES

Date of change[1]	% per annum	Date of change[1]	% per annum
Jan. 31, 1990	12.29	Aug. 28, 1991	8.80
Feb. 28, 1990	13.25	Sept. 25, 1991	8.68
Mar. 28, 1990	13.38	Oct. 30, 1991	8.17
Apr. 25, 1990	13.77	Nov. 27, 1991	7.69
May 30, 1990	14.05	Dec. 25, 1991	7.67
June 27, 1990	13.9	Jan. 29, 1992	7.08
July 25, 1990	13.59	Feb. 26, 1992	7.56
Aug. 29, 1990	13.01	Mar. 25, 1992	7.65
Sept. 26, 1990	12.61	Apr. 29, 1992	6.85
Oct. 31, 1990	12.66	May 27, 1992	6.50
Nov. 28, 1990	12.25	June 24, 1992	5.91
Dec. 26, 1990	11.78	July 29, 1992	5.50
Jan. 30, 1991	10.88	Aug. 26, 1992	5.11
Feb. 27, 1991	10.02	Sept. 30, 1992	5.69
Mar. 27, 1991	9.92	Oct. 28, 1992	7.37
Apr. 24, 1991	9.66	Nov. 25, 1992	8.82
May 29, 1991	9.07	Dec. 30, 1992	7.36
June 26, 1991	8.91	Jan. 27, 1993	6.81
July 31, 1991	8.94		

[1] On March 10, 1980 the Bank of Canada announced that beginning on March 13, 1980 and until further notice, its bank rate would be set at 1/4 percentage point above the latest average rate established in the weekly tender for 91–day treasury bills issued by the Government of Canada. The bank rates shown in the above tables are as at the last Wednesday of the month.

19.5 REFINERY OPERATIONS AT THE ROYAL CANADIAN MINT (TROY OUNCES)

	Gross weight		Refined gold (9999) produced		Refined silver (999) produced[1]	
	1990	1991	1990	1991	1990	1991
Deposits from Canadian mines						
Newfoundland	146,945	59,629	117,021	46,066	9,253	3,595
Nova Scotia	1,553	—	1,247	—	38	—
Quebec	1,494,174	1,564,553	1,024,744	1,186,277	280,034	258,563
Ontario	1,823,248	1,800,155	1,592,260	1,565,477	169,840	169,674
Saskatchewan	121,901	132,221	101,864	103,561	12,878	19,562
British Columbia	68,914	62,719	51,086	53,560	15,143	6,230
Northwest Territories	523,741	534,364	410,769	433,972	96,919	86,093
Yukon	49,483	839	42,872	691	3,578	139
Total	4,229,959	4,154,480	3,341,863	3,389,604	587,683	543,856
Deposits from all external sources	166,687	596,658	117,602	547,353	20,072	21,490
Total	4,396,646	4,751,138	3,459,465	3,936,957	607,755	565,346

[1] These figures refer only to the silver produced as a by-product of the refining of gold.

19.6 CANADIAN-OWNED CHARTERED BANKS, CONSOLIDATED STATEMENT OF REVENUE AND EXPENSE (MILLION DOLLARS)

	Financial years ending in			
	1986	1990	1991	1992
Interest income				
Loans, excluding leases	30,251.3	44,978.3	42,559.9	36,078.1
Lease financing	258.8	452.1	376.0	292.6
Securities	3,640.3	5,542.3	5,786.7	5,778.0
Deposits with banks	3,568.9	3,136.2	2,807.1	1,918.2
Total, including dividends	37,719.3	54,108.9	51,529.7	44,066.9
Interest expense				
Deposits	25,656.8	38,279.1	33,876.5	25,651.9
Bank debentures	598.9	821.2	924.0	931.0
Liabilities other than deposits	501.9	906.2	887.4	719.9
Total	26,757.6	40,006.5	35,687.9	27,302.8
Net interest income	10,961.7	14,102.4	15,841.8	16,764.1
Less provision for loan losses	−2,996.2	−1,692.1	−2,704.0	−6,034.7
Net interest income after provision for loan losses	7,965.5	12,410.3	13,137.8	10,729.4
Other income	3,600.7	6,321.0	6,821.2	7,560.7
Net interest and other income	11,566.2	18,731.3	19,959.0	18,290.2
Non-interest expense				
Salaries	4,596.6	6,761.0	7,176.0	7,566.9
Pension contribution and other staff benefits	344.9	672.4	793.7	925.6
Premises and equipment, including depreciation	1,605.6	2,539.2	2,910.2	3,282.3
Other	2,029.0	3,023.2	3,183.0	3,599.2
Total	8,576.1	12,995.8	14,062.9	15,374.0
Net income before provision for income taxes	2,990.1	5,735.5	5,896.1	2,916.2
Provision for income taxes	−854.4	−2,127.4	−2,086.5	−965.4
Net income before minority interest in subsidiaries and extraordinary items	2,135.7	3,608.1	3,809.6	1,950.8
Minority interest in subsidiaries	−10.8	7.0	−57.2	−60.1
Extraordinary items	−63.4	2.5	0.6	—
Special provision for losses on transborder claims	—	—	—	—
Net income[1]	2,061.5	3,617.6	3,753.0	1,890.7

[1] *Since 1965 all chartered banks have ended their years on October 31. The consolidated statements of revenue and expense and of shareholders' equity and appropriations for contingencies are based on the format prescribed in Schedules L, M and N of the 1980 Bank Act. The operations of all majority-owned subsidiaries are fully consolidated into income with the minority interest shown separately. Where a bank holds at least 20% but not more than 50% of a company's voting shares, the bank takes into its income an amount equivalent to its share of that company's earnings.*

19.7 CANADIAN-OWNED CHARTERED BANKS, STATEMENT OF SHAREHOLDERS' EQUITY AND APPROPRIATIONS FOR CONTINGENCIES (MILLION DOLLARS)

	Financial years ending in			
	1986	1990	1991	1992
Shareholders' equity				
Capital stock				
Balance at beginning of year	7,288.6	13,590.3	14,550.5	16,452.1
Changes in capital stock				
Common shares	1,216.6	531.1	641.8	516.8
Preferred shares	252.7	429.1	1,259.7	213.0
Transfer from (to) contributed surplus	—	—	—	—
Balance at end of year	8,757.9	14,550.5	16,452.0	17,181.9
Contributed surplus				
Balance at beginning of year	365.2	..	..	..
Additions from capital stock issue	110.2	..	..	..
Transfer from (to) capital stock	-	..	..	..
Transfer from retained earnings	−0.2	..	..	..
Balance at end of year	475.2	..	..	..
Retained earnings				
Balance at beginning of year	8,998.3	10,713.8	12,568.3	14,399.4
Prior period adjustments	—	—	—	−96.4
Net unrealized foreign exchange translation gain (loss)	17.8	−2.4	−117.5	144.7
Share issue expenses, net	−16.3	−11.8	−21.7	−13.9
Net income (loss) for year	2,061.5	3,617.6	3,753.0	1,890.7
Dividends				
Common	−771.9	−1,333.9	−1,180.5	−1,217.1
Preferred	−282.3	−410.7	−614.3	−658.7
Other	3.1	−4.3	12.1	12.7
Transfer from (to) appropriations for contingencies	−562.2	—	—	—
Income taxes related to above transfer	305.6	—	—	−1.8
Transfer from (to) general reserve	—	—	—	—
Transfer from contributed surplus	—	—	—	—
Balance at end of year	9,753.6	12,568.3	14,399.4	14,459.9
Total shareholders' equity at end of year	18,986.7	27,118.8	30,851.4	31,641.5
Appropriations for contingencies				
Balance at beginning of year	1,195.7	..	..	..
Net loss experience on loans	−3,530.6	..	..	..
Provision for loan losses	2,996.2	..	..	..
Transfer from (to) retained earnings	562.2	..	..	..
Deferred income taxes	6.5	..	..	..
Balance at end of year	1,230.1	..	..	..
Total shareholders' equity and appropriations for contingencies[1]	20,216.8	27,118.8	30,851.4	31,641.5

[1] *See note, Table 19.6.*

19.8 REVENUES AND EXPENSES OF TRUST AND MORTGAGE COMPANIES
(MILLION DOLLARS)

	Trust companies			Mortgage companies		
	1989	1990	1991	1989	1990	1991
Revenues						
Interest earned	11,916	13,994	13,225	11,954	14,896	15,575
Dividends	440	487	383	44	54	39
Fees and commissions	1,286	1,215	1,149	134	129	133
Other revenues	497	204	109	72	40	116
Total revenues	14,139	15,900	14,866	12,204	15,121	15,863
Expenses						
Interest	10,412	12,143	11,300	10,139	12,656	11,914
Depreciation and taxes	141	156	153	38	46	50
Income taxes	101	48	56	178	188	609
Other expenses	2,788	3,138	3,406	1,380	1,654	2,204
Total expenses	13,422	15,530	14,915	11,735	14,544	14,777
Net profit	697	370	−49	469	577	1,086

19.9 ASSETS, LIABILITIES AND SHAREHOLDERS' EQUITY OF TRUST COMPANIES
(MILLION DOLLARS)

	1989	1990	1991
Assets			
Cash and demand deposits	1,112	1,280	2,024
Investments			
Term deposits	965	694	572
Goverment of Canada	6,325	7,851	8,341
Provincial and municipal governments	671	951	1,618
Other	13,911	14,632	9,913
Loans			
Cash loans			
Personal	7,941	8,052	8,490
Corporations	7,695	8,305	8,210
Other	407	176	249
Mortgage loans			
Residential	63,929	68,153	66,968
Other	12,331	14,369	15,670
Allowance for doubtful loans	−306	−568	−947
Fixed assets (net)	727	906	1,228
Other assets	2,500	2,537	4,097
Total assets	118,208	127,338	126,433
Liabilities			
Accounts payable	3,873	4,311	4,193
Loans payable			
Banks	415	128	205
Others	1,778	1,748	1,474
Deposits			
Demand	26,268	26,762	25,702
Term	79,568	87,825	88,260
Other liabilities	704	601	741
Shareholders' equity			
Share capital	2,406	2,578	2,700
Contributed surplus	1,676	1,957	2,152
Retained earnings			
Appropriated	—	5	—
Unappropriated	1,520	1,423	1,003
Total liabilities and equity	118,208	127,338	126,430

19.10 ASSETS, LIABILITIES AND SHAREHOLDERS' EQUITY OF MORTGAGE COMPANIES[1]
(MILLION DOLLARS)

	1989	1990	1991
Assets			
Cash and demand deposits	802	429	563
Investments			
Term deposits	1,459	1,563	1,728
Goverment of Canada	3,832	4,467	5,080
Provincial and municipal governments	242	133	125
Other	5,818	6,423	6,131
Loans			
Cash loans			
Personal	7,964	8,013	6,464
Corporations	1,055	1,156	1,064
Other	11	—	—
Mortgage loans			
Residential	87,652	100,635	110,355
Other	6,786	8,059	8,586
Allowance for doubtful loans	−36	−69	−84
Fixed assets (net)	69	104	107
Other assets	1,481	1,160	1,162
Total assets	117,135	132,073	141,231
Liabilities			
Accounts payable	2,863	3,579	3,538
Loans payable			
Banks	46	103	95
Others	7,450	6,477	9,320
Deposits			
Demand	41,309	44,729	42,735
Term	60,036	71,055	78,949
Other liabilities	438	395	420
Shareholders' equity			
Share capital	3,257	3,565	3,591
Contributed surplus	721	767	166
Retained earnings			
Appropriated	1	2	2
Unappropriated	1,014	1.401	2,415
Total liabilities and equity	117,135	132,073	141,231

[1] *Includes mortgage subsidiaries of banks.*

19.11 LOCAL CREDIT UNIONS

	Credit unions chartered	Assets $'000	Loans granted to members $'000		Credit unions chartered	Assets $'000	Loans granted to members $'000
1981	3,448	31,657,404	23,716,793	1989	2,980	67,091,742	51,670,624
1986	3,072	48,780,160	37,523,834	1990	2,746	72,367,000	55,470,000
1987	2,975	55,060,268	43,362,991	1991	2,666	79,858,000	61,941,000
1988	2,987	61,106,287	48,017,904				

19.12   ASSETS, LIABILITIES AND SHAREHOLDERS' EQUITY OF LOCAL CREDIT UNIONS
(MILLION DOLLARS)

	1989	1990	1991
Assets			
Cash and demand deposits	5,639	5,911	5,507
Investments			
Term deposits	6,110	6,957	7,659
Goverment of Canada	371	212	358
Provincial and municipal governments	191	192	87
Shares in other credit unions	439	442	514
Other	974	1,288	1,720
Loans			
Cash loans			
Personal	12,809	12,205	14,517
Corporations	4,912	5,504	6,105
Other	1,125	1,225	1,036
Mortgage loans			
Residential	29,026	32,410	35,840
Farm	1,233	1,346	1,311
Other	2,566	2,780	3,132
Allowance for doubtful loans	−272	−320	−357
Fixed assets (net)	1,089	1,223	1,326
Other assets	880	992	1,103
Total assets	67,092	72,367	79,858
Liabilities			
Accounts payable	1,948	2,286	2,162
Loans payable			
Other credit unions	1,872	1,538	3,069
Banks	5	4	1
Others	830	696	557
Deposits			
Demand	24,332	26,559	28,529
Term	33,433	36,252	39,894
Other liabilities	390	374	565
Members' equity			
Share capital	2,120	1,924	2,439
Reserves	1,729	2,126	2,340
Undivided surplus	433	569	302
Total liabilities and equity	67,092	72,367	79,858

19.13 LIFE INSURANCE EFFECTED AND IN FORCE (MILLION DOLLARS)

Effected during the year	1990				1991			
	Canadian	British	Foreign	Total	Canadian	British	Foreign	Total
Individual	63,215	6,159	18,815	88,169	69,637	2,880	14,810	87,326
Group	33,525	9,311	11,933	54,770	41,296	1,680	7,292	50,268
Total	96,740	15,470	30,748	142,959	110,933	4,933	22,102	137,594
In Force — December 31								
Individual	377,237	29,294	92,586	499,117	425,857	17,838	94,289	537,985
Group	406,720	22,911	73,435	503,066	446,512	12,848	74,471	533,830
Total	783,957	52,206	166,020	1,002,183	872,369	30,686	168,760	1,071,816

19.14 LIFE INSURANCE PREMIUMS[1] (MILLION DOLLARS)

	1990				1991			
	Life			Accident and sickness	Life			Accident and sickness
	Ordinary	Group	Total		Ordinary	Group	Total	
Newfoundland	55	29	84	65	58	33	91	67
Prince Edward Island	20	7	26	16	22	8	31	16
Nova Scotia	134	60	194	120	139	65	204	136
New Brunswick	105	39	143	91	111	40	151	96
Quebec	1,001	249	1,251	663	1,065	258	1,324	697
Ontario	1,887	868	2,755	2,242	2,011	875	2,886	2,347
Manitoba	164	72	236	133	177	78	254	135
Saskatchewan	146	56	202	87	151	61	212	95
Alberta	443	169	612	413	483	187	669	435
British Columbia	462	192	654	442	507	209	717	464
Yukon and Northwest Territories	7	3	9	9	8	3	11	7
Miscellaneous	56	5	61	−1	51	5	56	−5
Total	4,479	1,747	6,227	4,281	4,783	1,824	6,607	4,490

[1] *Direct written.*

19.15 PROPERTY AND CASUALTY NET PREMIUMS WRITTEN AND NET CLAIMS INCURRED
(MILLION DOLLARS)

	Net Premiums Written				Net Claims Incurred
	Canadian	British	Foreign	Total	
1990					
Class					
Property	2,683	353	806	3,841	2,678
Automobile	4,779	316	1,307	6,402	5,448
Liability	735	92	348	1,175	734
Accident and sickness	171	69	11	251	144
Other casualty	264	42	99	406	274
Marine	44	12	30	86	70
Total	8,677	884	2,601	12,162	9,348
1991					
Class					
Property	2,807	367	754	3,930	3,219
Automobile	5,025	359	1,221	6,605	5,137
Liability	721	98	321	1,140	737
Accident and sickness	137	74	10	220	112
Other casualty	278	55	100	433	331
Marine	39	14	28	81	61
Total	9,009	967	2,434	12,410	9,597

19.16 BANKRUPTCIES

	Estates	Total Assets $'000	Total Liabilities $'000	Total Deficiency $'000
Business				
1990	11,642	1,436,816	3,342,576	1,905,760
1991	13,496	2,313,392	6,170,251	3,856,859
1992	14,317	2,044,520	7,374,212	5,329,692
Consumer				
1990	42,782	817,151	1,761,648	944,497
1991	62,277	1,606,084	3,265,719	1,659,635
1992	61,822	1,725,603	3,262,914	1,537,311

19.17 BUSINESS BANKRUPTCIES, 1992

Industry	Number of estates	Total assets $	Total liabilities[1] $	Total deficiency $
Agriculture and related service	421	43,742,700	84,945,465	41,202,765
Fishing and trapping	230	4,399,082	8,803,657	4,404,575
Logging and forestry	180	9,488,494	24,007,443	14,518,949
Mining, quarrying and oil well	67	26,845,233	201,367,045	174,521,812
Manufacturing	1,135	292,066,177	674,236,367	382,170,190
Construction	1,992	189,479,140	581,262,958	391,783,818
Transportation and storage	858	41,352,717	120,048,121	78,695,404
Communication and other utility	116	8,639,732	18,670,299	10,030,567
Wholesale trade	984	211,856,708	522,763,014	310,906,306
Retail trade	3,192	353,316,941	984,609,216	631,292,275
Finance and insurance[2]	173	129,676,046	2,249,558,807	2,119,882,761
Real estate operations and insurance agency	450	270,247,723	526,648,626	256,400,903
Business service	976	87,795,109	301,198,559	213,403,450
Government service	25	842,077	9,835,935	8,993,858
Educational service	34	1,004,923	4,789,326	3,784,403
Health and social service	249	49,044,571	125,304,547	76,259,976
Accommodation, food and beverage service	1,874	178,095,917	504,379,404	326,283,487
Other service	1,361	146,626,515	431,782,801	285,156,286
Total	14,317	2,044,519,805	7,374,211,590	5,329,691,785

[1] As declared by debtors.
[2] Includes the $1,295,000,000 liabilities of Castor Holdings Ltd..

Sources
Bank of Canada
Credit Union Central of Canada
Federal Business Development Bank
Office of the Superintendent of Bankruptcy
Office of the Superintendent of Financial Institutions Canada
Statistics Canada

CHAPTER TWENTY ECONOMIC PERSPECTIVES

INTRODUCTION

The Canadian economy of the early 1990s was dominated by a painful transition from recession to recovery. Indeed, many people viewed with scepticism the very notion that recovery was taking hold, pointing to ongoing unemployment and restrained domestic spending. Layoffs have remained a focal point of public concern and consumer confidence has been eroded and remains low. At the same time, many in Canada — and throughout the industrialized world — have felt that the pace of economic change is accelerating to unbearable levels and that sovereign nations are less and less in control of their economic destiny.

The recession that began in 1990 was particularly long and painful for many Canadians because it represented a cyclical downturn in tandem with an economy undergoing profound structural changes. To understand this recession completely, to separate the facts from the many myths surrounding it, these other changes require review.

Predictably, many of them were associated with the recession when it hit. The changes ran the gamut: from deep-seated unemployment and increased emphasis on skills and productivity, to rising taxes, ballooning government and foreign deficits and layoffs in many of our traditional industries.

Yet, while the recession admittedly aggravated these phenomena, they were all evident well before its onset.

To provide context and to explain them, this chapter reviews the structure of the Canadian economy, and offers a look at some of the fundamental forces at play. The spotlight is on unemployment, international trade, the services industry and the differences that marked the recession of the early 1980s and that of the early 1990s.

THE STRUCTURE OF THE CANADIAN ECONOMY

The Canadian economy is the seventh largest among the western industrialized nations, in terms of its total output of goods and services, the Gross Domestic Product (GDP). In 1992, total GDP amounted to $687.3 billion,

even after the recession of the early 1990s. On a per capita basis, this yielded Canadians the second-highest incomes in the world after the Americans.

However, economic growth has been slowing steadily in recent decades. From a peak average annual growth of 5.2% in the 1950s and 1960s, the volume of GDP grew on average by only 4.7% in the 1970s and 3.1% in the 1980s before the recession reduced the GDP in the early 1990s. The long-term trend of slower growth partly reflects a slowdown in population growth from over 3% to about 1%, as well as a reduction in productivity gains.

THE GROWTH OF SERVICES

In Canada, the post-war period has been marked by a steady shift away from the production of goods toward more emphasis on services. More than 7 out of 10 employed Canadians now work in the services industry, compared to only 5 out of 10 in 1960.

The growth in services has originated in such information-based industries as finance and communications. As well, the increased volume of international and interprovincial trade has helped to boost demand for transportation and trade services. A growing call for government services means that the government now accounts for almost 25% of employment.

The counterpart to this rapid growth in services has been a diminished industrial base. This was particularly true of manufacturing, where the share of jobs fell from 25% in 1960 to less than 15% in 1992. The shift can partly be explained by the ability of this industry to produce more with relatively fewer workers.

In fact, the shift from industry to services mirrors a similar shift from agriculture to industry that took place earlier in the century.

While agricultural output continued to rise in absolute terms, it certainly required dramatically fewer workers to produce the output. Part of the recent shift from industry to services probably also reflects an increased emphasis on contracting-out of services previously supplied in-house by firms engaged in industry.

Benjamin Rondel / First Light

Toronto business district.

GLOBAL OUTLOOK Canada's persistent current account deficits (deficits on all merchandise and non-merchandise transactions with other countries) and the corresponding growth of foreign debt have been a matter of concern for a long time. Since the early 1960s, the pattern has been surpluses on merchandise trade which are not sufficient to offset deficits on services and investment income.

From 1950 to 1992, Canada's cumulative current account deficit more than doubled every 10 years. From a small net surplus at the end of 1949, Canada was saddled with a deficit of $186 billion by the end of 1992.

A deficit on the current account leads to a net capital inflow from the savings of foreign countries. In Canada's case, this capital inflow took the form of investment by non-residents, adding to Canada's external net liability. From $4 billion at the end of 1950, Canada's net liability quadrupled in the 1950s, doubled in the 1960s and more than tripled in the 1970s. Growth was not as strong in the 1980s, the net liability slightly more than doubling in the decade. By

the end of 1992, however, the net external debt was a record $301 billion, made up of gross external liabilities of $540 billion which were partly offset by external assets of $239 billion.

Canada's relative dependency on the United States has diminished significantly as sources of foreign capital have become more diversified. Indeed, in the last 15 years, there has been a considerable global diversification which has significantly changed the composition of Canada's external debt. Up to the 1970s, the debt was overwhelmingly with the United States, Canada having generally a small net liability with other countries. From the early 1980s, Canada's net debt with the United States stabilized somewhat, and advanced sharply with other countries. By the end of 1992, Japan had become Canada's second largest creditor with a net claim of $59 billion, slightly less than half that of the United States' on Canada ($128 billion).

The trend toward globalization (the cross-border spread of products, production factors, firms and markets) has meant that the production of various components or activities for a given product may take place in more than one country. Often this gives rise at the firm level to a global organisation with activities such as research and development, sourcing, production and marketing being dispersed internationally.

In Canada, globalization has permeated the domestic economy. It has affected the origin of foreign capital, the type of foreign capital invested, as well as the Canadian sectors to which the investment flows. In fact, Canadian residents have started to build up assets abroad to an extent unknown in the past, and at a rate generally even faster than that of foreign investment into Canada.

Canada's external assets and liabilities are made up of a wide variety of capital which can be broken down into four major components: direct investment, portfolio investment, reserves and other capital. Through direct investment, an investor influences or has a voice in the management of a firm or enterprise. Through portfolio investment, the investor has a more passive role. Reserves refer to external assets of Canada's official monetary authorities.

Deficits

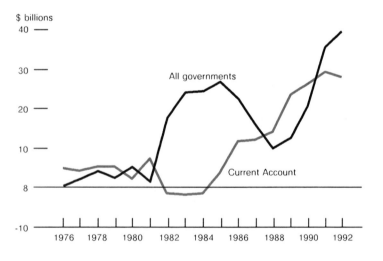

Canada's external liabilities amounted to $540 billion at the end of 1992, 25% of which was in the form of direct investment and 53% in portfolio investment, mostly Canadian bonds. The remaining 22% represents foreign capital which was widely spread in Canadian financial markets.

Foreign direct investment in Canada amounted to $137 billion at the end of 1992. This type of investment has been increasing steadily since the early 1950s and doubling in each of the following decades.

From the early 1950s, there was a continuous but moderate stream of foreign investment in Canadian bonds. However, in the mid-1970s, non-residents stepped up their net purchases of Canadian bonds considerably at the same time as the growth in foreign direct investment in Canada subsided. By the end of 1992, non-residents held $231 billion worth of Canadian bonds, or more than one-third of all Canadian bonds outstanding compared to 25% at the end of 1980.

Canada's external assets amounted to $239 billion at the end of 1992. Although most of the public focus has been on our growing external liabilities, Canada's assets in the last 15 years have grown more rapidly than our liabilities. Some 41% of our external assets are in the form of direct investment abroad and 27% as private holdings of foreign stocks, bonds and deposits.

By the end of 1992, Canadians had invested some $99 billion, or 41% of the country's assets, abroad. This compares to less than 30% up to the mid-1970s. In the intervening years, Canadians sharply increased their direct investment abroad by exporting very large sums of capital. The United States has been and continues to be the most favoured country, receiving some 58% of our exported capital.

Also by the end of 1992, Canadian residents held $46 billion worth of foreign stocks and bonds coupled with $18 billion worth of deposits abroad. Since the end of 1979, Canadian residents have virtually quintupled their holdings of foreign securities and of deposits abroad.

INTERNATIONAL TRADE Canada has often been yoked by the image of 'hewers of wood, drawers of water' in its trading relations with other countries. Much of Canada's early economic history was depicted in the staples theory of economic development: a dependency on resource exports starting with fur, then lumber and wheat and subsequently minerals.

Whatever the past merits of the staple theory, it has clearly become less and less relevant in recent decades. Manufactured goods increasingly dominate our exports. In 1965, we signed the Automotive Products Trade Agreement with the United States, which guarantees the free flow of automotive products and a certain share of production in Canada.

In the 1980s, other manufactured goods joined automotive products among our leading exports. The most obvious example is machinery and equipment. Throughout the 1980s, their share of export volumes doubled, surpassing automotive products by the early 1990s. Buoyant demand for goods such as telecommunications equipment, computers and aircraft led this surge.

Conversely, natural resource products have declined rapidly in importance over the past decade. Partly, of course, this reflects the collapse of oil prices in 1986. Export earnings that had been inflated through oil exports plummetted and allowed a greater spotlight on earnings from manufactured exports.

The shift in exports away from natural resources has paralleled an increased dependence on trade with the United States. In 1992, the United States accounted for over 77% of all our exports of merchandise, up substantially from less than half that amount in 1941.

MERCHANDISE TRADE SURPLUS Since 1926, Canada has run a merchandise trade surplus in all but a handful of years. In 1984, the surplus was as high as almost $20 billion. The lowest since then was $7.1 billion in 1989, before recovering to almost $10 billion in 1992. The usual pattern of surplus for Canada originates in substantial exports of our natural resource products, such as wheat, minerals, lumber and energy, while we import very

TRADING FOR A LIVING

Canada has been a trading nation since very early times, when Europeans traded tools and fabrics with native peoples for their much valued furs and meat. Today, Canada's trade patterns are more diverse — Canada now sells more than one-quarter of its goods and services abroad, and imports what it needs from countries around the world. Canada's total worldwide trade, based on Canada Customs data, amounted to $301.6 billion in 1992.

The United States is by far Canada's most important trading partner. In fact, the two countries share the largest trading relationship in the world, amounting to $215 billion Cdn in 1992 alone.

In recent years, this relationship has grown even more important. In 1992, Canada sold 77% of its exports to the US, compared to just 70% in 1972.

After the United States, Canada's largest trading partners in 1992 were Japan ($18.1 billion), the United Kingdom ($7.1 billion), Germany ($5.7 billion), France ($4.0 billion) and South Korea ($3.4 billion).

Fabricated materials such as lumber, plywood, wood pulp, paper, textiles, chemicals, iron and steel, petroleum products and non-ferrous metals accounted for 32.4% of all domestic exports in 1992.

End products such as machinery, transportation equipment and pharmaceutical products accounted for 44.3% of all domestic exports in 1992.

little of these products. The pattern for manufactured finished goods is mixed, as a surplus in our automotive trade is usually outweighed by a large deficit for machinery and equipment (including items such as computers and office equipment and industrial machinery).

In 1986, oil prices collapsed and at the same time there was an intensified competition for grain exports. From the developing countries recently has come an increased competition for mineral products such as aluminum and copper. Through much of this period, a higher exchange rate for the Canadian dollar helped to lower the price of imported goods, which fuelled an increased Canadian demand for them.

The merchandise trade surplus is often incorrectly viewed as a measure of our well-being. The rebound of the trade surplus in 1982 is a good case in point. In that year, the surplus jumped from $7 billion to over $17 billion. Most of the increase, however, originated in a steep drop in import demand, as consumers and business, deep in a recession, slashed spending. Meanwhile, exports stagnated as most of our trading partners found themselves in an economic slowdown. Neither performance reflects an improving economy.

On the other hand, the 1992 gain in our surplus was encouraging for sustained recovery. Exports leapt ahead by 11%, largely fuelled by increases to our key American markets. Meanwhile, imports recovered by almost 7%, led by rising business investment in machinery and equipment, which often is directly related to improving productivity.

THE GOVERNMENT IN THE ECONOMY

In some important ways, Canada represents a compromise between the European and American approaches to the economy, particularly in the role of government in the economy. In 1990, total government spending as a share of GDP was 47% in Canada, versus 37% in the United States and 49% in those European nations belonging to the Organisation for Economic Co-operation and Development (OECD). In Canada, government revenues were the equivalent of 42% of the GDP, compared to 32% in the United

States and 44% in Europe. The gap between the spending and revenues just cited, of course, represents government deficits. Since the 1970s, persistent annual government deficits in Canada have raised the accumulated government debt to about 90% of our GDP, the second highest of the major industrialized nations (second only to Italy). Increased foreign borrowing to finance this debt has also played a major role in raising Canada's current account trade deficit because of interest payments required to service this external debt.

REGIONAL GROWTH More than half of Canada's GDP is produced in the central provinces of Ontario and Quebec. In particular, these provinces house over 80% of Canada's manufacturing activities, partly because of their varied resource base and proximity to large American markets. The four western provinces account for more than 25% of the GDP, although their share has fallen from its peak in the early 1980s when the oil and gas industries in Alberta were benefitting from the peak in energy prices. The four Atlantic provinces have recorded little long-run changes in their share of GDP.

In per capita GDP terms, Alberta and Ontario are the richest provinces, at about $28,000. (In other words, if current incomes were divided among every man, woman and child within these provinces, each would receive $28,000.) At the other end of the scale, all of the Atlantic provinces have a per capita GDP of less than $20,000. Since 1961, regional differences in GDP per capita have narrowed slightly. The notable exception was Alberta which was more than 50% above the Canadian average during the energy boom in the early 1980s.

Regional inequalities are less pronounced if one looks at personal income instead of GDP. Partly, this reflects transfer payments from richer to poorer provinces, most explicitly under equalization payments. If one looks at GDP per capita relative to the Canadian average, provincial differences range from 113% in Alberta (implying 13% above the average) to 63% in Prince Edward Island. For personal incomes, on the other hand, the range is from 113% (Ontario) to 71% (Newfoundland).

UNEMPLOYMENT Throughout the 1980s, the unemployment rate has been persistently higher than that of the United States. In Canada, it averaged 9.3% versus 7.3% in the United States, with Canada ranging from a high of 11.8% in 1983 to a low of 7.5% in 1989, and the United States fluctuating between 9.7% and 5.3%. While the exact reasons for this are still being explored, two patterns of behaviour are worth noting. First, unemployment in Canada appears to be deeply-embedded in some regions and age groups, reflected in the repeat use of unemployment insurance. Secondly, the 1981-82 recession had a profound and lingering effect on unemployment in Canada throughout the decade, but not on our ability to generate jobs. The unemployed in Canada are more likely to stay in the labour force and look for a job.

Unemployment in the 1980s hit a low of 7.5% of the labour force in 1989. However, over 80% of the 1.8 million claims for unemployment insurance (UI) were made by people who had previously been on unemployment.

The repeat use of UI was heavily concentrated among men generally, and, east of Ontario, among all residents. In fact, nearly half the men who claimed in 1989 were on their fifth round of UI (48%, versus 30% for women). In Quebec and the Atlantic provinces, between 45% and 65% of claimants were on their fifth or more claim, versus between 28% and 38% in Ontario and western Canada. These regional differences show the structurally higher unemployment and lower GDP per capita east of Ontario.

Also of note is that the younger the claimant, the higher the chance of repeat use over a lifetime: a young man filing his first UI claim at age 16 has a 90% chance of a return to UI offices within five years. By contrast, a 30-year-old has a 60% chance of returning.

In the 1980s, the unemployed were less concentrated among the young. Throughout this decade, the share of all UI claims made by people between 16 and 19 years of age fell from 12% to almost 5%, while for those between 30 and 39 years old it jumped from 18% to 25%. Two developments are key here: the aging of the baby boom generation and a declining number of young people. However, the trend also points to structural shifts that were precipitated by the 1981-82 recession in labour markets.

GREENER GRASS SOUTH OF THE BORDER?

In 1992, the United States invited citizens of Canada and 36 other countries and territories to participate in a lottery to win a US immigration visa (also known as a 'green card'). Over 817,000 people applied worldwide, and Canada was the third-ranking country in successful applications, with more than 2,000 green cards awarded to citizens of this country. Canadians were again invited to participate in a green card lottery in 1993, the third and final such lottery to be held (the first, in 1991, did not involve Canada).

America has been called the 'land of opportunity'; clearly, it beckons to many Canadians, and some of the reasons for this attraction may be economic.

But is the grass really greener south of the border? Recent research comparing standards of living, poverty rates, and income distribution between Canada and the US says not necessarily. Although the average family income is slightly higher in the US (by about 2%), a smaller proportion of Canadians live below the poverty line, the income gap between rich and poor families is much smaller in Canada than in the US, and the majority of Canadian families have higher incomes than their American counterparts.

In the US, poverty is defined using a 'poverty line' based on calculation of needs. In Canada, poverty as such is not defined; instead, a 'low-income cutoff' defines a low-income family as one whose percentage of total income spent on the basic necessities of food, clothing and shelter is at least 20 percentage points higher than that of the average family. Applying either one of these methods to both countries yields a comparison of relative levels of poverty (or low income) in the two countries. Poverty was, in the early 1970s, slightly higher in Canada than in the US. But with strong economic growth in Canada the rate dropped and by mid-decade was lower than that of the US. During the recession of the early 1980s, poverty rose in both countries. Following the recession, poverty remained at recessionary levels in the US, but returned to its pre-recession level in Canada, thanks partly to more generous income transfer programs like unemployment insurance and social assistance (welfare) in this country. By 1987, the proportion of Canadians living in poverty was more than five percentage points lower than the US figure.

So Canada seems to have been kinder to the poor, at least in the recent past. But what of society as a whole, including low-income and middle-income earners and the rich?

Imagine an income scale representing the families that earn the least at one end, and those that earn the most at the other. It turns out that whether you would have a higher income in Canada or the United States depends on where you stand on this income scale. The majority of Canadian families (the first 60%, starting with those having the lowest incomes) make more than the American families occupying the same relative position on the scale. Only the top 40% of Canadian families (those earning the most) make less than the corresponding American families. How much less? — as much as 10%, depending on how close to the rich end of the scale the families are.

In other words, the gap between the rich and the poor is not as wide in Canada as in the US. What is more, it is in the US and not in Canada that family income inequality is increasing. Research suggests that, at least during the 1980s, income transfers were more effective in preventing income inequalities from increasing in Canada than in the US.

Now, suppose the first 20% of families (those earning the least) from either country were to pool their incomes. The Canadian families would, according to 1987 figures, account for about 5% of all income earned in Canada, but the US families would account for only 3.5% of all American income. At the other end of the scale, if the 20% of families who earn the most pooled their income, the American families would obtain 44.2%, the Canadians accounting for somewhat less — 41.5% — of total income in their respective countries. So the poorest families in Canada get a slightly larger share of all income than their American counterparts, while the richest get a slightly smaller share. Income is distributed somewhat more equally in Canada than in the US.

Finally, let's look at the two families in the dead centre of the scale, those who divide the scale in two equal halves, one half earning more and the other half earning less than these two particular families. Using purchasing power parities to convert Amercian dollars to Canadian dollars, the Canadian family would earn about 4% more than the American family.

So the grass is not necessarily greener; Canada's material standard of living is not significantly different from that of the United States, but poverty is less prevalent and income distribution is more equal. The 'land of opportunity' could, for the average person, just as easily be Canada.

RETIREMENT SAVINGS By 1991, Canadians had tucked away about $130 billion in Registered Retirement Savings Plans (RRSPs), up sharply from $22 billion a decade earlier. But for the first time, the number of contributors and the volume of contributions fell in 1990. This partly reflected tightened RRSP rules and the recession, which forced people to make early withdrawals. In 1991, however, contributors rose 14% and contributions rebounded by a remarkable 30%. These increases are directly attributable to new rules which raised contribution limits for high-income earners, who usually contribute the most to RRSPs.

Traditionally, the bulk of RRSPs are invested in low-risk savings vehicles such as guaranteed investment certificates and term deposits at banks, trust companies and credit unions. In 1992, only about 15% of funds were invested in mutual funds. This may change, as recent changes in legislation raised the foreign content permitted in RRSPs from 10% prior to 1990 to 20% by 1994.

HOUSEHOLD WORK An often unhonoured but essential work in the life of any country is its household work. In 1992, Statistics Canada updated its estimates of the value of household activities such as caring for children, cooking, and cleaning. Using

a variety of assumptions and calculations about the time involved in these activities and the value of this work, the estimates range from $160 billion to $199 billion for 1986. These estimates are equivalent to between 31.5% and 39.3% of GDP.

Overall, women produced from 40% to 50% more household work than men (or about two-thirds of the total). In fact, Canadians spend almost as much time doing household work (20.7 billion hours) as doing paid work (21.2 billion hours). Generally, for women, more than half their household chores involve cooking, cleaning and washing clothes, while men are to be found repairing or maintaining the home and shopping (which was shared almost equally between men and women).

The value of household work has been shrinking relative to GDP in recent years. As women continue to enter the paid labour force in greater numbers, the number of hours they clock on household work is inevitably down.

CANADA IN RECESSION

The recessions which began in 1981 and in 1990 have many points in common. Both are correctly perceived to be the two worst recessions (in terms of both length and severity) since the Great Depression of the 1930s, with widespread damage to many sectors including the previously immune services industry. Both these recessions were equally harmful to output and employment, at least initially, which is a new development in post-war business cycles. Both accompanied a worldwide economic downturn and higher real interest rates, partly because both ushered in a period of historically low inflation.

Yet, there were also surprising differences between the two. The recession which began in 1981 displayed the classic V-shape. Inventories played a dominant role. There was the lagged response of business investment, the counter-cyclical role of government finances, the retreat to financial caution by households, and the sluggish performance of productivity.

In 1990, however, the recession took on the unique L-shaped pattern of growth: it appeared to extend

Gross Domestic Product

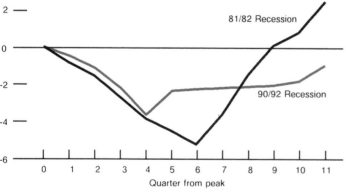

Per cent change from peak

over a longer period of time, notably for employment. The 1981 downturn was also faster; GDP dropped 5%, whereas in 1990, it dropped 3%.

These differences make it impossible to judge which was the worst recession anymore than one can say it is better to suffer a heart attack than to be afflicted by a long, lingering disease.

In the 1981 recession, inventories played the dominant role; they accounted for almost 90% of the drop in output (excluding inventories, GDP fell only 0.4%). In 1990, inventories played almost no role. This may reflect such new trends as 'just-in-time' inventory systems, computerized inventory control, and the high real interest rates in the 1980s and 1990s which raised the cost of holding inventories.

Instead, the 1990 recession began as a business investment recession. The initial drops in GDP in the second and third quarters of the year were led by outlays for plant and equipment. By contrast, in the early stages of the 1981-82 recession, business investment rose slightly, partly the result of the surge in energy projects after the second Organization of Petroleum Exporting Countries (OPEC) price shock. Thereafter, it fell at an accelerating rate, a classic lagged response by firms to slowing sales and dwindling profits.

What induced firms in 1990 to start cutting investment before sales started to decline? One of the early warning signals can be found in 1989, when the Canadian dollar began to rise sharply, squeezing the export earnings and profits of both manufacturing and natural resource based firms. The slump in profits also accompanied a deterioration in balance sheets, notably as long-term debt loads rose in response to higher interest rates.

The result of this retrenchment by firms in 1990 did not just affect investment, of course, but quickly manifested itself in layoffs and lower employment. This, in turn, quickly eroded real incomes and personal expenditure and by 1991, what had begun as an investment-driven downturn had turned into a full-blown consumer-driven recession.

In fact, in the 1990 recession, people were that much more vulnerable to job loss and rising taxes because

CONSUMER PRICE INDEX

The Consumer Price Index (CPI) is Canada's most widely-used measure of the inflation rate. The CPI measures monthly changes in the retail price of a selected basket of about 300 commodities, ranging from haircuts to dental fillings. These changes are published each month.

To understand a change in the CPI, imagine that the index was 100.0 in January, 1986 and 125.0 in January, 1991. This would mean that consumer prices had risen by 25% on average during that time.

The goods and services in the commodity basket are generally updated every four years to reflect changes in spending patterns. The base year (the year in which the CPI is given a value of 100.0) is changed less frequently. The importance of each item in the basket is defined by its share of family expenditures. These items' 'weights' are revised regularly to keep the CPI up-to-date. The measured prices include taxes such as the Goods and Services Tax (GST), provincial sales tax and property taxes.

Statistics Canada compiles the index for Canada and most major urban centres and first collected CPIs for the provinces in 1978.

their cushion of savings was dramatically low. Debt levels were much higher in 1990 than in 1981 (80% of incomes versus 60%). The savings rate was relatively low at 10% in 1990, versus 15% in 1981 and a peak of 18% in 1982. On top of this, over 90% of savings in 1990 were 'contractual' (such as RRSPs and trusteed pension funds) which were less accessible than the large piggy-bank of discretionary savings in 1982.

With little recourse to debt or savings, it was inevitable that the drop in real incomes, due to fewer jobs and higher prices, meant spending would drop. It did: almost 4% by early 1991.

The one sector that performed in a similar fashion in the last two recessions was housing. Moreover, this sector was also subject to the same speculative fever in the late 1980s, especially in Toronto, that affected so many areas of the economy in the early 1980s. In any event, both residential construction and housing starts fell to similar lows (despite the intervening period of population growth of almost 4 million people).

Throughout the 1981-82 recession and the first 12 months of the 1990 downturn, output and employment fell in lock-step, implying no significant change in productivity. This in itself marks an extraordinary departure from previous recessions, when output-per-employee (used here as a proxy of productivity) always fell. Economists for years have developed explanations on why firms let productivity fall during recessions, with the arguments usually centred on the costs of laying-off and then hiring new workers. Persistently higher rates of unemployment in the past decade probably helped to reduce these costs, implying as they do that a firm would not lose skilled laid-off workers to other firms during recessions.

What is particularly striking about the last recession, however, is the second stage of the drop in jobs from mid-1991 to mid-1992. It was this second period of declining employment (the 'double-dip' often referred to in the press) that appears to have delayed overall recovery, engendering as it did lower real incomes and shaky consumer confidence which checked the growth of consumer spending.

Manufacturing led this 'double-dip' in employment, shedding another 10% of its workforce even as output was stagnant. As a result, output-per-employee jumped by about 10%, the fastest rate of increase of any recent period except for the early stages of the recoveries in 1981 and 1983. The fact that productivity carried on much as it did in a recovery, despite the persistence of recession for manufacturing in 1991 and 1992, is a phenomenon without precedence in Canadian history. But it is consistent with the emphasis firms have placed on productivity-enhancing investment in machinery and equipment and it parallels similar developments in many industrialized nations in these times of record low profitability.

CANADA AND THE UNITED STATES Since World War II, recessions in Canada and the United States have been very closely synchronized. Downturns have begun, on average, within one month of each other in both countries and have ended at about the same time. A key reason is the large role that lower exports have played in our recessions, falling about 3% on average during recessions. Even in 1981-82, when exports directly played only a small role in the recession, other linkages between the two countries (notably in interest rates) led to an exact coincidence of the timing of recession and recovery.

In 1990, however, the Canadian economy appeared to contract in April, four months before a similar contraction in the American economy. In fact, the United States itself might have escaped a prolonged recession if not for the jump in oil prices and interest rates which accompanied the Iraqi invasion of Kuwait in August. Subsequently, employment in the United States recovered a good year (beginning in March of 1991) before Canada followed suit with an upswing firmly taking hold by mid-1992.

Despite the 1990-91 recession in the United States, Canadian exports grew steadily. While natural resource products and, to a lesser extent, automotive products remain sensitive to changes in American demand, the last decade has seen a rapid shift in our exports away from these traditional commodities to other products such as machinery and equipment. As in Canada, American demand for machinery and equipment has grown steadily through most of the recession. Higher oil prices early in the recession also buttressed our export earnings.

Ron Watts / First Light

Employment losses in the early 1990s were heavily concentrated among blue collar workers.

THE WORTH OF HOUSEHOLD WORK

Running a household takes a lot of work and virtually all of it goes unpaid. If Canadians were actually paid for the cooking, cleaning, shopping, repairs, gardening, pet care, and child care, what would be the size of the pay cheque?

*Statistics Canada estimates about $8,000 to $10,000 annually for every adult in the country. An experimental study called **The Value of Household Work in Canada, 1986**, published in 1992, has found that we spend almost as much time working in our households as we do at our paid jobs — about 21 billion hours a year. Women do roughly two-thirds of all household work, whether measured in time or by dollar value.*

For the country as a whole, that comes to about a third of Canada's Gross Domestic Product (GDP), or between $160 billion and $200 billion, depending on the way it's calculated. That means household work is an unpaid sector of the economy that produces more than Canada's entire manufacturing sector.

Putting a value on household work is getting more attention as economists acknowledge the value of unpaid work in national economies. In Canada, it is also becoming an issue in civil law, for instance, when courts set payments for divorce, child support, and compensation for earnings lost due to injury or wrongful death.

The importance of the issue is underlined by the attention it is receiving. This is the third study in two decades to try to value household work in Canada. While experimental, it is considered more accurate than attempts in the mid-1970s and 1980s. It used two ways to put a value on an hour of work at home: opportunity cost and replacement cost.

Opportunity cost is the amount of money a person gives up in potential wages when they work at home instead, based on average wages net of taxes in their area.

Replacement cost is what a professional would charge to do a particular household job. For instance, cooking is valued by using chefs' wages.

The resulting figures show similar trends.

Using opportunity costs, in 1986 each adult Canadian did an estimated $8,216 worth of work. On average, the work women did was worth about two-thirds more than the work men did.

Replacement costs averaged $10,246 a year. With this method, the average worth of women's work was almost twice that of men.

As well as working differing amounts of time, men and women tended to do different things in households. Preparing meals, cleaning and laundry made up more than half of women's tasks but less than a third of men's. In contrast, men did about two-thirds of all household repairs, maintenance and shopping, while women did about a third.

UNEMPLOYMENT IN THE 1990S

The 1990 recession was largely concentrated in central Canada, especially Ontario. But the Ontario of the 1990s bears little resemblance to the Ontario of the 1980s when buoyant exports and a speculative bubble in the Toronto real estate market helped lower its unemployment rate to only 4.9%, by far the lowest in Canada.

For Ontario, the results of the recession were devastating. The downturn in exports of manufactured goods that began in 1989 was the first sign of trouble for manufacturing jobs, largely concentrated here. Employment came next, followed by a collapse of both residential and commercial real estate values in the over-heated Toronto market. By 1992, the unemployment rate had more than doubled and employment had fallen by almost 7%. In fact, Ontario lost 70% of all jobs in Canada between 1990 and 1992 compared to its 25% share of jobs lost in 1981-82. Some provinces, such as Alberta and British Columbia, hardly experienced outright recession at all compared to Ontario.

In Canada, it seems that once one falls into the unemployment trap, it is especially difficult to escape it during recessions. About 65% of the increase in unemployment is due to a longer spell of unemployment for those without a job, and only about 35% is due to actual job loss.

Unemployment Rate

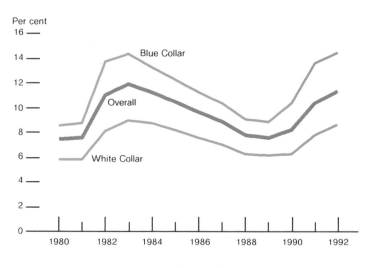

In the 1990-92 downturn, the duration of unemployment played a major role in raising unemployment. The average spell of unemployment jumped from 19.8 weeks in 1989 to 26.7 in 1992 and again, the most dramatic increase was in Ontario, which rose from 16.3 to 29.3 weeks.

The trend towards a longer duration began in the 1980s. Recent research has shown that the probability of finding a job in the first few months of unemployment rose in the 1981-82 recession, but never returned to pre-recession levels during the subsequent expansion of the economy.

The 1990-92 recession polarized unemployment even more. In fact, the chances of finding a job after only one or two months of unemployment were better in 1992 than during the previous recessions. However, job prospects were much worse for the longer-term unemployed, especially for older workers.

In the early 1990s, youth unemployment soared as firms sharply reduced hiring new entrants. In fact, hiring began declining in 1988, when corporate profits turned down. In the last four years, Statistics Canada's Help-Wanted Index has plunged to record levels, bearing testimony to this trend.

In 1992, the unemployment rate for young people peaked at just over 19%. This is slightly less than in the early 1980s, but only because youths left the labour force in record numbers during the early 1990s. As job prospects dried up, only 60.5% of young people were active in the labour force at the end of 1992; a 15-year low. The bleak job outlook seemed to send young people a message as the number of full-time students aged 15 to 24 years rose 4%, despite a drop in the youth population. The return to school appears well justified, as the unemployment rate for young people falls from 30% for those without high school to only 6% for those with university degrees.

After reaching a peak of 12.6 million early in 1990, employment fell steadily for four quarters. After a brief pick-up in the summer of 1991, the number of jobs began to fall again — the so-called double-dip — to a new low of 12.2 million in the second quarter of 1992. Growth since then has proceeded at an historically weak rate for a recovery.

A recurrent theme in the most recent recession is the sentiment that the changes in the economy have been more structural than in 1981-82. In labour markets, this is translated into a fear that job losses in the 1990s are permanent, and that recovery will not be as quick as in 1983.

In fact, there is little evidence that permanent layoffs played a greater role in the 1990-92 recession than in 1981-82. In manufacturing, about 40% of layoffs were permanent in both recessions. There was, however, a shift toward more permanent layoffs in other industries beginning in the mid-1980s.

The number of permanent jobs lost rose as the recession progressed, and had not yet begun to decline by the end of 1992. The increase of permanent, relative to temporary, layoffs reflects the diminished hope of firms for an imminent recovery of demand as the recession dragged on, and the cumulative toll of rising bankruptcies. As well, restructuring and cost-cutting efforts may have intensified as global competitive pressures have steadily increased.

WHITE COLLAR, BLUE COLLAR TRENDS

There has been widespread talk that part of the restructuring in the latest recession was an attack on white-collar jobs. The fact that white-collar job losses in the United States exceeded declines for blue-collar workers in the early 1990s has helped to fuel this speculation. On the whole, however, there is little evidence that white-collar jobs were unusually affected in Canada.

Employment losses and unemployment in the early 1990s were once again heavily-concentrated among blue-collar workers. While they represented only about one-third of the workforce, blue-collar jobs accounted for about two-thirds of the drop in employment — about the same as in 1981-82. This reflects hefty drops for the mining, construction, manufacturing, fishing and transportation industries. Overall, the unemployment rate for blue-collar workers rose from 9.3% to 14.5% during the recession.

White-collar workers have fared better. Unemployment in their ranks rose slowly from 5.2% to 7.5% but the impact of the recession was closely tied to their

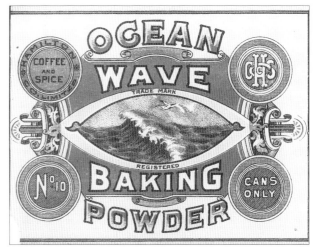

National Archives of Canada C 121149

Promoting a Canadian product at the turn of the century.

level of education. More highly-educated groups such as managers and professionals had unemployment rates persistently below 6%. The management group itself showed little or no employment loss, as widely-publicized cuts to middle managers at some companies obviously were not representative of the overall trend. Professionals meanwhile posted a net increase of 188,000 full-time jobs, led by growing demand in industries such as health and education.

Less skilled white-collar jobs such as service and clerical occupations saw some net decrease in the 1990s. In fact, their jobs were more at risk than during the 1981-82 downturn. Clerical workers in particular may have been victims of both technological change and cost-cutting.

PRICES AND WAGES

In 1992, price inflation fell to its lowest level in three decades. The Consumer Price Index (CPI), the most commonly-used measure of inflation, rose by only 1.5%. In 1991, the CPI had risen to a 10-year high of 5.6%, largely reflecting the introduction of the federal Goods and Services Tax on January 1, 1991 and a spate of provincial indirect tax increases.

The moderation of prices in 1992 reflected a number of factors. Perhaps most important was continued sluggish consumer spending in Canada, which limited the ability of retailers to pass on higher prices to consumers without aggravating the slump in sales. As well, the cost of many consumer products eased. Import prices were moderate as the Canadian dollar appreciated (which makes imports less expensive). Food prices edged down during the year, while energy costs were dampened by an excess of supply. Housing costs moderated in response to declining mortgage rates and the falling price of new homes. Prices regulated or controlled by government continued to rise faster than other prices, up 4.9% and 0.5%, respectively.

Exchange Rate

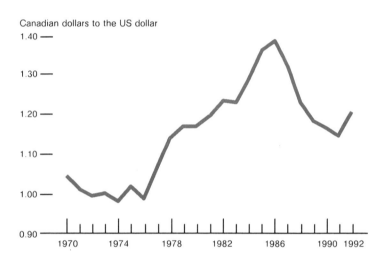

Canadian dollars to the US dollar

Prime Rate and Annual Change in the CPI

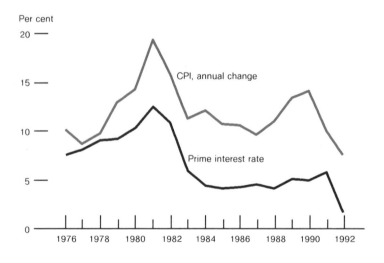

Per cent

Most other prices in the economy were also moderate in 1992. Prices for manufactured goods went up by only 0.5%, after a 1% dip in 1991. Unit labour costs were strictly controlled by manufacturing firms at a time of intensified foreign competition and low profit margins. The largest contribution came from a boost to productivity, as output per person employed surged ahead. Weak prices for most natural resources also contributed to moderate prices. Outside of a rally for wood, most raw material prices fell during the year, notably for commodities such as metals which faced increased competition from eastern Europe. These declines were reflected in a further drop in prices received for our exports. In fact, export prices in 1992 stood a full 3% below their 1986 average.

Wage increases were also slowed by the recession, falling below 5% for the first time since 1988. Average hourly earnings rose by only about 3%. Mounting unemployment led to the most pronounced slow-downs in the forestry, construction and retail trade industries. Public wage controls for the federal government and a number of provinces also slowed wage increases in this sector.

The number of labour disputes fell to the lowest level on record, despite the downward pressure on wages, with only about 2 million person-days lost to labour disputes in 1992. Real wages improved, despite the slowdown in nominal wages, as price inflation slowed even faster. Moreover, rising unemployment in virtually all regions accompanied a relatively light bargaining calendar.

INTEREST RATES AND THE CANADIAN DOLLAR Most short-term interest rates fell to 20-year lows in 1992. The prime lending rate, which is what banks charge their most credit-worthy customers, eased to an average of 7.5% during the year, while five-year mortgage rates dipped below 10% for the first time since the early 1970s. Both of these declines continued a downward trend evident since 1981, when rates peaked at about 20%. The steady decrease through the past decade mirrors a gradual reduction of inflationary pressures. Interest rates remained volatile on a monthly basis, however, as they rose sharply in the autumn when financial markets were engulfed in worldwide currency turmoil and uncertainties related to the constitutional referendum.

The value of the Canadian dollar eased against its American counterpart in 1992, after touching a 13-year high the year before. The exchange rate had appreciated for five straight years before its reversal in 1992. The dip in the exchange rate proved to be a boon to retailers, as it helped curb cross-border shopping. The lower dollar also helped exporters consolidate their recent gains, while raising the price of imports substantially by year-end. Recent movements in our exchange rate have been relatively muted by international standards. This was highlighted by the upheaval in the European Monetary System which forced the United Kingdom and Italy (along with some smaller countries) to abandon their goal of maintaining a fixed exchange rate with their other European trading partners.

The Toronto Stock Exchange drifted slowly downward throughout the year, closing with a loss of about 5% at year-end, then rallying to a three year high early in 1993. The market had edged up in 1991, but has not come close to matching its pre-recession high of about 4,000 (1975 = 1,000) set late in 1989. Firms did step up the pace of net new equity issues during 1992, in an attempt to raise funds and ease the burden of debt.

Both the downturns beginning in 1981 and 1990 were much more severe than any previous recessions in Canada. Why cycles have become more severe is unclear; the 1981 recession followed the shortest expansion on record, while 1990 followed the second longest. While it is true that inventories have come to play less of a role in this cycle, this did not brake the overall severity of the contraction. In fact, many of the management techniques applied to inventories have also increasingly been directed to labour needs as well, making employment and hence consumer incomes and spending more susceptible to declines during recessions. Similarly, the growing importance of services has defied the prediction of many analysts that this would mute the severity of cycles. Instead, services themselves have become increasingly sensitive to the overall business cycle.

SOURCES

Statistics Canada

FOR FURTHER READING

Selected publications from Statistics Canada

▲ *Canadian Economic Observer. Monthly. 11-010*

▲ *Canadian Economic Observer: Historical Statistical Supplement. Annual. 11-210*

▲ *National Income and Expenditure Accounts, the Annual Estimates. Annual. 13-201*

▲ *Income Distribution by Size in Canada. Annual. 13-207*

▲ *Provincial Economic Accounts. Annual. 13-213*

▲ *The Distribution of Wealth in Canada, 1984, 1986. 13-580*

▲ *Charting Canadian Incomes, 1951-1981, 1984. 13-581*

▲ *The Input-Output Structure of the Canadian Economy in Constant Prices. Annual. 15-202*

▲ *Aggregate Productivity Measures. Annual. 15-204*

▲ *Perspectives on Labour and Income. Quarterly. 75-001*

TABLES

20.1 PRICE INDEXES (1986 = 100)

	Consumer Price Index		Industrial Product Price Index	Raw Materials Price Index	New Housing Price Index
	All items	Annual percent change			
1961	23.9	1.0	25.3	..	..
1971	31.9	2.9	30.7	..	..
1981	75.5	12.4	83.6	104.0	95.8
1986	100.0	4.2	100.0	100.0	100.0
1987	104.4	4.4	102.8	107.3	113.8
1988	108.6	4.0	107.2	103.8	125.6
1989	114.0	5.0	109.4	107.2	142.2
1990	119.5	4.8	109.7	111.6	144.3
1991	126.2	5.6	108.6	104.7	134.3
1992	128.1	1.5	109.1	105.7	134.3

20.2 PROVINCIAL GROSS DOMESTIC PRODUCT PER CAPITA RELATIVE TO THE CANADIAN AVERAGE (PERCENT)

	Nfld.	PEI	NS	NB	Que.	Ont.
1961	50.2	49.4	65.3	60.2	90.6	120.2
1971	56.0	51.5	67.6	64.3	90.1	117.8
1981	58.0	56.8	61.4	60.6	86.0	102.7
1986	60.0	59.5	75.1	71.3	90.3	111.9
1987	60.6	58.2	74.2	71.2	91.8	112.7
1988	60.3	59.0	73.0	70.8	91.5	114.5
1989	60.0	59.0	73.0	71.1	90.0	114.8
1990	61.4	60.7	75.5	72.7	90.7	111.4
1991	65.0	63.7	78.6	75.6	91.5	109.6

	Man.	Sask.	Alta.	BC	Yt and NWT	Canada
1961	90.1	78.0	108.7	111.4	107.6	100.0
1971	89.1	83.3	107.0	106.0	118.6	100.0
1981	87.4	103.0	157.2	112.7	141.3	100.0
1986	86.5	85.4	121.4	99.9	151.3	100.0
1987	84.3	79.1	116.9	100.3	154.5	100.0
1988	85.2	76.6	111.5	100.3	151.8	100.0
1989	85.4	78.8	109.7	102.4	153.2	100.0
1990	86.6	81.7	115.2	103.7	153.9	100.0
1991	85.7	80.8	115.1	105.3	151.0	100.0

20.3 GROSS DOMESTIC PRODUCT PER CAPITA (DOLLARS)

	Nfld.	PEI	NS	NB	Que.	Ont.
1961	1,118	1,099	1,453	1,340	2,017	2,674
1971	2,501	2,303	3,024	2,873	4,027	5,267
1981	8,473	8,294	8,963	8,847	12,552	14,998
1986	11,934	11,833	14,923	14,186	17,965	22,244
1987	12,998	12,482	15,897	15,273	19,683	24,162
1988	14,132	13,829	17,103	16,597	21,436	26,820
1989	14,829	14,604	18,046	17,588	22,263	28,403
1990	15,390	15,203	18,912	18,210	22,732	27,927
1991	16,175	15,838	19,539	18,814	22,763	27,272

	Man.	Sask.	Alta.	BC	Yt and NWT	Canada
1961	2,004	1,735	2,420	2,480	2,394	2,225
1971	3,984	3,725	4,783	4,737	5,301	4,471
1981	12,757	15,034	22,948	16,458	20,624	14,597
1986	17,197	16,972	24,132	19,858	30,092	19,884
1987	18,065	16,954	25,052	21,506	33,111	21,437
1988	19,953	17,952	26,133	23,509	35,568	23,432
1989	21,126	19,497	27,128	25,330	37,895	24,736
1990	21,717	20,487	28,874	25,988	38,573	25,065
1991	21,327	20,102	28,620	26,179	37,558	24,873

20.4 GROSS DOMESTIC PRODUCT AT 1986 PRICES, EXPENDITURE BASED
(MILLION DOLLARS)

	Personal expenditure on consumer goods and services	Government current expenditure on goods and services	Government investment	Business fixed capital				Final domestic demand
				Total[1]	Residential construction	Non-residential construction	Machinery and equipment	
1961	102,669	36,968	6,610	23,239	10,179	11,192	4,835	167,551
1971	164,327	64,713	10,381	41,245	17,387	17,371	10,095	276,853
1981	257,129	90,916	10,489	86,006	25,155	31,525	29,369	445,833
1986	297,478	100,129	12,532	88,993	30,806	25,626	32,561	499,167
1987	310,453	101,857	12,812	99,693	35,843	26,400	37,450	524,852
1988	324,301	106,060	13,373	110,794	36,855	29,301	44,638	554,466
1989	334,765	109,963	14,461	117,047	38,409	30,709	47,929	576,237
1990	337,933	113,205	15,508	110,999	34,922	30,853	45,224	577,581
1991	332,337	115,326	15,878	105,810	30,808	29,573	45,429	569,383
1992	335,821	117,207	16,549	104,441	33,092	24,933	46,416	573,972

[1] For 1961, 1971 and 1981 components do not add to total because of various technical adjustments.

20.5 GROSS DOMESTIC PRODUCT AT 1986 PRICES, EXPENDITURE BASED
(MILLION DOLLARS)

	Business inventories			Exports of goods and services	Imports of goods and services	Statistical discrepancy	Gross Domestic Product at 1986 prices
	Total[1]	Non-farm	Farm and grain in commercial channels				
1961	1,493	1,871	80	25,755	23,798	−1,056	169,271
1971	1,332	1,193	290	60,664	49,866	−2,371	286,998
1981	1,209	830	379	101,853	105,313	−214	440,127
1986	2,592	1,745	847	138,119	133,369	−808	505,666
1987	3,259	3,682	−423	142,942	142,678	−1,608	526,730
1988	2,453	4,218	−1,765	156,528	162,385	1,834	552,958
1989	4,334	3,493	841	157,952	172,729	−14	565,779
1990	−3,096	−4,466	1,370	164,507	176,010	14	563,060
1991	255	−50	305	165,326	179,952	−1,523	553,457
1992	−2,731	−1,334	−1,397	178,874	189,886	−1,903	558,372

[1] For 1961 and 1971 components do not add to total because of various technical adjustments.

20.6 FINANCIAL MARKETS

	Bank Rate %	Prime Rate %	Conventional 5-year mortgage rate %	US exchange rate in $ Cdn	G-10 Index[1] 1981=100	TSE[2] Price Index 1975=1000
1961	3.06	5.60	. .	1.01	. .	646.2
1971	5.19	6.48	. .	1.01	122.9	967.2
1981	17.93	19.29	18.38	1.20	100.0	2158.4
1986	9.21	10.52	11.21	1.39	86.3	3010.6
1987	8.40	9.52	11.17	1.33	88.2	3567.8
1988	9.69	10.83	11.65	1.23	93.9	3302.7
1989	12.29	13.33	12.06	1.18	98.8	3801.5
1990	13.05	14.06	13.35	1.17	99.3	3421.1
1991	9.03	9.94	11.13	1.15	100.8	3469.5
1992	6.78	7.48	9.51	1.21	95.0	3402.9

[1] Trade-weighted exchange rate with Canada's 10 largest trading partners. A rise in the index indicates an increase in the Canadian dollar.
[2] TSE (Toronto Stock Exchange).

20.7 UNEMPLOYMENT RATES[1] (PERCENT)

	Canada	Nfld.	PEI	NS	NB	Que.	Ont.	Man.	Sask.	Alta.	BC
1966	3.4	5.8	. .	4.7	5.3	4.1	2.6	2.8	1.5	2.5	4.6
1971	6.2	8.4	. .	7.0	6.1	7.3	5.4	5.7	3.5	5.7	7.2
1976	7.1	13.3	9.6	9.5	11.0	8.7	6.2	4.7	3.9	4.0	8.6
1981	7.5	13.9	11.2	10.1	11.5	10.3	6.6	5.9	4.6	3.8	6.7
1986	9.5	19.2	13.4	13.1	14.3	11.0	7.0	7.7	7.7	9.8	12.5
1987	8.8	17.9	13.2	12.3	13.1	10.3	6.1	7.4	7.4	9.6	11.9
1988	7.8	16.4	13.0	10.2	12.0	9.4	5.0	7.8	7.5	8.0	10.3
1989	7.5	15.8	14.1	9.9	12.5	9.3	5.1	7.5	7.4	7.2	9.1
1990	8.1	17.1	14.9	10.5	12.1	10.1	6.3	7.2	7.0	7.0	8.3
1991	10.3	18.4	16.8	12.0	12.7	11.9	9.6	8.8	7.4	8.2	9.9
1992	11.3	20.2	17.7	13.1	12.8	12.8	10.8	9.6	8.2	9.5	10.4

[1] *Annual averages.*

20.8 MERCHANDISE EXPORTS AND IMPORTS ON A BALANCE-OF-PAYMENT BASIS

	Merchandise exports		Merchandise imports		Trade balance	
	Total $'000,000	Change from previous year %	Total $'000,000	Change from previous year %	Total $'000,000	With US $'000,000
1971	17,782	. .	15,314	. .	2,469	1,339
1981	84,432	10.1	77,140	13.6	7,292	3,323
1986	120,318	1.1	110,374	7.5	9,944	16,899
1987	126,340	5	115,119	4.3	11,222	17,620
1988	137,779	9.1	128,862	11.9	8,917	13,848
1989	141,767	2.9	135,347	5	6,420	11,631
1990	146,520	3.4	136,600	0.9	9,920	16,748
1991	141,728	−3.3	135,948	−0.5	5,780	13,884
1992	157,549	11.2	148,063	8.9	9,487	17,678

Source
Statistics Canada

HARPSICHORD ITALIAN 1596

RICHARD SWIECKI

GERA DILLON / *FIRST LIGHT*

CHAPTER TWENTY-ONE

THE ARTS

INTRODUCTION

In 1979, Acadian author Antonine Maillet's bestselling book, *Pélagie-la-Charrette*, became the first title by a non-French citizen to win France's coveted Prix Goncourt. Just over a decade later, British bookies were placing high odds on Michael Ondaatje's *The English Patient* as it ran for Britain's prestigious Booker McConnell prize. Ondaatje was named co-winner of the prize in 1992. These two international literary honours for Canadian writers stand as symbolic bookends for a period in which Canadian artists and other cultural producers have achieved unprecedented success at home and abroad.

The success of Canadian television productions has been another example of our growing international confidence. In a 1992 speech in Toronto, Jeff Sagansky, an executive with the Columbia Broadcasting System (CBS) network, spoke of successful US airings of Canadian productions such as "Love and Hate", "Conspiracy of Silence", and "Urban Angel". He pointed out that, unlike a decade ago when American co-productions in Canada meant that every effort was intended to hide their made-in-Canada status, today, "...amazingly, when [we] played these shows we were not inundated with angry calls from viewers protesting the loose use of [Canadian] terms like Queen's Magistrate and the Commonwealth of Toronto. Indeed, both "Love and Hate" and "Conspiracy of Silence" were among the best reviewed shows of the entire broadcast season."

The success and viability of contemporary Canadian culture is rooted in history. For over half a century, Canadian governments have helped develop a strong sense of Canadian cultural identity through funding cultural institutions and the arts. Two of the most important steps in this process happened in the 1930s: the Canadian Radio Broadcasting Corporation was founded in 1936 and the National Film Board (NFB) was established in 1939. After World War II, the federal government created other instruments, including, among others, the Canada Council (1957) and Telefilm Canada (1967). Today all three levels of government in Canada — federal, provincial, and municipal — work to support Canadian culture and heritage.

Government support for the arts and culture sector extends beyond funding. In 1992, as just one example, the federal government passed Bill C-7, the Status of the Artist Act. This new legislation is considered an important first step in recognizing the professional status and contribution of artists in Canadian society. Among other things, the legislation sets up regulations and a special agency to help artists working in areas of federal jurisdiction — including broadcasting, the NFB and the National Arts Centre — to improve their working conditions.

The fact is, contemporary Canadian culture is not an endless search for an elusive "Canadian identity". It involves a collection of dynamic cultural industries and institutions, each of which contributes significantly to the Canadian economy and to the social fabric of our society.

In the future, Canadian artists and cultural producers will continue to confront a unique set of challenges, including a small domestic market, a far flung population, increasingly diverse and demanding audiences, a rapidly evolving technological landscape, and a fiercely competitive international marketplace. It is equally clear, however, that Canadians have the talent, the creativity and the confidence to continue to take their place in the spotlight, at home and abroad.

FUNDING In 1990-91, federal, provincial and municipal governments spent a total of $5.9 billion on culture (including intergovernmental transfers of about $320 million). The federal share amounted to $2.9 billion, with more than three-quarters (77%) of this allocated to the operating budgets of cultural departments and agencies such as the Canadian Broadcasting Corporation. Capital expenditures accounted for about 8%, while the remaining 14% went to grants and contributions to artists and the cultural industries, institutions and organizations. Provincial and territorial governments devoted $1.8 billion to culture, while municipal governments spent $1.2 billion.

Malak / GeoStock

Dinosaur exhibit, Canadian Museum of Nature.

COOL SPACES

With an entrance that looks vaguely like it might descend into one of the more interesting parts of the historic Paris Metro, the new Canadian Museum of Contemporary Photography (CMCP) is unique in ways that go beyond its place as the first photographic museum in Canada.

And most of it is invisible from street level.

Dedicated in Ottawa in 1992, it has been described as a 32-storey highrise laid sideways. Some 166 metres long and only 17 metres wide, the museum has been artfully shoehorned into a long-disused Grand Trunk Railway tunnel between Parliament Hill and the historic Chateau Laurier Hotel.

The building's exterior is a period study in limestone and glass, its roof concealed under a hotel terrace complete with stone balustrades and copies of historic street lamps, and huge arched windows overlooking the locks of the Rideau Canal. The interior is another world, owing as much to high-tech as the exterior owes to history. The CMCP's director describes it as ''cool spaces and hard surfaces — a McLuhanesque environment. . . a place of energy and creation where things could be tried — a laboratory, not a salon.''

In this laboratory are displayed the visions of Canada's top photographers in two genres, social documentary and fine art — under lighting especially designed to exhibit photographic work.

More than half of the building is open to the public, consisting of gallery space, lobbies, a small theatre and a museum boutique. Densely packed behind the scenes lie a research centre, workshops and safe storage for 160,000 photographic transparencies, negatives, prints and photography-based works, including sculpture, installation and video.

The Museum houses more than 50 years' worth of the nation's best photography with the bulk of the collection added since the late 1960s. It was created in 1985 as an affiliate of the National Gallery of Canada, to take over the National Film Board (NFB) Still Photography Division's collection, mandate and staff.

During its first few years, the CMCP was a museum without walls, reaching the public through travelling exhibitions lent to galleries and museums across Canada. Even now the building is considered a symbol of something larger, serving as a home base and safe storehouse for a far-reaching program stretching beyond Canada's borders.

Since 1985, between 80 and 100 travelling exhibitions have been seen by over 3 million people in Canada and abroad. The CMCP also published catalogues, educational kits, a series of slide shows, and an anthology of essays on photography. Museum curators scout the country regularly, searching out Canadian photographers' work in galleries and private studios. Each year they see about 100 artists, evaluate another 100 photographic portfolios, and purchase more than 200 works for the museum's growing permanent collection.

Isolde Ohlbaum

Michael Ondaatje, winner of the 1992 Governor General's Literary Award for English fiction.

THE CULTURE SECTOR The direct impact of the arts and culture sector as measured by the contribution to the Gross Domestic Product (GDP) was an estimated $14.7 billion in 1990-91. This figure represents 2.4% of the national GDP. More than 330,000 Canadians work in the culture sector.

Although imported books, films, recordings and broadcast entertainment (series, drama and feature films for TV) still dominate the Canadian marketplace, there have been some important shifts in the last decade. For example, the market share of foreign-controlled companies involved in film distribution has been declining. Between 1986-87 and 1990-91, the foreign control share of total revenue in the home entertainment market dropped from 54% to 43% and from 87% to 83% in the theatrical sector. Canadian products appear to be holding their own in the marketplace — sales of Canadian-produced books, records and films are growing relatively quickly — while the demand for these products continues to grow. In foreign markets, sales of Canadian cultural products almost doubled through the 1980s, reaching $238 million in 1989. Although Canada still faces a large deficit in its cultural industries — the balance of trade between imports and exports was $7 billion in 1989 — this deficit is declining. Overall, Canadian-produced cultural products continue to find and expand their market niche and Canadian content is holding and sometimes increasing its ground.

THE PRINTED WORD: NEWSPAPERS, PERIODICALS, BOOK PUBLISHING AND LIBRARIES

PASTIME OR PASSION? In an age of electronic information, Canadians continue to demonstrate a healthy appetite for books, magazines and newspapers. According to a 1991 study of reading habits in Canada, we are a nation of print fans. Reading for pleasure ranks third after listening to music and watching TV. Indeed, we spend an average of seven hours a week reading for pleasure.

Canada's national reading habit is fed by vigorous newspaper, periodical and book publishing industries and a vast network of public libraries. In 1990-91, almost 1,100 periodical publishers produced a selection of more than 1,500 magazines. In the same period, Canada's 314 book publishers (companies earning $50,000 or more per year) published more than 8,100 books, bringing the total number of books in print to almost 59,000. By 1990-91, Canada's 854 public libraries boasted total holdings approaching 61 million books — in other words, everyone in the country could borrow two books at the same time and library shelves would still be well-stocked.

ADVERTISING Advertising sales are the major source of revenue for periodicals and newspapers. Magazines and newspaper publishers compete with radio and television broadcasters to capture precious advertising dollars. In 1991, the print media, including newspapers and magazines, were still winning this battle: over a five-year period, beginning in 1986, periodicals increased their advertising revenue by an average of nearly 6.0% each year, while newspapers upped their advertising revenue even more — with an average growth of 7.5% per year. At the same time, radio and television advertising revenues increased an average of only 3.0% and 6.7% per year.

DIFFERENT VOICES Canada's publishing industries have long served an ethnically and linguistically diverse population. Today, publications for the English and French language markets are still dominant — about 80% of published materials are in English — but the industry also produces more than 400 publications, including newspapers and magazines, catering to more than 40 different ethnocultural groups. These media often serve the particular needs of first-generation ethnic and language communities.

The long and distinguished history of Canada's ethnic press has helped shape the development of this country. Wherever groups of newcomers settled, they often founded newspapers to serve as their community voice. In Windsor, Ontario, the first black woman newspaper editor in North America helped found one such paper, the *Provincial Freeman*, in 1853. Mary Ann Shadd Cary was born in the United States and later moved to Canada, where her abolitionist paper became an outspoken champion of Ontario's early black community.

Sales of Books[1], 1991

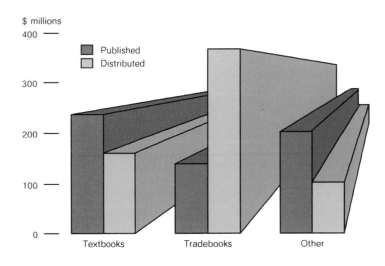

[1] Published and distributed by publishers and exclusive agents.

COMPETING FOR CANADIAN READERS Canadian book publishers face stiff competition from foreign-owned companies for markets within Canada. Publishers in the United States, Great Britain and France have larger domestic markets and print larger numbers of each book they produce. Their longer print runs make the cost of each book lower than for Canadian publishers, with their smaller markets and shorter print runs. Consequently, when foreign books are sold in Canada, they can be offered at a lower price and still make a profit. For example, an American, British or French book of fiction might sell in Canada for $19.95 while a Canadian book could be closer to $30.

In 1990-91, close to half of the $1.3 billion earned by book publishers and exclusive agents from sales in Canada came from importing, marketing and distributing foreign titles. In total, 110 publishers and 50 exclusive agents earned $654 million through the distribution of primarily imported books.

Though profits may be more difficult to come by for Canadian publishers, the number of books being published in Canada continues to rise each year. And an increasing share of these books are by Canadian authors.

Canadian book publishers have been looking to foreign markets to compensate for smaller markets and sluggish sales in Canada. Publishers either sell books directly to other English or French language markets, or sell publishing rights to foreign publishers. In 1990-91, book publishers in Canada earned $813 million from sales of their own releases, with one-quarter of these sales in foreign markets.

KIDSTUFF A 1991 study of reading in Canada revealed that Canadian parents have a firm belief in the importance of reading to their children. Throughout the past decade, Canadian publishers have responded with a rich harvest of quality children's books and magazines. And publishers around the world have taken notice. Each spring, at the International Children's Book Fair in Bologna, Italy, Canadian publishers sign international rights deals, putting Canadian children's stories into the hands of young readers all over the world. As just one

illustration, the books of Robert Munsch, a much-loved Canadian children's author, are now available in nine different languages (including four languages in Canada) and 12 different countries.

As children's books have met with international success, so too have our children's magazines, theatre, film and television productions. One successful example is *OWL* magazine, published by the non-profit Young Naturalist Foundation. In addition to two other magazines for young readers and their families, the foundation produces the popular ''OWL'' television series, which is broadcast in Canada, the United States, the United Kingdom and 22 other international markets.

TURNING THE PAGE Technology may soon change the way we read. Newspaper, periodical and book publishers all face the challenges of electronic publishing. As cable links and home computers spread, electronic publications will become even more accessible. Already, there are increasing numbers of reference books available on CD ROM. At work, many professionals routinely hook up via modem to sophisticated databases, such as *InfoGlobe*, to obtain the same information they may access through newspapers, magazines and journals. Some predict a technological future in which we may eventually browse through newspapers, books and magazines via our TV or computer screens more often than we venture out to the local newsstand or bookstore. Canadians' love for reading is likely to endure, but the future will determine how often we turn to the familiar printed page.

FILM AND TELEVISION

RAISED ON HOLLYWOOD Canadians have long been a major audience for Hollywood movies and American TV series. American productions run in our movie theatres, line the shelves of our video stores and dominate our TV screens. Despite the ubiquity of the American presence, Canadian film and television distributors and producers have made solid gains in recent years.

Pete Ryan / GeoStock

Actors, *Degrassi High* television series.

The Canadian penchant for high-budget American productions dates back to the 1920s, when the American movie industry began buying up control of the film distribution and exhibition system in Canada. Today, a small number of foreign-controlled distributors still bring in a steady stream of American products. For distributors, these popular imports remain a low-risk means of generating almost-guaranteed high profits from advertising and admission receipts.

Through the 1980s, a combination of technological change and Canadian broadcasting regulation began to change the distribution picture. Canadian-controlled distributors increased their share of distribution revenues. By 1990-91, 19 foreign-controlled

distributors earned only 53% of all film and video revenues in Canada, compared to 74% in 1982-83.

As Canadian-owned distributors increase their revenues, they are also making a small but growing share of their income from the sale and rental of Canadian films and videos ($74 million out of a total of $620 million in 1990-91).

Canadian-content productions earn varying proportions of distributors' income, depending on the market in which they are sold. Movie houses, for example, are still a limited market for Canadian productions. In 1990-91, distributors earned only 6% of their total revenue from Canadian feature films.

THE ENVELOPE, PLEASE...

Talented Canadians abound in the arts, as the number of award winners — and awards themselves — testify. A selective look at some of the winners shows the breadth and depth of ability in this country.

CANADA COUNCIL

Many of Canada's most prestigious awards in arts, sciences and the humanities fall under the aegis of the Canada Council, an independent agency created by Parliament in 1957 to assist, inspire and support cultural endeavours.

1992 GOVERNOR GENERAL'S LITERARY AWARDS

CATEGORY	WORK	NAME
FICTION	*The English Patient* (English fiction)	Michael Ondaatje
	L'enfant chargé de songes (French fiction)	Anne Hébert
POETRY	*Inventing the Hawk* (English poetry)	Lorna Crozier
	Andromède attendra (French poetry)	Gilles Cyr
DRAMA	*Possible Worlds* and *A Short History of Night* (English drama)	John Mighton
	Les petits orteils (French drama)	Louis-Dominique Lavigne
NONFICTION	*Revenge of the Land: A Century of Greed, Tragedy and Murder on a Saskatchewan Farm* (English nonfiction)	Maggie Siggins
	La Radissonie. Le pays de la baie James (French nonfiction)	Pierre Turgeon
CHILDREN'S LITERATURE	*Hero of Lesser Causes* (English text),	Julie Johnston
	Victor (French text)	Christiane Duchesne
	Waiting for the Whales (illustration)	Ron Lightburn
	Simon et la ville de carton (illustration)	Gilles Tibo
TRANSLATION	*Imagining the Middle East* (English text)	Fred A. Reed
	La mémoire postmoderne. Essai sur l'art canadien contemporain (French text)	Jean Papineau

Also administered by the Canada Council are the following prizes, listed with their 1992 winners:

GLENN GOULD PRIZE
(for an exceptional contribution to music) **Oscar Peterson**

PRIX DE ROME IN ARCHITECTURE
John McMinn

CANADA COUNCIL MOLSON PRIZES
(awarded to distinguished Canadians, one in the arts and the other in social sciences and humanities) **Douglas Cardinal**; **Fernand Dumont**

VIRGINIA P. MOORE AWARD
(given to a young Canadian classical musician, instrumentalist or conductor) **Corey Cerovsek**

THE ACADEMY OF CANADIAN CINEMA AND TELEVISION

1992 GENIES (motion pictures)

CATEGORY	WORK	NAME
BEST MOTION PICTURE	*Naked Lunch*	
BEST PERFORMANCE BY A LEADING ACTOR	*La Sarrasine*	**Tony Nardi**
BEST PERFORMANCE BY A LEADING ACTRESS	*Bordertown Café*	**Jane Wright**
BEST ACHIEVEMENT IN DIRECTION	*Naked Lunch*	**David Cronenberg**
BEST FEATURE-LENGTH DOCUMENTARY	*Deadly Currents*	**Simcha Jacobivici, Elliott Halpern, Ric Esther Bienstock**
BEST ANIMATED SHORT	*Strings/Cordes*	**Wendy Tilby**

1993 GEMINIS (television)

CATEGORY	SERIES	NAME
BEST DRAMATIC SERIES	*E.N.G*	
BEST COMEDY SERIES	*The Kids in the Hall*	
BEST VARIETY SERIES	*The Best of Just for Laughs*	
BEST INFORMATIN SERIES	*the 5th estate*	
BEST DOCUMENTARY SERIES	*The Valour and the Horror*	
BEST PERFORMANCE BY AN ACTOR IN A CONTINUING LEADING DRAMATIC ROLE	*Road to Avonlea*	Cedric Smith
BEST PERFORMANCE BY AN ACTRESS IN A CONTINUING LEADING DRAMATIC ROLE	*E.N.G*	Sarah Botsford

CANADIAN ACADEMY OF RECORDING ARTS AND SCIENCES

1992 JUNO AWARDS

CATEGORY	WORK	NAME
CANADIAN ENTERTAINER OF THE YEAR		Bryan Adams
ALBUM OF THE YEAR	*Mad Mad World*	Tom Cochrane
SINGLE OF THE YEAR	*Life is a Highway*	Tom Cochrane
FEMALE VOCALIST OF THE YEAR		Celine Dion
MALE VOCALIST OF THE YEAR		Tom Cochrane
GROUP OF THE YEAR		Crash Test Dummies
BEST VIDEO	*Into the Fire*	Sarah McLachlan
HALL OF FAME		Ian & Sylvia

1992 CANADIAN COUNTRY MUSIC AWARDS

CATEGORY	WORK	NAME
ALBUM OF THE YEAR	*Everybody Knows*	Prairie Oyster
SINGLE OF THE YEAR	*Take it Like a Man*	Michelle Wright
FEMALE VOCALIST OF THE YEAR		Michelle Wright
MALE VOCALIST OF THE YEAR		Ian Tyson
VOCAL DUO OR GROUP		Prairie Oyster
VIDEO OF THE YEAR	*Take it Like a Man*	Michelle Wright

1992 CANADIAN MUSIC VIDEO AWARDS

CATEGORY	WORK	NAME
BEST VIDEO	*She-la*	54•40

PEOPLE'S CHOICE AWARDS

BEST VIDEO	*Helluvatime*	Slick Toxik
BEST FEMALE	*Into the Fire*	Sarah McLachlan
BEST MALE	*Life is a Highway*	Tom Cochrane
BEST GROUP	*Lovers in a Dangerous Time*	Bare Naked Ladies

This is not a comprehensive list of all awards given to Canadian artists, nor of all categories in each award. It does serve, however, to highlight the accomplishments and talents of Canada's cultural community.

POTATO WITH A VIEW

Canadian couch potatoes aren't tuning in to television like they used to. In 1991, Canadians spent an average of 23 hours per week watching television — almost an hour less per week than in 1986.

Despite popular perception, teenagers spend the least amount of time watching television. In 1991, those aged 12 to 17 watched 18 hours of TV per week — about half of the time spent by those aged 60 and older.

The television habits of younger children have changed the most in recent years. In 1991, children under 12 watched 19 hours per week of television — down 2.5 hours from 1987.

Although Canadians throughout the country are spending less time glued to the tube, television viewership remains higher in some provinces than others. Albertans watched the least television in 1991 — only 21 hours per week. Newfoundlanders tuned in the most, watching more than 26 hours per week.

Generally, television viewership increases with age. Women tend to watch more television than men and francophones spend more time tuning in than anglophones.

The types of programs Canadians watch has also changed. Canadian-produced comedies and dramas have become far more popular in recent years and Canadians still get most of their news from Canadian-produced news and public affairs shows.

THE SMALL SCREEN Television, including pay TV and conventional TV, remains the most lucrative market for the distribution of Canadian productions. In 1990-91 distributors earned 12% of home entertainment revenues (including pay TV, conventional TV and the home video market) from Canadian productions. An encouraging trend for producers and distributors is our increasing willingness to watch Canadian productions. In 1990, Canadians watched three times more Canadian drama than they did six years earlier — Canadian drama shows accounted for 18% of TV viewing in 1990 versus only 6% in 1984.

LIGHTS, CAMERA . . . Despite the limitations of the distribution system, Canadian filmmakers and producers make a growing number of films and videos each year. In 1990-91, film and video producers put together more than 17,600 productions in Canada, including over 3,600 commercials.

NATIONAL FILM BOARD Canada is a world leader in producing animated films and documentaries. Indeed, it was John Grierson, the founder of Canada's National Film Board (NFB), who coined the word "documentary". Grierson later led the development of this Canadian art form, and generations of Canadian filmmakers have followed in his footsteps. By 1992, NFB productions had been nominated for 57 Academy Awards. Eight films had won Oscars, including four documentaries and three animated productions and one live action short film. In 1989, the NFB won a special Academy Award in commemoration of its 50th anniversary.

In the past 25 years the pace of film and video production in Canada has stepped up considerably. In 1967, the year Telefilm Canada was established, Canadians produced only four feature films. In 1990-91, 54 theatrical features were made in Canada, including 26 produced with the support of Telefilm Canada. Indeed, Telefilm Canada reports that in its first quarter century it supported the production of more than 500 Canadian feature films and more than 900 TV shows.

Arnaud Maggs / CMCP

Yousuf Karsh from the photographic series *48 Views*.

CO-PRODUCTIONS Co-productions have become the strategy of choice for Canadian film and television producers. By 1992, Canada had signed international co-production treaties with 23 countries. These agreements allow Canadian and foreign producers to form creative partnerships and access financial support and markets beyond their own borders. In 1992, Canadian filmmakers were involved in 37 co-productions with 10 different countries.

FILLING THAT NICHE Broadcasting technology is advancing at a terrific pace. Digitization, fibre optics, compression technology, interactive and high definition television all loom on the horizon. Through direct satellite broadcasting, for example, Canadians may soon have access to up to 200 different television channels. Some predict that broadcasters will need a huge supply of programming to attract viewers. Canadian productions may become even more appealing to networks and cable companies trying to satisfy an increasingly fragmented, niche-oriented marketplace.

Canadian television producers have already earned an impressive track record in the international marketplace. In 1992, Telefilm Canada reported that many productions have been sold to more than 30 countries and some have sold to more than 60 countries. In the United States, Canadian programs now represent one-third of all cable television programming.

Radio Listening[1] by Type of Station, 1989

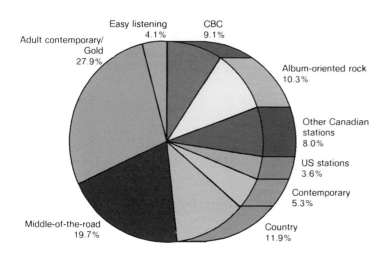

Easy listening 4.1%
CBC 9.1%
Adult contemporary/ Gold 27.9%
Album-oriented rock 10.3%
Other Canadian stations 8.0%
US stations 3.6%
Contemporary 5.3%
Middle-of-the-road 19.7%
Country 11.9%

[1] People aged 7 and over.

Sales of Music Recordings in Canada, 1990-91

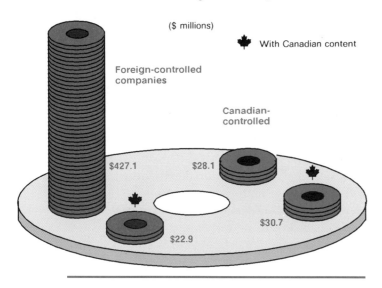

($ millions)

🍁 With Canadian content

Foreign-controlled companies

Canadian-controlled

$427.1 $28.1
$22.9 $30.7

Major American networks, in particular CBS, are increasingly relying on Canadian co-productions to entertain audiences. Notably, CBS has also purchased entirely Canadian-produced programming such as ''Kids in the Hall'', a renegade Canadian comedy produced by the Canadian Broadcasting Corporation (CBC).

TWO FOR THE MONEY . . . For Canadians who came of age in the era before VCRs and pay TV, going to the movies was a ritual experience, inextricably linked to the aroma of popcorn and the rustle of a crowd in a darkened theatre.

Back in 1952, Canadian movie admissions reached a peak of 256 million. When television arrived the next year, movie attendance dropped, averaging 100 million per year through the 1960s and 1970s. By 1990-91, with the arrival of VCRs and pay TV, movie admissions had taken another hit, dropping to 79 million.

Today, in some parts of Canada, going to the drive-in or the local cinema is becoming a thing of the past. Between 1980 and 1985, theatre and drive-in attendance in rural Canada dropped 46%. Theatre attendance has now levelled off to between 75 and 80 million per year, but drive-in attendance has continued to decline, dropping from 4 million in 1986-87 to 2.7 million in 1990-91. Many local theatres and drive-ins are simply closing up shop. In small-town and rural Canada, 40% of local theatres and drive-ins had closed by 1985-86 and, across Canada, another 17% of theatres and drive-ins had closed by 1990-91.

THE VIEW FROM THE COUCH

Nowadays, more and more of us are content to either grab a video at the corner video store and head straight for the living room couch, or settle for what's available on a pay TV channel. In 1990, for the first time, Canadian families spent more on movie rentals than movie tickets — an average of $72 at the movies, and $75 on videocassette rentals.

In the hectic early 1990s, despite the demands of our daily schedules, Canadians still spent a significant amount of time with their TVs. In 1991, virtually every home in Canada had at least one television, and more than 40% of Canadian households owned two or more colour TVs. On average, we spent at least three hours in front of the set each day (over 23 hours each week).

Throughout the 1980s, the percentage of Canadian drama and comedy shows on conventional television increased significantly, almost doubling for English television stations and tripling for French stations. By 1990-91 Canadian comedy and drama material made up one-fifth of all English programming and one-third of French programming on Canadian television stations.

We appear increasingly willing to watch home-grown shows. Although francophone viewers are still in the lead when it comes to watching Canadian shows, anglophone audiences are steadily increasing the amount of Canadian programming in their TV diet. Compared to 10 years ago, English-speaking audiences watch twice as much Canadian comedy and drama programming and francophones watch three times as much.

News is still our favourite Canadian content programming. English and French viewers alike turn primarily to Canadian programs for their news and public affairs reports rather than to their foreign counterparts.

RADIO AND SOUND RECORDING

In a busy world, Canadians treat their radios a little like old friends — they know what to expect so they don't always pay close attention. In fact, when their radios are on, Canadians are usually doing something else, like driving through rush hour traffic. In 1989, Statistics Canada found 94% of Canadians listened to the radio at least once per week. On average, we had the radio on for about three hours a day.

Canadians can tune into the country's public broadcasting network, CBC/Radio-Canada, from just about anywhere in the country. In addition, more than 500 other private radio stations serve local communities across the country. All radio stations in Canada obtain licenses from the Canadian Radio-television and Telecommunications Commission (CRTC), and FM stations are licensed by 'format'. FM formats are a guide to the type of music and programming radio stations offer. In recent years, Canadians under 45 have been particularly fond of the Adult Contemporary/Gold formats, stations that specialize in soft rock, pop and 'golden oldies'.

NEVADA OF THE NORTH

When many people think of gambling in Canada, they think of charity bingo and weekly lotteries. For the really big action — slot machines, roulette tables and blackjack — Canadians have traditionally flocked south of the border to giant gambling meccas such as Las Vegas, Nevada, another American city ''that never sleeps.''

While the Canadian gambling scene is still far tamer than in the United States, many provinces are taking steps to keep Canadian gambling dollars — and profits — on our side of the border.

Most recently, in 1992, Ontario and Quebec announced plans to open year-round American-style casinos. In the western provinces, charitable casinos have been successfully operated for years. Manitoba's government owned and operated casino, the Crystal Palace, opened its doors in 1989, earning more than $13 million in its first year of operation. All proceeds are used to support Manitoba's health care system.

Ontario's proposed new casino, to be located in Windsor — just across the bridge from Detroit — is expected to add more than $140 million to provincial coffers. With two casinos in the works, Quebec hopes not only to keep gambling dollars at home, but to attract tourist dollars as well.

When radio pioneered in Canada, it provided much more than background music. In the days before television, radio offered the excitement of the first live broadcasts. The family radio set was usually the focal point of Canadian homes.

The establishment of a national radio broadcasting system was seen as a way to tie this huge country together. The CBC radio and Radio-Canada networks have developed as a unique blend of private and public broadcasting. Historically, Canada's national radio system has nurtured the development of literature and plays in this country. Many of Canada's best-known authors began their careers writing radio plays and stories.

Today radio, including private stations and the CBC/Radio-Canada networks, is still an important outlet for new recordings released in Canada. The other key source is music video TV — an increasingly influential means of exposing Canadians to the latest in popular music.

SURROUNDED BY SOUND Each year, Canada's sound recording industry offers music consumers more diversity. While prestigious Canadian orchestras, such as the Montreal Symphony Orchestra, continue to make successful classical recordings, the Canadian music scene is rocked by Kashtin, a band that blends ancient native traditions and mainstream rock and roll — singing lyrics in the members' ancestral Montagnais (Innu) language. Sales of records, tapes and CDs in Canada increased substantially in the last few years, rising from $330 million in 1987-88 to $509 million in 1990-91. Rock recordings account for an ever-increasing portion of this income.

In 1990-91, record companies in Canada released almost 4,700 new releases, with more than 600 of these qualifying as Canadian-content material. To qualify as Canadian content, a recording must meet two of the following four requirements: the music must be composed by a Canadian, principally performed by a Canadian, recorded or performed wholly in Canada and broadcast live in Canada, and the lyrics must be written by a Canadian. In 1990-91 the Canadian content releases earned the industry $54 million, or just over 10% of total sales.

Like the film, video and book publishing industries, the Canadian music business is dominated by foreign-controlled companies. In 1990-91, 14 foreign-controlled companies garnered almost 90% of sound recording sales, including 43% of the sales from Canadian content releases.

Canadian recording companies struggle to compete. Often, smaller Canadian companies nurture Canadian artists who go on to find more lucrative recording and distribution deals with the large multinationals. In 1990-91, Canadian-controlled companies released almost three-quarters (71%) of all Canadian content releases. Although these releases brought in $31 million in sales, this represents only half their total sales revenue. Most Canadian record companies enter into license agreements to release foreign recordings in order to survive.

IN THE GLOBAL MARKETPLACE Although most Canadian musicians certainly don't get rich, a select group of Canadian performers continue to achieve international mega-stardom. The list now includes, among others, rockers Bryan Adams and Roch Voisine, pop artist Céline Dion, country singer k.d. Lang, children's performers Sharon, Lois and Bram and pianists Angela Hewitt and John Kimura Parker.

Like other Canadian musicians, these artists have benefited from the 30% Canadian-content airplay requirement in the radio industry. In fact, since the 1970s, the CRTC Canadian content regulations have been the foundation for the development of the Canadian music industry. Recently, the success of international musical partnerships has created the need for change. In 1993, the CRTC adjusted the Canadian content regulations, making it easier for international collaborations to qualify as Canadian-content material.

By 1990-91, vinyl records had virtually disappeared from the shelves, and compact discs had taken over their market share. In 1990-91, CDs generated 40% of total sales revenue ($203 million), while vinyl album sales fell to 2% of the total and standard cassettes held their own at 55%.

Just as they became accustomed to CDs, Canadian consumers were confronted with new formats, including mini-discs and digital compact cassettes. Despite the success of the CD format, however, the new sound carriers may not meet with the same response. In 1990-91, fewer families were willing to spend money on recordings, suggesting that cost may determine how warmly Canadians will embrace the new formats.

For Canadian music lovers, the choice between buying tapes or CDs, or tuning in to a favourite radio station, may soon become less relevant. The integration of technology could alter forever how Canadians listen to, purchase and record music.

In 1992, the CRTC received its first two applications for 'pay radio' — national satellite-to-cable digital music services to be delivered to cable TV systems across Canada. Using a new type of tuner hooked to a stereo system (similar to a television converter), listeners will be offered a huge selection of all-music channels representing every musical taste, from reggae to opera. Even relaxing environmental sounds — the cry of loons, the sound of rain, or the rhythmic washing of waves — could be on the menu. With their remote control units, listeners will be able to obtain information about their selections as the music plays, including the name of the performer and the song lyrics.

Some predict that with digitization, fibre optics and compression technology on the horizon, consumers may soon find themselves ordering and recording music selections on demand, much as they now select pay-per-view movies from their living rooms. Clearly, the new broadcasting technologies pose an enormous challenge to existing radio and sound recording formats.

The CRTC is re-examining its role within a rapidly evolving broadcasting environment. As a federal body charged with the protection and development of Canadian culture, the CRTC must develop new strategies which will work within an increasingly complex and competitive commercial environment. According to CRTC Chairman Keith Spicer, the coming changes are part of a global trend: ''Canadians — and I think they are following worldwide trends — want more choice in the number of services they are offered. They want more narrowly focused services to meet their individual needs. And they want a much higher level of personal control over what they buy and when and how they receive it.''

PERFORMING ARTS

The story of performing arts companies in Canada is one of a never-ending struggle to survive. From the earliest dance, theatre and music companies in pre-Confederation Canada to their contemporary counterparts, Canadian arts companies have defied the odds.

Over the past three decades, governments in Canada have established a tradition of providing arts funding, particularly through the Canada Council. Despite this financial support, however, most non-profit performing arts companies must rely on a resilient blend of artistic commitment and audience loyalty to survive.

The Statistics Canada survey respondents for 1990-91 included the professional and some semi-professional non-profit arts companies in Canada — a creative corps of 226 theatre companies, 100 music organizations, 54 dance companies and 15 opera companies. Together, these 395 companies gave almost 39,000 performances and reported $373 million in revenues. With expenditures of $381 million, the result is still a total annual deficit of $7.6 million. Although this debt level has somewhat stabilized in recent years (it was $7.5 million in 1989-90), it has increased 117% since 1988-89.

THE ART OF SURVIVAL Most arts companies perform a precarious balancing act when it comes to generating revenues. For every dollar brought in through ticket sales, advertising, bar and concession sales, investment incomes and facilities rental, companies must raise an additional dollar from public grants and private donations to keep deficits in line. Winning the support of private sector donors is critical. In 1990-91, arts companies brought in nearly $59 million through business and individual sponsorships and donations and fundraising activities, an increase of 9% over the previous year.

Ian Crysler / First Light

To add to their financial difficulties, total attendance dropped in recent years, from 15 million in 1988-89 to 13.6 million in 1990-91. Despite declining attendance figures, however, a recent survey offered some encouragement. According to the report, an overwhelming majority of Canadians (90%) say that when they go out, they want to go out to relax and be entertained. In fact, 67% of the respondents attend performances at least once each year. Two-thirds of Canadians said they'd like to get out more often. Their number one choice: attending a concert or performance in an auditorium or hall.

COMPETING FOR AUDIENCES

In recent years, big-budget commercial theatre productions have made headlines in many Canadian cities, attracting huge audiences and raking in astronomical profits. Toronto has hosted some of the longest-running success stories. In its first two-year run in Toronto in the mid-1980s, the musical *Cats* reportedly grossed $65 million and between 1989 and 1992, *Phantom of the Opera* garnered $220 million.

The success of these companies has met with mixed reviews from the Canadian theatre community; some

DANCE IN CANADA

The richness and depth of Canada's cultural life is nowhere more apparent than in the world of Canadian dance. In 1993, the Canada Council counted some 100 professional dance companies and more than 200 professional choreographers working in most of the country's major centres. These professionals are specialized in all forms of dance: ballet, modern, experimental, folk, ethnic, native dance and even ice dance.

Dance companies in Canada range in size from groups of 50 or more to solo performers. They also sustain a community of administrators, set and costume designers, lighting professionals and publicists.

Life can be a struggle for these groups, in terms of their financial well-being. They have not been immune to the effects of the recession. The Canada Council calculates that the dance companies it supports lost more than 130 weeks of work between the 1988-89 season and that of 1991-92. This has meant the loss of more than 1700 weeks of work, not only for the artists, but for the community of administrators and other professionals who work with them.

In its most recent Performing Arts Survey, Statistics Canada looked at some 50 professional non-profit dance companies operating across the country. It found that in 1990-91, these companies ran a collective deficit of $970,000, up from a deficit of $344,000 recorded five years previously.

In addition, the Canada Council calculates that for the entire dance community, the accumulated deficit in 1991-92 was as high as $6 million.

Despite their precarious balance sheets, Canadian dance companies persist, offering a repertoire ranging from the classic to the contemporary. Many of them tour throughout Canada, the United States, Europe and Asia and have drawn international acclaim in the process.

The National Ballet of Canada, the Royal Winnipeg Ballet, Les Grands Ballets Canadiens, La La La (Human Steps), la Fondation Jean-Pierre Perreault, O Vertigo, Ballet BC, to name only a few, have charmed their audiences, at home in Canada and around the world.

Canadian dancers are perceived to be innovative and dynamic. Whether they perform on pointe or barefoot, to classical themes or more contemporary sounds, the legacy of their trade in Canada is rich and varied, precise and graceful, and, it endures.

welcome the shows as a means of developing and encouraging a new audience of theatre goers. Others are concerned that mega-hits simply draw dollars away from existing companies and other local productions.

NATIVE RENAISSANCE Canada's independent choreographers and composers continue to dazzle audiences. As one example, in late 1992, the first native Canadian ballet, *In the Land of the Spirits*, met with enthusiastic reviews during a successful cross-country tour. The production was the brainchild of native composer John Kim Bell, who collaborated with leading modern dance choreographer Robert Desrosiers, among others, to create a new vocabulary of dance blending modern and native traditions. Intended as a showcase for the contribution of native performing artists, more than half the dancers were drawn from the native community.

Performing Arts Companies' Revenue, 1990-91

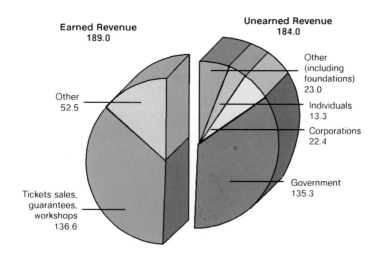

Earned Revenue
189.0

Unearned Revenue
184.0

Other
52.5

Tickets sales, guarantees, workshops
136.6

Other (including foundations)
23.0

Individuals
13.3

Corporations
22.4

Government
135.3

ON THE ROAD On the international scene, Canadian theatre, music and dance companies have distinguished themselves around the world. Our major dance companies have toured to critical acclaim in Europe. Some of our best-known orchestras have been signed to prestigious international recording contracts and are selling records worldwide. Canadian children's theatre companies have set standards for performance in the United States. And Canadian directors, such as Robert LePage and his Théâtre Repère, have brought down the house in London and Paris.

One of Canada's most unique contributions to the performing arts takes place in the circus ring. The dynamic performances of Quebec's *Cirque du Soleil* have vaulted the group into the international spotlight.

There is an element of historical irony in all of this. Whereas Canadian artists and musicians once believed they had to go to Europe to receive classical training, Canadian musicians now perform European classics on stages all over North America. Tafelmusik, for example, has taken its Baroque repertoire to Germany — the heartland of Baroque.

HERITAGE

When settlers first came to the Ottawa Valley, they were often surrounded by forest so tall they had to cut clearings around their cabins to allow more sunlight through. Today most of the ancient forests are gone, cleared by early logging and farming industries. But, thanks to a joint project of the Canadian Museum of Nature and the Nature Conservancy of Canada, visitors to the Shaw Woods Nature Preserve, near Eganville, Ontario can still walk through a section of the original forest, a protected stand of the towering trees that once covered this part of the Canadian Shield. Through hundreds of such programs, Canadian heritage institutions offer a nation-wide extravaganza of historical, cultural and scientific experiences.

Indeed, a traveller could spend several years wandering through Canada's observatories and planetariums (15), botanical gardens (22), zoos and aquariums (26), exhibition and other centres (105), archives (354),

David Neel / CMCP

British Columbia artist Bill Reid.

THE EYE OF THE BEHOLDER . . .

*Controversy and criticism are no strangers to the art world, and the National Gallery of Canada has had its share in recent years. The Gallery is charged with collecting new and old works of art, most but not all Canadian. Inevitably, some of the many works it acquires and exhibits in an average year will offend some people. And sometimes it displays a 'meat dress' or a **Voice of Fire** that provokes heated national debate.*

*Or, as the Gallery's director, Dr. Shirley Thomson, told the Wall Street Journal during the **Voice of Fire** controversy, ''Great works aren't always instantly appreciated — but at least people are talking about art.''*

*In 1991, the National Gallery displayed Jana Sterbak's **Vanitas: Flesh Dress for an Albino Anorexic**. Literally a dress of flesh, this work was made of salted flank steak, sewed into a sleeveless dress and draped over a wire dressmaker's form. Over a period of 12 weeks it dried from fleshy red to leathery brown, a comment on human vanity, aging and decay. Objections to the piece flew: some called it a health hazard (Health and Welfare Canada officials said it wasn't, as long as no one ate it), some said it was disgusting.*

Sterbak's work became nationally notorious, although it had excited only quiet praise in several earlier exhibitions, including one in Saskatoon, Saskatchewan. Sterbak herself said reaction to the dress indicated the power of the work.

*A year earlier, in 1990, the National Gallery had purchased Barnett Newman's **Voice of Fire** for $1.76 million. A storm of controversy followed the monumental canvas, which featured a red vertical stripe centred between two deep blue ones.*

From corner lunch counters to the House of Commons, people objected to the price given the work's apparent simplicity, and to the fact that Newman was an American painter. An often-repeated assessment was that anyone given a couple of cans of paint, rollers and 15 minutes could duplicate it.

In fact, several people tried — on barn doors and other surfaces in various places across Canada.

When Dr. Thomson eventually appeared before the Commons culture committee, committee members reaffirmed a long standing principle — that the National Gallery operates legally at ''arm's length'' from government, free from political intervention in its mandate.

Meanwhile, the Newman had become arguably the best-known modern work in the National Gallery's permanent collection.

Perhaps a sign of the public debate swirling around **Vanitas** and **Voice of Fire** was the flood of headlines in each case. A piece about the flesh dress, headlined ''Hereford today, gone Tomorrow'' joined numerous takes on ''Voice of Ire''; one wag advocated exhibiting the two pieces together and calling the result ''Bonfire of the Vanitas'' after a novel and movie of nearly the same name.

In fact, the National Gallery collected a six-inch thick pile of newspaper clippings just on these two pieces of art, and many of the writers came back to the definition of art itself.

One letter to a newspaper objected to **Vanitas**, saying, ''What most Canadians want is art that embodies beautiful and sensuous forms.''

But an interviewee in another paper said, ''It's not repulsive . . . it is shocking but daring. I like people who aren't afraid of saying something like this.''

Some in the art field have argued that public appreciation or dislike for a particular piece shouldn't affect National Gallery decisions — that its purpose as a national institution is to illustrate the development of civilization and of art by buying and displaying pieces that show important stages of that development.

Indeed, the history of art is of artists pushing personal and societal boundaries in their work. And history also records that even the Group of Seven, whose works are now Canadian icons, were rejected when they unveiled their then-revolutionary vision in the teens of this century.

Michael Torosian / CMCP

Toronto artist Robert Markle.

historic sites (371) and museums (1,228) in Canada. Altogether, there are more than 10 different types of museums in this country — everything from marine collections to sports museums and halls of fame.

In 1990-91, more than 57 million people (including some 270,000 researchers) visited Canada's heritage institutions. At the same time, the number of nature lovers who enjoyed the peace and serenity of Canada's 169 nature parks and conservation areas was over 56 million.

Protecting Canada's heritage and preserving it for future generations is the business of a huge network of federal, provincial, and local institutions, organizations and individuals. But the most revealing statistic is the number of Canadians who donate their own time to heritage preservation: in 1990-91 more than 42,800 Canadians volunteered at heritage institutions (not including nature parks) in their communities, an increase of nearly 11% over the previous year.

Heritage preservation is out on the street. Through initiatives such as the Heritage Regions and Mainstreet programs, entire communities are linking heritage preservation with economic development, and inviting visitors to participate in living history lessons. Visitors to the Cowichan-Chemainus Valleys in British Columbia, for example, can tour a local working sawmill. In Lanark, Ontario, tourists can take a first-hand look at the wool industry in operation.

With its potential for beefing up the tourist trade and sparking local economic development, heritage preservation and development has become big business in Canada. In Alberta, for example, investment in heritage facilities has increased tourism and stimulated regional economies. A dramatic example is the $28 million Royal Tyrrell Museum of Palaeontology in Drumheller. In 1989, 500,000 dinosaur-seekers injected $7.5 million into Drumheller's regional economy, a figure expected to rise to $10 million by 1990.

The heritage of Canada's First Nations peoples extends back thousands of years. Today, aboriginal artifacts form a significant part of many of Canada's institutional collections. But aboriginal communities across the country have raised concerns about the display and ownership of these items by museums. In response, the Canadian Museums Association and the Assembly of First Nations formed a task force to deal with the issues. Today museums and communities are working together to repatriate some artifacts. In the future, aboriginal communities will have a greater say in the decisions made by Canadian museums.

CONTEMPORARY VISUAL ARTS

In Canada, contemporary visual art stands for ideas and concepts. In a fantastic array of shapes and forms — from experimental music, film and video, to multi-media installations, to everyday household items — Canada's contemporary visual art reflects the mood of our times.

In large, metropolitan centres such as Montreal, Toronto or Vancouver, and in smaller regional communities from Newfoundland to Victoria, Canada's artists explore our social struggles, our political debates and our cultural identity. Whether their influences are regional or metropolitan, their ideas have become universal.

Indeed, if we can identify a post-modern Canadian tradition, it would be defined by a group of individuals whose goals are to change the way we see our world and ourselves.

ART FOR SALE A 1991 survey on the arts concluded that 16% of Canadians bought original paintings in the previous year and 25% had done so in the previous five years.

Although statistics are not available, Canadians have clearly developed a passion for wildlife art. The widespread popularity and commercial success of Canadian artist Robert Bateman is the leading edge of a phenomenon that now includes many other wildlife artists. For most Canadians, images of Canada's wilderness and its remaining inhabitants provoke a potent mixture of pride, awe and respect. This response may reflect our increasing concern for the fragility of the environment and our growing sense of responsibility for the creatures of this earth.

Karsh / Comstock

Canadian painter Jean Riopelle in his Paris studio.

Canada's North may be the most fertile artistic region in the country. In the Northwest Territories, for example, 5,500 people (or about 10% of the total population) work either part time or full time in the arts and crafts industry. Inuit sculpture and fine art prints account for three-quarters of the total production.

Dene, Inuit, Métis and non-native craftspeople also produce traditionally designed clothing and finely worked baskets and jewellery. Altogether, the arts and crafts industry is expected to contribute about $28 million to the economy of the Northwest Territories by 1993.

SOURCES

Canada Council

Canadian Association of Broadcasters

Canadian Conference of the Arts

Canadian Radio-television and Telecommunications Commission

Canadian Museum of Civilization

Canadian Museum of Nature

Department of Communications

Department of Consumer and Corporate Affairs

External Affairs and International Trade Canada

Heritage Canada Foundation

National Film Board

Statistics Canada

Telefilm Canada

Various provincial departments

FOR FURTHER READING

Selected publications from Statistics Canada

▲ *Focus on Culture*. Quarterly. 87-004

▲ *Sound Recording*. Annual. 87-202

▲ *Periodical Publishing*. Annual. 87-203

▲ *Film and Video*. Annual. 87-204

▲ *Government Expenditures on Culture in Canada*. Annual. 87-206

▲ *Heritage Institutions*. Annual. 87-207

▲ *Television Viewing*. Annual. 87-208

▲ *Performing Arts*. Annual. 87-209

▲ *Book Publishing*. Annual. 87-201

▲ *Selected Economic, Financial and Cultural Indicators for the Cultural Industries Sector*. Irregular.

Selected publications from Other Sources

▲ *Reading in Canada 1991*. Communications Canada, 1992.

▲ *Canadian Arts Consumer Profile 1990-91*. Communications Canada, 1992.

▲ *Proscenium; Canada's Arts and Culture Newsmagazine*. Canadian Conference of the Arts.

TABLES

21.1 GOVERNMENT EXPENDITURE ON CULTURE, 1990–91 (THOUSAND DOLLARS)

	Arts	Heritage	Libraries	Cultural Industries	Other[1]	Total
Federal						
Newfoundland	540	19,252	—	33,773	1,333	54,899
Prince Edward Island	459	7,141	—	6,244	496	14,339
Nova Scotia	1,976	46,781	—	46,159	2,928	97,846
New Brunswick	1,632	11,627	50	34,247	3,177	50,732
Quebec	24,091	156,469	25,386	630,165	41,400	877,511
Ontario	67,395	225,068	14,236	717,241	32,590	1,056,530
Manitoba	4,343	27,607	2,000	49,970	4,177	86,098
Saskatchewan	1,982	17,200	—	33,584	3,208	55,974
Alberta	5,826	77,503	—	59,942	8,052	151,325
British Columbia	8,258	35,588	—	91,515	8,833	144,194
Yukon	81	7,990	—	4,578	151	12,800
Northwest Territories	7	10,416	—	21,116	1,218	32,757
National Organizations	8,783	874	—	208,907	8,304	226,867
Foreign	36	4,301	59	12,543	—	16,939
Unallocated	3,678	—	—	1,901	4,837	10,416
Total	129,087	647,815	39,733	1,951,885	120,704	2,889,228
Provincial						
Newfoundland	6,402	3,021	13,825e	166	116	23,529,000
Prince Edward Island	1,481	4,658	3,857e	30	734	10,760,000
Nova Scotia	9,527	19,473	26,564e	1,722	3,157	60,444,000
New Brunswick	1,259	7,300	18,191e	294	586	27,631,000
Quebec	82,948	94,522e	165,331e	128,348	65,240	536,387
Ontario	54,477	139,197	215,555e	131,348	57,257	597,833
Manitoba	8,334	24,214	28,341e	2,700	15,609	79,198
Saskatchewan	2,543	23,507	27,728e	974	7,632	62,385
Alberta	38,461	28,574	54,045e	22,734	16,561	160,373
British Columbia	18,644	41,379	130,492e	13,380	5,568	209,463
Yukon	181	5,341	1,805e	—	417	7,744
Northwest Territories	1,892	5,938	2,691e	1,283	896	12,700
Total	226,149	397,123	688,425	302,979	3,773	1,788,447
Municipal						
Newfoundland	138	467	9,329	—	17	9,951
Prince Edward Island	246	26	1,004	—	45	1,321
Nova Scotia	—	69	23,551	—	1,800	25,420
New Brunswick	—	841	14,191	—	1,196	16,228
Quebec	11	10,104	167,340	—	94,390	271,845
Ontario	4,562	22,419	390,039	—	139,617	556,637
Manitoba	526	534	32,289	—	9,150	42,499
Saskatchewan	1,429	2,279	38,638	—	8,945	51,291
Alberta	1,959	4,555	68,444	—	5,599	80,557
British Columbia	7,848	7,039	149,989	—	11,992	176,868
Yukon	100	4	305	—	72	481
Northwest Territories	—	—	4,182	—	—	4,182
Total	16,819	48,337	899,301	—	272,823	1,237,280
All 3 Levels — Total	372,055	1,093,278	1,627,459	2,254,864	567,300	5,914,955

[1] *Includes expenditures related to heritage cultures component of multiculturalism.*

21.2 SUPPORT TO THE ARTS BY THE CANADA COUNCIL[1] (THOUSAND DOLLARS)

	1986-87	1987-88	1988-89	1989-90	1990-91
Dance	10,664	9,744	11,556	11,289	11,139
Music and opera	17,045	16,154	17,918	17,617	17,802
Theatre	18,079	16,547	18,837	18,423	18,659
Visual arts	8,380	9,382	9,718	10,086	9,923
Media arts[2]	4,512	4,003	4,929	4,929	4,985
Writing and publishing[3]	14,505	17,145	19,935	21,750	21,846
Other disciplines[4]	1,451	362	446	312	329
Art bank purchases	1,091	993	954	1,069	1,113
Explorations program	2,574	2,639	2,769	3,101	3,207
Touring office program	4,345	3,991	4,615	4,463	4,472
Total	80,646	80,960	91,677	93,039	93,475

[1] *Fiscal years ending March 31st.*
[2] *Media arts include film and holography, video and audio, and integrated media.*
[3] *Public Lending Rights Commission introduced in fiscal year 1986-87.*
[4] *Includes multidisciplinary work and performance art.*

21.3 CANADIANS OCCUPIED IN THE ARTS, 1986 AND 1991

Occupation	Total 1986	1991
Fine and commercial art, photography and related fields	72,190	87,115
Painters, sculptors and related artists	9,180	11,450
Product and interior designers	24,125	29,970
Advertising and illustrating artists	24,560	28,715
Photographers and camera operators	11,310	12,330
Other occupations in fine and commercial art, photography and related fields	1,030	1,075
Performing and audio-visual arts	46,585	52,240
Producers and directors	12,040	15,165
Conductors, composers and arrangers	1,330	1,640
Musicians and singers	12,205	11,650
Other occupations related to music and musical entertainment	1,255	1,240
Dancers and choreographers	1,490	1,445
Actors/actresses	3,635	4,125
Radio and television announcers	7,065	7,825
Other occupations in performing and audio-visual arts	6,100	6,990
Writing	42,775	53,510
Writers and editors	34,235	41,550
Translators and interpreters	7,200	9,615
Other occupations in writing	255	300

21.4 DIRECT CONTRIBUTION OF CULTURE TO THE ECONOMY, 1990–91[1]

	Jobs	Gross domestic products $'000,000
Written media	56,000	4,415
Film	36,670	749
Broadcasting	39,610	2,462
Recording	4,440	357
Cultural industries wholesalers	6,720	1,037
Cultural industries retailers	15,300	1,435
Performing arts	25,490	229
Heritage	77,890	955
Libraries	31,380	984
Cultural departments and agencies	20,030	1,359
Visual arts	21,500	688
Total	332,030	14,669

[1] *Fiscal year ending March 31st.*

21.5 MUSEUMS, 1990

	Number of institutions	Attendance
Art	184	5,931,338
Community	697	3,321,333
Fort and military	57	1,202,798
Maritime/marine	18	527,344
Human history	96	3,629,236
Science and technology	46	3,486,572
Natural history	41	1,603,117
Sport/hall of fame	17	663,033
Transportation	28	356,496
Multidisciplinary & other	44	4,250,447
Total	1,228	24,971,714

21.6 FILM AND VIDEO DISTRIBUTION REVENUES AND MARKET SHARE OF CANADIAN
PRODUCTIONS[1]

	1986-87	1987-88	1988-89	1989-90	1990-91
Total distribution revenues (million dollars)					
Theatrical	120.3	168.5	158.7	225.5	184.1
Home entertainment	226.8	288.2	306.4	398.2	486.1
Non-theatrical	30.4	23.8	25.4	25.7	24.3
Total	377.5	480.5	490.5	649.4	694.5
Market share of Canadian productions (percentage)					
Theatrical	5.0	4.4	4.9	4.3	6.1
Home entertainment	7.8	7.9	8.5	10.2	12.0
Non-theatrical	16.0	25.6	40.9	24.8	21.1
Total	7.5	7.5	9.0	8.7	10.8

[1] Fiscal years ending March 31st.

21.7 NUMBER OF CANADIAN FILM, VIDEO AND AUDIO-VISUAL PRODUCTIONS[1]

Type of Production	1986-87	1987-88	1988-89	1989-90	1990-91
Theatrical features	26	34	46	48	54
Productions under 30 minutes	6,380	6,069	6,939	6,511	7,210
Productions 30-74 minutes	1,430	3,222	3,865	3,363	4,970
Non-theatrical 75 minutes or over	117	127	474	568	577
Music videos	105	92	80	157	217
Television commercials	3,733	4,065	4,366	4,728	3,619
Other	1,552	2,423	3,032	1,806	987
Total	13,343	16,040	18,802	17,181	17,634

[1] Fiscal years ending March 31st.

21.8 MOTION PICTURE THEATRES

	Number of theatres		Number of paid admissions ('000)		Average admission price[1] $
	Regular	Drive-ins	Regular	Drive-ins	
1960	1,427	232	107,705	10,029	0.61
1970	1,156	279	80,826	11,489	1.38
1980	1,037	287	88,980	11,991	3.05
1990	633	109	76,275	2,732	5.56

[1] *Admission receipts excluding amusement taxes divided by number of paid admissions (regular theatres only).*

21.9 DISTRIBUTION OF TELEVISION VIEWING HOURS, 1991 (PERCENT)

Type of program	Canadian	Foreign	Total
News/public affairs	17.2	5.6	22.7
Documentaries	0.8	0.8	1.6
Instruction	2.4	0.8	3.1
Religion	0.2	0.1	0.3
Sports	5.0	2.4	7.3
Variety/games	4.5	5.0	9.5
Music & dance	0.6	0.5	1.1
Comedy	1.4	15.6	17.0
Drama	4.5	24.7	29.2
Others	—	8.2	8.2
Total	36.5	63.5	100.0

21.10 PERFORMING ARTS COMPANIES BY TYPE[1]

	1984-85	1990-91
Theatre		
Companies	146	226
Attendance	6,771,165	8,651,199
Performances	25,182	31,999
Music		
Companies	62	100
Attendance	2,455,318	3,070,439
Performances	2,568	4,046
Dance		
Companies	32	54
Attendance	1,180,761	1,311,435
Performances	1,803	2,028
Opera		
Companies	9	15
Attendance	475,836	554,265
Performances	571	616
Total		
Companies	249	395
Attendance	10,883,080	13,587,338
Performances	30,124	38,689

[1] *Fiscal years ending March 31st.*

21.11 PERFORMING ARTS COMPANIES BY PROVINCE, 1990–91[1]

	Number of companies	Total performances	Total attendance	Total revenue $	Total expenditure $	Surplus/ deficit $
Newfoundland	6	270	53,652	1,477,142	1,561,635	−84,493
Prince Edward Island	5	601	122,621	2,980,005	3,363,503	−383,498
Nova Scotia	8	1,141	357,162	5,706,994	5,807,042	−100,048
New Brunswick	5	502	204,103	2,522,677	2,363,426	159,251
Quebec	129	10,602	3,803,217	101,367,335	104,585,972	−3,218,637
Ontario	124	12,956	5,025,269	161,134,693	163,639,402	−2,504,709
Manitoba	15	1,556	798,751	21,479,429	21,908,439	−429,010
Saskatchewan	5	498	138,337	3,514,474	3,412,313	102,161
Alberta	46	4,763	1,358,209	36,756,361	37,500,739	−744,378
British Columbia	51	5,750	1,721,017	36,259,429	36,680,464	−421,035
Yukon	1	50	5,000	66,675	68,062	−1,387
Canada	395	38,689	13,587,338	373,265,214	380,890,997	−7,625,783

[1] *Fiscal year ending March 31st.*

21.12 CANADIAN AUTHORED AND PUBLISHED BOOKS, 1990–91[1]

	English language firms				French language firms		Total	
	Canadian controlled		Foreign controlled		No. of firms	Net sales $'000	No. of firms	Net sales $'000
	No. of firms	Net sales $'000	No. of firms	Net sales $'000				
Textbooks								
Elementary and secondary	36	43,230	16	85,670	41	68,768	93	197,668
Postsecondary	26	6,406	13	30,004	22	12,554	6 1	48,964
Total	51	49,636	19	115,674	53	81,322	123	246,632
Tradebooks								
Mass-market paperbacks	18	14,918	2	[2]	13	1,851	33	16,769
Trade paperbacks	121	44,411	7	9,350	54	24,431	182	78,191
Trade hardcovers	66	19,328	10	6,300	14	1,911	90	27,538
Total	127	78,657	10	15,649	60	28,192	197	122,499
Scholarly	27	5,118	—	—	10	1,346	37	6,464
Reference	36	24,847	6	78,227	21	4,181	63	1 07,255
Professional and technical	30	78,623	7	17,097	12	9,605	49	105,325
Total	178	236,882	24	234,647	107	124,645	309	588,174

[1] *Fiscal year ending March 31st.*
[2] *Confidential.*

21.13 BOOK TITLES PUBLISHED IN CANADA[1,2]

	1987-88	1988-89	1989-90	1990-91
Number				
Textbooks	1,643	1,700	2,020	2,012
Tradebooks	4,125	4,671	4,813	4,505
Other	1,079	1,246	1,525	1,609
Total	6,847	7,617	8,358	8,126
Percentage Canadian-authored				
Textbooks	92	95	98	97
Tradebooks	50	50	57	53
Other	92	90	90	94
Total	67	67	73	72

[1] *Includes Canadian-controlled and foreign-controlled companies.*
[2] *Fiscal years ending March 31st.*

21.14   ORIGIN OF A TYPICAL CANADIAN PERIODICAL ISSUE[1] (PERCENT)

Origin of editorial content and artwork	1986-87	1987-88	1988-89	1989-90	1990-91
Text					
In-house	53.3	51.8	50.9	51.3	50.4
Outside the organization					
Canadian-authored	39.5	41.2	42.2	41.5	42.0
Foreign-authored	7.2	7.0	6.9	7.2	7.6
Illustrations and photography					
In-house	48.6	45.6	44.8	44.0	44.0
Outside the organization					
Canadian-authored	44.7	48.0	48.8	49.6	49.4
Foreign-authored	6.8	6.4	6.4	6.4	6.6

[1] *Fiscal year ending March 31st.*

Sources
The Canada Council
National Film Board of Canada
Statistics Canada

RON WATTS / FIRST LIGHT

FITNESS AND SPORT

INTRODUCTION

IN STEP WITH THE TIMES...
On any given morning or evening in shopping malls across the country, crowds of late middle-aged and older people may be seen walking past shop windows, some strolling in talkative groups and some pacing faster and alone. They're not chasing bargains — they're participating in organized mall-walking, for exercise and their health.

It's a sign of the times. Fitness is becoming increasingly important to Canadians of all ages, and more of us than ever before are not just walking, but gardening, swimming, dancing and playing golf.

One indicator, Statistics Canada's 1991 General Social Survey, found that some 32% of Canadian adults (6.7 million) considered themselves "very active" based on the amount of energy they spent on leisure activities, compared with 27% in 1985.

As well, more than a million Canadians take part in voluntary fitness agencies as organizers and coaches, with many millions more participating in everything from marathons to team sports. Fitness and amateur sporting activities are organized at the local community, provincial and national levels. The Young Men's Christian Association (YMCA) and Young Women's Christian Association of Canada (YWCA), particularly influential in developing fitness programming, have been joined since the early 1980s by an increasing number of health clubs. Professional and semi-professional sports teams are also found in many larger Canadian cities.

SPORTS HISTORY

In Canada, sporting competitions have been a part of life since colonial days. In fact, it was from the indigenous peoples that Canada's settlers learned to snowshoe, canoe, play lacrosse and toboggan, activities they added to those they brought from their homelands: cricket and rugby from England, golf from Scotland, and so on.

The role of climate in Canadian sport showed in the popularity of another Scottish game, curling, ideal in this land of often-frozen ponds and lakes. Another game developed to entertain during the long winter months, hockey, was first played under formal rules in 1875 in Montreal. Before long, amateur hockey leagues formed from coast to coast.

During the final decades of the 1800s, hockey became a national pastime, and lacrosse and baseball gained popularity too.

In 1891, another important game entered the Canadian sporting scene — basketball. In that year, a Canadian psychology student, James Naismith, developed it as part of his studies in Springfield, Massachusetts. Basketball is now played in virtually every country in the world.

With the start of the 20th century, Canadian athletes began increasing their international profile. Since fielding its first official Olympic team in 1908, Canada has competed in every Olympics except the 1980 Moscow Games, which we boycotted to protest the Soviet invasion of Afghanistan.

In the 1920s, Canada's amateur boxers, rowers and track and field competitors numbered among the stars of international amateur competition. By the 1930s, however, it was clear that other nations were supporting their amateur athletes more vigorously — and reaping corresponding rewards.

GOVERNMENT SUPPORT To help promising Canadian athletes reach their potential, the federal government undertook a commitment to support amateur sport, beginning in 1943 with the Canada National Physical Fitness Act. The Fitness and Amateur Sport Act followed in 1961, and in 1969 the Task Force on Sport in Canada recommended greater government support, which resulted in increased funding for amateur sport. By the 1980s, the government's annual budget to support amateur sport exceeded $50 million.

SPORT CANADA Today, the federal government provides leadership, overall policy direction and financial support to Canadian amateur sport at the national and international levels through Sport

Lionel Stevenson / Camera Art

Mill River, Prince Edward Island.

Canada. Sport Canada, which works to stimulate excellence in Canada's athletes at the international level, has also helped to develop a strong domestic sport system to encourage all Canadians to participate in sports. To do this, it funds and facilitates the activities of about 85 national and other sport organizations. Some are national sport governing bodies. Others provide important support services such as coaching and sport medicine.

Through its core support program, Sport Canada helps pay for professional, technical and coaching staff, and defrays the costs of meetings, coaching clinics and seminars, training program development and national and international competitions.

THE GAMES . . . This kind of backing has helped Canada place strong teams at major international sporting competitions such as the Olympic, Paralympic, Pan-American, Commonwealth, and World University Games.

A Canadian athlete first competed in the Summer Olympics in 1900 as a member of the American team; this country's first official team went to London in 1908. Canada has been at every Summer Olympics since, except in 1980 when it joined other nations in boycotting the Moscow Games to protest the Soviet invasion of Afghanistan. Canadians have competed in every Winter Olympics since the first in 1924.

The Canadian Olympic Association estimates that Canada will field about 110 athletes in 11 sports for the 1994 Winter Olympics in Lillehammer, Norway. While no team had been assembled for the 1996 Summer Olympics in Atlanta at publication time, Canada's summer games teams have had between 300 and 440 members for the past two decades. At publication, 30 sports were on the Atlanta program.

In addition to participating, Canadians also have a tradition of hosting such major games, most recently the Winter Olympics in Calgary in 1988 and the 1976 Summer Olympics in Montreal. The Calgary Olympics remain the largest-ever Winter Games held, in terms of numbers of athletes and of demonstration sports. Canada's next major event will be the 1994 Commonwealth Games, set for Victoria, British

Columbia in August, 1994, featuring 3,200 athletes from 66 Commonwealth nations.

In addition to major games, Canada hosts other world-class competitions. For instance, in 1995, the World Nordic Ski Championships, involving some 500 athletes from 30 countries, will take place in Thunder Bay. It is the first time this country has hosted the event, which occurs every two years.

Since 1980, Canadians have been world champions or world record-holders in alpine skiing, speed skating, figure skating, yachting, track and field, equestrian events, swimming, synchronized swimming, rowing, trap shooting, boxing, wrestling, pentathlon, softball, ringette, hockey, swimming for amputees, and wheelchair discus.

Sport Canada's Best Ever winter program was initially established in 1983 to prepare Canada's Best Ever team for the 1988 Calgary Olympics, and has since been renewed in five-year blocks for subsequent Games. The latest five-year renewal, after Canada's success at Albertville, was in April, 1993. Some $31 million in funding will be spread over the five years to support Olympic-calibre athletes preparing for the 1994 Winter Olympics in Lillehammer, Norway, and the 1998 Winter Olympics in Nagano, Japan. In addition, the program focuses on increasing participation in winter sports at home among young Canadians — the next generation of Olympians.

A matching Best Ever summer program was created after the success of the original winter program, to develop the Canadian team for the 1988 Seoul Olympics. Beyond ensuring that Canadian athletes received the best possible preparation for the Summer Games, Best Ever helped to develop a sound administrative foundation on which to build future sport programs. The Best Ever summer program has since been rolled into Sport Canada's base budget.

IN THE CARDS . . . Day-to-day living and training expenses can be costly for the amateur athlete in pursuit of sports excellence. Sport Canada's Athlete Assistance Program financially assists between 800 to 900 of the country's top international-calibre amateur athletes.

Called 'carded athletes' for the identification card they receive as program members, they receive a monthly allowance, the amount linked to their athletic performance, that helps defray living and training costs. The program may also provide tuition support if they enrol in a Canadian college or university. Payments to carded athletes total about $5 million per year.

WOMEN IN SPORT Opportunities in sport have not always been open for women. Indeed, it was not until 1928 that Canada included women in its Olympic team. These days, women figure in many of the country's most memorable sports stories: rower Silken Laumann's gritty comeback to medal status in Barcelona after a catastrophic leg injury; Kerrin Lee-Gartner's impressive Olympic alpine skiing victory; and hockey goalie Manon Rhéaume's unprecedented move into major league play.

In the aftermath of Silken Laumann's victory, Canadian rowing appears to be undergoing a renaissance, with more interested potential competitors now than at any time during the previous half-century. The miraculous bronze she won carried as much weight as her rowing teammates' golds in women's pairs, fours and eights, and men's eights.

Kerrin Lee-Gartner's apparent overnight gold-medal success story is as impressive. Aside from Canada's Olympic hockey team, she was only the seventh Canadian to win Winter Olympic gold, and it seemed to be a warmup for what followed. A month later, she took second place in a World Cup downhill race at Panorama, BC, and by the end of 1992, she was the first woman in 25 years to win three successive Canadian women's downhill ski titles.

Few people have what it takes to stop a 160-kilometre-an-hour slapshot. Manon Rhéaume is one of them. In 1992, this 20-year-old from Quebec City became the first female to play in a major league hockey game, goaltending a period for the Tampa Bay Lightning in an exhibition game against the St. Louis Blues.

Her prior career included stints as goaltender when the Canadian women's hockey team won their gold medal at world championships earlier in 1992, a half-hour practice with the Montreal Canadiens that

John de Visser / CMCP

Speed skaters, Quebec.

THE PARALYMPIC GAMES

In the summer of 1992, in the shadow of the Olympic spotlight, a smaller but equally determined group of athletes from around the world met in Barcelona to compete for the gold. In the ninth-ever Paralympic Games, Canada's athletes with disabilities shone brighter than ever, bringing home a total of 75 medals.

The Paralympic Games, held every four years, is the world's most elite competition for athletes with physical and sensory disabilities. Participants include wheelchair athletes, amputees, those with cerebral palsy and the blind and partially sighted. In terms of complexity, duration and the number of athletes, the event is second only to the Olympic Games. In 1992, more than 4,000 athletes and staff from 96 countries participated.

There were 15 events in the 1992 Summer Paralympics, ranging from the long-jump to volleyball. Many of the sports are exclusively designed for athletes with physical disabilities. In cycling events, for example, visually impaired athletes compete on tandem bicycles — the athlete and a sighted guide or a pilot.

In total, the 137-member Canadian team participated in 11 of the 15 events, earning a total of 28 gold, 21 silver and 26 bronze medals. Canada's medal count was sixth overall among competing nations.

Two Canadian athletes were among the top medalists in the Games. Swimmers Joanne Mucz from Winnipeg and Michael Edgson from Victoria raced their way to five medals each, collectively earning nine gold medals and one silver.

Two other athletes — Frank Bruno and Joanne Bouw — earned three gold medals each, winning each competition they entered. Joanne Bouw, who won in shotput, discus and javelin, added the medals to the three she had already won at the previous Paralympics.

The Paralympic Games traces its origin to the Games For People With Spinal Injuries, first held in Aylesbury, England, in 1948. The Games, which were organized to coincide with the London Olympic Games, were originally part of a rehabilitation program for those with spinal injuries.

Today's modern counterpart — the Paralympic Games — was first held in Rome in 1960. Since then, there have been eight other Paralympic competitions. While the first Paralympics focussed on wheelchair sports, the Paralympic Games now emphasize a wider array of events. Participants compete in a variety of sports, many of which are only open to those with specific disabilities. The judo competition, for example, is only open to the blind and partially sighted. The key elements of judo are balance, touch, sensitivity and instinct — all qualities which are highly developed in the blind.

Generally, the Paralympic Games and the Olympic Games travel the globe together. In 1988, for example, both the Olympics and the Paralympics were staged in the city of Seoul, South Korea. In 1984, both events were held in the United States — the Olympics in Los Angeles and the Paralympics in New York.

Lionel Stevenson / Camera Art

Young boxers.

impressed players and coaches, and, late in 1991, play with a Quebec men's Major Junior League team.

Managers for the Lightning admitted it was partly publicity that prompted them to place the 5-foot-6 Rhéaume in the net in the first place. However, Rhéaume's drive, skill, and record won her a three year contract in the Lightning's farm system, with the Atlanta Knights.

To support such individual success stories and inroads, Sport Canada's Women's Program encourages women to become involved as athletes and leaders in sport at the national level.

To this end, the program lends financial support to several ventures: national sport organizations working on projects designed to improve opportunities for girls and women; the National Coaching School for Women; and the Canadian Association for the Advancement of Women and Sport. The program has also given financial assistance to set up pilot projects: one to introduce community-level, low-cost, low-skill team sports for girls, one for school gender equity initiatives, and one to set up workshops on gender equity with national and provincial sport organizations.

ATHLETES WITH DISABILITIES

Reflecting a growing trend in society in general, athletes with disabilities are entering more sports and becoming less segregated from the mainstream. For the first time in 1993, the Canada Games, held in Kamloops, BC, were scheduled to include events for national-calibre athletes with disabilities. And in another, international first, six demonstration events for athletes with disabilities have been scheduled for the 1994 Commonwealth Games in Victoria.

Sport for athletes with disabilities is an area where Canadians play a lead role. In fact, in 1993, both the Sport Science and Medical Officer, and the President of the International Paralympic Committee were Canadians. Another example of Canada's leadership was the hosting of Vista '93, the first international congress about high-performance athletes with disabilities. Sport scientists, technicians, coaches, athletes and medical experts from 27 nations discussed issues related to training, assessing athletes' physiological performance, concerns about performance-enhancing drugs, injury patterns, a functional classification system, technology and equipment and inclusion in the Olympic Games.

In 1992, the first year that the Organizing Committee of the Paralympic Games became part of the larger Olympic Organizing Committee, the Canadian government also honoured Paralympic and Olympic athletes together for the first time at a single post-Games reception after Barcelona.

Canadian Summer Paralympic athletes had won 75 medals, including 28 gold, 21 silver and 26 bronze.

Canadian stars at the games for athletes with disabilities included Joanne Mucz (5 gold medals in swimming for amputees); Mike Edgson (4 gold, 1 silver in blind swimming); Jacques Martin (gold in wheelchair discus, silver in wheelchair javelin, bronze in wheelchair shotput); and Chantal Petitclerc (bronze in women's 200 metre and 800 metre in wheelchair athletics).

In 1992, as part of Canada's National Strategy for the Integration of Persons with Disabilities, Fitness and Amateur Sport paid $4 million to support programs that ensure Canadians with a disability have a fair opportunity to participate in sports and physical activities.

The Program for the Disabled helps Canadians with disabilities to excel at sports and fitness-related activities. Fitness and Amateur Sport assists the many projects carried out on behalf of athletes with disabilities through financial contributions to the Canadian Paralympic Committee and six other national sport organizations for athletes with disabilities.

AFTER THE DUBIN COMMISSION... In 1988, the Canadian government set up the Dubin Commission. The commission was a consequence of the discovery that sprinter Ben Johnson had used anabolic steroids to enhance his performance at the Summer Olympics in Seoul. In the aftermath of the discovery, the gold medal Johnson had won was stripped by Olympic organizers. The Dubin Commission was the most extensive investigation ever undertaken of the use of banned substances or practices in sport. It has since influenced regulation and attitudes toward drug abuse in sport, not only in Canada, but around the world.

Justice Charles Dubin was asked to investigate the extent of the use of banned substances, such as anabolic steroids, by Canadian athletes and by athletes from other countries. After months of testimony from athletes, coaches and sport medicine experts, Justice Dubin made 70 recommendations.

By 1991, the federal government had acted upon 62 of them, including scheduled and no-notice drug testing of athletes, stricter controls on the supply and distribution of anabolic steroids, and better education.

In the aftermath of Seoul and the Dubin Commission, Canadian sport has tightened up.

The independent Canadian Centre for Drug-free Sport was created to research doping, investigate alleged drug abuse, test athletes, handle appeals, and educate athletes and coaches.

As well, Canadian athletes and trainers face escalating penalties for using banned substances. Athletes caught committing major doping infractions for the first time are banned from participating in sports for four years and cut off from direct federal sport funding for life. A second infraction, and they're banned from participation for life. Anyone found helping athletes to obtain or use illegal substances is banned from sport for life.

In 1992, anabolic steroids were reclassified under the federal Food and Drug Act, which imposed stiff new legal penalties for illegally possessing, importing or producing the drugs for non-medical purposes. Now, anyone giving anabolic steroids to athletes commits a criminal offence, and doctors prescribing steroids

CITIUS, ALTIUS, FORTIUS

The Olympic motto is "Faster, Higher, Stronger" and for Canadians at the 1992 Winter and Summer Olympics, the motto appeared to have special meaning. At the Winter Olympics in Albertville, Canada competed against 64 countries, winning more medals than it has at any other Olympics since 1932. In Barcelona, at the Summer Games, Canada competed against 170 other countries, earning 18 medals, almost double its previous performance in Seoul, South Korea, four years earlier.

Much of the drama of the Olympics was captured at Estany de Banyoles in Barcelona, when Canadian Silken Laumann won the bronze for women's single sculls in rowing. Laumann had suffered a devastating leg injury just 10 weeks before the Olympics. Somehow, as she pulled to the finish line, the Olympic creed seemed particularly apt:

> *The most important thing at the Olympic games is not to win but to take part, just as the most important thing in life is not the triumph but the struggle. The essential thing is not to have conquered, but to have fought well.*

> *Pierre de Coubertin*

EVENT	MEDALIST	TOP 15 MEDAL STANDINGS
Canadian medalists at the 1992 Olympic Winter Games:		**ALBERTVILLE OLYMPIC GAMES:**
Women's alpine skiing downhill:	Kerrin Lee-Gartner (Gold)	**Germany:** 10 Gold, 10 Silver, 6 Bronze
		Unified Team: 9 Gold, 6 Silver, 8 Bronze
Women's short track speed skating 3 000 metre relay:	Sylvie Daigle, Angela Cutrone, Nathalie Lambert, and Annie Perreault (Gold)	**Austria:** 6 Gold, 7 Silver, 8 Bronze
		Norway: 9 Gold, 6 Silver, 5 Bronze
		Italy: 4 Gold, 6 Silver, 4 Bronze
		USA: 5 Gold, 4 Silver, 2 Bronze
		France: 3 Gold, 5 Silver, 1 Bronze
Hockey:	National Team (Silver)	**Finland:** 3 Gold, 1 Silver, 3 Bronze
		Canada: 2 Gold, 3 Silver, 2 Bronze
Men's short track speed skating 1 000 metre:	Frédéric Blackburn (Silver)	**Japan:** 1 Gold, 2 Silver, 4 Bronze

(continued on next page)

EVENT	MEDALIST	TOP 15 MEDAL STANDINGS
Men's short track speed skating 5 000 metre relay:	Frédéric Blackburn, Michel Daignault, Sylvain Gagnon, and Mark Lackie (Silver)	**ALBERTVILLE OLYMPIC GAMES:** **South Korea:** 2 Gold, 1 Silver, 1 Bronze **Netherlands:** 1 Gold, 1 Silver, 2 Bronze **Sweden:** 1 Gold, 0 Silver, 3 Bronze
Figure Skating pairs:	Isabelle Brasseur and Lloyd Eisler (Bronze)	**Switzerland:** 1 Gold, 0 Silver, 2 Bronze **China:** 0 Gold, 3 Silver, 0 Bronze
Women's Biathlon 15 kilometre:	Myriam Bédard (Bronze)	**BARCELONA OLYMPIC GAMES:**
Demonstration Events:		
Men's Freestyle skiing aerials:	Philippe LaRoche (Gold) and Nicolas Fontaine (Silver)	**CIS:** 45 Gold, 33 Silver, 29 Bronze **USA:** 37 Gold, 34 Silver, 37 Bronze **Germany:** 33 Gold, 21 Silver, 23 Bronze **China:** 16 Gold, 22 Silver, 16 Bronze **Cuba:** 14 Gold, 6 Silver, 11 Bronze
Women's Curling:	Julie Sutton, Jodie Sutton, Melissa Soligo, Karri Willms, and alternate Elaine Dagg-Jackson (Bronze)	**Spain:** 13 Gold, 7 Silver, 2 Bronze **Korea:** 12 Gold, 5 Silver, 12 Bronze **Hungary:** 11 Gold, 12 Silver, 7 Bronze **France:** 8 Gold, 5 Silver, 16 Bronze **Australia:** 7 Gold, 9 Silver, 11 Bronze **Italy:** 6 Gold, 5 Silver, 8 Bronze **Canada:** 6 Gold, 5 Silver, 7 Bronze **Great Britain:** 5 Gold, 3 Silver, 12 Bronze **Romania:** 4 Gold, 6 Silver, 8 Bronze **Czechoslovakia:** 4 Gold, 2 Silver, 1 Bronze

EVENT	MEDALIST

Canadian medalists at the 1992 Summer Olympic Games:

Women's rowing pairs:	Marnie McBean and Kathleen Heddle (Gold)
Women's rowing fours:	Kirsten Barnes, Brenda Taylor, Jessica Monroe and Kay Worthington (Gold)
Women's rowing eights with coxswain:	Kirsten Barnes, Brenda Taylor, Megan Delehanty, Shannon Crawford, Marnie McBean, Kay Worthington, Jessica Monroe, Kathleen Heddle, and Lesley Thompson (Gold)
Men's rowing eights with coxswain:	John Wallace, Bruce Roberston, Mike Forgeron, Darren Barber, Robert Marland, Michael Rascher, Andy Crosby, Derek Porter and Terry Paul (Gold)
Men's 100 metre backstroke:	Mark Tewksbury (Gold)
Men's 110 metre hurdles:	Mark McKoy (Gold)
Light welterweight boxing:	Mark Leduc (Silver)
Solo synchronized swimming:	Sylvie Fréchette (Silver)
Duet synchronized swimming:	Penny and Vicky Vilagos (Silver)
20 kilometre racewalk:	Guillaume Leblanc (Silver)
Super heavyweight wrestling:	Jeff Thue (Silver)
Middleweight boxing:	Chris Johnson (Bronze)
Men's individual sprint cycling:	Curt Harnett (Bronze)
Middleweight judo:	Nicolas Gill (Bronze)
Women's single sculls rowing:	Silken Laumann (Bronze)

EVENT	MEDALIST
Men's swimming 400 metre medley relay:	Mark Tewksbury, Jon Cleveland, Marcel Gery, Stephen Clarke and Tom Ponting (Bronze)
Women's track and field 3 000 metre:	Angela Chalmers (Bronze)
Yachting:	Ross MacDonald and Eric Jesperson (Bronze)

Demonstration Events:

Women's taekwando middleweight:	Marcia King (Silver)
Men's taekwando bantamweight:	Sayed Youssef Najem (Silver)
Men's taekwando featherweight:	Woo Yong Jung (Silver)
Women's taekwando welterweight:	Shelley Vettese-Baert (Bronze)

Participation in Physical Recreation Activities

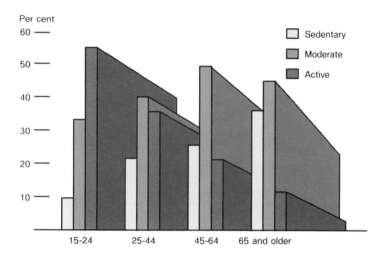

for athletic rather than medical reasons are liable to prosecution. Maximum penalties range from 18 months for summary convictions to 10 years in prison for indictable offenses.

This reclassification was considered a temporary stopgap. By 1993, the nation's lawmakers were working on a proposed federal Psychoactive Substance Control Bill, which would include penalties for misusing anabolic steroids. At publication time, the bill had received the second of three readings needed to pass through Parliament and become law.

Finally, to look at the broader implications of the Dubin Commission report, the federal Minister's Task Force on Federal Sport Policy was set up. Its wide-reaching report, released in 1992, examined the place of sport in Canadian society, sport's underlying values and ethics, and the government's future role in sport policy and funding.

SHAPING UP: FITNESS FOR ALL CANADIANS

Physical activity is part of daily life for millions of Canadians who think of it as gardening, walking to appointments or hitting the dance floor, although others may don spandex or sweats for aerobics,

marathon running, or cycling. Not everyone wants to be a top athlete, but more and more Canadians are realizing that sports and other physical activities are key to improving overall health.

Generally speaking, the younger we are, the more active we say we are. As well, men are more active than women.

But whatever Canadians' age or sex, and whatever activity we choose, more of us say we are exercising. Statistics Canada's General Social Survey found that in 1991, some 6.7 million Canadian adults (32%) labelled themselves ''very active'' based on the amount of energy they spent on leisure activities, compared with 27% in 1985.

The survey also found that, generally, the number of healthy choices Canadians say they make about their lifestyles increases as they become older and better educated. However, it is the youngest part of Canada's adult population that is the most physically active. Physical activity tends to fall off with age. In 1991, more than half of 15 to 24 year-olds were physically active, compared with a third of people aged 25 to 44, a fifth of those aged 45 to 64 and a tenth of those over 65.

Men were more likely to be active (29%) than women (26%), but both sexes increased their activity from the previous survey in 1985.

Between 1985 and 1991, the percentage of active women grew in every age group.

Among men, the picture was different. While there was a higher proportion of active men than women in every age group, between 1985 and 1991, only men aged 25 to 64 became substantially more active. Those aged 15 to 24 became only moderately more physically active, and the proportion of physically active men over 65 actually declined.

FITNESS CANADA

The federal government promotes fitness through Fitness Canada. In 1992, Fitness Canada provided $9.7 million in federal funding to dozens of organizations and special projects, and continued to

RACQUET CLUB

Lynne Cohen / CMCP

collaborate with groups such as the Canadian Parks and Recreation Association, YMCA Canada and YWCA of Canada.

Canada's Fitweek has become an important spring event for many Canadians, with 8 million participating in more than 17,000 events in communities across the country in 1992, the program's tenth anniversary. Other programs which Fitness Canada wholly or partly supports include ParticipACTION, Winteractive International, Vitality (a joint physical

activity and nutrition program) and the Quality Daily Physical Education Program.

In 1990, Fitness Canada focused attention on developing the concept of Active Living, a milestone in the evolution of a new approach to physical activity. Active Living integrates physical activity in all dimensions of everyday life, encouraging people to bicycle to work, and to play sports rather than watching them on television.

A MALL AFFAIR

In scores of the brightly-lit, self-contained worlds normally populated by Canadian consumers, a fitness revolution is taking place. Throngs of predominantly 50ish and older people, some with canes or walkers, are pacing past indoor shops, benches and fountains as members of the organized mall-walking phenomenon.

Walking is a physical activity in which most people may safely participate. For some, it's ideal. Walking benefits the heart and lungs and can lower cholesterol levels. And it's inexpensive — basic equipment is a pair of comfortable shoes.

Organized mall-walking often takes place in the low-traffic hours when stores are closed, so walkers, some of whom may have limited mobility, don't have to dodge the press of shoppers. Everyone moves at their own pace, untroubled by weather or season. They follow a marked and measured indoor course, and each person walking records their 'laps' on their own chart. Once a week, they meet to tally distances, enter them on a club chart, and compare their progress.

Many malls actively promote mall-walking, providing financial or human resource help. Individual stores and restaurants may offer free juices after a session, and prizes or discounts to walkers who reach important milestones.

Typical mall walkers are adults older than 50 years, likely retired. Until recently, most were women, but the number of men is increasing. For those at work, lunch hour walking groups inhabit company health clubs.

During the past few years a profusion of mall-walking groups have sprung up in Canada, and some don't even walk in malls — community centres, school gymnasiums and Legion halls serve as well.

In early 1993, Fitness and Amateur Sport combined a number of separate active living bodies into a single organization called Active Living Canada. Designed to unify the active living environment while cutting overlaps and costs, it uses a 'bottom-up' approach to meet needs in different communities, provinces and territories.

One popular Active Living program is the Canadian Active Living Challenge, formerly the Canada Fitness Award. The Canadian Active Living Challenge for children and youth now stresses participation rather than performance, but carries on its goal of encouraging Canadians from ages 6 to 18 to develop habits of regular physical activity that will benefit them throughout their lives.

To promote the Active Living concept, Fitness Canada has developed, or is developing, several **Blueprints for Action**, aimed at children and youth; people in the workplace; persons with disabilities, under the National Strategy for the Integration of Persons with a Disability; and older adults, among others.

SPORT MEDICINE

Sport medicine covers everything from delicate and complex knee surgery, to the physiotherapy that rebuilds muscles after a lay-off or accident, to studies aimed at preventing common injuries, to nutrition during training... to as simple a thing as sending along drinking water from home with athletes who compete abroad, to safeguard their health.

Issues with which sport medicine experts have dealt during the past two years range from implications of the Human Immuno-deficiency Virus (HIV) for sport competitors to iron deficiencies among high-performance athletes, to safety issues in hockey and cycling.

In Canada, the Sport Medicine and Science Council of Canada (SMSCC) oversees all of this activity. Within it are four member organizations: the Canadian Academy of Sport Medicine, the Canadian Athletic Therapists' Association, the Sports Physiotherapy Division of the Canadian Physiotherapy Association and the Canadian Society of Exercise Physiologists.

Pete Ryan / GeoStock

Skydome stadium, Toronto.

Their programs involve an array of disciplines, including physicians, physiotherapists, exercise physiologists, scientists, and nutritionists, all directed toward aiding athletes. The SMSCC also oversees several programs — a medical monitoring program for high performance athletes who compete in international events, a sport nutrition program, an athlete insurance program, and an accreditation service for sport medicine clinics.

HELMETS IN SPORT Under some conditions, even a light blow can cause unseen harm to the surprisingly delicate human brain. Helmets have become standard for players in many sports — football, hockey, boxing, competitive skiing, even baseball where batters switch their soft caps for harder headgear at the plate. In each case, the helmet is designed to pad the parts of the head most at risk in a particular sport.

Although bicycle helmets have been gaining a following in Canada, recently there have been moves to further increase their use.

The Canadian Medical Association (CMA) urged mandatory helmet laws for cyclists in 1992, estimating that in 1990 more than 100 people were killed and 15,000 injured riding bikes. Close to half of the deaths were children aged 5 to 14.

The CMA suspects the actual number of cycling injuries may be three times higher than are reported.

Head injuries account for 70% to 80% of cycling deaths. A study published in the New England Journal of Medicine in 1989 suggested wearing helmets reduced the risk of serious head injury by 85% and the risk of serious brain injury by 88%.

CANADA'S WORLD SERIES CHAMPIONS

On October 24, 1992, Canadians from coast to coast celebrated into the wee hours of the night, cheering Canada's first-ever World Series champions, the Toronto Blue Jays. In Toronto alone, some 350,000 fans took to the streets, partying and cheering with friends and strangers alike.

The World Series is the championship competition of professional baseball in North America. It first began in 1903, and since then, there have been 89 World Series. In 1992, when the Toronto Blue Jays beat the Atlanta Braves, they made World Series history as the first team outside the United States ever to win this event.

As baseball's most prestigious prize, the road to the championship is a long and rigorous one. Contenders are divided into two leagues — the American League and the National League — which are each divided into eastern and western divisions. In the 1992 regular season, the Blue Jays played some 160 games before they won their division, the American League East. By then winning a best-of-seven games series against the American League West champions, the Oakland Athletics, the Blue Jays won the right to represent the American League.

Meanwhile, the National League West champions, the Atlanta Braves, beat the National League East champions, the Pittsburgh Pirates, to secure their berth in the 1992 World Series.

The Jays began major-league life in the spring of 1977, when they played their first major league game in Toronto's Exhibition Stadium. Since then, the Jays have struggled and endured, with a franchise record preceding the 1992 World Series of 1160 wins, 1211 losses and 2 ties. In recent years, however, the Blue Jays have become one of the most successful franchises in major league baseball.

The first game of the 1992 World Series, played in Atlanta, went to the Braves by a 3-1 score. The second game, also played in Atlanta, began ominously. During the singing of the national anthem, American marines marched an upside-down Canadian flag onto the field during the pre-game ceremonies. The Blue Jays won, nonethless, by a 5-4 score.

The third game was held in Toronto's Skydome and in itself made baseball history as the first World Series game ever to be held outside the United States. This time, the Americans carried the Canadian flag back onto the field, but the right way up. The Jays won 3-2, giving them a two-games-to-one series lead.

By winning the following game, also at the Skydome, by a 2-1 score, the Jays were just one win away from the World Series title. They lost their next game, however, 7-2.

On October 24, the Blue Jays returned to Atlanta for game six. It was a white-knuckle event. Up by one run with two strikes and two outs in the bottom of the ninth inning, the Blue Jays were just one pitch away from winning it all. Then, amazingly, the Braves' Otis Nixon hit a single to left field to bring in the tying run.

With a score of 2-2, it was on to extra innings.

The story finally concluded in the 11th inning. Down 4-3 with two outs in the bottom of the inning, the Braves had the tying run on third. In an incredible gamble, the Braves' batter laid a soft bunt down the first base line. The Jays' pitcher Mike Timlin, expecting the move, fielded the ball quickly and threw it to first base for the final out, just a split second ahead of the base runner.

The game was over. The World Series was over. The Toronto Blue Jays had made baseball history and the celebrations began.

CANADA TAKES UP AEROBICS

Aerobics is becoming a popular sport in Canada. This rigorous form of calisthenics to music first came to light in the late 1970s, as a kind of 'new wave' exercise fad out of California. Popularized by such proponents as Jane Fonda, it quickly became a mainstream form of exercise in countries around the world.

Today, aerobics is established as a competitive sport. In 1983, the National Aerobic Championship was founded in the United States and since then more than 25 countries have established national championships. Winners move on to the World Aerobic Championship, which has been held three times since its inception in 1990.

Canada has drawn attention at the World Championship with a Canadian from Quebec, Natalie Tomaro, winning the gold medal in the women's singles competition in the inaugural 1990 event. The next World Championship, to be held in 1993 in New Orleans, had not yet occurred when the **Year Book** *went to print.*

The most recent survey to look at Canadian fitness trends was the Campbell Survey, carried out in 1988. It found aerobics to be the 14th most popular sport, out of some 18 activities in which 5% or more of Canadians participated. Interestingly enough, this survey found the number one fitness activity for Canadians to be walking, followed by gardening and then swimming.

Since then, however, unofficial estimates have put the number of Canadians who do aerobics at some 2.9 million, with a growing interest in competitive aerobics at the novice and elite levels. The annual Canadian National Aerobic Championship attracts athletes from across the country.

To date, the only province to consider mandatory cycle helmet legislation for all riders is Ontario. It had not been made law when this *Year Book* went to press, but the Ontario provincial legislature was expected to give the bill for the law third reading by mid-1993. Manitoba has a helmet law, but requires them only for children under 6 in mounted cycle carrier seats.

THE MAJOR LEAGUES

At the turn of the century, most sporting events were contested by amateurs, but since then, Canadians have become used to paying to view feats of athletic ability. Technological advances have also helped professional sport advance: air transportation has made city-to-city travel by teams (and their more avid fans) easier; and television has increased visibility and revenues to the point where major-league players can earn millions of dollars each year.

HOCKEY Canada's greatest contribution to world sport has been hockey. If it is well-played, this game is fast, graceful, and physical. However, a recurring issue of the past decade has been violence among players.

In the 1992 off-season, the National Hockey League (NHL) moved to address some of the professional game's stormier aspects with a package of new rules. One of the most important was a new game misconduct penalty for anyone instigating a fight, and during the first season the rules were in force, major penalties for fighting dropped 31% to 1,067, compared with 1,544 the season before.

The beginning of recorded hockey history can be traced to the pen of J.G.A. Creighton, a student at McGill University who wrote down the first set of hockey rules in 1875. By 1886, the Amateur Hockey Association of Canada had formed. By 1917, the NHL had formed, and professional teams began to dominate the league.

The NHL moved into the United States, adding the Boston Bruins, New York Americans (1925), Pittsburgh Pirates (1925), New York Rangers (1926), Chicago Blackhawks (1926) and Detroit Cougars

David Nunuk / First Light

Stanley Park, Vancouver.

(1926). After rapid expansion, the league dwindled to six teams, with only the Montreal Canadiens and Toronto Maple Leafs in Canada.

A rival professional league, the World Hockey Association (WHA) began play in 1972, but eventually merged with the NHL in 1979. The NHL continues to expand, and now comprises over 20 teams. The Canadian teams are: Montreal Canadiens, Toronto Maple Leafs, Vancouver Canucks, Edmonton Oilers, Winnipeg Jets, Quebec Nordiques, Calgary Flames and the Ottawa Senators.

Hockey has also been gaining a following south of the border. Of five expansion teams signed up by the league in the early 1990s, the Senators were the sole Canadian organization. The others, based in the United States, were the Tampa Bay Lightning, Florida Panthers, San Jose Sharks, and the Mighty Ducks of Anaheim, California.

The NHL relies heavily on Canada's amateur youth hockey leagues as a source of talent. However, amateur hockey attracts players of all ages. About 450,000 Canadians play on more than 27,000 teams in organized leagues, and still more play in informal pick-up games.

Although Canada continues to supply most of the talent for the National Hockey League, an increasing number of European players as well as Americans now play in the NHL.

FOOTBALL In the 1990s, the Canadian Football League (CFL) faced down a financial squeeze caused by shrinking crowds, rising costs and growing team deficits, with a new game plan of financial streamlining and expansion.

Cash flow problems were no stranger to the league during the 1980s. Until 1987, the Canadian Football League, the only professional league in Canada, had nine teams, but the Montreal team folded due to financial problems, leaving eight. In the years that followed, some of the survivors were shaky, too.

Just prior to 1993, each of the league's eight football clubs had a $3 million salary cap, but each was allowed to exempt the pay of one big-ticket 'marquee' player, so called because of their expected box-office draw, from this cap. Because of this, a single player could add hundreds of thousands of dollars to a team's payroll, and many clubs lost money when the box-office take fell short.

For 1993, the league and its clubs imposed a $2.5 million salary cap on each team. Clubs across the country pushed players to take pay reductions to meet it. Some teams spoke of wage rollbacks as large as 25%, and even marquee players took hefty cuts.

Then the league's executive and team owners looked south, with expansion in mind. The hope was that growth, especially cracking the American football market with the Canadian version of the game, would help the bottom line and showcase the brand of football some call the most exciting in the world. However, the move also raised the question of whether the league would be able to keep its Canadian player quota for teams. Of four proposed expansion teams, three were American — the sole Canadian city to be considered was Montreal.

Canadian football, while similar to American football, is played on a slightly longer and wider field, and some of the rules differ. CFL officials and team owners hoped the differences would intrigue American fans. Eventually a single new California team, the Sacramento Gold Miners, was franchised to begin CFL play in the 1993 season.

The most coveted prize in Canadian football is the Grey Cup, won in the 1992 season by the Calgary Stampeders. Before 1925, the Grey Cup game usually involved at least one university team. Thereafter, city-based teams with some professional players began to dominate the sport. The professional CFL eventually took responsibility for the cup, and retains it today.

Football isn't solely a professional game, though. It is also played at the community, university and college levels and, unlike baseball, is played in organized high-school leagues across the country. In early 1992 about 112,000 players, coaches and officials were involved in amateur tackle football and two low-contact derivatives, touch and flag football.

BASEBALL Each year, the 'kids of summer' show up on countless baseball diamonds across the country, in organized leagues and pickup teams, to play the game and inhale its subtle perfumes —

newly-mown grass, clay dust on the pitcher's mound, a leather glove in the hot sun.

Baseball's Canadian history is lengthy. A game similar to the modern version was played in Beachville, Upper Canada, in 1838 — seven years before the New York Knickerbockers are said to have codified baseball's rules and diamond design. By 1868, large financial prizes had introduced professional status to the game, something avoided by other sports such as hockey until the 20th century.

In 1876, the first Canadian professional league was born, with teams from Kingston, Toronto, Hamilton, Guelph and London. For much of the 20th century, both Toronto and Montreal had Triple-A professional teams, a league of major-league farm teams in Canada and the United States.

The first major-league franchise to be awarded outside the United States went to Montreal in 1969, when the Montreal Expos joined the National League. The Toronto Blue Jays followed in 1977, joining the rival American League. The Expos have drawn crowds of over 2.3 million in one season. In 1992, the Blue Jays, playing in the Skydome, set an American League record of just over 4 million while becoming the first professional team outside the United States to win the coveted World Series.

National television coverage of these teams has greatly increased the popularity of baseball as a spectator sport, but baseball has always been a popular amateur activity. There are about 300,000 registered amateur Canadian baseball players, and about 37,000 certified coaches; when estimates of unregistered players and coaches are included, the total approaches a million. Nearly 420,000 registered players, coaches and umpires play softball, a derivative of baseball, and the total number of Canadian softball players and officials is estimated at 2.5 million. While baseball players are predominantly men, many softball players are women.

Despite its popularity, only about 180 Canadians have played in the major leagues. Notable among them is Ferguson Jenkins, the only Canadian inducted into the Baseball Hall of Fame in Cooperstown, New York.

SOURCES

Canada's Sports Hall of Fame

Canadian Academy for Sport Medicine

Canadian Amateur Hockey Association

Canadian Centre for Drug-free Sport

Canadian Federation of Sport Organizations for the Disabled

Canadian Fitness and Lifestyle Research Institute

Canadian Football League

Canadian Hockey Hall of Fame

Canadian Medical Association

Canadian Olympic Association

Fitness and Amateur Sport

Fitness Canada

Football Canada

Montreal Expos

National Hockey League

National Walking Campaign

Softball Canada

Sport Canada

Toronto Blue Jays

Statistics Canada

TABLES

22.1   AVERAGE TIME SPENT[1] ON ACTIVITIES, 1992

	Total Population[2] Minutes per day			Participants[3] Minutes per day			Participation rate[4] Percent		
	Total	Male	Female	Total	Male	Female	Total	Male	Female
Paid work and related activities	214	270	160	497	526	457	43	51	35
Paid work	193	243	144	461	489	423	42	50	34
Activities related to paid work	4	5	3	35	40	28	10	12	9
Travel to/from work	18	22	13	47	50	44	37	44	31
Household work and related activities	192	134	248	224	172	265	86	78	93
Cooking/washing up	47	22	70	71	45	86	66	49	81
House cleaning and laundry	39	13	65	105	79	113	37	16	58
Maintenance and repair	12	19	4	161	165	149	7	12	3
Other household work	24	28	19	84	105	66	28	27	29
Shopping for goods and services	45	37	53	116	109	122	39	34	43
Primary child care	26	15	36	123	94	139	21	16	26
Civic and voluntary activity	23	23	24	130	1313	129	18	18	18
Education and related activities	35	35	35	387	384	351	9	9	10
Sleep, meals and other personal activities	631	617	645	631	617	645	100	100	100
Night sleep	483	474	491	483	475	491	100	100	100
Meals (excluding restaurant meals)	73	74	72	77	78	77	94	95	94
Other personal activities	76	68	82	79	72	85	96	95	96
Socializing	109	107	112	175	180	171	62	59	65
Restaurant meals	18	19	17	91	90	92	20	21	19
Socializing (in homes)	76	68	82	150	154	147	50	44	58
Other socializing	16	19	12	164	175	150	10	11	8
Television, reading and other passive leisure	168	183	153	198	210	185	85	87	83
Watching television	131	146	117	173	184	161	76	79	73
Reading books, magazines, newspapers	30	28	31	83	82	83	36	35	37
Other passive leisure	7	8	5	72	80	64	9	10	9
Sports, movies and other entertainment events	8	8	8	202	204	200	4	4	4

22.1 AVERAGE TIME SPENT[1] ON ACTIVITIES, 1992 (concluded)

	Total Population[2] Minutes per day			Participants[3] Minutes per day			Participation rate[4] Percent		
	Total	Male	Female	Total	Male	Female	Total	Male	Female
Active leisure	59	63	54	158	173	145	37	37	37
Active sports	27	35	20	125	142	104	22	25	19
Other active leisure	31	28	34	158	162	155	20	17	22
Residual	1	1	1	65	64	66	1	1	2
Paid work and related activities/unpaid work	430	427	432	450	458	443	95	93	97
Unpaid work	216	157	272	246	195	288	88	81	94
Free time	343	360	327	354	370	338	97	97	97

[1] Averaged over a 7 day week.
[2] The number of minutes per day spent on the activity averaged over the entire population aged 15 years and over (whether or not the person reported the activity).
[3] The number of minutes spent on the activity averaged over the population having reported the activity on diary day.
[4] The proportion of the population that reported spending some time on the activity on diary day.

Source
Statistics Canada

LARRY J. MCDOUGALL / FIRST LIGHT

STATISTICS CANADA REGIONAL REFERENCE CENTRES

Atlantic Region

Serving the provinces of Newfoundland and Labrador, Nova Scotia, Prince Edward Island and New Brunswick.

Advisory Services
Statistics Canada
Viking Building, 3rd Floor
Crosbie Road
ST. JOHN'S, Newfoundland
A1B 3P2
Toll free service: 1-800-565-7192
Fax number: (709)772-6433

Advisory Services
Statistics Canada
North American Life Centre
1770 Market Street
HALIFAX, Nova Scotia
B3J 3M3
Toll free service: 1-800-565-7192
Local calls: (902)426-5331
Fax number: (902)426-9538

Quebec Region

Advisory Services
Statistics Canada
Guy Favreau Complex
200 René Lévesque Blvd. W.
Suite 412, East Tower
MONTREAL, Quebec
H2Z 1X4
Toll free service: 1-800-361-2831
Local calls: (514)283-5725
Fax number: (514)283-9350

National Capital Region

Statistical Reference (NCR)
Statistics Canada
R.H. Coats Building Lobby
Holland Avenue
OTTAWA, Ontario
K1A 0T6
If outside the local calling area, please dial the toll free number for your province
Local calls: (613)951-8116
Fax number: (613)951-0581

Ontario Region

Advisory Services
Statistics Canada
Arthur Meighen Building, 10th Floor
25 St. Clair Avenue East
TORONTO, Ontario
M4T 1M4
Toll free service: 1-800-263-1136
Local calls: (416)973-6586
Fax number: (416)973-7475

Prairie Region

Serving the provinces of Manitoba, Saskatchewan, Alberta and the Northwest Territories.

Advisory Services
Statistics Canada
MacDonald Building, Suite 300
344 Edmonton Street
WINNIPEG, Manitoba
R3B 3L9
Toll free service: 1-800-563-7828
Local calls: (204)983-4020
Fax number: (204)983-7543

Advisory Services
Statistics Canada
Avord Tower, 9th Floor
2002 Victoria Avenue
REGINA, Saskatchewan
S4P 0R7
Toll free service: 1-800-563-7828
Local calls: (306)780-5405
Fax number: (306)780-5403

Advisory Services
Statistics Canada
Park Square, 8th Floor
10001 Bellamy Hill
EDMONTON, Alberta
T5J 3B6
Toll free service: 1-800-563-7828
Local calls: (403)495-3027
Fax number: (403)495-5318

Advisory Services
Statistics Canada
First Street Plaza, Room 401
138 – 4th Avenue South East
CALGARY, Alberta
T2G 4Z6
Toll free service: 1-800-563-7828
Local calls: (403)292-6717
Fax number: (403)292-4958

Pacific Region
Serving the provinces of British Columbia and the Yukon Territory

Advisory Services
Statistics Canada
Sinclair Centre, Suite 300
757 West Hastings Street
VANCOUVER, British Columbia
V6C 3C9
Toll free service: 1-800-663-1551
Local calls: (604)666-3691
Fax number: (604)666-4863

Telecommunications Device for the Hearing Impaired: 1-800-363-7629

Toll Free Order Only Line (Canada and United States): 1-800-267-6677

METRIC CONVERSION

In view of the degree of metric conversion in Canada almost all quantities in this edition of the *Canada Year Book* appear only in SI metric or in neutral units such as dollars or dozens.

Following are conversion factors for units used in the present edition and some others in common use. Conversions are from SI metric to traditional units. The same number of significant digits is used in these conversion factors as in the *Canadian Metric Practice Guide*. If users do not need this level of accuracy, they can round off figures at any number of digits, either in the calculations or in the results. It is a requirement in SI metric to use spaces instead of commas to separate groups of three digits; a space is optional with a four-digit number. Although this practice is not imperative with neutral units, it is taking place in many cases now and will undoubtedly come about generally through standardization. In all Statistics Canada publications, a period is used as a decimal marker.

Relative weights and measures:
SI Metric, Canadian Imperial and United States units

Area

1 km² (square kilometre)	=	0.3861022 square miles
1 ha (hectare)	=	2.471054 acres
	=	10 000 m²
100 ha	=	1 km²

Length

1 m (metre)	=	39.37 inches
	=	3.281 feet
	=	1.094 yards
1 km (kilometre)	=	0.6213712 statute miles = 3,280.840 feet
	=	0.5399568 nautical miles = 2,850.972 feet

Volume and capacity

1 L (litre)	=	0.0353147 cubic feet
	=	0.4237760 board feet (for lumber)
	=	0.0274962 Canadian bushels (for grain)
	=	1 L (litre) (for liquids or, in some cases, for fine solids which pour)
	=	0.2199692 Canadian gallons
	=	35.1951 fluid ounces
	=	0.8798774 quarts
	=	1.75975 pints
	=	0.264172 US gallons
	=	1.05669 US quarts
	=	2.11338 US pints

1 imperial proof gallon	=	1.36 US proof gallons
1 m³ (cubic metre)	=	6.289811 barrels (oil barrel: 42 US gallons)
	=	0.3531466 register tons (in shipping)*
	=	35.31466 cubic feet
	=	1 000 dm³

Mass (weight)

1 g (gram)	=	0.03527396 ounces (avoirdupois)
	=	0.03215075 ounces (troy or apothecary)
1 kg (kilogram)	=	2.20462262 pounds (avoirdupois)
1 t (metric tonne)	=	1.10231131 tons (short)
	=	0.98420653 tons (long)

(For register ton, see Volume and capacity, and footnote *)

Length and mass

1 t.km (tonne kilometre)	=	0.6849445 short ton miles

Volume and mass

$1\ m^3$ of water weighs 1 tonne
(approximate)

Temperature

Fahrenheit temperature	=	1.8 (Celsius temperature) +32
Celsius temperature	=	5/9 (Fahrenheit temperature –32)

At sea level water freezes at 0°C (32°F) and boils at 100°C (212°F) (approximate)

The following weights and measures are used in connection with the principal field crops and fruits:

Crops	Pounds per bushel	Kilograms per bushel	Bushels per 1 000 kg (1 t)
Wheat, potatoes and peas	60	27.215 5	36.7437
Wheat flour	43.48	19.722 2	50.7043
Oats	34	15.422 1	64.8418
Barley and buckwheat	48	21.772 4	45.9296
Rye, flaxseed and corn	56	25.401 2	39.3683
Mixed grains	45	20.411 7	48.9916
Rapeseed, mustard seed, pears, plums, cherries, peaches and apricots	50	22.679 6	44.0925
Sunflower seed	24	10.886 2	91.8593
Apples	42	19.050 9	52.4910

Strawberries and raspberries 1 kg	=	1.47 quarts in BC
	=	1.76 quarts in all other provinces

To produce 100 kg of flour it takes 138 kg of wheat.

*Gross register tonnage of a ship, as used by Lloyd's Register of Shipping, is a measurement of the total capacity of the ship and is not a measure of weight. Net register tonnage equals gross register tonnage minus space used for accommodation, machinery, engine area and fuel storage, and so states the cargo carrying ability of the ship.

COLOUR PHOTOGRAPHY

COVER
John de Visser / CMCP
Horseshoe Falls Niagara, Ontario at dawn.

David Reede / First Light
Barley and canola crops near Holland, Manitoba.

Darwin Wiggett / First Light
Car tail lights, Drumheller, Alberta.

CHAPTER 1
Bob Herger / Image Finders
Tranquil sunrise and mist, lower mainland British Columbia.

CHAPTER 2
David Nunuk / First Light
Spawning sockeye salmon on the bed of Adams River, British Columbia.

Thomas Kitchin / First Light
Canada leads the world in softwood lumber exports.

CHAPTER 3
Brian Milne / First Light
The spirit of the west lives on at this Alberta cattle ranch.

Brian Milne / First Light
Young Hutterite girls, Alberta. Hutterite colonies are spread across Canada's western provinces.

CHAPTER 4
Canapress Photo Service
Advanced diagnostic equipment provides early warning signals on varied health problems.

CHAPTER 5
Thomas Kitchin / First Light
Discovering the wonder of beluga whales at the Vancouver Aquarium.

CHAPTER 6
Larry Goldstein / Image Finders
In Canada, blue-collar workers were hard-hit during the last recession.

CHAPTER 7
Pete Ryan / GeoStock
There were slightly more than 10 million occupied dwellings in Canada in 1991.

CHAPTER 8
J. Cochrane / First Light
The War Memorial, Ottawa, Ontario. Canada has long recognized the sacrifice of veterans in war and peacekeeping with social programs to respond to their needs.

CHAPTER 9
Ron Watts / First Light
Tulips on Parliament Hill: a rite of spring in Canada's capital, Ottawa.

CHAPTER 10
Ron Watts / First Light
On guard for thee. Canada's national police force is the Royal Canadian Mounted Police.

CHAPTER 11
John Sylvester / First Light
Rural Route #1, Canada.

CHAPTER 12
Thomas Bruckbauer / Image Finders
City pace: Water Street, Gastown, Vancouver.

Dave Reede / First Light

CHAPTER 13
G. Krasichynski / First Light
In 1992, some $10 billion in research and development took place in Canada.

CHAPTER 14
Eric Aldwinckle / National Archives of Canada C 87430
Recruitment poster, World War II.

CHAPTER 15
Al Harvey / Masterfile
Sea of cranberries at harvest time in the Maritimes.

Ron Watts / First Light
Over time, Prairie winds tilt an abandoned shed in southern Saskatchewan.

Dave Reede / First Light
Wind swirls the flowers of flax plants, a staple crop on the Canadian prairies.

CHAPTER 16
Peter Christopher / Masterfile
Roughnecks wrestle a drill stem on an oil drilling rig in Canada's Northwest Territories.

CHAPTER 17
Hans Blohm / Masterfile
Microphoto: gypsum, the chalky mineral used to make plaster of Paris and wallboard, takes on unaccustomed beauty under a high-powered microscope.

CHAPTER 18
Darwin Wiggett / First Light
Edmonton's central business district reflected in the waters of the North Saskatchewan River.

CHAPTER 19
W. Cody / First Light
Engraved robins grace the back of Canada's $2 bill, the lowest denomination of paper currency in circulation.

CHAPTER 20
Canapress Photo Service
Frantic trading pace on the Toronto Stock Exchange.

CHAPTER 21
Richard Swiecki

Gera Dillon / First Light
Poetry in motion: the Toronto Dance Theatre

CHAPTER 22
Ron Watts / First Light
Canadian fitness and sport — ''there's no finish line.''

END LEAF
Larry J. McDougall / First Light

production, 530, 531
shipments, 517, 533
uses, 517
See also Metals
Leather industries, 538, 557
employment, 557
shipments, value, 554, 555
Lee-Gartner, Kerrin, 663, 668
Legal system, 313
Legislation
enactment process, 279
Legislature
federal, 276, 283
provincial, 284
LePage, Robert, 642
Lester B. Pearson International Airport, 371
Liberal Party of Canada, 277
Libraries, 627
Licences and permits, 301, 307
Lieutenant-governors, 284
Life expectancy, 87, 111, 128, 131, 148
Lightburn, Ron, 630
Liquor Licence Act, 325
Literacy, 159
Literature
See Books
Livestock
See Cattle
Loans
Bank of Canada, 573
credit unions, 578
Local government, 284
aboriginal, 285
arts and culture, 622, 650
assets and liabilities, 308
debt, 308
employment, 295, 296, 309
remuneration, 309
revenues and expenditures, 152, 167, 307, 308
Logging, 50, 74
Lone-parent families, 97, 121, 122, 190
income, 190, 195, 198, 217
Longest highway, 374
Low income, 216, 217, 602
and health, 128, 140
Lowest annual amount of precipitation, 14
Lowest temperature, 14

Macdonald, Sir John A., 423
Machinery and equipment, 545, 600
exports and imports, 424, 441, 442, 599, 600, 606
shipments, value, 555
Magazines
See Periodicals
Mail, 353
electronic, 347, 353
hybrid, 353
Maillet, Antonine, 4, 622
Main demographic indicators, 110
Major Industrial Accidents Council of Canada, 372
Major, John Charles, 332
Manitoba
agents and brokers, 561, 562
agriculture, 455, 466, 470, 471, 474, 476, 481
alcoholic beverages, 566, 567

arts and culture, 650, 655
construction, 238, 239
economy, 16
education, 176, 177, 178, 180, 181, 182, 183
employment, 208, 209
energy, 504, 507, 510
ethnicity, 108
fertility rate, 113
fishing industry, 60, 75, 76
forest industry, 72, 73
gambling, 637
health, 152
highways, 385
housing, 222, 228, 242
income and earnings, 214, 216
income supplements, 247
injuries and workers' compensation, 212, 213
land area, 36, 115
language, 122
manufacturing, 538, 554, 555, 558
marriage and family life, 120, 121, 122
minerals, 516, 525, 528, 532, 533, 534
motor vehicles, 386, 387
parks, 46
physical features, 16, 36, 38
police, 335
population, 89, 112, 114
ports, 391
research and development, 412
service industries, 559
sport, 678
therapeutic abortions, 151
transportation, 388, 389
wholesale and retail, 560, 563
wildlife management, 67
Manufacturing, 538
companies, 556, 557
employment, 207, 541, 557, 596, 606
provinces and territories, 540
research and development, 409
shipments, value, 538, 554, 555
Marine Search and Rescue Program, 380
Maritime law, 317
Maritime Telegraph and Telephone Company, 163
Marketing
agricultural products, 463, 464, 465
Markle, Robert, 646
Marriages, 82, 92, 93, 104, 111, 120
rate, 92, 93
Martin, Jacques, 667
Maternity leave, 204
McKoy, Mark, 670
McLachlan, Sarah, 632
McLachlin, Beverly, 332
McLuhan, Marshall, 338
McMinn, John, 631
Meat
consumption, 461
Media, 338, 652
support, 651
See also Broadcasting
See also Newspapers
Medical Council of Canada, 290
Medical Research Council, 137, 396, 406
budget, 137
expenditures, 408
Medical sciences
research and development, 399, 406

Medicare
See Health
Meech Lake Accord, 274
Mental disorders, 151
Merchandise trade, 423
See also International trade
Merchandising, 544
Merchant Navy Veteran and Civilian War-related Benefits Act, 254
Metals, 13, 20, 516, 523, 524, 540, 557
employment, 557
exports and imports, 441, 442
production, 516, 528, 530, 531
research and development, 409
shipments, 538, 540, 555
shipments, value, 554
See also Minerals
Métis, 285
See also Aboriginal peoples
Mexico
imports and exports, 459
main demographic indicators, 110, 111
median age, 82
population, 82
trade, 426
Mighton, John, 630
Migrants
interprovincial, 119
Migration, 82, 110
See also Immigrants
See also Immigration
Migratory birds, 63, 66
Milk
See Dairy products
Mineral and Energy Technology (CANMET), 226
Minerals, 16, 20, 514, 540
aggregates, 522
employment, 514
environmental problems, 526
exports and imports, 514, 519
production, 514, 528, 530, 531
research and development, 409
shipments, 538
See also Metals
See also Mining
Mining, 20, 514, 524, 529
employment, 210
expenditures, 303, 514
research and development, 409
See also Minerals
Ministère de la Justice (Quebec), 324
Mink farms, 67
Mint
See Royal Canadian Mint
Missing Children's Network Canada, 328
Missing Children's Registry, 328
Missing Children's Society of Canada, 328
Mitchell, W.O., 4
Mobile Servicing System, 403
Monetary aggregates, 583
Monetary policy, 572, 573
Montgomery, L.M., 350
Montreal Expos, 680
Montreal Protocol on Substances that Deplete the Ozone Layer, 31
Morbidity, 132
Mortality
See Deaths
Mortgage Loan Insurance Program, 228

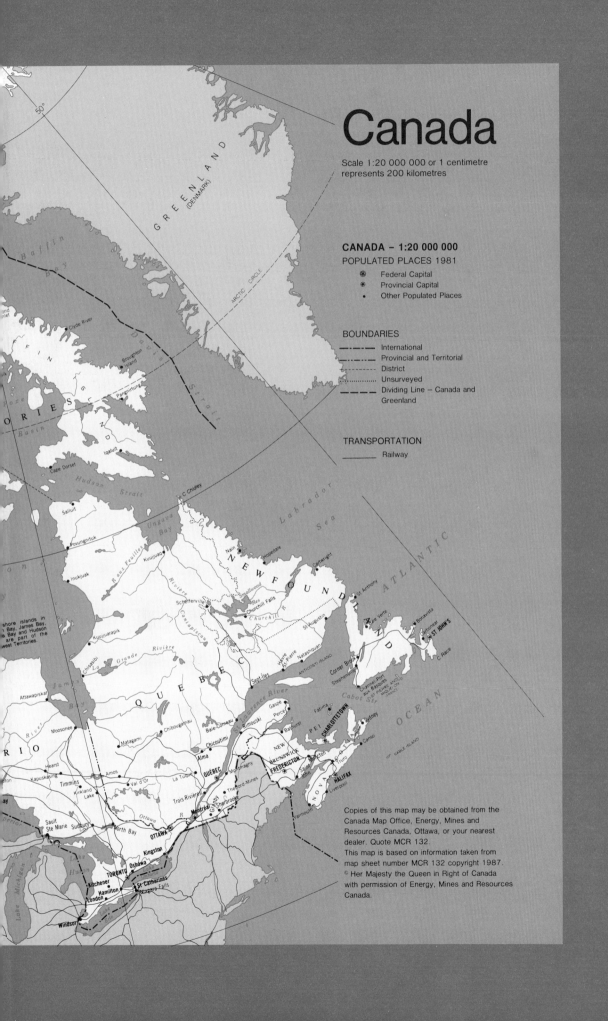

Canada

Scale 1:20 000 000 or 1 centimetre
represents 200 kilometres

CANADA – 1:20 000 000

POPULATED PLACES 1981

⊛   Federal Capital
✸   Provincial Capital
•   Other Populated Places

BOUNDARIES

—·—·—   International
—··—··—   Provincial and Territorial
———————   District
·············   Unsurveyed
— — — —   Dividing Line – Canada and
            Greenland

TRANSPORTATION

—————   Railway